BEYOND BORDERS

Edition Angewandte
Book Series of the University
of Applied Arts Vienna

Edited by
Gerald Bast, Rector

edition:'ʌngewʌndtə
Universität für angewandte Kunst Wien
University of Applied Arts Vienna

BEYOND BORDERS

Conservation Goes International

Gabriela Krist
(Ed.)

DE GRUYTER

Contents

p.14 India

p.116 Mongolia

p.172 Myanmar Thailand

Considering that parts of the cultural or natural heritage are of outstanding interest and therefore need to be preserved as part of the world heritage of mankind as a whole...

Considering that, in view of the magnitude and gravity of the new dangers threatening them, it is incumbent on the international community as a whole to participate in the protection of the cultural and natural heritage of outstanding universal value, by the granting of collective assistance which, although not taking the place of action by the State concerned, will serve as an efficient complement thereto...

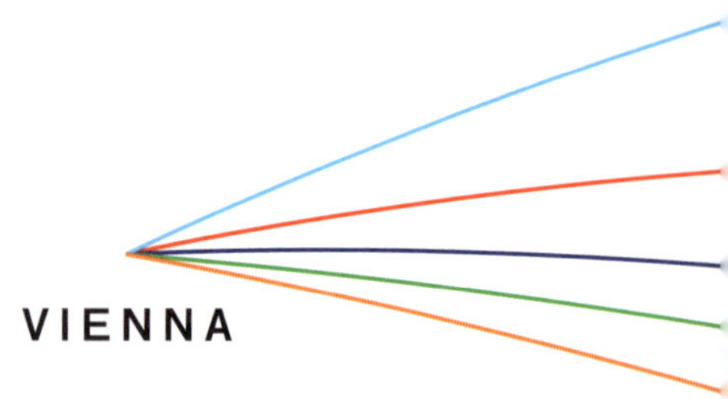

Extracts from the Convention Concerning the Protection of the World Cultural and Natural Heritage, 1972

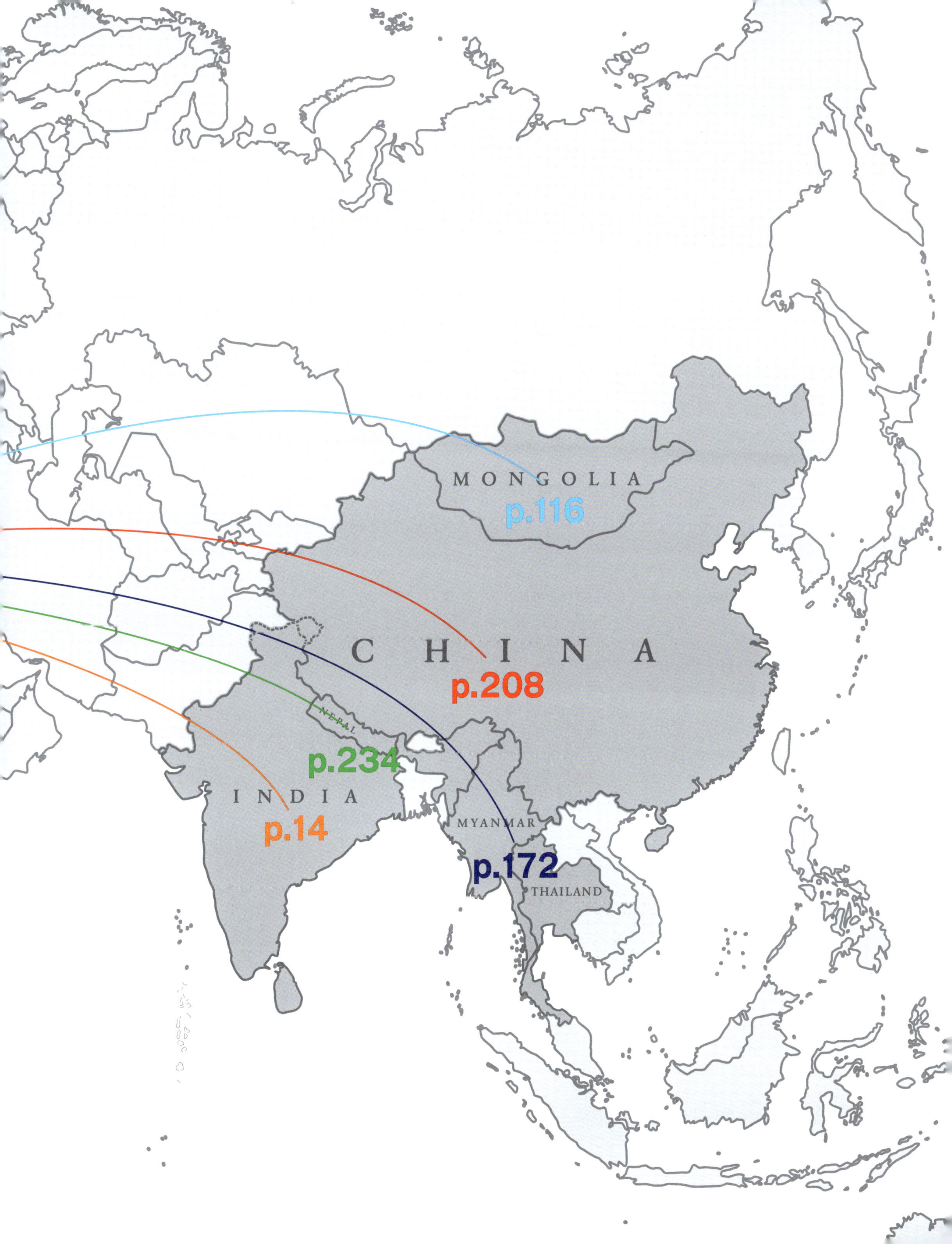
MONGOLIA
p.116
CHINA
p.208
NEPAL
p.234
INDIA
p.14
MYANMAR
p.172
THAILAND

Foreword

GERALD BAST

Rector of the University of Applied Arts Vienna

Bringing out a book about the multifaceted projects of the Institute of Conservation in the Vienna University of Applied Arts (the "Angewandte") is an idea that excited Anja Seipenbusch and me some time ago. The Institute has been headed by Gabriela Krist since 1999 and is internationally renowned for its practice-oriented conservation studies; it has also – and especially – made a name for itself through its international projects in India, Nepal, Mongolia, China and most recently in Thailand.

Gabriela Krist has succeeded in using these projects not only for the benefit of students of conservation studies and graduates of the Angewandte, but also of the teaching staff and team of associates. Research in the conservation sciences is intensifying abroad in the form of theses, dissertations, diplomas and pre-diplomas, guaranteeing progress in further education. It also means that development work is being done and cooperative ventures are being implemented with important institutions in the key countries, which are now initiating their own conservation study programmes. As regards this last point, it is incumbent on us to provide assistance. Until now, nine students from Mongolia, China and India have been enrolled at the Institute so that within the scope of scholarships they may further continue their PhD work (ÖAD-Ernst Mach). Austria has been in the fortunate situation since the middle of the last century of having academic conservation programmes at its disposal. The Angewandte has taken on a pioneering role in this, most notably in the field of metal conservation.

The Institute's international activities all started in the north of India, in Nako at the Tibetan border. Between 2004 and 2010, a project was ventured on here and successfully accomplished the research and conservation of a Buddhist temple complex. Integrated into a FWF research project – two associates completed their doctoral thesis – many students, graduates and staff members took part in the annual campaign on site and gathered important experience. The project was immortalised in 2016 in the brilliantly illustrated publication *Nako – Research and Conservation in the Western Himalayas*. Today, the Institute is primarily active in the south of India, at Trivandrum, Kerala. The agenda here includes the development of preservation strategies for collections in sub-tropical regions and the support of the Napier Museum in the creation of a modern storage for its collections and the updating of their exhibition concept. Since 2016, four missions – workshops – have been organised in Trivandrum together with the Institute's team; more than sixty people from all over India took part. The Institute's activities in India were further supported and reinforced on state level by a MoU between the Federal Chancellery and the Ministry of Culture of the Republic of India, which explicitly provides for cooperation in the field of conservation.

The Institute has been active in Nepal since 2010, mainly at the Royal Palace and Durbar Square in Patan, a UNESCO World Heritage Site. Immediately after the earthquake in 2015, together with Gabriela Krist, I appealed to the Foreign Ministry, the Austrian Development Agency (ADA) and the Federal Chancellery (BKA – Bundeskanzleramt) to organise our support to help this natural catastrophe. Since then, the team and students of the Institute, together with local institutions and artisans, have implemented substantial projects, thus contributing to the reconstruction and conservation of Nepal's important cultural heritage.

Thirteen work campaigns by the Institute's team have taken place in Nepal since 2010.

In China, Liangren Zhang, at that time from the North West University Xian (NWU), Gabriela Krist, Brigitte Winklehner (EPU) and Sabine Ladstätter (Austrian Archaeological Institute, Academy of Sciences) developed the concept for a conference series with the title "Archaeology and Conservation along the Silk Road". The first international conference took place in May 2014 in Xi'an, the second in May 2016 at the Nanjing University, as Liangren Zhang had switched to this institution. Last month the Nanjing conference postprints were published in the Institute's own series of publications that deal with the wide range of current research projects on the Silk Road and acknowledge the archaeologists and conservators in this interdisciplinary cooperation. The next Silk Road conference was held in November 2018 in Iran.

In Mongolia the main activities concern the setting up of a relevant programme of studies and the training of conservation specialists, which have been supported by the Angewandte for several years now. Six workshops have been organised since 2014. The focus here is on stone conservation and the revival of lost painting techniques and traditions within the framework of the pilot project "Analysis and Conservation of Polychromy in the Bogd Khan Palace, Summer Residence of the Mongolian Dalai Lama."

Thailand and the Silpakorn University in Bangkok wish to establish a position for themselves as a centre and contact point for conservation studies in Southeast Asia. Here, too, the Institute is offering aid in setting up and equipping a Conservation Centre and in the training of specialists and teachers. At present the Angewandte is working together with the Silpakorn University on a new Joint Master's Study programme which will come into force in October 2019 and open up new perspectives in the international conservation of cultural assets.

A further international project also involved our Chinese and Indian partners, likewise East European universities with programmes devoted to conservation: the International Conservation Summer Schools, as yet taking place annually at the Institute since 2014; up until now, 58 students from the partner countries have been able to gain insights into conservation practices at the Angewandte. As of next year, the Summer Schools will take place on a rotating basis in China, India, Mongolia and Austria; in 2019 the NWU in Xi'an will host our students.

We have to thank the university networks Eurasia-Pacific Uninet (EPU) and the European Academic University Network (ASEA), also the Austrian Exchange Service (OeAD), which all these years have provided the financial basis for the international cooperation and manifold projects of the Angewandte's conservation institute, also the Republic of Austria, which has supported the Angewandte's commitment after the earthquake catastrophe in Nepal. The Angewandte also wishes to thank the many international partners from the multifarious institutions that have worked with us: Northwest University Xi'an (NWU), Nanjing University, Central South University of Forestry and Technology China, National Museum Institute New Delhi (NMI), Indian National Trust for Art and Cultural Heritage (INTACH), government of Kerala, National Centre for Cultural Heritage Mongolia, the Bogd Khaan Palace Museum, the Mongolian State University of Arts and Culture, the Kathmandu Valley Preservation Trust, the Patan Museum and Silpakorn University Thailand. All these institutions are associated with us through valid MoUs.

The Institute will be endowed this year with a UNESCO Chair, giving the University of Applied Arts – the Angewandte – visible presence within the World Heritage conservation campaign, and enabling it to accomplish an international contribution here. In this book project we have encouraged the Institute to venture beyond the academic framework of conservation research and to present personal contributions about the multifaceted projects: from members of the Institute, from graduates and from partner organisations. This gives us an opportunity of sharing their personal insights, which they have won in the long years of commitment to the international conservation of cultural assets and to cooperative ventures.

Foreword

BRIGITTE WINKLEHNER

former President of Eurasia-Pacific Uninet

University of Applied Arts Vienna: A Strong Partner in the Internationalisation of the Austrian Universities with Asia within Eurasia-Pacific Uninet

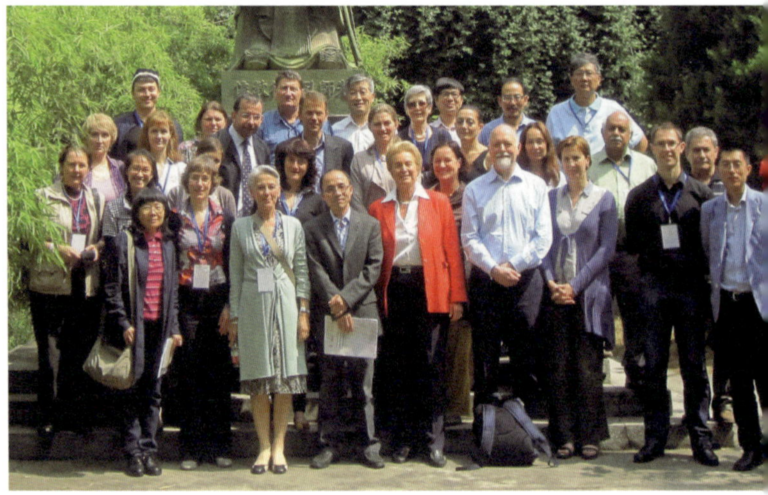

Fig. 1: First Silk Road Conference "Archaeology and Conservation along the Silk Road" in 2014: Gabriela Krist, Liangran Zhang and Brigitte Winklehner in the centre.

Eurasia-Pacific Uninet (EPU) was founded in 2000 with financial support from the Austrian Ministry of Education, Science and Culture (BMBWF) and the former Austrian Board of Science and Technology Development as an autonomous network under one single body for the scientific cooperation of Austrian universities with partner institutions in East Asia, Central Asia, South Asia and the Pacific Region. Since its official start in 2003, the network has grown very quickly, adding 80 members, including 32 Austrian and 48 members in six Asian countries (mainly in China and Central Asia) by 2005.

According to a 2010 study of the European Commission and its European Union Delegation in China, the Eurasia-Pacific Uninet had become the largest autonomous network of single member states of the European Union that targeted cooperation with China and other Asian countries in the field of education, science and research. At this point the cooperation comprised 140 member institutions from 13 Asian countries. As one of the smaller countries in the European Union and its governmental entities, Austria has been very much in favour of such a coordinated and unified approach to international higher education and research cooperation.

From the beginning of EPU, the University of Applied Arts Vienna – with long-term president Gerald Bast and the University's Institute of Conservation headed by Gabriela Krist – has always been an appreciated partner of the Eurasia-Pacific Uninet. Gabriela Krist has been a very strong and most creative and insistent EPU-institutional coordinator, setting up manifold sustainable activities such as joint research projects, conferences, faculty and student exchanges, training activities and summer schools in several different Asian partner countries.

Gabriela Krist, as a scientist and expert in conservation and scientific documentation of objects of art and architecture of very diverse materials, has not only been a most committed teacher and scientific trainer to her students at her institute, but also a highly respected expert for teaching and training activities in research, documentation and practical conservation work in Asian partner countries. For many years, she has cooperated with partners in China, Mongolia, Nepal and India and succeeded in setting up long-term partnerships of mutual understanding and scientific and cultural policy benefits for the countries and institutions she has been working with.

The activities of Gabriela Krist were partially financed with Eurasia-Pacific Uninet budgets granted to the network by the Austrian Ministry of Science and Research and the support of the Austrian Agency for International Cooperation in Education and Research (OeAD). Some co-funding was provided by the University of Applied Arts Vienna and Asian partner institutions. Her most precious projects always managed to obtain interest and support from Austrian embassies and specific ministries in Asian partner countries.

Since 2004, when her team engaged in the conservation of a temple complex in Nako, Himachal Pradesh, India, Gabriela Krist has stressed the importance of getting feedback, not only from local authorities and persons in charge, but also from the local population in order to address the needs of monument protection and sustainability in tourism activities. Due to Krist's work in India and Nepal, her expertise has been requested and valued by local communities following some of the natural disasters in years past. Respect is also due to Gabriela Krist Summer School projects, organised in cooperation with the National Museum Institute, a renowned conservation training and research institution in New Delhi, India.

In 2012, the Chinese government discussed a "New Silk Road" and planned a revitalisation of the ancient cultural and commercial links between Europe and Asia via the Silk Road countries by building a large commercial linkage over the ancient tracks through Central Asia; accordingly, questions of preservation and protection of cultural heritage along the road also arose. Since its foundation, the Eurasia-Pacific Uninet was able to successfully crosslink its activities in China with the interests of its Central Asian partner institutions. When asked by Northwest University in Xian, in 2011, to set up links for archaeological and conservation research in the said area, we turned to partners in Central Asia and Austrian institutions, namely the Austrian Institute of Archaeology (ÖAI) and the University of Applied Arts Vienna, to cooperate in the field of "Archaeology, Preservation and Conservation of Cultural Relics along the Silk Road Countries".

We are most grateful to Gabriela Krist for taking up this initiative by starting a very successful series of conferences on this topic, the first held in 2014 at the Northwest University in Xian, together with renowned archaeologist Liangren Zhang (Fig. 1). The second conference took place at Nanjing University, again organised by Gabriela Krist and her Chinese partner Liangren Zhang in 2016. The third conference on behalf of this important topic, initiated by the Iranian Research Institute of Cultural Heritage and Tourism (RICHT) took place in November 2018 in Tabriz, Iran. It was organised with the cooperation of RICHT, Nanjing University and the University of Applied Arts Vienna.

EPU also appreciates Gabriela Krist and her Institute's important cooperation with Mongolia, a significant partner country within the network. On the occasion of the Austrian Days in Mongolia in June 2015, the Institute of Conservation held a workshop on "Cultural Heritage and Conservation Science", which resulted in a new partnership for Eurasia-Pacific Uninet with the Mongolian State University of Arts and Culture in Ulaanbaatar. This year, the team from the Institute has started with practical conservation work on some cultural relics in Mongolia.

All these examples of the many contributions of the University of Applied Arts Vienna and its Institute of Conservation to the activities of Eurasia-Pacific Uninet show how the tireless efforts of a very dedicated partner and network institutional coordinator, Gabriela Krist, have contributed to the overall success of Eurasia-Pacific Uninet in Austria and its partner countries in Asia. Gabriela Krist and her team, with their activities, have truly gone beyond borders and have contributed to the international reputation of the University of Applied Arts Vienna in Asia.

India

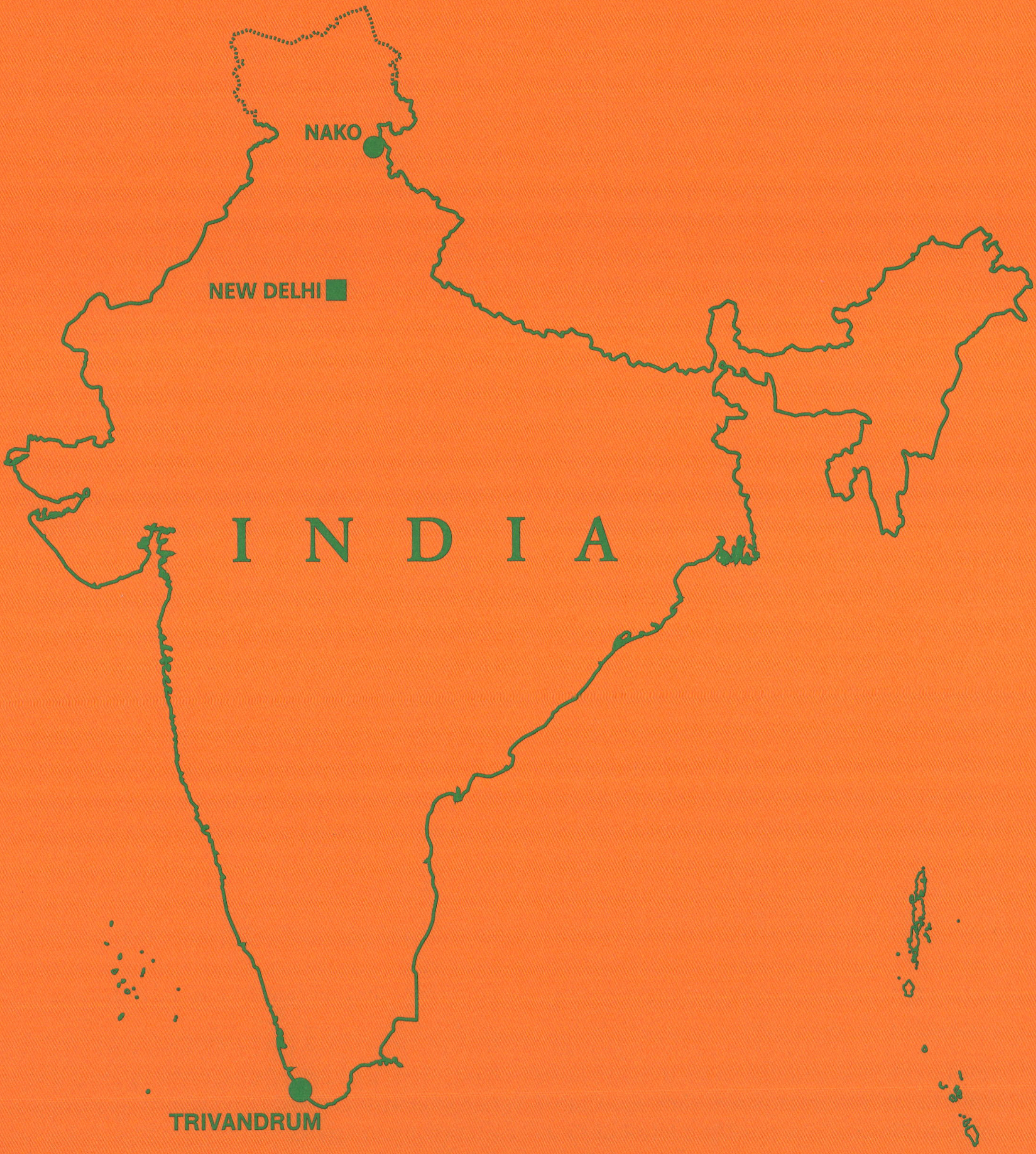

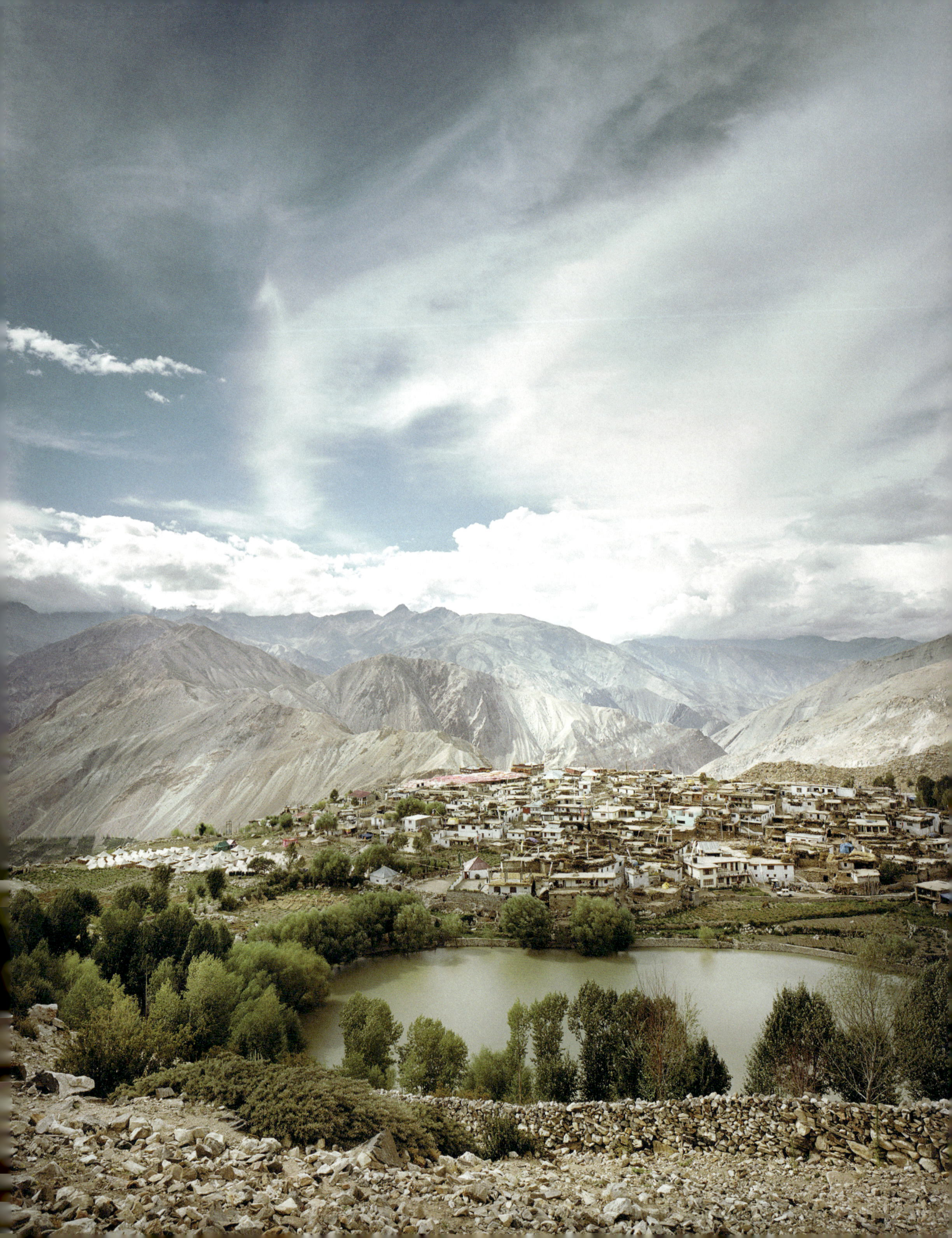

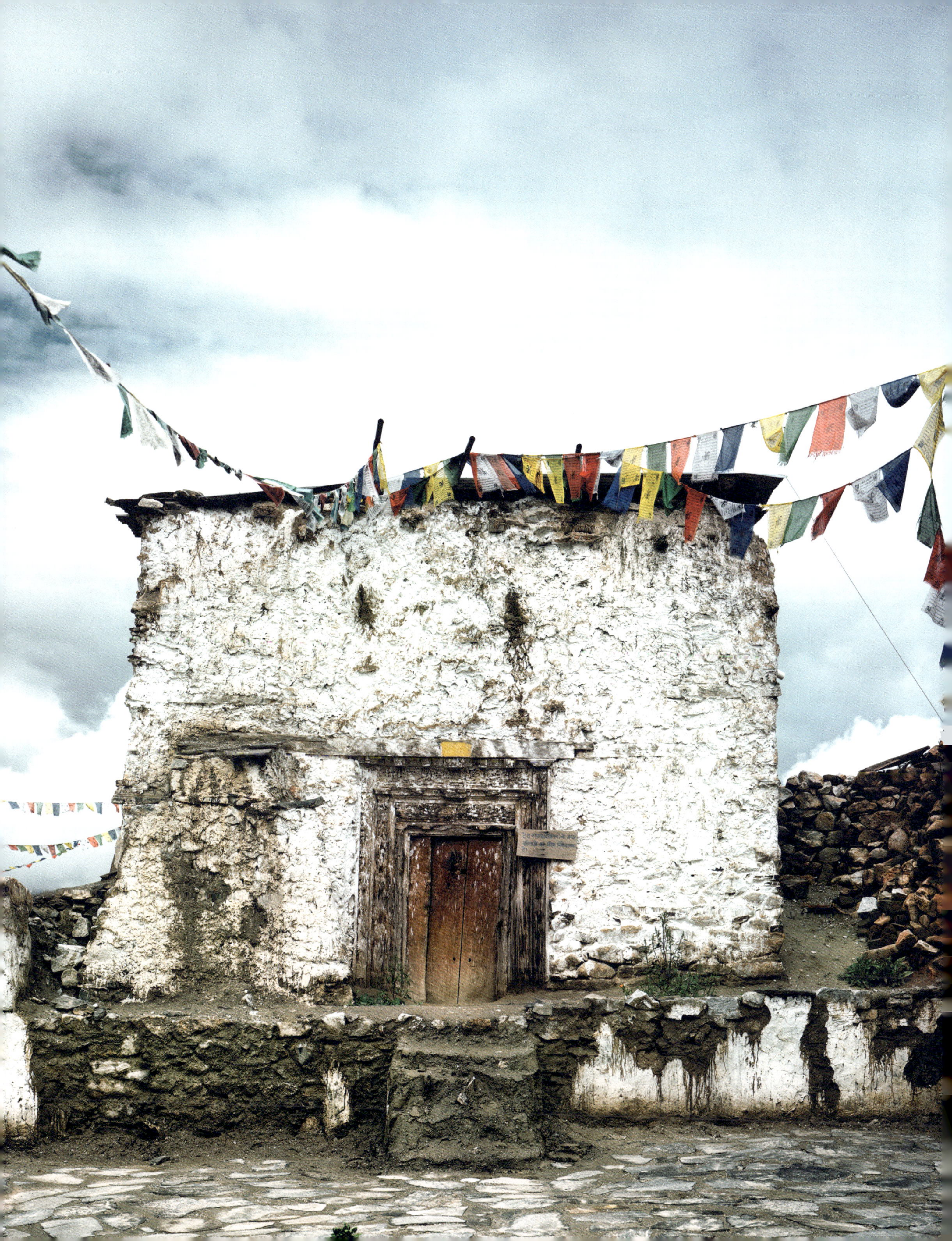

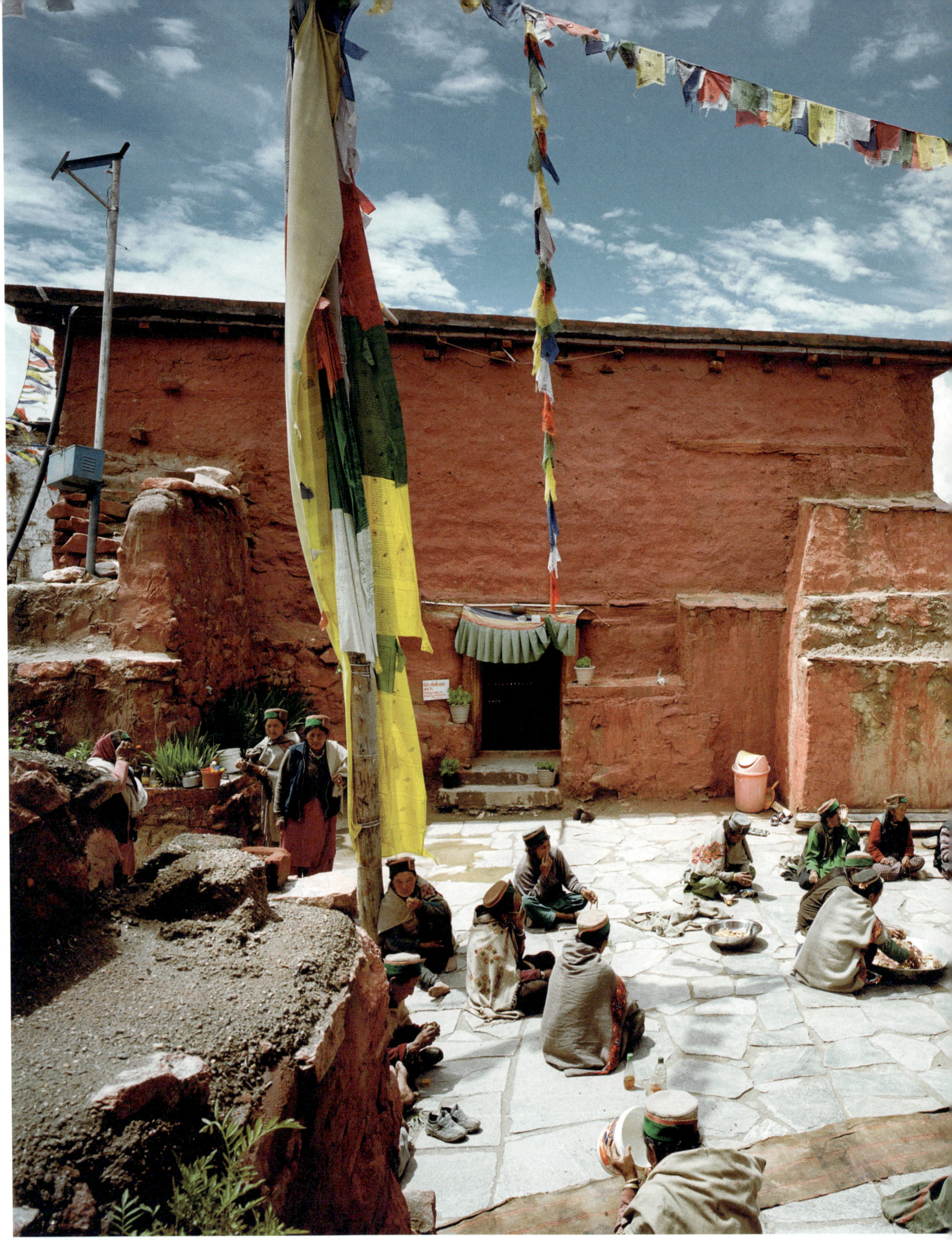

previous pages:
Fig. 1: Nako village, embedded in the southwest slope of the Himalayan mountain massif, 2007
Fig. 2: “White Temple” Karchung Lhakhang, one of the four temples of the complex, 2007

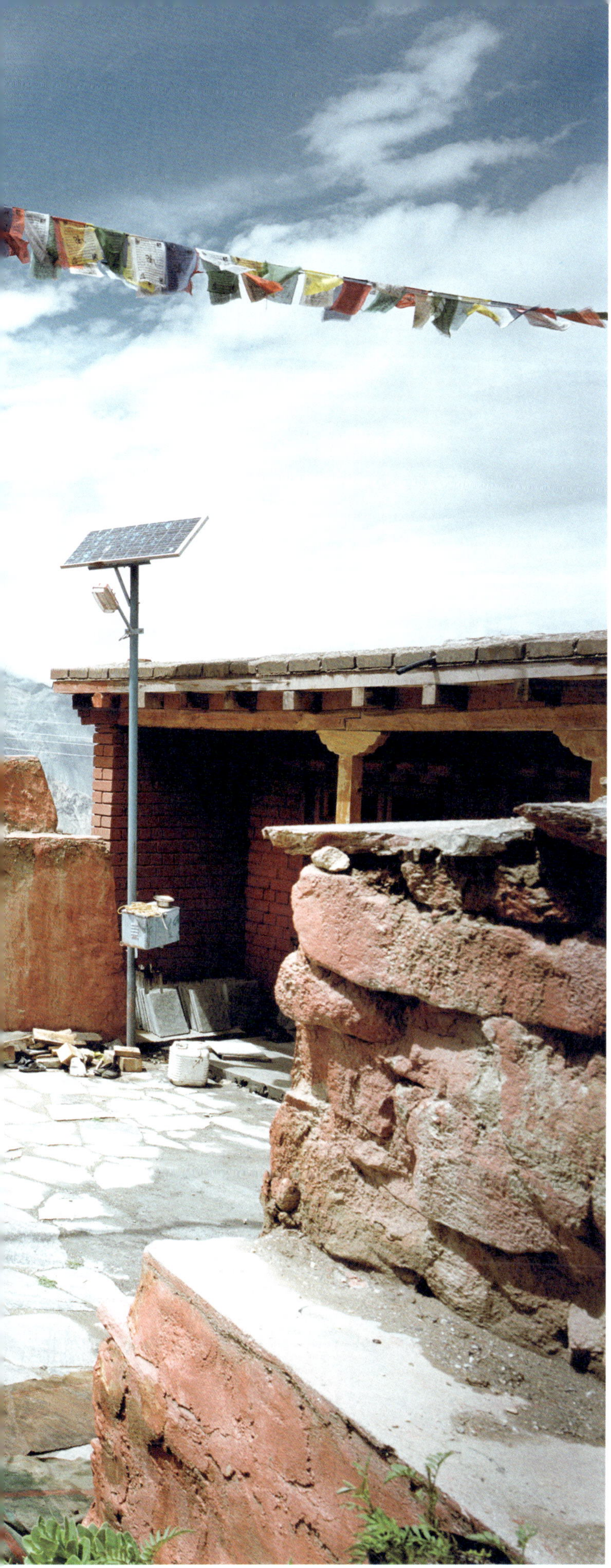

Fig. 3: Courtyard in front of the “Main Temple” or “Translator’s Temple” Lotsawa Lhakhang, 2007

Incredible India!

GABRIELA KRIST

About Nako "…at the ends of the earth with nothing beyond…"

Taking Francke's famous quotation from his work *Antiquities of Indian Tibet* as the beginning of my introduction to the Nako project – our most challenging international undertaking so far – indicates how much I felt like this great researcher and world traveller when I approached the village for the first time in May 2005. On our long journey, in Jeeps, from New Delhi, passing Shimla and Rampur, the drivers wished to smoke a last cigarette on this final and very hazardous leg, about 40 km from the Sutlej River Valley on the National Highway 22, always climbing up and up in never-ending curves — I called it "the long and winding road…" after the famous Beatles song. We were standing on a stone block in the middle of nowhere with the most incredible view of the Himalayan mountains, and it was breathtaking (Fig. 1). Never before or since have I had this feeling of being so far away from home, in a completely different world, not mine but very close to my heart — a child's dream come true. A heavy snowstorm was our welcome at Nako; cold rooms, frozen water at the newly opened Reo Purgil Hotel (the top address in town) – a nearly 10-year-long adventure began.

What awaited us the following day, when we first entered the Nako Gompa, was even better. The four temples around the courtyard offered an unspectacular view from the outside (Fig. 2-3), but what could we see in the dark interiors? Fine, delicate wall paintings together with clay sculptures and colourful polychrome wooden ceilings formed the most beautiful cultural ensemble ever seen (Fig. 4). We knew that it would be hard, but a privilege to work there.

Since then, that first exposure to a new culture and region, much has changed. We came every summer from 2004-2010 onwards (Fig. 5-6), and Nako had a strong and sustainable impact on all of us, not only professionally but also personally. We gained our own experiences, met friends, learnt about the hard mountainous life and got involved in the most stimulating, most difficult and challenging conservation project ever.

Ernst Bacher, then Conservator General of the Austrian Bundesdenkmalamt (Federal Monuments Office), brought us to Nako. He was the chairman of the "Nako Research and Preservation Project" (L335-N19), which started in 2002 and was directed by Deborah Klimburg-Salter. Bacher had the difficult task of establishing a conservation masterplan for the Buddhist temple complex at Nako; the team around Klimburg-Salter was responsible for art-historical research, Romi Khosla, the chief architect, involved for architectural conservation, and we — the Institute of Conservation at the University of Applied Arts Vienna — received the opportunity and challenge to undertake the preservation and conservation of the temple interiors.

The Austrian Science Fund (FWF) sponsored our project "Scientific Study of the Artwork at Nako 2007-2011", which enabled us to carry out primary conservation research, laying the foundation for subsequent conservation work. In the framework of two dissertations, three diploma theses and four undergraduate theses, important aspects of the building and artistic materials and techniques used at Nako were studied and appropriate conservation methods developed.

Additional support for the project was given by the Austrian Development Agency (ADA), the Eurasia-Pacific Uninet (EPU), the University of Applied Arts Vienna and the Cultural Forum of the Austrian Embassy in New Delhi.

The National Research Laboratory for Conservation of Cultural Property in Lucknow and later the National Museum Institute (NMI), Conservation Department, New Delhi, in the capacity of my old friend M. V. Nair, and the various Committees at Nako, e.g. The Buddhist Society, the Nako Youth Club, were the helpful and supporting local partners.

His Holiness, the 14th Dalai Lama Tenzin Gyatso came to Nako in summer 2007 to deliver his teachings on the "Thirty-Seven Practices of a Bodhisattva" to 8,000 pilgrims of the Hangrang Valley, an unforgettable event (Fig. 7). He reconsecrated the Nako Gompa and opened the museum. This gave us the chance to speak with him about our work and to introduce the audience to the conservation projects we had completed so far.

What has been achieved from 2004 to 2010? Conservation of the Translator's and the Upper Temple (Lotsawa Lhakhang and Lhakhang Gongma), and documentation of the two smaller temples, which were secured as much as possible. Wall paintings, clay sculptures and painted wooden ceilings received treatment. After unsuccessful trials and tests with modern concepts, our conservation philosophy favoured local traditional materials – learnt and experienced in Nako – and minimal intervention. This was a different approach from other sites of the region, where reconstruction measures and overpainting dominate the conservation results.

With the help of the locals, a museum could be established; furthermore arrangements were made for a workshop on building maintenance and a training course for monks for the handling and storage of thangkas. The thangka collection of the village was surveyed, documented, secured and properly stored; some objects underwent exemplary conservation at our workshops in Vienna. In addition two documentary films were produced by Austrian State Television (ORF) filmmaker Gundi Lamprecht. A Nako photo exhibition at the National Museum in New Delhi, and four similar events in Vienna, contributed to the public awareness of Nako's most beautiful but fragile natural and cultural landscape.

For years we worked on our Nako book, finally published in 2016 with the sponsorship of the FWF. The book does not pretend to be complete and illustrate all aspects of the complex Nako village and site. Moreover, owing to the interdisciplinary nature of the authors, several aspects are highlighted, others only touched on. Sometimes there are different opinions, e.g. in dating or contributions to different styles and schools, but I believe that this will encourage and stimulate future research and in-depth studies. The conservation work done by our team is surely put in focus, as research and practical conservation work at Nako kept us busy for nearly one decade.

For professional help and the hard work in Nako, I wish to thank my team, first of all my staff at the institute – Tatjana Bayerová, Marija Milchin, Kathrin Schmidt and Manfred Trummer – and furthermore my former colleagues, especially Stefan Oláh for his wonderful photographs, Martina Griesser-Stermscheg for her work for and at the Nako museum, and Marie Gruber for her continuous help to coordinate Nako missions. Without the commitment, full involvement and professional expertise of each individual, the project would not have been possible. Sincere thanks go also to a long list of our former students who worked with us on the site.

At last, my thoughts go to Ernst Bacher, who initiated the project and who left us much too early in 2006. I speak for my whole team in saying that we are grateful for his always wise and knowledgeable advice and for his kindness as teacher and friend. Our work at Nako is dedicated to him.

Francke, A.H., *Antiquities of Indian Tibet, Part I: Personal Narrative, Archaeological Survey of India, New Imperial Series, Vol. XXXVIII*, Calcutta 1914.

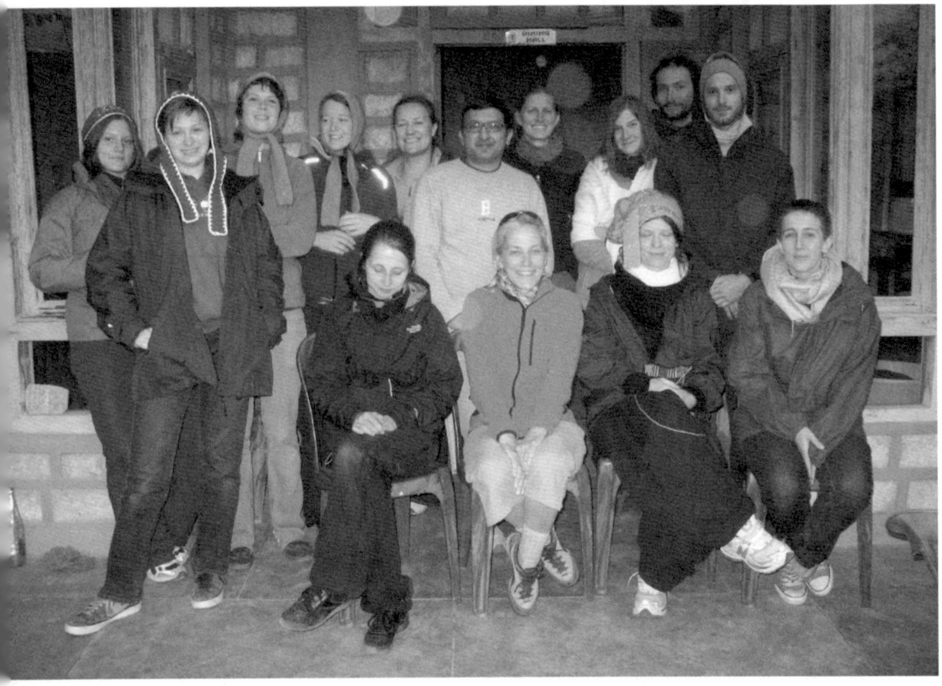

Fig. 5: The Institute's team in Nako 2008

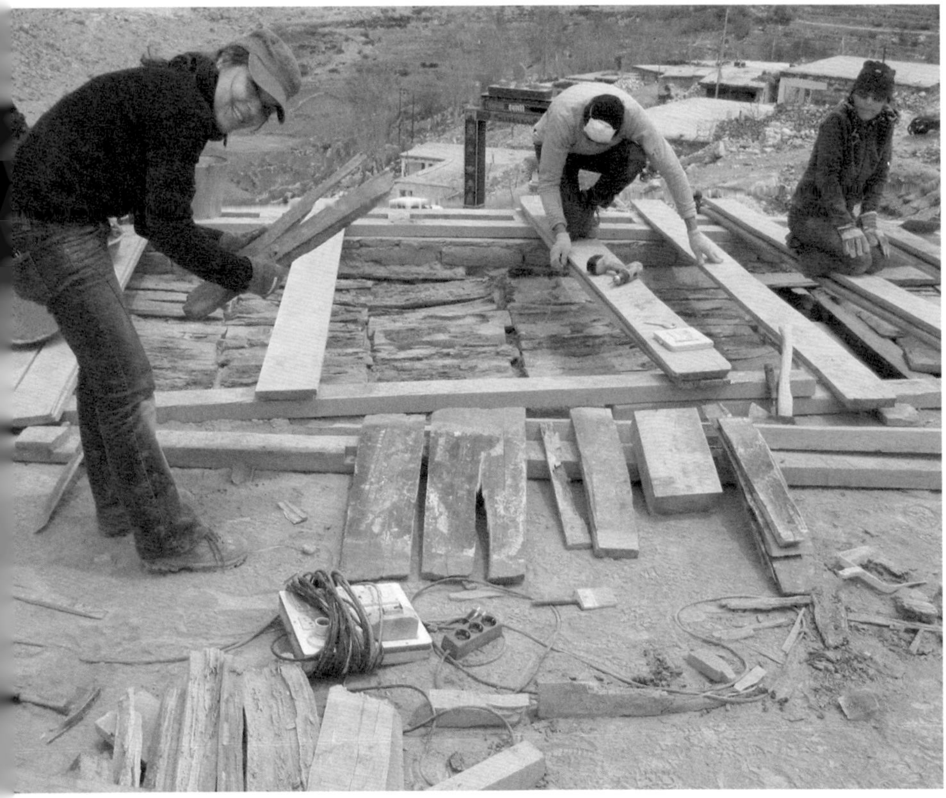

Fig. 6: Redistribution of polychrome ceiling panels of the “Upper Temple” Lhakhang Gongma, May 2005

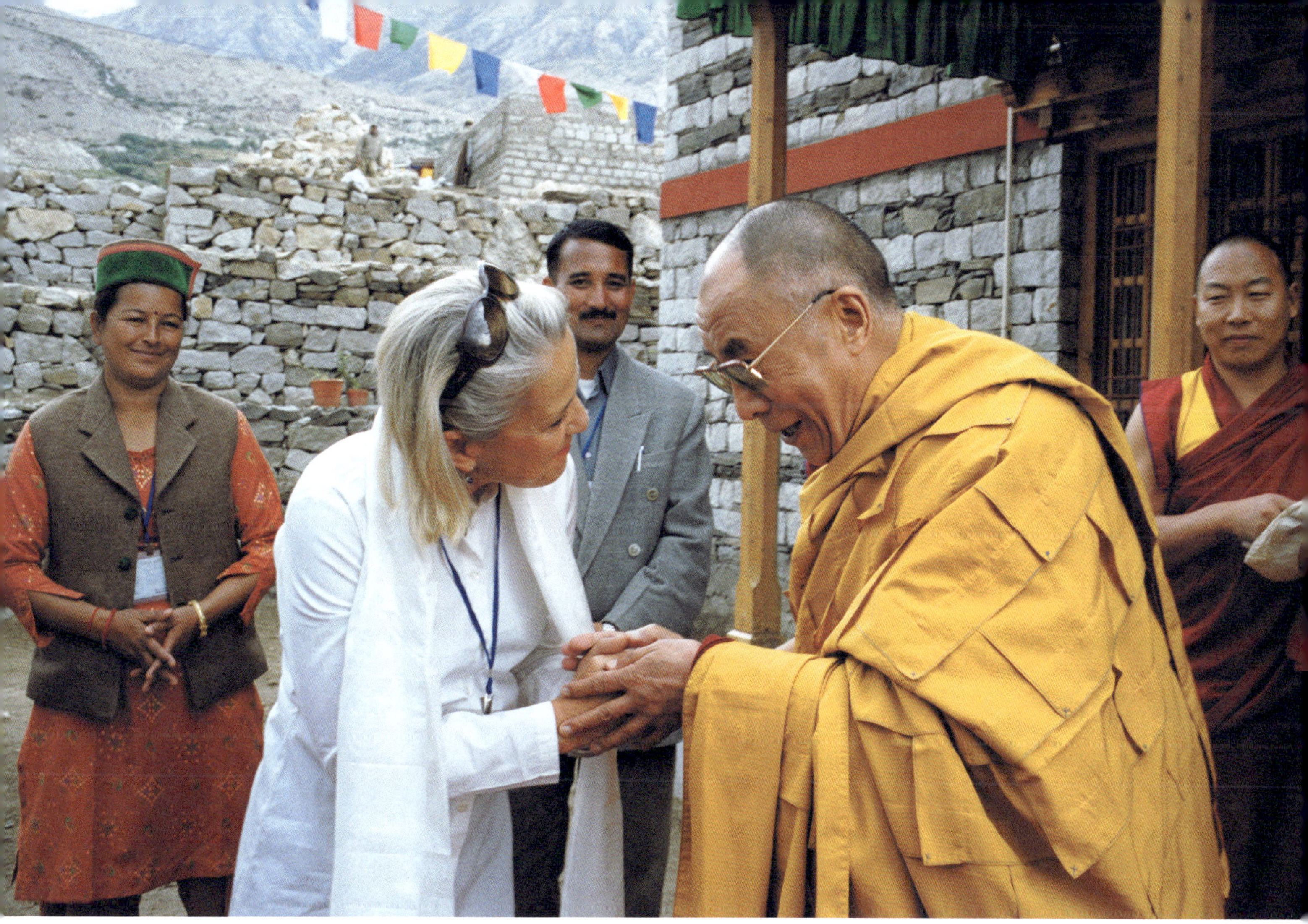

Fig. 7: Meeting His Holiness, the 14th Dalai Lama Tenzin Gyatso in 2007

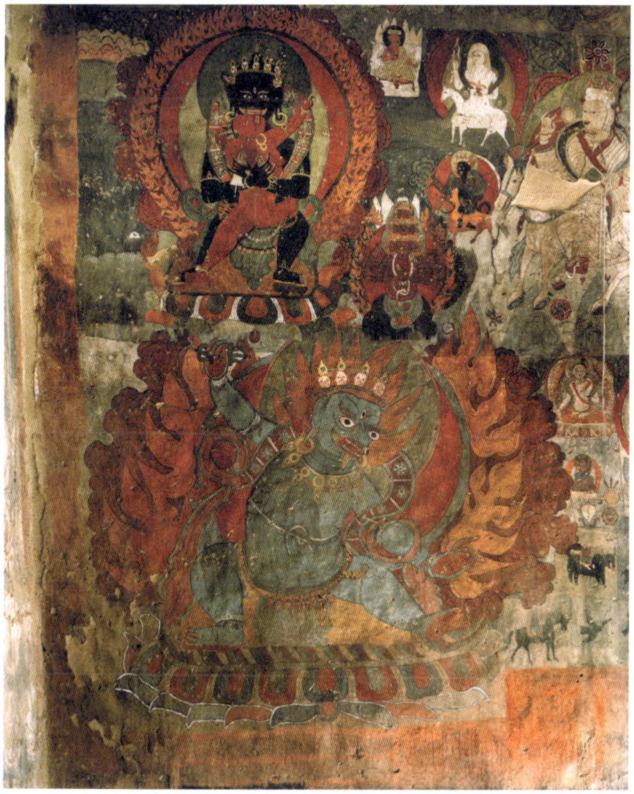

Fig. 4: Delicate wall paintings inside Lotsawa Lhakhang, 2007

next page: Fig. 8: Interiors of Lhakhang Gongma, 2007

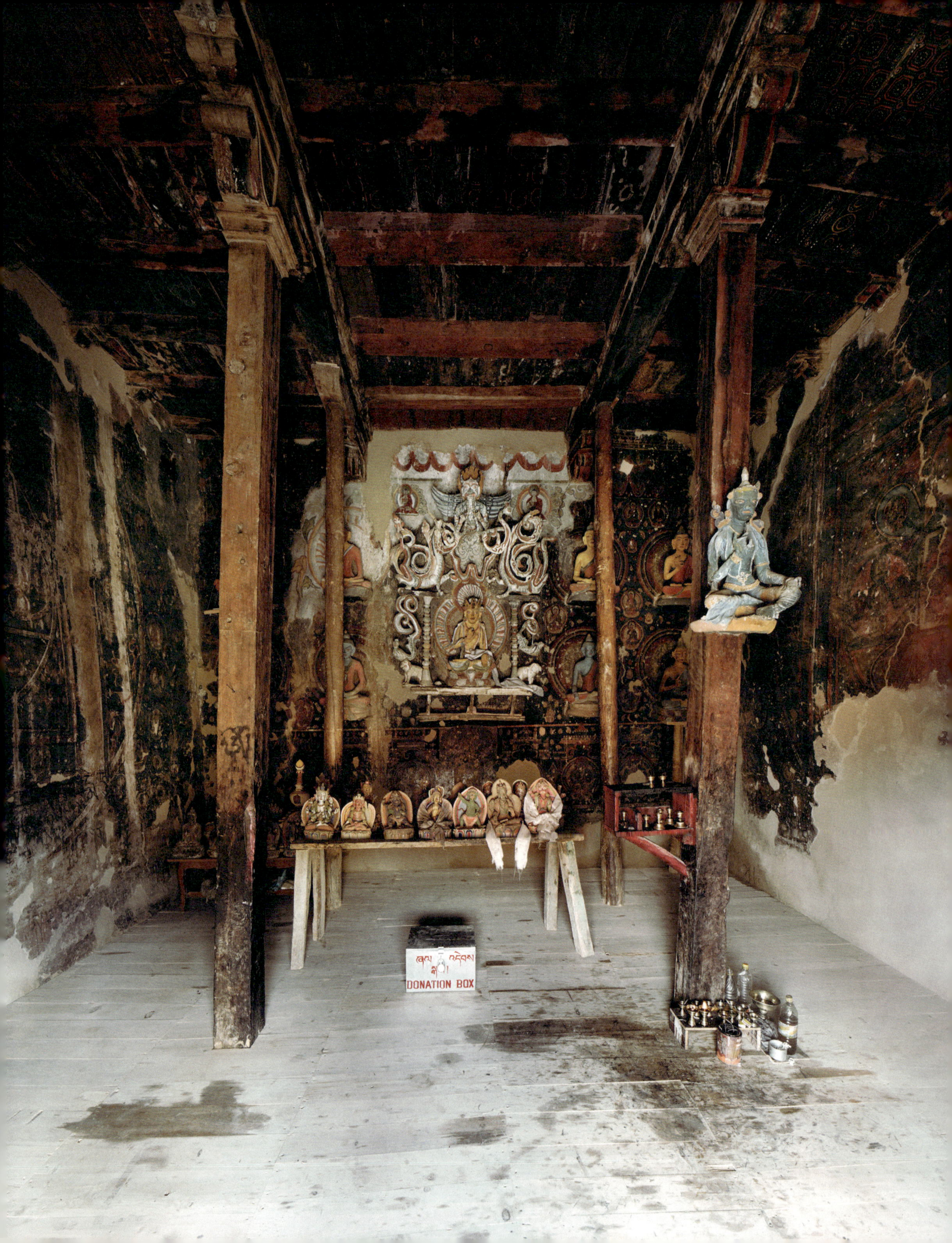
DONATION BOX

Factsheet Nako

PROJECT	NAKO: Research and Conservation in the Western Himalayas	DURATION	2004-2010
HEADED BY	Gabriela Krist	INITIATED BY	Ernst Bacher

PARTNER INSTITUTIONS

Austrian Cultural Forum New Delhi
Hangrang Organisation
Nako Youth Club
Nako Tsug Lakhang (Nako Buddhist Society)
National Museum Institute New Delhi (NMI), Department of Conservation
National Research Laboratory for Conservation of Cultural Property Lucknow (NRLC)
University of Vienna, Department of Art History
Visva-Bharati, Department for Indo-Tibetan Studies
World Monuments Fund (WMF)
Geological Survey of Austria, Department Mineral Resources
Institute of Applied Geology, University of Natural Resources and Life Sciences Vienna
STRABAG Societas Europaea
Chair of Geology and Economic Geology, Montanuniversität Leoben
Conservation Science Department, KHM Vienna
Department of Geography and Regional Research, University of Vienna
Department of Geodynamics and Sedimentology, University of Vienna
Faculty of Philological and Cultural Studies, University of Vienna
Department of Ecophysiology and Functional Anatomy of Plants, University of Vienna
Department of Art History, University of Vienna

FUNDED BY

Austrian Science Fund (FWF)
Austrian Development Agency (ADA)
Eurasia-Pacific-UniNet (EPU)
University of Applied Arts Vienna

TEAM MEMBERS

Ernst Bacher, Tatjana Bayerová, Susanne Beseler, Charu Chodry, Florian Flicker, Eva Götz, Lisa Gräber, Martina Griesser-Stermscheg, Maria Gruber, Michael Höflinger, Stefan Kainz, Regina Knaller, Gabriela Krist, U.S. Laal, G. Laal, Gundi Lamprecht, Marija Milchin, Birgit Müllauer, M.V. Nair, Hary Narain, Helmut Neumayer, Georg Oberlechner, Stefan Oláh, Roberta Renz, Sandeep Sikka, Kathrin Schmidt, Christoph Tinzl, Manfred Trummer

STUDENTS INVOLVED

Matea Ban, Andrea Hackel, Charlotte Holzer, Stefan Karacsonyi, Judith Kern, Katharina Kohler, Susanne Leiner, Katherina Mergl, Maria Perwög, Martin Pliessnig, Gunn Pöllnitz, Edgar Skomorowski, Susanne Spornberger, Bettina Unterberger

The Nako Story

TATJANA
BAYEROVÁ

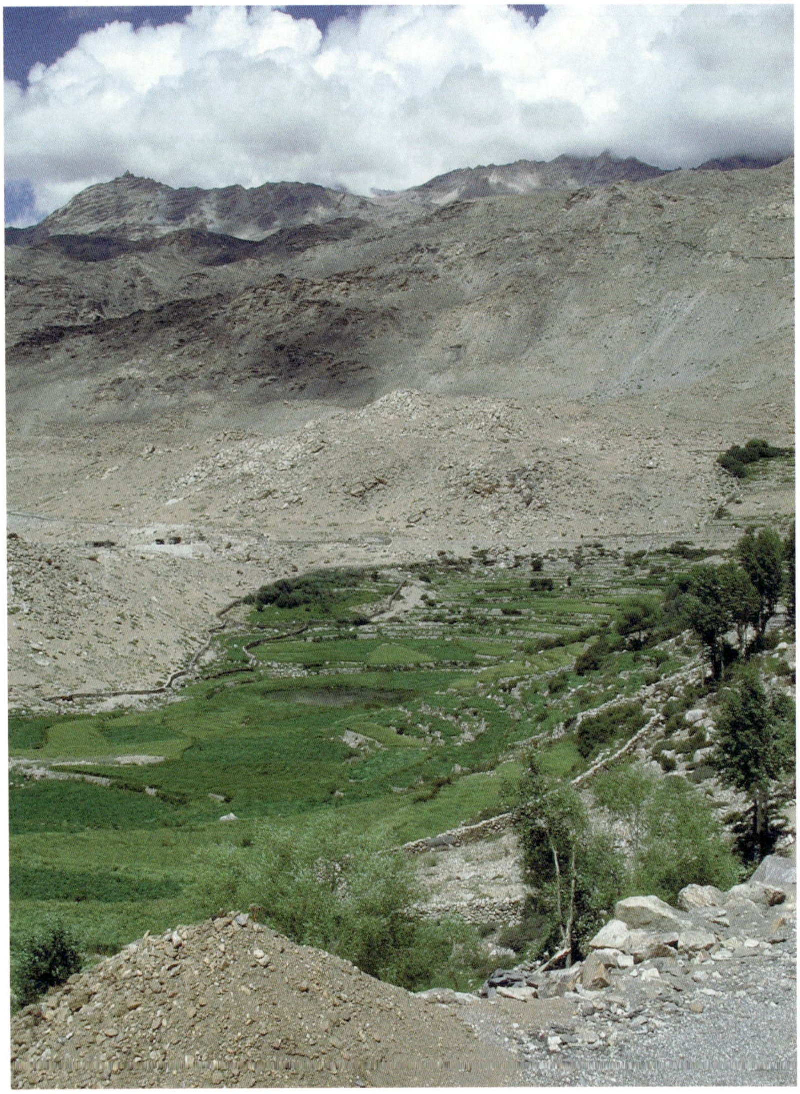

Fig. 1: Emerald green fields around Nako

Working Missions and Experiences

Nako…I close my eyes and in one second I see dozens of images…bright green fields (Fig. 1), dark and mysterious temples, Manish´s flowers on the table, Prajnaparamita statue with her hand missing, the Milky Way, white scarves around our necks, the smell of daal, the grumble of the generator, snowy Reo Purgyil, a bizarre depiction of the realm of hungry ghosts, colourful prayer flags…Nako, a small village nestled in Himalayan Mountains in the middle of nowhere, for decades not known to any one of us, but leaving an indelible mark for ever in all of our hearts.

Nako lays in the Indian part of the Western Himalayas at an altitude of 3,660 m (12,007 feet) above sea level, in the Kinnaur District of the North Indian state Himachal Pradesh, a stone's throw from the Chinese border of the Tibetan Autonomous Region (TAR). The village settlement consists of a historic village centre with traditional dwellings, farm buildings, communal and religious structures that were, and still are, built using vernacular stone/earth/wood building techniques. In the south-western corner there is the Buddhist Temple complex. The Tibetan-Buddhist faith is the cultural factor which determines all aspects of life of the approximately 600 village inhabitants (Fig. 2-3).

The temple compound was once one of the main Buddhist centres in the Western Himalayas and today is an important source for the study of early and later Buddhist culture in the Himalayan region. It was founded in the territory of the former Purang-Guge kingdom during its golden age in the 11th/12th centuries, and the Purang-Guge rulers were the ones who initiated the period of the re-introduction of Buddhism, today known as the second propagation of Buddhism in Tibet. One of the most important historical figures from this time is Rinchen Zangpo, the "Great Translator", who became a driving force of the teaching and spreading of Buddhism. His life is rich in legends, and one of those legends says that Rinchen Zangpo founded 108 temples (a sacred Buddhist number), among which Nako was included. However, there is no evidence that Rinchen Zangpo ever reached Nako. The complex was erected under the patronage of a local prince on an ancient pilgrimage route leading from Mount Kailash via Ladakh to northern Pakistan, which was used at least since the early 13th century. Later, Nako was not an active monastery for a long period of time, but the complex was maintained by villagers and the Nako Buddhist Association. Nevertheless, the temples continuously served as a place of worship for the villagers and inhabitants of the whole valley. The Chinese "Cultural Revolution" from 1966 on led to the destruction of the majority of Tibetan religious buildings in Tibet and a lot of the artwork and evidence of Indo-Tibetan history was lost. Fortunately, the Nako temple complex on the Indian side has survived. Its proximity and strong cultural connection to Western Tibet makes it a valuable living record of the social and cultural history of the region in the 12th century. Also because of its artistic qualities, the temple complex is thus one of the most important and unique art works of its kind in the world. The year 2007 was an important turning point in the modern history of the complex. In August 2007, His Holiness the 14th Dalai Lama visited Nako and reconsecrated the temple complex. Since then, two lamas from the Drukpa Monastery in Bhunter, Kullu Valley, permanently reside in the Nako monastery, which now belongs to Venerable Somang Rinpoche, a Nako-born lama and tulku.

The compound consists of four temples that form a courtyard space in the centre: the Lotsawa Lhakhang (Translator's Temple or Main Temple), the largest and most important one, the Lhakhang Gongma (Upper Temple), and two smaller temples, the Gyaphagpa Lhakhang and the Karchung Lhakhang (Small White Temple). The temples are built in a purely West Tibetan architectural style; all of them are simple single-storey buildings made of unfired earthen bricks, with one door opening, flat earthen roofs and, besides the largest temple, they are of an almost cubic shape. Their simple exterior is in sharp contrast to the rich interior decoration: both larger temples are embellished with marvellous original wall paintings from the 12th century, polychrome clay sculptures and painted wooden panel ceilings. In two smaller temples, solely large-scale, 16th century overpaintings are visible today, under which the original decoration can still be traced.

This wonderful architectural jewel in the Himalayas has recently started showing alarming signs of deterioration. Changing climatic patterns, rising ground water, frequently occurring earthquakes and constant human interventions have posed a serious threat to the existence of this living cultural heritage. The extensive damage and deterioration the site had suffered resulted in an urgent need for a comprehensive conservation programme and further preservation.

Our Nako story, lasting until 2010, started in 2004, when our institute got the chance to fulfil the conservation master plan for the Buddhist temple complex drafted by Ernst Bacher, former Conservator General of the Austrian Bundesdenkmalamt, and, after his unexpected death, finished by Gabriela Krist. The plan was based on the conservation and preservation of the complex as a whole, which was designed to consider all individual elements equally, so that the character of the complex would be preserved in its entirety. Because of the extreme geography and unfavourable working conditions – the remoteness of the site in the high mountains with no electricity, no infrastructure, and no transportation facilities – this task became a difficult, exciting, partly dangerous, but unforgettable challenge.

Each summer for seven years, the team, composed of members, students and alumni of the Institute and invited experts from Austria and India, spent some weeks in Nako to complete the work programme that was planned and prepared in Vienna prior to each work campaign. After the flight to New Delhi and comfortable transport with modern taxi cars to Shimla, an opening gate to Himalayas, the adventure started. When we looked at the non-existent tyre-tread patterns of the terrain Jeeps that were supposed to bring us to Nako, the first doubts were triggered as to whether we would ever reach the spot. The journey using National Highway 22, the most dangerous road in the world, accompanied by never-ending horn-honking before each curve, lasted more than twelve hours. The time spent in the Jeeps was an adventure on its own: the admirable skill of experienced mountain drivers, the amazing view of the panorama of the surrounding Himalayas and the deep canyon of the wild Sutlej River on one hand, the dread when looking at broken or completely cut-off road from landslides on the other. These mixed feeling were not comforted by reading signboards put up by the Border Roads Organisation (BRO) along the road – "Drive slow, not to heaven!", "Feel the curves, do not test them", "After whisky driving risky" and many more (Fig. 4). After successfully reaching our destination, some of us suffered from diarrhoea, some from mountain sickness, but all of us were glad and thankful to the Himalayan gods that we were alive.

Now the working programme could start. Each morning breakfast awaited us in the dining room decorated with flowers from Manish, a small boy working in the hotel where we were accommodated. Then we filled bottles with water purified with tablets and moved to the Sacred Gompa, which was approximately 700 m from the hotel. To reach the place we could take various footpaths through the village. We walked around the traditional houses with small courtyards, from which we were silently observed by the big and tender brown eyes of cows. Sometimes a group of village children surrounded us with their traditional request "one photo, one pen, one chocolate". Those of us who reached the temples as the first immediately started the diesel Powerking generators, which often worked only thanks to Manfred Trummer's patience and skilled hands. Then we dispersed to our various working spots on scaffolding built by Nepal helpers and started our nine-hour working day interrupted only by a lunch break and discussions with villagers, using our grimaces and gesticulations to overcome the language barrier (Fig. 5). Each member of the group had his or her particular task: mason work to secure the structural cracks together with the local mason Tashi, cleaning of wall painting surfaces, filling of numerous lacunae in murals and their consolidation, dismantling, cleaning and consolidation of the wooden ceiling panels in the Lhakhang Gongma, sieving of earth and preparation of earthen mortar necessary for partial plastering, cleaning and consolidation of polychrome clay sculptures in both bigger temples, safeguarding conservation intervention and proper storage of the temples´ thangka collection, stabilisation of the highly endangered murals in the Gyaphagpa Lhakhang and many more smaller daily routine tasks. Parallel to the conservation works there was also an on-going research programme. It included a comprehensive mapping of wall paintings in all four temples, their photo documentation and detailed description, climate monitoring, various on-site measurements and tests, collecting of samples and small trips to the quarries and places of origin of raw materials used. Subsequent material analyses addressed several scopes of research: the historic material and material technology, as well as parameters for material alteration and decay, and for applied conservation science. All these varied activities were sometimes accompanied with small conflicts, such as who, in which temple and for how long, needs the power source, prolongation cables or the best camera or who would clean the Hoover. Nevertheless, in the late afternoon all of us relaxed. We enjoyed tea breaks on the scaffolding, where Lamaji daily served us his delicious lemon tea. From time to time, villagers or small groups of tourists came to temples and observed our work, occasionally we were accompanied by little goats that had lost their way. Around six p.m. we started to stumble back to the hotel, tired but satisfied with the working progress, looking forward to the luxury of having a shower. After dinner, usually composed of different kinds of daal, sometimes refreshed by momos from the opposite buffet or pieces of salami and hard cheese that some of us still had carefully hidden in our backpack, we discussed what had been achieved by which group during the particular day. Enjoying the cold (but expensive!) Kingfisher beer, we typed the records and notices into our laptops, we selected and ordered the working photos shot during the day – this documentation later served as basis for our working reports. But, for two summers, there were other late evening work activities going on as well (Fig. 6). When the temples became dark and empty, a small group of us worked there to document the interior decoration using ultraviolet and infrared lights. Those nights belong to other unforgettable moments; we alone on the "Roof of the World", omnipresent silence interrupted only by the monotone noise of generator, the peak of Reo Purgyil in moonlight and stars that, never before and never since, seemed to be so close.

In the evenings, there were sometimes festivities organised by the Buddhist Association, Nako Youth Club and villagers. Local boys and girls dressed in the colourful costumes, embellished with the typical turquoise-coral headdress and jewels, performed their traditional dances, to which we were also dragged. The cultural input from our side was delivered mostly in the form of singing that was sometimes not only listenable but also really good (Fig. 7).

Despite a working week usually lasting seven days, we managed to take one or two weekend days off and explore the neighbourhood (Fig. 8), or visited some other Buddhist sites such as monasteries in Tabo, Lhalung or Dangkar.

The first days seemed extremely long, but as time went by, days became shorter and shorter, and suddenly it was the last day. This was marked by the cleaning of work tools, packing, careful recording of what stays in the local storage and what is necessary to be brought for the next year's campaign. And then, in the late afternoon, the last heart-touching ceremony started, when the whole team was decorated with white scarves – a symbol of respect and gratitude.

The next morning we got into jeeps and after the usual spill of a bucket of water on each jeep – the tradition for promising you would come back – we started the adrenaline-filled journey back. Exhausted, tired, but more or less satisfied with the job delivered, full of various experiences and memories, we were happy to go home and hoped to return again next year.

Writing this article and looking back from a distance of about ten years, I ask myself what were the most important, valuable aspects achieved, besides, of course, the essential core conservation, preservation and research programme. Conservation is usually considered to be an interdisciplinary field; I think that the whole Nako project proved the necessity and showed the fruits of tight collaboration that gradually developed between the various disciplines – conservators, conservation scientists, art historians, architects and other professionals. We learned that successful work demanded a constant willingness of all participants to compromise not only in a professional way but also in human behaviour. All of us were enriched professionally and all of us returned with our own personal stories, experiences and memories that will never be forgotten.

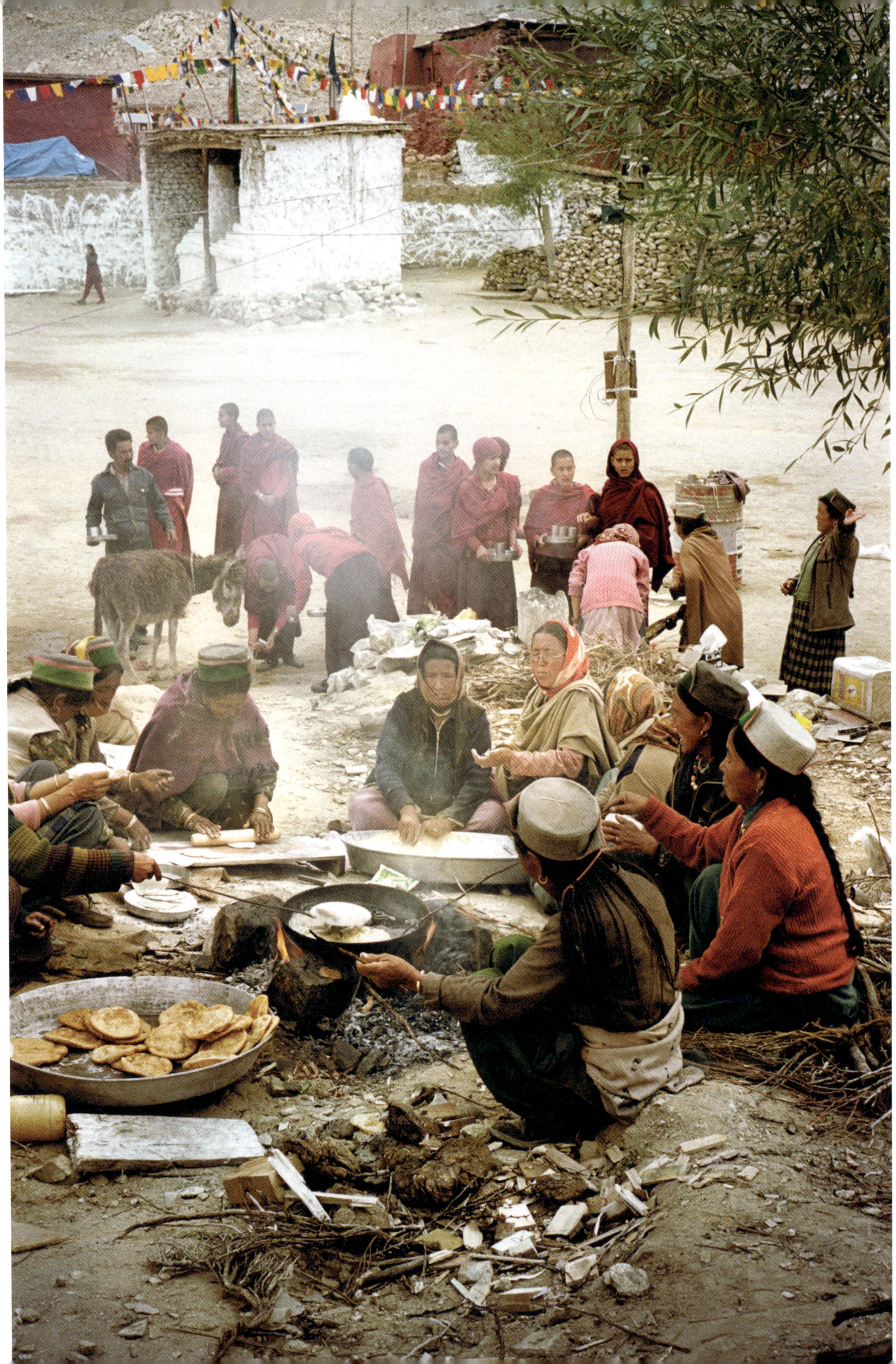

I
N
D
I
A

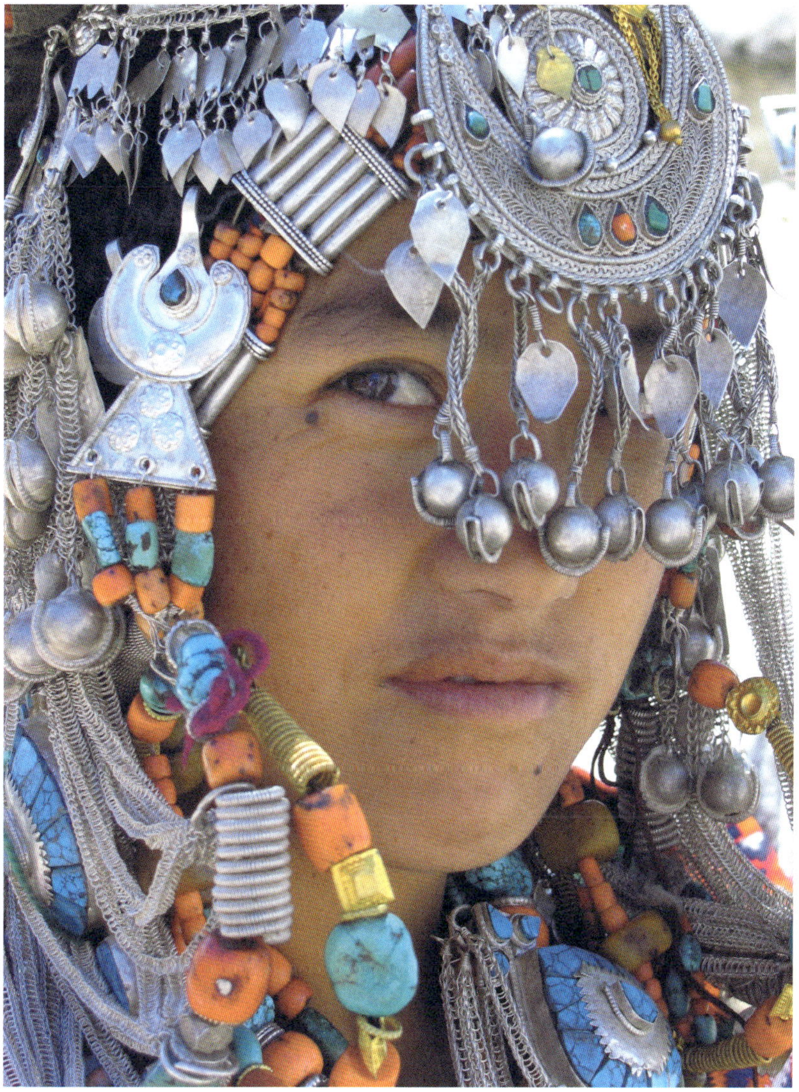

Fig. 3: Young girl wearing traditional ornamental headdress

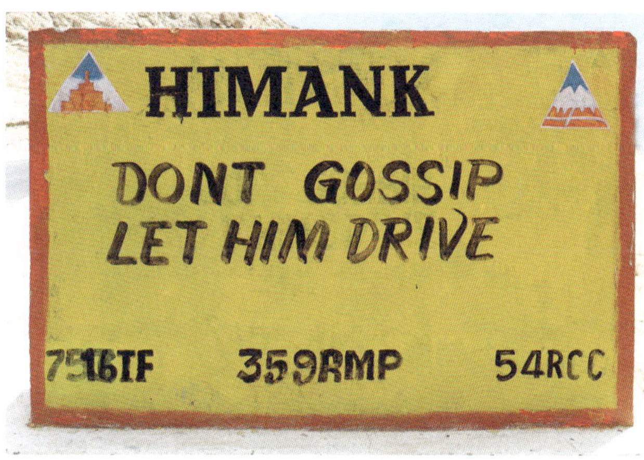

Fig. 4: Signboard along National Highway 22

left: Fig. 2: Baking of chapati for the whole village

EPILOGUE

Brief citations of deepest impressions of some Nako-project participants (all the expressions are published in the book)...

Katharina K.: A place where quiet and peace can be found. We construct a new Roof on the Roof of the World.

Stefan K.: The Buddhist "third eye" has become a reality and does not only exist as an empty symbol.

Marija M.: Fantastic landscape, new culture, breathing difficulties, rocks and pebbles, cold and dust, cabin fever, marvellous objects. Invaluable experiences! "Yes Mam/ Sir, that´s Nako!"

Tatjana B.: Simply unforgettable.

Kathrin S.: "Nako" to be transferred into words is difficult, almost impossible. One team of various people who despite their differences always pull together. An exploration of one's own limits and the experience of growing beyond oneself.

Birgit M.: Experience from many stories in a small village in the great mountains - meagre wealth.

Edgar S.: Smells. This crops up first when I think of Nako. Kitchen vapours, gas and diesel. Omnipresent smell of mud in temples mixed with scent from butter lamps and offerings. Deep black exhaust gases from burned diesel of Powerking. All these smells form the characteristic perfume of the working campaigns in Nako.

Charlotte H.: In India, a new, unknown world has opened up for me: extreme living conditions, rich world of fabrics, exotic dishes and landscapes, everyday life in Nako...

Regina K.: Meeting people, breathtaking land - impressions that will never be forgotten.

Gunn P.: Nako is a place where you can silently chuckle and learn, and I am happy I could be there.

Susanne S.: Nako is for me a very special place.

Bettina U.: Prior to the work campaign, we obtain advice from the experienced Nako-specialists, e.g. that Nako as well as the whole of India "is a bit different" and everything is simply slower. Something was confirmed on spot, something not.

Martina G.-S.: Nako - something that makes sense. Living heritage instead of dying nation.

Gabriela K.: Simply unforgettable!

Maria G.:
"Well I gotta say
Yeah I gotta say
Goodbye.
Goodbye.
Goodbye."
*(from Nick Cave,
More News from Nowhere)*

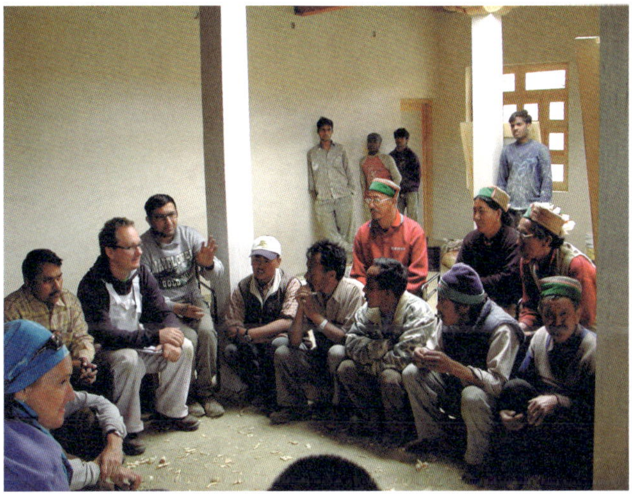

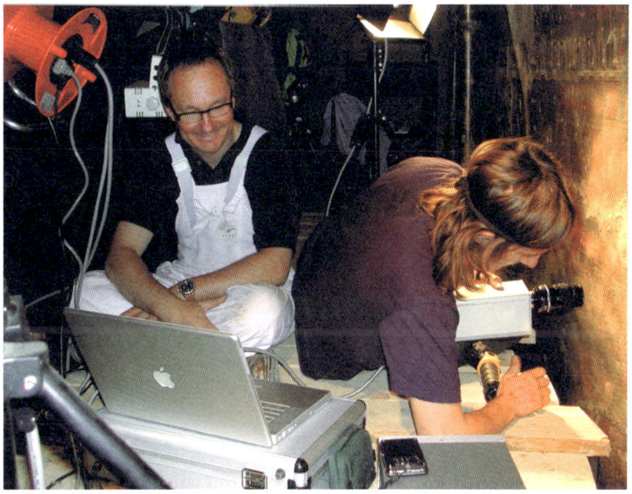

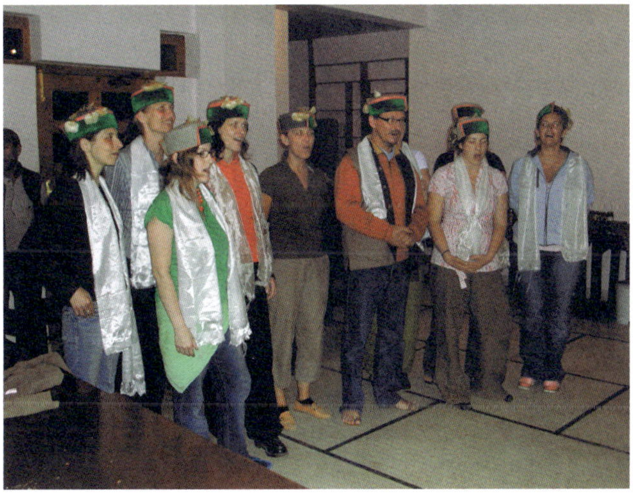

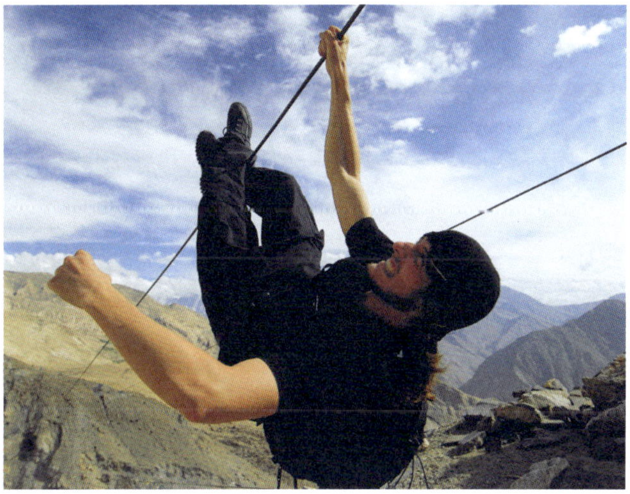

top left: Fig. 5: Discussion with villagers
top right: Fig. 6: Night measurements with infrared light
bottom left: Fig. 7: Austrian group singing/Austrian cultural input
bottom right: Fig. 8: Outdoor activities

The Nako Museum

MARTINA GRIESSER-STERMSCHEG

From the Foundation of the Collection to the "Permanent Changing Exhibition"

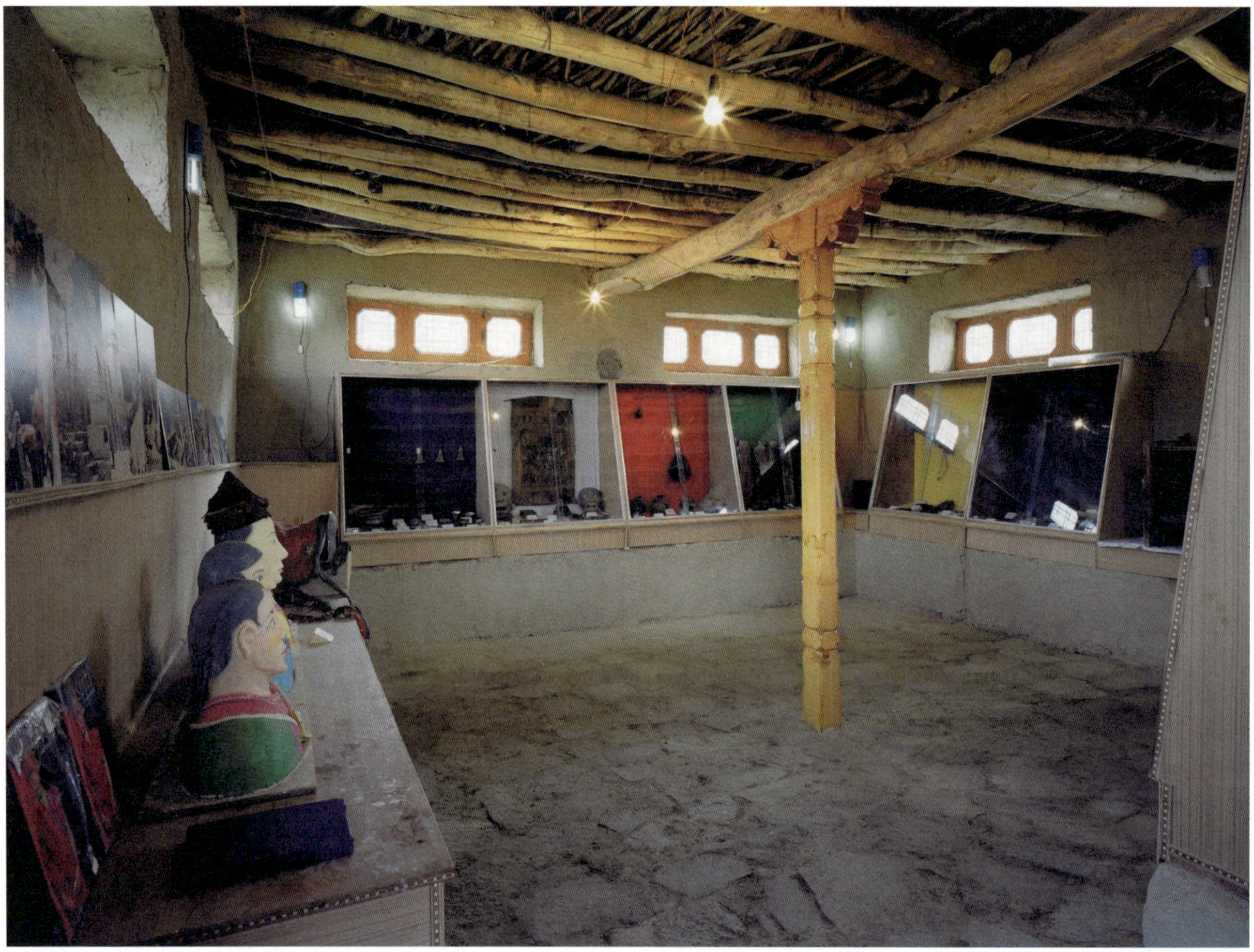

Fig. 10: The Nako Museum at the opening

"...the museum as a contact zone, in which the collection should become part of an on-going historical, political, moral relationship between different cultures."
James Clifford (Routes, 1997)

PREHISTORY

It is 2007. Nako needs a museum. The visit of His Holiness the Dalai Lama is imminent. The village is in a fever of excitement. The historic village centre of Nako, a labyrinth of stone houses and prayer wheels that has grown ever denser over the centuries, was extended for this occasion on the village outskirts by adding spacious assembly grounds harbouring a new temple and a residence for the Dalai Lama. Opposite is the new museum building, a small house in traditional architectural style with stone walls, loam rendering, wooden roof and floor space of around forty square metres. We find ourselves in the Western Himalayas at an altitude of 3,800 metres (approximately 12,500 feet) (Fig. 1).The idea of founding a museum here seems foreign and unexpected. According to Western theory, museums are founded only when there is pressure to enhance a location's image, when there is the urge to establish an interior cultural identity, or to communicate it to the world outside. Experience has shown that the representation of visible traditions, the collecting and exhibiting of material cultural heritage in a museum contribute to the shaping of identity. Thus the Western model. But does this apply to the little village of Nako?

All are of the opinion that the museum is a momentous thing for Nako. Through the Dalai Lama's visit and the presence of His Holiness – which will also attract thousands of pilgrims to the tiny community – a general feeling is being generated that the occasion should be represented through some kind of official and prestigious gesture. Around 20 people from the local Buddhist youth club volunteered to work together to establish the museum and to run it afterwards. No women have volunteered. Most of the young men are farmers. Only one of them has ever been to a museum. Uncertainty and enthusiasm weigh in equal balance among the young people. What shall we exhibit, and who will come to our museum? What will the exhibition room look like? How much admission should we demand?

We should get an expert in. We could surely ask "the Austrians", couldn't we? Meant here are the students and teachers of the University of Applied Arts Vienna, Institute of Conservation, who travel to Nako every year to work on conserving the local temple complex.

THE FOUNDING OF THE COLLECTION

The first gathering with the youth club representatives, the mayor and the village elders, provides the opportunity for round-table talks on the museum and its future functions. The Austrian advisory team arrives in Nako faint with altitude sickness and digestion problems. The discussion is multilingual, four languages to be precise: English, Hindi, the local dialect of Boti and now and then German. In all this Babylonian linguistic confusion, one thing becomes clear: the Nako Museum has as yet no objects at its disposal, and it is supposed proverbially to open the day after tomorrow. But "objects" are indeed necessary or not? What do we want to collect?

These days, collection profiles are usually shaped based on existing collections. But it turned out that founding a collection on a theoretically created profile was far more difficult. Both sides are unsure of themselves: owing to lack of experience with the institute of the museum per se, the villagers' inhibitions are too great for them to propose "inappropriate objects". The advisory team, resolved not to act in any way redolent of "cultural imperialism", ensconce themselves as much as possible behind generally held recommendations. The discussions make no progress and days pass by one after another, waiting for potential museum objects.

Objectivity is needed in the truest sense of the word. Time is running out; then, at last, the advisory team makes a concrete suggestion. Twenty wooden planks, fragments of the wooden ceiling of the main temple that were not classifiable in the conservation of 2004, are laid out in the temple courtyard. The young future curators are invited to choose five to ten planks, which would then be presented in the museum (Fig. 2). In the meantime, several spectators have gathered on the scene. An elderly man, fascinated by the respect shown to the historical wooden planks, asks if his grandfather's shoes might be appropriate for

right: Fig. 11: The Nako Museum and its visitors

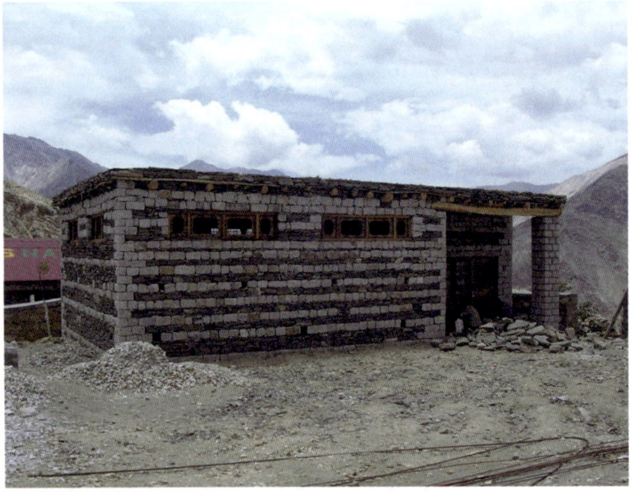

Fig. 1: The Nako Museum shortly before completion of the construction works

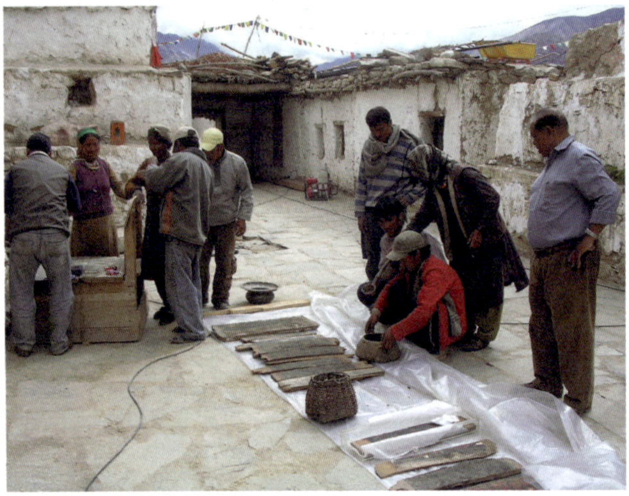

Fig. 2: The first objects arrive in the temple courtyard

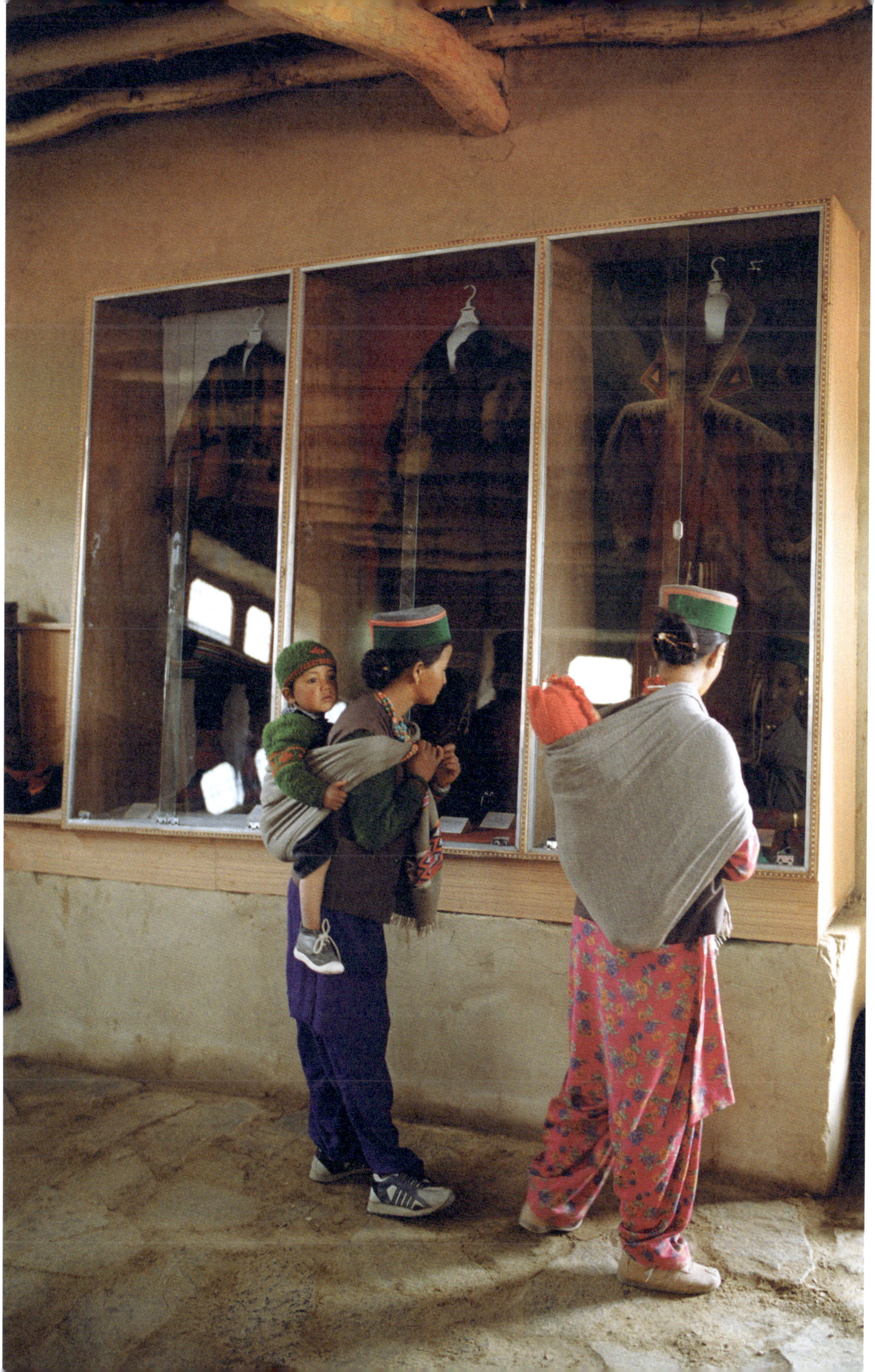

BY MARTINA GRIESSER-STERMSCHEG

the museum. He comes back with Tibetan snowshoes from the late 19th century; woven and embroidered over-knee boots with distinct signs of wear and tear (Fig. 3). Encouraged by the unanimous enthusiasm over the snowshoes, other objects belonging to the villagers follow; butter scales used for generations for preparing Tibetan butter tea (Fig. 4); a carved cooking spoon, a hammered copper alloy bowl for hand-washing (Fig. 5), and a basket for work in the fields. At the end of a long day we can make an inventory list of seven objects. After two weeks it has already grown to 70. The objects stem almost exclusively from private homes in Nako. Time and again, the donors insist that if they had known earlier that the museum declares old and worn-out items as valuable and collectable, they would have brought their objects out much sooner. The question arises as to whether a fifty-year-old object is already ancient enough for the museum. Age alone is no criterion, but now it was time to formulate guidelines and make the criteria of collecting transparent for everybody.

THE GUIDELINES

Over one of the many cups of tea and probably without realising what was happening, members of the youth club set up the guidelines of the Nako Museum: "We want to show what we have and how we live." Even after the Dalai Lama's visit, the residents of the neighbouring villages ought to keep visiting the museum and spending time there. Thus the chairman of the youth club stresses that it shouldn't be a permanent exhibition, but a "permanent changing exhibition". Acquisitioning would be pragmatic: a winter coat or shawl might be on display in summer, but is replaced by another object with the outbreak of the cold weather in autumn, one that is not needed so urgently in winter. The museum should be a regional museum, perhaps even a "museum of local history" showing the customs, habits of life and objects of the Tibetan village of Nako. The target group consists of neighbouring villages and day-trippers. The museum will be run by the youth club, and of course there is hope in the air of lasting extra revenue – a shop and "café" are planned as well.

Many objects are donated to the museum as gifts. But several objects are placed at its disposal only as temporary loans. These include the objects that are still in use when needed, for example the aforementioned winter clothing (Fig. 6–7). Nor should the jewellery so typical of the region (Fig. 8–9) be missing from the show, or so the youth club thinks. Nevertheless, not one private person was willing to hand silver jewellery over to the museum, not even on loan. The enthusiasm for the museum evidently stopped at the prospect of providing valuable items made of precious metal. In the end, the youth club decides to purchase from a travelling tradesman, who advertises himself as selling "historical jewellery" from regional production. Admittedly, there is no budget set aside for purchases, but the future revenue from the museum shop would surely guarantee credit from the tradesman.

INVENTORYING

A thick ledger was acquired to set up inventory lists for the collection, growing daily. A small step, but a great day for the museum: writing is power and collective documentation means institutionalisation. The inventory book made the Nako Museum into a "serious museum" and enormously intensified the acceptance and respect of the villagers. Entry numbers acting simultaneously as inventory numbers are added to all objects in the inventory book. The name of the former owner comes straight after the inventory number. Inventorying involves measuring all objects, listing materials, collecting data for identification, and marking the function of each of the objects. This always refers to the actual (!) assigned function: for instance, a small hand drum is not used for drumming and making music, but solely for praising Buddha and for prayer. The new inventory book is hugely popular. Its date column teems with spectacular date specifications, including "700 yrs old" or "250 yrs old". This is based on estimating how long the object must have been in family ownership, or simply guessed at. Western dating such as "c. 1950" or "late 18th century" meets with incomprehension. These are rejected simply because they do not express enough. Our objection that the inventory book also ought to remain up to date in maybe fifty years from now, by which time a 250-years-old object is already 300 years old is encountered with a shake of the head. They feel sorry for us because of our lack of relation to the present. Attaching inventory numbers to the objects likewise turns out to be impossible. There is (still) too little trust in the institution of the museum. Apart from which, this contradicts the concept of the "permanent changing exhibition", which assumes that the donors are able to withdraw their objects from the museum and bring replacements. In this case the mark "on loan" is noted in the inventory book. Loan contracts are not planned.

CONSERVATION

Most visitors in the improvised conservation workshop next to the museum had a key question: how do we know that the objects are better kept in museums than at home, where they have been safely kept for generations? This is without doubt a legitimate question when founding a museum – and this in a village without a museum tradition. The conservation of the collected objects was organised as a conservation show, and the "open studio" became a meeting point for young and old in Nako. Materials and tools flown in from Austria or acquired at Delhi markets on arrival aroused great interest. There were admiring and encouraging comments on such self-evident conservation skills as the care bestowed on each individual object, no matter how small or "unimportant", the careful handling, the photo documentation, the mild cleaning with small brushes and the precise work with scalpels. And above all the use of dental implements brought from Austria for particularly fine tasks kept stimulating positive associations in giggling children about a "hospital for old objects": conservation work as a mean of creating trust in the institution of the museum, a quality that is frequently underestimated in the West. Over a period of two weeks, a total of 70 objects was documented, inventoried, cleaned, conserved and, if required, restored. The aesthetic goal was a neat appearance with traces of age and usage. Committed villagers contributed their help, after initial training. But cleaning measures that were much too radical and that had the aim of attaining a good-as-new appearance were often prevented only at the last moment. The cleaning and conservation work aspired to the qualities cultivated in European regions of "ageing" and "patina" and their maintenance; they were consistently argued for (even risking the danger of acting in a culturally imperialist way) and communicated as goal of the endeavours.

THE EXHIBITION ROOM

He wanted to travel just to the next town. It took four days for the carpenter to return with the timber and glass for constructing the display cases. The design planned for wooden display cases with sliding glass doors, all around the room. For the free exhibition of larger objects, the row of display cases was interrupted with wooden tableaux raised on plinths. When looking for a creative metaphor for Nako and its museum, Buddhist prayer flags were found as the smallest common denominator for everything. The village landscape is alive with fluttering prayer flags. These can be found on houses and mountain ridges and, despite being assigned to the Buddhist prayer cult, they are a unifying, omnipresent attribute for the multi-denominational community of Buddhists, Hindu believers and Christians. So it was mutually decided to line the display cases with polychrome lengths of fabric in the colours of the prayer flags (Fig. 10). The ordering and simultaneous hierarchy of the flag colours – blue, white, red, green and yellow – were reflected in the set-up of the display cases. The colours were assigned to the exhibits according to their value: religious and liturgically important items were presented on white fabric, household items and cooking utensils, for example, in the red display case. At the wish of the youth club members, precious metals were given the most prominent place on blue fabric and thus – significantly – were valued higher in comparison to the religious items.

THE MUSEUM SHOP

One of the project's declared aims was the establishment of a museum shop. To this end, 3,000 postcards were made in Vienna and transported to Nako. The motifs stemmed from the Austrian photographer Stefan Oláh, who had produced a photographic portrayal of the village in 2005. The postcards were a gift to the museum as basic stock for budgeting the enterprise. Sale of the postcards proved to be a great inspiration for the youth club. The price per postcard was continually discussed and altered daily. Other things planned for sale were Tibetan socks. Sock-knitting was a rather helpless attempt on our part to involve the women of Nako in the museum project. This proved difficult to organise, because "we only knit socks for people we know personally. Pattern and colour are related to the owner." At any event, socks were on sale at the museum opening: in a great variety of patterns and colours.

THE OPENING

During the festivities surrounding the Dalai Lama's visit, the little Nako Museum could count thousands of visitors. The Dalai Lama spoke of Tibet as a "dying nation" and thanked the Austrian delegation for their efforts to preserve the "living heritage" in the Tibetan-Buddhist temples and the museum of Nako. After the prayers, "Tibetan families queued in the museum and reflected on their history", reported the author and theatre/film director Florian Flicker, who was fortunate in experiencing the newly opened museum and its visitors. Parents demonstrated the devices and tools used by their grandparents to their children and put a piece of Tibet on show. Kunzang Tripley, a young Buddhist monk from Nako, wrote in a letter: "The exhibition was become very famous and good. Lots of people are interesting towards it and come to visit, and could not stop praising for it. Now the committee of the youngester is looking after it."

THE FUTURE

The impetus for founding the Nako Museum was mainly triggered by the visit of the Dalai Lama and the urge this inspired to create a representative image for the little village. The Western idea of a museum doesn't seem in any way to be rooted in Nako and is nurtured at best by superficially imported clichés. In order to keep the Nako Museum attractive for its operators and visitors also after the Dalai Lama's visit, the profile of the existing guidelines should continue to be enhanced, or rethought for alternatives. What does the "permanent changing exhibition" mean in the long term, and doesn't this model offer an opportunity for a really unique concept which is able to emancipate itself clearly from the Western ideas of a museum?

Special thanks in the phase of the museum founding go to: Mag. Manfred Trummer, Austrian Museum of Applied Arts/Contemporary Arts (MAK Wien) and Dr. Hari Narein, National Research Laboratory for Conservation Lucknow, India.

Fig. 8: (From the museum's inventory) "Silver Ornaments for Gents (Chhuktu), period: 150 years, place: Nako, purpose: worn by gents around throat during dance sessions"
Fig. 9: (From the museum's inventory) "Silver Ornaments for Ladies, Period: 150 Years, Place: Nako, Purpose: Worn by ladies during dance sessions"

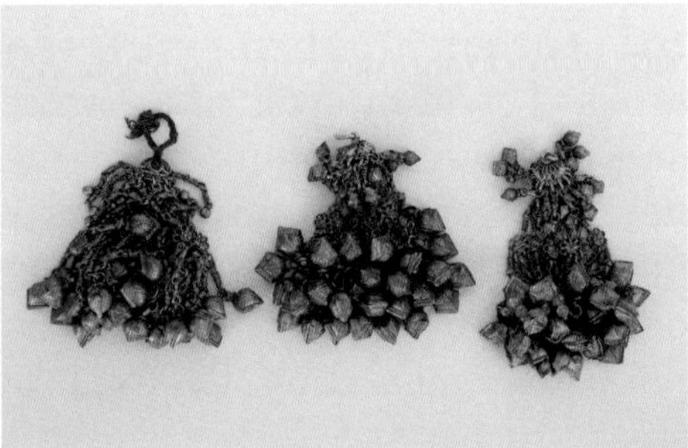

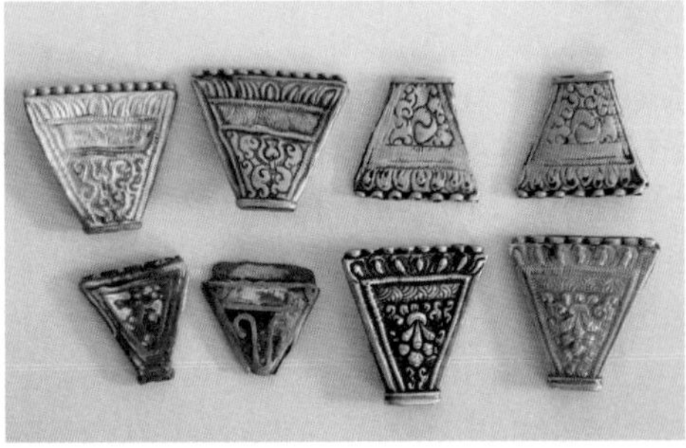

Fig. 6: (From the museum's inventory) "Woollen Coat, period: 120 years, place: Nako, purpose: for wearing in winter season and at festivals"

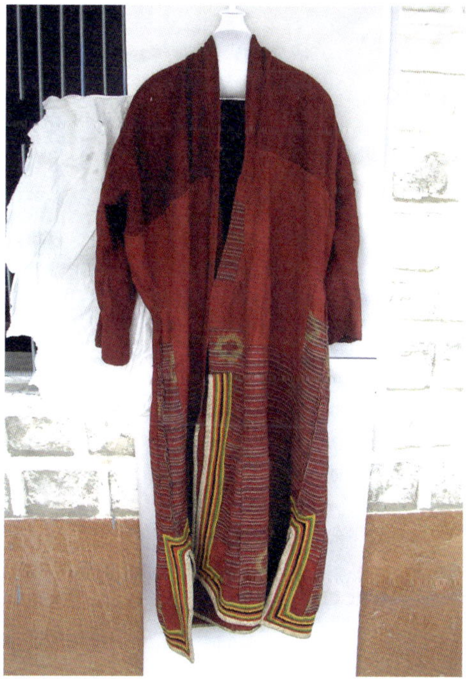

Fig. 7: (From the museum's inventory) "Woollen shawl, period: 50 years, place: Nako, purpose: for wearing in winter season"

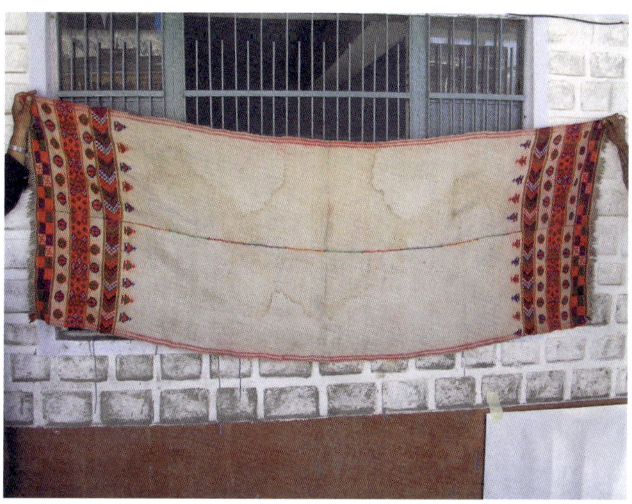

Fig. 3: (From the museum's inventory) "Pair of Leather and Woollen Shoes, period: 120 years, place: Nako, purpose: for wearing in winter season"
Fig. 4: (From the museum's inventory) "Traditional Scales, period: 109 years, place: Nako, purpose: for weighing butter"
Fig. 5: (From the museum's inventory) "Metal Pot (copper alloy), period: 80 years, place: Nako, purpose: for washing hands of guest"

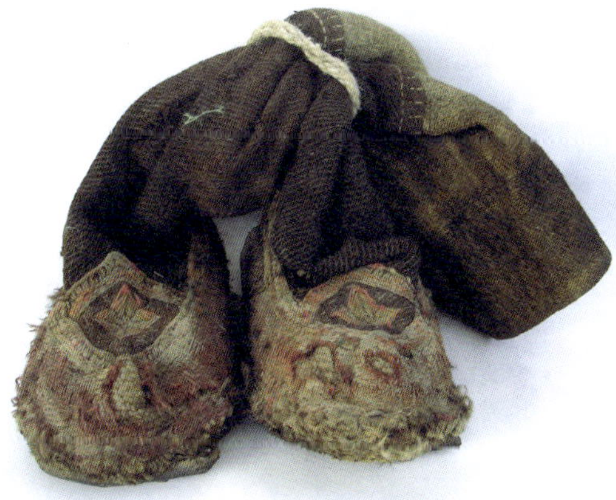

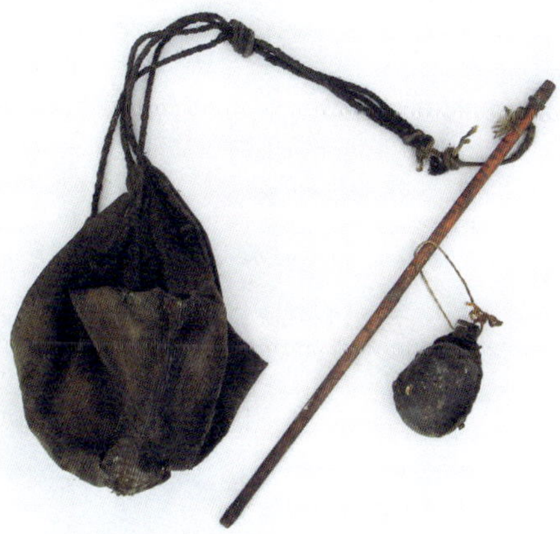

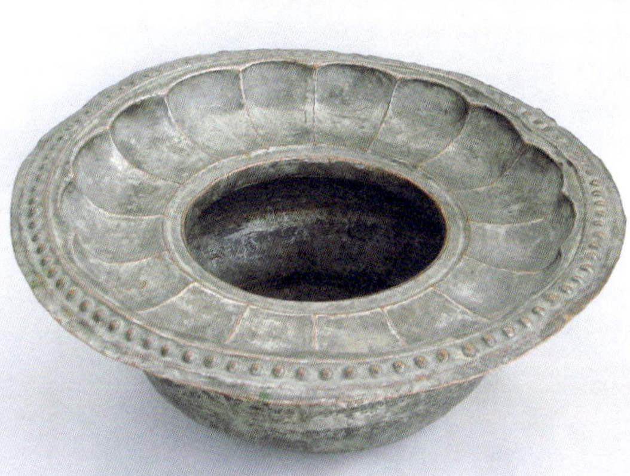

A Wild and Wonderful Journey

STEFAN
OLÁH

From Delhi via Shimla to Nako

Glimpses into Stefan Oláh's Photographic Travel Log

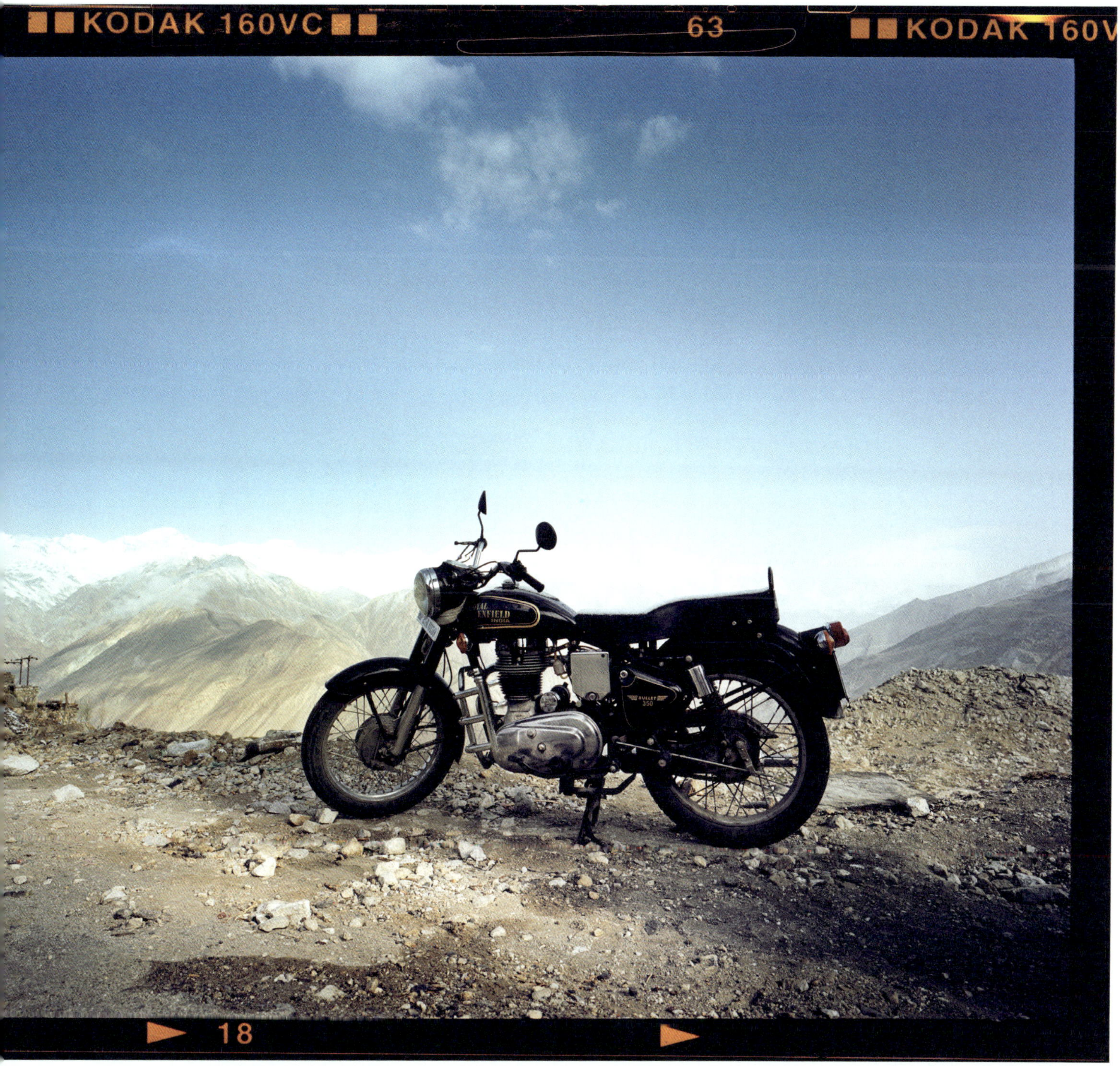
KODAK 160VC
63
18

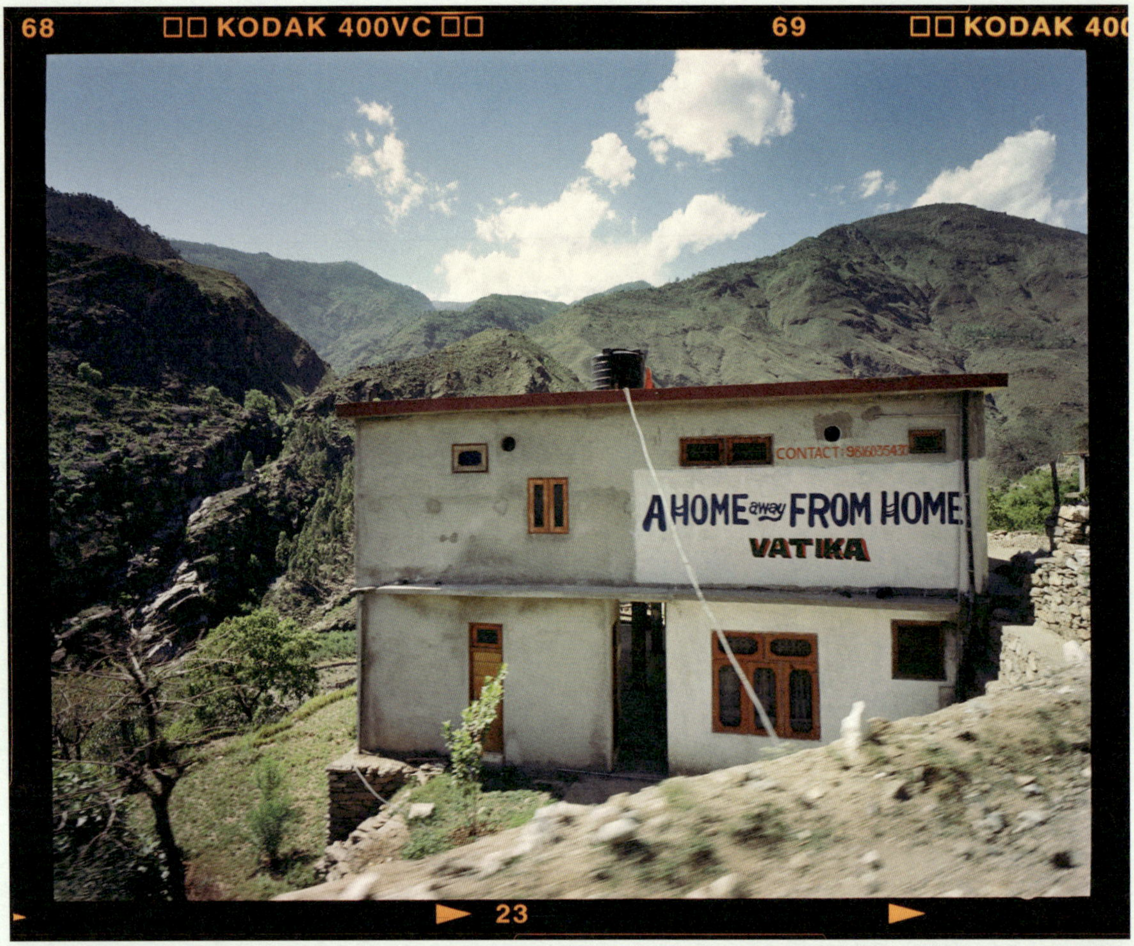
68
KODAK 400VC
69
A HOME away FROM HOME
VATIKA
23

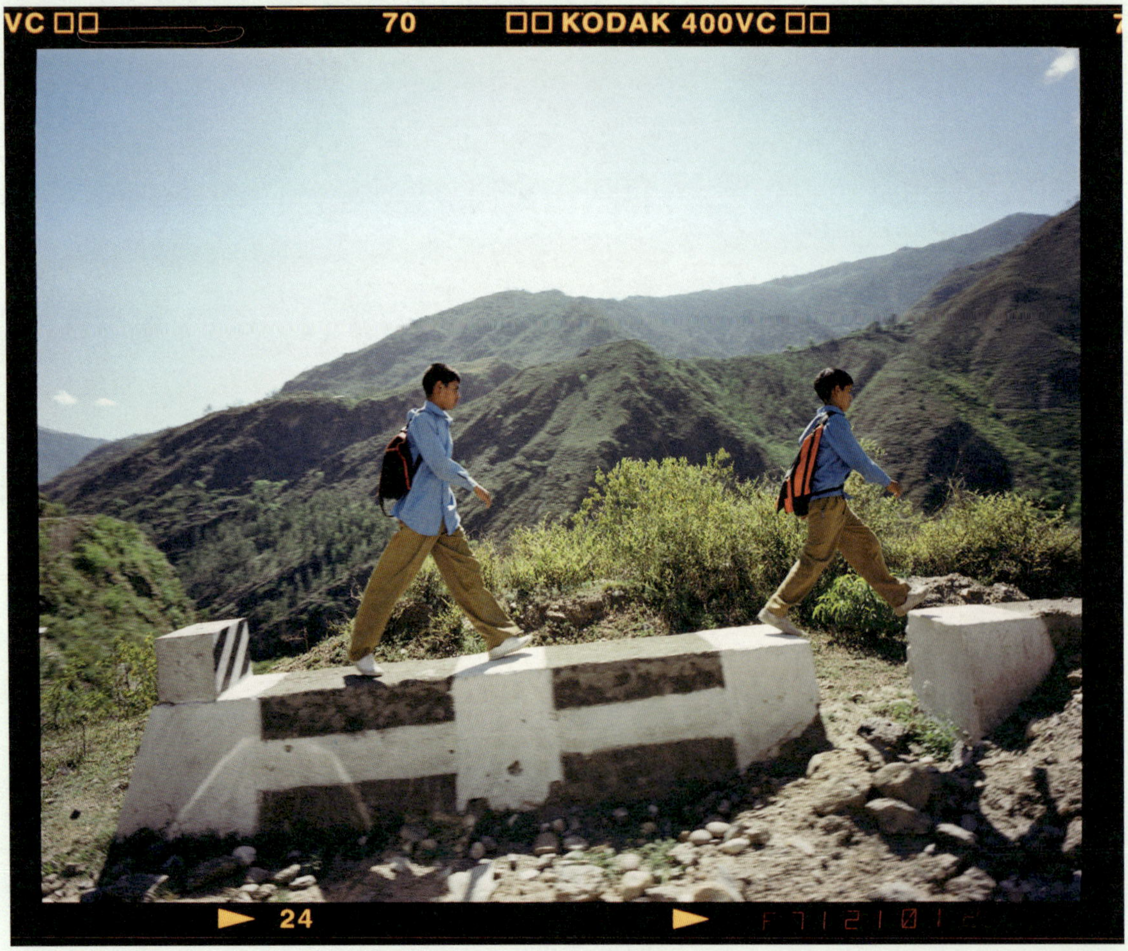
70
KODAK 400VC
24

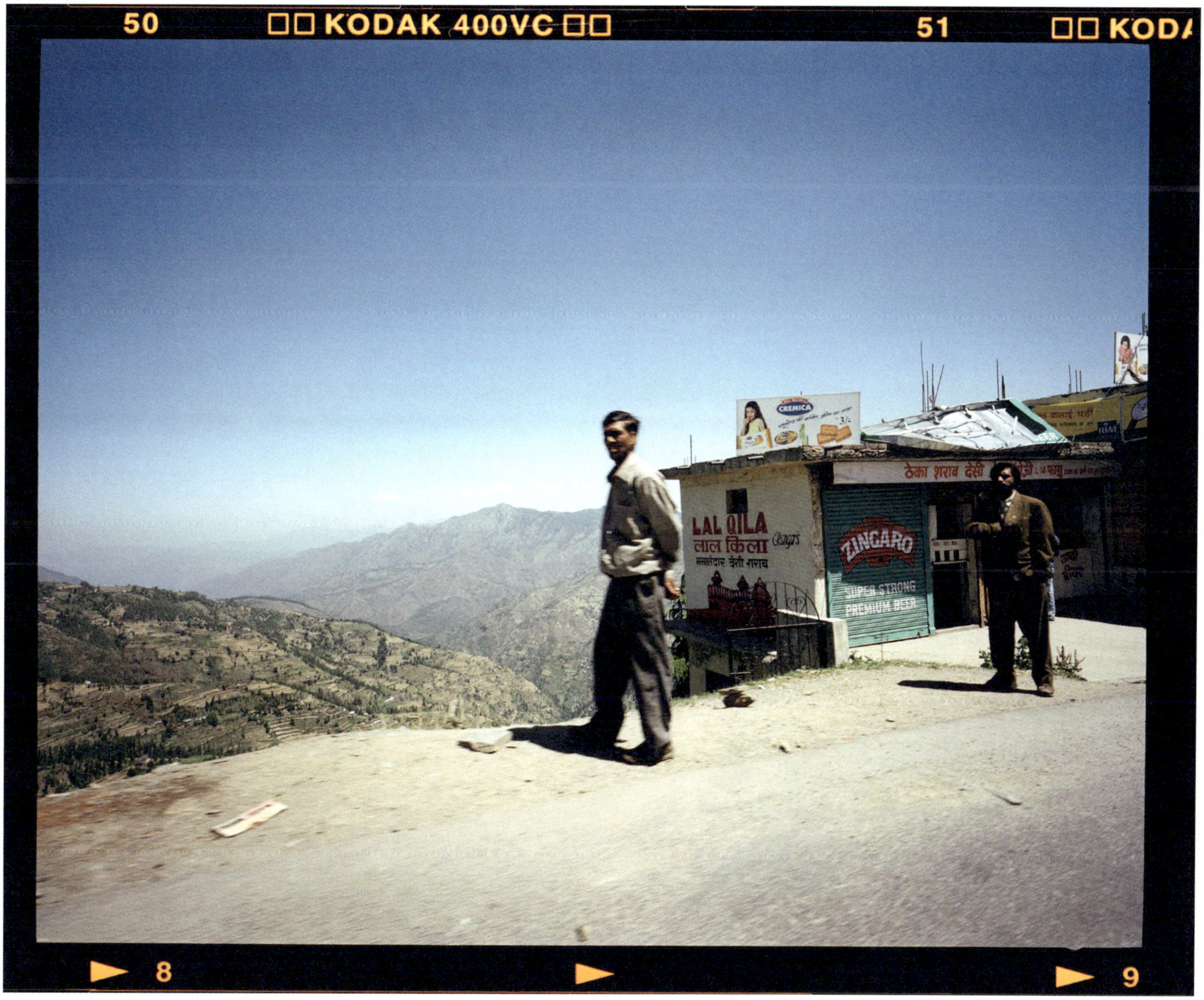

BY STEFAN OLAH

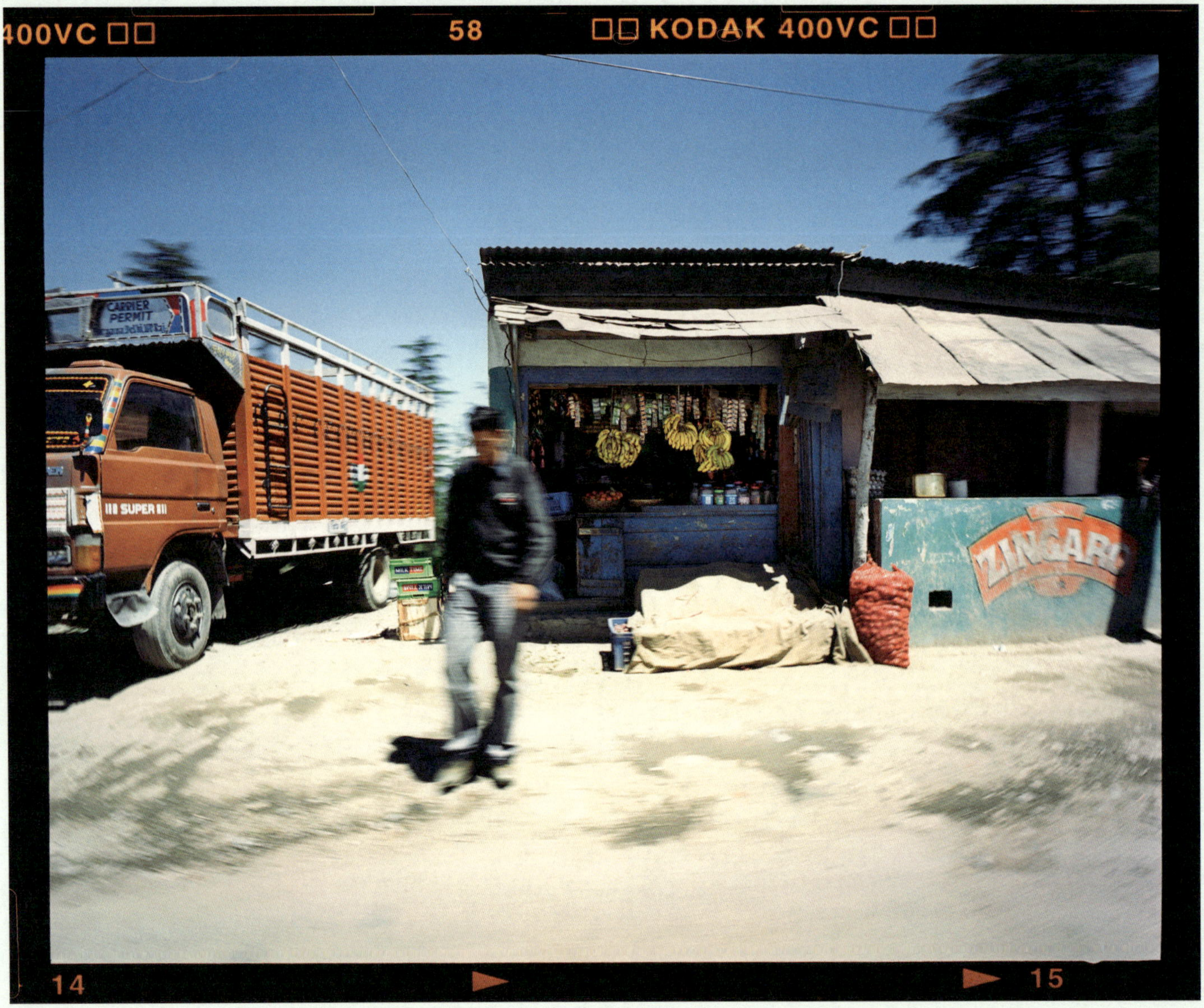
400VC
58
KODAK 400VC
CARRIER PERMIT
SUPER
14
15

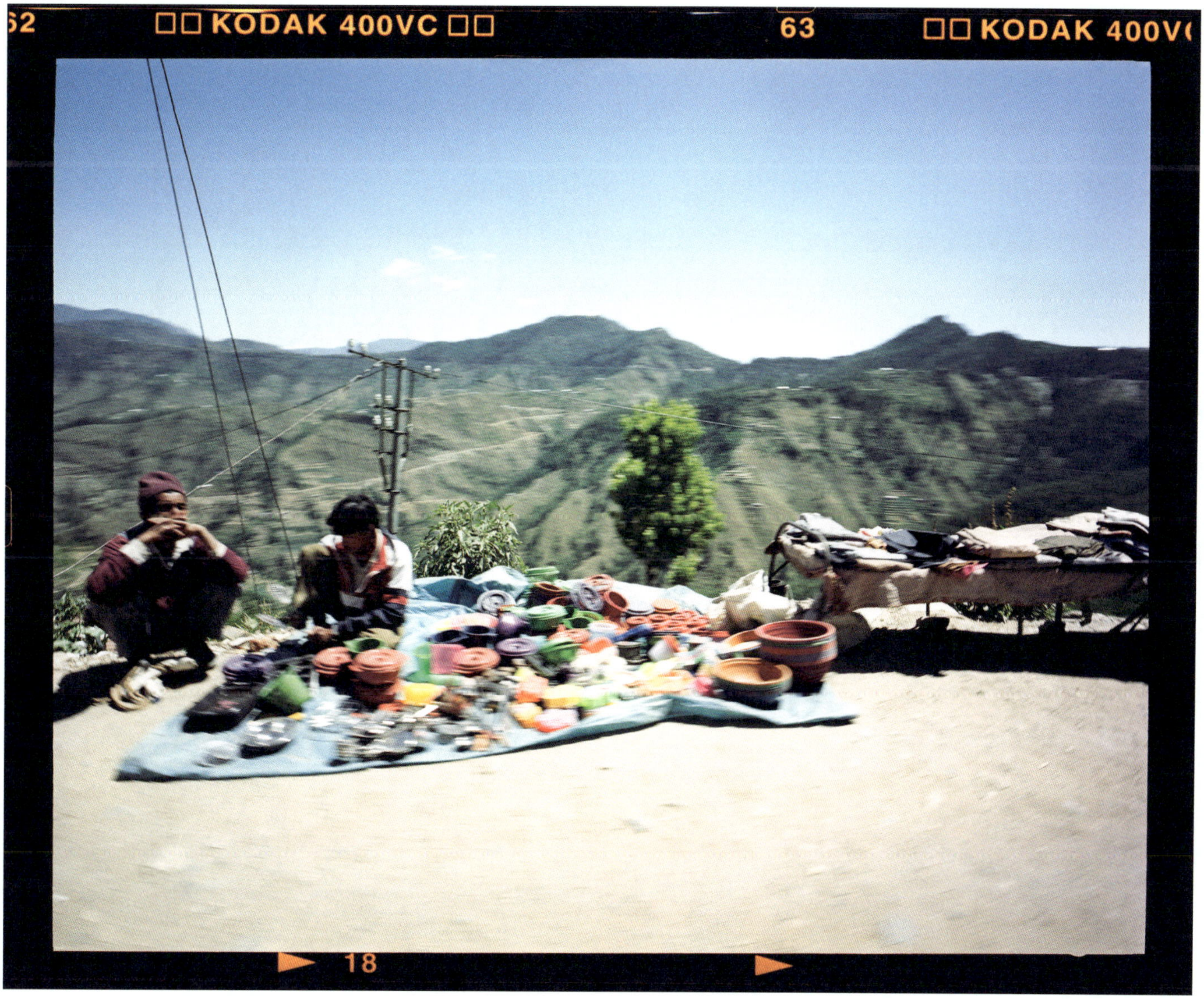

BY STEFAN OLAH

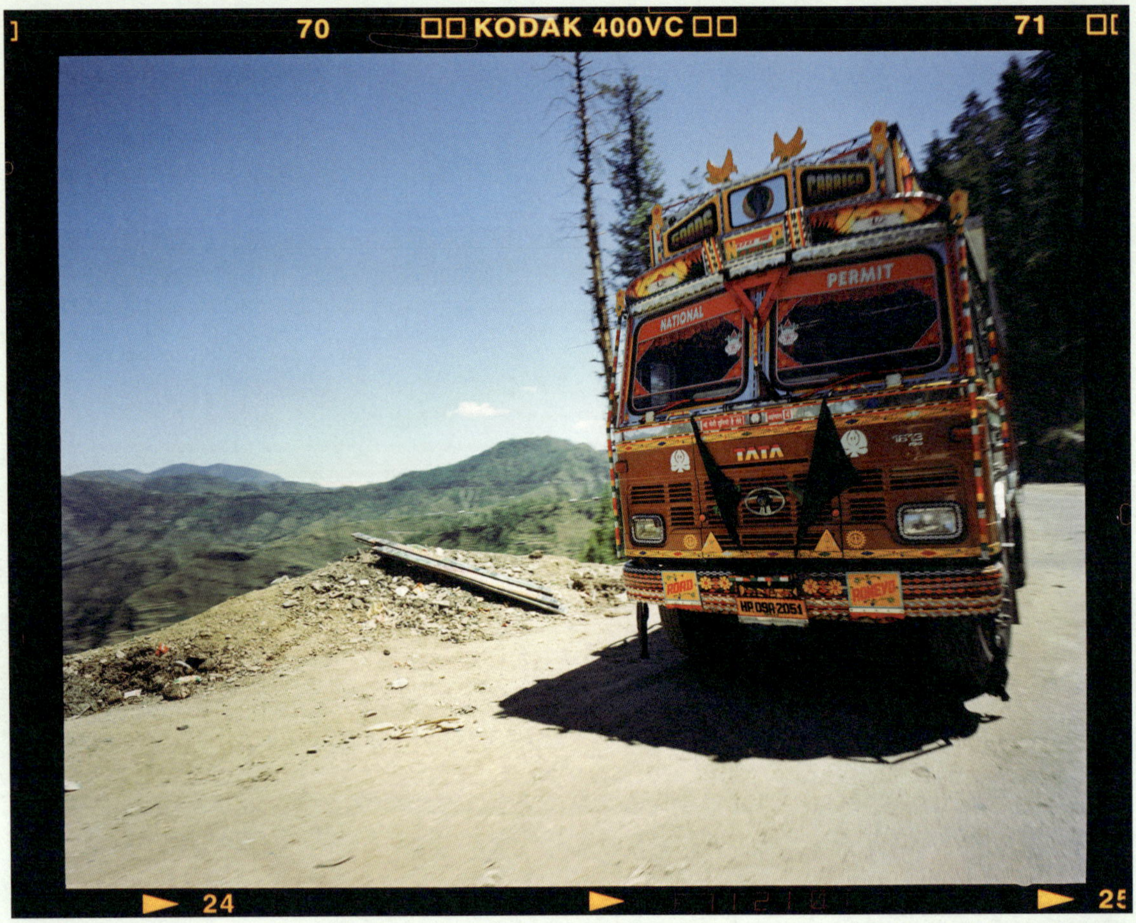
70
KODAK 400VC
71
PERMIT
NATIONAL
24
25

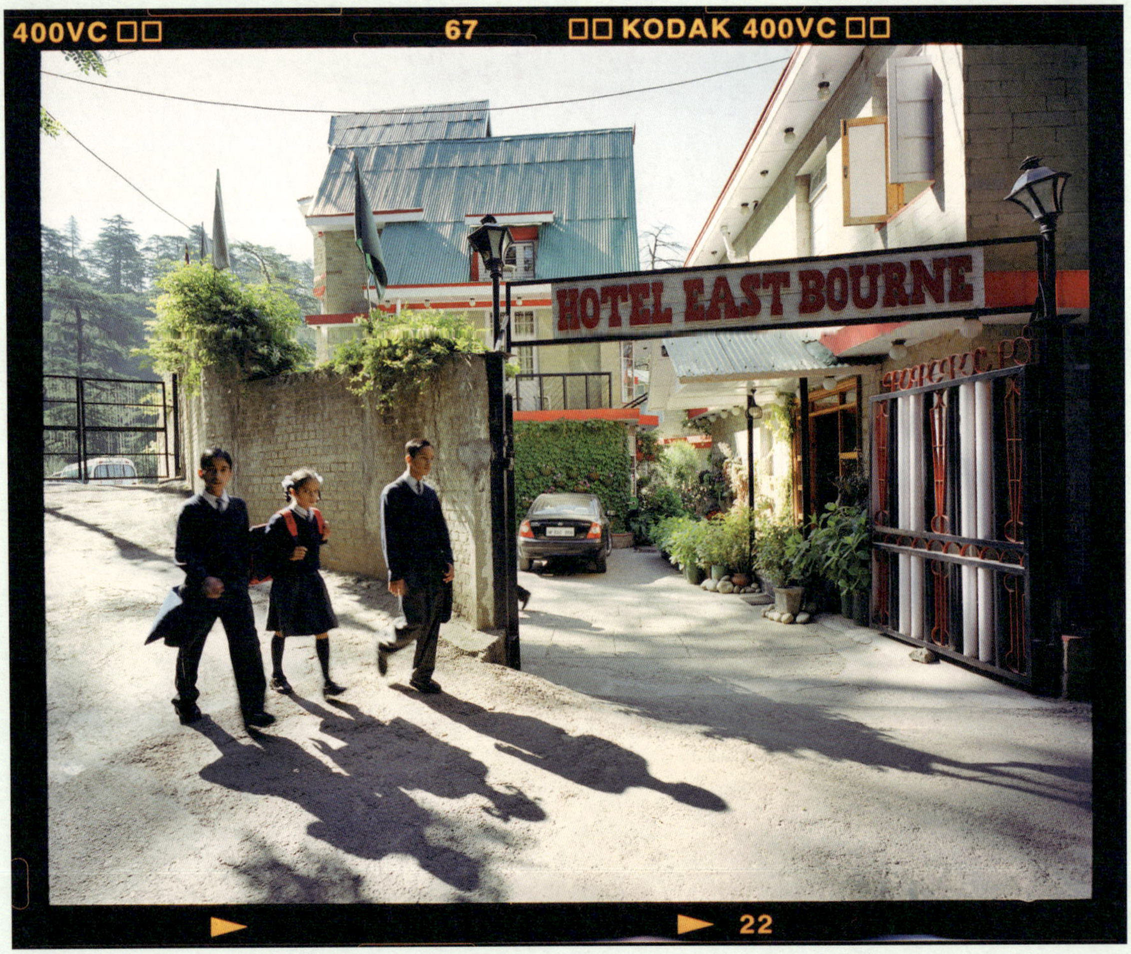
400VC
67
KODAK 400VC
HOTEL EAST BOURNE
22

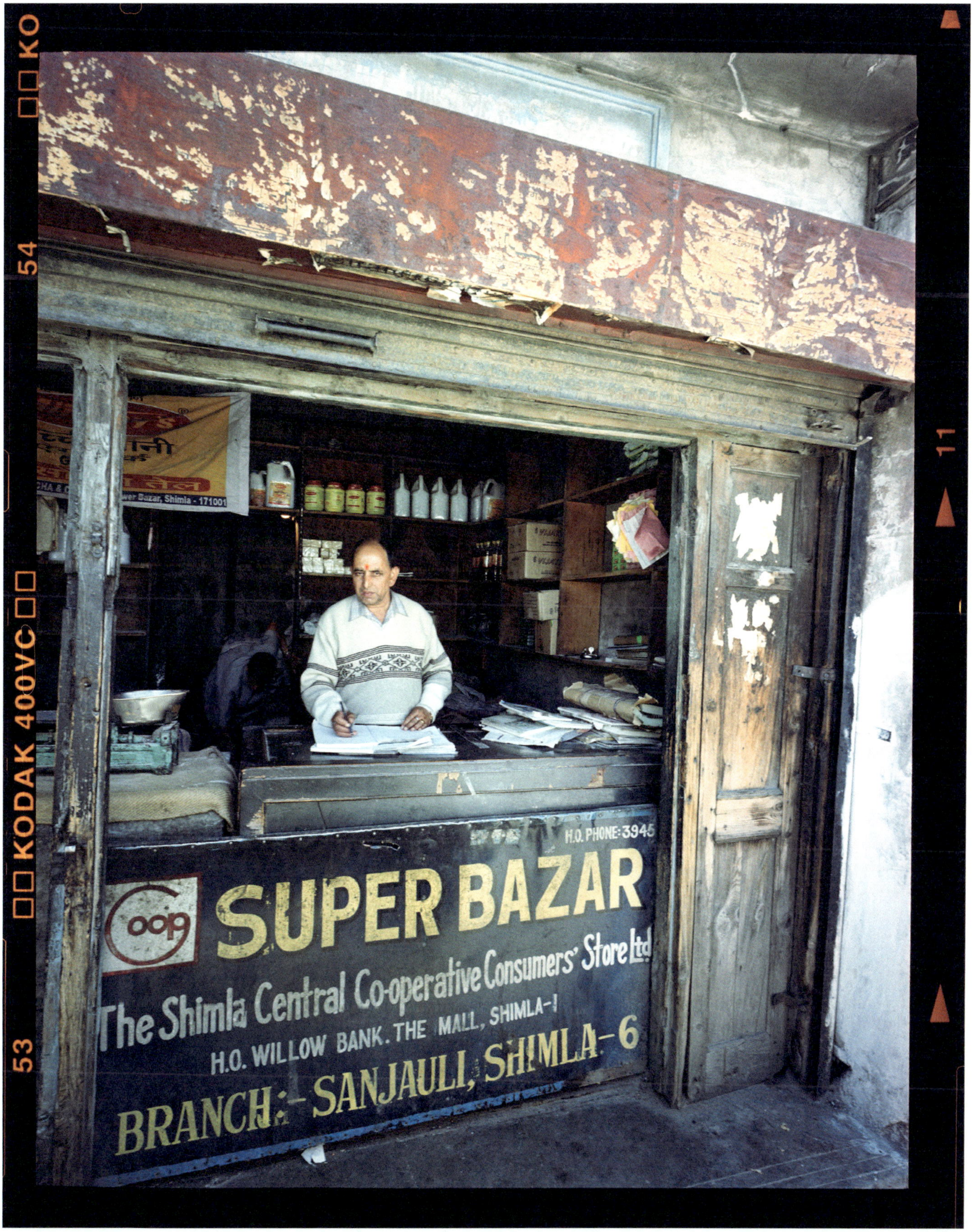

BY STEFAN OLAH

This All Belongs to Tibet

GUNDI LAMPRECHT

It was in the year 2007 that I twice travelled to Nako along with experts from the Institute of Conservation of the University of Applied Arts Vienna to make a documentary film for ORF/Austrian Television; a journey I shall never forget for a variety of reasons. For a start, there was the unforgettable journey up to an altitude of 4,000 metres (13,000 feet): if you get a kick out of curves and don't have vertigo, the Hindustan-Tibet Highway is just the thing for you, but most people are scared stiff. That's the way it is with me. And it's not only the overhanging rock faces and deep gorges that terrify me, but the unconventional driving skills of the Indians. "Drive left" and "stronger and louder have priority" – two rules that are religiously kept. But the minute you arrive in Nako, you quickly forget this trip through hell. The idyllic village of four hundred people on the border to Tibet reminded me a great deal of the fabled paradise "Shangri La", so wonderfully described by James Hilton in his novel *Lost Horizon*. For centuries, people have lived here in harmony with nature and completely cut off from the outside world, but the visit of the Dalai Lama, who had announced his presence for a week of his "teachings", as he calls them, was to change the village and its people forever. I was quite sure of this. 10,000 pilgrims were expected at the time, mostly from Kashmir, Ladakh and India. Quite a few Western devotees of the Dalai Lama had turned up as well. What impressed me so much was the fact that exactly the same residence was put up for His Holiness with exactly the same rooms as his main residence in Dharamsala. The Dali Lama should feel at home here, the villagers were all in agreement. Of course, I was very curious to see him. I have long been a devotee of him and his Buddhist teaching, and now I had the opportunity to get to know him personally. That's what I love about my work. As a journalist you often come in contact with fascinating, impressive personalities you would never meet in "normal life".

In over-hasty devotion, a helicopter landing pad was now built at the entrance to the village; everyone thought the Dalai Lama would come by helicopter (Fig. 1). Far from it. He came by car – and disappeared for quite some time into his domicile. When we heard that we, the experts from the University of Applied Arts and I, were to have an audience with him, I don't need to say how nervous we were. Let's hope and pray the sound equipment would function, the camera work; all these thoughts spun through my head. And then he came, the Dalai Lama, whose "wisdom is as great as the ocean". He handed us the obligatory white shawl and said to us Austrians: "The entire cultural heritage belongs to this land, I mean Tibet. But today Tibet is a dying nation and is going through very, very difficult times. The precious Tibetan heritage and the rich Buddhist tradition are doomed." His words sounded sad. But as long as the Dalai Lama lives he will work for his Tibetan people, for peace and justice, of that I am certain. He travels the world unstintingly even today and makes it aware of the problems in Tibet.

The audience didn't last very long, but it will stay in my memory for ever. I was able to film him during his teaching sessions and "delight" in his presence (Fig. 2). In conclusion, I would like to include a few quotes of the Dalai Lama, which express his deep wisdom and inspire us all so much:

> I believe that to meet the challenges of our times, human beings will have to develop a greater sense of universal responsibility. Each of us must learn to work not just for oneself, one's own family or one's nation, but for the benefit of all humankind. Universal responsibility is the key to human survival. It is the best foundation for world peace.
>
> Every human being should realize that the future of humanity is dependent on their present action and thinking.
>
> Meditation is the key to spiritual growth.
>
> I myself feel, and also tell other Buddhists, that the question of nirvana will come later. There is not much hurry. If in day-to-day life you lead a good life, honestly, with love, with compassion, with less selfishness, then automatically it will lead to nirvana.
>
> According to Buddhism, individuals are masters of their own destiny. So our future is in our hands. What greater free will do we need?
>
> As long as we are alive as human beings, there is something we can do about it. It is a great mistake to regard this life as fruitless. We have such a wonderful opportunity. We need a little bit more patience and determination. There is no point in engaging in foolish anxiety.
>
> Without inner peace it is impossible to have world peace. Through compassion, through love, it is possible to become a true human family. Through love we can have true happiness, real disarmament.
>
> In the East, we need more material goods and development. In the West, you need to develop the mind to sustain happiness and peace, so I think we can benefit from an exchange.
>
> In the interests of everyone, of humanity, the artist has a responsibility to use his medium well. In the Tibetan culture, most of the paintings are of deities or Buddhas and they try to send a message of value of the spiritual.
>
> A young man caught a small bird, and held it behind his back. He then asked: "Master, is this bird I hold in my hand alive or dead?" the boy thought this was a grand opportunity to play a trick on the old man. If the master answered "dead", it would be let loose into the air. If the master answered "alive", he would simply wring its neck. The master spoke: "The answer is in your hands."
>
> I always believe that it is much better to have a variety of religions, a variety of philosophies, rather than one single religion or philosophy. This is necessary because of the different mental dispositions of each human being. Each religion has certain unique ideas or techniques, and learning about them can only enrich one's own faith.

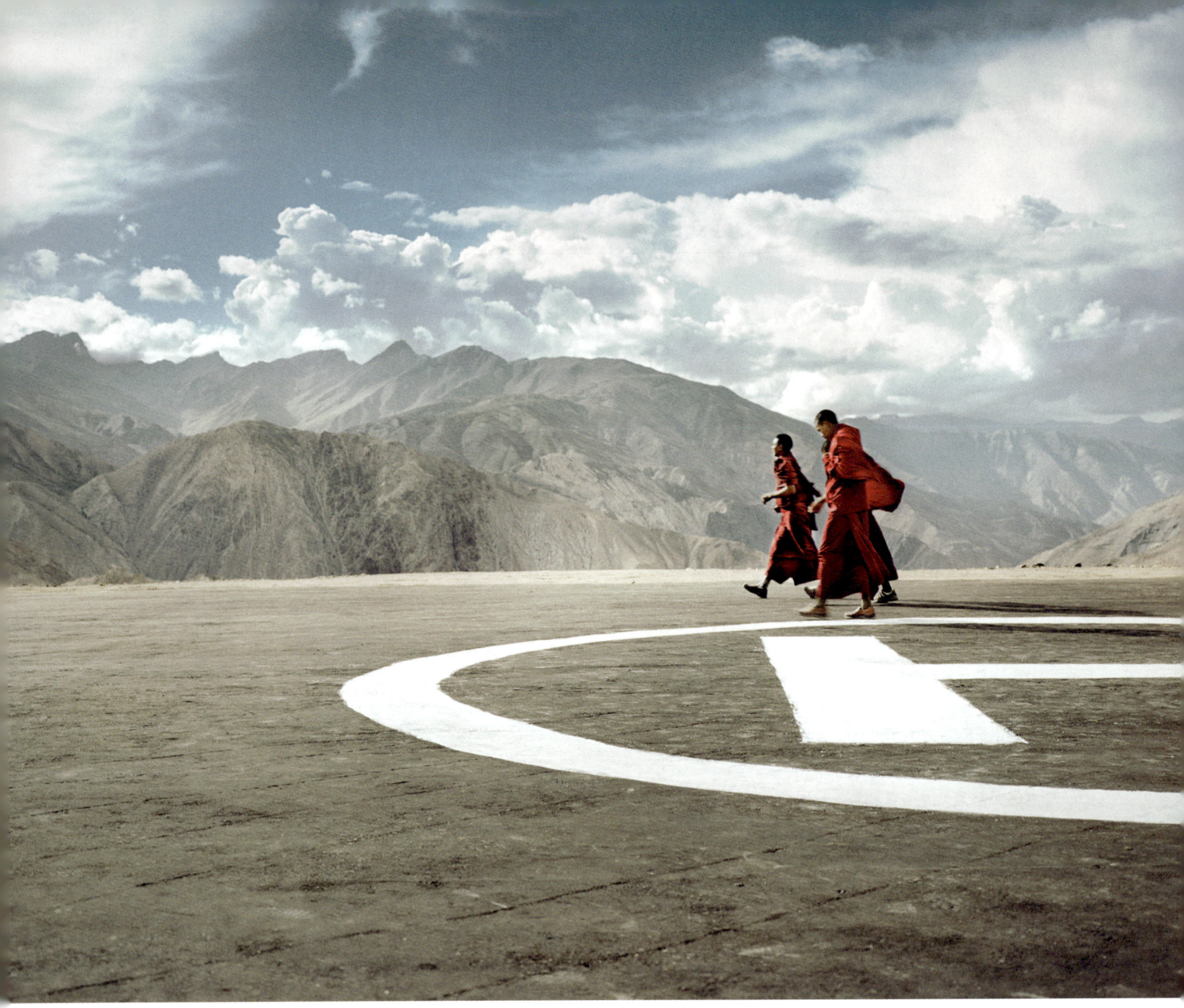

I
N
D
I
A

Fig. 1: A helicopter landing pad was built in Nako for the Dalai Lama, 2007

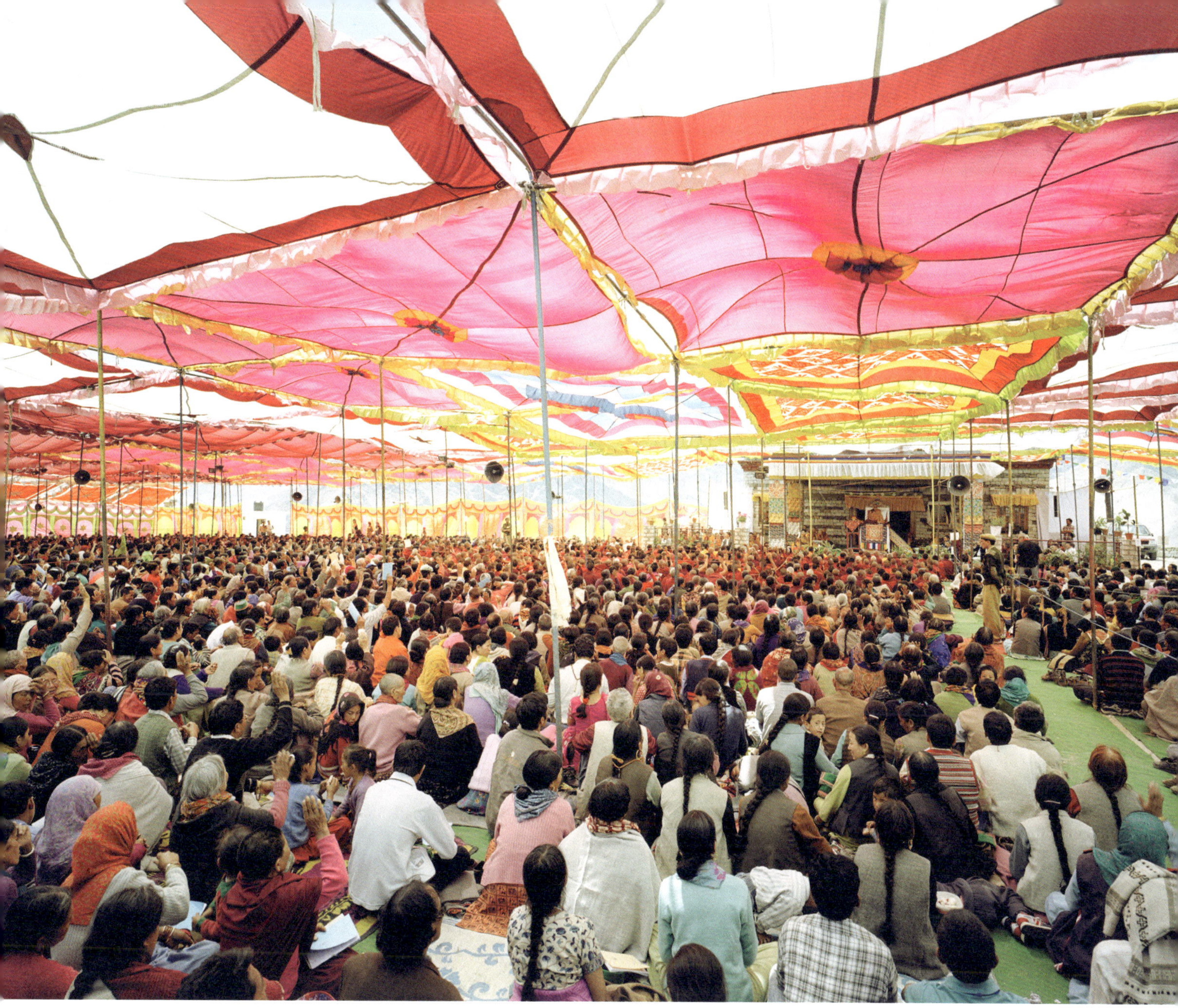

Fig. 2: Celebrations for the visit of the Dalai Lama in Nako, 2007

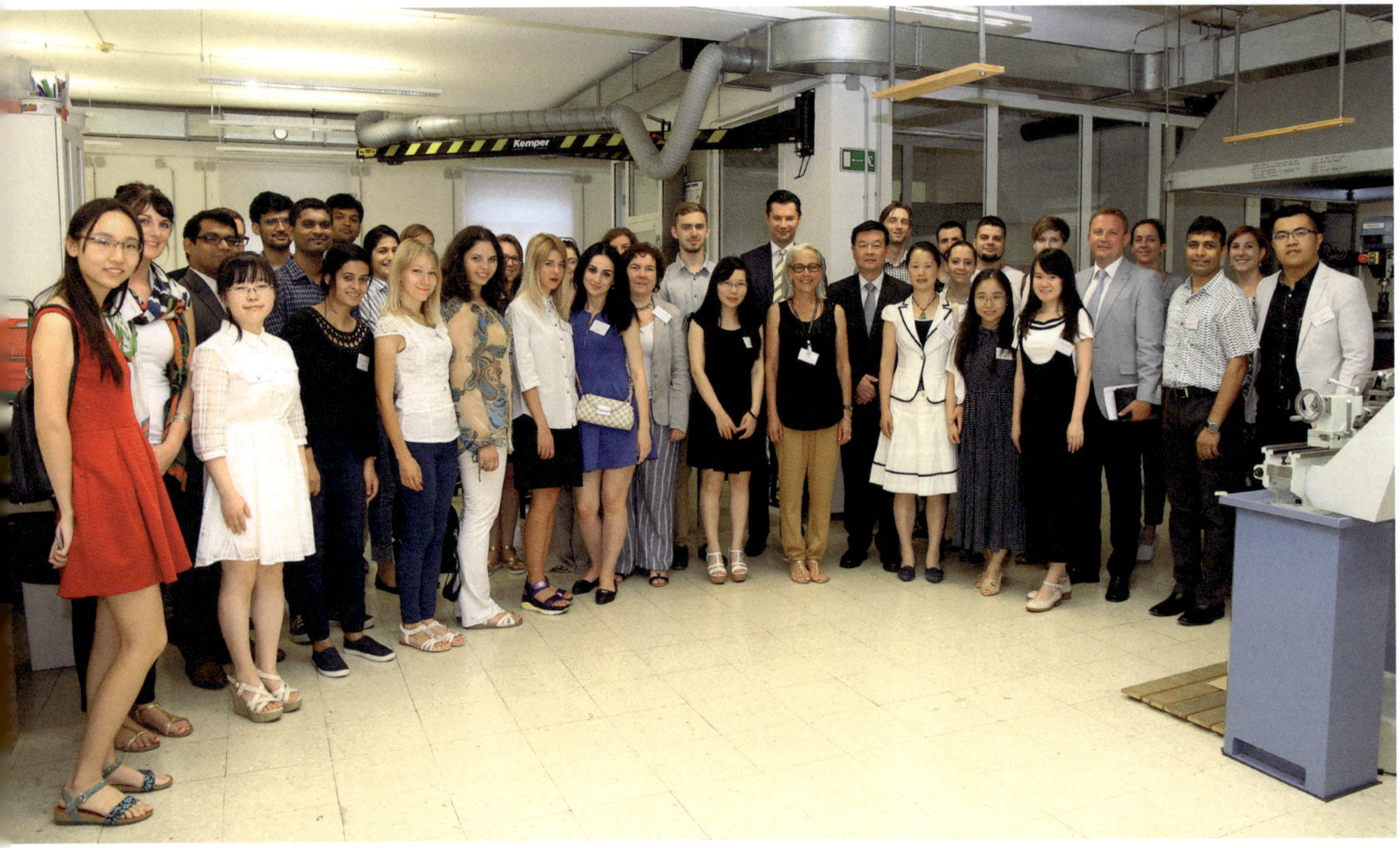

Fig. 9: Group picture of Summer School 2016

Fig. 10: Group picture of Summer School 2017

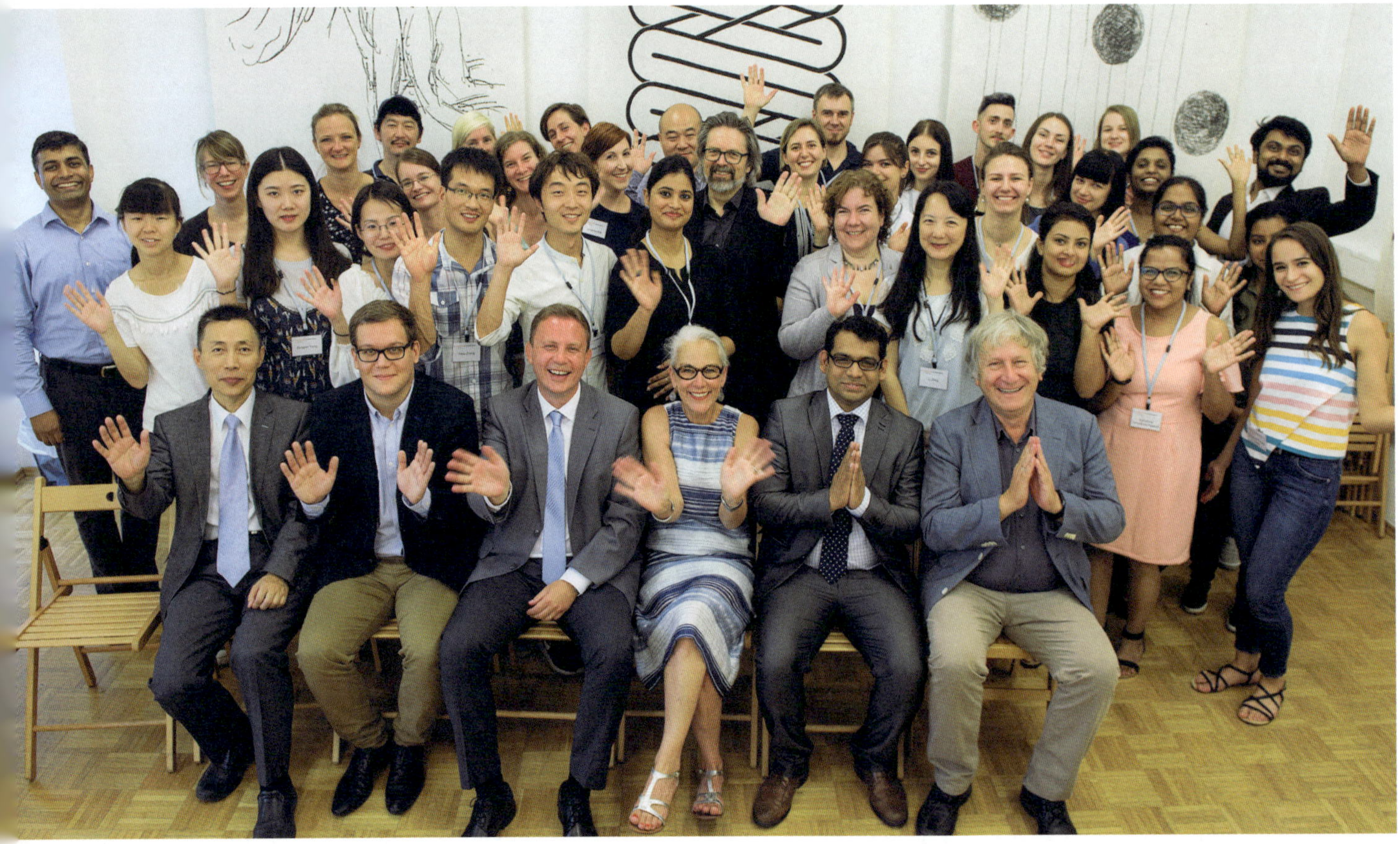

Factsheet Summer Schools

PROJECT	International Summer Schools - Training in Conservation for 76 Guests from all over the World		
HEADED BY	Gabriela Krist	DURATION	Since 2014 until 2017, continuation in 2019
COORDINATED BY	Johanna Runkel	INITIATED BY	Gabriela Krist, M. Velayudhan Nair
PARTNER INSTITUTIONS	National Museum Institute of History of Art, Conservation and Museology, New Delhi (NMI) Belarusian State Academy of Arts, Minsk, Belarus Northwest University, Xian, China (NWU) Polytechnic Institute, Lviv, Ukraine		
FUNDED BY	Eurasia-Pacific Uninet (EPU) Austrian agency for international mobility and cooperation in education, science and research (OeAD) Impulse programme University of Applied Arts Vienna		
TEAM MEMBERS	Tatjana Bayerova, Barbara Eisenhardt, Caroline Göllner, Tanushree Gupta, Martina Haselberger, Ava Hermann, Tanja Kimmel, Philippine Lagardere, Eva Lenhart, Veronika Loiskandl, Marija Milchin, Caroline Ocks, Stefan Oláh, Marina Paric, Gercilene Pinheiro-Chagas, Susanne Sandner, Christoph Schleßmann, Kathrin Schmidt, Britta Schwenck, Ana Stefaner, Agnes Szökrön-Michl, Manfred Trummer, Li Zeng		
PARTICIPANTS	Smita Singh, Nitin Kumar, Rini Hazel Templeton, Abdur Rasheed, Kalpana Singh, Imrana Wasi, Amira Sultan, Anshu, Eisha, Priya Kapoor, Aditya Prahash Kanth, Ali Nasir, Anuja Mukherjee, Ritu Garima, Shashi Ahuja, Prerana, Ashna Rawat, Nivedita Dilip Dhage, Bhawana Kathuria, Siarhei Ashuka, Ales Bagdanau, Taras Kuchynski-Paravy, Alesia Skarabahataya, Fei Fu, Meixian Kong, Yun Zhang, Boxiang Shi, Mamchur Olha, Hoshovska Mariia, Stefaniv Khrystyna, Khrystsina Vysotskaya, Mitchenko Liudmyla, Fondov Bohdan, Harshita Upreti, Divya Yadav, Isha Chaturvedi, Rahul Sharma, Shivanand Dilip Trimbakkar, Xiaoying Zhang, Anaka Asokan, Karishma Selvadurai Rakesh, Aparajita Sengupta, Prathamesh Laxman Pawar, Bhasha Shah, Oksana Lekhniak, Bohdan Novosad, Yulija Andriiv, Alona Ochkovska, Ganzam Sumberraz, Aliaksandra Bahaleisha, Katsiaryna Ivanisenia, Katsiaryna Karanets, Yana Voitsik, Jing He, Weijia Mao, Zengxin Yang, Yaxu Zhang, Yingpei Zhu		
VISITING PROFESSORS	M. Velayudhan Nair, Satish C. Pandey, Bipin Kumar Thakur, Olena Stasyuk, Lijuan Sun, Valery Malakhau, Xue Ling		

International Summer Schools in Vienna

JOHANNA RUNKEL

International Summer Schools took place each year from 2014 to 2017 at the Institute of Conservation, University of Applied Arts Vienna. The programme aimed at fostering knowledge transfer and mutual learning in the field of conservation and focused on hands-on conservation in a full-time, intensive course. Each year a group of students and teaching staff from different international partner institutions came to Vienna to participate. The duration varied throughout the years from four to two weeks in July.

Human resources are among the most crucial factors in promoting development in the conservation profession. Therefore, such training programmes are among the most efficient forms of international cooperation in the field. In the future, the International Summer Schools are going to be expanded. They will take place not only in Vienna, but also in partner countries. This programme will merge the best of the know-how and characteristics of each participating institution - mutual learning rather than one-sided knowledge transfer.

HOW DID THE IDEA COME UP?

The Summer Schools in Vienna started through the personal friendship and joint efforts of Prof. M.V. Nair and Prof. Gabriela Krist, head of the Institute of Conservation, in 2014. Dr. M.V. Nair was at first Director of the National Research Laboratory for Conservation of Cultural Property (NRLC) in Lucknow and then professor and Head of the Conservation Department at the National Museum Institute (NMI), New Delhi. In these positions, he always strongly supported the planning and implementation of joint projects. The activities of the Institute of Conservation in India began in 2004, starting with the conservation project in the temple complex of Nako in the Himalayan region. Subsequently, the Institute of Conservation organized joint conferences, publications and several workshops in cooperation with the NMI. Both institutions signed a Memorandum of Understanding to facilitate academic collaboration and updated it several times throughout the years of cooperation.

In 2016, a Memorandum of Understanding, on a governmental level, was signed between India and Austria with the desire "to strengthen the cooperation of both countries in the fields of arts and culture". In Article 4 of the document, conservation is emphasized. It states that India and Austria welcome "the organization of bilateral seminars, symposia and conferences on an expert level, to study issues related to the preservation of cultural heritage and to promote other forms of cooperation in the field of heritage protection, conservation and development of museums". These ideas, formulated on a governmental level, run parallel to the idea of an International Summer School on Conservation in Vienna that was born through the friendship of two professors.

Moreover an International Summer School perfectly meets the aim of the development plan (*Entwicklungsplan*) of the University of Applied Arts Vienna. In 2013–2014, internationalization was defined as one of the main goals of the university: a world-wide exchange of artistic and scientific knowledge is intended to build the basis for innovation and promote quality in art, science, research and teaching, and dealing with other cultures. In the framework of these ideas and values, International Summer Schools were planned to enable knowledge transfer, mutual learning and horizon-expanding experiences for everybody involved.

WHAT ABOUT THE MONEY?

In the beginning, from 2014 to 2015, the Summer Schools were funded by Eurasia-Pacific Uninet (EPU). EPU is an Austrian University network that aims at establishing contacts and scientific partnerships between Austrian universities and member institutions in East Asia, Central Asia, South Asia and the Pacific region. With a total of 162 member institutions, the network promotes multilateral scientific cooperation, joint research projects, conferences and also faculty and student exchange. The National Museum Institute New Delhi (NMI) and the University of Applied Arts Vienna are both members of the network; therefore an application for funding of the Summer School was successful in 2014 and 2015. In these years, participants came only from the National Museum Institute New Delhi to Vienna. The training programme was free because the workforce, teaching staff, organization, ateliers and material were provided by the Institute of Conservation. Financial support also came from the University of Applied Arts Project Management Department and President Gerald Bast. This additional budget made it possible to enrich the programme and reduce the staff's workload by engaging student helpers. However, attending the Summer School involved some costs for the Indian partners – travel to Austria and living costs in Vienna had to be covered National Museum Institute itself in 2014 and 2015.

In 2016, a new funding programme enabled the Institute of Conservation to develop the Indo-Austrian Summer School further, into an International Summer School. The Institute successfully applied to the IMPULSE programme of the Austrian funding agency OEAD (Austrian agency for international mobility and cooperation in education, science and research). The overall objective of this funding was for the start-up and the strengthening of partnerships between Austrian Higher Education institutions and universities from Central and East European countries. IMPULSE stated that at least one partner must come from a CEE-country and that the other partners can be selected from all geographic destinations around the world. Therefore, the decision was made to apply for a summer school programme which includes partner universities from all over the world: China, Belarus and Ukraine and again – India. The application of the Institute of Conservation was successful – all in all only 9 of 60 applications were accepted.

In the following, the increased budget caused the number of participants to increase rapidly: in 2014, all in all, 14 students, and in 2015, 12 students came from India. Then, in 2016, there were 26 participants, and in 2017, 24 participants from all over the world. These numbers also include long-term interns at the Institute of Conservation who came through the "OeAD Ernst Mach" programme from Mongolia, China and India, and were also included in the Summer School programme. With the help of IMPULSE, the Institute was able to lower

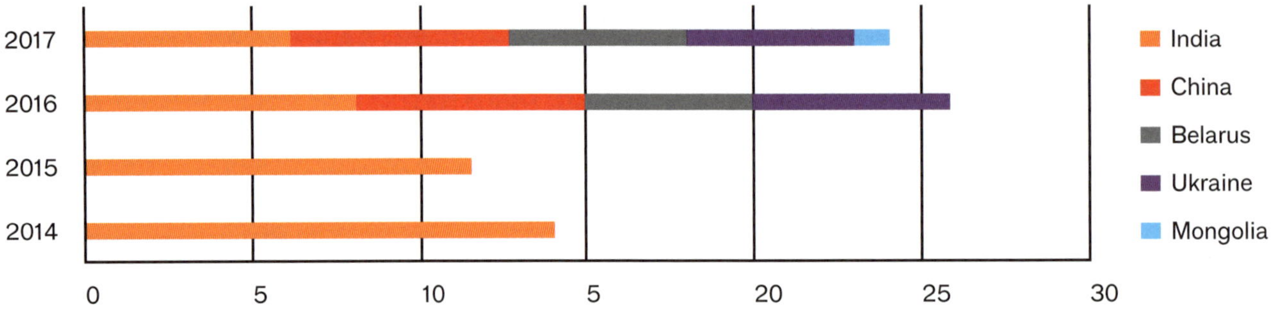

Table 1: Participants of the International Summer School in Vienna from different countries in numbers from 2014-2017.

the costs for the international partner universities to nearly zero. From 2014 to 2015, the participants lodged in a student dormitory in the outskirts of Vienna, then from 2016 to 2017, a more central hostel could be afforded, only a ten-minute walk from the Institute of Conservation. Additional funding from the President and the University of Applied Arts Project Management Department was again used to pay student helpers.

WHO PARTICIPATED IN THE SUMMER SCHOOLS?

Mainly four different institutions sent participants to the Summer School in Vienna: the National Museum Institute New Delhi, the Belarusian State Academy of Arts, Minsk, Belarus, Northwest University, Xian, China and the Polytechnic Institute, Lviv, Ukraine.

The two participating Eastern European countries, Belarus and Ukraine, have a strong artistic tradition. The Belarusian State Academy of Arts in Minsk is the only higher education institution in the country preparing students for a career as conservator. The study programme is still in an early phase of development – in 2016 the conservation programme only took one year. The first conservators, educated in Belarus, graduated from the Academy in 2014. Therefore, most of the Belarusian students that came to Vienna for Summer School were artists who wanted to learn more about conservation.

At the Lviv Polytechnic Institute, conservation is a master's study programme called "Restoration of Works of Art of Stone", which belongs to the architecture department. As the name suggests, it focuses on stone, and the production of high-quality reconstructions is an important aspect of the study programme. The Lviv Polytechnic Institute, Ukraine, has had a long-lasting relationship with the Institute. In 2010 – 2012, mutual work visits were supported by the EU-project ROCARE. In the framework of this programme, the inventory of façades in selected quarters of Lviv, as well as workshops for staff and students, were conducted together.

At Northwest University Xian, conservation is aligned with the School of Cultural Heritage and called "Preservation Technology for Cultural Heritage". The other main study field is archaeology. Therefore, conservation mostly focuses on archaeological findings. There are master and doctoral degree programmes. Together with the Northwest University in Xian, the Institute of Conservation already organised two conferences in China with the title "Archaeology and Conservation along the Silk Road"; the next one is about to follow. The National Museum Institute, New Delhi, as already mentioned, was the first international partner of the Institute of Conservation Summer Schools. There the conservation study is a two-year master's programme. It is possible to continue with a PhD.

WHY SUMMER SCHOOLS IN VIENNA?

The partner universities included in the Summer School all have different traditions and curricula. In most partner universities, conservation studies are rather young, and, respectively, possibilities for practical training of conservators and advanced staff training are still limited. As the University of Applied

Arts has a very long tradition of academic conservation education, well-equipped ateliers and trained staff, the idea of the Summer School was to share these assets and provide a role-model for partner universities. This way, the partners can further develop their study programme and built up similar structures at home.

HOW WAS THE TRAINING ORGANISED?

Summer School was held in July at the Institute of Conservation, University of Applied Arts Vienna. The programme included academic tuition, excursions and social events. The 2014 Summer School took four weeks; 2015, three weeks; and 2016 and 2017, two weeks. Tutors were drawn from the university's staff and from graduates of the Institute. Following the regular system at the Institute of Conservation, teaching took place in small groups (about 12 students). A student of the Institute of Conservation was included in the Summer School team, dedicated to ensure that the participants enjoy their stay in Vienna. His or her role was mostly pastoral, guiding the students through Vienna and giving them advice on where to go and what to do in their free time.

The programme was improved each year according to experiences and feedback. In general, the courses started with a welcome reception, where students and tutors could quickly get to know each other. After the introduction, the hands-on part of the programme started with practical tasks. The workshops were always divided into different fields, according to the specialisations in the Institute: stone, textile, metals, ceramic, painting conservation and chemical investigation of objects have been topics so far in all these years. The training schedule then comprised lectures, discussions and practical demonstrations. The theoretical knowledge was imparted by hands-on activities and exposure to historical art objects.

Short introduction lectures and demonstrations about the handling of art objects marked the start. How to carry a painting? What do I have to think of when touching an object made of silver? Moreover, the students learned about materials that are used in museums and storages like special foams, foils, papers... They were introduced into the simple examination of art objects, their manufacturing techniques and condition, also the identification, extent and nature of alterations and the evaluation of the causes of deterioration. Fig. 1 shows students doing a condition survey in the objects class about a classical golden object of the Christian liturgy.

Under the supervision of tutors, the students had the possibility to conduct conservation measures. They explored different cleaning methods for metals: from dry methods to solvents to the usage of a brew of a plant called "soap root" – soap root is one of the commonest, and very traditional, mediums in metal conservation in Austria. In the course on ceramic and glass conservation, the participants put together broken objects, filled the gaps and retouched the surface (Fig. 2). In the paintings class, they were introduced to surface cleaning as well as to consolidation procedures of paint layers with natural and synthetic materials (Fig. 3). In the field of textiles, the participants learned about dry and wet cleaning, also sewing techniques and labelling (Fig. 4). Fig. 5 shows the stone workshop, where students explored methods for cleaning and for putting broking parts together with glue and reinforcements and therefore explored how to drill stone. Twice, the scientific analysis of paint layers was also included in the Summer School programme. It was taught in the hands-on chemistry workshop delivered by the chemist of the Institute. Also covered were taking samples, preparing cross-sections for investigation, and techniques of microscopic and chemical spot tests for material identification.

Apart from this, study trips to renowned museums, institutions and monuments were organised to show Vienna in all its facets and give an impression of how conservation is carried out in Austria. Every year, Prof. Krist led a tour through the city centre of Vienna, where the students were given an inside view of the history of the city and the care of monuments in Austria (Fig. 6). A visit to Schönbrunn Palace and the Kunsthistorisches Museum Vienna was a must. In the Vienna Museum of Applied Arts, the students had the opportunity to look behind the scenes and could visit the storage facilities.

Apart from the courses and study tours, social events were organised, such as the visit to a traditional Viennese *Heuriger* to drink wine and have some local food.

At the end of the Summer School, there was a presentation of students' work and a feedback session. Then certificates were awarded to the participants.

EXPERIENCES

The structure of the International Summer School in 2016 and 2017 inevitably involved heterogeneity among the participants. On one hand, heterogeneity reduced the efficiency of the training schedule, as the teaching had to be adjusted to the individual level of knowledge. On the other, the participants obtained a great deal of inspiration because of this very heterogeneity. As a side effect, the social life parallel to the courses was most active when students from four different countries participated. A kind of international "campsite atmosphere" arose and the people connected. The Summer School offered students and staff a valuable opportunity for building international networks.

It was not easy to make sure that the participants had enough knowledge of the instruction language of the programme (English). As a simple test, we introduced the handing in of a short letter of motivation from each student before Summer School, to verify that he or she was able to write and understand English.

Finding their way in Vienna was a challenge to some of our participants – therefore student helpers were included in the programme to accompany them when necessary. Moreover, the Indian participants at first could not believe that Vienna is a "safe place". To their own surprise, they found out that they could go out in the evening without anything untoward happening.

Summer School showed that even though we are living in a globalised world, the needs, requests and ideas of the participants were very different from one another – depending on what they were used to at home. Each year, new, surprising challenges came up – all of them could be solved. However, this showed that we ourselves as organisers have specific concepts in mind as to how things can work, or not, what people need, or not – which are perhaps not applicable to everyone or everywhere in the world. Therefore, organising Summer Schools required a great deal of flexibility, but thinking outside the box also gives some kind of freedom. It is a revealing experience to recognise that there are hundreds of ways – you just have to find one.

OUTCOMES

For the participants, the Summer School is a valuable experience abroad. This international experience is becoming increasingly important in the job market. The participants of today will be the new conservators of tomorrow, and therefore they can influence the development of the conservation profession in their countries. Because teachers of the partner universities were also present at the Summer School, they could draw inspiration from the training methods in Austria and bring home new ideas to their institution. Of course, the Institute's Summer School was not only about the academics but also offered the opportunity to get to know fellow students and colleagues from all over the world, improve language skills, meet locals and experience a different culture.

As the conditions of preservation of art objects are different in each part of the world, depending on specific climate, culture and materials, participating and contributing to the Summer Schools was of great benefit for everybody involved, also for the Austrian side (Fig. 7–10).

In the future, the International Summer Schools are going to be expanded. They won't only take place in Vienna but also in partner countries. This programme will merge the best of the know-how and characteristics of each participating institution – mutual learning rather than one-sided knowledge transfer. In 2019 the first of these "new" Summer Schools will take place in Xian, China, and will be organised by the School of Cultural Heritage of Northwest University. New partnerships with

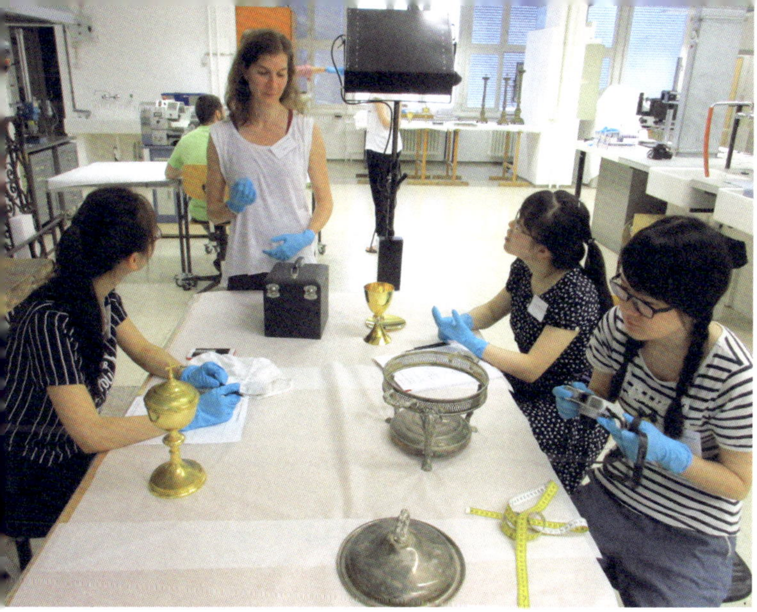

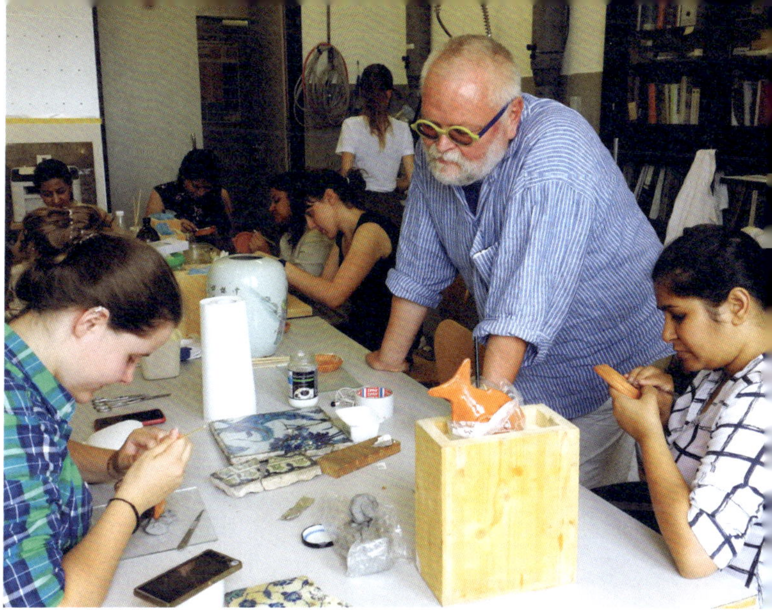

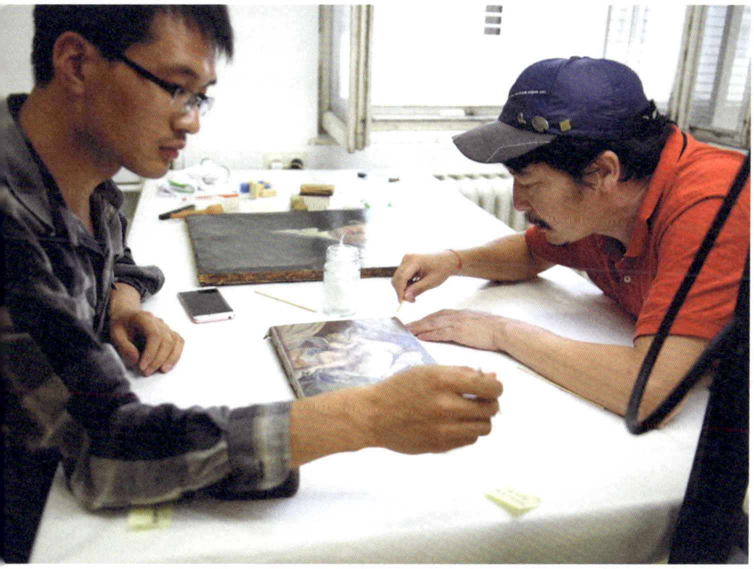

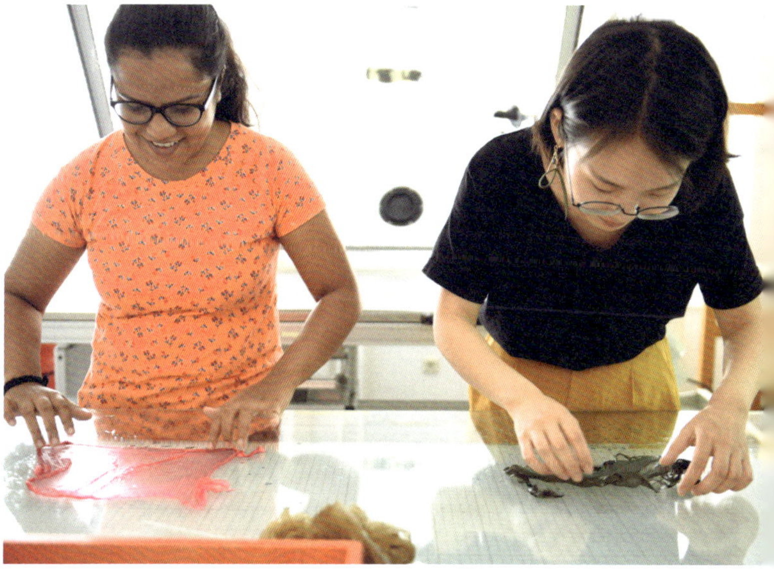

top left: Fig. 1: Doing a condition survey in the objects class, Summer School 2016
top right: Fig. 2: Ceramic conservation workshop with Manfred Trummer, Summer School 2015
bottom left: Fig. 3: Hands-on conservation pf paintings class, Summer School 2016
bottom right: Fig. 4: Hands-on conservation in the textile class, Summer School 2017

Mongolian and Thai universities are being explored right now.

In the end, the main idea of all of these training programmes stays the same: It is the responsibility of all of us to take care of the cultural heritage of the world over and above national borders, as it is stated in the UNESCO Convention concerning the Protection of the World Cultural and Natural Heritage: "...it is incumbent on the international community as a whole to participate in the protection of the cultural and natural heritage of outstanding universal value, by the granting of collective assistance[.]" All Summer Schools and follow up programmes are dedicated to this idea.

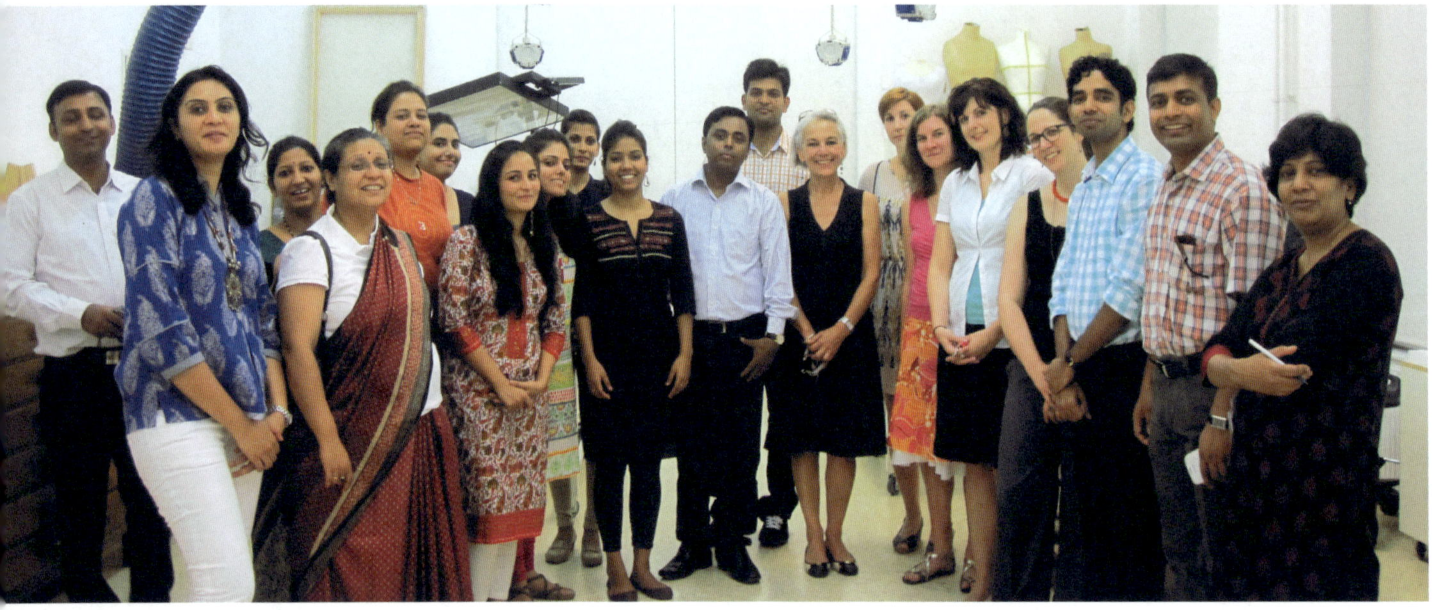

Fig. 7: Group picture of Summer School 2014

left: Fig. 5: Hands-on conservation in stone class: drilling, Summer School 2017
below: Fig. 6: Visit to Vienna with Gabriela Krist, Summer School 2016

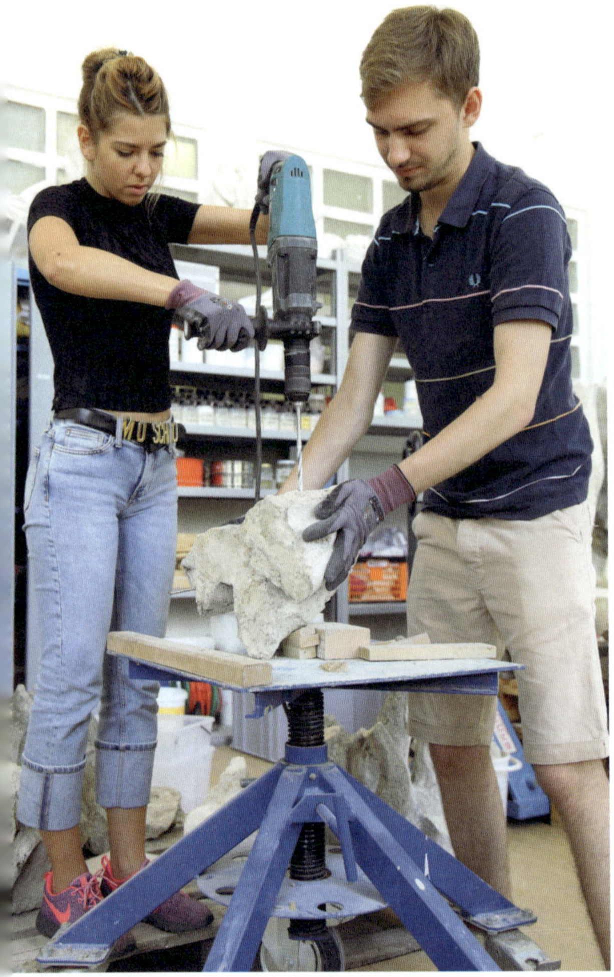

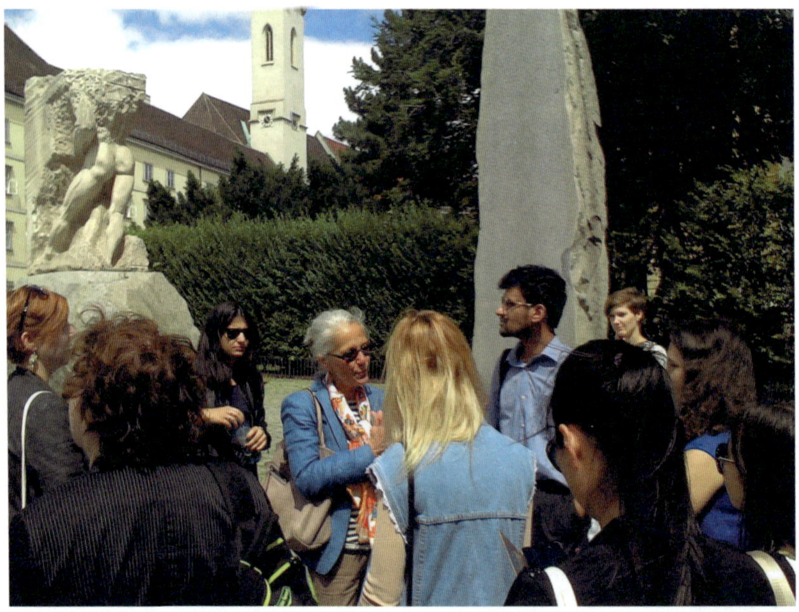

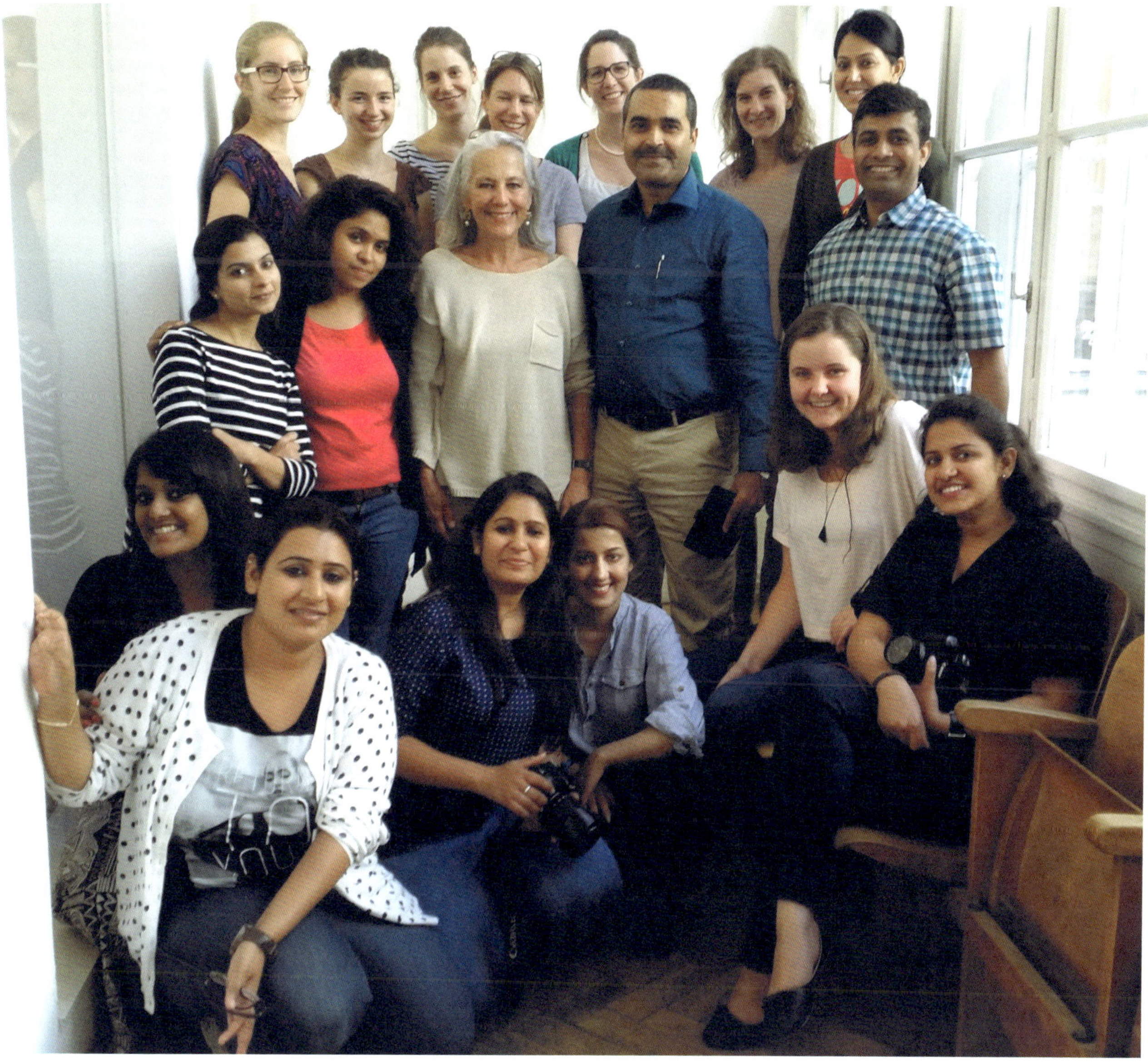

Fig. 8: Group picture of Summer School 2015.

Factsheet Workshops

PROJECT	Conservation Workshops at National Museum Institute New Delhi, 2009-2016
DURATION	17–22 August 2009: “How to Care for Textile Collections: Methods and Practical Approaches” 13–15 September 2011: “Preventive Care of Metals in Collections” 28–30 November 2011: “Investigation and Analysis of Paintings” 9–12 April 2012: “Painting Materials – Theory and Practice” 11–15 February 2013: “Historical Textiles in Museums: Displaying Textiles (Conservation) & Education Strategies in Textile Collections (Museology)” 22–26 February 2016: “Structural Conservation of Canvas Paintings”
HEADED BY	Gabriela Krist, M. Velayudhan Nair, Anupa Pande, Manvi Seth, Satish Pandey
INITIATED BY	Gabriela Krist, M. Velayudhan Nair
FUNDED BY	Eurasia-Pacific Uninet (EPU) Austrian Cultural Forum New Delhi University of Applied Arts Vienna National Museum Institute New Delhi
TEAM MEMBERS	Gabriela Krist, Tatjana Bayerova, Barbara Eisenhardt, Martina Griesser-Stermscheg, Beatrice Jaschke, Tanja Kimmel, Regina Knaller, Marianne Nowotny-Kargl, Britta Schwenck, Nora Sternfeld
PARTICIPANTS (numbers and institutions)	28 participants in 2009 20 participants in 2011 12 participants in 2012 42 participants in 2013 11 participants in 2016 National Museum Institute New Delhi, Gurusaday Museum, Government Museum Chennai, Salarjung Museum, Indian Museum, Victoria Memorial Hall, Goverment Museum and Art Gallery, National Museum, UGRMS, National Gandhi Museum, Maharaja Sawai Man Singh II, NIFT Hyderabad, Museum of Folk and Tribal Art, Chandrahari Museum, INTACH, Kala Bhawan Museum, Pearl Academy of Fashion, Weavers Studio, Chatrapati Shivaji Maharaj, Rajasthan University in Jaipur

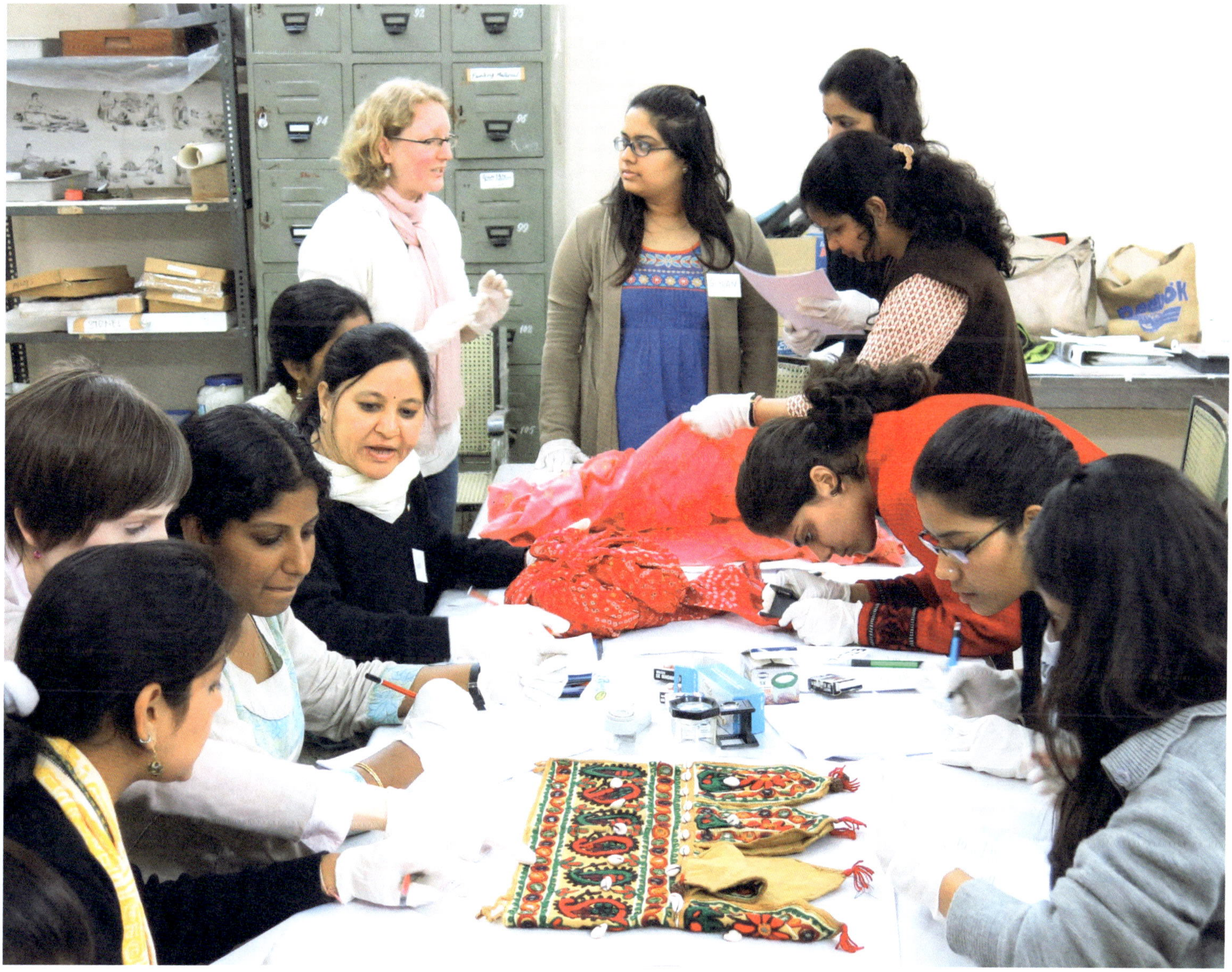

Fig. 5: Visual examination and documentation of textile objects during the workshop “Historical Textiles in Museums; Conservation and Display, Museology and Education” in 2013

Conservation Workshops

JOHANNA RUNKEL

at National Museum Institute (NMI), 2009-2016

Hands-on conservation workshops at the National Museum Institute New Delhi (NMI) marked the beginning of Indo-Austrian training programmes, initiated by Prof. M. V. Nair and Prof. Gabriela Krist (Fig. 1). These workshops are an important tool for doing training on specific topics in an intensive "crash" course. So far, these workshops have taken place six times for one to two weeks in New Delhi, supervised by members of the Institute of Conservation and supported by external lecturers from different Indian Institutions. The Austrian Cultural Forum, the Austrian Embassy in India, and Eurasia-Pacific Uninet (EPU) have always supported these training programmes.

The workshops mainly consist of individual lessons divided into theoretical parts and practical exercises. If possible, original art objects were integrated into the programme, for example from the collection of the National

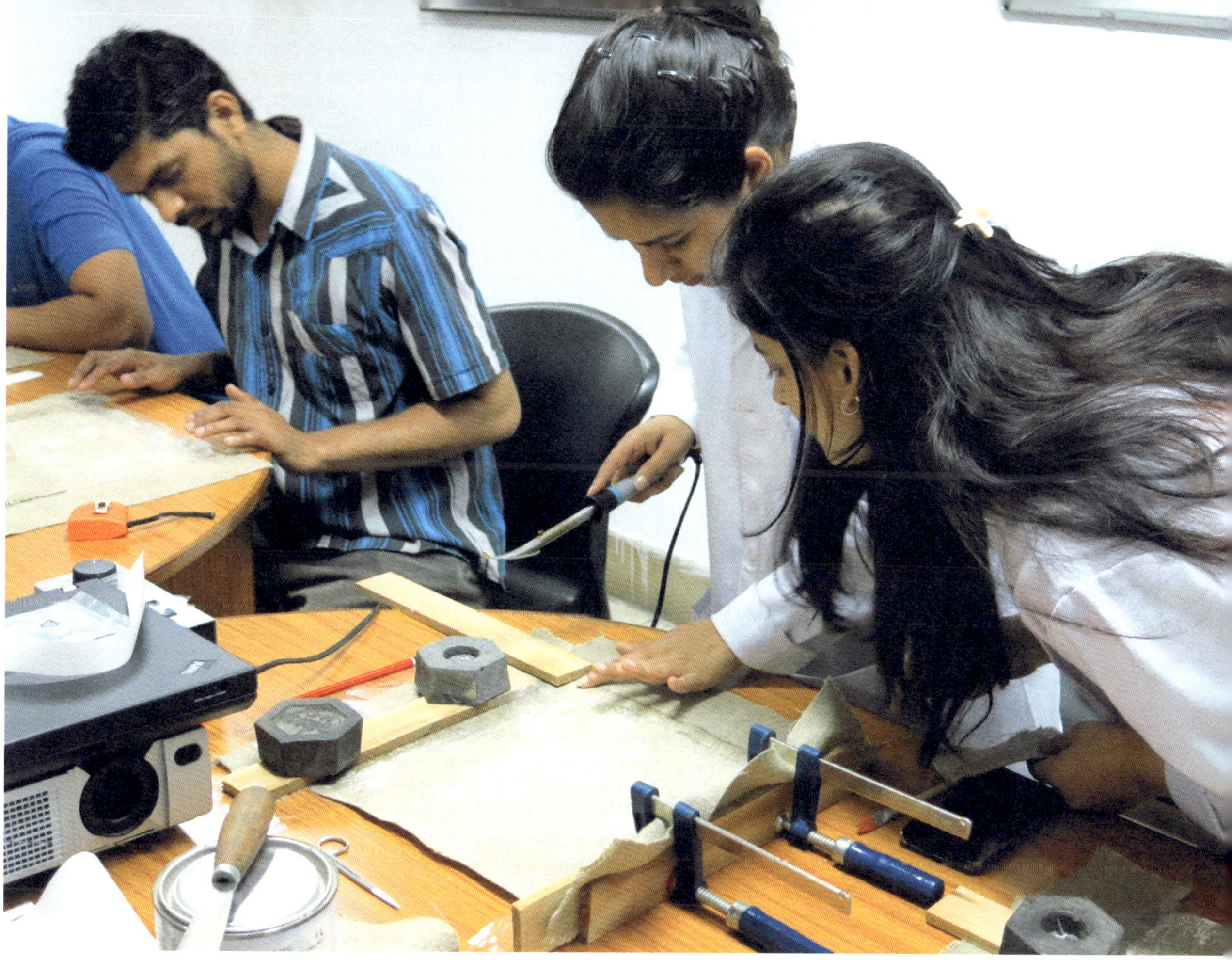

Fig. 4: Hands-on work in 2016

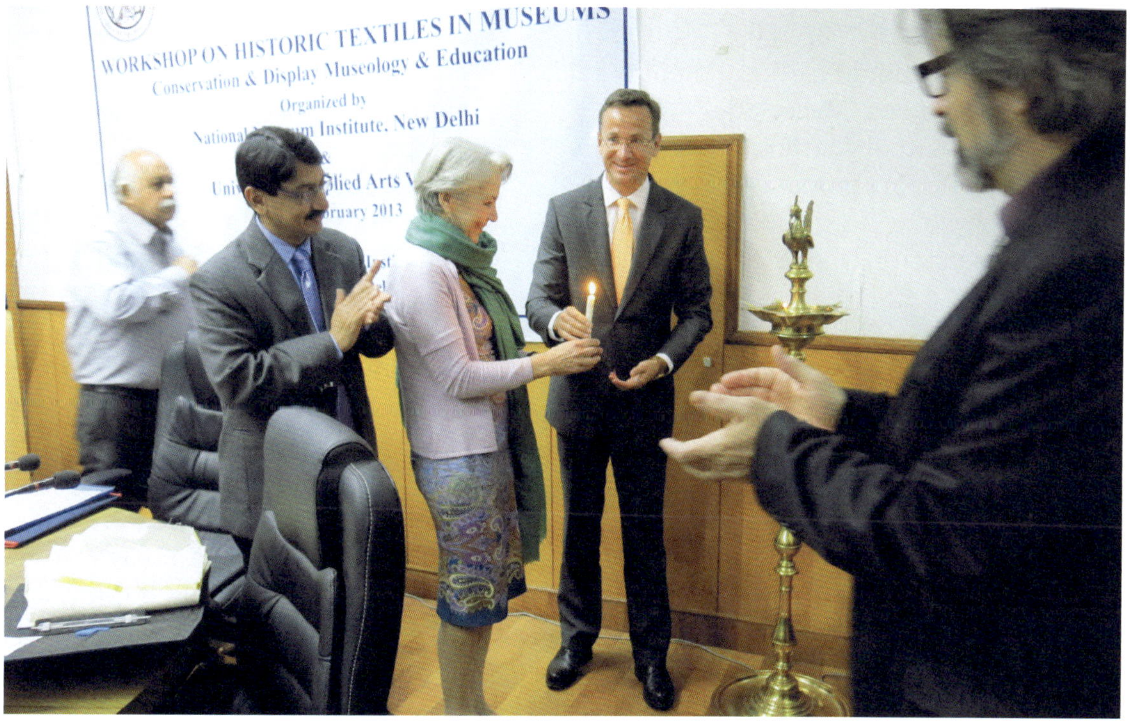

Fig. 1: Most workshops were opened with an official ceremony, where representatives light a lamp. From left to right: M. V. Nair, Venu V., Gabriela Krist, Raimund Magis, Gerald Bast, inauguration ceremony at NMI in 2011

Museum New Delhi. The workshop programmes were supplemented by study tours and the input of the participants (Fig. 2).

The participants were mainly students of the Conservation Department, but also from the Department of Art History and Museology at the National Museum Institute. In 2009, the first workshop also addressed representatives of Indian museums and cultural institutions who care for textile collections in their daily work, as well as conservators, curators and registrars from all over the country. The workshop was the first of its kind and provided the initial impetus for a long history of joint projects and training programmes of the University of Applied Arts Vienna with the National Museum Institute New Delhi (as described in numerous other contributions in this book).

PREVENTION IS BETTER THAN CURE

17–22 August 2009:
"How to Care for Textile Collections: Methods and Practical Approaches"
13–15 September 2011:
"Preventive Care of Metals in Collections"
11–15 February 2013:
"Historical Textiles in Museums: Displaying Textiles (Conservation) & Education Strategies in Textile Collections (Museology)"
Team: Gabriela Krist, Martina Griesser-Stermscheg, Tanja Kimmel, Regina Knaller, Marianne Nowotny-Kargl, Britta Schwenck, Barbara Eisenhardt, Nora Sternfeld, Beatrice Jaschke,

So far, three workshops at National Museum Institute have put the focus on preventive conservation. According to the definition of ICOM-CC, preventive conservation includes all measures and actions aimed at avoiding and minimizing future deterioration or loss. They are carried out within the context or on the surroundings of an item or a group of items. These measures and actions are indirect – they do not interfere with the materials and structures of the items and they do not modify their appearance. To apply preventive conservation in an appropriate way, knowledge about the materials and manufacturing techniques of each object and about mechanisms of decay is essential. Analysing the objects and also the surroundings (for example the museum building) builds the basis of decision-making in preventive conservation. The goal is to find simple and easy-to-maintain measures to improve the situation in storage and display. Preventive conservation can build a sound basis for the preservation of collections; therefore it was the focus of all in all three workshops of the Institute at the NMI.

In two of the workshops, in August 2009 and February 2013, textiles were a priority topic, since they are an integral part of Indian culture and tradition. India is the only country today that holds a "Ministry of Textiles" in its government. Textiles play an important role in everyday life in India: on one hand as an essential economic factor in textile industries, on the other, in keeping outstanding textile collections in museums all over India, which still serve as a source of inspiration for crafts people, designers, artists and the industry. About 116 museums in India have textiles in their collection. Every region in India produces textile objects of a distinct quality and design, made in modest village dwellings or organized craft centres. When it comes to textiles, the need of preventive conservation is evident, as they rank among the most sensitive objects in collections. Textiles as organic materials are very fragile in nature and deteriorate quickly under unfavourable environmental conditions. They are prone to pest infestations, dust and dirt, mechanical stress and also light damage. Often, textiles are already weakened by years of intensive use. Unfortunately, much damage also comes from negligence in handling, storage and display.

The third preventive conservation workshop focused on metals, as the National Museum New Delhi houses a rich collection of bronze sculptures from the Chola period, from the southern part of India. Indian sculptures like "Nataraj" (the dancing Shiva) are famous worldwide for their intricate work. An important treasure is the arms and armour collection which has inscriptions engraved on the daggers and swords. Exquisite pieces of armour coats including from the Mughal period and made in precious metals are kept in the National Museum.

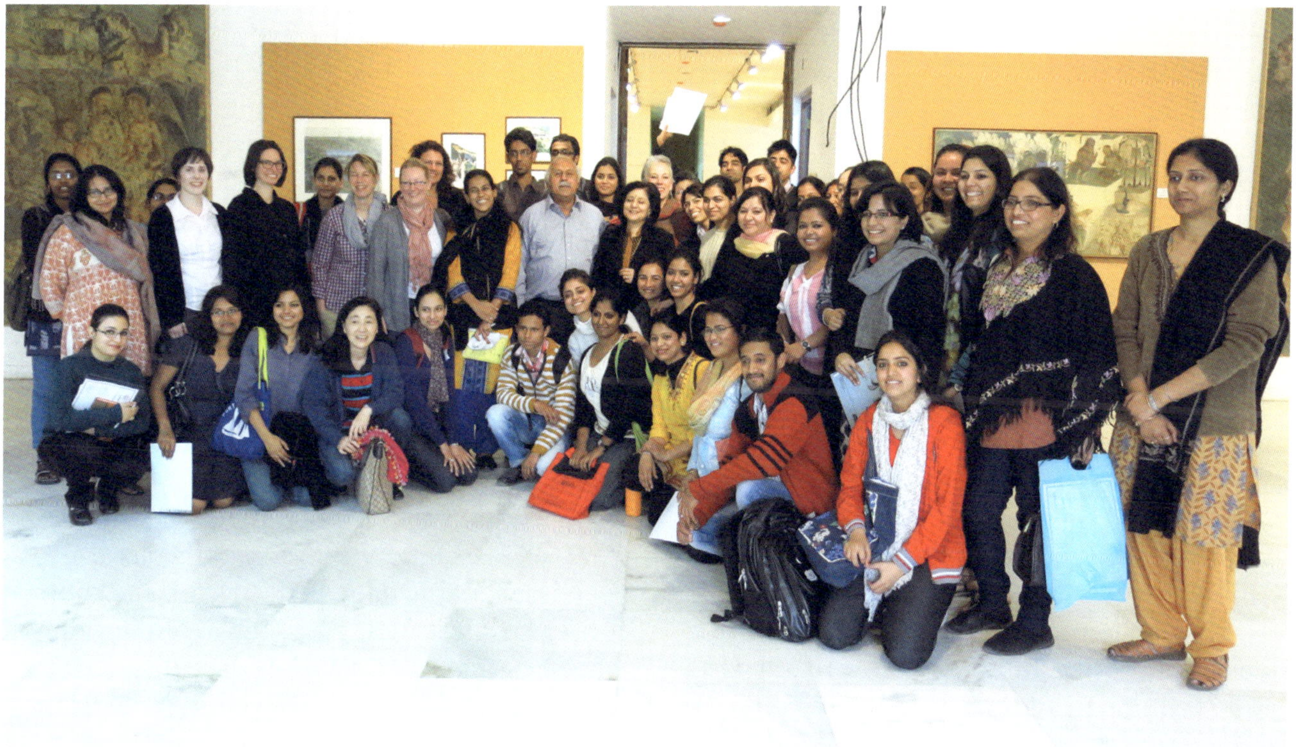

Fig. 2: Group shot
(all participants) 2013

Fig. 3: Preparation of textile
objects for display in 2013

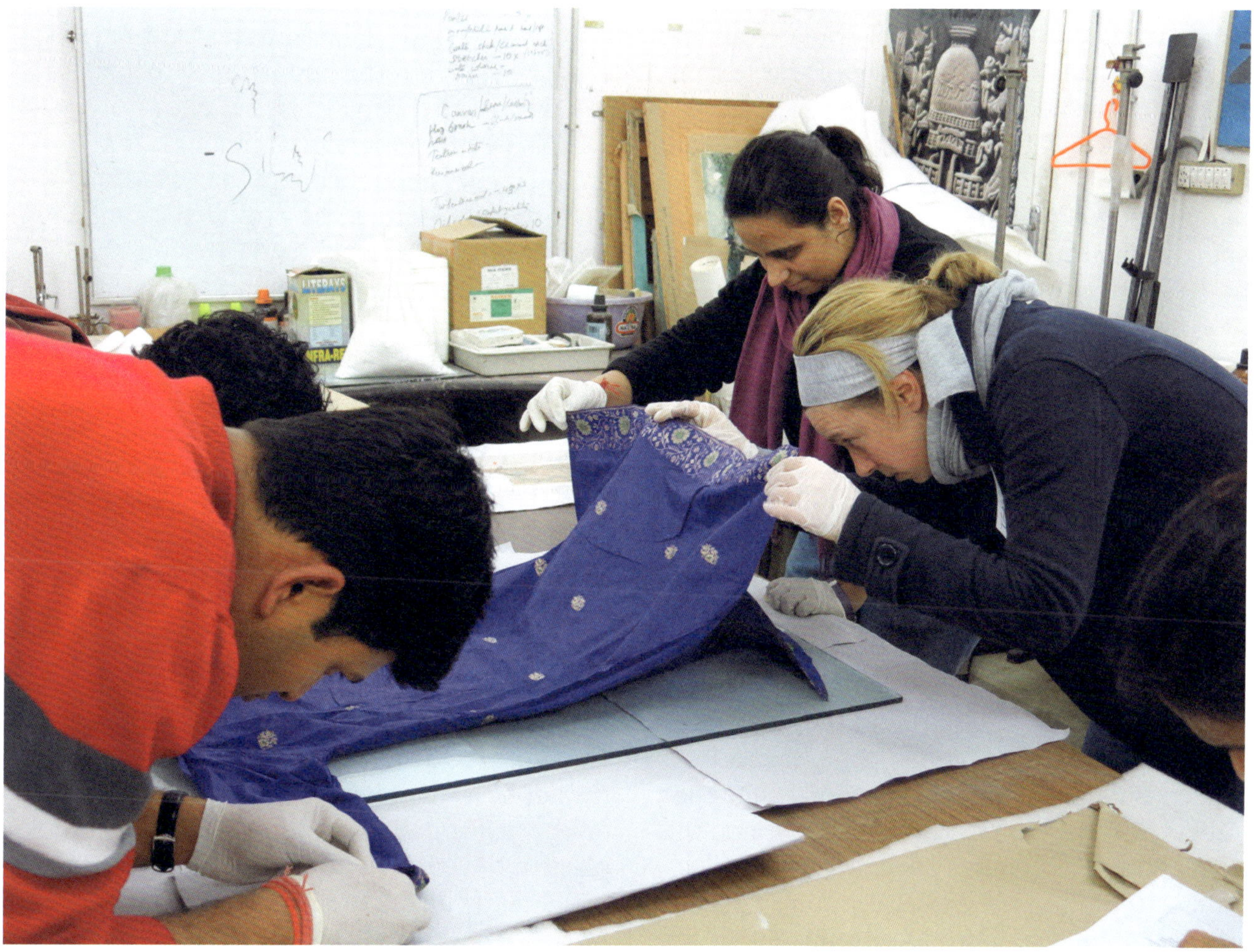

The Buddhist gallery also has beautiful works executed in gold. The collection of coins in different metals depicts the entire history of different rulers in India. Starting with the punch-marked coins in silver from the 6th to the 4th century B.C., the National Museum has a vast collection of coins in gold and copper as well. Metals are especially prone to tarnish and corrosion in high relative humidity. Considering the fact that the climatic conditions of India and Austria are completely different in terms of temperature and humidity, a workshop about preventive conservation for metals was a horizon-expanding experience and knowledge exchange for both the Indian and the Austrian team.

The teaching of condition surveys and documentation techniques were integral parts of the training in all three preventive conservation workshops at NMI. Techniques of documentation of objects were demonstrated and then carried out by the participants on real art objects, mainly from the collection of the National Museum New Delhi. Here, the participants learned to determine their materials and techniques and causes of damage. These lessons were always combined with theoretical introductions and an introduction to the appropriate ways of handling objects.

In 2009 and 2013, risk assessment, respectively museum survey – an important tool of preventive conservation – was taught in the workshops programme. Risk assessment means that conservators quantify all risks that might endanger a collection and then determine the best means of reducing these risks to that collection. In 2009 the storage of the National Museums and the textile gallery of the National Handicrafts and Handloom Museum were the key focuses in the group work. The storage and exhibition areas of the two museums offered an ideal field of learning for the participants, which enabled questions, discussions and exercises under real conditions in the surroundings of an Indian museum. In 2013, museology and conservation students together visited the Albert Hall Museum in Jaipur and repeated this work with focus on the valuable carpet collection. Attempting the exercise among a group of students and staff produced valuable results. The participants were made aware of the range of risks affecting collections. The overall surveys (from the building outside to the inside storage) helped them to understand the broader context in collection care. By doing the surveys "our eyes were opened for the things we tend to ignore" (quotation of one participant) (Fig. 3).

In 2013, the focus was also put on the display of textiles. The display can be an important factor in preventive conservation, as poor display conditions will accelerate deterioration and shorten the textile's useful and/or decorative lifespan. By the time you see visible changes, such as colour fading, yellowing, tears, or insect activity, the textile has already been irreversibly damaged. In the workshop, conservation students learned about various materials that can be used for the display of different types of textile objects. Then two days were dedicated to practical work in finding easily applicable solutions for displaying pre-selected textile objects (Fig. 4). The results were finally presented in a small exhibition by the students. The workshop also included a visit to the textile gallery in the National Museum and offered the opportunity to analyse and discuss the display.

In 2013, the ecm master course for exhibition, theory and practise of the University of Applied Arts Vienna also provided a contribution in the field of museology. The museology students were working on education strategies in textile collections. In small groups, the students prepared their own guided tour of the textile gallery in the National Museum.

28–30 November 2011:
"Investigation and Analysis of Paintings"
9–12 April 2012:
"Painting Materials – Theory and Practise"
Team: Tatjana Bayerová

It is not possible to think about conservation without the support of natural sciences. Therefore, two workshops in India dealt with the application of natural sciences with focus on the investigation of paintings. The first took place in November 2011 and a follow-up that was directly linked to the first one took place in April 2012.

First, the participants were introduced to the chemistry of pigments and their identification in theoretical and practical sessions. The theoretical part comprised painting structures, the general properties of pigments and the overview of artists' pigments. In the intensive practical training, the students could learn how to take samples from a mock-up object and how to prepare the samples, for example as cross-sections. One focus was put on the documentation. At the end of this session samples were taken from the real objects that are currently under restoration at the NMI, and the readymade cross-sections were taken to Vienna where they were photographed in the polarised light microscope. The results were sent back to representatives of the museum. In the second part of the practical session basis of the spot tests (microchemical reactions), heat and colour flame tests for pigment identification were explained and practically demonstrated. Students practised the full range of tests on the reference pigments.

22 - 26 February 2016:

"Structural Conservation of Canvas Paintings"
Team: Veronika Loiskandl, Caroline Ocks

The workshop in February 2016 dealt with an important topic of remedial conservation: the structural conservation of canvas paintings. The structural treatment of deteriorated oil paintings on canvas is a major concern of paintings conservators. In the past, the attachment of a second canvas to reinforce the weakened original was universal practice. This was called re-lining or lining. Now, a less interventionist approach is taken and emphasis is on preserving the original state of the canvas support and applied paint film.

The workshop aimed to provide an overview of current methods and techniques of structural conservation of canvas paintings. The teaching program included mostly hands-on sessions and demonstrations on mock-ups (Fig. 5), supported by short lectures and discussions. In the first session, an overview was provided about different kinds of textile supports, wooden strainer and stretcher systems, and their properties. The second session was dedicated to the adjusting of support frames for optimising the painting's tension. In the third session, the team discussed historical and up-to-date lining methods with the participants in terms of their reasonable use in conservation. One method, strip-lining, was then performed in the hands-on session on the mock-ups. Next, the Institute team introduced methods for tear-mending in canvas, such as thread-by-thread tear-mending, reweaving and the insertion of fabric. Moreover, the advantages and disadvantages of historical linings and up-to-date systems were discussed. A main point was to underline the importance of using proper materials in terms of long time stability. As a conclusion of the week, a joint discussion and evaluation with all of the participants took place.

CONCLUSION

The hands-on conservation workshops at the National Museum Institute New Delhi (NMI) marked the beginning of a long history of joint projects and training programmes of University of Applied Arts Vienna with the National Museum Institute New Delhi. They were further developed year by year and then resulted in the organisation of international summer schools on conservation at the Institute of Conservation in Vienna. In the future, summer schools as well as workshops in Delhi are planned, and the National Museum Institute and the University of Applied Arts Vienna will continue to learn from each other.

REFERENCE

Gupta, T./Nair, M. V., "Collection Care – The Topic of Focus at the National Museum Institute of History of Art, Conservation and Museology, New Delhi", in: Krist, G. (ed.), *Sammlungspflege - Collection Care*, Vienna 2015, pp. 557-563.

Institute of Conservation, University of Applied Arts Vienna, Reports to Eurasia-Pacific- Uninet of 2009, 2012, 2013 and 2016.

Jain, K. K./Dalela, N., "Academic Conservation Training Programmes in India and International Networking", in: Krist, G./Bayerová, T. (eds.), *Heritage Conservation and Research in India. 60 Years of Indo-Austrian Collaboration*, Vienna 2010, pp. 139-146.

Kimmel, T., "Workshops zur Pflege und Erhaltung textiler Sammlungsbestände in Indien und der Mongolei – ein Erfahrungsbericht", in: Krist, G. (ed.), *Sammlungspflege - Collection Care*, Vienna 2015, pp. 547-556.

Research in Vienna

TANUSHREE GUPTA,
NOOR JAHAN

Perspectives, Experiences and Learning Effects

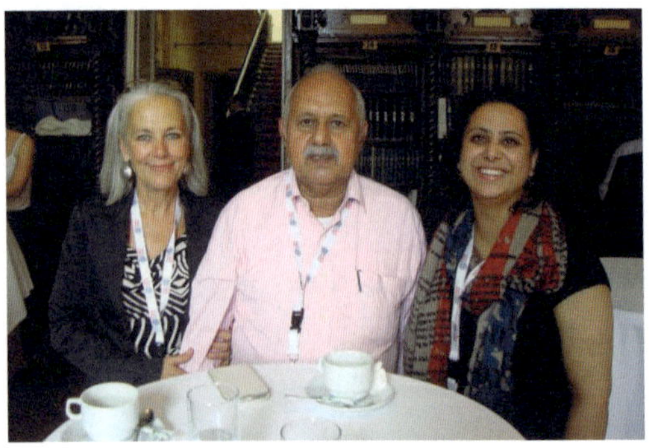

Fig. 4: Attending the fifth Eurasia-Pacific Uninet plenary meeting (Gabriela Krist, M. Velayudhan Nair and Deepakshi Sharma)

The Institute of Conservation, University of Applied Arts Vienna, held its first workshop in the National Museum Institute of History of Art, Conservation and Museology (NMI), New Delhi in August 2009 on "How to Care for Textile Collections: Methods and Practical Approaches". The event was enthusiastically joined by students, researchers and practising conservators from across India. The practical knowledge imparted in the workshop was unique, since this was one of the rare opportunities that theoretical knowledge from books could be learnt hands-on. This was possible because formal studies in conservation were established much earlier in Europe as compared to India, which led to advanced expertise in practical conservation. In the following years, both institutions signed a Memorandum of Understanding, planned more workshops in addition, also organised summer schools, and opened up research possibilities for Indian PhD students in Vienna.

The Institute of Conservation offers a five-year diploma course with specialisation in one of its sections – textiles, stones, objects and painting conservation. After these studies, the students are eligible to apply for their PhD. In India, conservation education begins at the Masters level. NMI is the only one in India that offers a full two years' Masters course in conservation and in addition offers a PhD. The course is theoretically sound, but limits sufficient practical exposure and specialisations, partly because of the lack of time and partly owing to unavailability of facilities. The co-operation between India and Austria has been beneficial in bridging this gap.

The University Grants Commission, which comes under the central government, conducts National Eligibility Test for Lectureship – Junior Research Fellowship (NET-JRF) with written exams twice a year for all study disciplines in India. From the second year on of the master's course, the student is eligible to take this exam. Those who qualify for the exam become eligible for lectureship in universities in India, and those who secure top marks additionally receive a fellowship for a maximum of five years for a PhD, first as Junior Research Fellow and then as Senior Research Fellow. In this way, funded PhDs are possible in India. All PhD interns who came to Vienna have been holders of this fellowship in India. Selection for internship is made on the basis of interview and written application. Starting in 2011, there have been eight PhD internships so far, financially supported by the Austrian Federal Ministry for Science and Research within the framework of the Eurasia-Pacific Uninet (EPU). The Austrian Agency for International Cooperation in Education and Research (OeAD) and Centre for International Cooperation & Mobility (ICM) are the authorities awarding the scholarships – Technologiestipendien Ost-/Zentral-/Südasien (TOZS Doktorat) and Ernst Mach Grant, Ernst Mach – worldwide.

At the Institute of Conservation, students work on original objects under the supervision of Professor Gabriela Krist and university assistants. This approach of practice linked with investigative studies is introduced to interns as well. Depending upon the area of interest, interns learn practical skills twice a week. This knowledge is complemented in their research. Other days are devoted to carrying out the research work in the conservation science laboratory. As all laboratories are technically equipped with the essential facilities, it is possible to accomplish different experiments under one roof. When any further requirement arises, the Institute collaborates with other organisations to carry out analytical studies. In addition, interns take part in a project week, which takes place in the first week at the beginning of each semester. Project weeks are dedicated to on-site implementation of collection care in museums and monasteries. This gives the opportunity to learn the know-how of working with big collections using high-end, conservation-grade materials for storage and exhibition. Interns attend all lectures, which are held in English, and can appear for the exams and obtain marks as they register in the university. Interns are always made part of all ongoing activities in/of the Institute, e.g. summer schools, workshops, conferences and excursions (Fig. 1); for many of these, interns get to travel in Austria as well as abroad. Additional learning is facilitated by the richly equipped library of the Institute and the assignments of fellow students. As publication remains an essential part for documentation of research, the Institute helps interns to develop effective and systematic scientific writing.

OeAD regularly organises social events for all its scholars, who are enrolled in different courses and come from different nations, and offers everyone help in dealing with the new system. In the Institute, too, students and faculty, as well as fellow interns from different countries, form a mutual bond. In between numerous cross-cultural talks, similarities bring us together and diversities make us more curious. The city of Vienna with its historic buildings, magnificent museums, beautiful gardens, natural landscapes, clean surroundings, traditional cuisines, and a walk along the Danube always make the weekends worthwhile.

The internships have been fulfilling in carrying out the research work for a PhD, gaining practical skills and, more importantly, in developing an informed approach to conservation. The result and experience of internships is disseminated in the form of presentations in jour-fixes, at the Indian Embassy in Vienna, and then, back in the home country, in association with the Austrian Embassy in New Delhi; and also in the form of training other students. Interns also report their outcomes in the annual magazine of the Institute.

Research fellow from NMIHACM, New Delhi	PhD duration	PhD Title	Internship period at Institute of Conservation, University of Applied Arts Vienna
Tanushree Gupta	September 2010 – December 2016	"Scientific Studies on Conservation Issues of Acrylic Paintings"	October 2011 – March 2012 October 2013 – January 2014 October 2015 – June 2016
Deepakshi Sharma	January 2012 – August 2018	"The Technical Analysis of Different Varieties of Palm Leaf Manuscripts in India"	September 2015 – December 2015
Md. Ali Nasir	January 2012 – ongoing (thesis submitted and under review)	"Indo-Islamic Carpets: A Study of Materials, Motifs and Techniques from a Conservation Perspective"	October 2013 – January 2014
Nitin Kumar	June 2012 – ongoing (thesis submitted and under review)	"Study of Natural Materials Application on Vegetable-Tanned Leather as Potent Fungicide"	October 2013 – January 2014 November 2015 – July 2016
Noor Jahan	April 2014 – ongoing	"A Technical Study of Wall Paintings and Other Decorative Art Features in Hunder Zimskhang, Nubra"	October 2017 – August 2018

Table 1: List of interns from India (2011 – 2018)

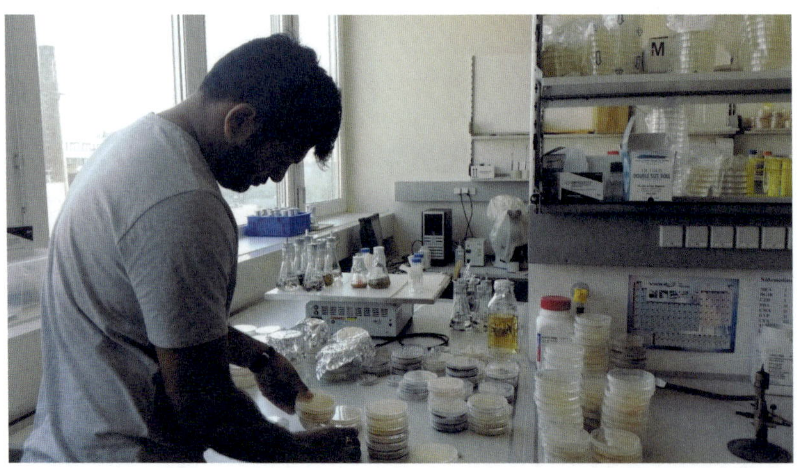

Fig. 6: Working in the laboratory at the Institute of Biotechnology (Nitin Kumar)

“Conservation of acrylic paintings is a challenge worldwide. My research attempts to understand the behaviour of ‘Camel’ acrylic emulsion paint films when applying selected cleaning solvents. In my first internship, I worked on the conservation of four modern paintings from the collection of the Museum auf Abruf (MUSA) and learnt basics of investigative studies in conservation science. In my second internship, I performed experiments for material research using in-house facilities as well as scanning electron microscope – energy dispersive x-rays, fourier-transform infrared spectroscopy and differential scanning calorimetry studies from other institutes. In my third internship, I worked on my research publications. Simultaneously, I participated in various on-site collection care projects, and attended many workshops and conferences (Fig. 2). Approach and methodology learnt during my internships for research and practice have expanded my knowledge and endowed me with better decision-making skills. These internships have not only had a major influence on my research work, but have also provided the opportunity to experience the grandeur of Austria.”

Tanushree Gupta

“It was indeed a great opportunity to receive an Ernst Mach Fellowship for carrying out the research work on ‘Technical analysis of different varieties of palm leaf manuscripts in India’ at the Institute of Conservation, University of Applied Arts Vienna. The main motive for my applying here was because its laboratory is fully equipped; hence this institution has played an essential role in my research work (Fig. 3). I had brought leaf samples from different parts of India for analysis such as structural characterisation under polarised light microscope, pigment analysis under scanning electron microscope – energy dispersive X-rays and finally, binding media analysis under gas chromatography mass spectrometry. Simultaneously, I also got an opportunity to attend the 5th plenary meeting of EPU (Fig. 4) and hands-on practical work with the team of the Institute at a monastery in Wiener Neustadt. Finally, I got accessibility and prepared detailed condition reports of a rare collection of palm leaf manuscripts in the Austrian National Library.”

Deepakshi Sharma

Fig. 2: Poster presentation at the IIC conference in Turin 2018 (Tanushree Gupta)

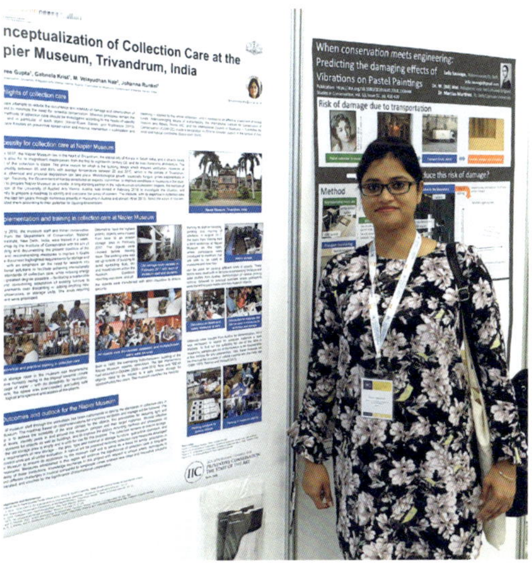

Fig. 3: Working in the laboratory (Deepakshi Sharma)

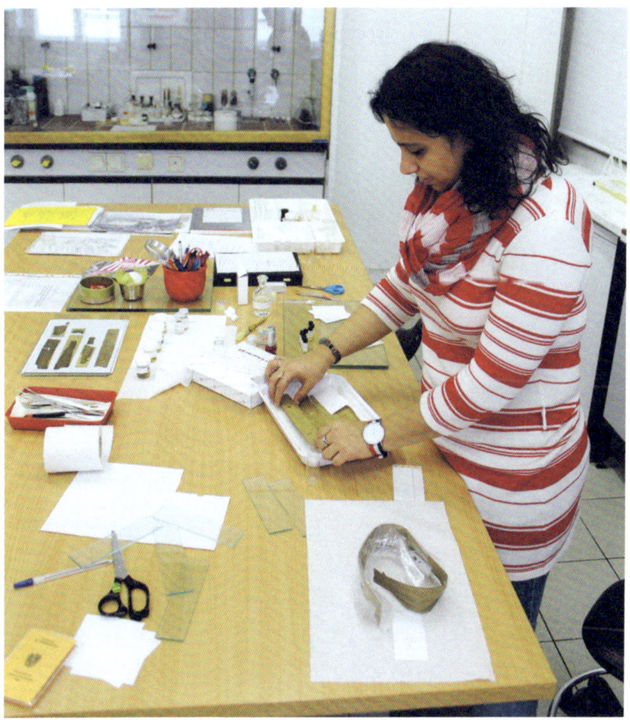

"This thesis pioneers the exploration of natural dyes in 17th–19th century carpets. To study the constituents of natural dyes, samples from five different carpets were collected. For the morphological study, fibres were analysed using scanning electron microscope and scientific analysis of natural dyes were done using liquid chromatography – mass spectrometry, UV spectroscopic measurements and fourier-transform infrared spectroscopy. During the internship, I worked on fragments of 20th century carpets. They had several problems, including insect remains, deposition of dust and dirt, tears on the border and loss of weft. Before starting conservation work, I examined the fibres of the carpet using a microscope. I started careful dry cleaning by using a special vacuum cleaner. After dry cleaning I also did wet cleaning (Fig. 5). Most of the time, the carpets needed some stitching work for consolidation. So, I learnt different techniques of stitching and supporting and implemented it on the carpets. There was also the chance to work with textile conservators of two museums in Vienna, the Museum of Applied Arts and the Kunsthistorisches Museum Vienna."

Md. Ali Nasir

"Art Conservation has struggled to tackle the problem of fungi, and the impact of chemicals is harmful not only for the object being treated, but is also detrimental to human health. Thus, my aim was to find if natural materials could be exploited to treat fungi. I carried out tests to study the behaviour of oils as anti-fungal agents and their impact on leather. For my tests, the Institute of Conservation approached the Institute of Biotechnology, University of Natural Resources and Life Sciences, Vienna, to conduct fungi-related experiments (Fig. 6). During my stay in Vienna, I got the opportunity to work in the textile conservation studio. I was also part of the Summer School and took part in the stone conservation studio activities. I will always be thankful to the Institute of Conservation for trusting me till the last moment. Ultimately I was able to find natural materials that can be used to fight the problem of fungi in an eco-friendly manner and with less side-effect."

Nitin Kumar

"Hunder Zimskhang is a traditional aristocratic house that served as the residence of the aristocratic family of the Hunder village from the early 16th to the middle of the 20th century. The house accommodates a number of wall paintings which are non-typical for the region. The main goal of the research is to perform a comprehensive scientific study on the artistic techniques and materials used for executing the artworks present in this house. In the frame of the internship, cross-section, dispersion and thin-section samples of the paint and plaster layers were prepared and analysed by the means of optical microscopy (Fig. 8), polarised light microscopy and scanning electron microscopy equipped with energy dispersive X-ray. Spot tests were done for preliminary identification of the binding media and simultaneously data sheets were prepared for all the samples (Fig. 9). The Institute approached the Kunsthistorisches Museum Vienna for the gas chromatography mass spectrometry analysis. I had the opportunity to attend practical classes on textile conservation and present my work updates in the jour fixe of the Institute (Fig. 10). The continuous support of the Institute allowed me to successfully complete the analytical work for the research."

Noor Jahan

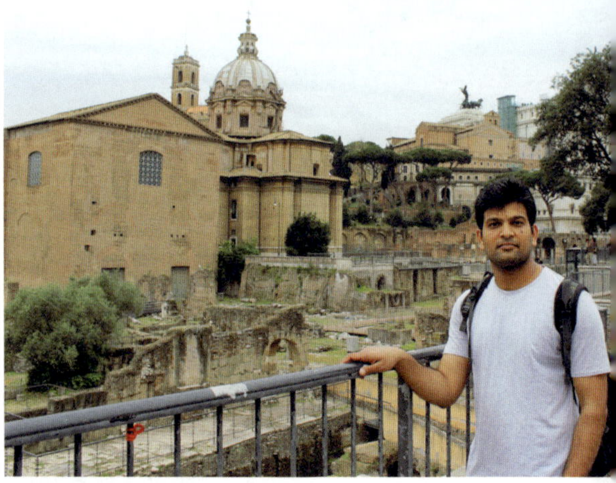

Fig. 7: During the excursion in Rome (Nitin Kumar)

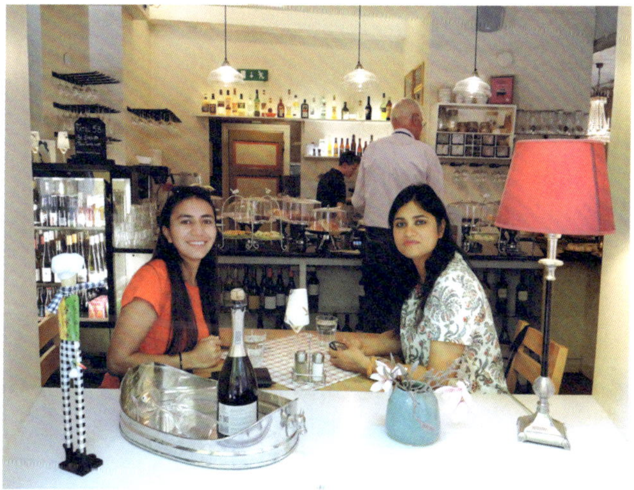

Fig. 1: During the excursion in Stockholm (Noor Jahan and Tanushree Gupta)

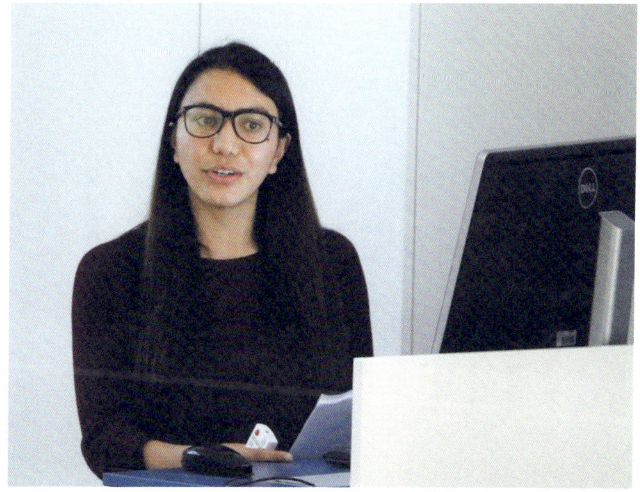

above: Fig. 10: Presentation at the workshop organised by the institute (Noor Jahan)
right: Fig. 5: Wet cleaning of a carpet on the suction table (Md. Ali Nasir)

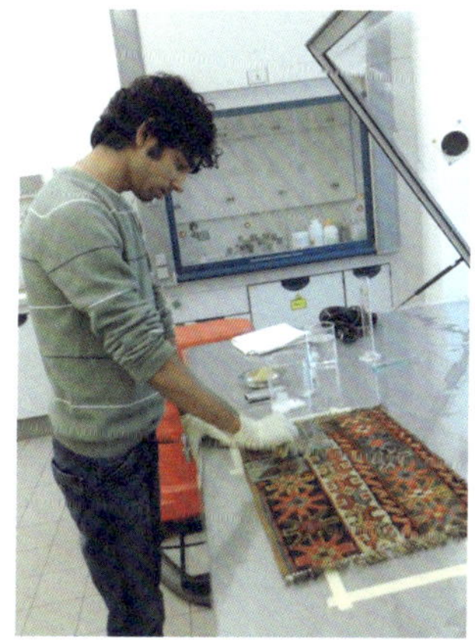

Fig. 8: Working on the optical microscope (Noor Jahan)

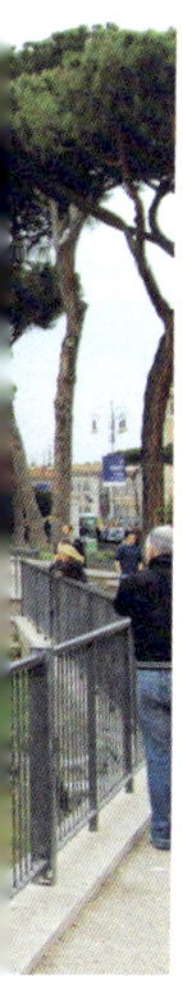

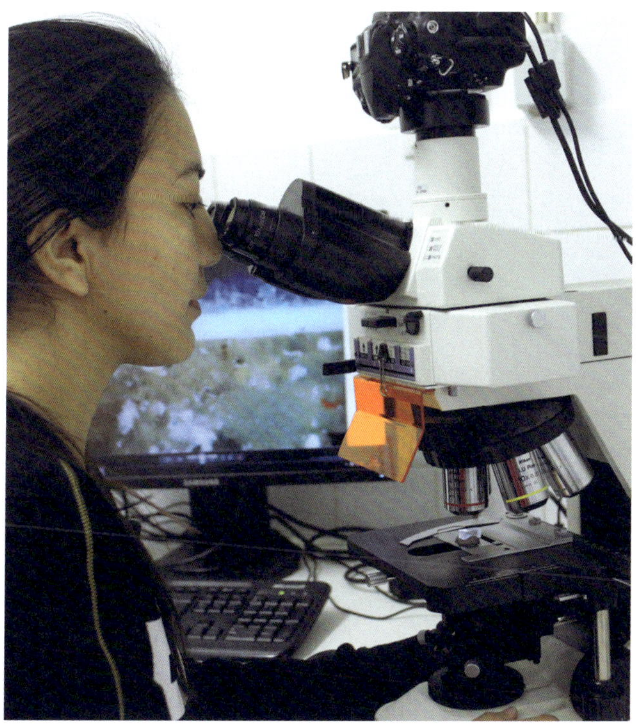

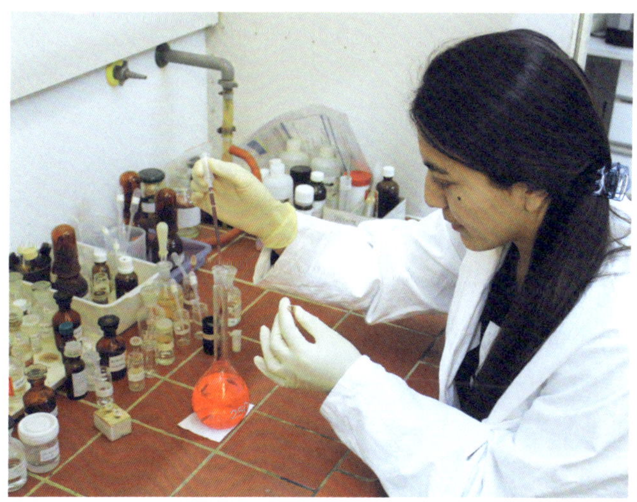

Fig. 9: Performing micro-chemical tests on pigment samples (Noor Jahan)

Art Conservation in India

TANUSHREE GUPTA

Reviving the Cultural Richness

India is a land of diversity. Long before the Indus Valley civilisation, India was home to humans, evidence of which remains even today in the prehistoric caves of Bhimbetka in Madhya Pradesh. In the past, India was ruled in smaller kingdoms, and often attacked by neighbouring powers. The Mauryan Empire (321–187 B.C.) is believed to have conquered the largest area under the reign of Emperor Ashoka, whose lion capital on the pillar at Sarnath has been adopted now as National Emblem of India. There are multitudes of such examples from the past which still carry significance for present-day society. The long history, influenced by diverse regional and religious features, led to the rich culture which we experience today.

The government of India operates with the Ministry of Culture to ensure the significance of tangible and intangible heritage to society. Each state of India has its own Department of

Cultural Affairs encompassing various bodies devoted to showcasing and reviving cultural assets. Some organisations work directly under the central government. This paper presents the recent efforts invested by the union government in the field of conservation of tangible cultural heritage, which have been remarkable in raising standards within the profession.

The tradition of caring for objects to preserve them for future generations has always existed. As for other subjects, ancient texts also contain examples of art conservation practice, as documentation was necessary for the continuation of knowledge that was developing in society. In 1930, the first laboratory for conservation of museum objects was established in the Government Museum, Chennai, and from then on in many more museums. Over time, the government has undertaken various steps to develop expertise in the country. The staff members of pioneer laboratories were sent abroad to receive training, because at this point, India did not have any formal training or academic courses in art conservation. With the efforts of the founding members, the field excelled in various divisions.

The establishment of the National Research Laboratory for Conservation of Cultural Property (NRLC), originally in New Delhi in 1976 before moving to its present headquarters in Lucknow in 1978, was a milestone in the history of conservation in India. This scientific institution was founded with the support of the United Nations Development Programme (UNDP) and the United Nations Educational, Scientific and Cultural Organization (UNESCO). It is responsible for researching and developing methods and materials for carrying out conservation with reference to the climatic conditions of India. As part of education and training, the NRLC conducts training courses for in-service and early-career professionals. With a regional centre in Mysore, Regional Conservation Laboratory (RCL), the NRLC also undertakes multidisciplinary field projects across the length and breadth of the country.

In India, training in conservation was for a long time practised "on the job" in government institutions. In 1983, diploma courses in "History of International and Modern Art and their Sources" and "Restoration of Oil Paintings" were started in the National Gallery of Modern Art, New Delhi, which was shifted to the National Museum, New Delhi in 1985. These courses were expanded into MA and PhD programmes and the Society of the National Museum Institute of History of Art, Conservation and Museology, New Delhi (NMI) was established with the three departments as mentioned in its name. The NMI is housed within the National Museum and was registered on January 27, 1989 under the Societies Registration Act, and since April 28, 1989 has had the status of "Deemed to be University" by University Grants Commission, the Ministry of Human Resources Development, Government of India. The Department of Conservation offers 15 places for MA every year and possibility of further research in its PhD programme. There are many other universities in India which offer studies in conservation as one subject or semester, but none as a full degree course. In addition, including the NMI, many museums and conservation organisations offer short certificate courses to enhance understanding of art conservation and to promote public awareness and appreciation of cultural heritage. There are two major international associations in the conservation of artworks – the International Council of Museums – Committee for Conservation (ICOM-CC) and the International Institute for Conservation of Historic and Artistic Works (IIC). The NMI hosted the ICOM-CC conference in 2008 and will host the IIC conference in 2020. The NMI will shift to a new and bigger campus in Noida in the near future.

The blueprint for establishing the National Museum was prepared in 1946, with the aim of having an institution for disseminating knowledge on historical, cultural and artistic excellence through its collection. The museum was inaugurated in the President House in 1949. It was then moved to its present building in Janpath, which was founded by Pandit Jawaharlal Nehru, the first Prime Minister of India, in 1955. The central location and the exquisite collection of the National Museum make it a prominent attraction to art admirers and researchers. The National Museum has an in-house conservation laboratory which takes care of the preservation of its collection, as well as extends services to other institutions. The laboratory also engages in research and capacity-building programmes. Moreover, the National Museum has numerous in-house publications communicating appreciation of the cultural property, and a library devoted to the collection of rare literature on heritage.

To bring art from different parts of the country to a common platform, the Indira Gandhi National Centre for the Arts (IGNCA) was established. The IGNCA is an autonomous institution under the Ministry of Culture, constituted in 1987 in memory of the late Prime Minister Indira Gandhi. This organisation encompasses study and experience of all forms of arts. Based in New Delhi, the IGNCA has a dedicated conservation laboratory which takes care of books, manuscripts, paintings and objects. It has devoted units for preventive conservation and conservation science research. With various national and international collaborations, the IGNCA is an active centre for arts and art conservation in the country.

Besides art objects, important documents from various offices across the country receive advice for proper care. The National Archives of India (NAI), established in 1891, functions as an Attached Office of the Ministry of Culture. As per the Public Records Act 1993 and the Public Records Rules 1997, after every 25 years, records from ministries and departments as well as public sector undertakings of the central government are transferred to the National Archives of India in New Delhi. The holdings of records in the archives run into forty km of shelf space and contain series from the year 1748. Documents to be added in the archives are at first cleaned, fumigated and checked for any insect infestation before they enter storage. All records are kept under controlled climate conditions with appropriate measures of fire prevention and fire-fighting systems. The NAI established a conservation laboratory in 1941, and it avails of a research and development unit equipped with various paper testing machines. The NAI also offers short training courses in paper conservation.

India has 32 World Heritage properties – 25 cultural and 7 natural. The Archaeological Survey of India (ASI) was founded in 1861 to undertake archaeological research and protection of cultural monuments of India. It is the key national survey organisation with a team of archaeologists, conservators, epigraphists, architects and scientists, and puts more than 3,650 ancient monuments, archaeological sites and remains of national importance into 24 circles for maintenance. With expertise of structural as well as chemical conservation, ASI is not only taking care of the monuments in India but has been working also with Afghanistan and Cambodia.

In addition to assigning various museums and organisations the responsibility of conservation – preventive and remedial – the ministry also focuses on reviving culture through endorsing various research projects. The Ministry of Culture is dedicated to many important missions. With the mandate of promoting and preserving art and keeping society connected to its culture, the National Mission on Cultural Mapping and Roadmaps aims at achieving social harmony through cultural growth and revival. There are many monuments and antiquities in India which still needs to be documented and preserved for next generations. The National Mission on Monuments and Antiquities is responsible for promoting awareness and extending training facilities for preservation and documentation in this regard. India is a proud owner of approximately ten million manuscripts in a variety of illuminations and illustrations in different languages made with different materials. One of the most popular missions – the National Mission for Manuscripts – aims at identifying, documenting, conserving and making accessible the manuscript heritage of India. To commemorate the Father of the Nation, the Gandhi Heritage Sites Mission focuses on preserving important sites visited by Mahatma Gandhi by creating guidelines for maintenance of physical structures and by properly storing documents and objects. The idea is to form an electronic library of Gandhi's life and achievements and to promote research. Furthermore, the National Cultural Fund also supports culture-related endeavours in the country by accepting institutions and individuals as equal partners of the government.

To carry out research in conservation, the Ministry of Culture offers two types of grants for the duration of two years. One is the "Award of Senior/Junior Fellowships to Outstanding Persons in the Fields of Culture", under which every year two hundred senior and two hundred junior fellowships are awarded to applicants with graduation as minimum qualification. Various fields related to culture, with special mention of "Scientific and Technical aspects of Conservation", can be opted for as study. Another option is the "Tagore National Fellowship for Cultural Research Component" for which fifteen fellowships are paid per annum. In collaboration with Andrews W. Mellon Foundation, the government of India has been able to organise international fellowships for Indian mid-career conservation professionals to receive short training abroad.

Acknowledging the need for harmonisation in the professional practice of conservation, the National Cultural Heritage Conservation Policy is being prepared. This task is being undertaken within six sub-committees: pre-paper; paper; monuments, murals and antiquity; movable antiquities; modern visual materials; and audio-visual materials, which are administered by various organisations. Although this is only a "policy", not a "law", this document would enable the custodians of arts to have a better understanding of standards and ethics of the profession.

India is active internationally on the cultural front; it has partnered with seventy countries, and cooperation is proceeding with most of them – Armenia, Australia, Austria, Belarus, China, Cyprus, Greece, Iran, Italy, Japan, Malaysia, Mali, Mauritius, Morocco, Myanmar, Netherlands, Portugal, Russia, Rwanda, Saudi Arabia, South Africa, Thailand, Turkey, Uganda, and the United Kingdom.

A developing country of large size with huge and remarkable cultural assets always offers scope to improve further. To save and revive the tangible heritage of the country, the field of art conservation has advanced exponentially in past years. With the ever increasing number of trained conservators in the field, the future of art conservation in India is promising, and the future of the past is bright.

FURTHER READING

Archaeological Survey of India, in: http://asi.nic.in/, access 19.11.2018.

Dhar, S., "Addressing Cultural Diversity: Challenges, Meaning and Consequences", in: ICOM-CC (ed.), *ICOM-CC Conference Preprints 2008*, New Delhi 2008, pp. 1035–1040.

Gupta, T./Nair, M.V., "Collection Care – The Topic of Focus at the National Museum Institute of History of Art, Conservation and Museology, New Delhi", in: Krist, G. (ed.), *Sammlungspflege - Collection Care*, Vienna 2015, pp. 557–563.

Indian Association for the Study of Conservation of Cultural Property, Golden Jubilee Celebrations, New Delhi 2016.

Indira Gandhi National Centre for the Arts, in: http://ignca.gov.in/, access 12.10.2018, update 12.10.2018.

Jain, K.K./Dalela, N., "Academic Conservation Training Programmes in India and International Networking", in: Krist, G./Bayerová, T. (eds.), *Heritage Conservation and Research in India. 60 Years of Indo-Austrian Collaboration*, Vienna 2010, pp. 139–146.

Ministry of Culture, Government of India in: https://indiaculture.nic.in, access 12.10.2018.

Nair, M.V., "Status of Conservation Research in India", in: Krist, G./Bayerová, T. (eds.), *Heritage Conservation and Research in India. 60 Years of Indo-Austrian Collaboration*, Vienna 2010, pp. 121–127.

National Archives of India, in: http://nationalarchives.nic.in/, access 12.10.2018, update 10.08.2018.

National Museum Institute of History of Art, Conservation and Museology, in: http://nmi.gov.in/, access 12.10.2018, update 09.10.2018.

National Museum, in: http://www.nationalmuseumindia.gov.in/, access 12.10.2018.

Pandey, S.C./Nair, M.V., "Research and Training in the Field of Cultural Heritage Preservation – First Indian Austrian Summer School 2014 in Vienna", in: Krist, G. (ed.), *Sammlungspflege - Collection Care*, Vienna 2015, pp. 565–570.

Factsheet Napier Museum

PROJECT	Collection Care at Napier Museum, India	DURATION	Since 2016 until now
INITIATED BY / LEAD BY	Gabriela Krist, M. Velayudhan Nair		
PARTNER INSTITUTIONS	Napier Museum, Department of Museums and Zoos, Government of Kerala National Museum Institute of History of Art, Conservation and Museology, New Delhi (NMI)		
FUNDED BY	Eurasia-Pacific Uninet (EPU) Government of Kerala University of Applied Arts Vienna		
TEAM MEMBERS	Gabriela Krist, Johanna Runkel, Tanushree Gupta, Manfred Trummer, Tanja Kimmel (Institute of Conservation, University of Applied Arts Vienna) K. Gangadharan, P.S. Manjula Devi, R. Sajeev (Napier Museum, Department of Museums and Zoos, Government of Kerala) Satish C. Pandey (Department of Conservation, National Museum Institute of History of Art, Conservation and Museology, New Delhi)		
PARTICIPANTS AND STUDENTS INVOLVED	Abhay T., Abhijeet Shrivastava, Ajith M., Ajithkumar, Amina B., Anaka Asokan, Anjali V.S., Anjana Sivan, Anju Vijayan, Aparajita Sengupta, Aswathy K.S., Aswathy U., Bhasha Shah, C.S. Ajithkumar, Chinnu G., D.N.V.S. Seetharamaiah, Deborah Thiagarajan, Deepakshi Sharma, Dheeraj Kumar, G.R. Rajagopal, Gireesh Babu K.K., Gopal Sharma, Gopika J., Indu Sathyendran, J.S., Jalajakumari P.K., Jessin Kabir, K.R. Sona, Karthika Mohanan M.J., Komal Singh, Liji B.R., M. Nandakumar, M.A. Rajendran, Madhusoodanan C.C., Md. Ali Nasir, Meera Natampally, Mohamad Gasnafar, N. Ramaswamy, Nandakumar M., Natarajan P.N., P. Biju, P.M. Joy, P.N. Natarajan, P.S. Priyarajan, P.V. Binukkuttan, P.V. Vijaya Lekshmi, Pankaj Modi, Pradyun Nair, Prathamesh L. Pawar, Praveena S. Nair, R. Gireesh Kumar, Rajeev R., Rajesh V., Rekha Biju, Renju S., S. Abu, S. Jaikumar, S. Unnikrishnan, S.R. Karishma, Sanjeev Kumar Singh, Sathya Jacob, Sheeja K.P., Sheena V.R., Shikha Bansal, Sindhu K.K., Sinitha G.S., Sochipui Shinglai, Sugathan L., Sunthu S. Mohan, T.V. Anilkumar, V.K. Suresh, V.S. Satheesh, Vineesh T.S.		

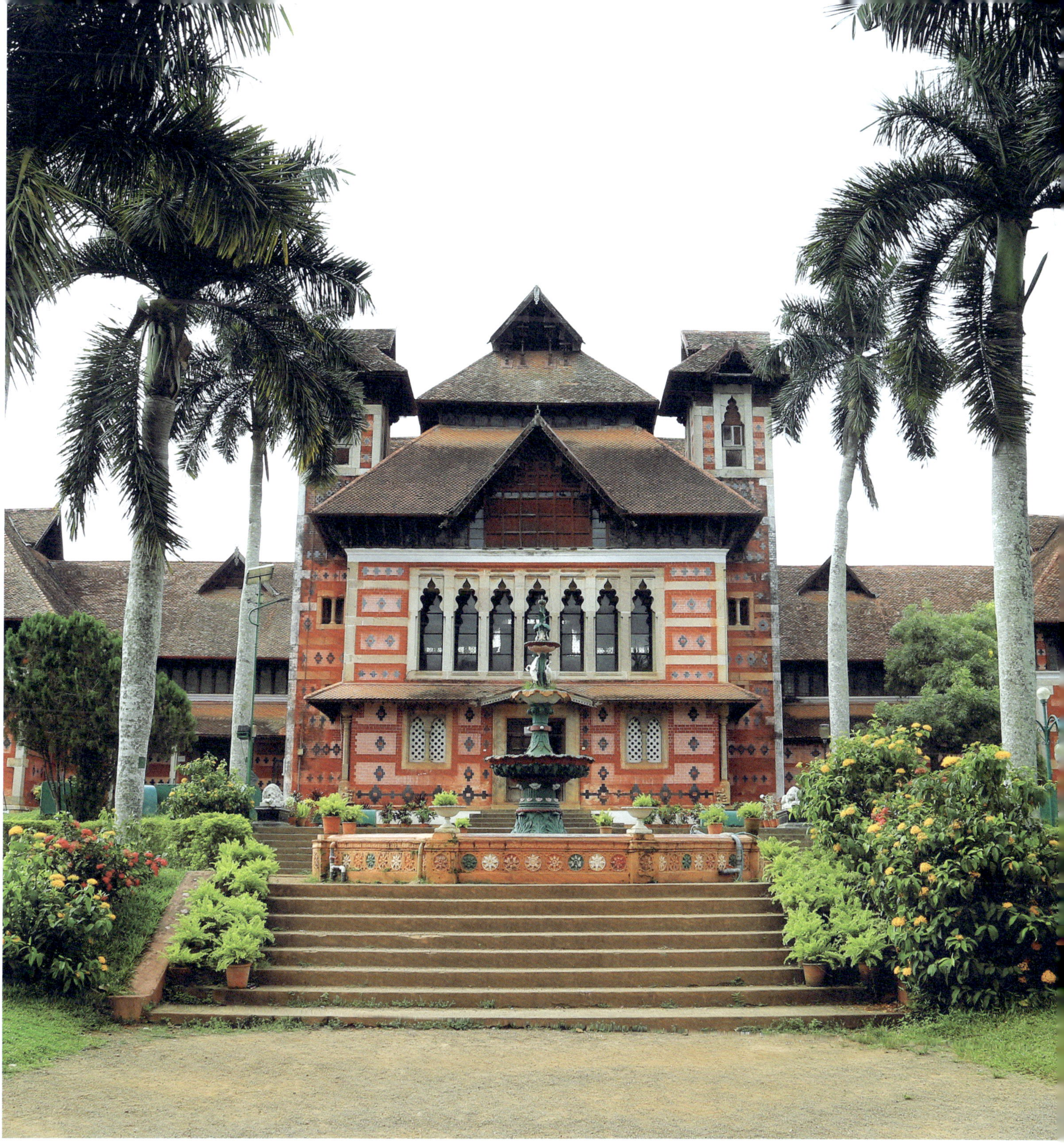

Fig. 1: Napier Museum,
Trivandrum, India

India and Austria

TANUSHREE GUPTA,
GABRIELA KRIST,
M. VELAYUDHAN NAIR,
JOHANNA RUNKEL

Together for Napier Museum

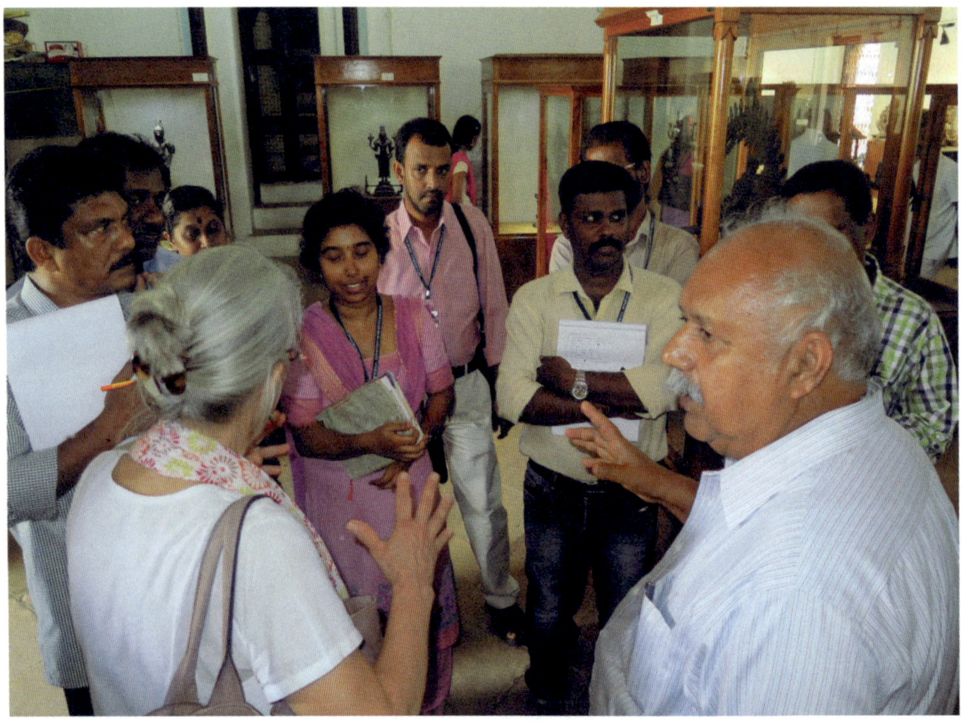

Fig. 4: Survey of the museum to identify areas requiring improvements, 2016

INTRODUCTION

Properly implemented measures of collection care in a museum allow long-term survival of its artefacts and identification of case-specific areas requiring research in preventive conservation. Stable conditions so achieved minimise the deteriorating factors that may incur need of remedial conservation. Concepts of collection care comprise simple, easy and often cost-effective solutions that can detect and prevent potential problems at their inception, allowing time to make corrections before they could affect the collection. As objects adapt to their local climatic conditions, practices successful in one geographical location need to be re-assessed for suitability in another. Similarly, materials used for storing and exhibiting objects should suit the given environmental condition.

Established in 1857, with a collection comprised of artefacts from the 1st to the 18th century, the major part of the Napier Museum collection is in a stable condition, even though it lacks formal measures of conservation. Lately, the government of Kerala constituted an Experts' Committee to improve conditions of museums in the state and chose to begin with the Napier Museum. Longstanding partner in the Indo-Austrian collaboration projects, the Institute of Conservation, University of Applied Arts Vienna, was then invited in February 2016 to help prepare a roadmap to identify and overcome the areas of concern. The Institute of Conservation works on-site in collection care projects in Austria and abroad.

Subsequently, several specialised work missions by the Institute have taken place in the Napier Museum from 2016 to 2018, while more are being planned for the coming years. The principle of these workshops is to research the needs of the collection in the given tropical climate and formulate a bespoke plan for its upkeep. All sessions are designed to impart hands-on training to the museum staff with supporting lectures in essentials of collection care and – more importantly – to carry out practical collection care measures.

This text features the progress towards implementing principles of collection care in the Napier Museum, scope of research in defining sustainable ways of conserving the collection, future plans, and significance of international cooperation in developing innovative solutions.

PREVENTIVE CONSERVATION AND COLLECTION CARE

Ageing is a law of nature and deteriorating agents are present everywhere. When left on their own, art objects are bound to deteriorate owing to intrinsic properties of the material and the action of external factors. Whereas some damage can be "fixed" by remedial conservation, others may be permanent. Therefore, it is better to prevent the encounter of deteriorating agents with the objects. Aimed at achieving "ideal" conditions to prolong the life of the objects, preventive conservation and collection care thrive best in avoiding and minimising foreseen risks of damage and deterioration to the collection.

Preventive conservation aims to establish and revise standards for long-term preservation of both object and collection by bringing change into the surrounding conditions. Per definition of ICOM-CC (International Council of Museums – Committee for Conservation) measures and actions of preventive conservation are indirect and do not interfere with the materials and structures of the items or modify their appearance. Some of the examples of preventive conservation are appropriate measures and actions for registration, storage, handling, packing and transportation, security, environmental management, emergency planning and public awareness. Preventive conservation can, to the greatest extent, avoid and minimise deteriorating factors (direct physical forces, pests, contaminants, pollutants, light, temperature, relative humidity, fire, water, and vandalism). In practice, some of these solutions may require high-energy maintenance and budgets that do not always comply with sustainable development and are often not feasible for museums with limited finances at their disposal.

Collection care refers to understanding and prioritising requirements of the given collection. It includes preventive conservation as well as conservation measures such as surface

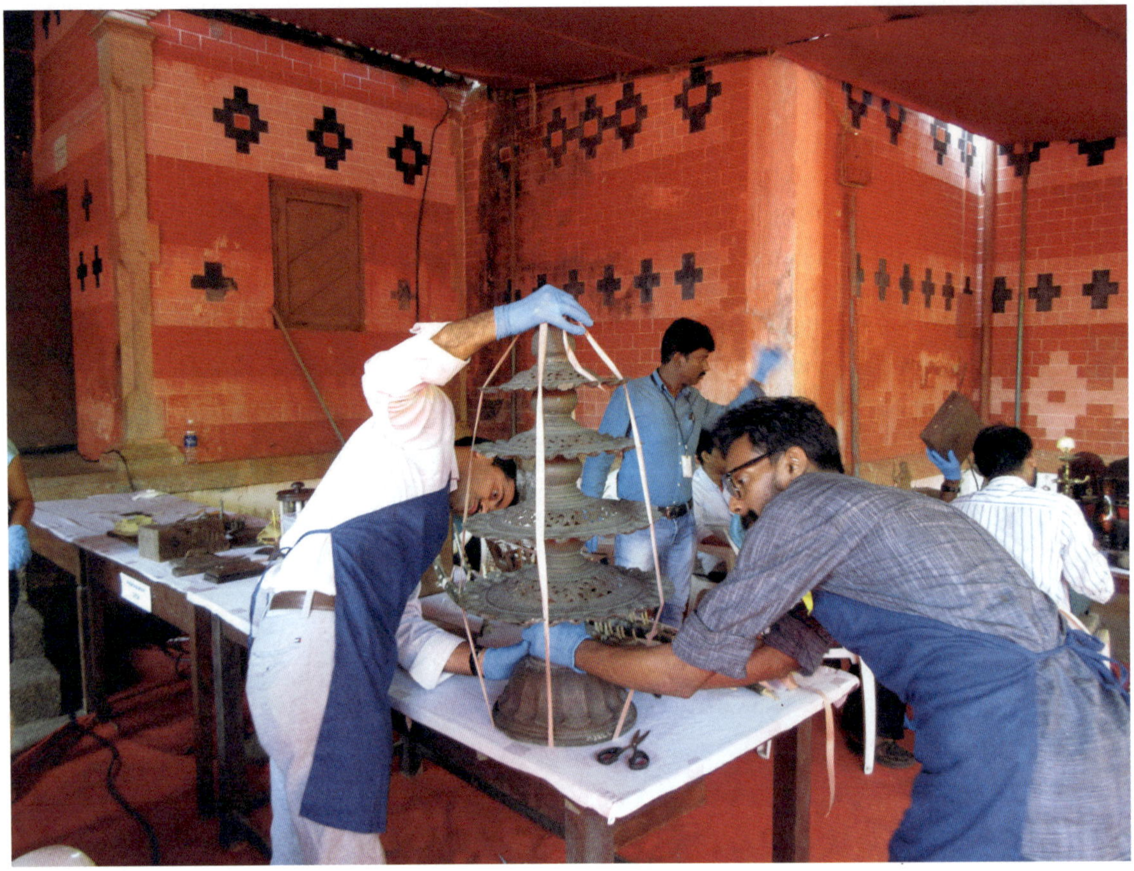

Fig. 5: Securing various parts of the object using cotton ribbon, 2017

Fig. 2: Historic fountain in the garden in front of the Napier Museum

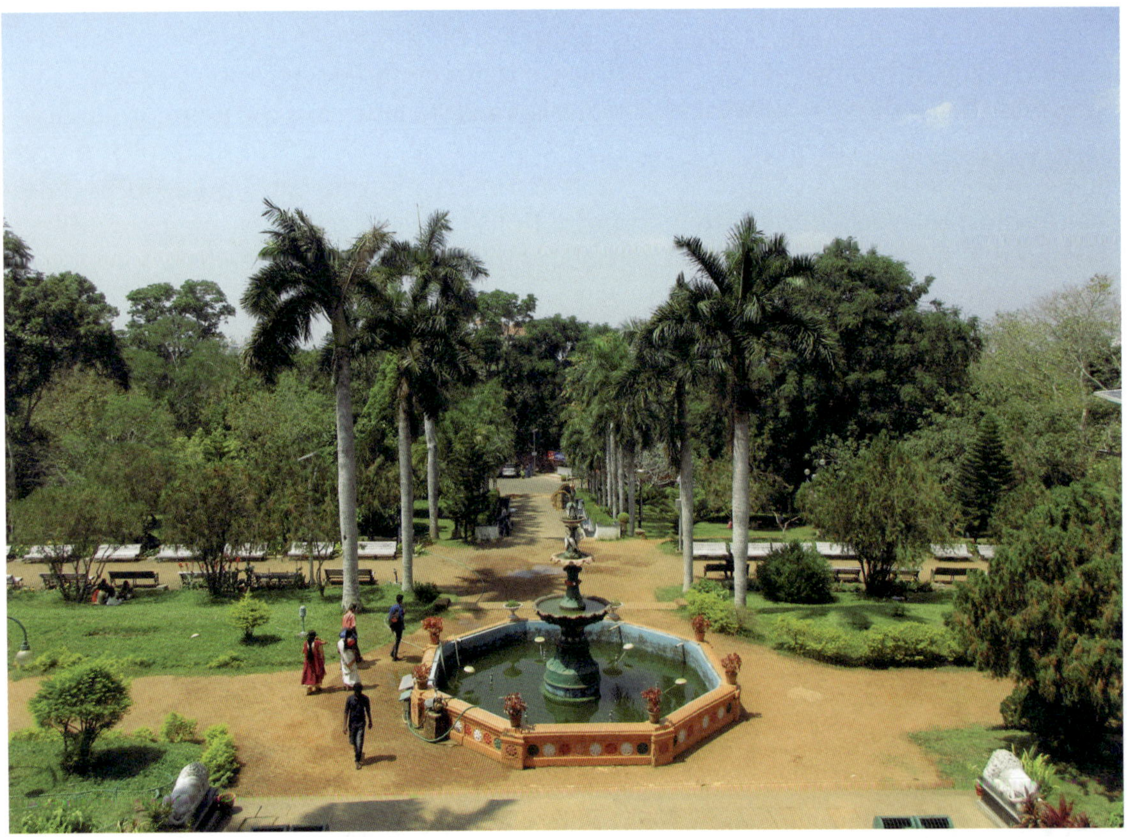

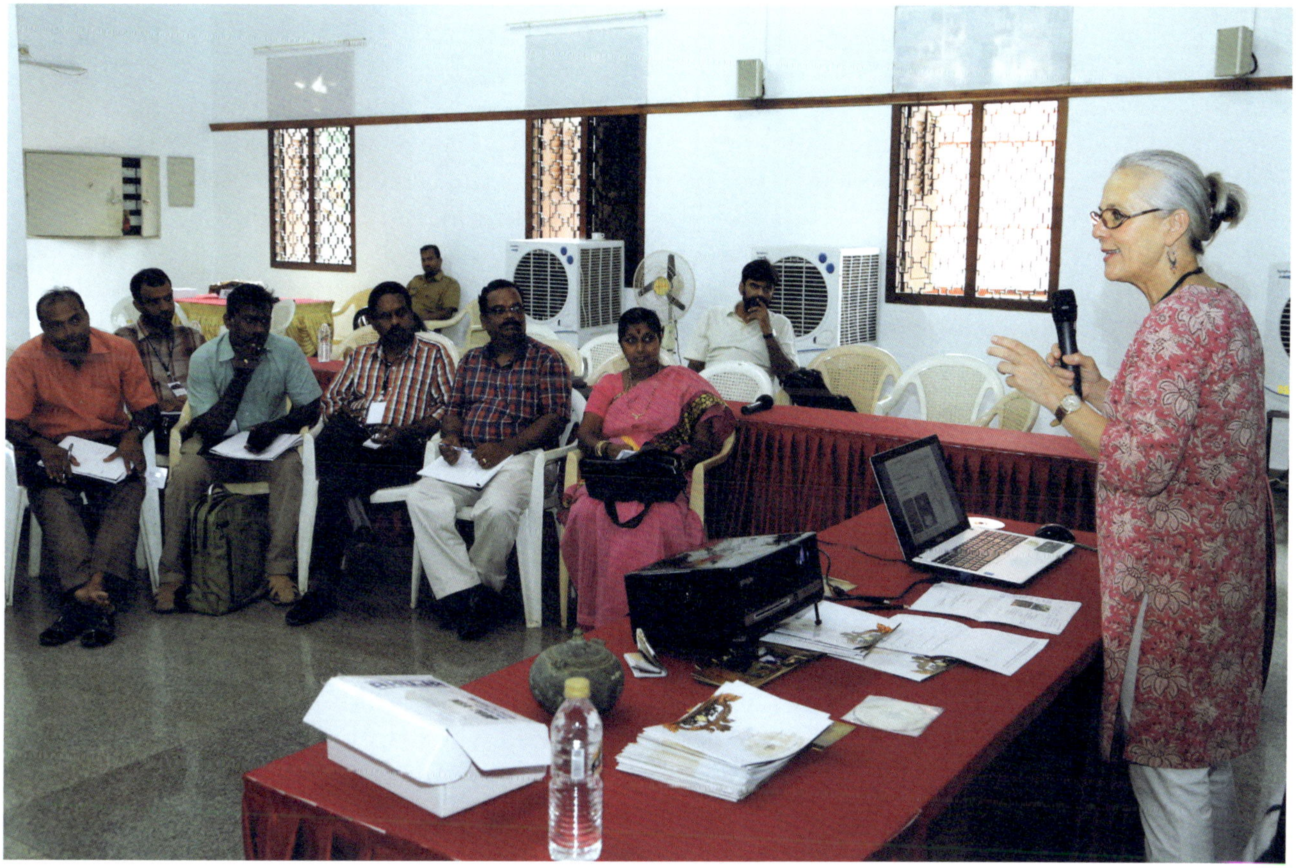

Fig. 3: Gabriela Krist talks about the essentials of collection care, 2016

Fig. 8: Museum objects packed in ventilated box for storage, 2017

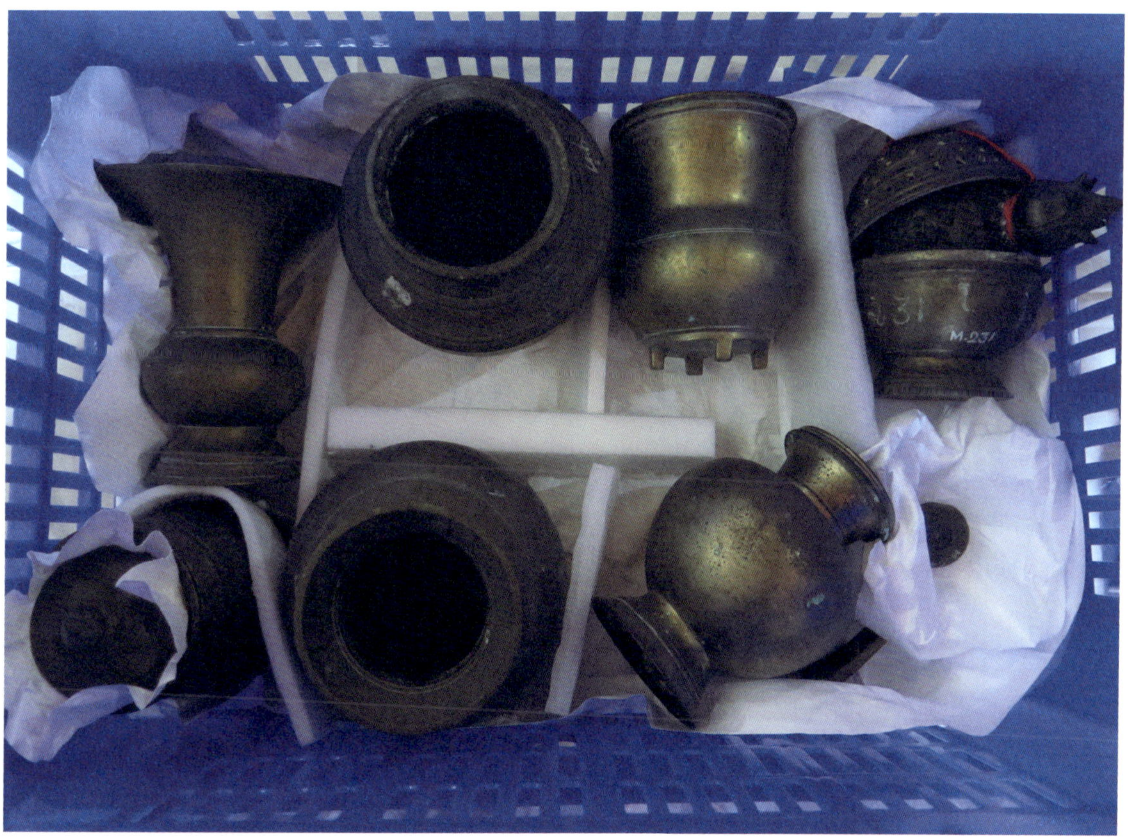

cleaning, consolidating and securing. Collection care attempts the minimal intervention necessary to keep the collection stable. The measures are applied to ensure that maximum number of objects can benefit, and their effectiveness is continually observed.

Ideally, collection care and preventive conservation focus on finding simple practicable solutions, and consider using locally available materials and traditional knowledge. To achieve sustainable development, investment of energy should be kept to a minimum. This is an integral step in reducing costs, reviving traditional culture and enhancing the involvement of local community.

THE NAPIER MUSEUM, TRIVANDRUM

The Napier Museum, Trivandrum, one of the early establishments in Kerala, was opened to public in September 1857, when J.A. Brown, then Director of the Trivandrum Observatory, and General William Cullen, then British resident, incepted the idea of encouraging arts and crafts by exhibition of artworks in Kerala's capital from India and abroad. The government approved launching the museum first in a bungalow of J.A. Brown, and appointed him as its director. To place the museum on a stronger and more satisfactory basis, the government also formed a society, with Brown as its secretary, the Maharaja of Travancore, Sri Uthram Thirunal as patron, General Cullen as president and the Elaya Raja as vice-president. From 1866 to 1872, Lord Francis Napier served as governor of Madras. He sent British architect Robert Fellowes Chisholm to the government of Madras, to Travancore, to design a building for the museum. He promoted Indo-Islamic elements of native art in his architecture and combined it with Gothic revival and Neo-Classical styles that were favoured in the Victorian era and incorporated Indo-Saracenic elements into the building. This architectural style was favoured in British India in the late 19th century. The high cost involved in the construction of such elaborate buildings could only be allowed in those of esteemed importance. Housed in the building of highly prized architecture in 1880, the Napier Museum received its name after the then-governor of Madras, Lord Francis Napier. The building has double walls with ventilators to allow the exchange of air, which is important for Kerala because of its tropical climate. Moreover, the ornamented structure makes the building an interesting exhibit in itself (Fig. 1-2).

The collection of the Napier Museum represents various facets of Indian art in metal, wood, stone, textile, ivory, papier mâché, and leather, etc. The bronze collection has South Indian style of sculptures from the 8th to the 18th century, which include Hindu gods and goddesses following iconographic details and rules from *Silpa Sastras* (a text from the Gupta Period c. 320–550 AD; meaning – science of arts and crafts). The lost-wax technique for casting metal sculptures is popular in Kerala. Highly esteemed sculptures like dancing Siva (Hindu god associated with creation, protection and transformations of the universe) Nataraja (depiction of Siva as a cosmic dancer), Vishnu (Hindu god considered as preserver of the universe), Parvati (Hindu goddess of fertility, love and devotion) and Lakshmi (Hindu goddess of wealth and prosperity) are fine examples of this technique. The art of wood-carving in this region is manifested in relief works of temple cars, mandapas (a porch-like structure through the gateway to the inside of the temple) and central shrines of the temples. Furthermore, ivory and stone carvings, inlaid and outlaid kuftgari (art of damascening) work with silver wire on both metal and wood, lamps, jewellery, coins and musical instruments form the collection of the museum. The sword of Velu Thampi, the prime minister of the kingdom of Travancore from 1802 to 1809 and one of the first martyrs of India's struggle for freedom, has been on display ever since it was handed over to the government of Kerala by the National Museum, New Delhi in 2010. In addition, colourful masks, headdresses, Javanese shadow play and Balinese calendars represent the collection of the former Maharaja of Travancore made during his visit to the Far East in 1937.

Centrally located in the capital city of Kerala, the Napier Museum lies in a complex with other museums and a zoological park, which attracts locals and visitors alike for its magnificent masterpieces and artistic ambience. For more information about Napier Museum, visit: http://www.napiermuseum.org/.

IN COLLABORATION WITH THE INSTITUTE OF CONSERVATION, UNIVERSITY OF APPLIED ARTS VIENNA

Austria and India have a bilateral agreement to work in cooperation in the field of culture and the arts. Within this framework, the University of Applied Arts Vienna, the Napier Museum and the government of Kerala have a Memorandum of Understanding in the following areas of interest – training workshops in the field of cultural heritage conservation and collection care – joint research and conservation projects – scholarships/ internships for students/ professionals.

Since the inception of Napier Museum in 1857, there have not been enough conservation measures to take care of the collection, which is a problem common to museums in India because of the lack of trained people. Lately, authorities expressed concern about the long-term stability of the collection. On an urgent note, the government of Kerala constituted an experts' committee, with M. Velayudhan Nair, chief advisor to the government of Kerala for Museums, as its head, to improve conditions of museums in the state, and chose to prepare the Napier Museum as a model example in the country. Longstanding partner in the Indo-Austrian collaboration projects, Gabriela Krist, Head of the Institute of Conservation of University of Applied Arts Vienna, was invited in February 2016 to investigate the situation and subsequently prepare a roadmap to identify and overcome the areas of concern. Key areas requiring intervention were identified and training on collection care has begun in the Napier Museum since then.

WORK MISSIONS FROM 2016 TO 2018

Organising and teaching team:
M. Velayudhan Nair (Government of Kerala),
K. Gangadharan, P.S. Manjula Devi,
R. Sajeev (Napier Museum),
Gabriela Krist, Johanna Runkel, Tanushree Gupta, Tanja Kimmel (Institute of Conservation, University of Applied Arts Vienna),
Manfred Trummer (Museum of Applied Arts Vienna – Department of Conservation),
Satish C. Pandey (National Museum Institute New Delhi - NMI)

"Conservation of Tangible Heritage with Special Reference to Napier Museum Trivandrum" (18-21 February 2016)

The Institute of Conservation held the first workshop in 2016 with the objective of understanding the existing condition of exhibition and storage in the Napier Museum collection and recommend measures to improve it. This included addressing the essentials of collection survey and preventive conservation, including risks and causes of damage, handling and care of objects and various options of labelling in the form of lectures, demonstrations and hands-on exercise. A session dedicated to condition reports for objects provided the experience of real problems in the museum. Participants were given an overview of the effects of climate and light on the collection. Problems of pests and their monitoring were also covered, as these are very serious issues faced by tropical museums all the year round. Participants were familiarised with materials that could be used for better storage and display of objects. Based on this, in the final exercise, the participants worked in groups to identify strong and weak points in the exhibition and storage areas and presented their recommendations on improving the situation of the Napier Museum in the future (Fig. 3-4).

The resulting document highlighted necessities in storage and exhibition. The largest part of the collection was found to be rather stable, but some objects were in danger and needed immediate action. Climatic extremes, biological agencies and improper placement are the high-risk factors of the collection. Organic items, like Balinese calendars and parchment figures, are inherently sensitive to fluctuations and extremes in climate. Several objects, such as a Temple car, stand directly on the floor, which makes them prone to accidental damage. In the showcases, the biggest problem is inadequate mounting and support of the exhibits. Based on the degree of deterioration potentially caused by each factor, a prioritised list of action was developed to be followed in future.

"Hands-on Storage Improvement in Napier Museum" (8-13 February 2017)

The storage room of the Napier Museum is a later addition, since the original plan did not reserve any space for storage. As the collection grew, so did the need for more space; the side porch was turned into a storage room. Major problems in this room were high humidity owing to tropical savannah climate and seepage, and lack of ventilation, which resulted in visible signs of corrosion and mould growth. Furthermore, space was overcrowded on shelves as well as on floor, preventing any possibility of safe disposition and access of the objects, leading to risk of accidental damage. As highest priority, objects were moved from here to an interim storage in 2017 where these problems could be overcome. The museum building is under special security from the government, which means that the objects could not be transferred to any other location. The only possibility was to prepare an interim storage space at one side of the exhibition hall until the museum gets a sanctioned and secured space for making a new storage room.

The week before the workshop, a working area was prepared in the open air outside the museum and the interim storage was set up. All materials needed were purchased in local shops so that extra import and tax costs could be avoided. Moreover, this exercise allowed the museum staff to gain a better understanding of supplies in their vicinity for needs in the future. Also, the requirement of materials was adapted according to local availability, for example, washed cotton cloth was used instead of acid-free tissue paper, since the former is more economical in India.

All objects needed to be moved from the existing to the interim storage space. Each object was cleaned in the open air to ensure ventilation while working with the mouldy objects, and assessed for its condition before transfer so that unwanted depositions that are a source of deterioration could be removed, and necessary stability could be provided; for example, objects with broken pieces, loose or multiple parts, were tied together with cotton ribbon to avoid misplacing them. First, objects were moved outside the old storage in trolleys, then they were dry-cleaned in the working space using soft brushes, polyurethane sponges and micro-fibre cloth, and were secured wherever necessary (Fig. 5). Thereafter, condition reporting was done where objects were categorised into: unstable, degraded but stable, stable and not degraded (optimal) (Fig. 6). In particular, objects with biological infestation were highlighted to be kept in isolation to avoid spreading of biodeteriogen to nearby sound collection. Objects were then shifted to the interim storage. All object movements were recorded and verified at three checkpoints – old storage room, working area, interim storage hall – under museum security. The last record tells exactly where the objects are now in the interim storage – precisely, the exact cupboard and shelf. During the workshop, all collection items of the old storage could be moved to the interim storage. In the interim storage, all objects are kept in almirahs, showcases and on tables lined and covered with pre-washed cotton cloth. As this arrangement is temporary, no money was invested in buying new furniture. Instead, extra almirahs, showcases and tables in the museum complex were utilised. Health and safety were important issues, since dust, dirt and mould are not only a cause of damage to objects but also a threat to health. Therefore, masks with FFP3 filters, powder-free gloves and aprons were used by all participants all the time. The collection is now easily accessible.

"Collection Management – Planning and Practice" (25 August – 1 September 2017)

In the coming years, the museum building will undergo renovation and a new storage and exhibition plan will be conceptualised. Therefore, for approximately two years, the art objects from the exhibition and the interim storage will need to be moved to another building. In order to train museum staff for this assignment, focus of the workshop "Collection

Management – Planning and Practice" was set on handling, packing, transport and storage of art objects. All the while, museum staff were introduced to materials that are safe to be used in museums and how they can be used for packing different kinds of objects. These topics were dealt with in lectures encompassing literature and case studies from Austria, demonstration of various packing options, followed by practical exercises where participants were trained to pack imitation objects (Fig. 7). Afterwards, the museum staff and resource persons packed selected exemplary objects of the collection for safe movement and storage (Fig. 8). Packing materials were partially brought from Austria and the rest were procured from local markets of Trivandrum. To find out suitability of use of the latter in museums, samples were put in the storage space to be checked after a few months for any deterioration. (These materials were removed accidently by the cleaning staff and hence the results could not be seen.) Also, these materials underwent Oddy-testing to ensure that they are not off-gassing volatile compounds. The materials procured from the local market failed the Oddy test. Therefore, more appropriate materials still need to be searched. All materials used for packing museum objects were brought from the Institute of Conservation so that only tested materials come in contact with the objects.

"Discussion and Seminar – Planning of Exhibition and Storage at the Napier Museum" (16-24 February 2018)

After renovation of the building, an improved exhibition plan will be executed in Napier Museum. The collection and present display methods were analysed and areas for improvement have been presented. As an example, one showcase with the problem of over-crowding and wrong methods of display was improved. Before the improvement, ten fragile textiles were vertically held on display with metal pins which caused continuous damage. While smaller pieces were shown in full, larger pieces were folded to accommodate all of them in the given showcase. Historical textiles should not be folded, to avoid cracks and tears caused by the mechanical stress. Also, if they are hanging, the textiles carry their own weight, which can cause tears and deformations. The appropriate method is flat and rolled storage. In February 2018, these textiles were taken out of the showcase and examined for their condition. In addition to stress leading to tears from improper mounting and stains caused by now corroded metal pins, these textiles faced damage from dirt, dust and insect attack. Two textiles have been retained on display with secure and stable mounting. They were rolled and then part of them was supported by a board, so that they are still visible for the visitors. Others have been packed to be kept in storage. Larger textiles are rolled and smaller textiles are stored flat (Fig. 9-10). From the local market, stainless steel tubes with a diameter of 8 cm were purchased according to the width of the textiles. These tubes were cleaned once more with ethanol in the museum and then covered with polyethylene foam, which was fixed with polyethylene tape. The textiles were then rolled onto them with an intermediate layer of polyethylene fabric Tyvek®. Afterwards, the rolled textile was covered once again with Tyvek®. The rolls were equipped with stands of polyethylene foam, so that the textiles are not pressed. Small textiles were put on boards covered with a layer of polyethylene foam. Then a cover of Tyvek® was fixed on the top. The label of each textile was fixed to the packed objects – either it was bound to the rolls or it was glued to the boards of the textiles in flat storage. In the future, a decision based on the general content and concept of the exhibition, shall be taken as to which textile shall be shown in the exhibition and what information shall be given about them.

Plans for new storage were discussed further and more areas requiring attention were identified. To improve the labelling and marking system on the objects, a one-day workshop on various labelling options that can be applied on different kinds of museum objects were demonstrated and practised on dummy objects.

OUTCOME AND OUTLOOK

Over the years, the collection of the Napier Museum has acclimatised to the local humid conditions. This climate accelerates ageing in all types of materials, and potential threats like fungal attack and corrosion can drastically destroy the target collection and therefore cannot be overlooked. Attempts are being made to attain stability using both scientific and traditional knowledge.

Plans of collection care are being established according to the specific needs of the Napier Museum and practical training is being carried out to ensure inclusion of these parameters in day-to-day activities. So far, the work missions have been successful in:

- identifying areas requiring improvement and making a prioritised list of action
- imparting practical training to museum professionals, researchers and students
- discovering and reviving locally available materials and traditional methods for/of collection care to achieve internationally accepted standards
- identifying areas of research in preventive conservation and collection care
- finding simple, easy, low-energy investing, cheaper and sustainable solutions
- planning of new storage and developing new concept for display

Following the same principle, the next missions will cater to the immediate needs of the Napier Museum. A manual will be prepared on collection care in the Napier Museum for quick reference and implementation. The exemplary improvements in the Napier Museum are believed to encourage other limited-budget museums in the surrounding region to check applicability and adaptability of this research in saving their collection. The project aims to integrate the traditional practices and materials with a scientific attitude to collection care. The challenges in tropical climate are different from those in temperate ones. In addition, solutions successful in Austria always have to be researched for their effectiveness in India, owing to the contrast in the two climates. Thus this project enables Austrian and Indian partners each to learn from the expertise of the other and develop innovative ideas by combining experiences of working in two extreme climatic zones.

ACKNOWLEDGEMENTS

The authors would like to thank Dr. K. Gangadharan, Director and Ms. P.S. Manjula Devi, Superintendent, Napier Museum, Trivandrum and their staff for joining forces and to Eurasia-Pacific Uninet and the government of Kerala for supporting the programme.

FURTHER READING

Gupta, T., "Improving Preservation Parameters at the Napier Museum", in: *IIC News in Conservation*, June 2016, pp. 10–12, in: https://www.iiconservation.org/system/files/publications/journal/2016/b2016_3.pdf.

Gupta, T./Wilk, J., "Präventive Konservierung im Napier Museum", Trivandrum, Kerala, in: *India Spectrum*, June 2016, pp. 1–2, https://issuu.com/indemb/docs/india_spectrum_vol.6.

Gupta, T., "Collection Care in Kerala – International Workshop on Conservation of Tangible Heritage, Napier Museum Kerala", Jahresbericht 2016, Institut für Konservierung und Restaurierung der Universität für angewandte Kunst Wien, 2017, pp. 118–119.

Gupta, T., "Collection Care in Kerala – Workshops in Napier Museum", Jahresbericht 2017, Institut für Konservierung und Restaurierung der Universität für angewandte Kunst Wien, 2018, pp. 114–117.

Gupta, T./Krist, G./Nair, M.V./Wilk, J., "Conceptualization of Collection Care at the Napier Museum, Trivandrum, India", in: *Studies in Conservation*, 63(sup 1)/2018, pp. 359–361, in: https://www.tandfonline.com/doi/abs/10.1080/00393630.2018.1504511. doi: 10.1080/00393630.2018.1504511.

Krist, G. (ed.), *Sammlungspflege – Collection Care*, Vienna 2015.

Krist, G./Runkel, J. (eds.), *Depotoffensive: Wiener Neustadt – Zwettl – Eggenburg – Purgstall – Korneuburg – Retz*, Vienna 2019.

Runkel, J./Krist, G./Gupta, T., "Collection Care in Napier Museum in Trivandrum, India" in: *IIC News in Conservation*, October 2018, pp. 10–12, https://www.iiconservation.org/system/files/publications/journal/2018/b2018_5.pdf.

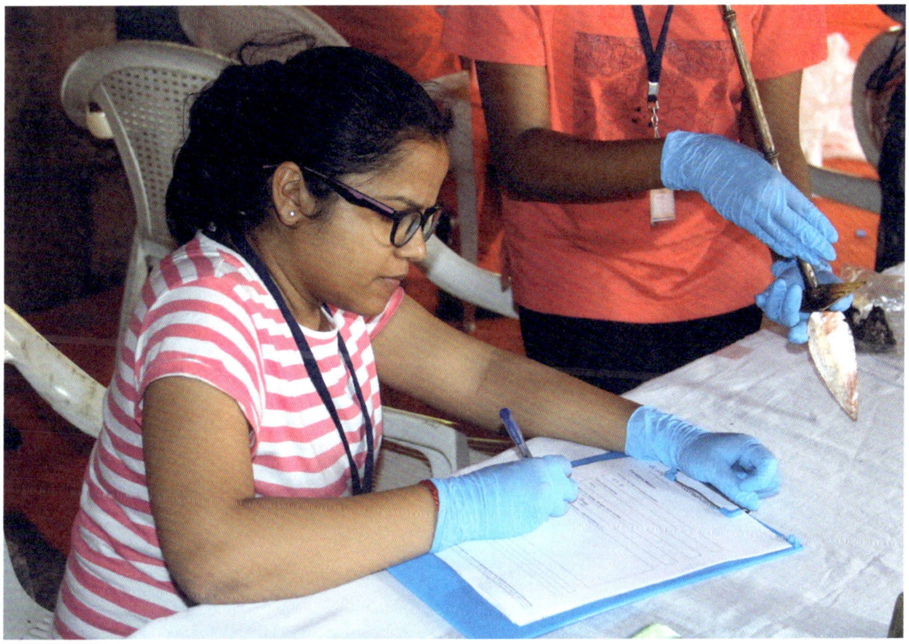

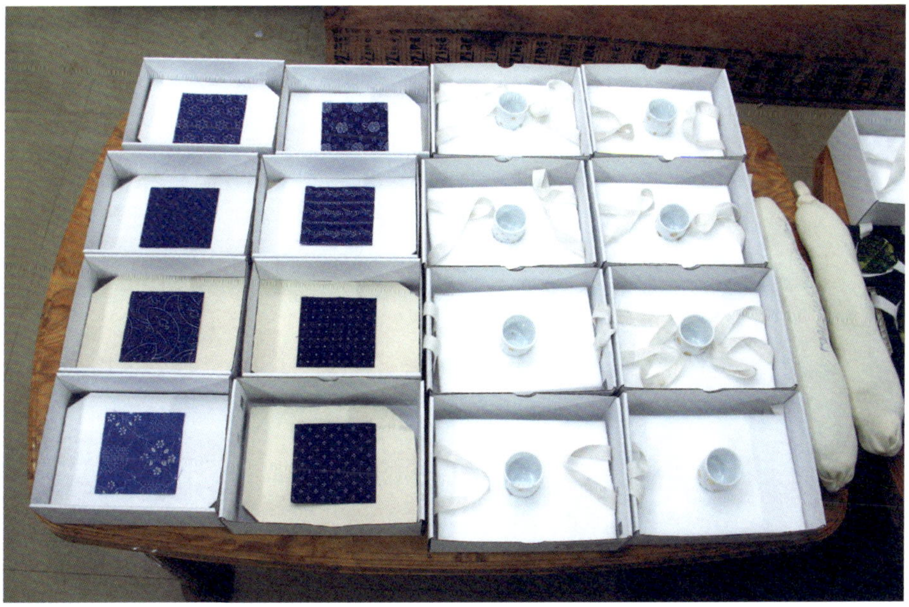

Fig. 6: Condition report prepared for each object, 2017
Fig. 7: Packing solutions prepared for dummy objects, 2017

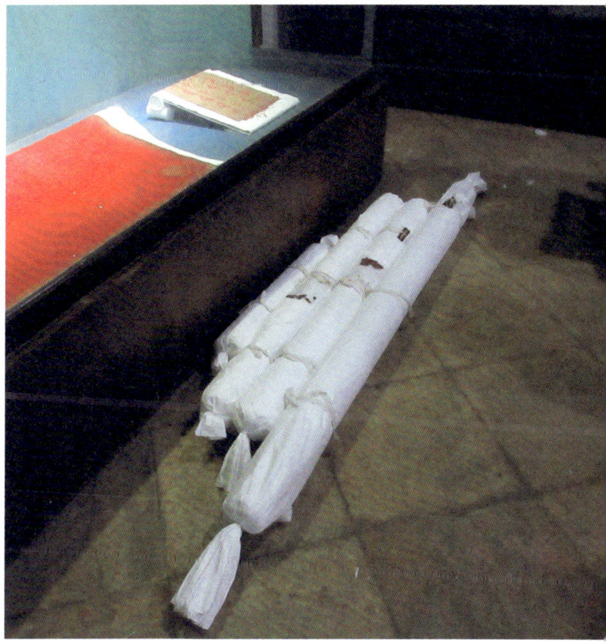

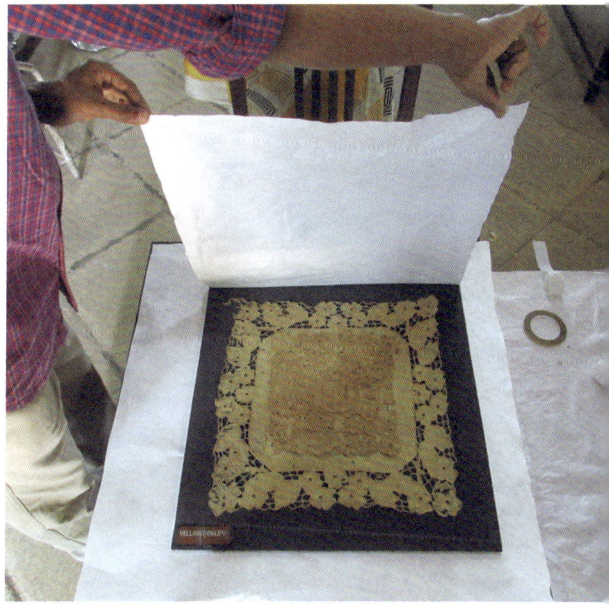

Fig. 9: Two textiles prepared for display and other textiles rolled to be kept in storage, 2018
Fig. 10: Small textile packed for flat storage, 2018

Kerala

JOHANNA RUNKEL

A Photo Story

The scientific and professional aspects of our project in Napier Museum in Trivandrum, Kerala are already extensively described in this book. Here I would like to add some impressions of our/my "Kerala experience" in pictures and words to give an understanding of "God's Own Country" Kerala and about the hands-on collection care with the team in Napier Museum. This photo-story is dedicated to Kerala and the people involved.

Prof. Nair, the chief advisor to the government for museums in Kerala and Prof. Gabriela Krist, head of the Institute of Conservation of the University of Applied Arts Vienna are the initiators and the driving forces for the collection care project in Napier Museum. Their personal, long-lasting friendship laid the foundation for this rich collaboration in Kerala, that started in February 2016 (Fig. 1–2). Team members from the Institute of Conservation throughout the years have been Johanna Runkel, Tanushree Gupta, Manfred Trummer and Tanja Kimmel, who brought in their expertise and workforce in their fields of specialisation: preventive conservation, exhibition, pest management and textile and object conservation. They built a team with the museum staff of Napier Museum, amongst them Manjula Devi, superintendent of the Napier Museum; Gangadharan, head of museums and zoo director; and Abu S., head of the Natural History Museum.

What is the Kerala experience like? First of all, every stay there is characterised by the tropical climate of the region – hot and humid all year long and you can immediately understand why the local people prefer wearing light, cotton fabrics and silk. The traditional dress of Kerala is marked by dhothi or mundu and shirt, for men, as you can see on Prof. Nair in one of the first pictures (fig 2). Women mostly wear saris.

One very important fact that you can feel in daily life is that Kerala is one of India's most progressive states in terms of social welfare and quality of life. Different from the rest of the country, they have a tradition of matrilineal inheritance, where the mother is the head of the household. As a result, women in Kerala have had a much higher standing and influence in society than in the rest of India. In the street life, women are very present (Fig. 3).

Kerala lies on the sea and also offers some beautiful beaches and very good fish meals. Moreover, festivals and celebrations are an important part of life and happen very often – also during our work missions of course. Some of the age-old rituals and traditions of Kerala involve the presence and combined efforts of people from different religious faiths: Hindu, Moslem and Christian.

One of the most famous folk traditions in Kerala is the Kathakali dance (Fig. 4), which we could experience when we first went to Trivandrum in 2016. By dancing and very expressive face movements the mostly male actor-dancers show folk mythologies, religious legends and spiritual ideas from the Hindu epics. They wear colourful make-up, costumes and facemasks.

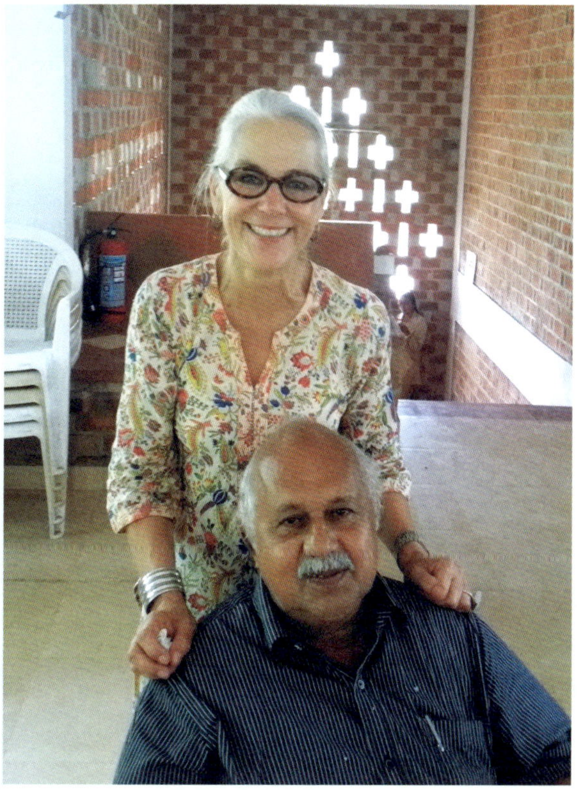

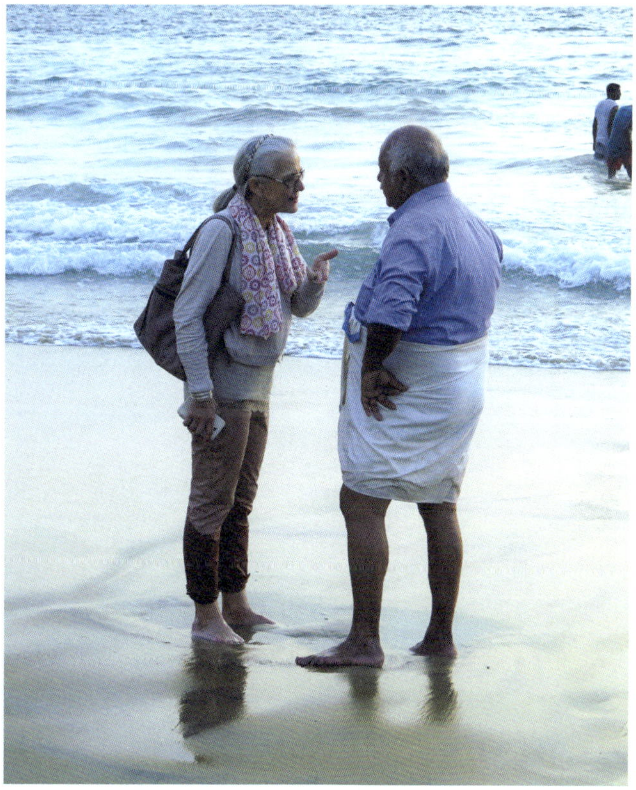

Fig. 1-2: Prof. Krist and Prof. Nair meet in Kerala and work together – in Napier museum and at the seaside

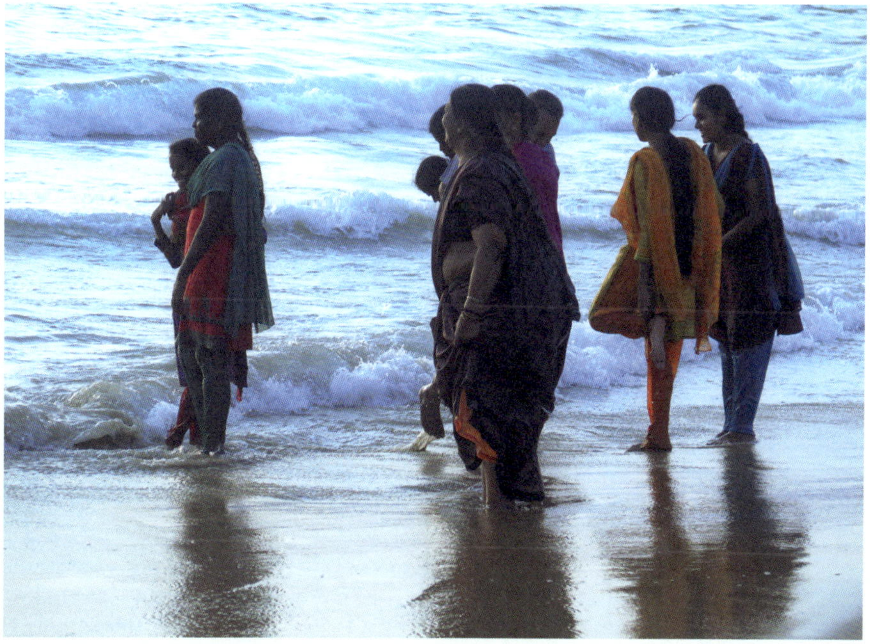

Fig. 3: Women in Kerala enjoying the seaside at Kovalam Beach near Trivandrum

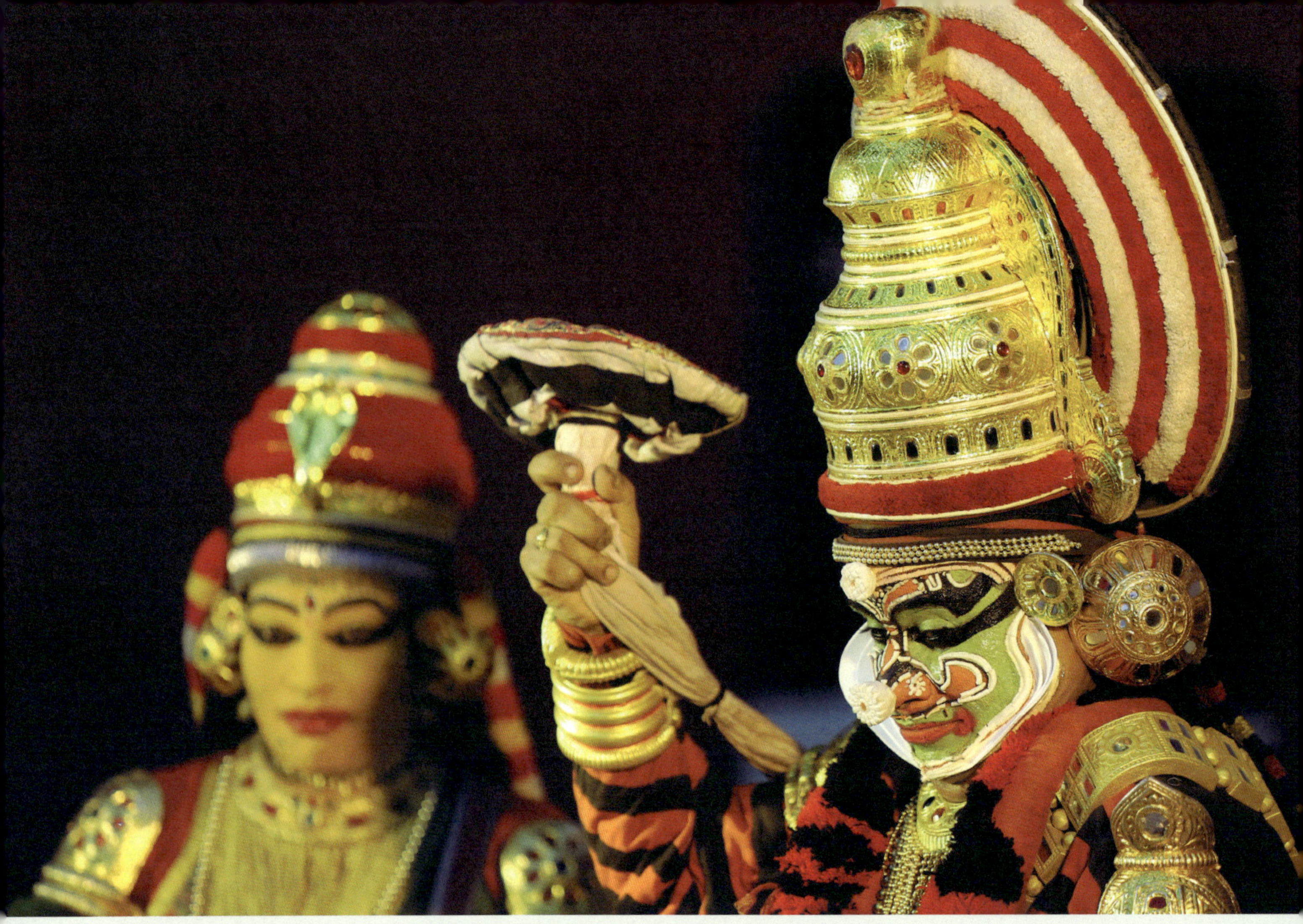

Fig. 4: Kathakali Dance

Woodworking has an age-old tradition in Kerala. In 2018 we visited an atelier, where artists produce wonderfully detailed wooden statues of Hindu gods in hard tropical woods (Fig. 5). The working conditions and tools have not changed for the last centuries. Now the profession is slowly dying because woodworkers cannot earn enough money. Most of them are already old and their children have turned to other ways of life and earning their living.

Padmanabhaswamy Temple is the central temple of Trivandrum (Fig. 6). The temple is built in a fusion of the indigenous Kerala style and the Tamil style of architecture. Only those who profess the Hindu faith are permitted entry to the temple – this is why this picture had to be taken from outside. The name of the city of Thiruvananthapuram, in Malayalam, translates to "The City of Lord Ananta", referring to the deity of the Padmanabhaswamy Temple. The temple bears a large treasure of gold that was found in 2011.

Last but not least, I have to mention tuk tuks. These three-wheeled auto rickshaws are the best way to move around in the city of Trivandrum. They can get through nearly any traffic and cost very little (Fig. 7).

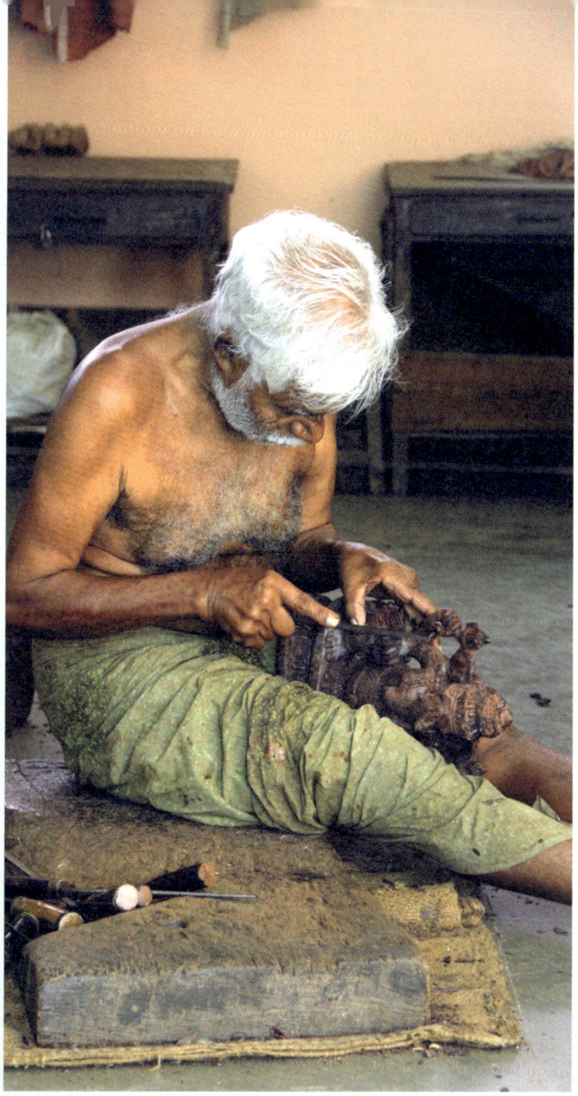

Fig. 5: Woodworker in Trivandrum

below left: Fig. 6: Padmanabhaswamy Temple in Trivandrum
below: Fig. 7: Seeing the world through a tuk tuk window

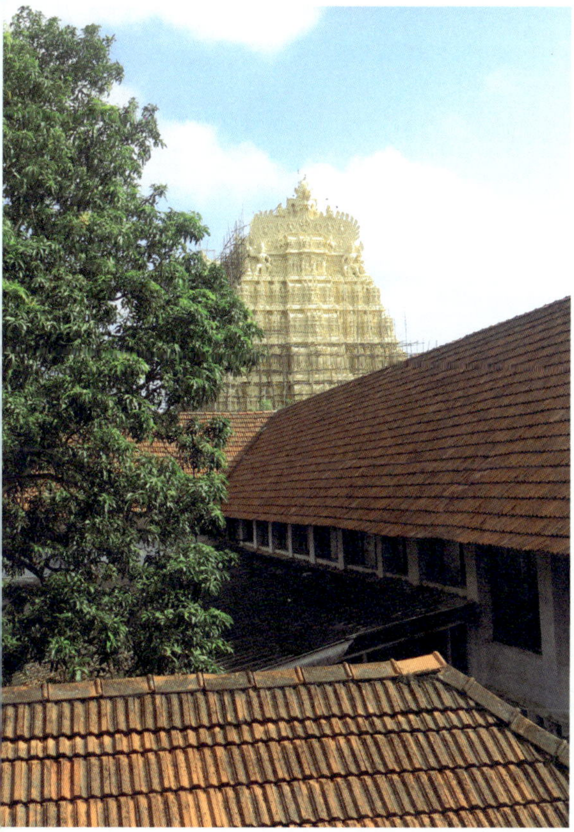

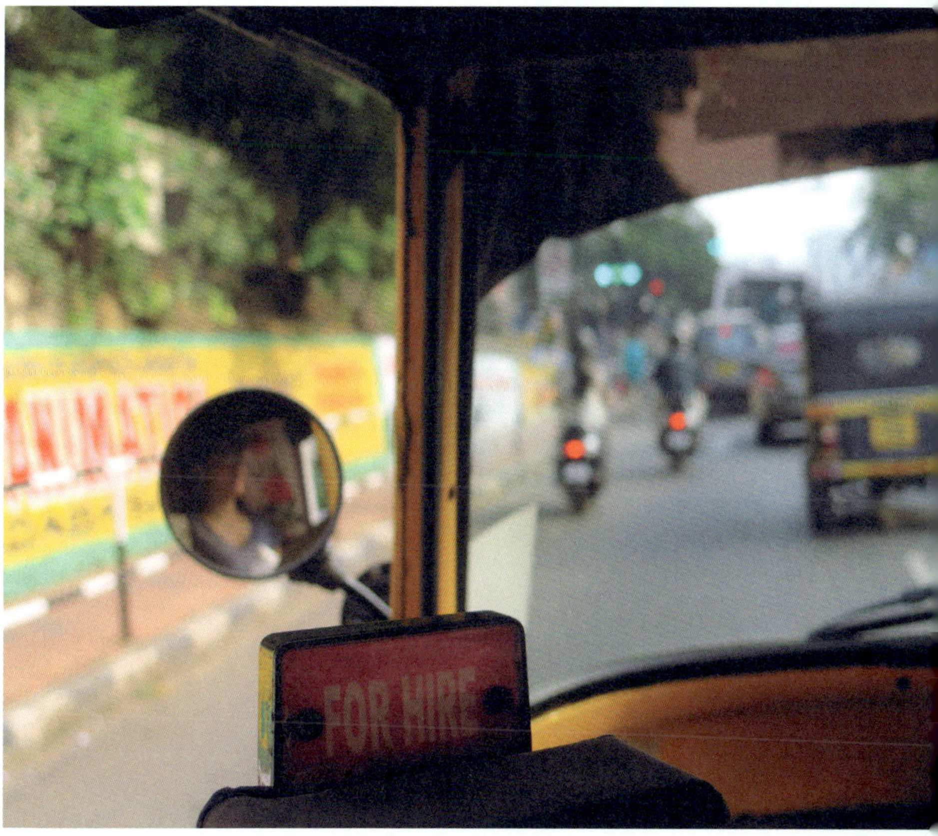

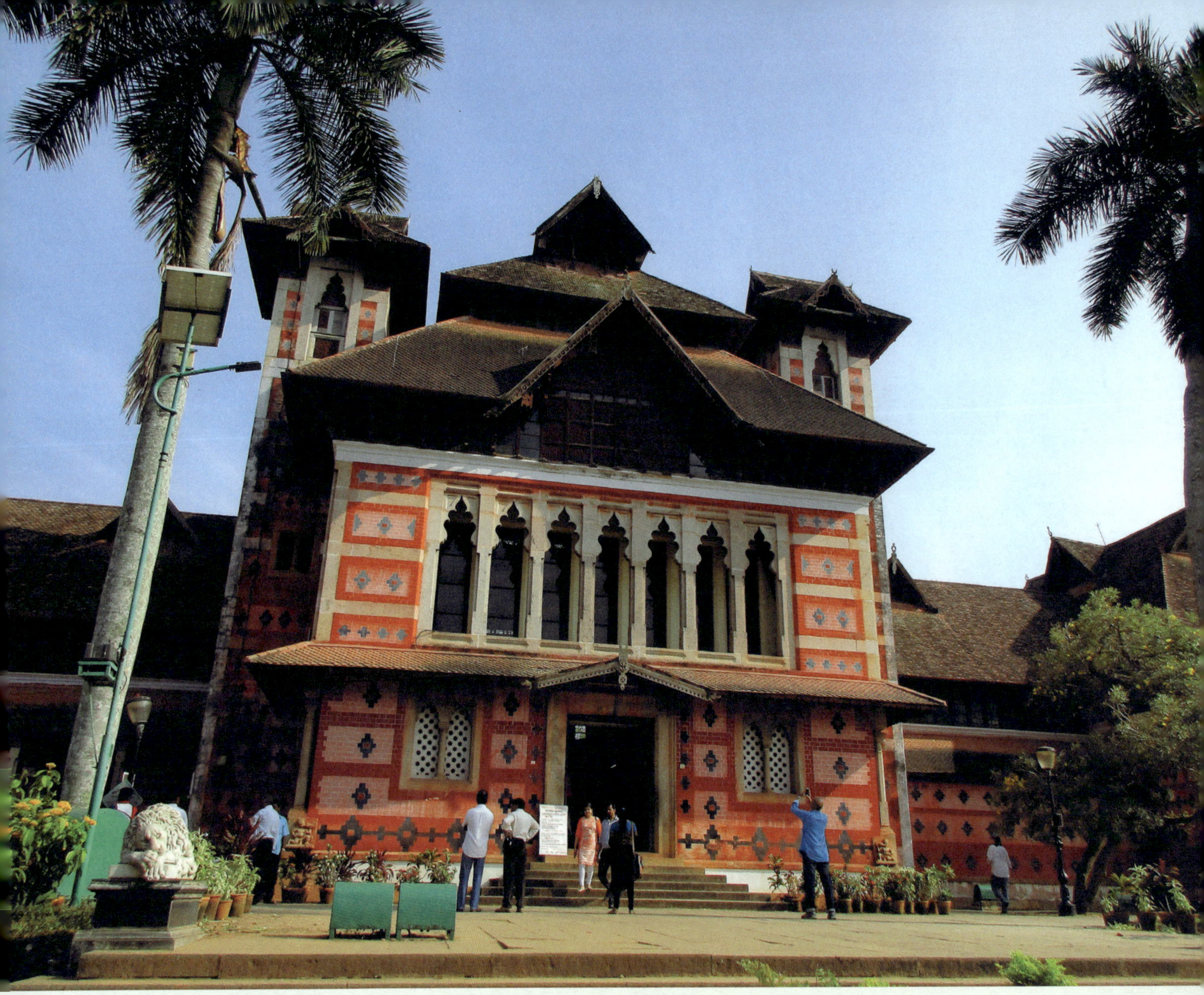

Fig. 8: Napier museum, the team's workplace - it is a cultural landmark in the region

THE MUSEUM COMPLEX

The museum complex of Napier Museum in the centre of the city of Trivandrum does not only avail of different art galleries but also a natural history museum, a zoo and a wonderful garden. The local people use it to relax and spend evenings and free days. The building was completed in 1880 and designed by British architect Robert Chisholm.

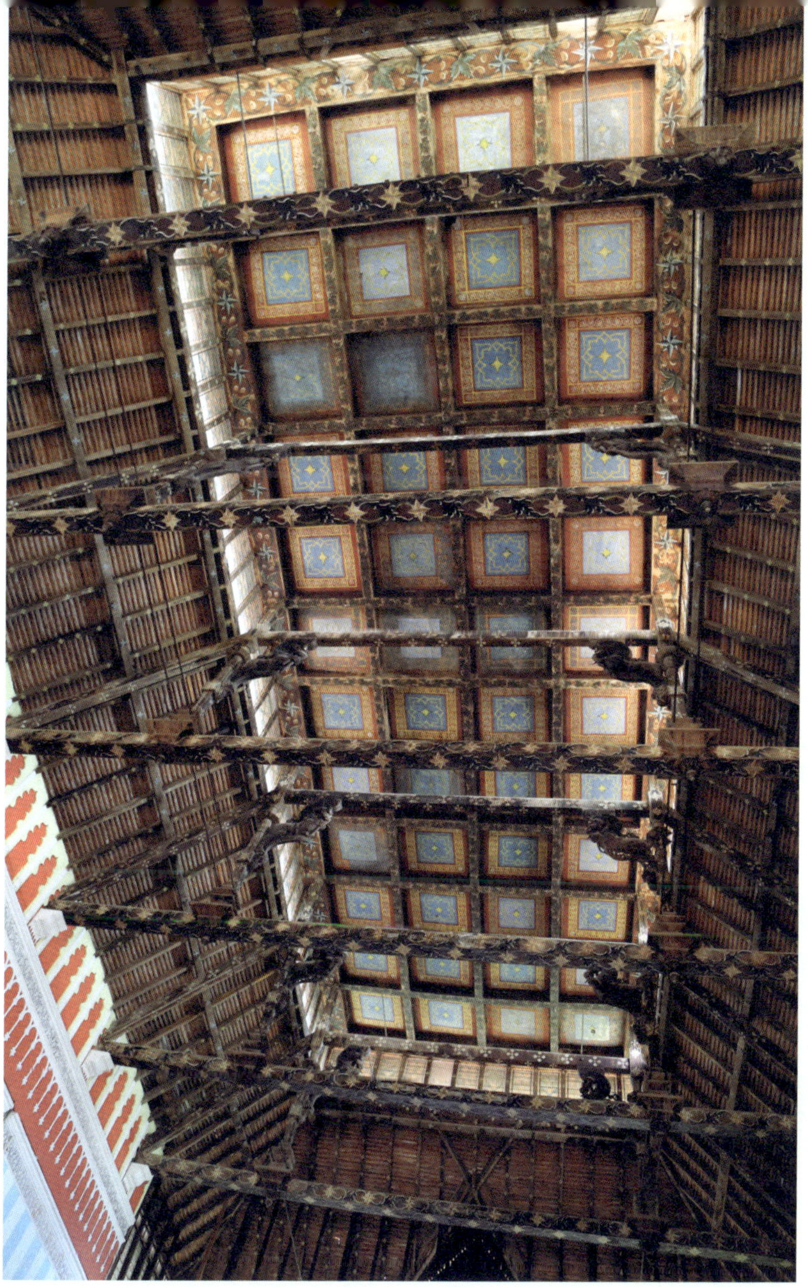

Fig. 9: The museum ceiling with rich decoration including ivory inlays

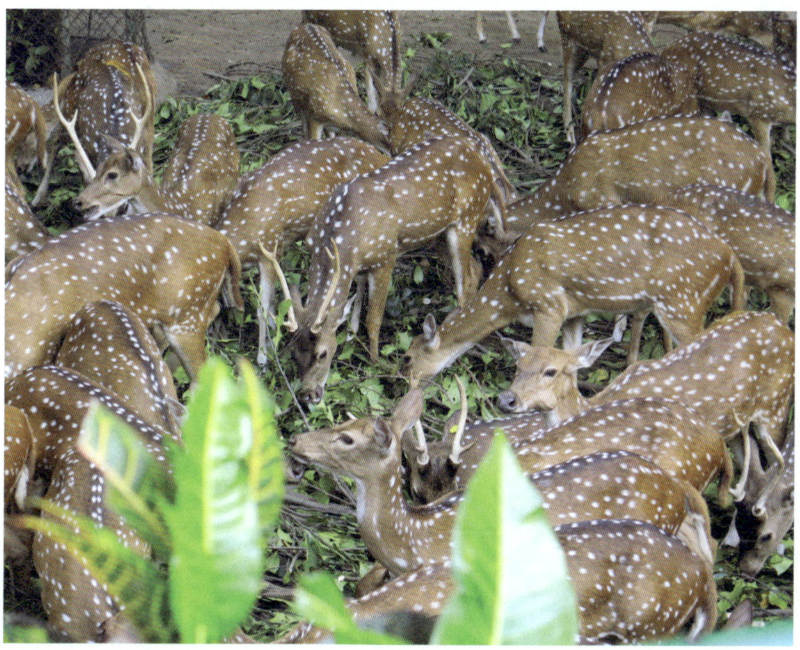

Fig. 10: A glimpse into the zoo

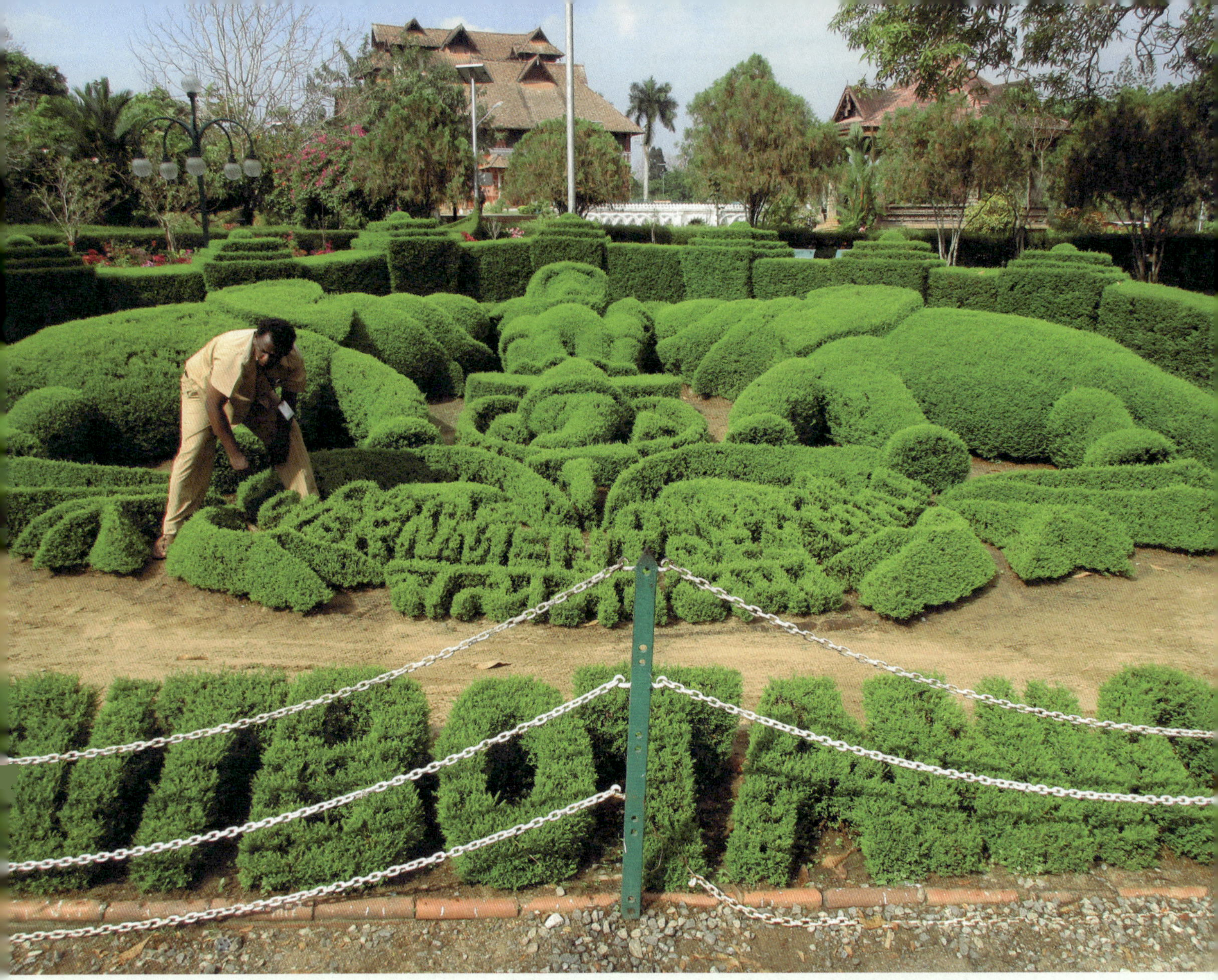

Fig. 11: Gardener in the park around the museum complex

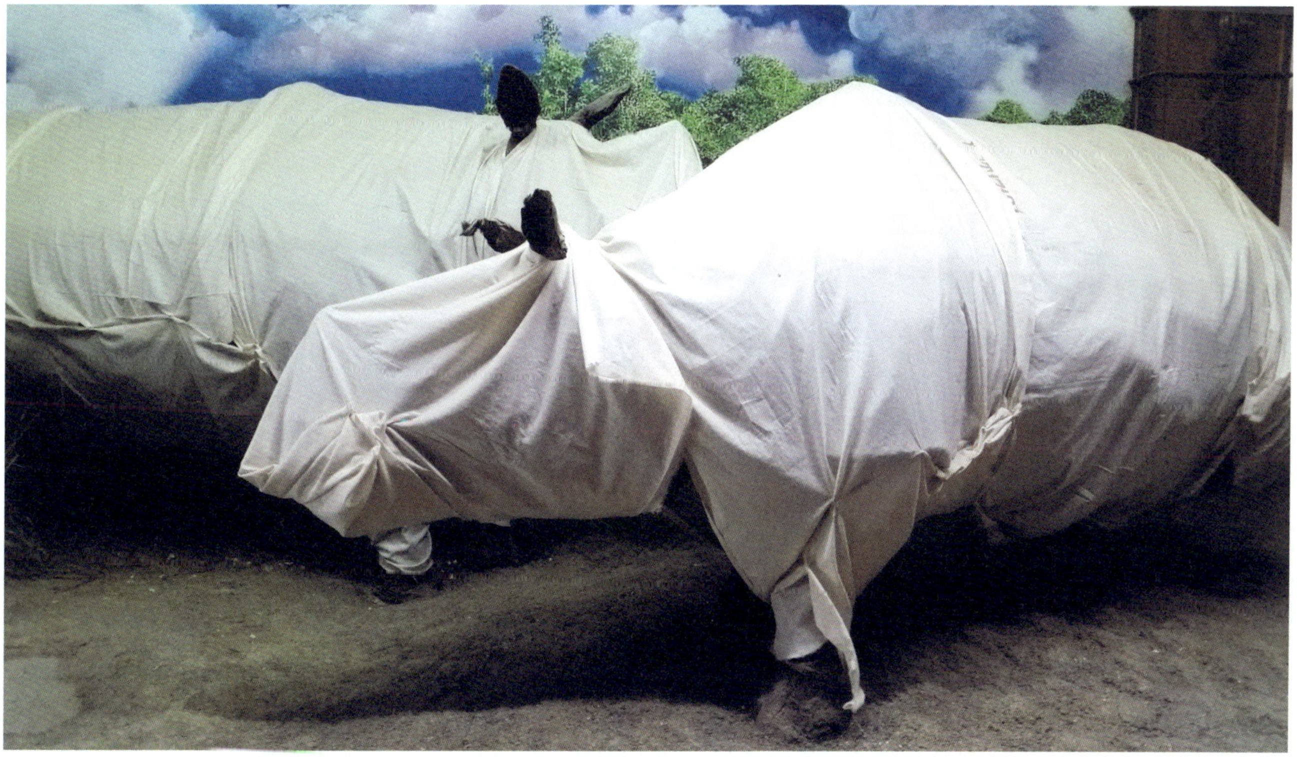

Fig. 12: The natural history museum in 2017 – these are stuffed hippos, that were covered because of construction work

WORKING MISSION FEBRUARY 2016 (18/02/2016 – 21/02/2016)

February 2016 marked the start of the project in Napier Museum. Experts from all over the country came together to identify the status quo of collection care in Napier Museum and develop a roadmap for the future, the next steps that should be taken. The developing of the roadmap generated extensive media activities in the region, from newspapers to television.

Apart from work, Manjula, the chief curator and our direct partner, made great efforts in this first working mission to equip the Austrian team with saris and tailored-to-fit sari blouses (Fig. 17). The white saris are a modern version of the so-called "mundum neriyathum", a traditional costume of women of the Malayali community. Characteristic are the gold borders contrasting with the plain white cotton.

Fig. 13: Team to develop the road map for Napier Museum, posing in front of the museum

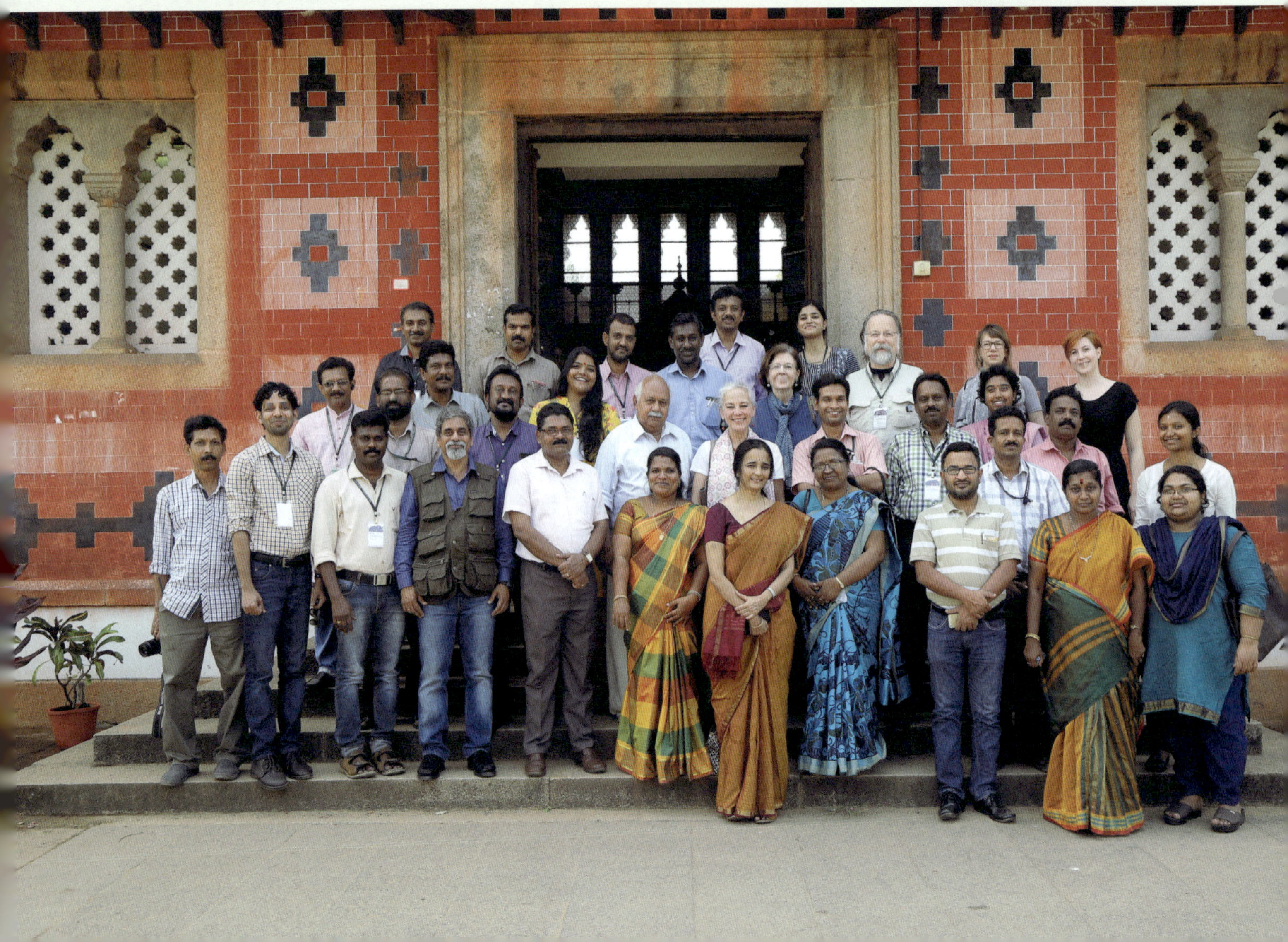

Fig. 14: Tanushree inspects Napier museum upside down

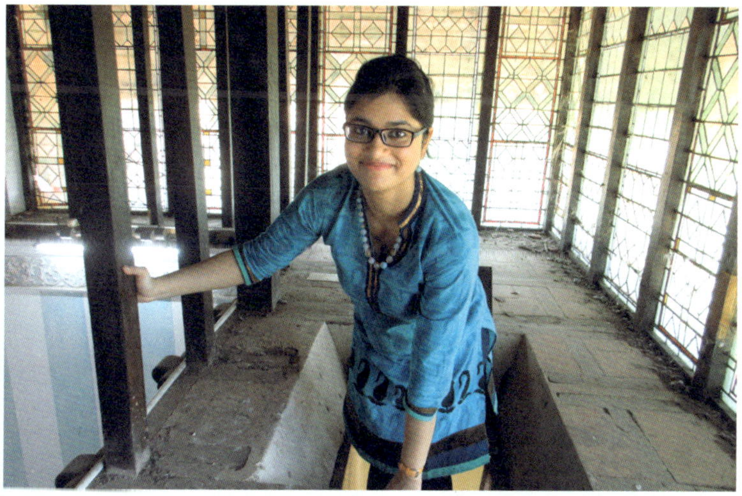

Fig. 15: Prof. Krist summarizes the results of the workshop in February 2016

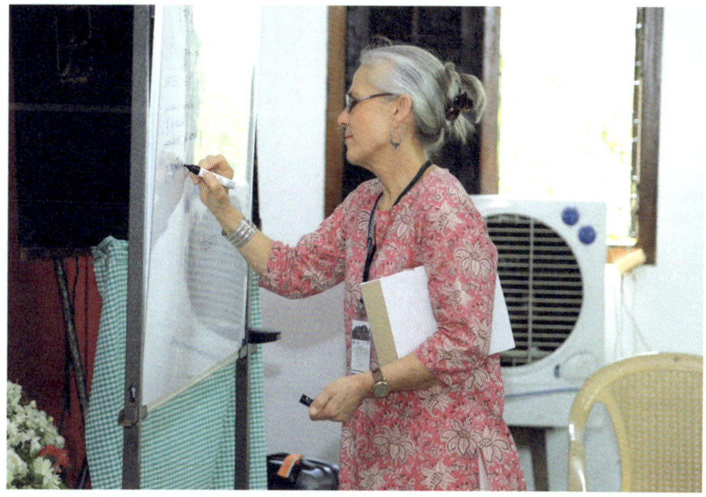

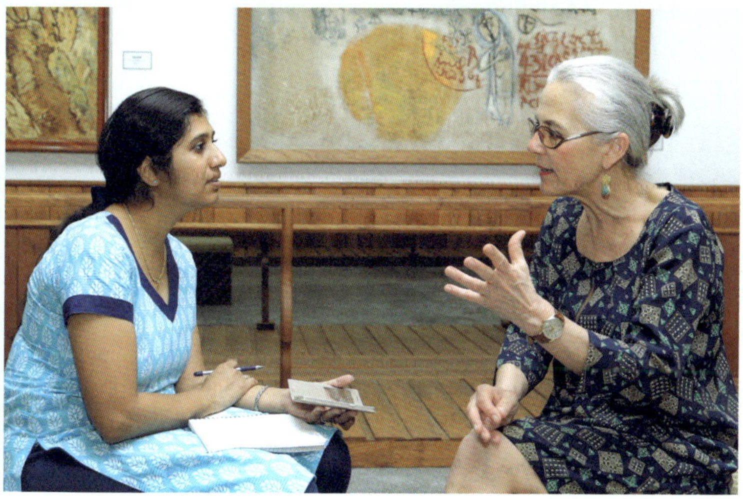

Fig. 16: Prof. Krist gives an interview for a local newspaper

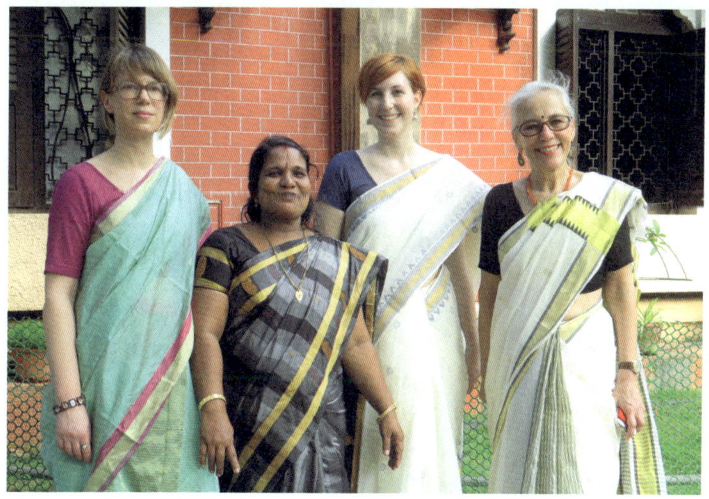

Fig. 17: Tanja Kimmel, Manjula Devi, Johanna Runkel and Gabriela Krist fully equipped with saris

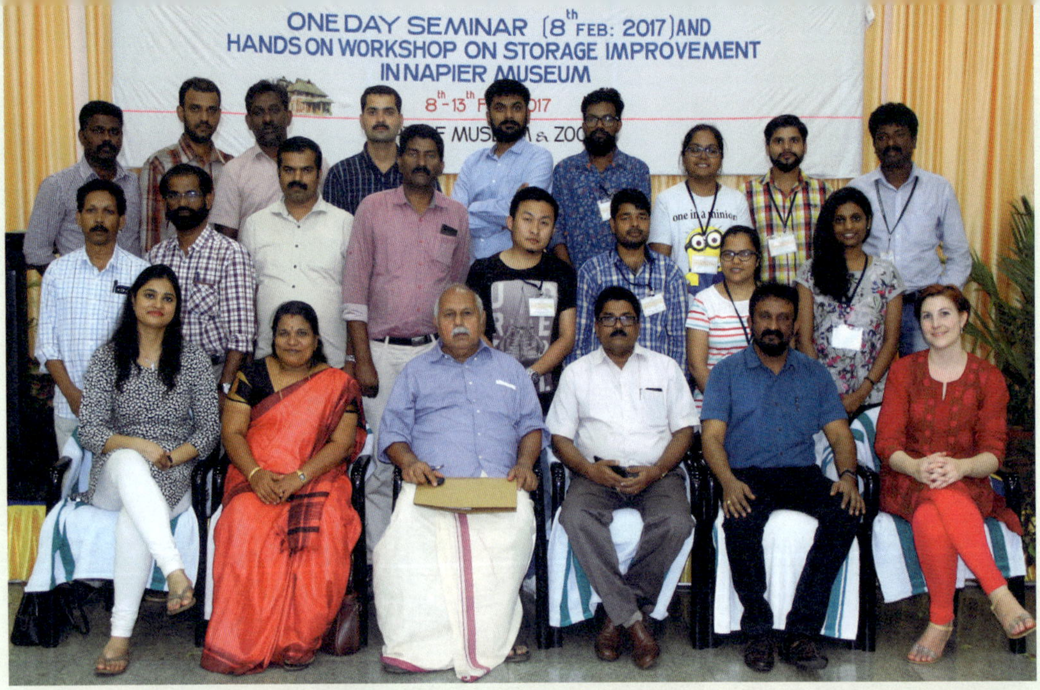

Fig. 19: The working team of 2017, ready to clean and move

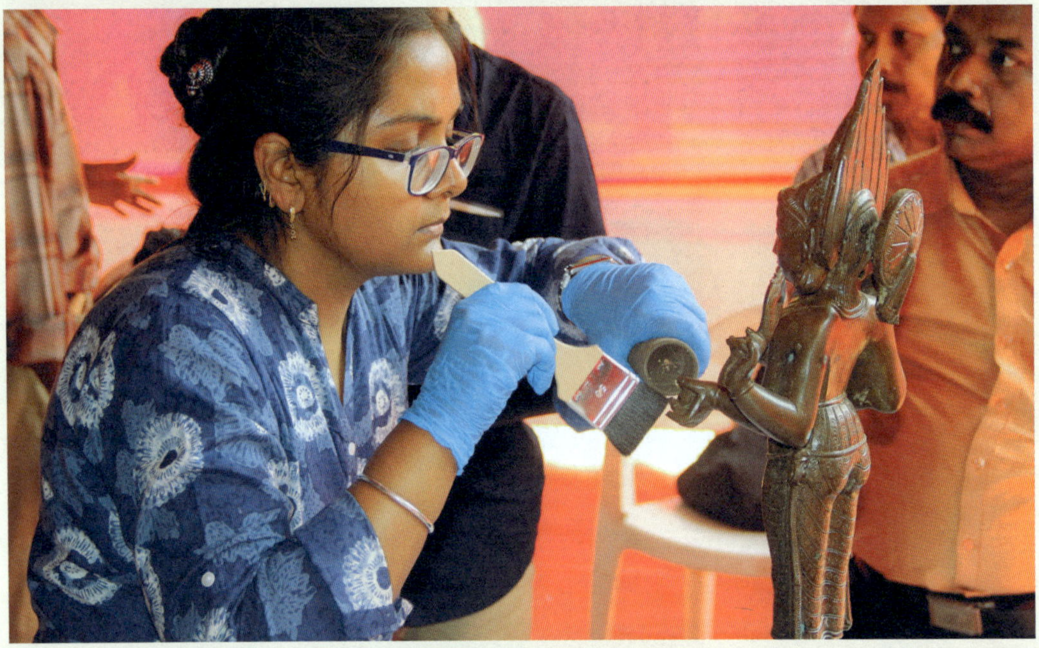

Fig. 21: A student of the National Museum Institute New Delhi dry-cleans a bronze sculpture with brush and vacuum cleaner. The suction opening of the vacuum cleaner is covered with a part of nylon stocking to prevent accidentally soaking up of small loose parts of objects.

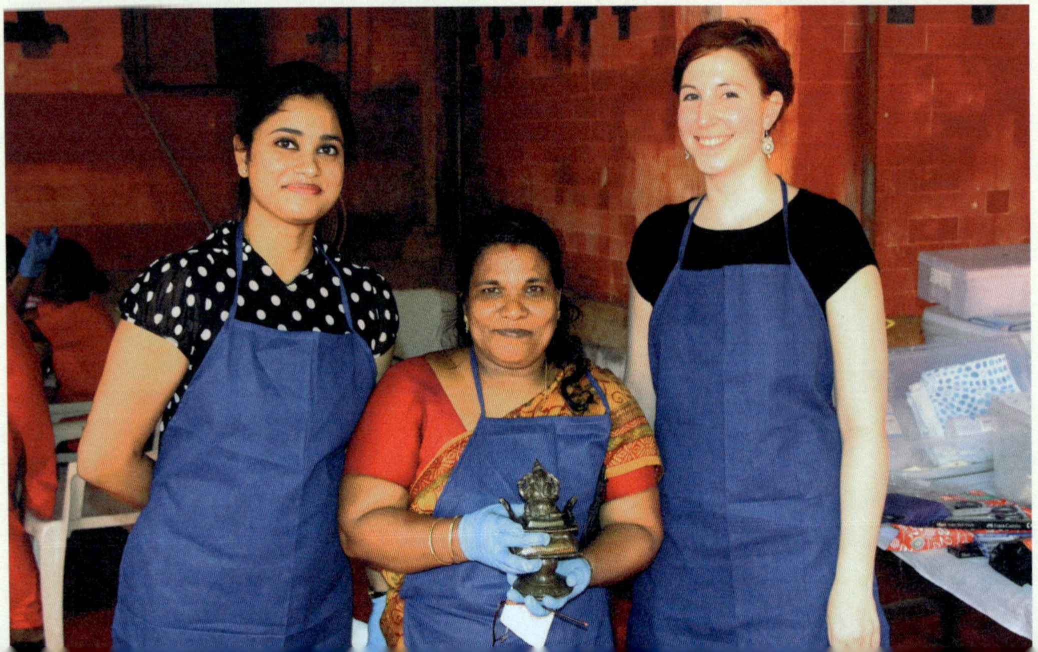

Fig. 23: Manjula, Tanushree and Johanna with Ganesha. Ganesha is the Lord of Obstacles, both of a material and spiritual order and in this case he was asked for help for the project to remove all obstacles in our way. And indeed, it worked out.

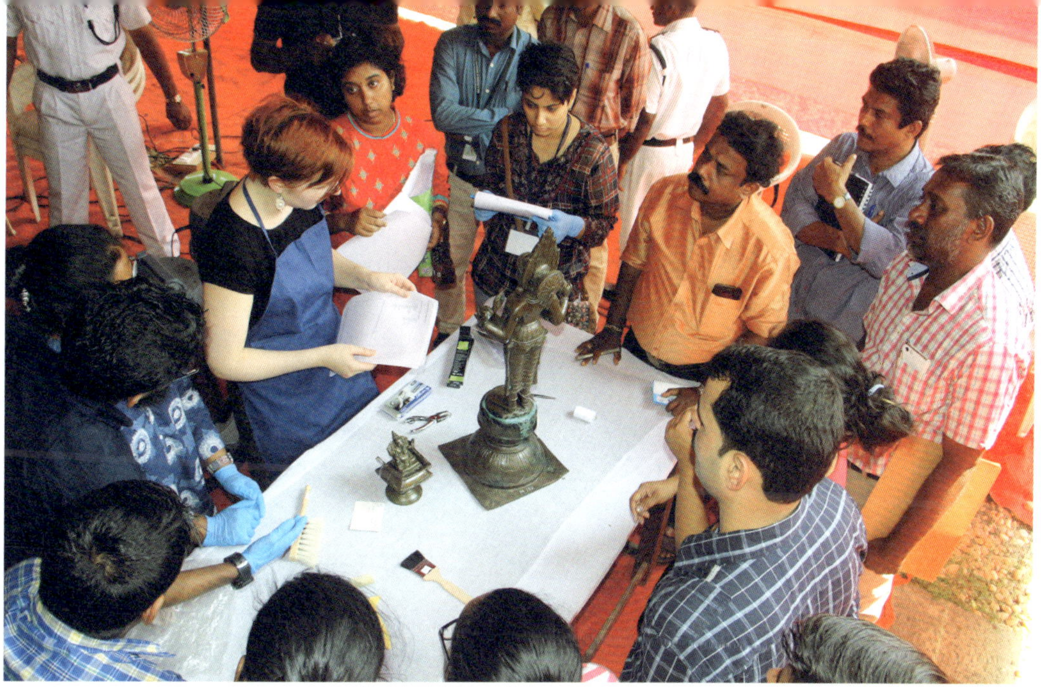

Fig. 20: Johanna explains how to do condition reporting on the museum objects

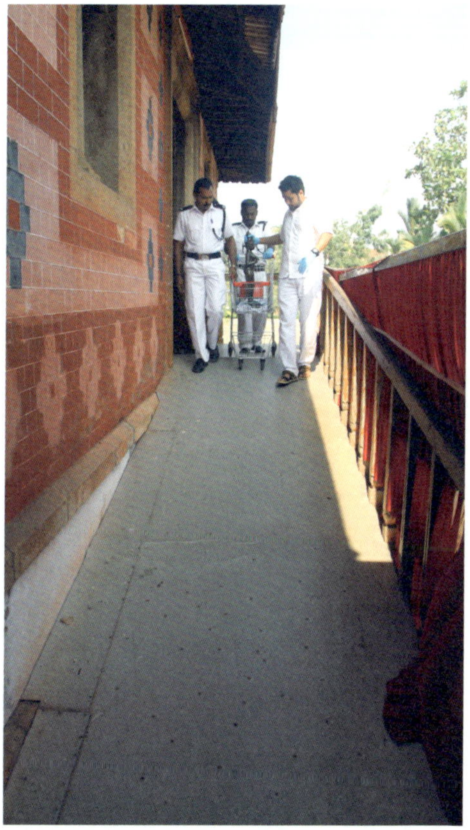

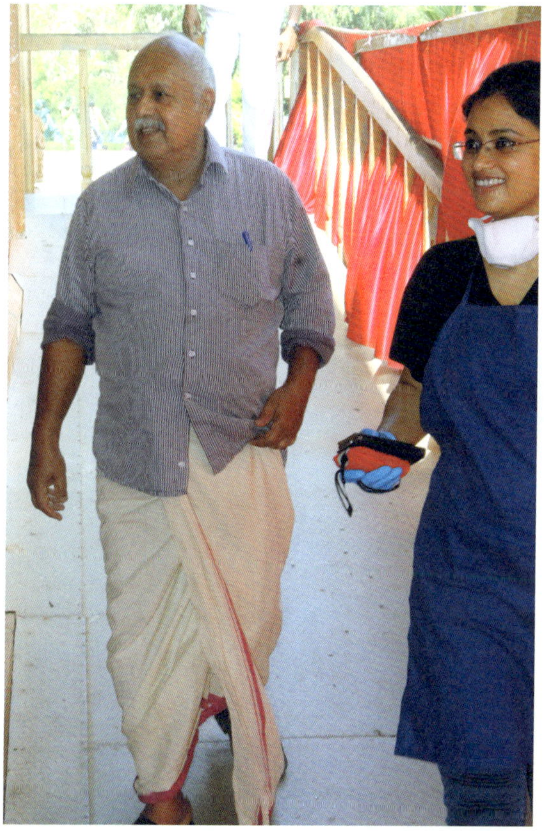

right: Fig. 18: Members of the museum's security team move a sculpture from the old storage to the working space with the shopping cart
far right: Fig. 22: Prof. Nair inspects the working space and happily realises that work is going on quickly

WORKING MISSION FEBRUARY 2017

In February 2017, a team of students of the National Museum Institute New Delhi, museum staff, and Johanna and Tanushree were ready to implement the first steps in collection care that were defined in the road map. The storage of Napier Museum was emptied, all objects were cleaned, a condition report was made and then all objects were brought to a safe interim storage. The working space was installed outside of the museum to ensure enough ventilation. For lack of other devices, moving of objects was partly done with a shopping cart.

WORKING MISSION AUGUST/SEPTEMBER 2017

In August 2017, the next workshop held by the Institute of Conservation at Napier Museum was all about handling packing and moving of objects. As the renovation of the museum building will start soon, the whole collection had to be moved out of the future construction site and the topic was of high importance to the museum staff.

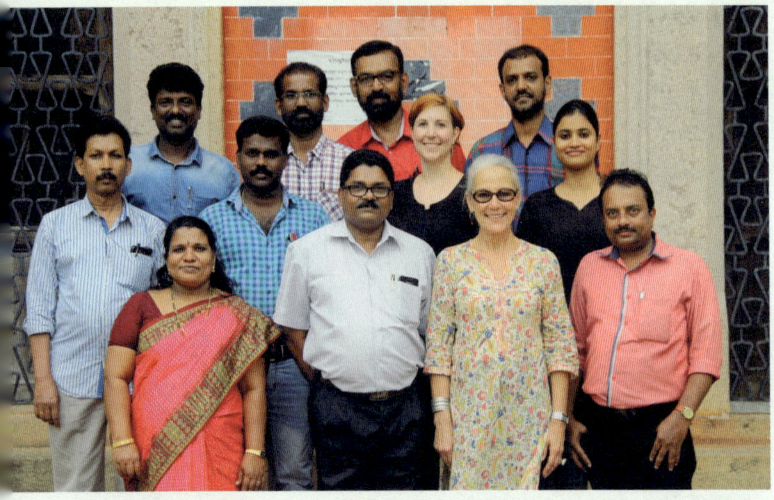

Fig. 24: Team and participants of the Workshop in August/September 2017

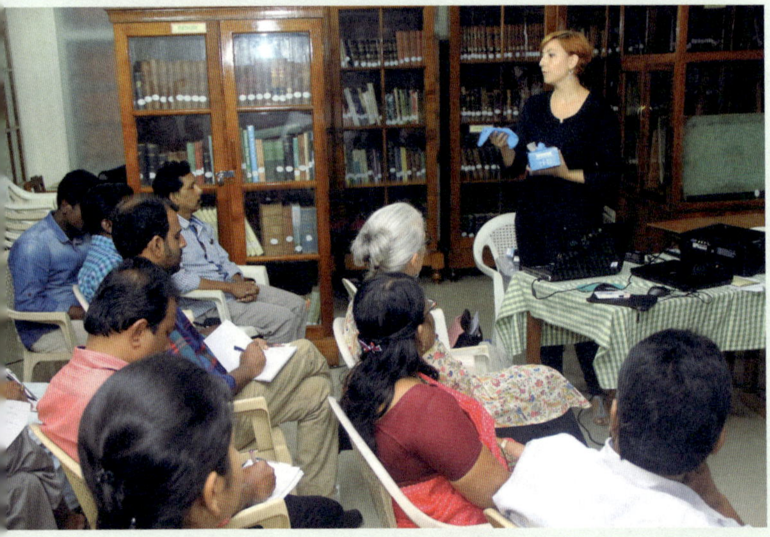

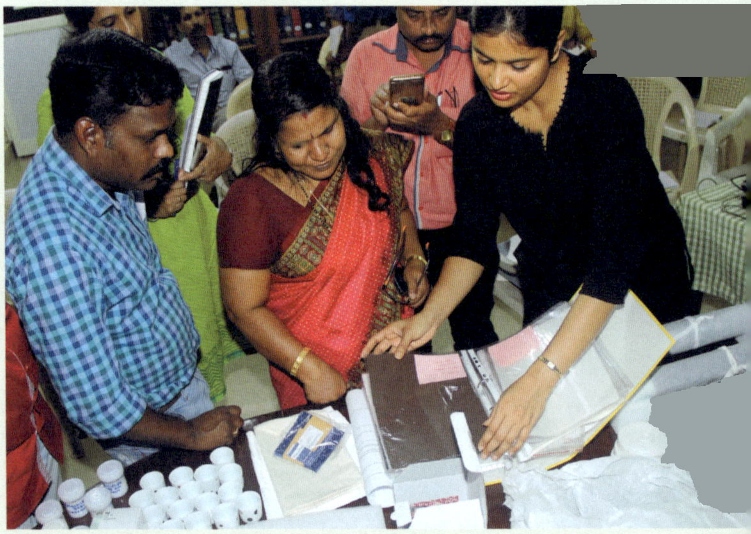

Fig. 25: Johanna presents how to handle objects and which kind of gloves can be used to protect the art objects from grease and acids of human touch

Fig. 26: Tanushree hands over a map with different sample materials, which are proved to be suitable for museum use

WORKING MISSION FEBRUARY 2018 (16/02/2018 –24/02/2018)

In February 2018, Johanna and Tanushree dived into the packing of the most fragile objects in the museum, together with the museum staff. This involved also a lot of shopping for material and carrying it in suitcases. In the end, the fragmented textiles of the museum were all adequately packed. If possible, they were rolled on stainless tubes and with inlays of Polyethylene fleece and sheets. At the same time Johanna and Manfred Trummer, head of conservation at the Museum of Applied Arts Vienna, discussed and worked on a new exhibition concept for the museum, including the design of the showcases, visitor paths and lighting.

WHAT HAPPENS NEXT?

In the course of the next two years the museum building will be renovated and a new depot erected. In February 2019 the Institute of Conservation will again be at the museum's disposal with practical workshops and planning aids for further steps and progress, whether in the depot or in the exhibition.

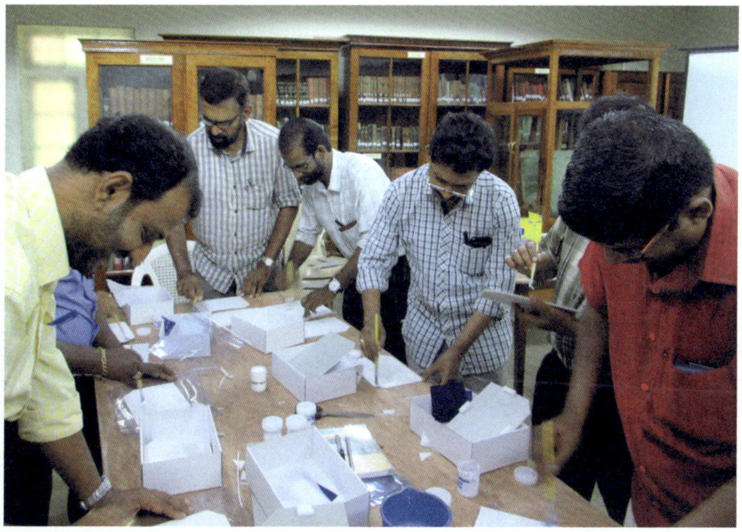

Fig. 27: Museum staff of Napier museum conducts practical exercise with dummy objects to get to know the museum packing materials and how to use them

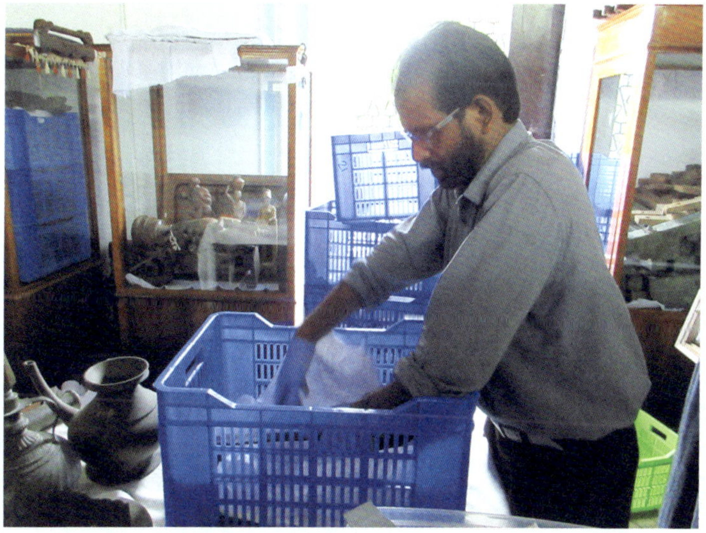

Fig. 28: After the workshop, Rajendran starts packing real museum objects in the interim storage

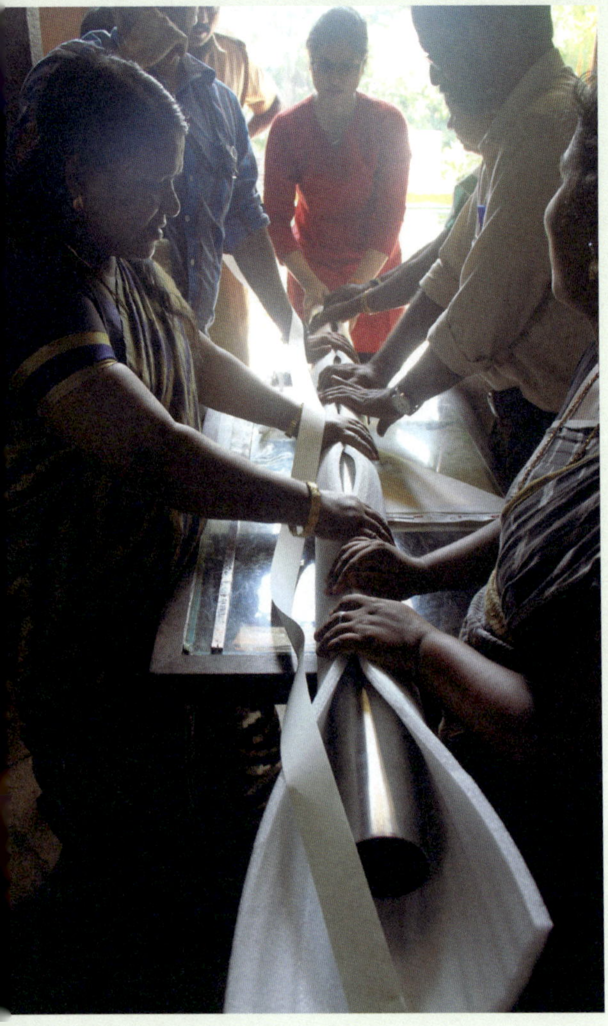

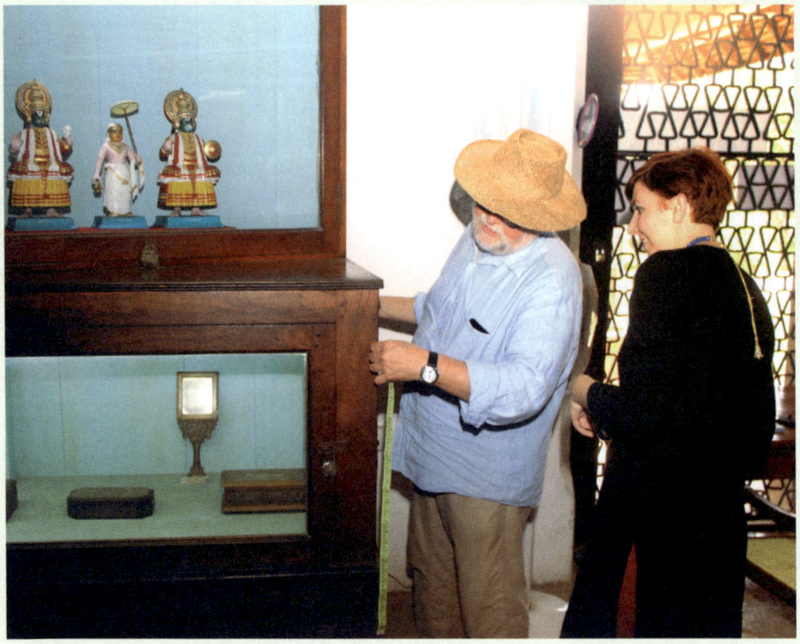

Fig. 29: Preparation of the stainless-steel tubes for rolling the textiles on them

Fig. 31: Manfred and Johanna inspect the furniture in the museum

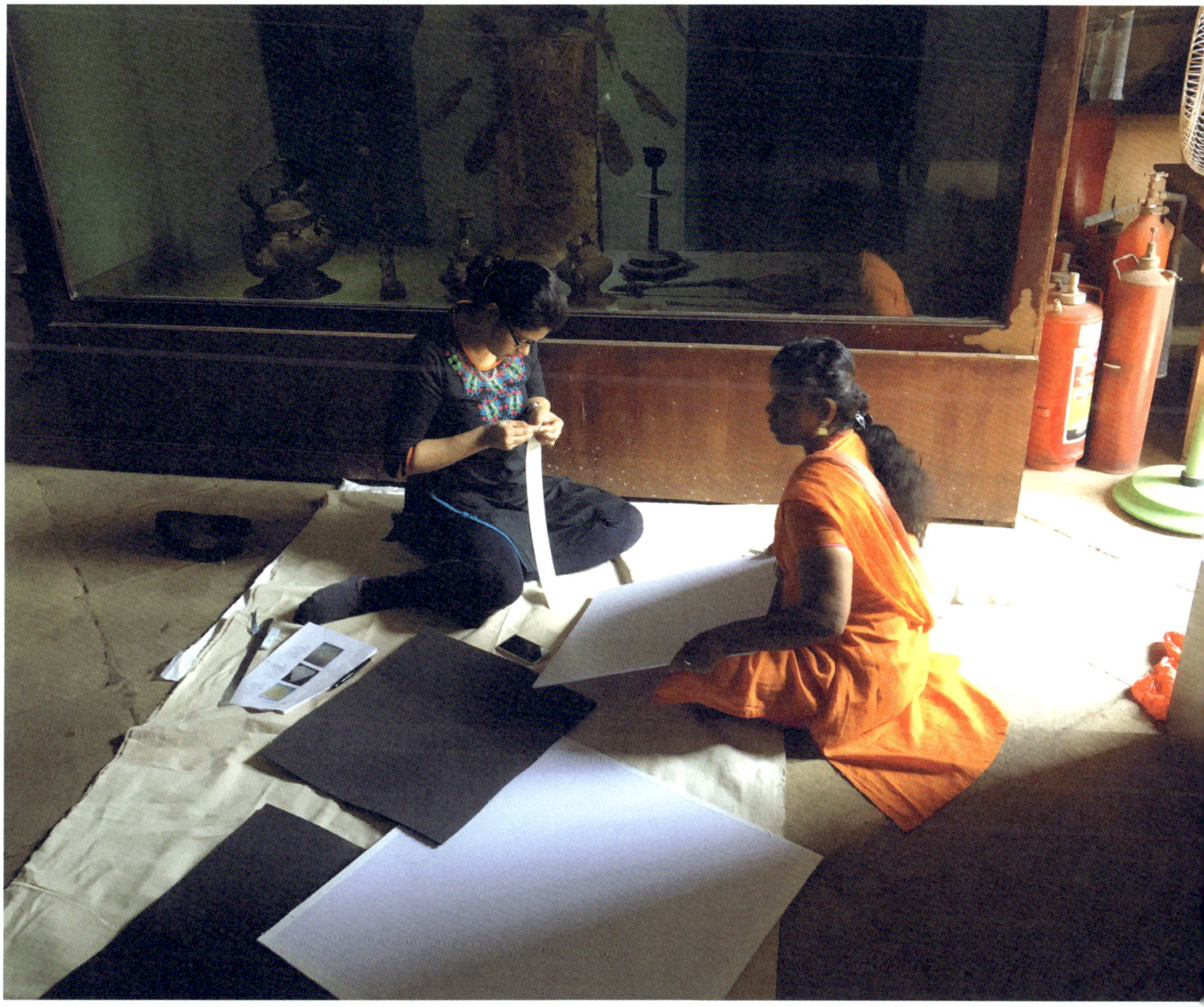

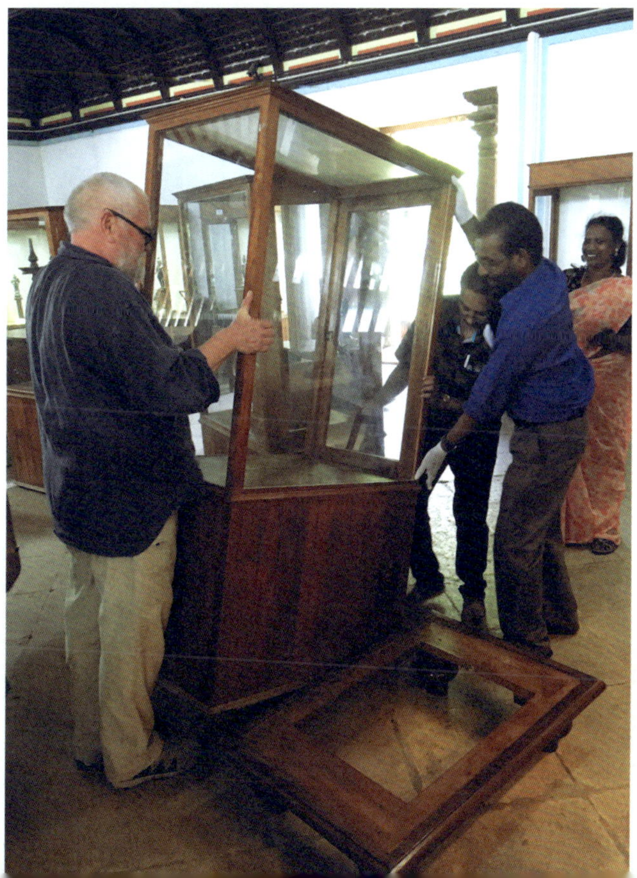

top: Fig. 30: Our packing place within the museum: Sometimes conservators have to work on the floor
left: Fig. 32: Manfred develops new ideas and immediately tries them out. What if the showcases are a little bit higher? Don't you have a suitable pedestal somewhere? Here we go

India is different. Don't rush for conservation.

INTERVIEW M. VELAYUDHAN NAIR

BY ROMAN TRONNER

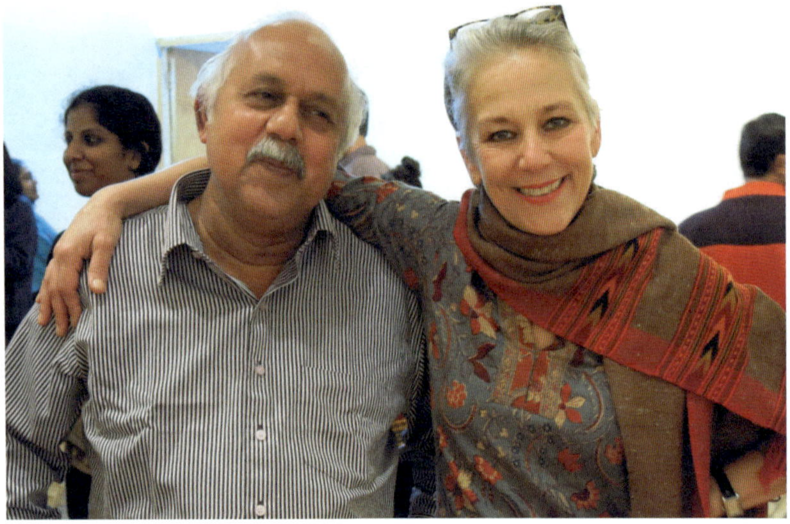

Fig. 1: Prof. M.V. Nair and Prof. Gabriela Krist in New Delhi 2013

India owns a rich and manifold cultural heritage. Preservation strategies differ from the West. Not only because of difficult climate conditions, explains Prof. M.V. Nair, conservation specialist and former vice-president of ICOM-CC.

Velayudhan Nair is professor emeritus at the National Museum Institute (NMI), Conservation Department, in New Delhi, India. In 2003 he was elected vice-president of ICOM-CC (UNESCO) – the International Council of Museums, Conservation Committee. From 1991 to 1995 and 2005 to 2010 he was director of the National Research Laboratory for Conservation of Cultural Property (NRLC). He studied chemistry at the Indian Institute of Technology in Madras. Today he is chief adviser and responsible for the museums in his home country, Kerala.

What does cultural heritage in general mean to people in India?

Basically, cultural heritage in India is something which is our ancestor's property. For Indians it is the way of life: my father's, my forefather's property, even if it is a pen, even if it is a cloth.

Are there any differences to western countries?

In India, even if you notice a monument, say 150 years old, it may not become so important because there is such a large quantity of cultural property in this huge country. But if you go to the US or another country you see it is very valuable and much care is given to it. Of course, preservation is also a matter of how much money and manpower you can spend and whether there is trained manpower for such an intervention. In India, the standards are very different because you have such an abundance of cultural property. This is the only difference I see among the approaches to cultural property. It is the question of how relevant it is, because even if you want to make it important, sometimes you may not be able to achieve this in India because you don't have resources to take care of everything even if it becomes relatively important. In Austria, for example, or in Europe, it is totally different. You will get the attention. In India it is a matter of recognition, how much importance you are giving to an object and how much money you spend for its preservation. For example, in India, if you live in a house that is five hundred years old, sometimes people think it is cursed, I cannot renovate it. When you come to Europe it is a matter of pride that "I am living in a house that is a few hundred years old." That is the difference in approach. Of course renovation of such a house can be very expensive, and in India you may not be able to afford it. In other countries like in the UK there are tax exemptions for renovating old buildings; you have trained conservators, qualified professionals. So there should be more incentives given by the state to protect cultural properties.

How does India as a state protect its cultural heritage?

India has a national legislation with regards to cultural property. Ancient monuments are subject to the Monument Sites Act of 1952, of the government of India. In addition, there is further legislation at the level of the federal states. For example in Kerala, where I work and live, ancient monuments remain subject to the Monument Sites Act, which was enacted two years after the national act. All these acts basically work the same. Before federal state legislation was enacted, most of the cultural property was government controlled. Today, protected monuments are governed by India if they are of national importance. If it is of regional importance, it becomes protected by the federal state and once it is protected, the upkeep becomes a duty of the Indian government. Often there won't be any conservation or refurbishment because if it is a living monument, it will continue to live and if it is a temple, it will continue to function as a temple. But there will be restrictions on its preservation because you won't be able to alter the temple in any way. Preservation becomes the responsibility of the owner and also of public authorities. Sometimes an agreement is signed between the owner and the government.

What policies in conservation does India follow?

India follows the ICOM and the UNESCO conventions. UNESCO defines cultural property and what a museum object is. But the policies of conservation in India may be different to Europe. For example, we don't want to imitate the original artist because we hold him in high esteem. We believe that no other paintings made by different people can reach the quality of the original. Take the Ajanta paintings. There are so many patches in there, but that doesn't mean that India has no conservators. This is a tick of conservation we follow, the fact that we cannot do anything with the creations of the original artist. We preserve, but we cannot restore to the extent that it looks original. This is the difference to Europe.

The approach in Europe is indeed somewhat different.

Yes, you can see that, even if you go to the Vatican Museum, all the paintings look brand new, the mural paintings also look brand new, which means they have attained an emulation of the original, but in India we don't do this. And we have restrictions, we all follow different aesthetics and it will probably remain so. But preventive conservation should be carried out. Because if for example one leg of a sculpture is missing, I fix the equilibrium and the strength of the object. The conservator should not misunderstand it as original so we resort to recursion, even if you have to conserve it to some extent. We have to ensure that all applied measures remain reversible. Reversibility in that sense is a principle everywhere: if a better technique emerges, the worse one won't stand in the way of improving the object Everything should be reversible; we follow this principle, we cannot add something which is permanent to the object.

What is the role of museums and collections in preserving cultural heritage?

Of course, there is a collection policy for all the museums. They should collect objects and care for them; in India, faking is one of the problems. We had the case of 24 Mughal paintings in a museum in Calcutta. The museums found out that the paintings were faked. The High Court of Calcutta intervened to discover whether they were genuine or fake. We could easily identify the fake because the technique of faking was not intended for faking, but for making a duplicate of these paintings about fifty years ago.

To give a proper identification of authenticity is the duty of a qualified conservator and a laboratory that can identify it correctly. If it is a painting, they may use old canvas; fakers really do use these things as well. But who is going to carry out the search for fakes in the collections? Only conservators can do that. Therefore, collection care becomes very important. And objects have to be authentic, particularly before they go for exhibitions.

You are pointing to the prevalent need in India to bridge the gap between knowing preventive conservation measures and applying them to the collections. What is so challenging in this respect?

Preventive conservation is very important in India because of the tropical climate. In the Indian climate, conditions vary a lot, from the Himalayan region and Kashmir to the tropical south. In the northwestern areas humidity levels are very low, that means everything can be more easily preserved. If you come to Central India, like Delhi, there will be many variations in the climate, temperature and humidity. There you have hot summers and hard winters. In the south of India, like Kerala, temperature variations might not be high but the humidity variations will be very prominent, whereas in the desert in Rajasthan, humidity will be very low and the temperature variations are very high.

Conditions such as in Kerala are ideal for the growth of fungus, insects, and bio-deterioration is high. Another problem is precipitation. A few years back, there used to be no rain in Leh, a city in Ladakh; there was only ice, but that caused a lot of problems to the monasteries there because they were not equipped for such climate conditions, which are quite barren.

Therefore, preventive conservation and risk assessment should now deal with everything. We cannot allow disasters to happen only because we did not take precautions. So, we have to be aware of those challenges for preventive conservation, which has become very relevant in a country like India.

You've been collaborating with the Institute of Conservation in Vienna for many years. How did this cooperation evolve?

The starting point dates back to 2004 in Nako. In that year I was the director of the National Research Laboratory of Conservation of Cultural Property in Lucknow under the Ministry of Culture. This is a national laboratory of India. Therefore, we collaborated with Gabriela Krist`s team from Vienna in conserving and working on many of our problems concerning the Buddhist temples in the Nako village. We enjoyed working with the Austrian team.

But today the main subject of your cooperation is the exchange of students and expertise?

Yes, we had students from the University of Applied Arts and staff members, they worked in the laboratory in Lucknow and started with analyses. Our first thing in analysis was how to investigate cultural property, like a doctor intervening a patient. First you should know what the disease is, how the patient reacts to the chemicals.

How can the Institute of Conservation in Vienna support preventive conservation in India?

When we started the collaboration in Kerala for Napier Museum, the first thing we had to do was to deal with the climatic variations in different seasons. First we had to collect data about the climate variations and data of organic objects, various types of wood, paintings, leather, and textiles and how these materials are affected by the climatic variations. What we need here is collection care, which is what the Institute of Conservation in Vienna is concentrating on. In 2016, we had a workshop on how to establish a roadmap to be prepared for conservation strategies in Napier Museum. The first thing Gabriela Krist and we discussed was the study of the effects of climate and how preventive conservation can be achieved. This is a prerequisite for adopting any type of conservation.

Students from India come to Vienna to be trained particularly in this practical hands-on type of work. Was that the main experience that your students gained?

Of course, but it is a mutual exchange, because the techniques followed in Vienna were not working in Delhi and in Trivandrum. For example, when you take a mud painting, the painting has been done on a mud plaster. Therefore, you have to use the traditional techniques to conserve this. You have to take a decision to what extent non-conventional chemicals can be used. You have to examine how conservation methods behave in the specific climate in India, whether pigments are affected and so on. If these things aren't carried out successfully, conservation has no meaning.

The experience from such analyses was mutually profitable because our chemists and scientists do not know the latest chemicals that are used in Vienna, for example ethyl silicate they use in Vienna – it was very new to our scientists and conservators.

What in your opinion was the most important contribution of Gabriela Krist`s crew during their work in India?

Gabriela`s colleagues have become very important because they are very well organized. Sometimes in India the laboratories are not that organized. Sometimes the museum people in India are not fully aware of the conservation problems and conservation standards and also the needs of a museum. India is a very large country, it has so much cultural property and so many museums, so sometimes there are no fixed standards. So, it is essential that custodians of the cultural property follow the standards. This is why we organized joint workshops on the right practices with a large group of museum professionals. Therefore, this collaboration with Vienna is very useful for India, and in Kerala we feel that this cooperation is very important.

You talked about standards. Do you believe there should be one world-wide standard of conservation training and if so what has to be done to achieve such standards?

I think the standards should be different, particularly because of the problems you face. The training should not be universal, it should be for the particular case, the particular collection. For example, if somebody is trained in Vienna for the preservation of paintings – curatorial and preventional – it may not work under other climatic conditions. When I was council member of ICCROM, I was responsible for a wall painting training course; we took equal number of South-east Asian people and Indians. First of all, we asked them to bring materials from their own places and we made some analyses. You have to know which technique was originally used. Of course, the standards and syllabus can be internationally fixed. But how can that be achieved? You always have to take into account the specific situations and challenges, for example climate conditions.

We have to decide about the practical standards in the training. The training should be to know the object, to know the climate, to know your problems, and the first thing in the training is that you should use common sense in understanding the object, and you should see the object in its particular state. If there is any intervention, you should plan where you are doing it, whether the intervention is essential, whether you can avoid it as far as possible – the conservation ethics say: minimum intervention for an object; whether you fulfil these criteria, the minimum intervention and reversibility, whether you are able to achieve this. You should repair and conserve that object. To go for conservation for conservation sake – that should not be the criteria. It is saving the object. This is the training one should give to students to make them qualified conservators.

What would you recommend to a conservator from Europe to take into account before starting a conservation campaign in India?

I would recommend: don't immediately start in India. First you should understand the problems. Because if you apply chemicals to objects that are prevalent in Europe and use them for preservation or consolidation, it may be a disaster for the cultural property in India. An historical example: the paintings of the Ajanta caves are world heritage. In 1940, Italian qualified conservators did the conservation of the paintings. They came and put shellac on it, which made the paintings shiny. This was the work style of the Italians that time. But the paintings which were preserved from the second century B.C. until 1940 didn't have many problems in the beginning. The problem was, however, that the expansion properties of shellac are totally different from the paintings. The paintings, which were safe until 1940, started to crumble and to fall down from the wall. The intention was good but they didn't consider the variations in climate. Therefore, it should be a lesson for all the other conservators coming from Europe – they should learn this lesson and before attempting anything in India – India is different. You should not rush for conservation in India, one should have proper understanding before attempting anything.

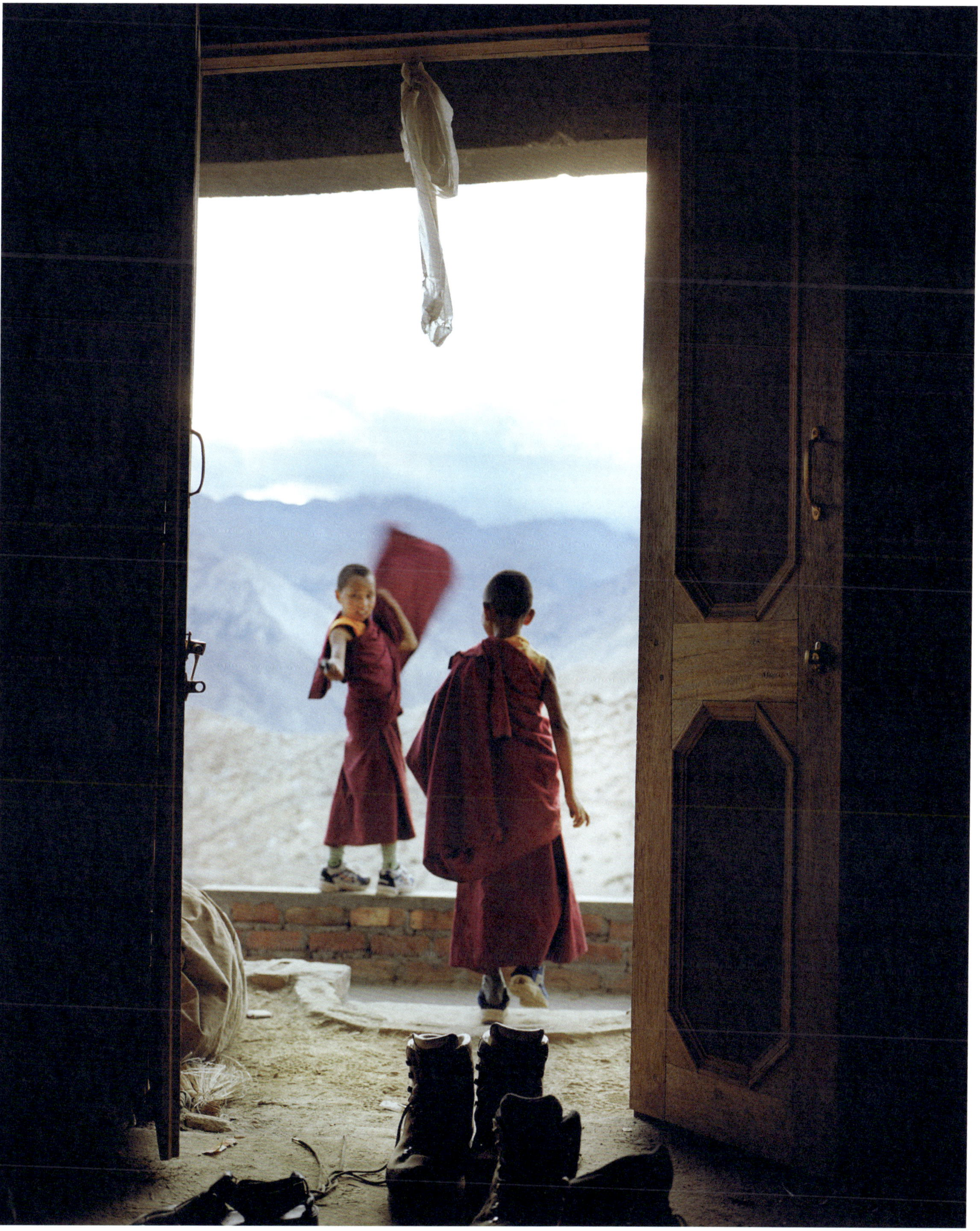

Fig. 2: Nako, where it all started

Mongolia

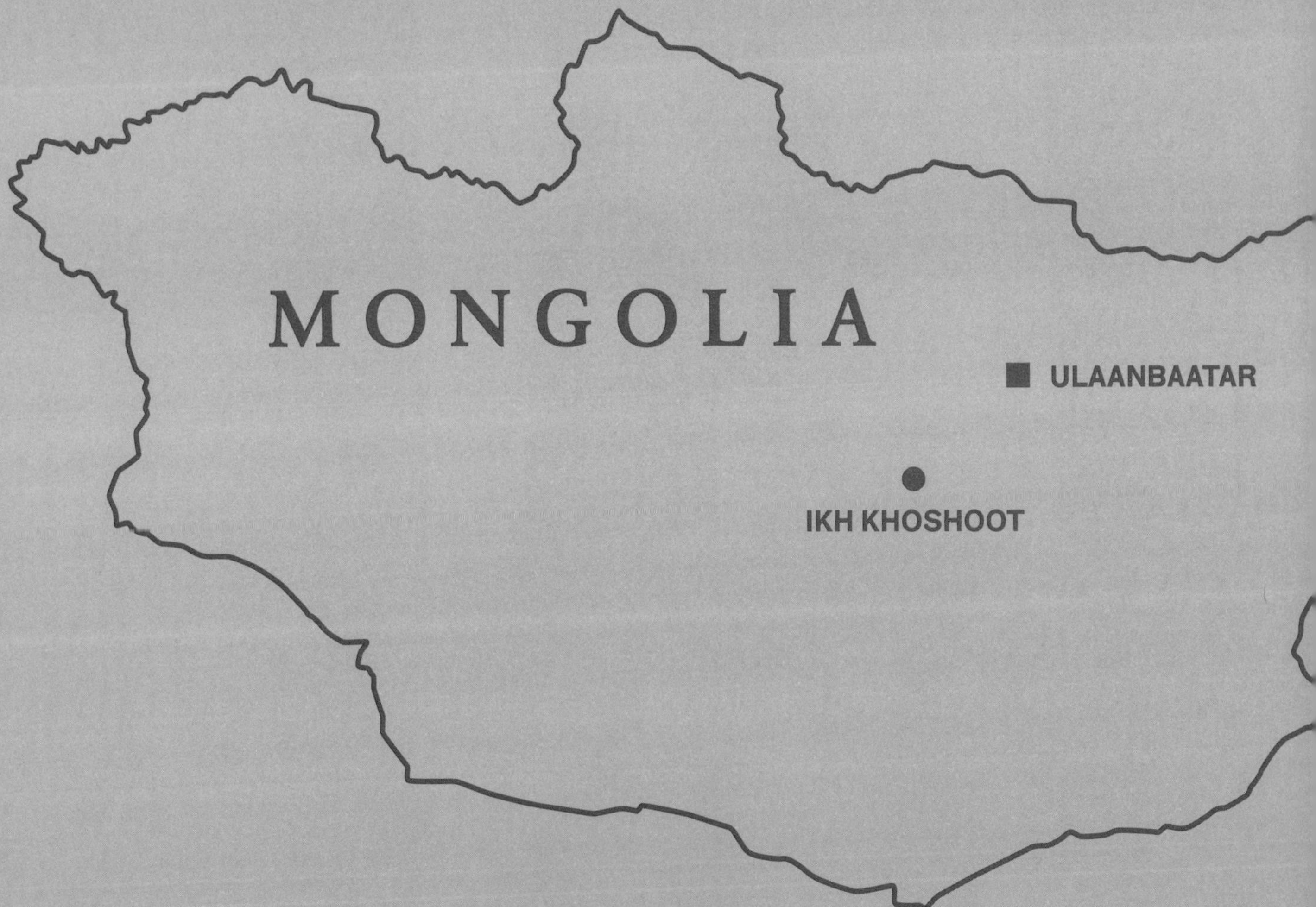

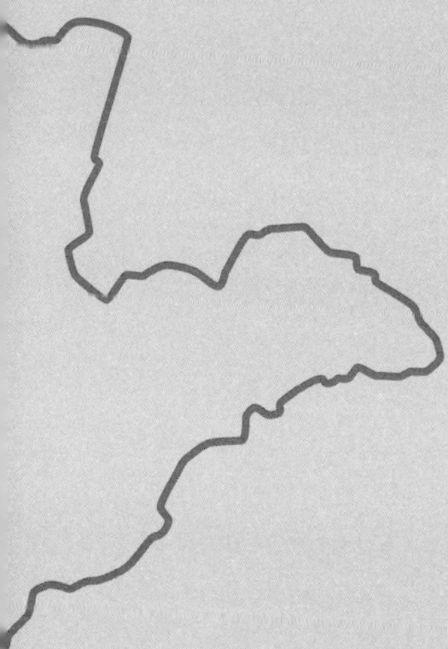

The Dog Who Travels Comes Back with the Bone

(Free After Khosbayar Narankhuu, Khosoo for Short)

GABRIELA KRIST

MONGOLIA 2014–2018

When I asked my Mongolian friends, at lunch in Ulaanbaatar in August 2017, whether they could quote a proverb for me that was typical of their country, Khosoo chipped in spontaneously: "The dog who travels comes back with the bone". Well, this is what I want as my banner headline right at the start of my report on Mongolia and the Mongolians, as a motto, which puts our activities in this extraordinary country into a nutshell. We are "the dog", the employees of the Institute of Conservation, who after every visit to Mongolia come back home showered with gifts and finds, enriched by the professional and human experiences that made these journeys possible. The Mongolians are "the dog" as well; they like travelling, they are still nomads; they love moving around – anything rather than staying in the same place – and they love their country and especially their steppe, the freedom offered by this phenomenon of nature with its never-ending sky, its breathtaking landscape and animals (Fig. 1), horses, Kashmir goats...and of course the cultural assets and art treasures that are inseparably connected to the steppe landscape, the focus of the following essays and reports. I am so happy and grateful to have had the privilege of seeing Mongolia several times now, and am all the more grateful to have become acquainted with so many wonderful people there.

It all started in 2013. Two people – the former president of the Eurasia-Pacific Uninet (EPU) Brigitte Winklehner, and Gudrun Hardiman-Pollross, whom we knew very well from New Delhi and at the time was head of the Kulturforum, the Cultural Forum, of the Austrian Embassy in Beijing and also responsible for Mongolia – promoted the setting up of a workshop for the first time in Ulaanbaatar (Fig. 2). We appealed to our EPU as financing partner. The Mongolians need support in the preservation of cultural assets; priority was to be given to textile collections, costumes and textiles, which we know are very important to them. The Bogd Khaan Palace, the former residence of the Mongolian Dalai Lama Bogd Khaan, was an excellent option as an event location (Fig. 3). Here at the Winter Palace, today a museum and premier tourist site, will be the setting for exhibiting his magnificent robes, also personal items, furniture...and, very important for every Mongolian, his *ger* (yurt). Contacts were established and we got ready for Mongolia.

It was February 2014 when we – our textile conservators and myself – arrived in Mongolia for the first time, it was forty degrees below freezing, bitter cold; a fine covering of snow covered the city, light and powder-like, quite different from at home (Fig. 4). We had prepared ourselves for the winter journey – bought thick winter coats, fur boots, thermal underwear. We checked in at the Ulaanbaatar Hotel, a house of rich tradition in the centre of town. I was indeed ready for Mongolia as far as coping with the cold was concerned – but not for the food. Meat is the thing here, lots of meat, only meat, mountains of meat…(Didi told me that meat is the most important thing for Mongolian men. When they arrive in a new town, the first thing they ask is, "Where can I get good quality meat?"). I was somewhat groggy after India and felt incapable of eating anything. This was the main problem on my first visit to Mongolia.

The first day of our workshop in Bogd Khaan Palace: office building, overheated, wobbly chairs, improvisation, many – too many – participants from the various collections in the city and throughout the country, ostensibly textile conservators, an interpreter, the director and his team. We discussed collection care, treatment of delicate textiles, how they are handled, stored and cared for (Fig. 5). We received examples to practise on from the collection: Mongolian headgear, embroidered leather boots, wonderful objects. It was a pure delight to instruct the highly motivated participants, to prepare the pieces for exhibition and storage, to support, to pad out, to package…communication presented no problem, although many participants hardly spoke English or German, and the interpreter had her hands full. The collective work provided the bond between us, and it all went very well (Fig. 6).

What a surprise when, on the last day of our workshop, the intern textile conservator took us into the museum depot in the basement. Perfectly correct, simple, but everything exemplary and state of the art, both equipment and storage aids, just as in Austria – although the country doesn't have a training system for conservation, we were told, not yet; but they have creative, motivated people who love their cultural assets and care for them as well as they are able.

Supper…every day a dinner in excellent Mongolian restaurants was organised. But I've already mentioned this problem. I still felt sick and there was lots of meat. One time I wasn't hungry, the next time I had a migraine, then the excuses gradually ran out.

One evening Gudrun invited all the museum directors in Ulaanbaatar and the director of the National Center for Cultural Heritage to the Buffalo Grill Restaurant in the city centre on Sükhbaatar Square, formerly Chinggis Square. Oh yes, I forgot to say that Genghis Khan is omnipresent in the country, monuments to the Mongolian hero grace every square (Fig. 7). He's sung about, danced about and portrayed in every museum…Well, everyone sat around a large table; this time I could order what I wanted myself, no meat. Genghis Khan vodka came and came and kept coming. Another thing I forgot to mention; the Mongolians can drink, and can drink a lot. So can we Austrians, but the Mongolians are better at it, much better. After several vodkas we were invited to sing an Austrian song, "Das Wandern ist des Müllers Lust" (from Schubert's *Schöne Müllerin*; we couldn't agree on anything else, the lyrics were the problem). We failed miserably. Now it was the Mongolians' turn; what a show, Khosoo was wonderful, a real Mongolian tenor, one song followed the next, one Genghis Khan vodka after another. It was a fantastic evening, unforgettable, and still a great memory.

To continue: our textile workshop was held in June 2015 as part of the Austrian Days in Mongolia (Fig. 8), and another on pigment and bonding agent options, and in 2016 a stone conservation training session in the far-flung steppe (Fig. 9). You might know of those famous engraved and relief-adorned stones, graves formed like steles, littered as if by chance across the landscape (but the Kashmir goats like rubbing against them); there will be a separate report about them, also about the follow-up in June 2018, where hands-on conservation work was carried out, a real adventure (Fig. 10)! And further training programmes in 2017 and 2018, analysis, documentation and maintenance of the polychrome works of the Bogd Khaan Palace – this, too, will be the subject of a report, a project that will also be the topic of a doctoral thesis (Fig. 11).

Today we have Memoranda of Understanding with all our Mongolian partners, the National Center for Cultural Heritage, the Mongolian State University of Arts and Culture, which has also joined the EPU, and the Bogd

Khaan Palace (Fig. 12). These contracts pave the way to cooperation on various levels. On one hand, we are interested in supporting the Mongolian colleagues in developing a course of conservation studies at the University of Arts and Culture in Ulaanbaatar. In 2017, Ganzam Sumberraz attended our painting class for four months; he is a thangka painter and will be trained as a teacher for painting conservation. In October 2017, we had Chinbat Magsar with us on an Austrian Exchange Service (OeAD) scholarship; he worked in our object conservation department and learned about our methods of metal and ceramic conservation. He, too, will join the future teaching staff of the conservation department in the Mongolian University. And then there is Khosoo, already mentioned several times and the chief conservator at Bogd Khaan, also a practising traditional painter. He joined us in winter 2016 and in February 2018 passed our entrance exam, thus he will start regular conservation studies in autumn (Fig. 13). And then there is Erdene Batjargal, our English-speaking "model participant" of the last workshop run by the National Center for Cultural Heritage; he is presently working on the application for an OeAD scholarship for studying conservation with us, something he really wants to do...I think this might be a way to sensitise Mongolians who would rather be artists than conservators for the preservation of cultural assets and to show them that conservation can (also) be a rewarding and above all useful profession in Mongolia. There are so many cultural assets that need conservators, and the Mongolians are aware of this.

My thanks go to Brigitte Winklehner and Wolf-Dieter Rausch, EPU presidents, who made our research and training activities in Mongolia possible. The Eurasia-Pacific University Network really is a fantastic organisation.

Finally, my warmest thanks go to all my Mongolian friends, Sara, Tsolmon, Didi, Khosoo, Ganzam, Chinbat, Director Mendsaikhan Otgonbileg and Director Enkhbat Galbadrakh, President Sonintogos Erdenetsogt, also my colleague Uranchimeg. Thank you for the support and thank you for the many insights – histories, stories and facts – that we were privileged to experience through you about your fascinating country.

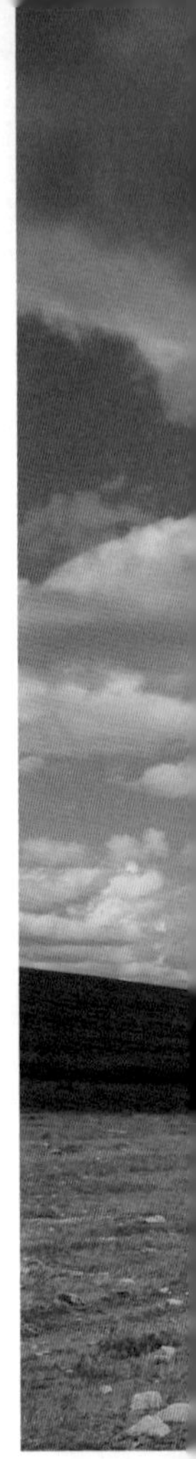

Fig. 1: The breathtaking Mongolian steppe with its never-ending sky

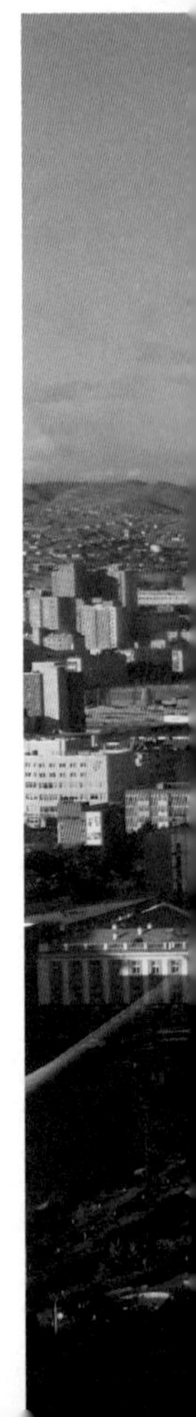

Fig. 2: Ulaanbaatar, Mongolia's capital

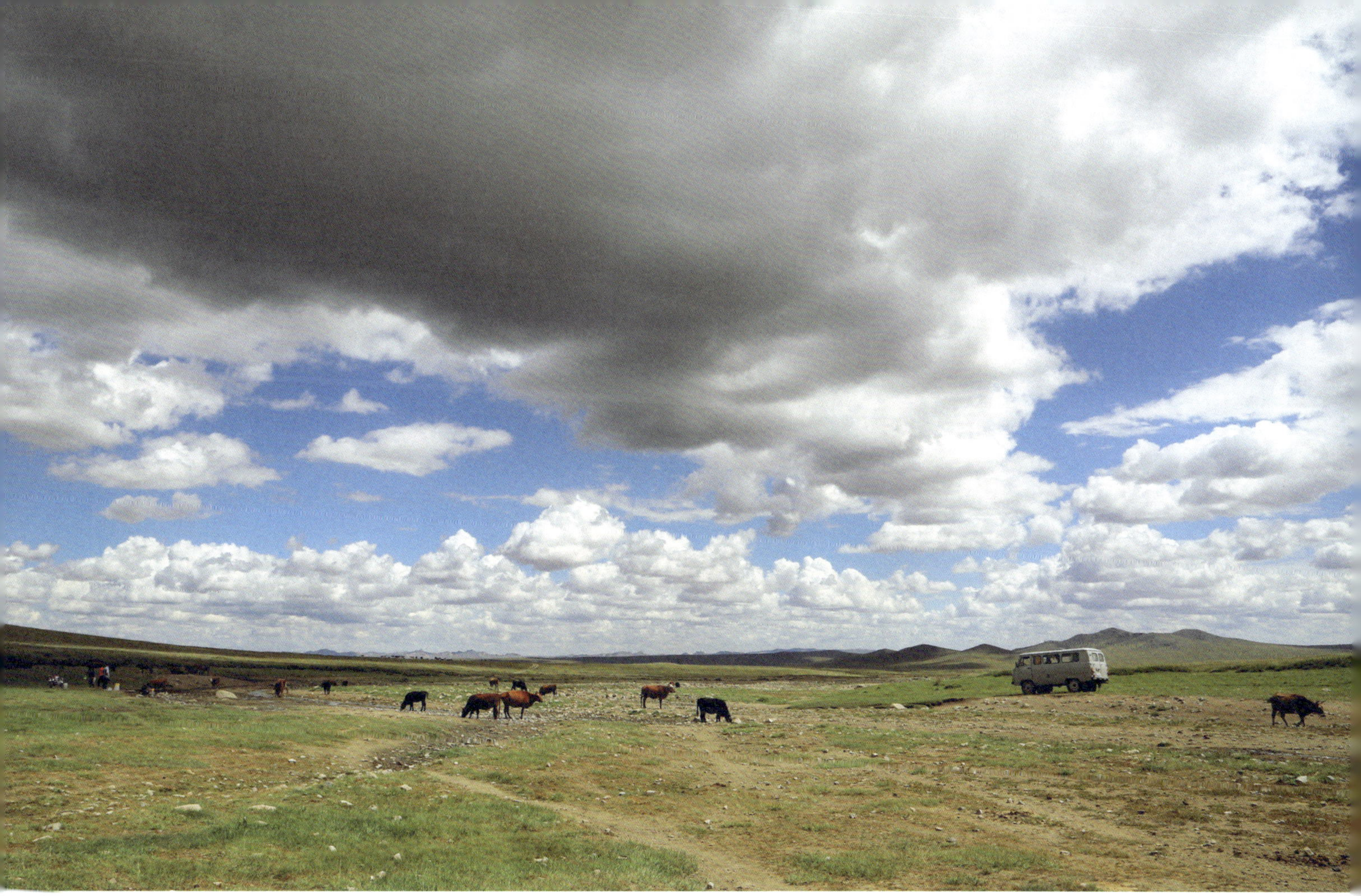

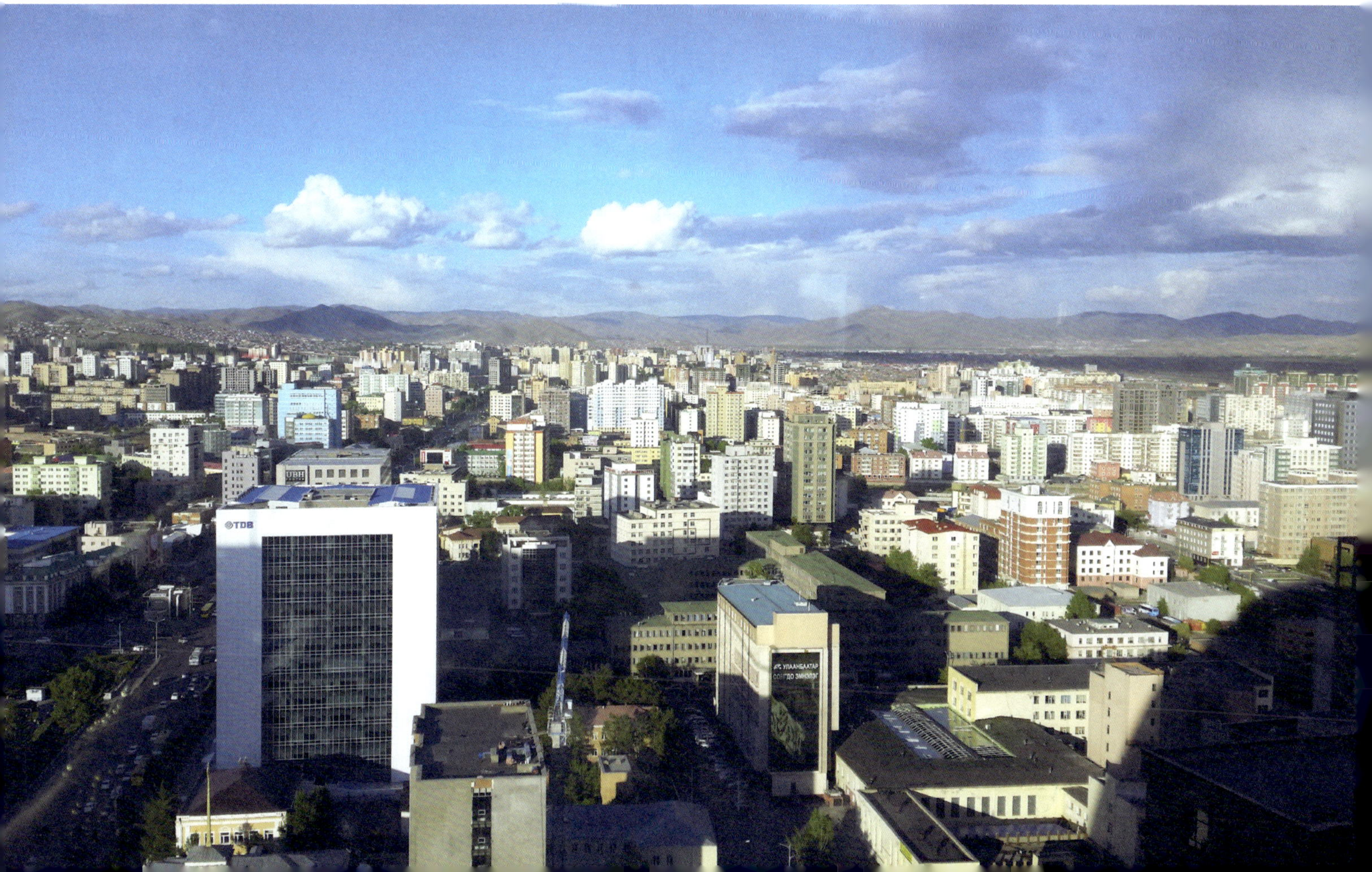
TDB

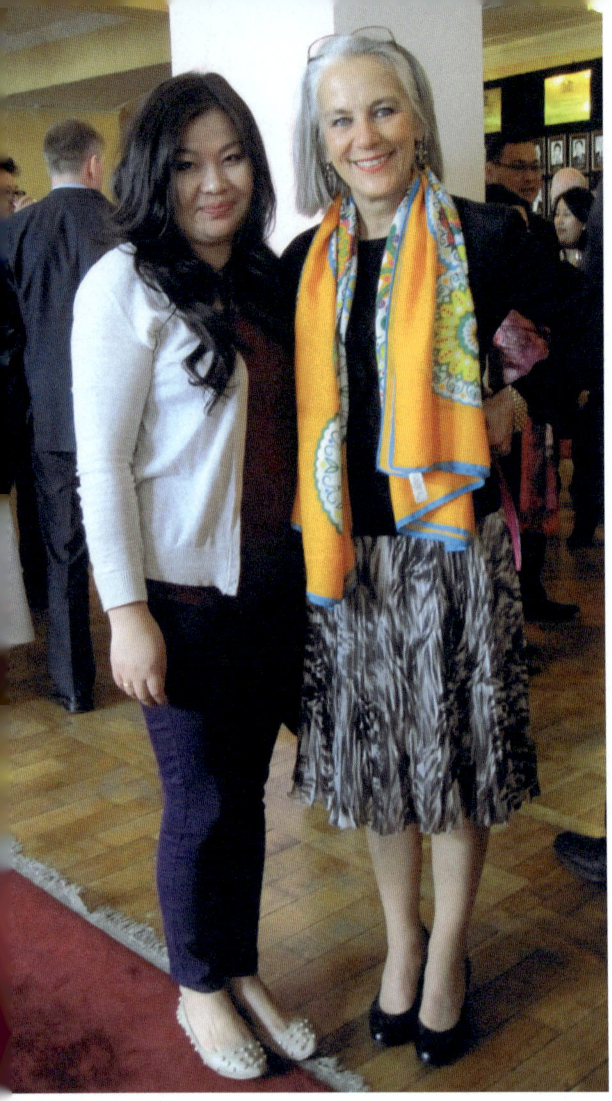

Fig. 8: With my friend Tsolmon (left) at the "Austrian Days in Mongolia", June 2015

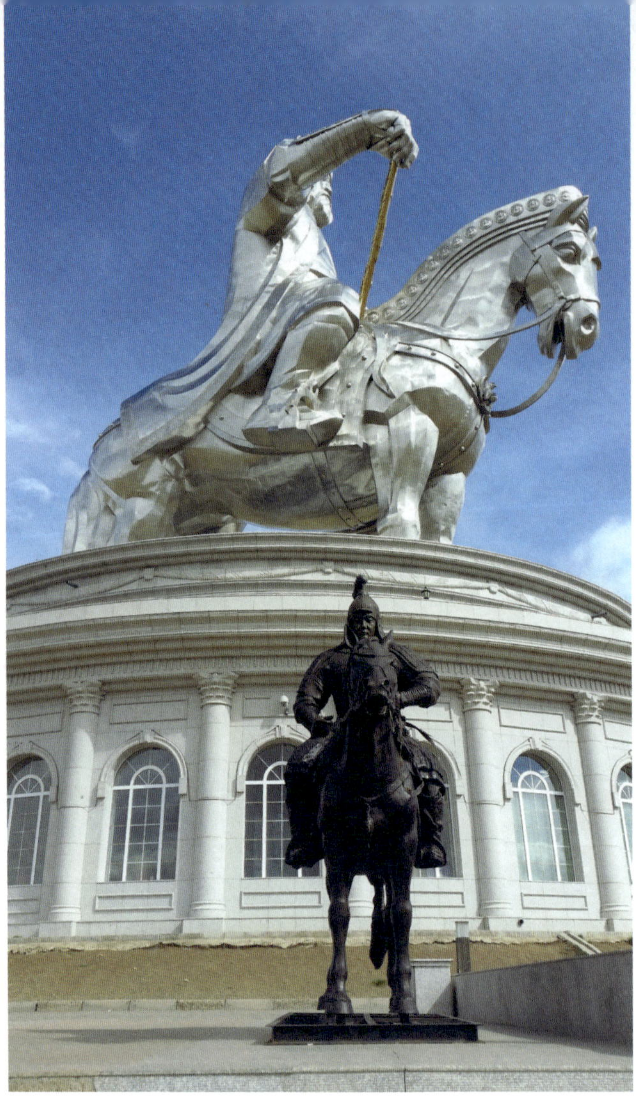

Fig. 7: Monument of the omnipresent Genghis Khan

right page:
Fig. 10: "Stone Conservation Workshop", June 2018
Fig. 3: Bogd Khaan Palace

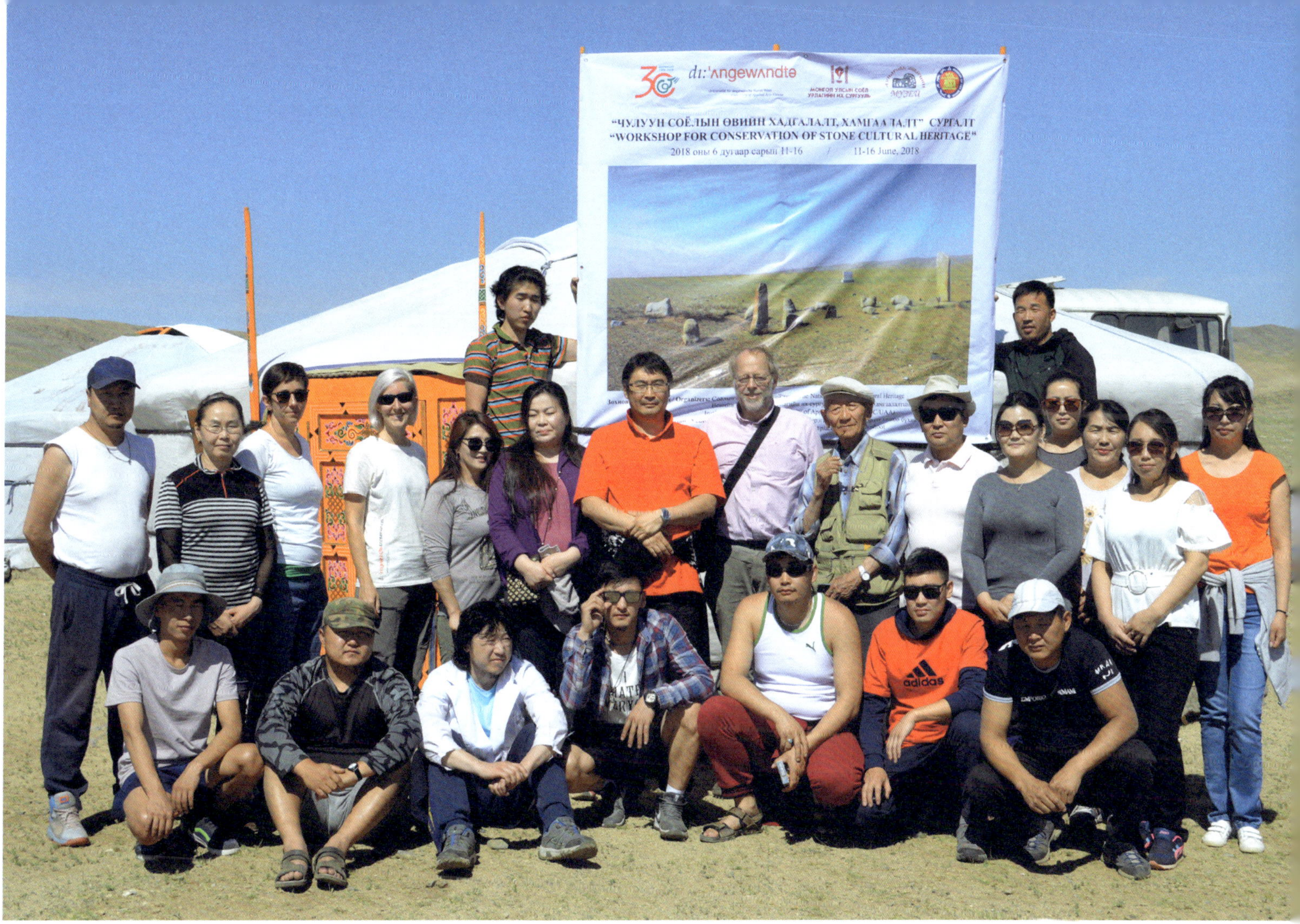
di:'ʌngewʌndtə
МОНГОЛ УЛСЫН СОЁЛ УРЛАГИЙН ИХ СУРГУУЛЬ
"ЧУЛУУН СОЁЛЫН ӨВИЙН ХАДГАЛАЛТ, ХАМГААЛАЛТ" СУРГАЛТ
"WORKSHOP FOR CONSERVATION OF STONE CULTURAL HERITAGE"
2018 оны 6 дугаар сарын 11-16 / 11-16 June, 2018
adidas

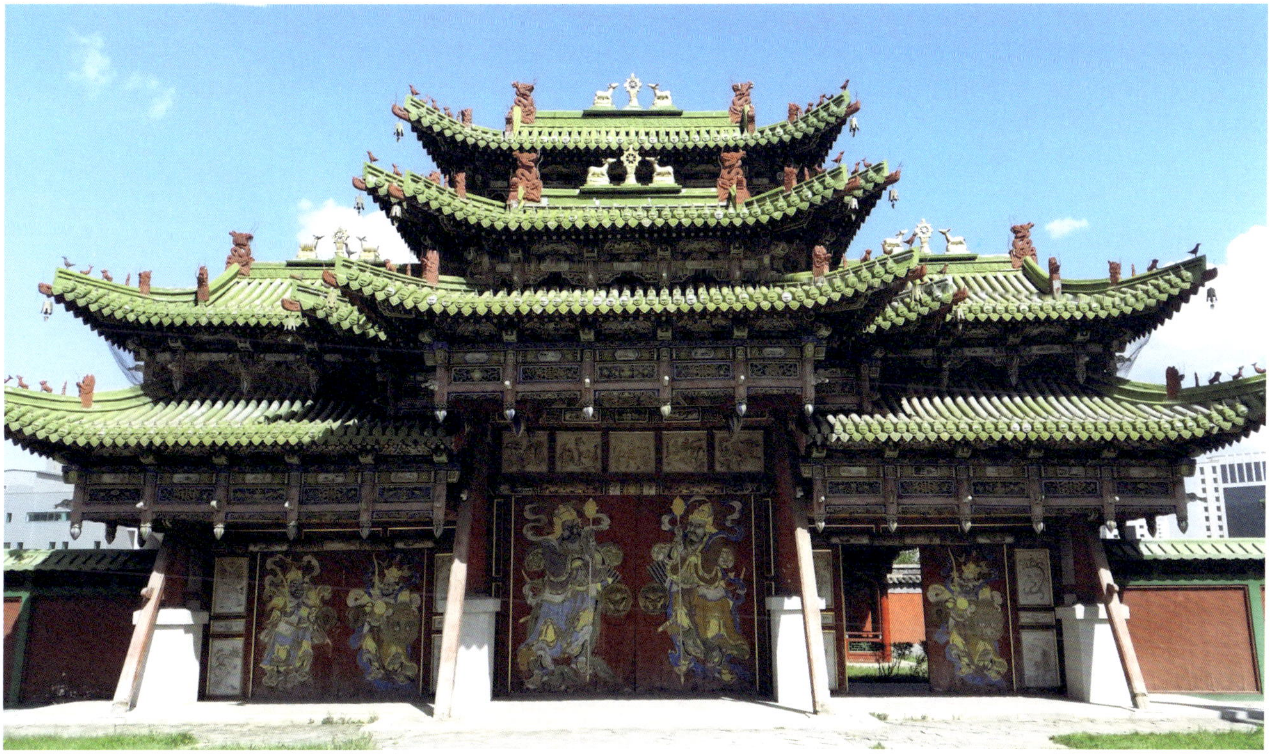

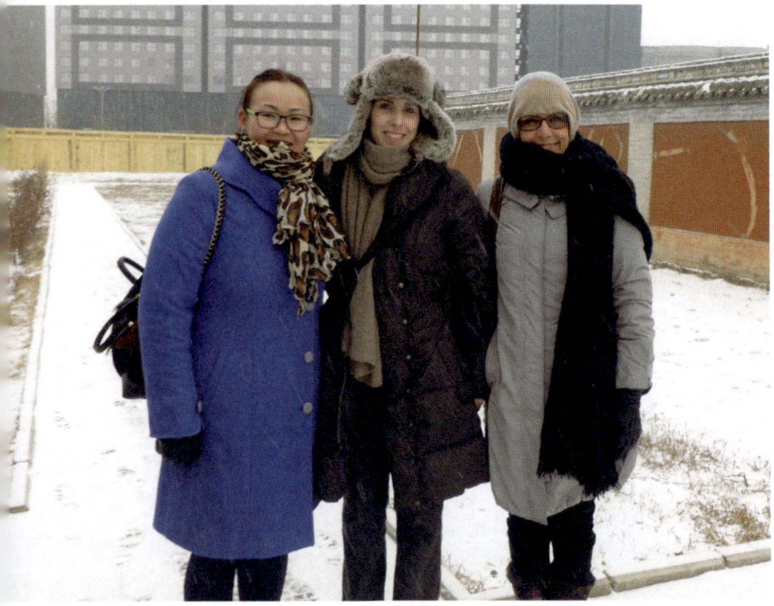

Fig. 4: With textile conservator Britta Schwenck and our interpreter, at 25 degrees below zero, February 2014

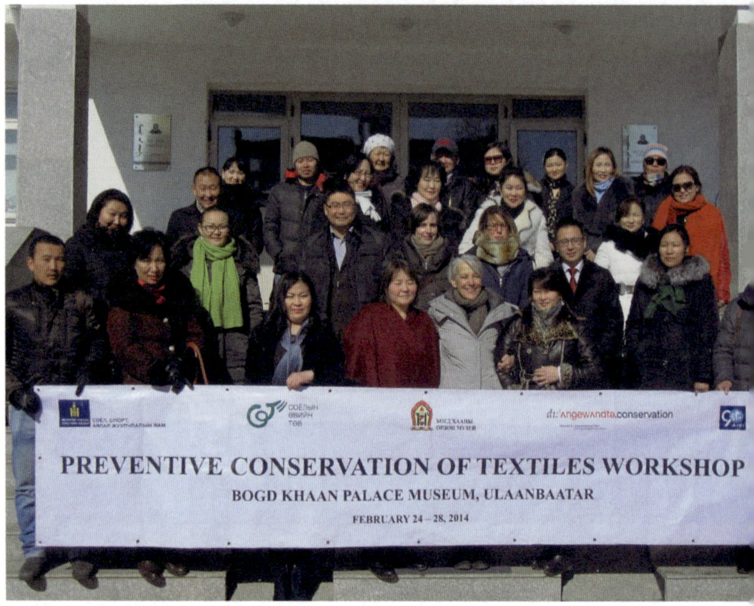

Fig. 5: Training activities at Bogd Khaan Palace, Workshop “Preventive Conservation of Textiles”, Ulaanbaatar 2014

Fig. 6: “Preventive Conservation of Textiles” Workshop at Bogd Khaan Palace Museum, February 2014

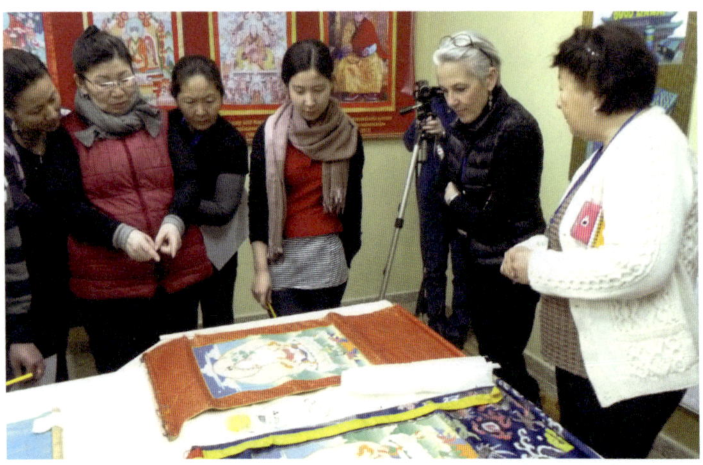

Fig. 11: Training activities at Bogd Khaan Palace, building survey, Ulaanbaatar 2017

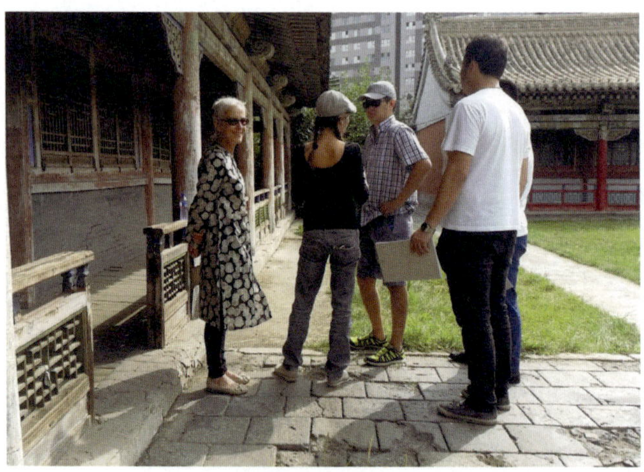

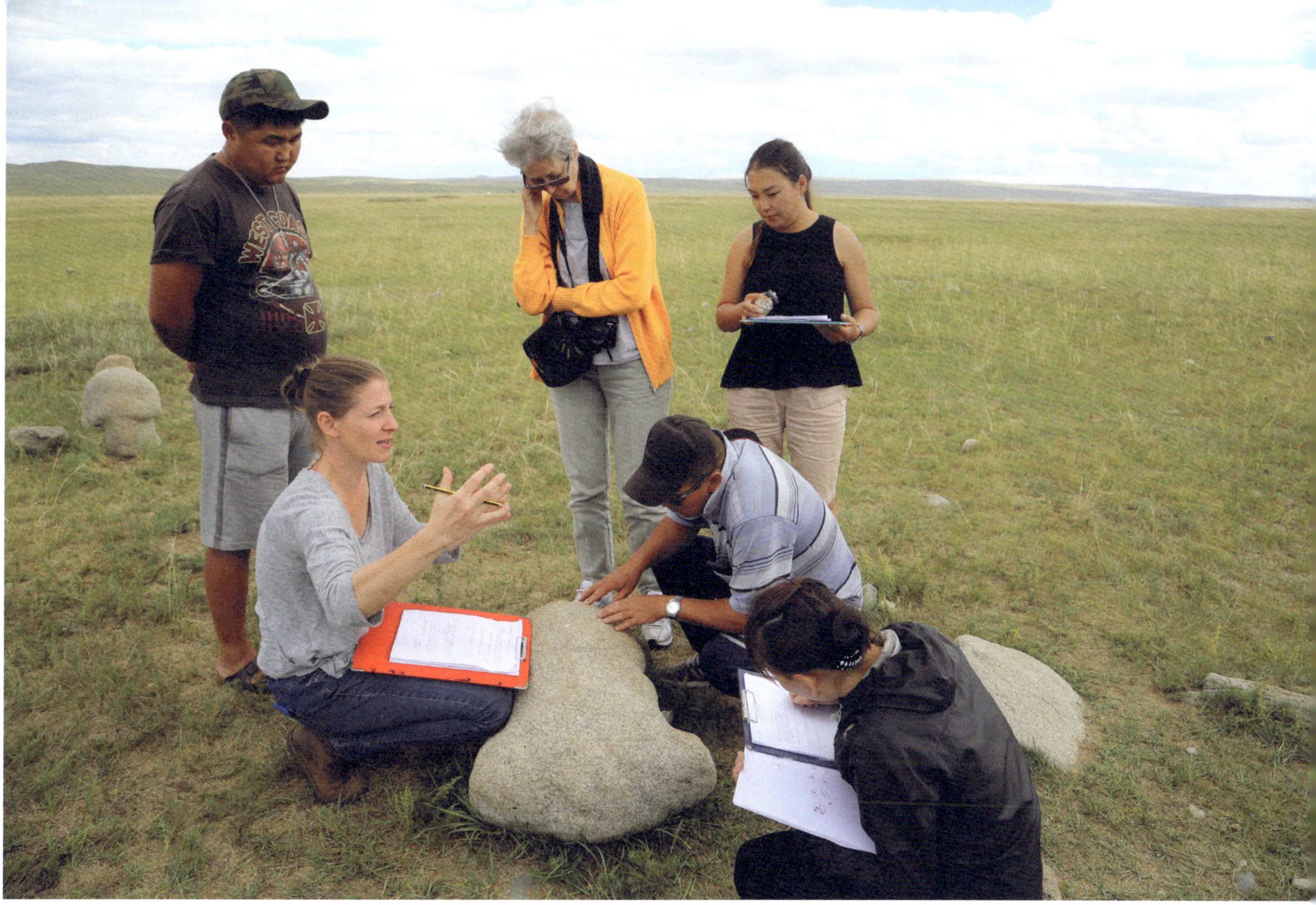

Fig. 9: Conservation
training at Ikh-Khoshoot,
August 2016

Fig. 12: Signing of MoU with Director Enkhbat
of the National Center for Cultural Heritage,
in presence of Gudrun Hardiman-Pollross
and Brigitte Winklehner, 2015

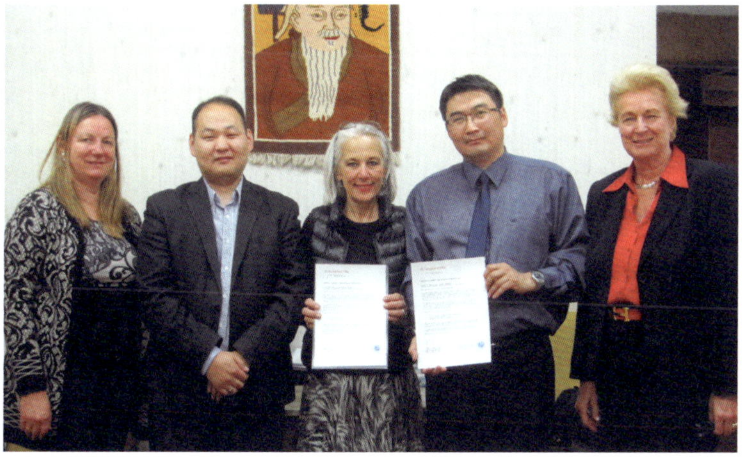

Fig. 13: Our interns from
the Mongolian State University of Arts and Culture,
Khosbayar Narankhuu
and Chinbat Magsar, and
their supervisors, 2018

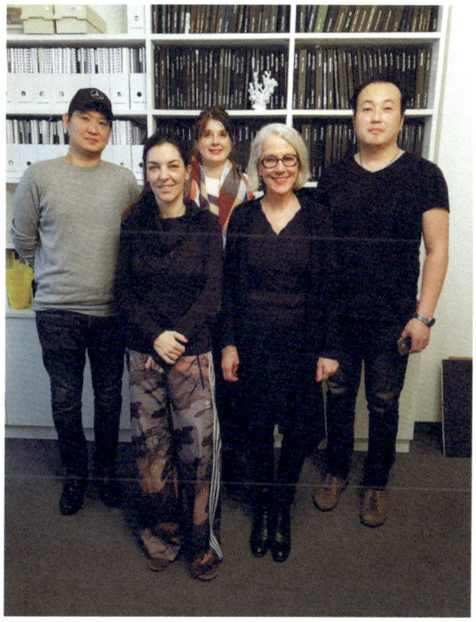

Factsheets Mongolia

PROJECT	Workshops on Investigation and Conservation of Architectural Polychromy (former Workshop on Cultural Heritage Conservation in Mongolia)		
INITIATED BY	Gabriela Krist, D. Uranchimeg, N. Khosbayar	HEADED BY	Gabriela Krist
DURATION	14–19 August 2017 18–22 June 2018	WORKSHOP ORGANISER	Katharina Kohler, Gabriela Krist
PARTNER INSTITUTIONS	Bogd Khaan Palace Museum (BKPM) Mongolian State University of Arts and Culture (MSUAC) National Center for Cultural Heritage, Mongolia (NCCH)		
FUNDED BY	Eurasia-Pacific Uninet (EPU) Austrian agency for international mobility and cooperation in education, science and research (OeAD) University of Applied Arts Vienna		
PARTICIPANTS	N. Enkhmanlai, N. Khosbayar (BKPM) S. Ganzam, M. Chinbat, D. Anand, B. Soninbayar (MSUAC) E. Batjargal, G. Uuganchimeg, A. Mongontsooj (NCCH) T. Jamyansuren		

PROJECT	Stone Conservation Workshops	DURATION	15–19 August 2016 11–16 June 2018
INITIATED BY	Gabriela Krist, G. Enkhbat	HEADED BY	Gabriela Krist

WORKSHOP ORGANISER	Gabriela Krist, Martina Haselberger, Marisa Laurenzi Tabasso, Marija Milchin, Susanne Sandner (Institute of Conservation, University of Applied Arts Vienna) Johannes Weber (Department of Conservation Sciences, Institute of Art and Technology, University of Applied Arts Vienna)
PARTNER INSTITUTIONS	National Center for Cultural Heritage, Mongolia (NCCH) Mongolian State University of Arts and Culture (MSUAC) Bogd Khaan Palace Museum (BKPM)
FUNDED BY	Eurasia-Pacific Uninet (EPU) University of Applied Arts Vienna
PARTICIPANTS	G. Enkhbat, S. Chinzorig, A. Mongontsooj, D. Nyamdorj, N. Bat-Erdene, B. Badar-uugan, E. Batjargal, G. Ankhsanaa, B. Lhamsuren, S. Davaadari, G. Uuganchimeg, T. Tsolmon (NCCH) S. Ganzam, G. Amarsanaa, A. Delgermaa, B. Davaajargal, B. Batbold, D. Anand, B. Soninbayar (MSUAC) B. Sukhbaatar, E. Oyun, T. Altantogs, G. Dagmidmaa, Ts. Tsetsegjargal, B. Amgalanbat, B. Mendbayar (Tov province museum) M. Byambajav, A. Batjargal, U. Monkh-Erdene (Dundgovi province museum)

Workshops on Cultural Heritage Conservation

KATHARINA KOHLER

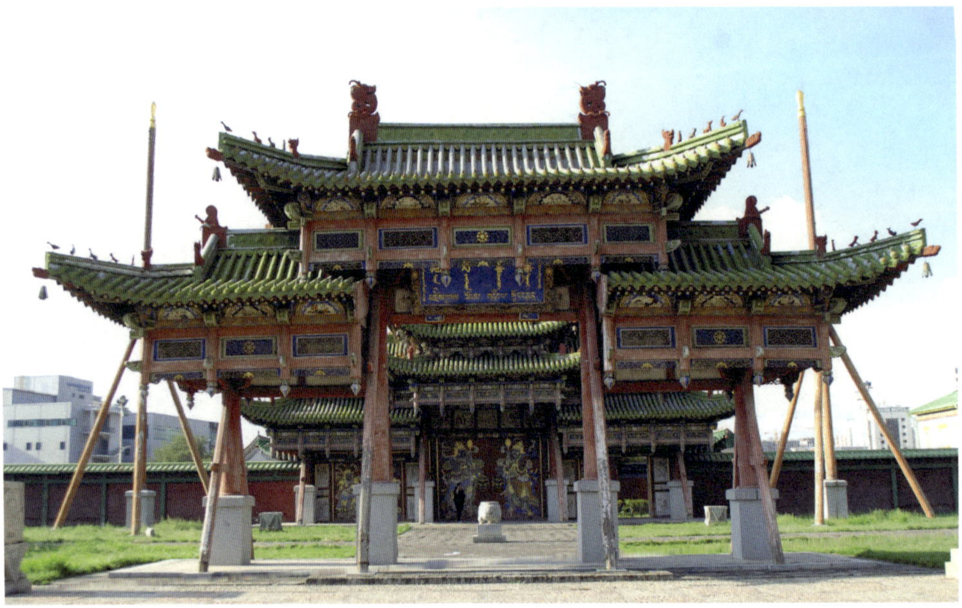

Fig. 1: Front Square of Bogd Khaan Palace

at Bogd Khaan Palace in Mongolia: Training, Activities and Research

Following the successful workshops since 2013, the workshop "Cultural Heritage Conservation in Mongolia" has been organised by the Institute with their Mongolian partners. The workshop was held from 14–19 August 2017 at the Bogd Khaan Palace Museum in Ulaanbaatar (Fig. 1–3). It focused on the documentation and investigation of polychromy on wood.

Bogd Khaan Palace is an important cultural heritage site of universal significance. As it is in critical condition, a preservation and maintenance concept and also capacity building is urgently needed.

The traditional painting technique is lost, according to Mongolian experts. An academic conservation training programme is still in the development phase in Mongolia, so conservators and restorers are rare and cannot cope with the workload.

Researching outdoor polychromy on wood in the framework of a doctoral thesis at the Institute of Conservation, I had the honour of guiding the workshop.

It was my first journey to Mongolia and I was accompanied by Gabriela Krist.

Upon reaching the destination, we were greeted with a wonderful green expanse. A grassy landscape of gently rolling hills opened up in front of us. White patches turned into small white tents when approaching: the so-called yurts. We arrived in Mongolia, the largest landlocked country with the lowest population density.

We were picked up at the airport by two staff members of the Bogd Khaan Palace Museum. After a warm welcome we drove into the city. The yurts amass into districts and turned into bigger and bigger houses. Ulaanbaatar. As sublime as I previously felt on looking at the landscape, I suddenly felt small when we arrived in the centre (Fig. 4): a city, powerful, modern, which seems to offer everything. We were brought to the traditional UB hotel, a 1959 restored landmark in downtown Ulaanbaatar. Suddenly, during breakfast, we noticed the promising announcement of our training programme in the Mongolian newspaper.

After a short rest we were brought to our place of work to get an overview.

The palace complex was erected in three phases between the late 19th and early 20th century. It includes seven summer temples, a winter palace, a wall surrounding the temple district, another wooden wall enclosing the Winter Palace, and several gates of different sizes, in a mixture of Chinese, Tibetan, Mongolian and European building traditions. The ensemble complex largely consists of multi-coloured painted and gilded wood with filigree carvings. It is the only remaining residence of the last religious leader in Mongolia, the so-called Bogd Khaan. After the Bogd Khaan passed away, the complex was turned into a museum. Opened in 1926, it is the oldest museum in Mongolia. Today it is one of the tourist hotspots in UB.

On 14 August the workshop started with a visit of the site, guided by the director of the Bogd Khaan Palace Museum. Participants were conservators from the National Center for Cultural Heritage, artists from the Mongolian State University of Arts and Culture, as well as the Bogd Khaan Palace Museum conservators, and a renowned artist (Fig. 5). Many more participants turned up than estimated, all male, inquisitive and with great expectations. This did not abate over the days, as an unexpected press conference also attracted other interested people to visit and join us.

After an introduction on building surveying, I showed the participants how to manage documentation. During the workshop, we could already collect various preliminary information on the history, technology, manufacturing, previous interventions and conservations of the site.

Today, this important cultural heritage site is in a critical condition. The paint is flaking off, the colour is heavily bleached and water trickles through the roof directly over the paintings. Wooden architectural elements are in some places strongly distorted and can no longer fulfil their static purpose. The inconsistent preservation status caused by different complex alteration processes and inadequate methods of conservation is disrupting the overall appearance of this historic building complex. The development of a long-term preservation and maintenance concept is urgently needed (Fig. 6-8).

The teamwork has been very good. There have been fruitful discussions, interactions and contact with other specialists or witnesses.

From English to Mongolian and reverse, the translations by a staff member of the museum were a real blessing.

As a vegetarian I was worried about having difficulties with the food in a country where meat is said to be almost the only available food. In the end, this was not a problem at all. The city seems to offer everything in food. We even found a vegan restaurant. Once we went to a very small traditional canteen. After a short conversation between one of the Mongolian participants and the waitress, they prepared something vegetarian for me specially. We went to many fancy restaurants.

I noticed that the locals are all well-dressed and stylish, and I even thought I recognised tourists from their lack of taste in clothing.

During the last two days, the participants were introduced to sampling. Everybody received a toolbox so they could take samples on their own. Nearly twenty samples were taken by the group. They seem to be natural talents in sample-taking. It was fun!

During wintertime, I analysed these material samples together with our experts in the laboratory at our university in Vienna, in part accompanied by two Mongolian interns who studied with us.

After analysis, long-term plans are to be elaborated for conservation and restoration efforts for the whole palace complex, also a concept for maintenance.

The demand for further training led to another workshop on the investigation and conservation of architectural polychromy with the Mongolian partners at the Bogd Khaan Palace Museum, from 18–22 June 2018. Participants were again conservators from the Bogd Khaan Palace Museum and National Center for Cultural Heritage, also teachers and first restoration students from the Mongolian University of Art and Culture (Fig. 9).

This follow-up focused on the development of a conservation concept, and conservation methods of polychrome structures at the Bogd Khaan Palace.

Now, the second time in Ulaanbaatar, I already knew what to expect. But life is always full of surprises. As my airport pickup service came one hour late, I thought I had been forgotten and took a taxi to the centre. I have not seen many official taxis in Ulaanbaatar. Everybody seems to take unofficial ones, which are simply locals picking up people. This can be anybody. Feels like paying for hitchhiking. I preferred to be driven by colleagues. By the way, Mongolians drive in a downright dangerous way. Following the slogan – the stronger will win.

Same hotel, same room, it seemed like I have never been away.

In the afternoon I went to meet the director of the National Center for Cultural Heritage. I was accompanied by a representative of the Bogd Khaan Palace Museum. The centre is in a large building with many small floors. People were working on Sunday.

Next morning I was picked up by car by one of my Mongolian colleagues. Cosy. But there is so much traffic in Ulaanbaatar!! You never know how long the ride will take. So people are always late or too early. This year, traffic was even worse. Because of road works, they say. Sounds familiar. Spending a long time in the car, I found myself listening to the same music that is also on the Austrian charts, in a Japanese car, in the middle of Mongolia. A huge board computer screen showing the status display of the hybrid drive with rolling tyres and Japanese characters attracted my attention. Time and again, we meet the same people walking because of the traffic jam. In the afternoons I sometimes walked back home. It took me the same time. This is not so common here. My hosts didn't like it so much, as they wanted me to arrive safely and comfortably.

On the first day, the workshop started with an introduction and a presentation of the preliminary investigation results from 2017, which were carried out by Tatjana Bayerová, Marta Anghelone, Johannes Weber, Andreas Heiss and myself.

The wood species of one used beam was identified as Mongolian Scots pine, maybe combined with another type of wood for the carvings. The painting technique is oil-based. First, a protein containing grey preparation ground with a layer of fibres was applied, followed by the final painting layer. Red painted architectural elements have an additional white ground under the paint layer containing red organic pigment. Leaf metal was also used for decoration purposes. Different treatments have taken place in the palace complex buildings' history. In this context, examinations have to check what transformations and changes in materials there have been. So far, only beams, columns and fences seem to be overpainted, but some buildings have more overpaintings and marginal original paint layers underneath. For more precise information further samples need to be taken and further investigations are required.

This was a good opportunity to also introduce the new participants to the theory and practice of sample taking. They liked it.

The first workshop was a well-prepared impromptu without any gadgets, so the second time I arrived equipped with a computer-based presentation for a projection. It worked very well on the first day, but on the second I was without computer or suitable cables to connect mine. So I returned to the easy speaking way and my laptop was like the miracle presentation case. The second workshop day started again with a short introduction to condition survey for the new participants and as refresher for last year's (Fig. 10). All spread out. I found everyone busy documenting and discussing. Based on the collected information of materials used, damages and changes, a first conservation concept was developed with the group.

On day three, the participants were introduced to different cleaning methods used in conservation. Afterwards we also tried them practically on site (Fig. 11).

Dry cleaning with pencils and different sponges, water and aqueous systems was tested. Solvents seem to be difficult to get in Mongolia. For the workshop, only alcohol and acetone were available. Well...either too strong or too soft, but not solving what we wanted.

Next time we must order materials long in advance, maybe from abroad.

Contrary to the expectations, a real enthusiasm for cleaning developed – only with water.

On the last two days, consolidation materials used in conservation for outdoor polychrome wood were presented and discussed. We also tested them on site (Fig. 12). This small test series was preliminarily evaluated and will be controlled during the coming year(s).The participants could get insight into different materials and their handling. As they didn't want to stop, I think it seemed to appeal to them.

This familiar smell in the air, a brewery, close to the palace, they told me, made me remember things back home in Vienna. During the week, my watchful eyes sighted water drops and puddles. But there was no rain??! On the last day I discovered the sprinkler! This year's dryness is also visible in Mongolia. The grass is watered, and the sprinkler was too close to the building. Start of the maintenance program!

The workshop was rounded off by meetings with different important people. I had excellent food in fancy bars and restaurants in the midst of hospitable and party-loving Mongolians, unexpected welcomes and photo shootings.

The people enjoy the few summer months on lively playgrounds, parks and the view from restaurant gardens or verandas. If possible, people go to the countryside in summer, where they also live in yurts or lovely treehouses. But until now I have only seen the countryside from the plane.

Things don't seem cheap to me in Mongolia. The people seem to value quality.

Also, as regards preservation, while being together it has become more important for the group to do more precise research, planning and tests, than to make hasty decisions.

On the last morning of my journey and Saturday, I had breakfast with the National Coordinator of EPU in Mongolia. Afterwards I had to go back to the palace to take some more samples and more photographs.

It is not a bad idea to wear work clothes, clearly identified as such, like "conservator at work". The guards in the Bodg Khaan Palace Museum, and even tour guides, turned out to be attentive and strict.

My camera broke.

It started to rain cats and dogs.

This joint collaborative project was not only a further step to deepen the cooperation between Mongolia and Austria, but a valuable means of learning from each other and a much needed step forward in understanding and protecting one of Mongolia's few remaining important historic buildings.

The workshop contributed to building up and enhancing capacities among conservators in Mongolia in the fields of conservation and conservation science. Austrian conservators can improve their knowledge of Mongolian sites, teaching skills, and benefit from extended expertise in general.

All project partners emphasised their interest in follow-up workshops at the palace.

For me the trip was enrichment in every way. Do I maybe have to mention that it was the year of the Football World Cup in Russia?

It was, of course, also a buzzing event in Mongolia, and I flew over Moscow!

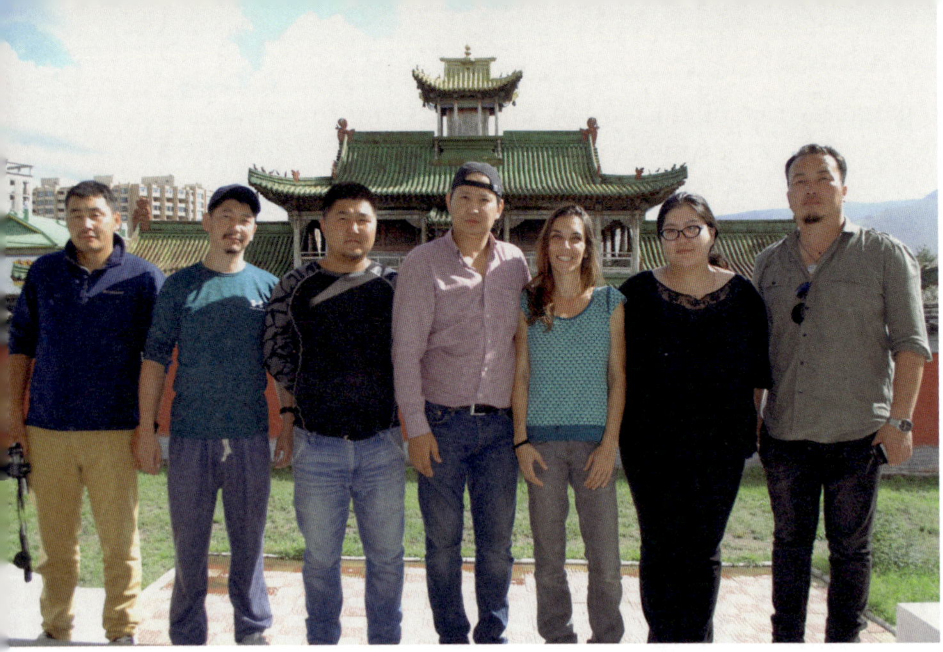

Fig. 4: Group photo, Workshop 2017

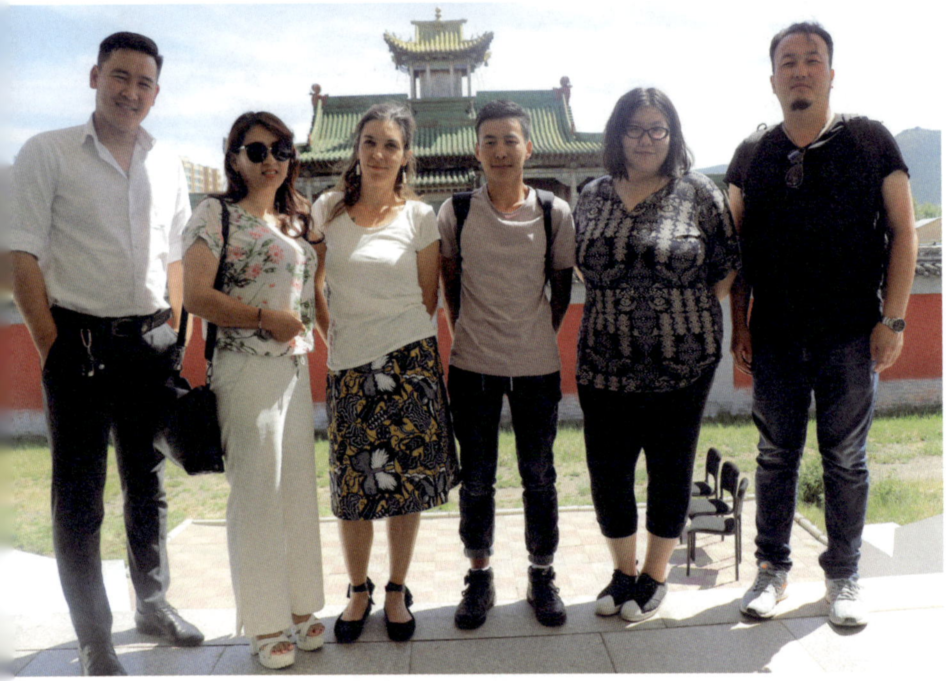

Fig. 8: Group photo, Workshop 2018

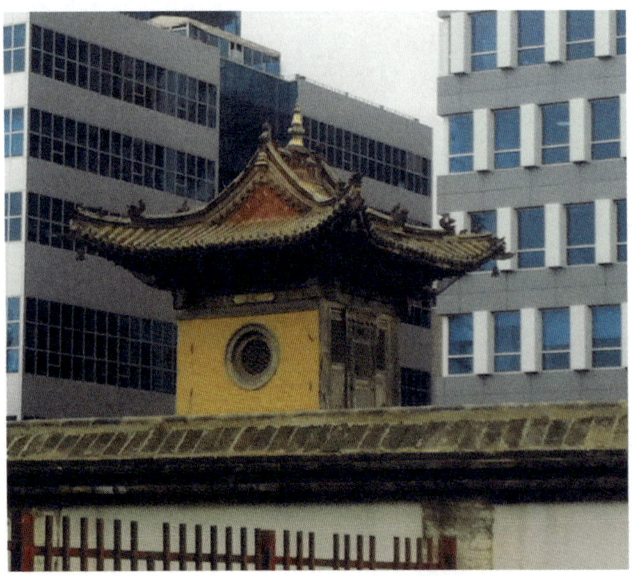

Fig. 3: Choijin Lama Monastery surrounded by skyscrapers in central Ulaanbaatar

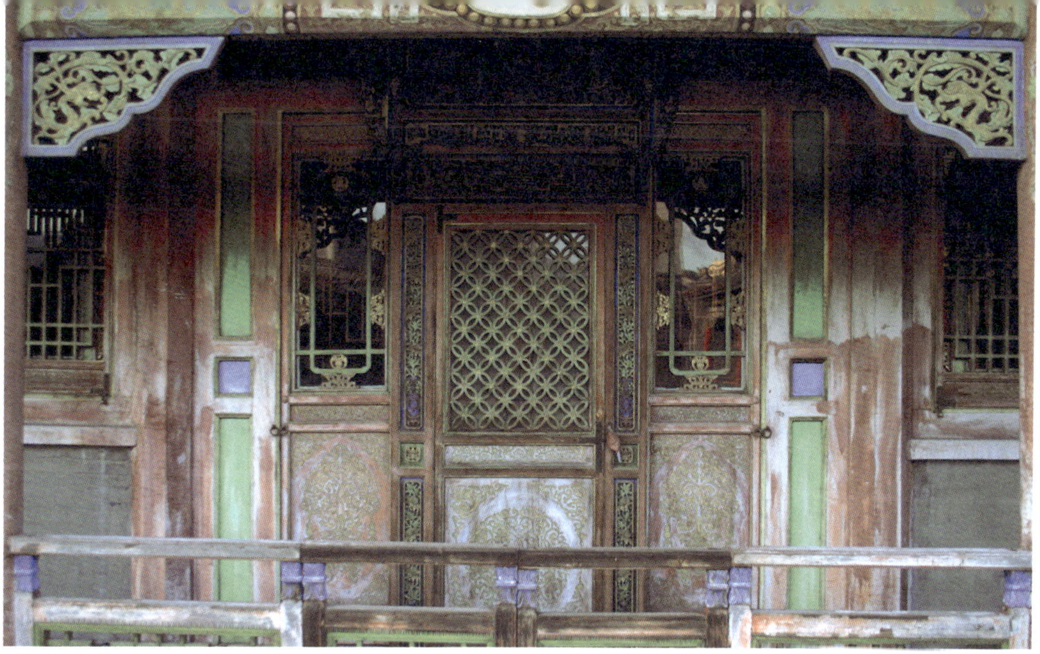

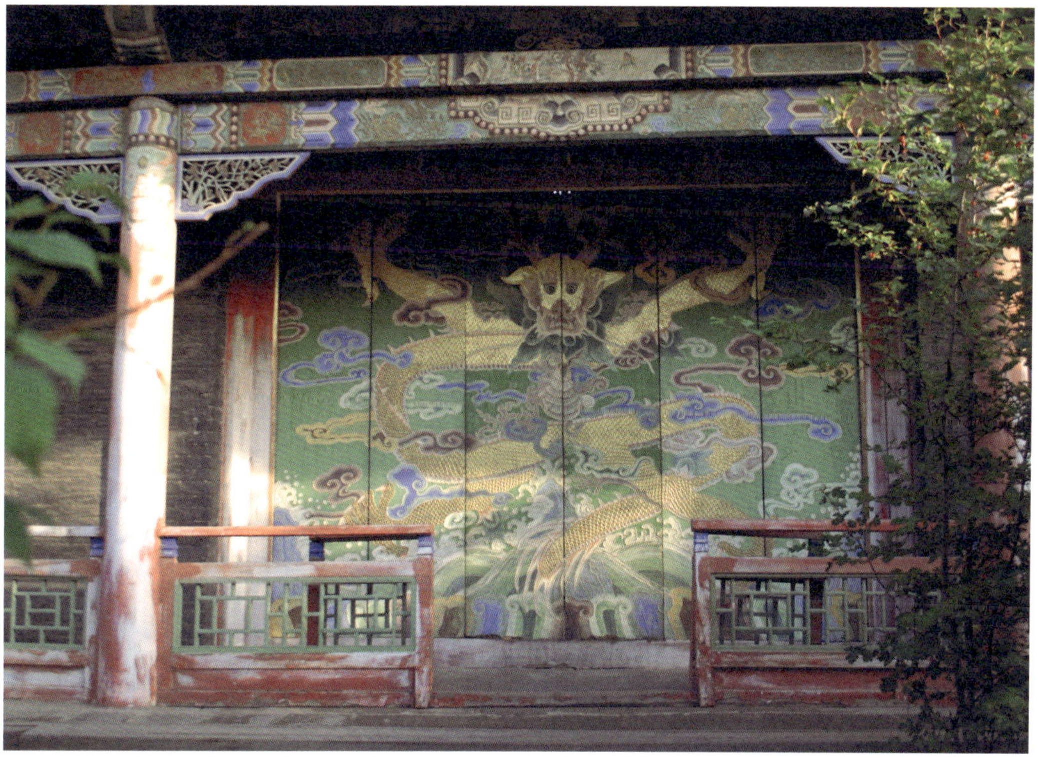

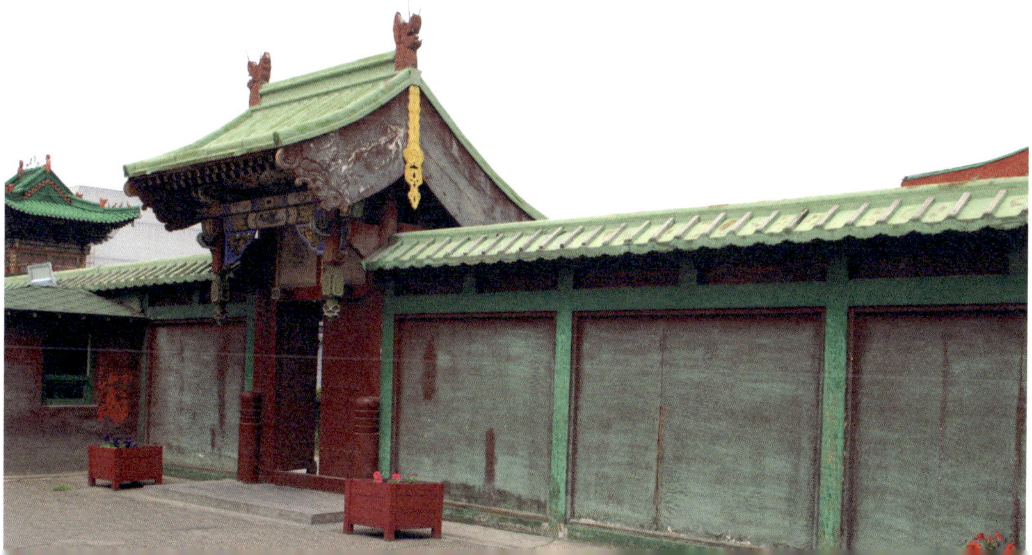

top: Fig. 5: Main door of Labrang Temple
middle: Fig. 6: Temple of Confidence in Learning, northern gate
bottom: Fig. 7: Extreme colour degradation at painted wooden surround

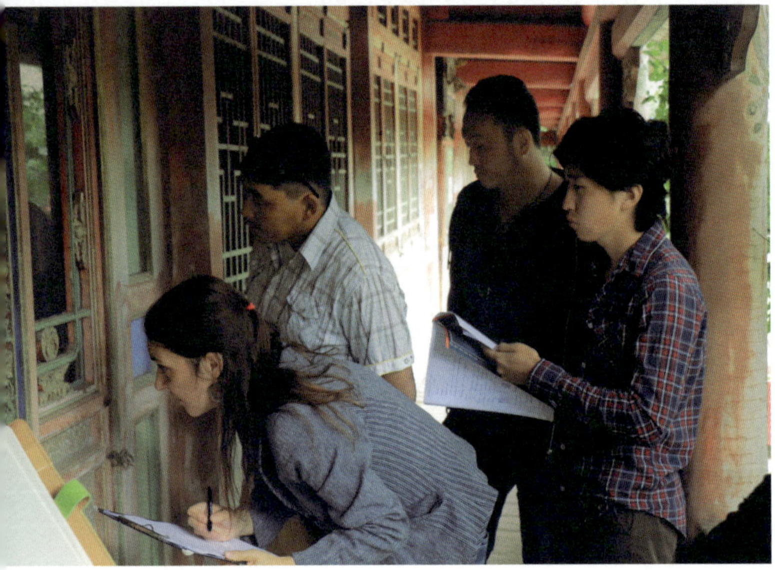

Fig. 9: Condition Survey in 2018

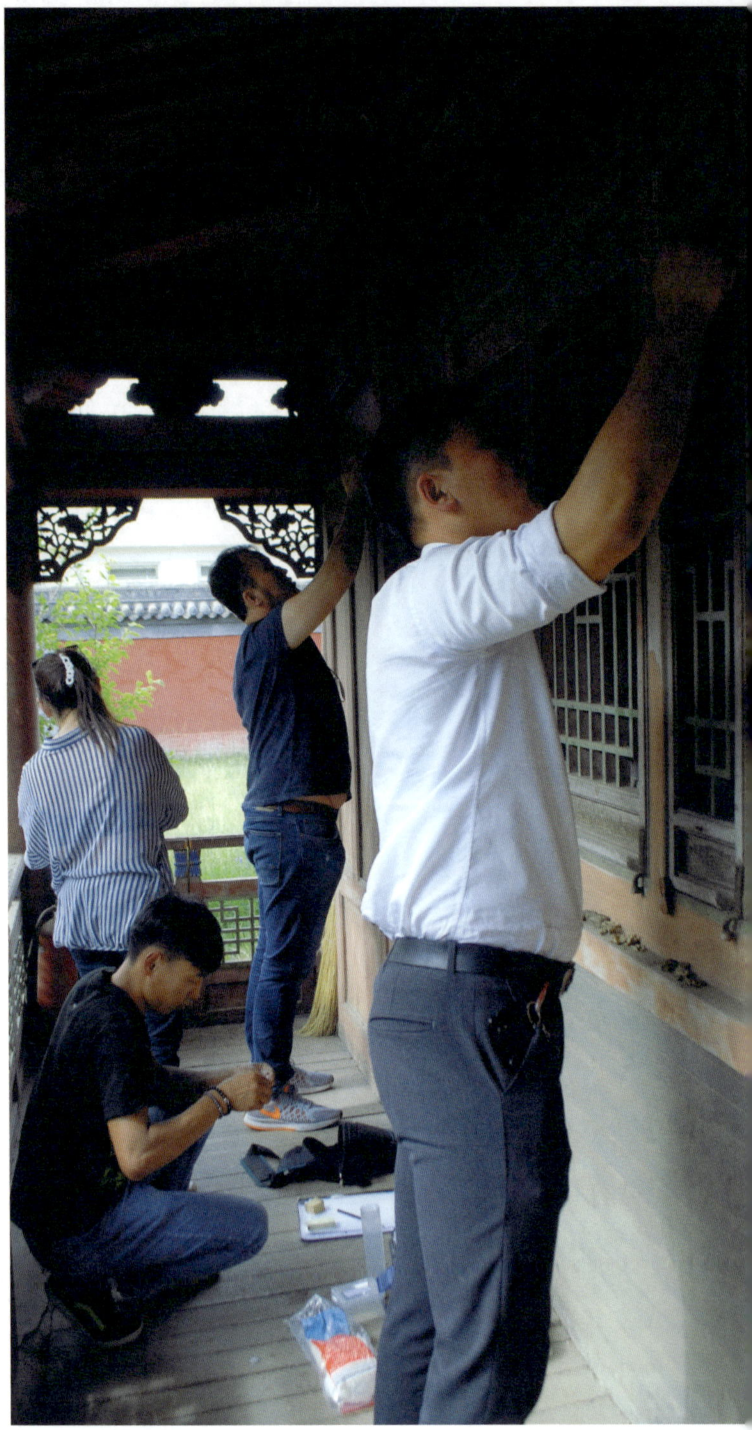

Fig. 10: Practical work: cleaning test at Labrang Temple

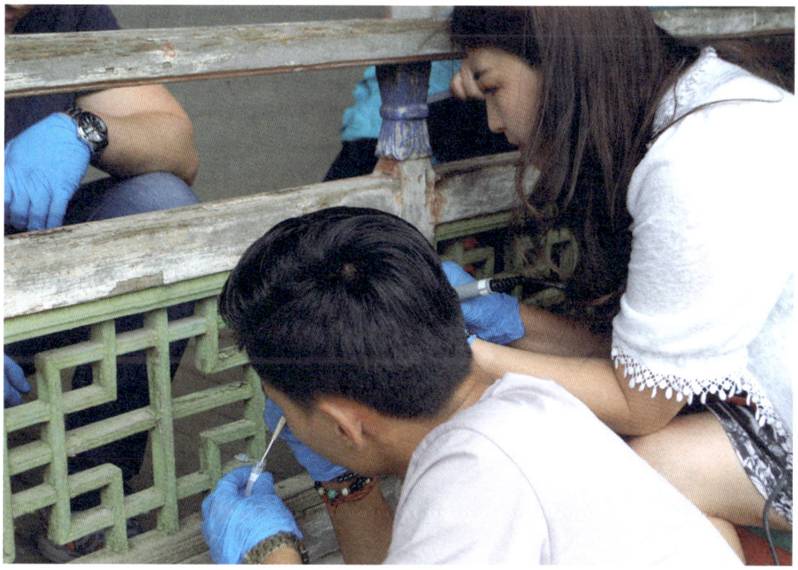

Fig. 11: First consolidation tests at Labrang Temple

Fig. 2: Peace and Happiness Gate, eastern door

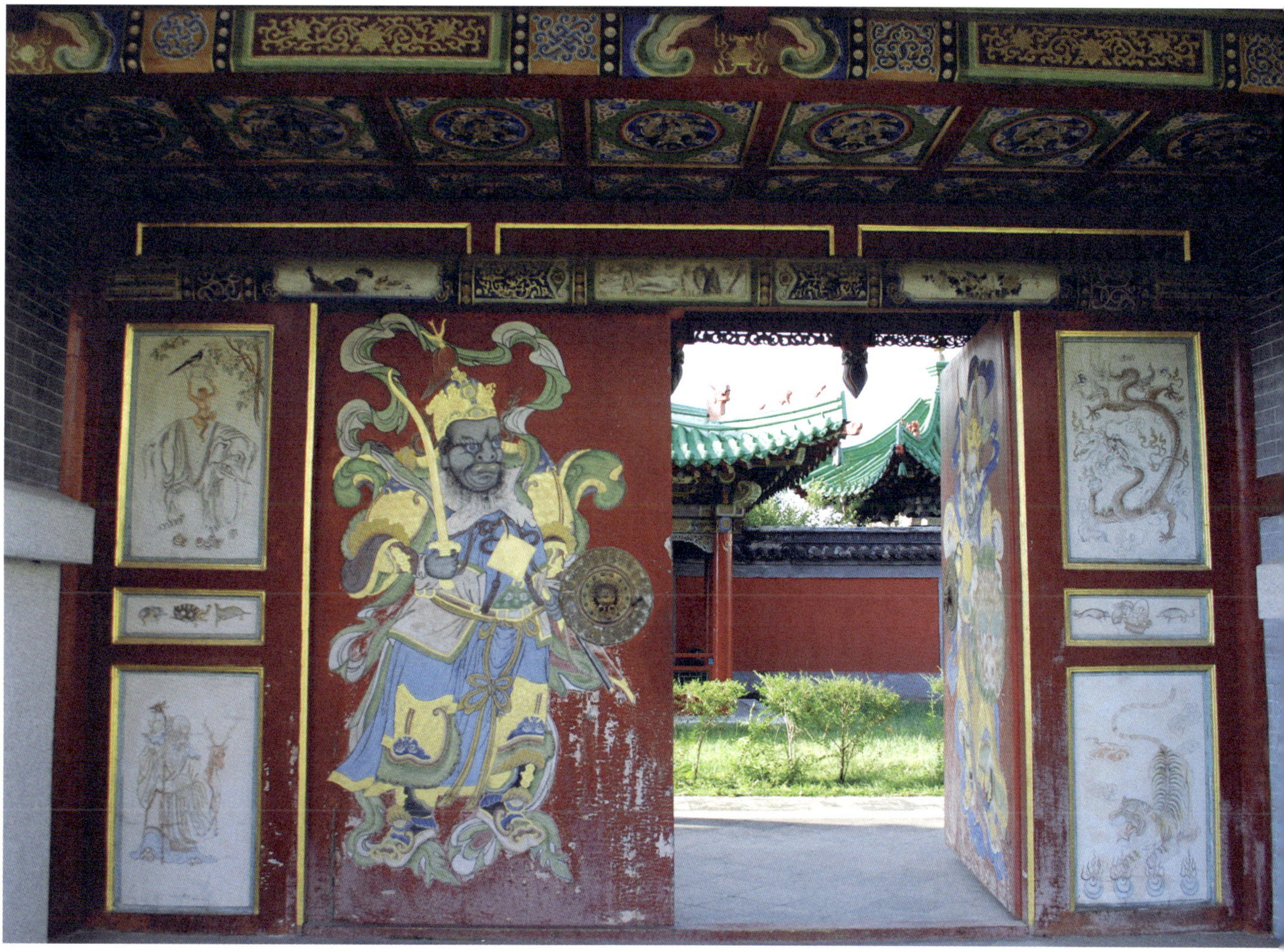

My Mongolian Experience in 2016

MARISA LAURENZI TABASSO

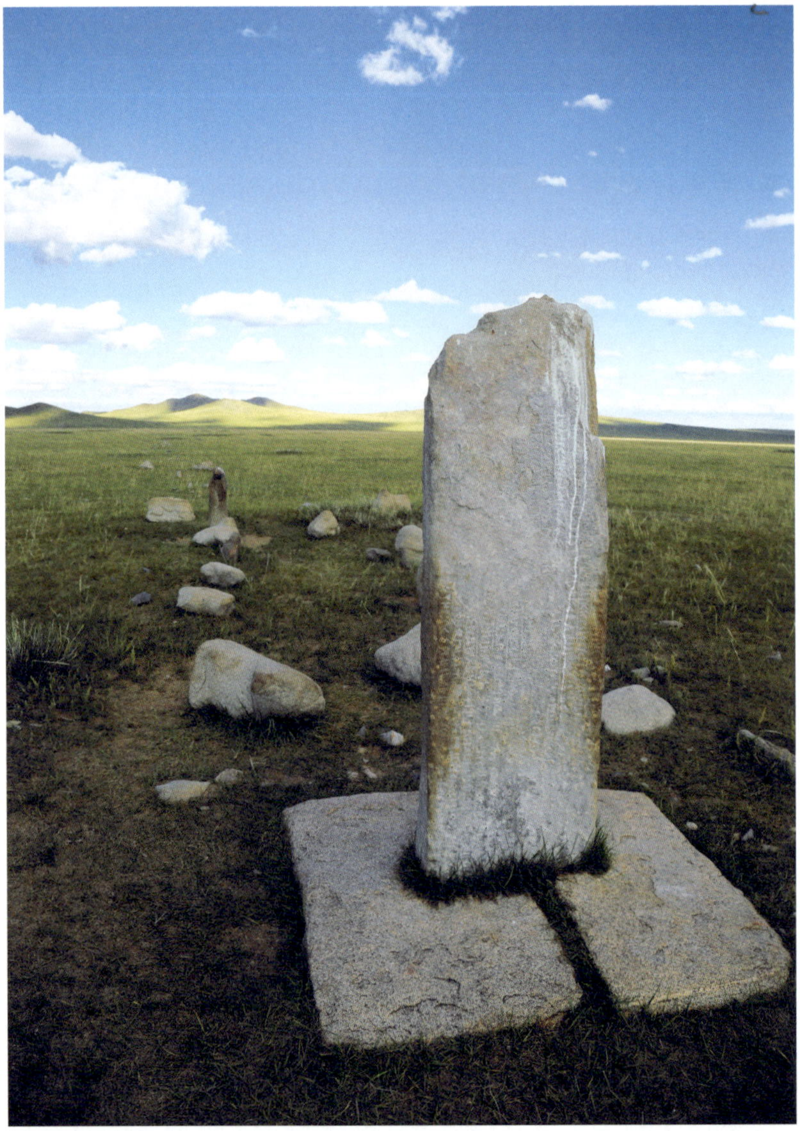

Fig. 1: Monument of Tureg's Kul-chur at Ikh-Khoshoot

If I were to summarise my Mongolian experience in just one word, I would use the word *"challenge"*. In fact, it was a challenge to visit a country not only very far from mine and from all the other Asian countries I had the chance to visit in my life, but also because I had just a very vague and "romantic" idea of Mongolia, derived from the beautiful book by René Grusset on Genghis Khan, *Le Conquérant du Monde, Vie de Gengis-khan*. It was a challenge, but it was a fantastic challenge, and this is the reason why I accepted the invitation by Gabriela Krist to join a colleague of the Institute of Conservation, Susanne Sandner (senior conservator), in a mission dealing with the conservation of stones.

The first part of the mission took place in Ulaanbaatar, the capital of the country, and was dedicated to training activities based around the conservation of stone monuments. The task was to deliver basic information on the scientific principles that must be foundational for conservation activities. It was the easiest part of the job but, to a certain extent, even this part had some difficulties to overcome since the audience, mostly composed of archaeologists and painters, was not very much at home with this kind of chemistry, and was rather inhibited about it. However, this was a very useful lapse of time during which I could start getting acquainted with the Mongolian colleagues, the town centre and its museums, and could acquaint myself with people in the institutions and even people in the streets. I remember once Susi and I met a young couple strolling nearby the art academy (where we were lecturing): they asked us where we were from and, knowing that we were from Europe, offered us ice cream. I've never come across such a warm sign of welcome by people I didn't know in any other country!

But it is not too hard to imagine that the most exciting and challenging part of the mission was the trip to the steppe, to examine the ruins of the Tureg's Kul-chur Memorial Complex at a place called Ikh-Khoshoot located around 350 km southwest of the capital (Fig. 1).

The visit to the memorial was the second part of our Mongolian workshop. Five of the participants of the theoretical course came with us to put part of the information received in Ulaanbaatar into practice. And actually this was a very good training ground for them, considering the very poor condition of the memorial's stones.

The memorial is dedicated to a military chief of a Turkic-Mongolian population and is dated to the eighth century A.D. It is very important for the history of Turkic people, especially because it is one of the still surviving Turkic monuments and has four dedicatory inscriptions carved on its four sides.

It is still a thrill for me to remember the journey to the site – the emotion of being in the steppe was really intense and unique. For a person who normally lives in a very crowded city like Rome and in a densely populated country like Italy, the green and endless landscape of the steppe was simultaneously exciting and moving: the herds of cows, sheep and horses strolling quietly or running about with no limits or fences gave me a tangible image of freedom.

Along the way to Ikh-Khoshoot we stopped to pay a visit to a Mongolian family (Fig. 2) who live there in a yurt (they call it *ger*) during the summer period. It was a large and pleasant yurt with a wooden and painted central pillar and pretty carpets covering the circular wall of the tent. We, as the guests, were invited to sit on the left side, while the relatives of the family sat on the right side of the yurt and the father sat cross-legged on the floor between the two groups (Fig. 3). He poured in a bowl some *airag* from a large white ceramic vessel with blue decorations; this is a traditional, slightly fermented drink made from mare's milk, very popular among the Mongolians. The bowl with airag was offered at first to the oldest Mongolian male guest, who took a sip and then passed the bowl to the following guest sitting at his right side, and so on. After a whole tour, the bowl, now empty, returned to the hand of our host, who filled it again with airag, and another tour started. The ceremony went on several times, to everybody's huge pleasure.

A further sign of friendly hospitality was the offer to ride one of their horses which were grazing just outside the yurt: I admit, and regret, that I did not accept the offer because I was too afraid of falling off the horse's back (Fig. 4)!

At last, after a one-day journey, we arrived at the site at sunset, and our Mongolian colleagues rapidly set up camp and prepared dinner. Once again, it was a challenge for me to be in a very small tent (I never had this experience, even when I was young!) and sleep in a sleeping bag under a wonderful starry and silent sky.

I come now to the greatest challenge of my mission in Mongolia, the poor condition of the stones still surviving on the site: the challenging question was "How to conserve them in that environment, so singular and hard?" Not all parts are still visible in the memorial: two stelae (one of them with the precious inscriptions), a large carved slab, broken in few places, the relics of sculptures probably representing human and faunal figures, a large number of

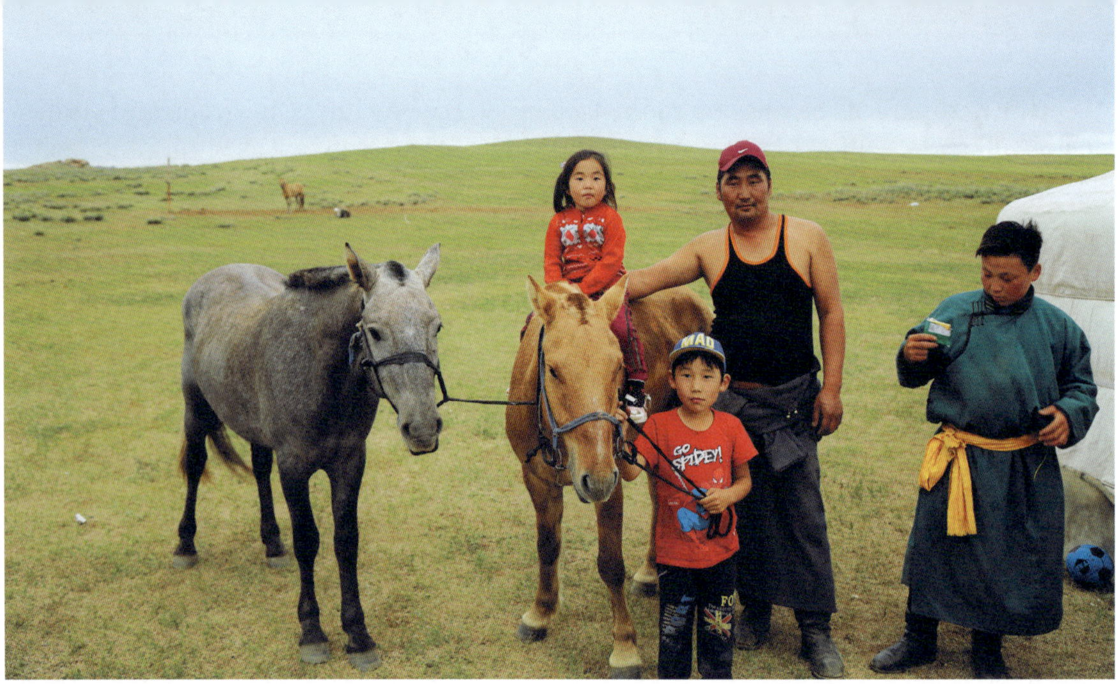

Fig. 2: Our host with some of his children and horses

smaller fragments spread along a line (about 1 km) which could have been the road to the memorial. The large majority of them comprise granite-like stones. The conditions of the stone objects are very poor and many significant parts are already lost (Fig. 6–7).

All around, only the green steppe with its mint scented grass, horses, cows and sheep.

Johannes Weber (Department of Conservation Sciences, University of Applied Arts Vienna) and student Katharina Breunhölder (Institute of Conservation, University of Applied Arts Vienna) analysed the samples we collected during the mission. Quoting their report, we can say that the "studied rocks represent granitoids of varying colour, grain size and accessory mineral content". As for the condition of the stones and the products of decay, Weber and Breunhölder noted that an almost complete granular disintegration and network of cracks running around each single grain were present in many of the samples; the higher degree of biotite orientation could possibly contribute to the surface- and sub-parallel cracks. Lichens and other biological agents (birds with their dropping, herds of animals) also contribute to the decay of the monuments (Fig. 8).

It is not too hard to understand, even for those who are not experst in stone conservation, that the survival of this memorial really is at risk, also considering the severe environmental conditions and the lack of monitoring for a major part of the year. To propose provisions to mitigate the velocity of the decay process is a challenge for any professional.

However, the Institute of Conservation sent a second team of conservators in 2018 to implement the most urgent measures to slow the decay, and this is certainly of great advantage. Their experiences and stories are told in another chapter of this book.

To make the results achieved by this second mission durable, regular monitoring of the stone conditions after treatments and frequent maintenance are fundamental and indispensable. But how to implement these activities in the steppe?

Two alternative proposals could be formulated: the first proposes transferring the original monuments to a more suitable, better protected place, and replacing them with replicas. The other option is to build a shelter which protects the stones but is not too invasive for that unique environment. Each of these proposals has considerable drawbacks, which demand conscientious discussion among the archaeologists and the authorities responsible for the site.

This is the reason why I used the word "*challenge*" so many times in my short account.

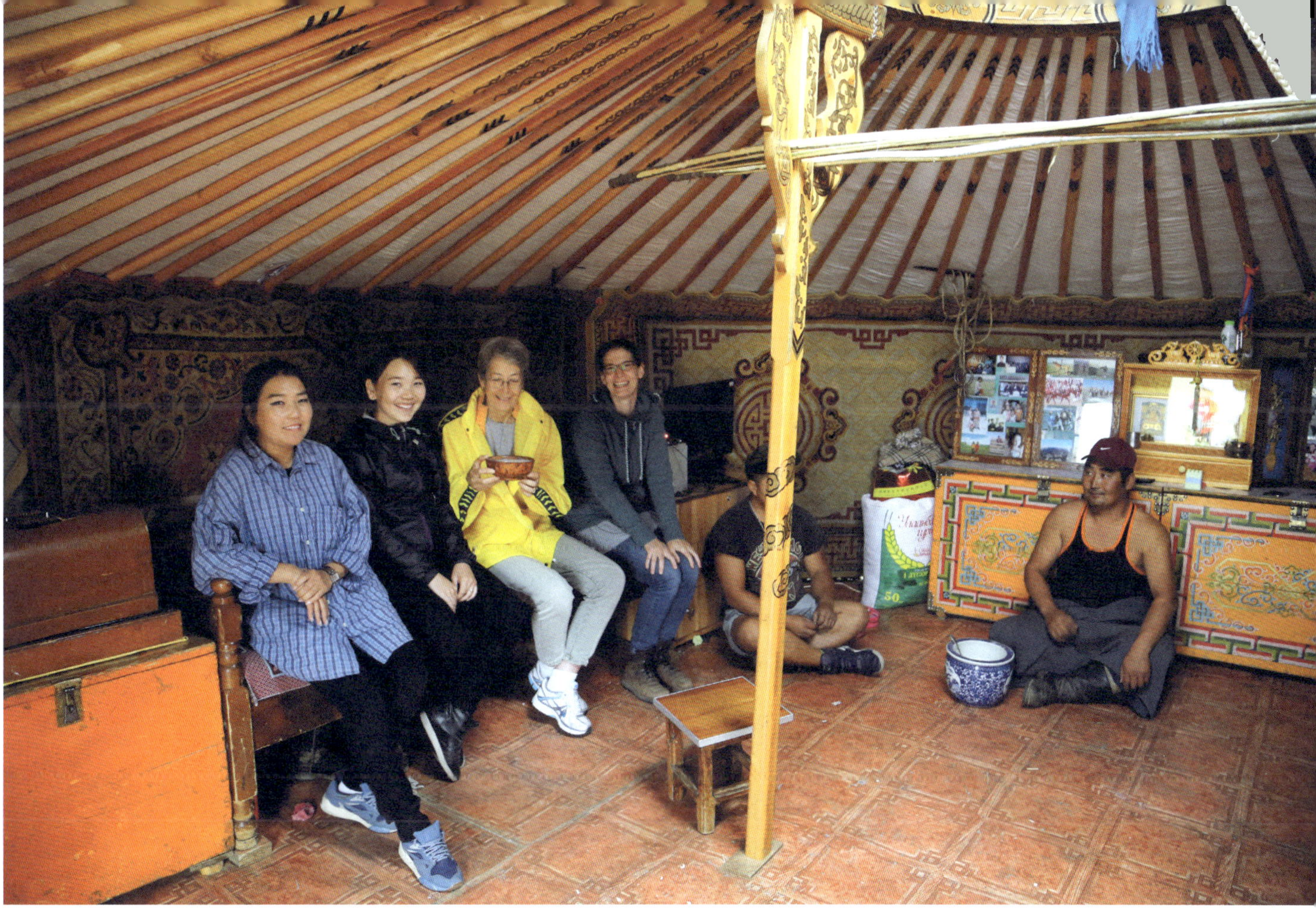

Fig. 3: The offering of *airag* in the yurt

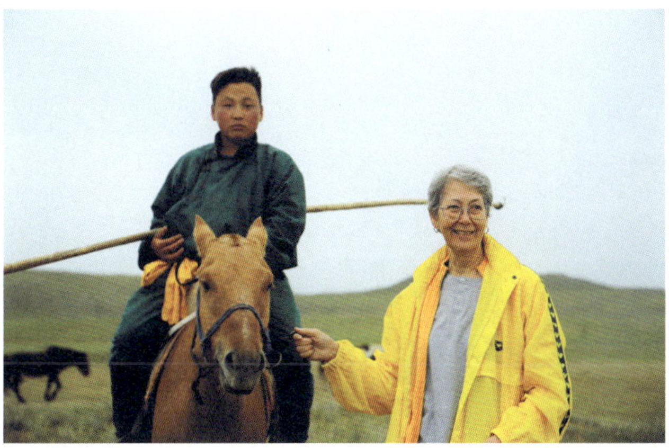

Fig. 4: The horse-riding offering

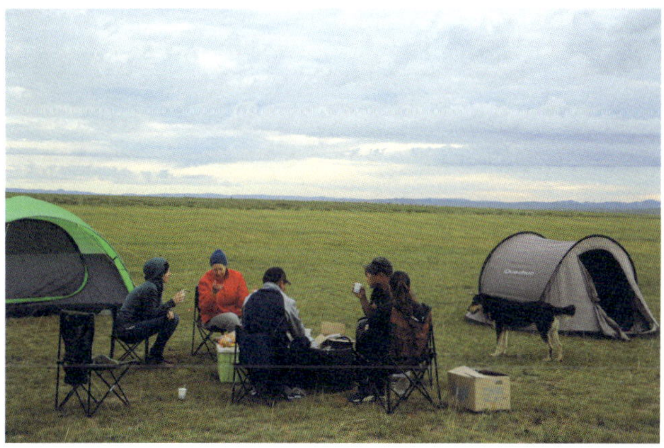

Fig. 5: Our campsite

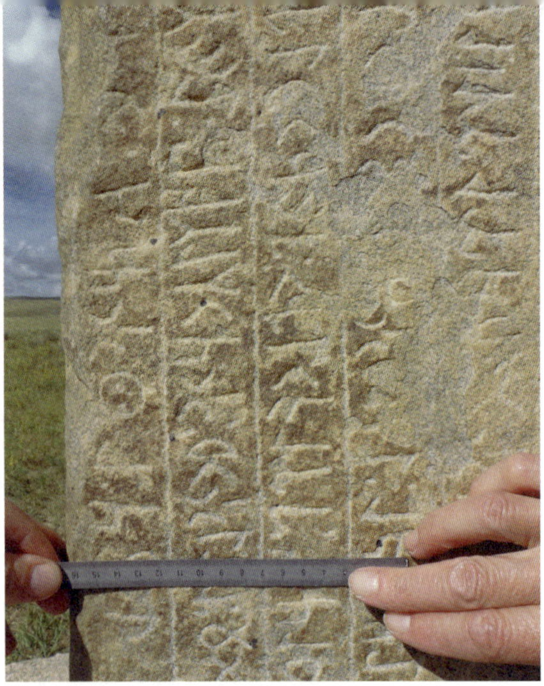

Fig. 6: Inscriptions on the monument

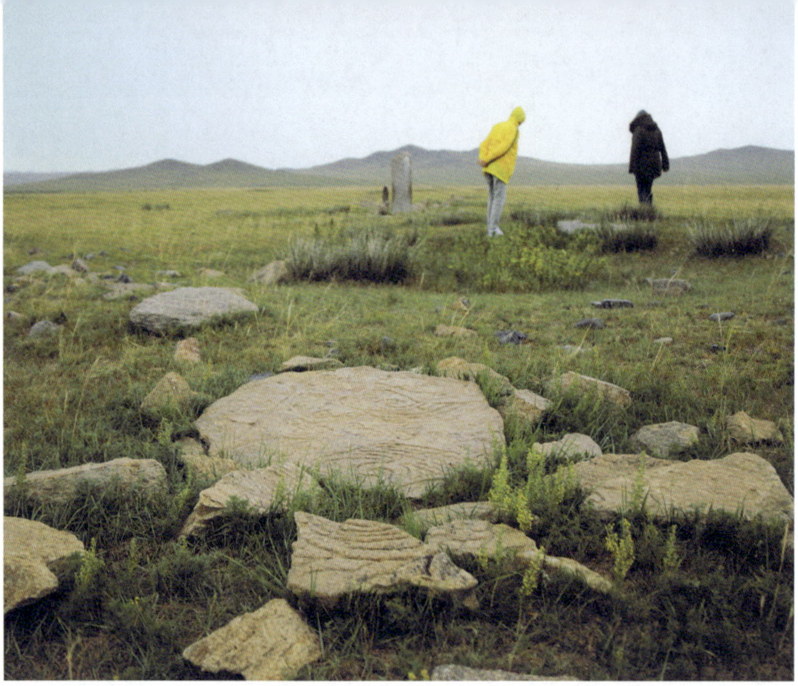

Fig. 7: Fragments of the monument

Fig. 8: Herds of animals "visiting" the monument

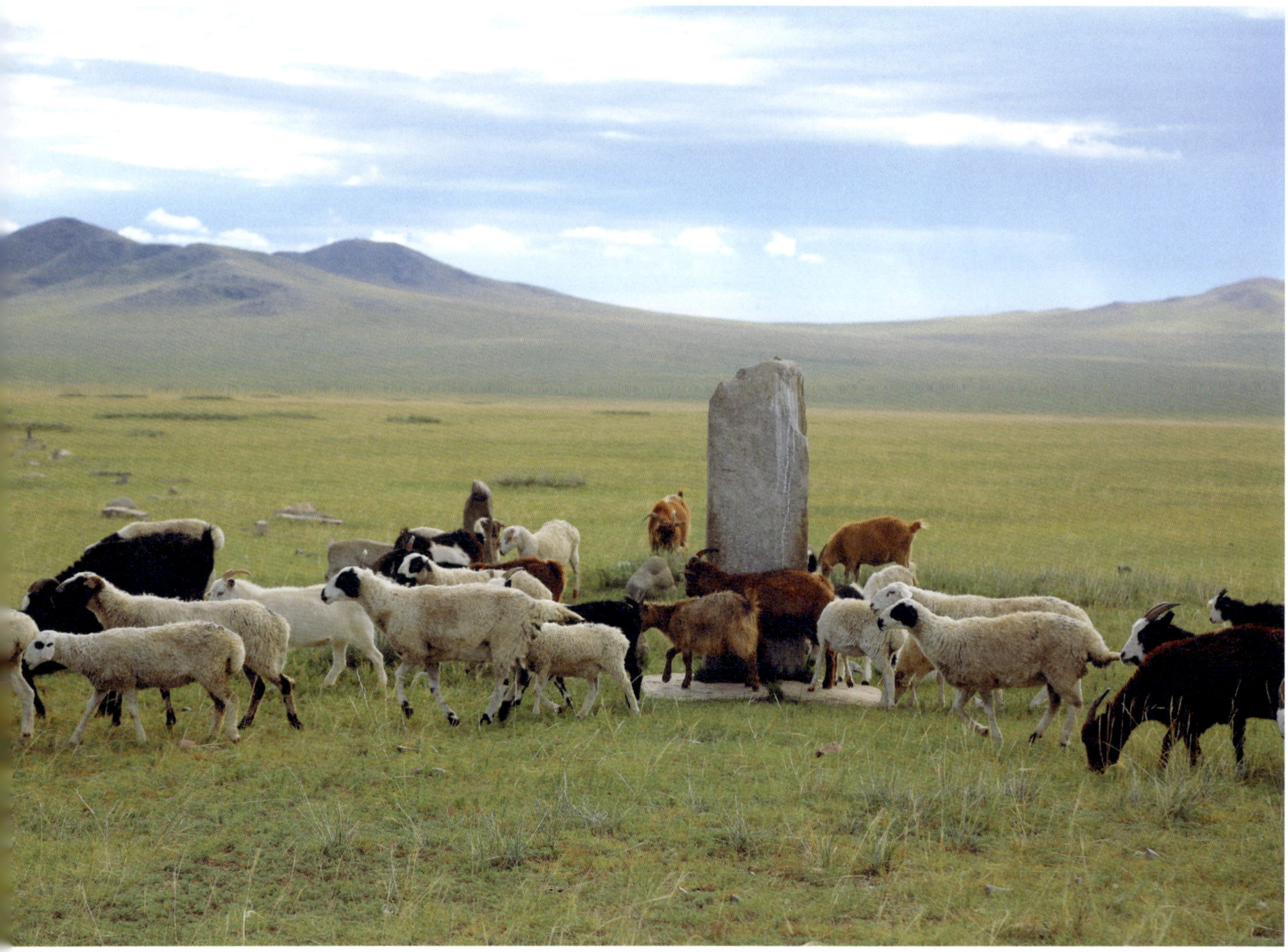

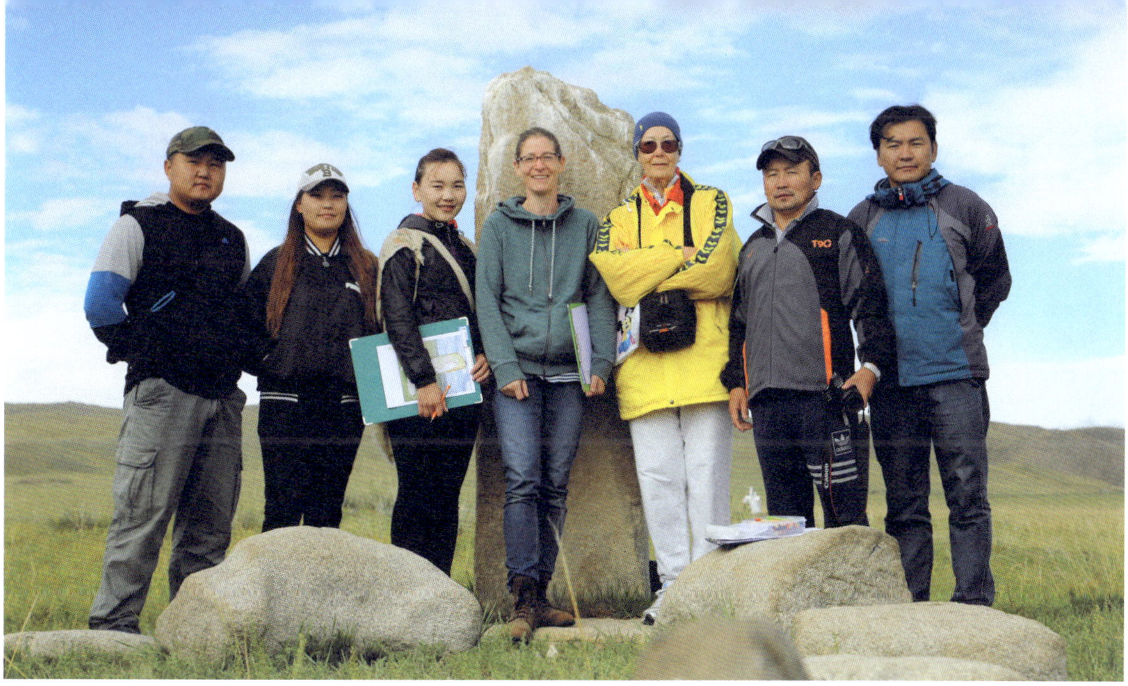

Fig. 10: Participants of the "Stone Conservation Workshop" in front of the monument at Ikh-Khoshoot

Fig. 9: Susi and me working

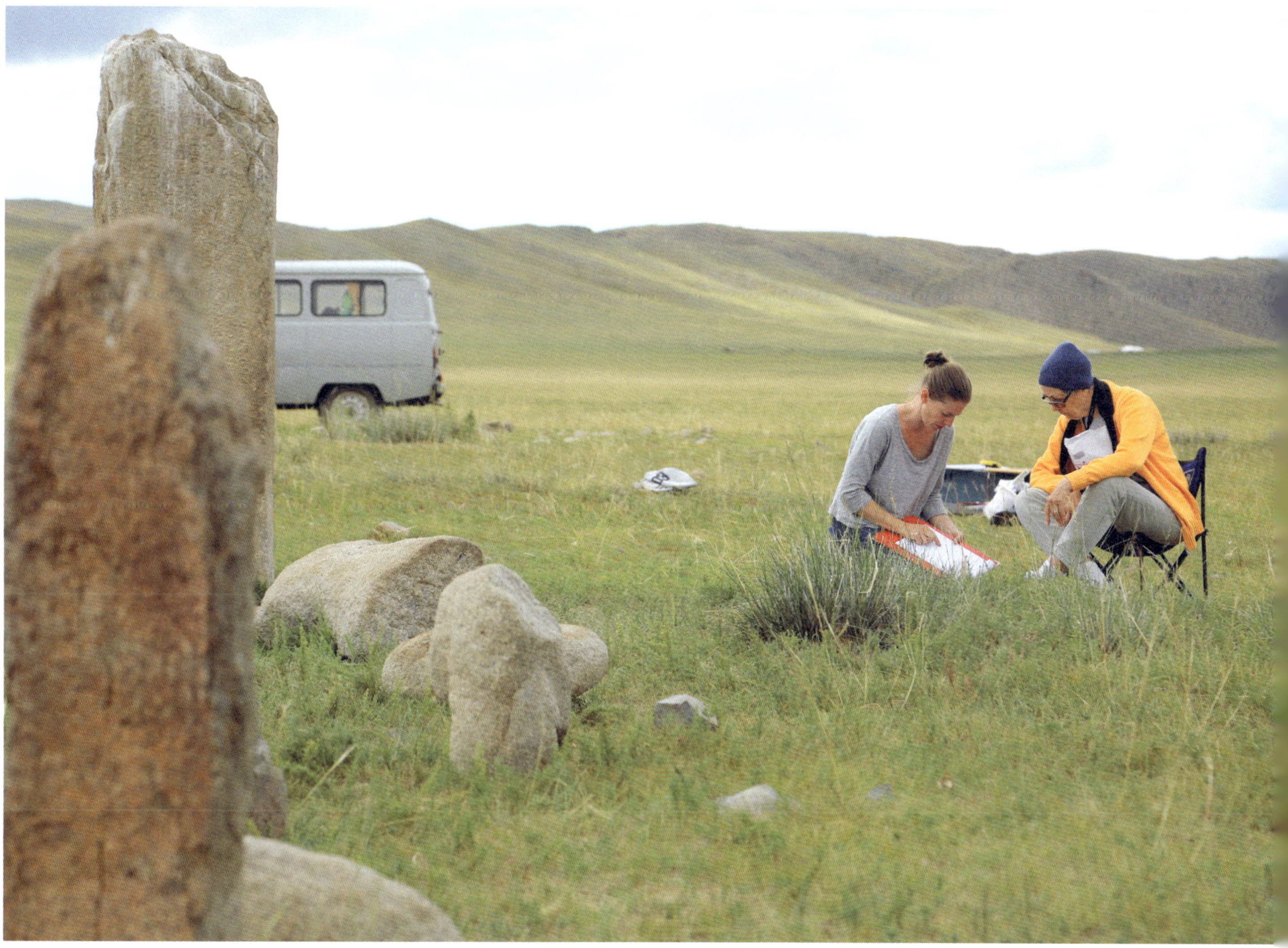

Joining Forces in the Field of Cultural Heritage Preservation

G. ENKHBAT,
E. BATJARGAL,
TS. TSOLMON

Workshop on the Conservation of Stone Heritage

According to the MoU between the National Center for Cultural Heritage, Mongolia (NCCH) and the Institute of Conservation, University of Applied Arts Vienna, and following the visit of G. Enkhbat, director of the NCCH, the training workshop for "Conservation of stone cultural heritage" (Stone Conservation Workshop) was successfully held in Mongolia from 11-16 June 2018.

This workshop was organized in two phases. The first phase was held in Ulaanbaatar city for conservators from the NCCH, curators and research workers from the National Museum of Mongolia, the Fine Arts Museum, the Bogd Khaan Palace Museum, teachers from School of Fine Arts in the Mongolian State University of Arts and Culture (MSUAC), and research workers from the Institute of History and Archaeology, and the Institute of Physics and Technology under the Mongolian Academy of Sciences. Lectures and presentations were given on geology, weathering processes and non- and low-invasive methods of diagnosis (including microscopy) by conservation scientist Johannes Weber – further on stone conservation and investigation results of the previous stone conservation workshop by senior stone conservators Martina Haselberger and Marija Milchin.

The second phase of the workshop, structured in theoretical and practical parts, was held at the complex monument of Kul-chur belonging to the Tureg period, located at a place called Ikh-Khoshoot in Delgerkhaan soum of Tov province Mongolia. This site comprises human- and animal-shaped sculptures, fragments of a sarcophagus and two stelae, partly showing Turkic runic inscriptions, from the 8th century A.D., all made of different types of granitoids. The main decay patterns are delamination, cracks, breakage, soiling and surface deposits (mainly bird droppings and remnants of animal rubbings). Besides conservators from the NCCH, museum workers and directors of the Tov province museum, the Dundgovi province museum, and students from the School of Fine Arts at MSUAC attended the on-site workshop.

Participants carried out cleaning measures in accordance with theoretically introduced principles and methods of cleaning of stone surfaces in conservation (lecture by Marija Milchin), the application of test series was demonstrated by the Austrian senior conservators. Another topic was the practice of backfilling and micro-pointing. Along with lectures imparting basic knowledge on this field, available binding media and aggregates were discussed and test series carried out using inorganic binders and different pigments. Finally, backfilling and micro-pointing was jointly done at the main stele (Fig. 1–2). Methods and materials for gluing and pinning were also discussed in theory and then exemplarily carried out on a dummy (rock found in the surrounding area). Thereby correct drilling and use of epoxy resin and glass-fibre rods was demonstrated and practised by the participants.

A half-day trip to the complex of Tsogt taij in the place called Duutyn Khar Chuluu in the territory of Delgerkhaan soum rounded up the workshop. The site is famous for its rock formations covered by black crusts (also called desert varnish, rock varnish or desert lacquer), which show historical inscriptions from the 17th century (1624) and engravings depicting humans and animals dating back to 1500 B.C. The Institute of Conservation was approached for professional advice with regard to cracks, visible on some rocks, partial chipping of the black crust and present signs of vandalism (new scratching). Under discussion were such topics as the potential of the damage patterns to cause loss of original inscription and engravings and also long-term preservation strategies for the site. The Institute of Conservation is proposing regular monitoring and recording of cracks and chipping by photos, measurements and drawings (changes in number, propagation and depth of cracks). In order to detect any sub-parallel layers that might cause loss of original surface, samples of the stone material and black crust were taken for further analyses to be done in Vienna. With regard to the newly made scratching, the Institute of Conservation suggested retouching them. Now that they are less visible, the overall appearance is more homogenous and visitors are less motivated to add new scratching.

After this enriching workshop, we now look ahead for 2019. Follow-up training programmes are amid preparations. Work at the complex monument in Ikh-Khoshoot has just begun. Further research is needed not only on still-open questions on present deterioration processes and the condition of the complex monument request but also important elements such as the fragmented sarcophagus, the small stele and the human- and animal-shaped sculptures are in need of conservation treatment. In the long run, a monitoring and maintenance plan should be elaborated to contribute to the long-term preservation of the site.

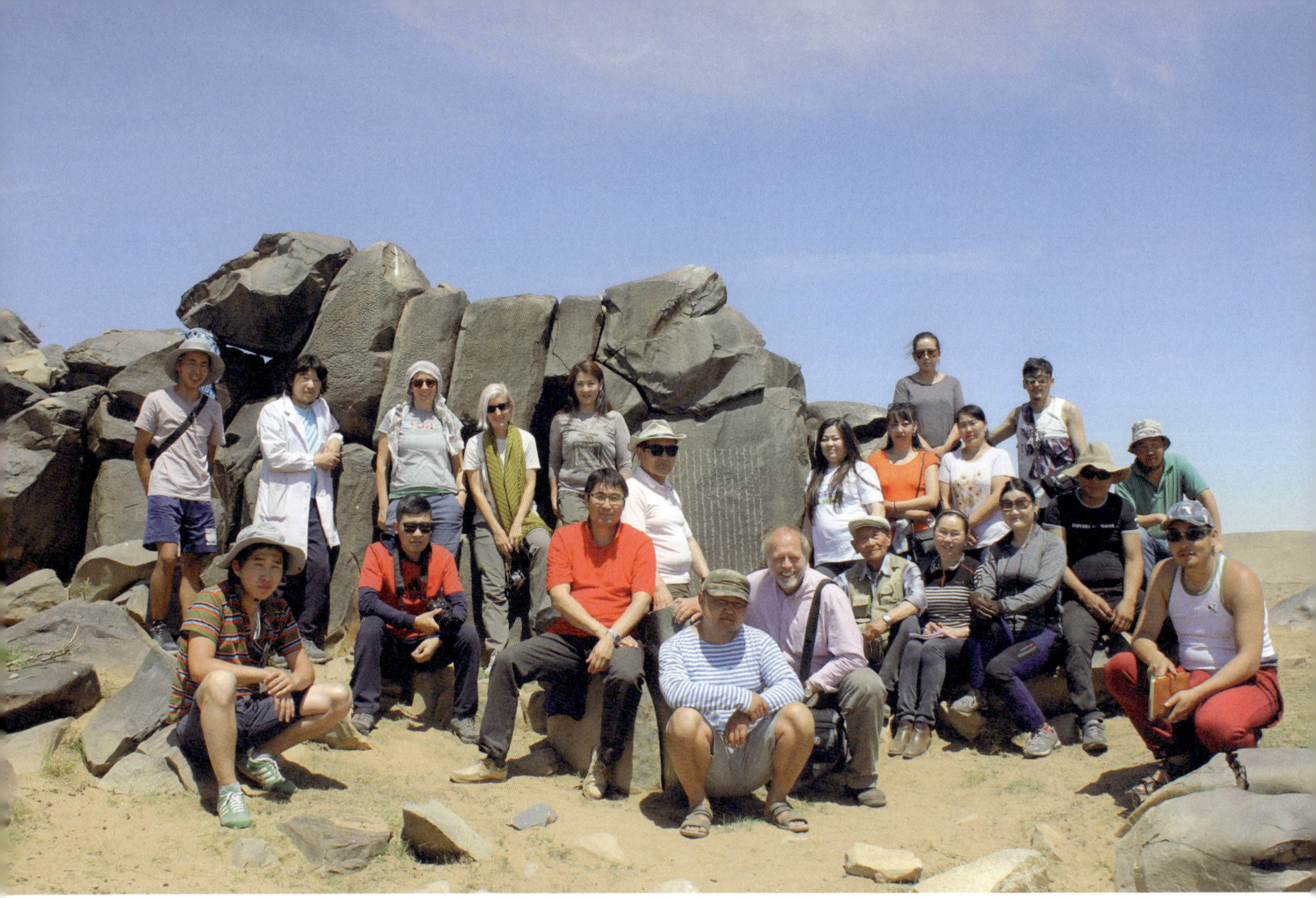

above: Fig. 3: Workshop participants
right: Fig. 1-2: Backfilling at main stele

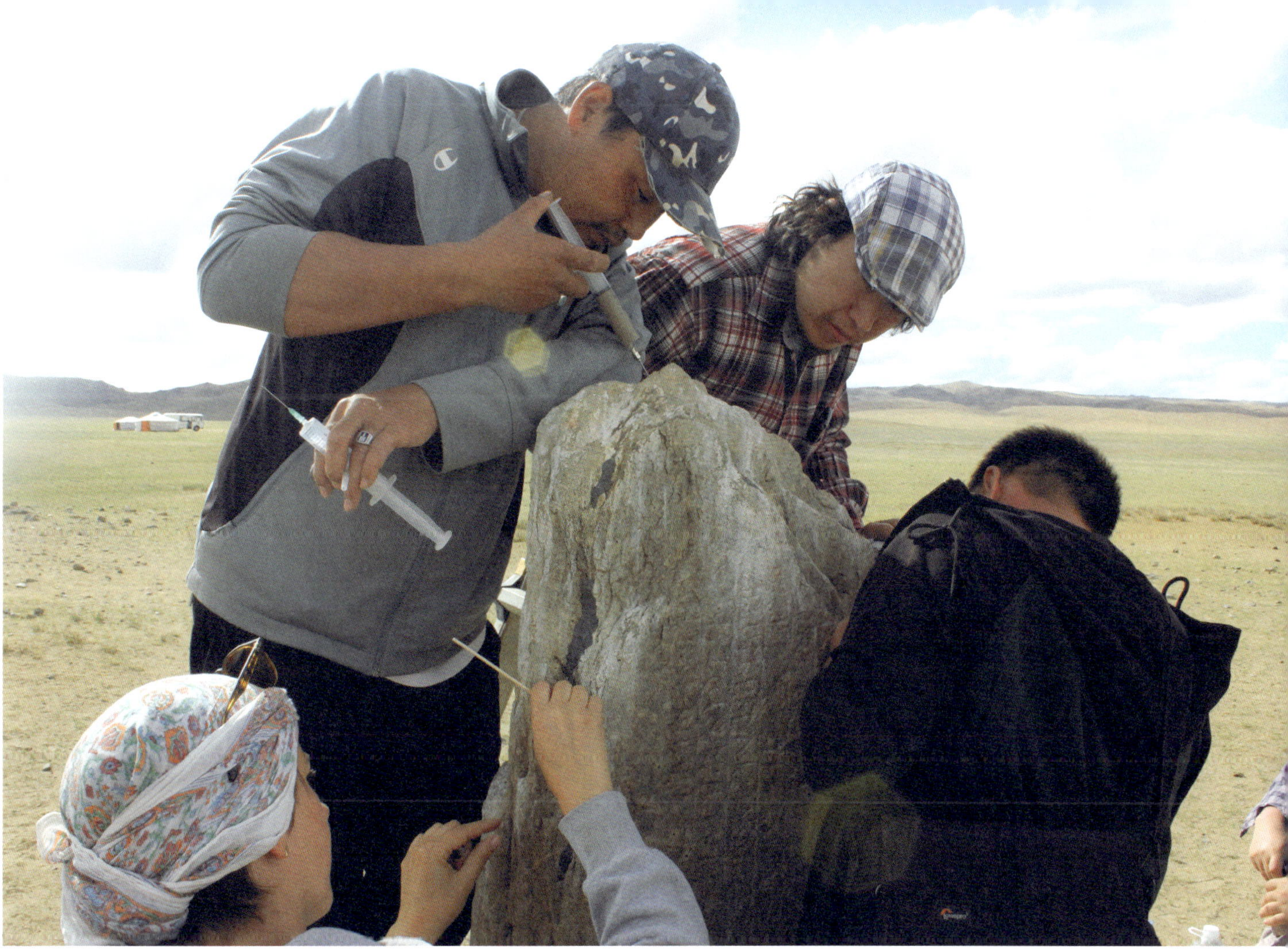

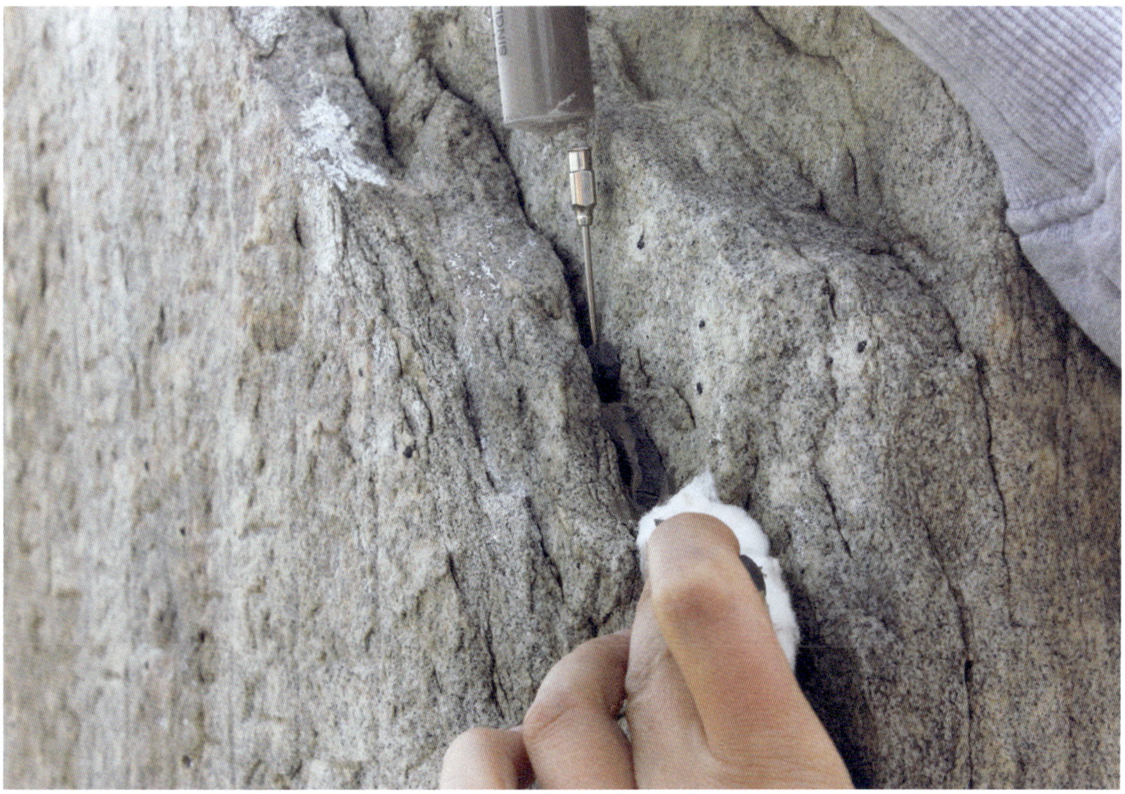

Cultural Heritage Conservation in Mongolia: Stone Monuments

MARTINA HASELBERGER, MARIJA MILCHIN

JUNE 2018

Experiences, Training, Activities

After the first stone conservation workshop in Mongolia in 2016, a follow-up was held in June 2018 by senior stone conservators Marija Milchin and Martina Haselberger from the Institute of Conservation together with conservation scientist Johannes Weber from the Department of Conservation Sciences, Institute of Art and Technology, both at the University of Applied Arts Vienna.

The workshop in 2018 aimed to provide further theoretical and practical knowledge in the field of stone deterioration and conservation. Its main focus was on hands-on conservation of the important monument of Tureg's Kul-chur at Ikh-Khoshoot (along with theoretical lectures on this topic). Workshop participants comprised conservators and staff from the National Center for Cultural Heritage (NCCH) and two province museums as well as students from the Mongolian State University of Arts and Culture (MSUAC).

Altogether the Austrian team spent a week in Mongolia, mainly on site in the Mongolian steppe. The first impressions and experiences in the country, whose name triggers pictures of wide-open spaces, sparse population and obviously Genghis Khan, are captured in the following (Mongolian) diary...

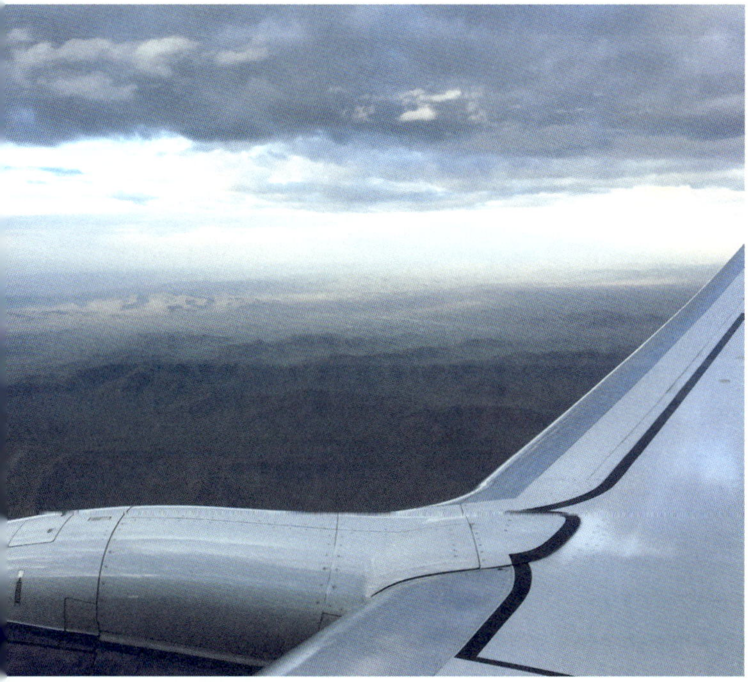

Fig. 1: A first glance out of the airplane window

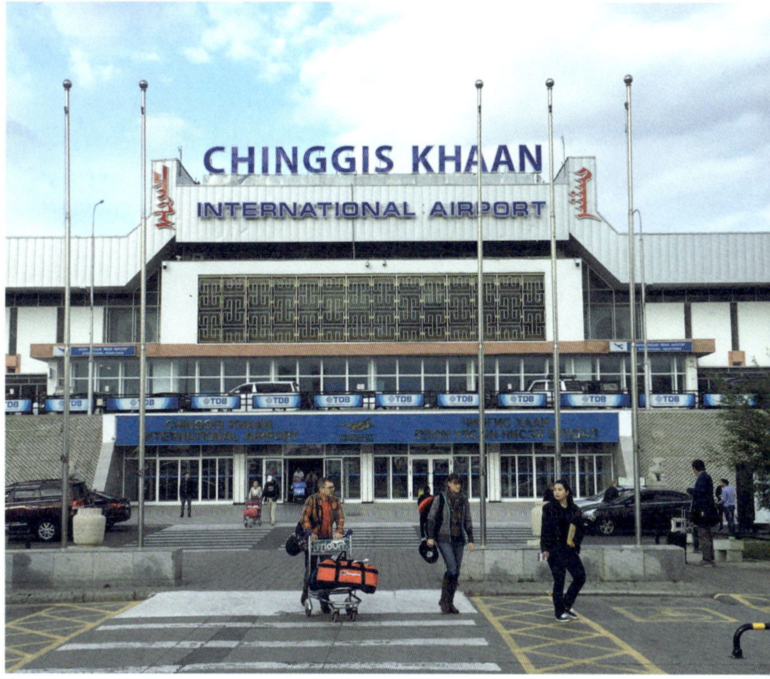

Fig. 2: Arrival at Chinggis Khaan Airport

SATURDAY, 9 JUNE 2018

Marija: I am totally uninformed...I am flying to Mongolia without knowing anything about the country apart from what I have seen and heard from Susi and Marisa. Typically I would take the time to get informed but this time I really didn't have any. It is in the middle of the semester and I have my family...which also means I don't have time, but hey it will all be fine. I love meeting new people and getting to know new cultures and most important I have Martina and Johannes, we will do great, I am sure!

SUNDAY, 10 JUNE 2018

Martina: Welcome to Mongolia!

Tomorrow our stone conservation workshop starts! In the footsteps of Susi and Marisa, who held the first workshop in 2016, I feel quite lucky to be part of the follow-up now. Our institute has been actively involved in conservation training programmes in Mongolia since 2014, so we – my colleague Marija, our conservation scientist Johannes and I – can benefit from the experiences of our colleagues. All their briefings, presentations and lectures in the recent years gave me a good impression of Mongolia, the current state of conservation education and the skills of local conservators. All in all I think I am prepared!

And, although I am only here for less than three hours now, some of the things I got to know already proved true: First, it is REALLY one of world's least crowded places. I was lucky and had a window seat in the plane which is why I could already catch a first glimpse of Mongolia during the flight (Fig. 1): What I saw was grassland – or was it steppe or desert? Doesn't matter...In any case, vast nearly-empty lands, literally nothing, no trees, no bigger cities, hardly streets, some rivers. The few white yurts, the traditional portable round tents used as dwellings by Mongolians nomads, appear like dashes of colour on the otherwise homogenous greenish to yellowish surface. Sometimes they are gathered into some kind of "villages" – although much smaller than what I would call a village in Austria. And in the distance – some mountains. The view was totally different from the one I am used from the Kathmandu Valley in Nepal with its densely populated areas.

Second, meat plays an important role in the diet of Mongolians. Although Susi and Kathi informed me in detail on the local eating habits, although I prepared myself mentally for a meat-based cuisine, it still was strange to hear the attendant in the plane asking: “chicken or beef?”…no vegetarian…

And third, Genghis Khan, history identifies him as the man who ruled over the largest contiguous empire in history, he is omnipresent. Starting with the Chinggis Khaan International Airport – what else? – over the Chinggis Khaan Avenue and Chinggis Khaan Hotel to the numerous Genghis Khan memorials you meet almost at every street corner (Fig. 2-3).

I am so curious to explore this country in the upcoming days! But now I will take a rest, the flight was exhausting.

P.S. There are better airlines than Aeroflot. Seven hours flight without any entertainment programme is quite boring.

Marija: So now we are here, I am wondering about many things…I did know that Genghis Khan was Mongolian, but I didn’t know that Marco Polo was here too. We saw a statue of him close to our hotel. I also knew that Mongolia used to be part of the SSSR but I didn’t know that they actually use Cyrillic letters even though they don’t speak a Slavic language. So I can sort of read, but cannot understand anything, it makes me smile all the time. Mongolians are mainly Buddhists but I have never been in a country that eats more meat…They are very honest and direct (I enjoy this a lot), one does not have to waste energy on reading the subtext; people here smile when they are friendly and laugh when they find something funny, they also tell you when you do or say something inappropriate. I guess this honesty and direct way has to do with the nomadic culture and the rough weather and landscape.

MONDAY, 11 JUNE 2018

Martina: First day successfully finished! Today our introduction lectures were on the agenda. I was a little bit nervous as the audience was bigger than expected. The lecture room in the National Modern Art Gallery was quite crowded. There were representatives from our main partner, the National Center for Cultural Heritage, short NCCH, Mongolian museums, universities, research institutions, and even from the ministry. In my lecture I summarised the activities of the first stone conservation workshop in 2016 and presented the results of the condition survey and the scientific analyses of the stone samples taken at that time. In this way we intended to bring all participants to an equal level of knowledge on which we could base our workshop.

And what did I learn today? On one hand, that lecturing with simultaneous translation is not as easy as I thought. As some of the people from the audience don’t or hardly understand English, Tsolmon, of the NCCH, translated our lectures. At the beginning it was difficult to choose the right amount of information to say before to stop for a break and let Tsolmon repeat. But I think after today’s 90-minute lecture Tsolmon and myself are a well-coordinated team – ready for the forthcoming teaching.

On the other hand, I know how my name is written in (Mongolian) Cyrillic now: our name tags were bilingual (Fig. 4). I hope I will find some time to learn the language, or at least some words, better in the upcoming days.

Marija: First day of action: Johannes had a very intensive start, he spoke for hours. He gave an overview on the science of stone, a bit of geology and mineralogy, chemistry and physics. I enjoyed it a lot…it is always nice when one can sit and listen, you always learn something new, or at least get reminded of facts that got buried in your brain…Afterwards Martina presented the results of the past workshop and the analyses on stone samples conducted in Vienna. The hall in the National Gallery of Modern Art was full.

TUESDAY, 12 JUNE 2018

Martina: Today in the afternoon we arrived at the site – the monument of Tureg’s Kul-chur. Although only roughly 250 km away from Ulaanbaatar, it was a long drive, more

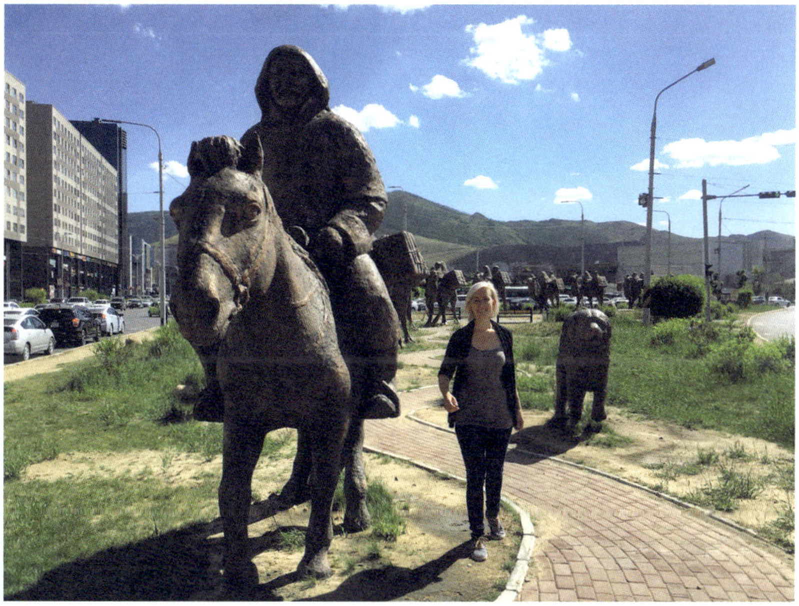

Fig. 3: Going for a walk in the shadow of Genghis Khan

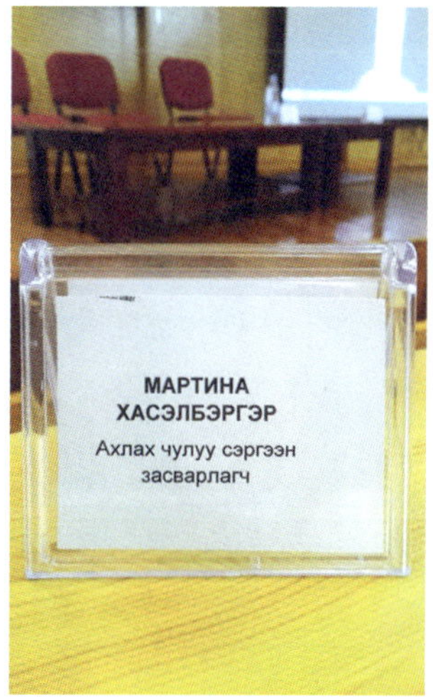

Fig. 4: Name tag in Mongolian

than six hours towards the southwest, across the Delgerkhaan sum (sum = district). The first two hours we were driving on an asphalt road, one lane in each direction, speed limit at 100 km/h, always straight ahead. At the beginning I was really fascinated by the stunning landscape and the clouds looking like candy floss. But after two hours with unchanged hills and plains on a dead straight street, overtaking a truck, passing small "Wild West"-like cities and petrol stations or herds of sheep and goats roaming the steppe and crossing the road were a welcome change (Fig. 5-6).

And then after these rather "easy" two hours we went off-road. It was fascinating that Director Enkhbat, the director of the NCCH, found the way to the site. No signs, numerous crossings and junctions leading in all directions (Fig. 7). Sometimes the only thing we could do to find the right way: ask a local. But they were rare. At least the few ones we met were very friendly and supportive.

So, we finally managed to arrive with a short delay and very hungry at the site (Fig. 8). Luckily, we immediately got a delayed lunch – stew with meat, what else.

After this refreshment we went straight into action and started with our lectures in the yurt (Fig. 9). Yes, I gave my first lecture in a "tent"! Considering the circumstances, the setting was quite professional. We had a beamer and a screen, chairs and desks.

And how did we conclude our first day in the steppe? With a big welcome party! Hereby we can certainly learn something from our Mongolian friends...they know how to celebrate.

There was dancing and laughing, vodka was flowing in huge amounts, all under the starry sky. I have never seen more stars – even the Milky Way was visible. And there was singing...which is to say mutual auditions of folk songs from home. And here we're in a fine mess. First, I am not a gifted singer. Singing together or in front of others is limited, in my case, to Singstar and Christmas Eve. Second, I hardly know Austrian folk songs by memory. Apart from some carols my pool is exhausted. Thank god, Johannes proved to be a very skilled singer!

Note: if I come back to Mongolia I have to practise some folk songs at home!

P.S. I already saw my first wild camels! I feared that I won't see any as Ganzam (our former intern in Vienna) told us yesterday that they live more in the south, in the Gobi Desert.

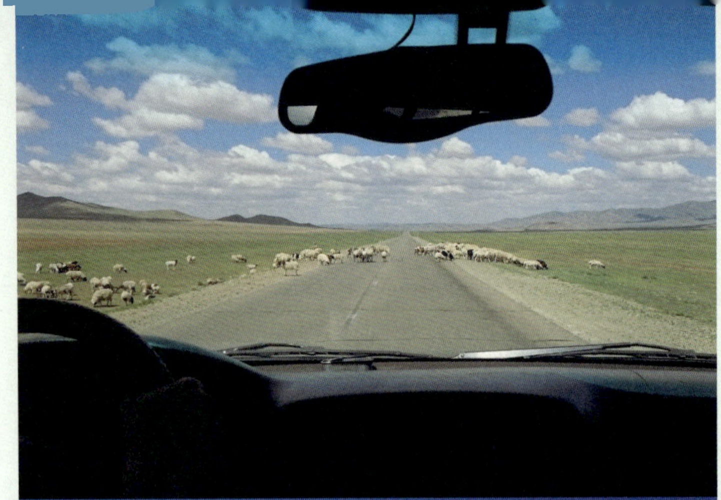

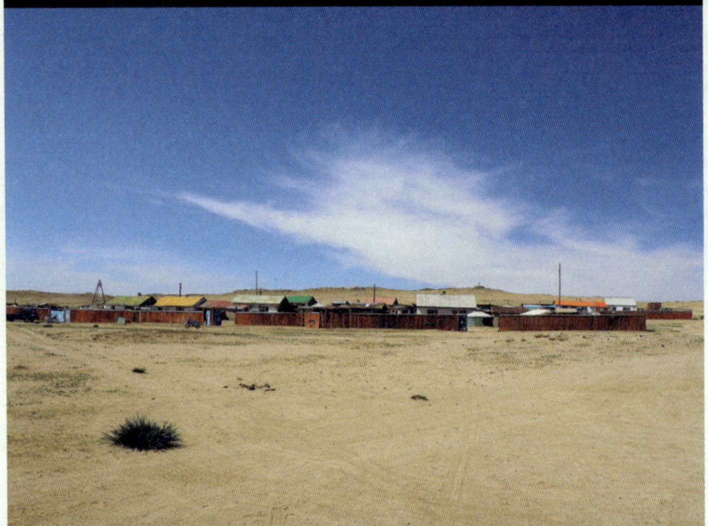

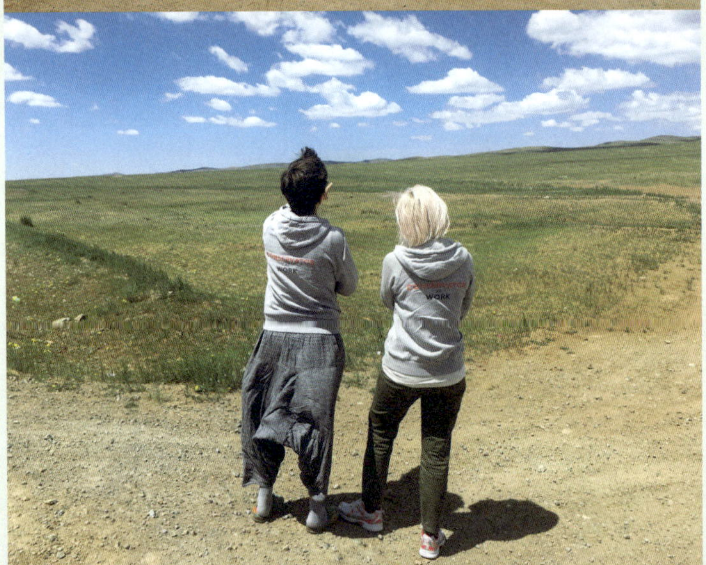

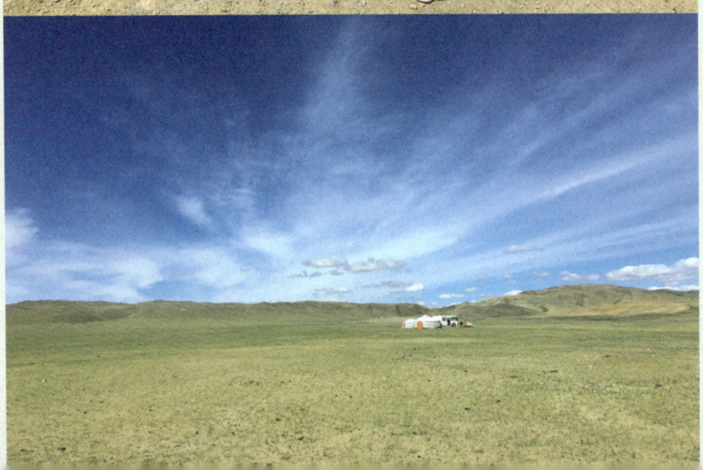

from top to bottom:
Fig. 5: Herds of sheep and goats crossing the dead straight road
Fig. 6: "Wild West"-like cities embedded in the plains of Mongolia
Fig. 7: Two conservators in search of the right road in Mongolia
Fig. 8: Our yurt camp in the middle of nowhere

Fig. 9: Our yurts – place for sleeping, eating and giving lectures

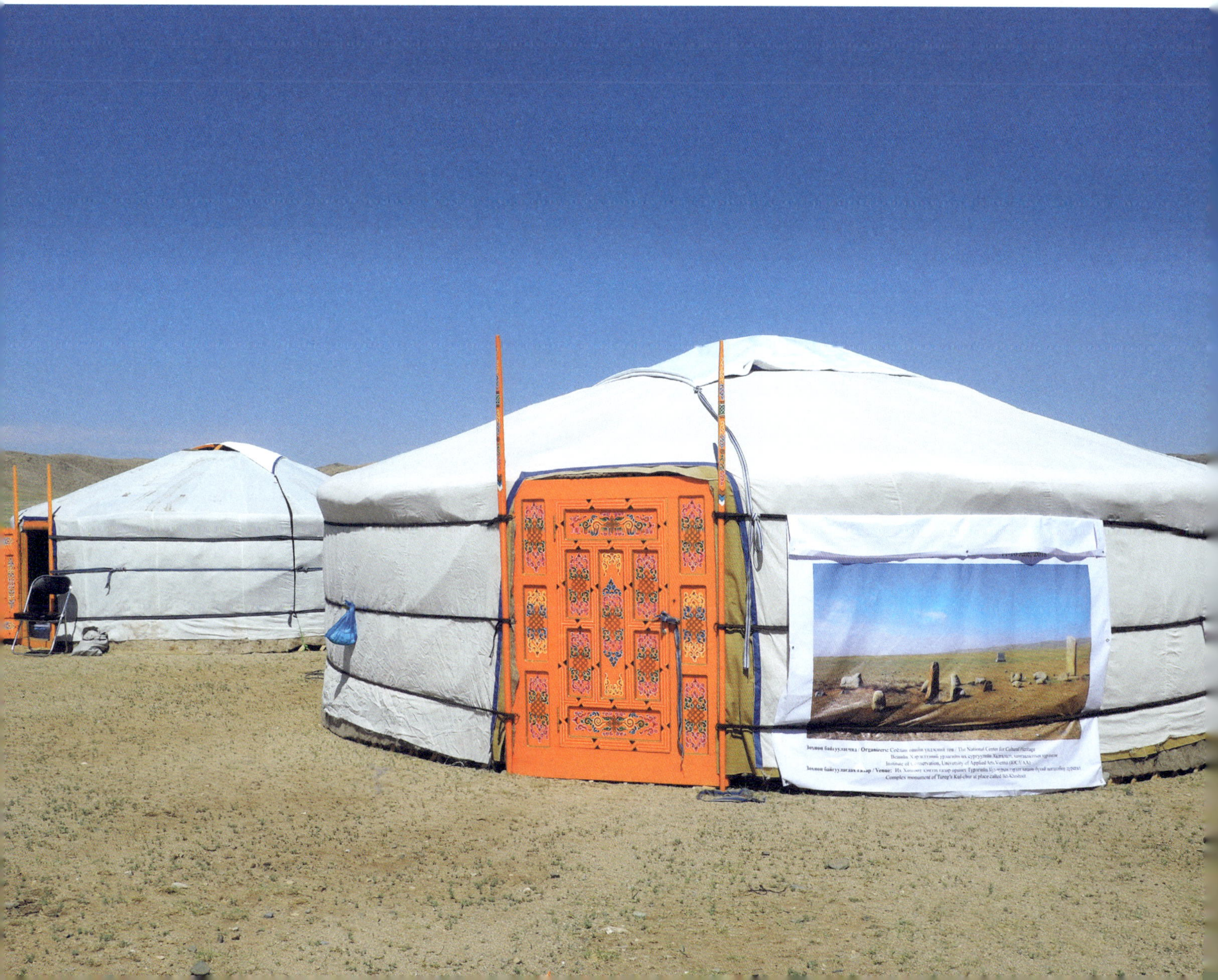

But we were lucky on our way to the site! Director Enkhbat even was so kind to leave the path and drive a bit closer so that we could take some pictures – I felt like a real tourist (Fig. 10).

Marija: We head to the site, for our hands-on workshop. I love car drives, I find it very meditative. One can relax and look through the window. This time it is so meditative that I fall asleep even though we are not yet out of Ulaanbaatar, or what our Mongolian friends would say: UB. When I wake up I am looking at endless plains...in every direction, it is boundless...nothing on the horizon, I don't think I have ever seen further away, at least on land... it is very calming. We stop for a break, I leave the car and realise the whole scenery is not that calm at all, the wind is very strong and it messes up hair and clothes, it brings dust and sand with it...on moments it feels a bit like sandblasting. Ok so, harsh climate and peaceful landscapes, I can get used to Mongolia.

After lectures in the yurt (the same as in UB) I ask: "What do we do now?"

Director Enkhbat answers: "We go to bed!"and smiles...

Vodka and beer, different sweets and a music system appear from somewhere and the party can start. Mongolian people sing and dance and consume big quantities of vodka. Johannes has to put some traditional Mongolian clothes on; he looks funny.

WEDNESDAY, 13 JUNE 2018

Martina: Today, Johannes and I used a time slot before our excursion to the complex of Tsogt Taij in Duutyn Khar Chuluu to inspect the site in more detail. We wandered from stone to stone, surveyed the stones varieties and the damage patterns once afar and then up close. The complex monument is somehow smaller than expected. The focal element is certainly the rectangular, life-size stele showing Turkic runic inscriptions. Towards the east several animal- and human-shaped sculptures are arranged in pairs. Their surfaces have been considerably reduced and their edges rounded, therefore it is hard to determine their former shape. Probably they depicted lions, sheep and warriors' torsos? It seems furthermore as if they are flanking a kind of path leading towards the main stele. In the distance there are several bulky stone blocks laid out in a row like "bread crumbs", which guide the visitor to the complex (Fig. 11).

But I shouldn't interpret too much into this current arrangement. We already compared the current condition with photos and plans of former expeditions and site visits in the 20th century and quickly recognized that the objects have been repeatedly dislocated – it will be impossible to reconstruct the original arrangement and positioning of each object.

On the west side of the complex a fragmented relief is lying on the ground (Fig. 13). I counted more or less 35 single pieces. On the biggest preserved fragment, with a bit of imagination, peacocks and plants are visible. I have done a bit of research. It seems like it is a side panel of a former sarcophagus. This would go with the assumption that the site is a tomb for a Turkic military leader. Perhaps the sarcophagus was damaged by a grave robber, who visited the site in former times.

Anyhow, the relief will be certainly a focus of forthcoming workshops. The single pieces should be re-adhered to prevent them from getting lost. At the moment, they can be easily carried awa...and in this remote area one never knows what a tourist will do in an unobserved moment.

The more time I spent at the site, the more I understand the relevant deterioration mechanisms.

It seems that the thermal dilatation plays a decisive role. At the site we have no trees, no shadow. So, from sunrise on, sunrays hit the stone surface and heat it up. I checked the weather conditions in Mongolia beforehand: up to 40°C in summer – the stone will get even hotter. During the heating up the highest temperature gradient we naturally have on the east side – here the stone, cooled off during night, is heated up quickly by the direct sunlight. Accordingly, also the east side of the main stele is most affected: it shows big detachments of the surface and surface-parallel cavities. In contrast the west-side scales are much smaller in size. I think it would be interesting to measure how fast and to what extent the stone at the site is really heated up during the day. Next time we have to take some infrared measuring device with us!

Another damage factor, which we considered, are freeze-thaw cycles. They are a very important deterioration mechanism in Austria but in Mongolia it seems that they play only a minor role. First, it hardly rains in winter, only 5 mm per month, and second, although we have to face almost minus 40°C in winter (I immediately get goose bumps when I imagine these low temperatures), it is uncertain how often the available water changes its condition between liquid and solid – the detrimental situation.

Furthermore, the properties of the stone material itself, the granitoids, seem to favour the decay. The stone variety used for the main stele for example has a distinctive layering. Combined with the unfortunate positioning of the stele – the layering is orientated in right angle to the ground – the creation of cracks on the top owing to water accumulation and solution processes is obviously favoured. Then deposits, water, earth, bird droppings and so on accumulate in these open and gaping cracks – solution processes increase and cracks deepen – we have come full circle.

Marija: Today is my first lecture in a yurt (Fig. 13). It is about soiling, deposits, cleaning and uncovering. I enjoy it. I think the participants enjoy it as well. Some of them are more interested than others.

After the lectures we visit another site in the province. On the way we make two short stops: the first one is a site with tumuli. We climb on the middle one and can see the rectangular structures in the low vegetation of the steppe. One of the few plants that cope with the harsh climate is a kind of wild thyme, Martina and I recognise it, but our Mongolian colleagues don't know it and they don't use it for cooking either...strange. The next stop is a very green patch of land with many horses on it, as we approach I realize that in the middle of the green there is water running (Fig. 14). Springs! The two students from the art university take out their sketch books and start drawing immediately, no time to lose!

Then we move further, the site that we visit is the complex of Tsogt Taij in Duutyn Khar Chuluu, a natural rock formation with engraved inscriptions and pictograms (Fig. 15). The earliest lithoglyphs show different animals and are supposed to be 3,500–4,000 years old. Other inscriptions are dated in the 17th century and written in Mongolian (Fig. 16). One of them tells the sad story of a brother that is looking for his lost sister. Our Mongolian colleagues want to know our opinion on the preservation state and if we think they should do some consolidation. It is all too fast for me, I need some time to understand the situation, I don't even under stand why or how the inscription from the 17th century can look so sharp still. Or did somebody make some "conservation" work on it in the past years...A politician from the nearby village says that he would know if some work had been done. Ok, so concentrate and try to understand...Which kind of stone is this? I have never seen anything similar...Johannes? Also no clue...We also have a local petrologist...but he can´t help either. I look at the surface and at the working marks. I look at the 17th century and at the prehistoric lithoglyphs, and then from somewhere deep in my memory...Desert varnish...of course! We are in an arid climate with loads of sun and wind, in such circumstances manganese and iron ions move towards the surface and build a dark, sometimes shiny patina. The process is very slow and the patina rather thin. If you scratch the patina, you can write and draw on these stones, a bit like a natural stone scraffitto. I have learned about this phenomenon but have never seen it – live, I am overwhelmed. That is also why one can see the inscriptions from the 17th century very clearly, whereas the prehistoric lithoglyphs are not as sharp anymore – the new desert varnish is slowly covering the depicted animals.

After the site visit we are invited for lunch in the school of the nearby village. We have a typical Mongolian lunch with loads of meat and a few potatoes (they are very, very good). There is vodka also, of course. After lunch, Martina and I have some problems finding the toilet in the village but that is a totally different story.

Back at the camp we say goodbye to Johannes and Director Enkhbat; they are going

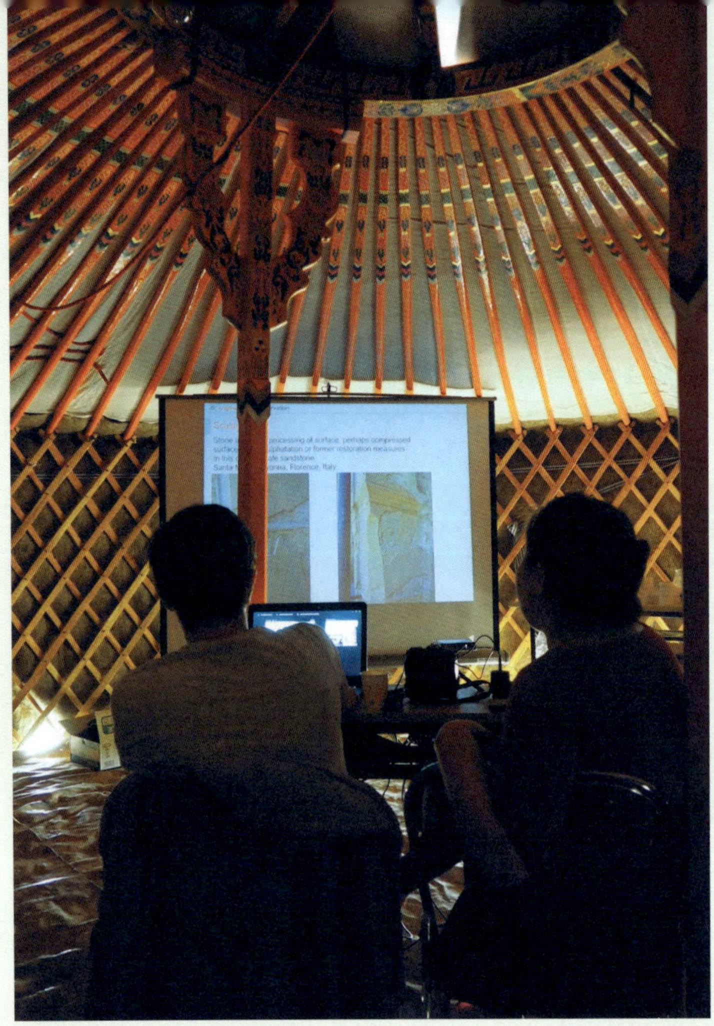

Fig. 13: Marija gives her first lecture inside a yurt

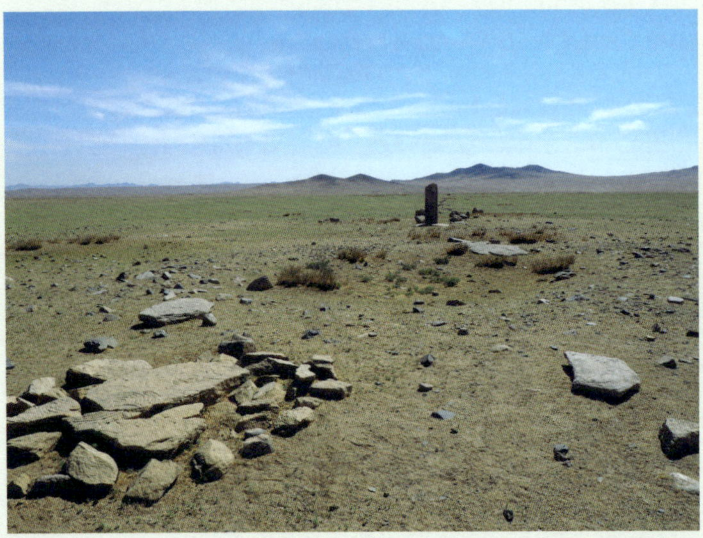

Fig. 12: The monument with the fragmented peacock sarcophagus in the foreground

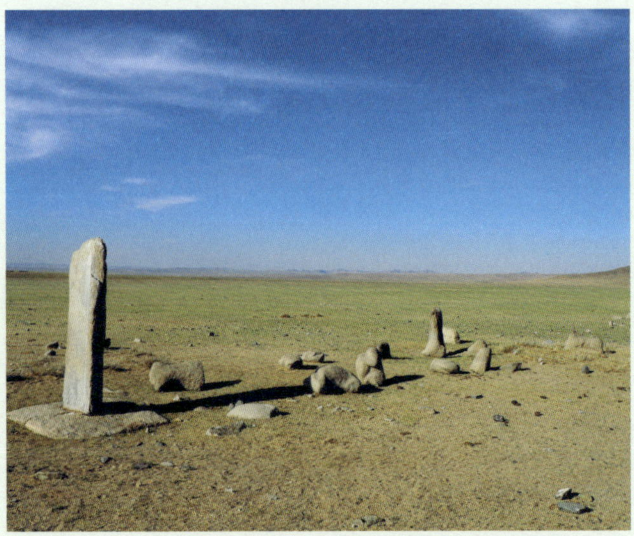

Fig. 11: The monument of Tureg's Kul-chur at Ikh-Khoshoot comprising stelae and animal- and human-shaped sculptures

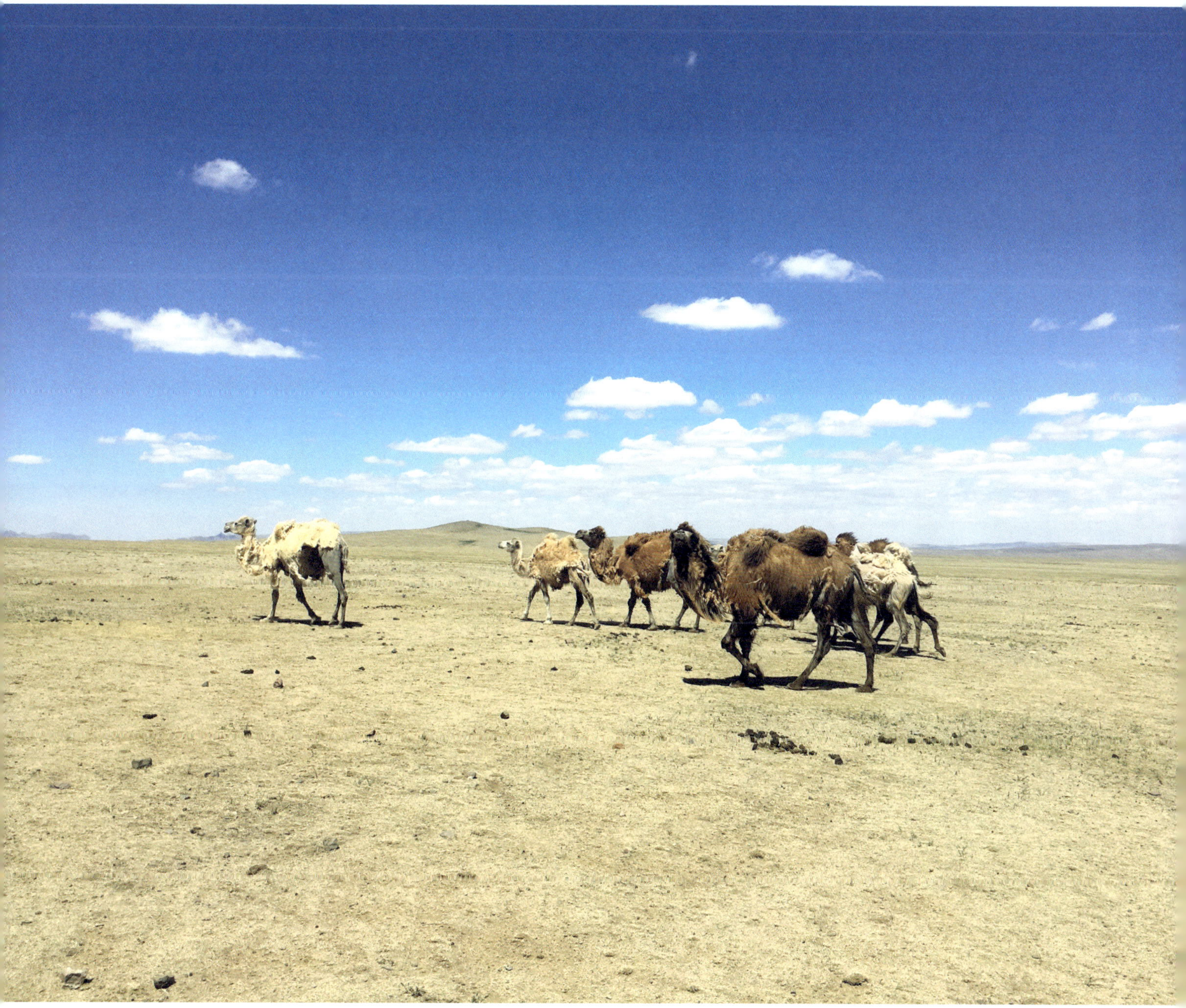

Fig. 10: Camels crossing the desert-like Mongolian steppe

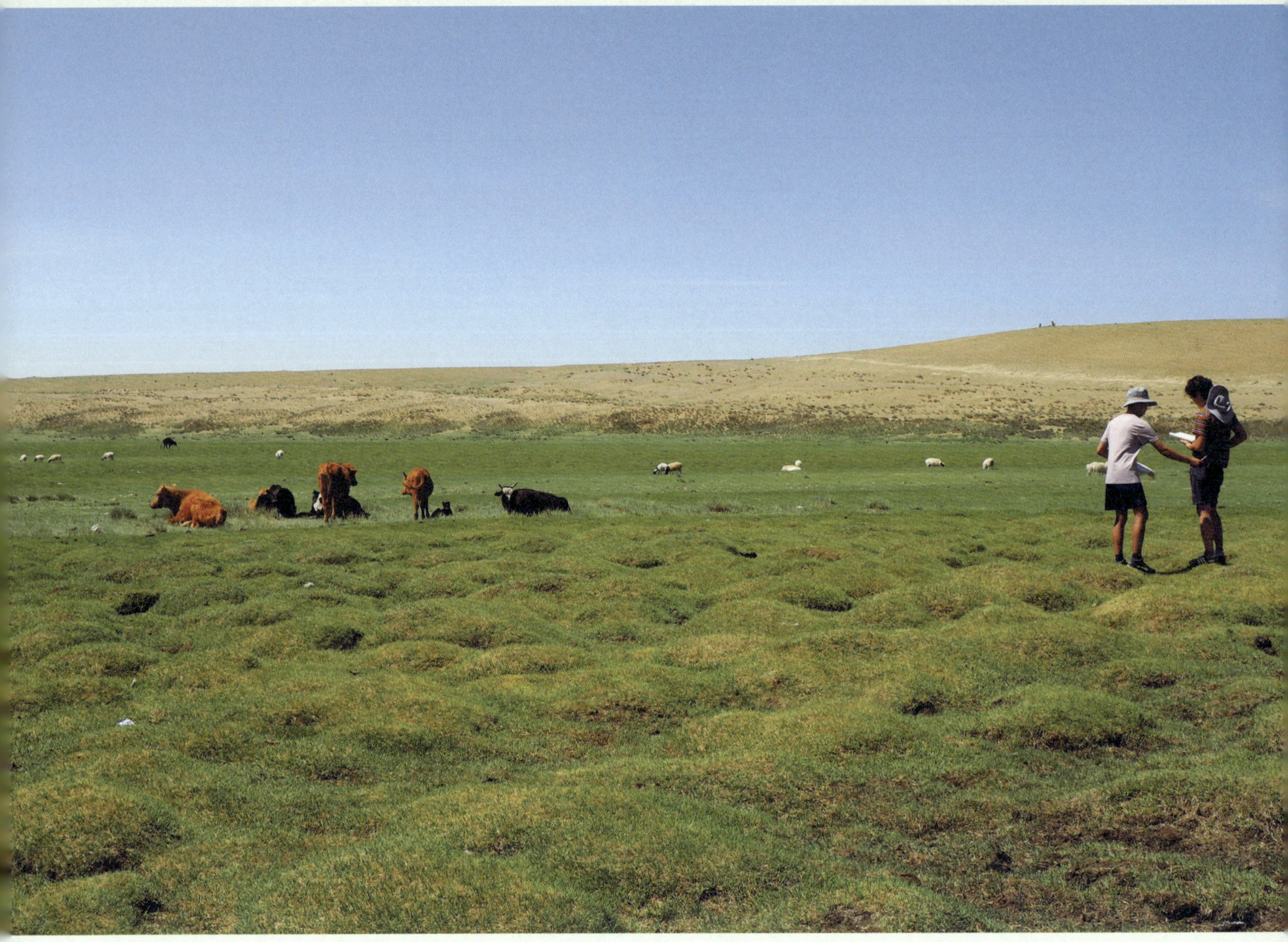

Fig. 14: On the way to the complex of Tsogt Taij – a green oasis in Mongolia

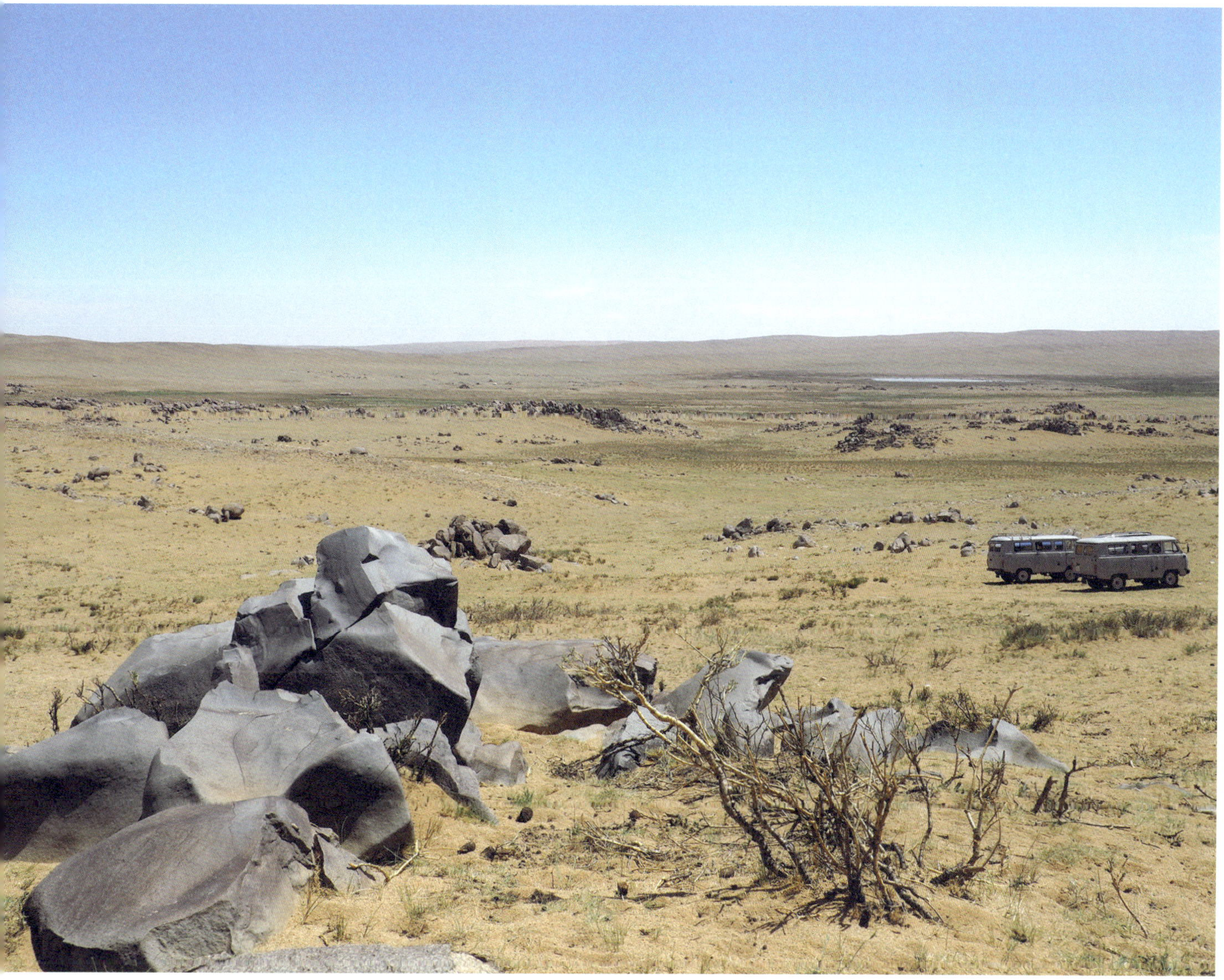

Fig. 15: A completely different landscape – the complex of Tsogt Taij in Duutyn Khar Chuluu itself

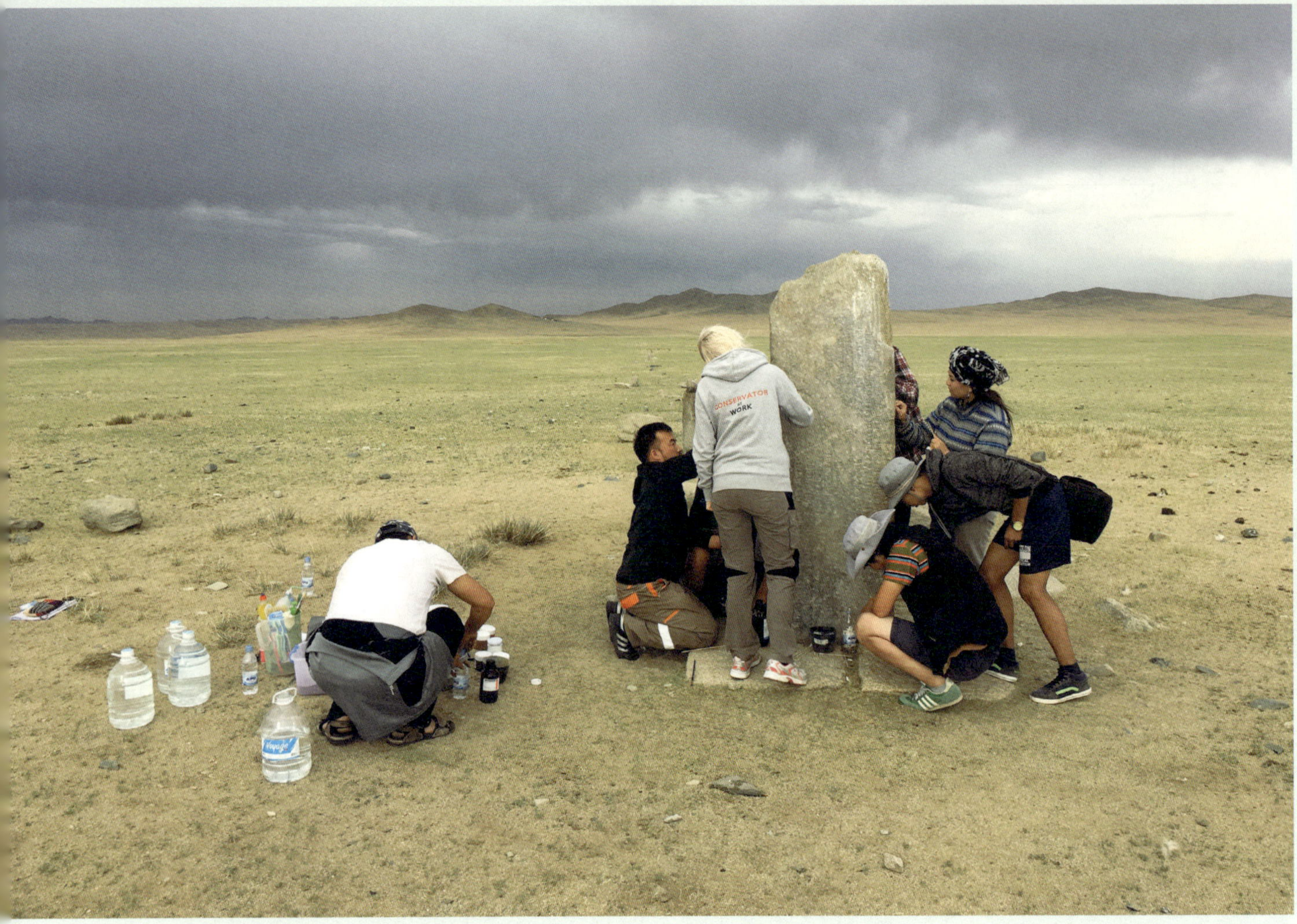

Fig. 17: The cleaning of the main stele is highlighted in the workshop

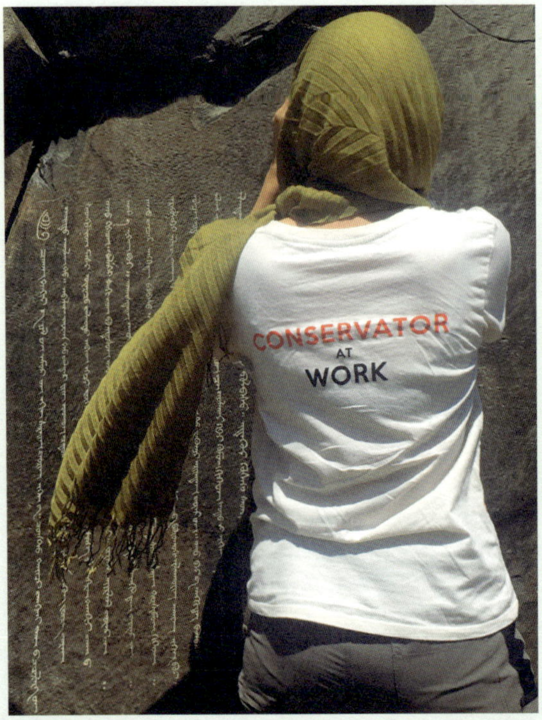

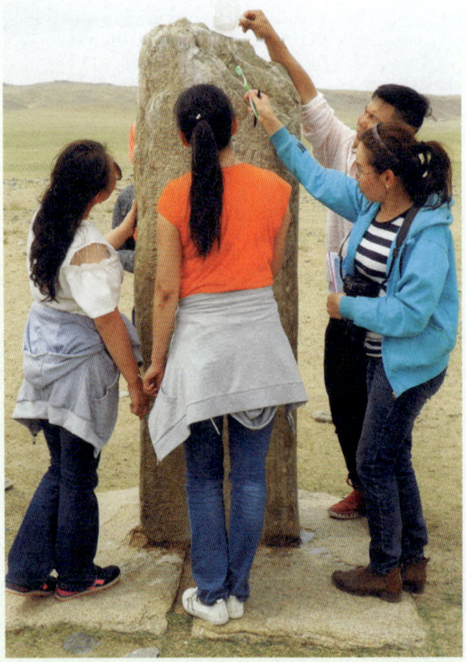

left: Fig. 16: Documentation of the engraved inscriptions and pictograms on the natural rock formation
right: Fig. 18: Enthusiastically, the workshop participants collect around the main stele and start cleaning

back to UB. We also add a session that was not planned, it is on consolidation. We think we have to do this, because we realised that the site was consolidated last year with an ethyl silicate but that the conservators do not have any experience with the material and are not really sure why and how to implement it. So I talk about consolidation and about TEOS (ethyl silicate) till late in the night. After that all I need is a good sleep.

THURSDAY, 14 JUNE 2018

Martina: Today's workshop emphasis was on cleaning (Fig. 17). The removing (or at least considerable reduction) of deposits like bird droppings, dust and dirt and remnants of animal grease from rubbings were on the agenda. I had the task to supervise more than 20 participants, which was not easy as all of them were very motivated and curious, frequently asking questions. I had to have my eyes everywhere.

We started simple, with dry and wet cleaning. It was a pleasure to see how enthusiastic the participants joined. Some immediately grabbed a brush, others the wooden spatulas and water bucket. I was not aware how many people can work on one object simultaneously – the main stele was hardly visible behind the eight people eagerly brushing, rubbing and washing (Fig. 18).

The results were quite satisfactory, although we were not able to remove the bird droppings on top, which already converted to a compact and thick crust. Despite our rather "harsh" cleaning trials (we tried pure lime, hydrogen peroxide, solvent poultices), the removing of the crusts will remain a challenge for future workshops. I have never experienced such a resilient bird dropping before...but who knows what decades-long exposure to dry air and high temperatures does to them?

Then we dedicated ourselves to the more comprehensive challenge – the reduction of the brownish discolouration at the lower half of the stele.

They reach up to a height of approximately 60 cm – exactly the shoulder height of small domestic animals. As there is no fence around the site and herds roaming wild, it can be assumed that the stains result from animals rubbing at the rough stones. This means that we are confronted with greasy substances from the animal skins combined with dust and dirt. With all this in mind, I normally know what kind of solvents to test but on behalf of the learning effect and the workshop-environment we made a comprehensive cleaning trial series with the participants. We worked from polar to nonpolar, from water, ethanol and acetone, to benzine. Finally, we chose acetone for the cleaning to avoid an over-cleaning of areas. And it was also for the learning effects and for the better control of the level of cleanliness, that we used cotton swabs... It was a funny image...cleaning stone surfaces with cotton swabs in the middle of nowhere (Fig. 19).

P.S.: Today I solved the riddle regarding first name and family name of our Mongolian friends: in contrast to Austria, Mongolians predominantly use their first name to address each other and to introduce themselves. Also on their business card their first name is written in capital letters. Quite unfamiliar for me (as an Austrian), but it made everything more amicable, more collegial.

Marija: The programme today: Martina is working on the practical cleaning with the participants. After yesterday's lecture, I hope they will better understand the way we approach these kind of problems. My task today is teaching theory on injection, backfilling, micro-pointing and gluing. As I am giving the lecture I realise the participants have little knowledge about mortars and mineral binders. So we squeeze in a block on mortars and binders; we discuss lime and NHL, cements and puzzolana. In the afternoon, the participants from the local museums leave; we stay alone with the conservators from the National Center. Tomorrow will be easy, small team of skilled conservators, perfect for the work with mortars and glues.

FRIDAY, 15 JUNE 2018

Marija: It was a very successful day. We did loads of hands-on work today. After the test series for an injection grout and micro-pointing mortar we concentrated on the main stele. The vertical cracks were filled and closed with a micro-pointing (Fig. 20–22). I find that the work looks very good. We also did some gluing and pining on a dummy. I realised that our colleagues from Mongolia are very good when it comes to practice, but they lack some knowledge in the theory i.e. deterioration mechanisms and conservation materials; this is something that we can teach them. In return we can learn many things from them, not only directly connected to conservation but things that can come in very handy in different situations. For example, I am trying to learn a very handy knot today. It is one that does not loosen at all. They use this knot here a lot, to tie horses (most of the time there is nothing to tie the horse to, so they tie the two front feet of the horse to each other), to build the yurt, to keep two pieces of stone together while gluing…I am really amazed and it is not that I have never used knots myself – I was a scout for years – but what nomads can do with a rope is true art. And in the evening we discuss eating habits. Martina and I find it very cool how the Mongolian can "clean" the bone when they eat, they do not leave anything eatable. We love the idea of not throwing food away, it is very sustainable, so we try to do it also…we are miles away from the polished bones of our colleagues, but at least we try. After dinner they make a pipe from one of the bones, so we have a drag of a cigarette using the pipe and make funny photos, of course.

SATURDAY, 16 JUNE 2018

Martina: Only five days in the steppe, away from civilisation, and I already have the feeling I've been here for weeks. I fell in love with the eternal blue skies, with Mongolia's undisturbed beauty. I got used to the silence, the remoteness…and lack of mobile coverage. Currently I am only using my phone for the alarm in the morning. I wonder how it will be, being back in Vienna with my phone beeping or ringing every couple of minutes.

Marija and I were kidding today that we should perhaps stay here and become "Conservation Nomads" following the so-called "Modern Nomads", today's shepherds on motorcycles.

An hour ago we concluded the practical session of our workshop in the steppe. We were able to finish the conservation of the main stele yesterday. Overnight it was wrapped in a tent tarpaulin to keep the freshly applied mortar moist for a longer period (Fig. 23). Today we only did some finishing, moisted the mortar once more and made some final photographs (Fig. 24–25).

Currently I am watching our Mongolian colleagues dismantle the whole camp (Fig. 26). They said it will only take two hours, and then we will head back to Ulaanbaatar.

Reviewing the past days, I am pleasantly surprised by the practical skills of the workshop participants, how tough they are in the application of various conservation methods and materials (Fig. 27). At the same time we had the feeling that specific knowledge on underlying chemical reactions, long-term behaviour, ageing processes, compatibility and degradation phenomena is sometimes only at the beginning – probably due to the fact that there is no education or training in the field of conservation or conservation science in Mongolia. Some Mongolian conservators got their education abroad, others are trained in the field of fine arts and are autodidacts.

I hope that they can apply lessons learnt from our workshop in their demanding work routine. The few conservators working in the National Center for Cultural Heritage are confronted on a daily basis with a broad range of materials and works of art. Particularly, the conservation of stone is a rather new topic in Mongolia. And they have to cover thousands of kilometres per year to carry out inspections and conservation treatments of immovable cultural heritage, distributed over the whole country (1,566,000 m^2). I think they do a great job.

And last but not least, what I am very thankful for was the delicious food! Uuganchimeg, actually textile conservator at the NCCH, but during our workshop also cook, conjured up a range of tasty dishes like stews, soups, salads, dumplings and pasta out of a small range of ingredients. And she always took care that there are enough vegetables for us Austrians.

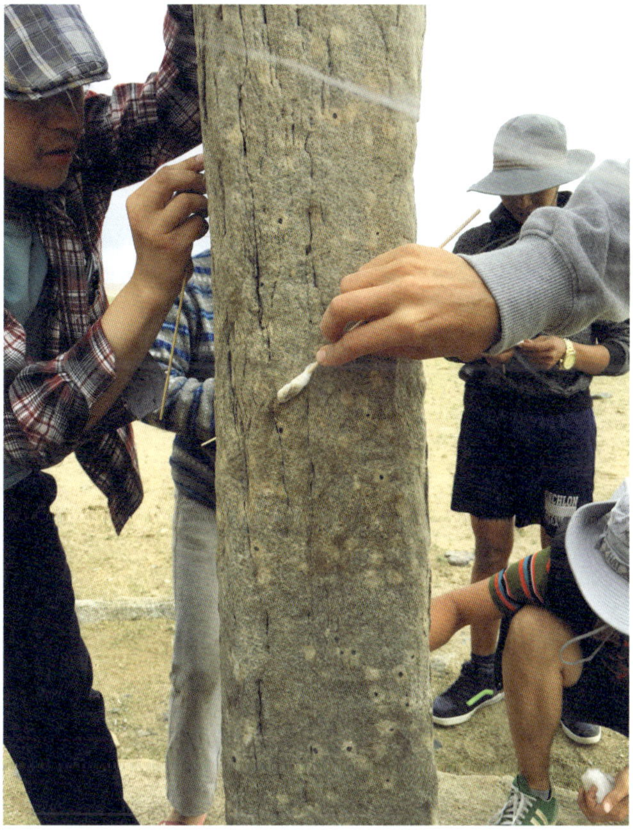

Fig. 19: Cleaning with cotton swabs

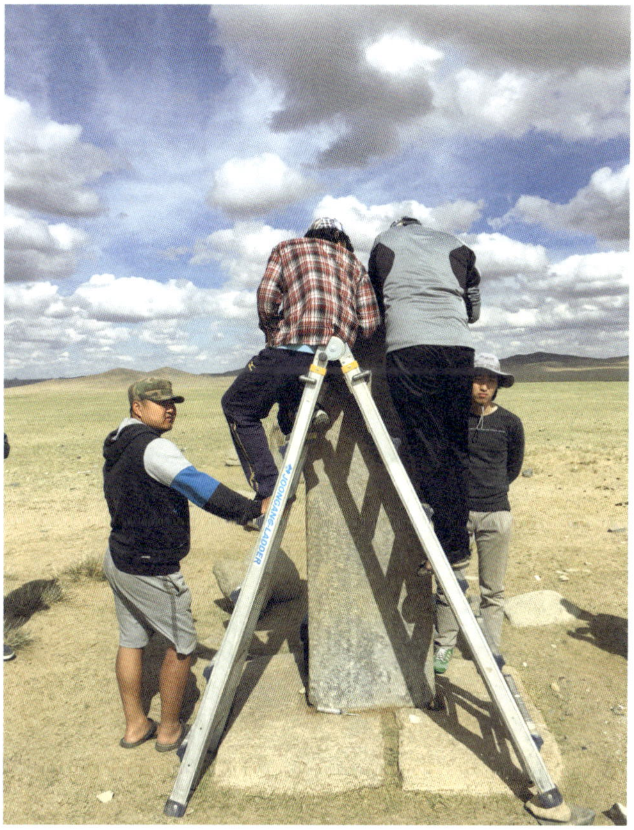

Fig. 20: Injecting a grout in the cracks

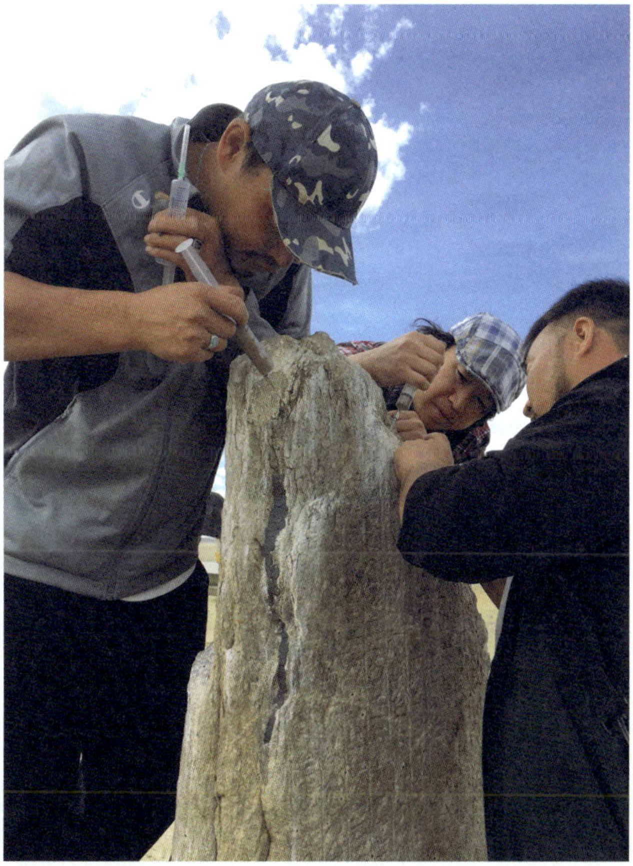

Fig. 21: Injecting a grout in the cracks

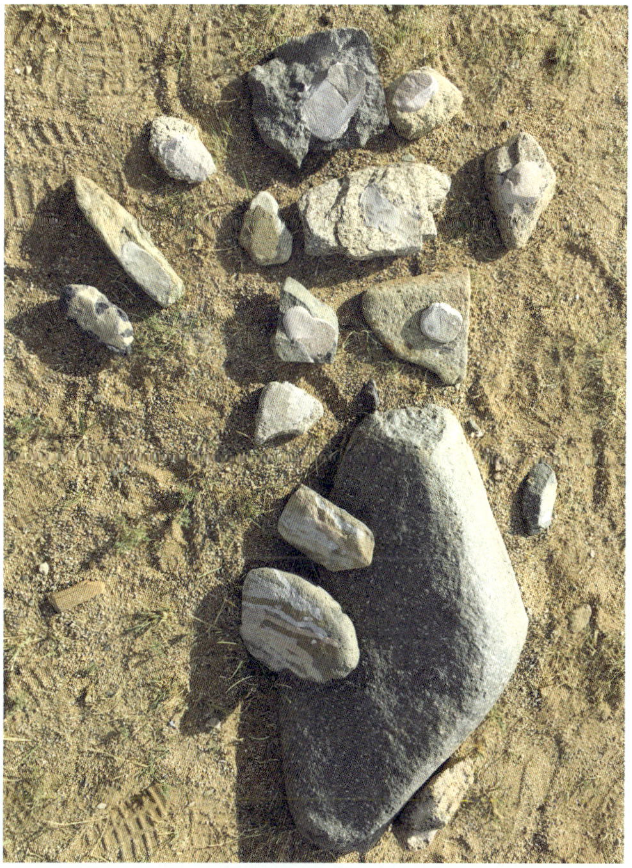

Fig. 22: Trials for injection grout and micro-pointing mortar

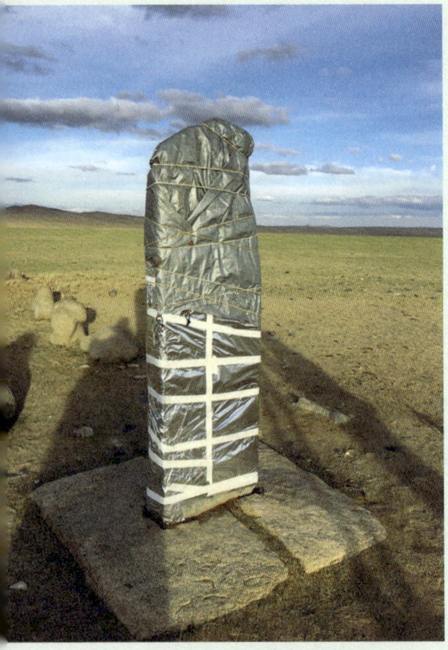

Fig. 23: The main stele, wrapped in a tent tarpaulin over night to enable curing of the applied mortar

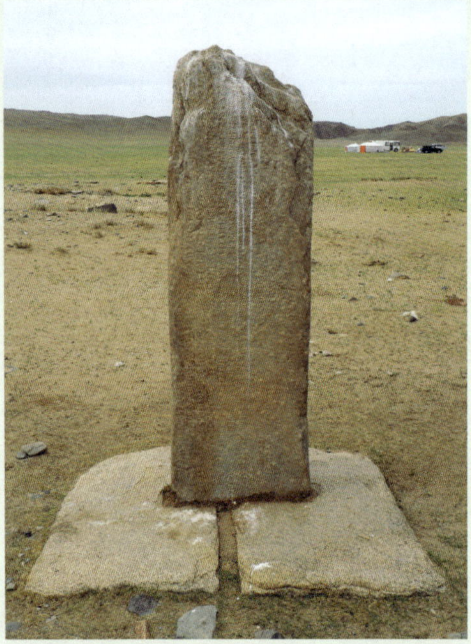

Fig. 24: The main stele before conservation

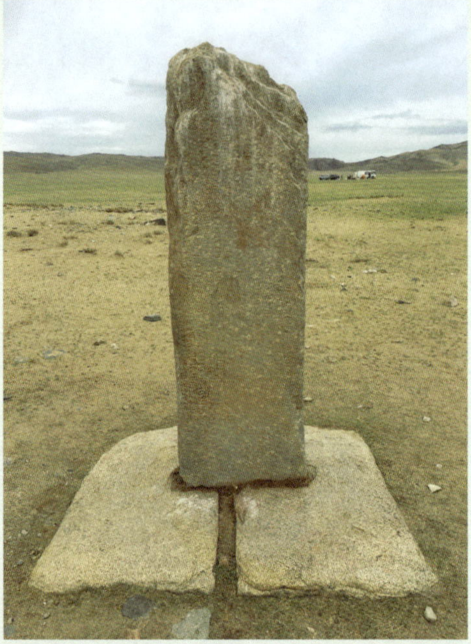

Fig. 25: The main stele after conservation

Fig. 27: Austrian conservators together with their colleagues from the National Center for Cultural Heritage in Mongolia – after one week a well-coordinated team!

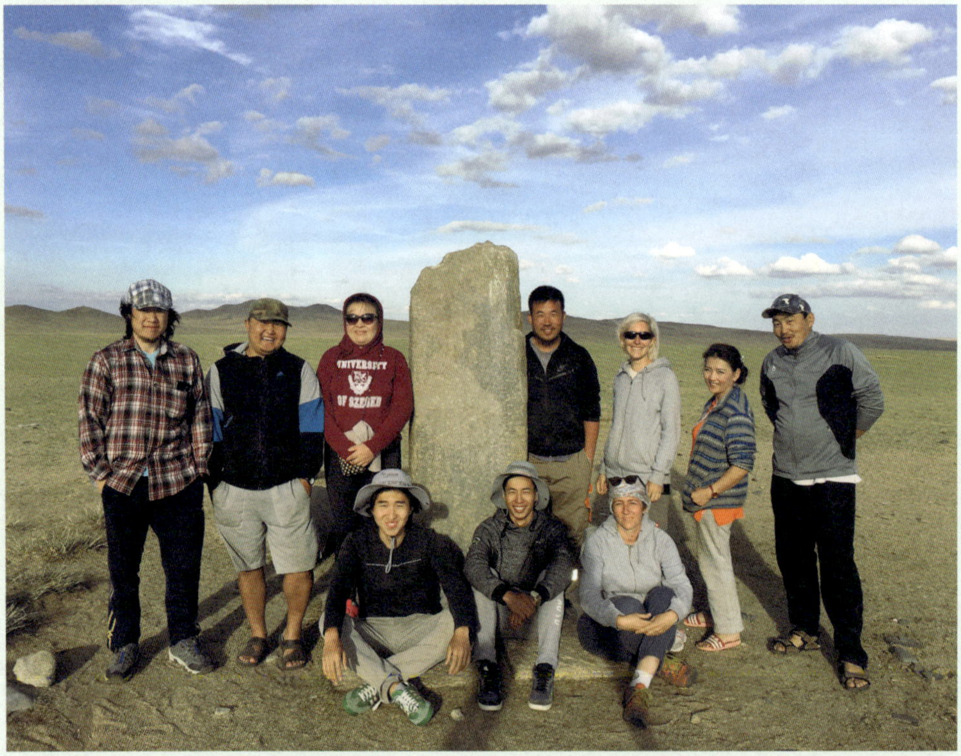

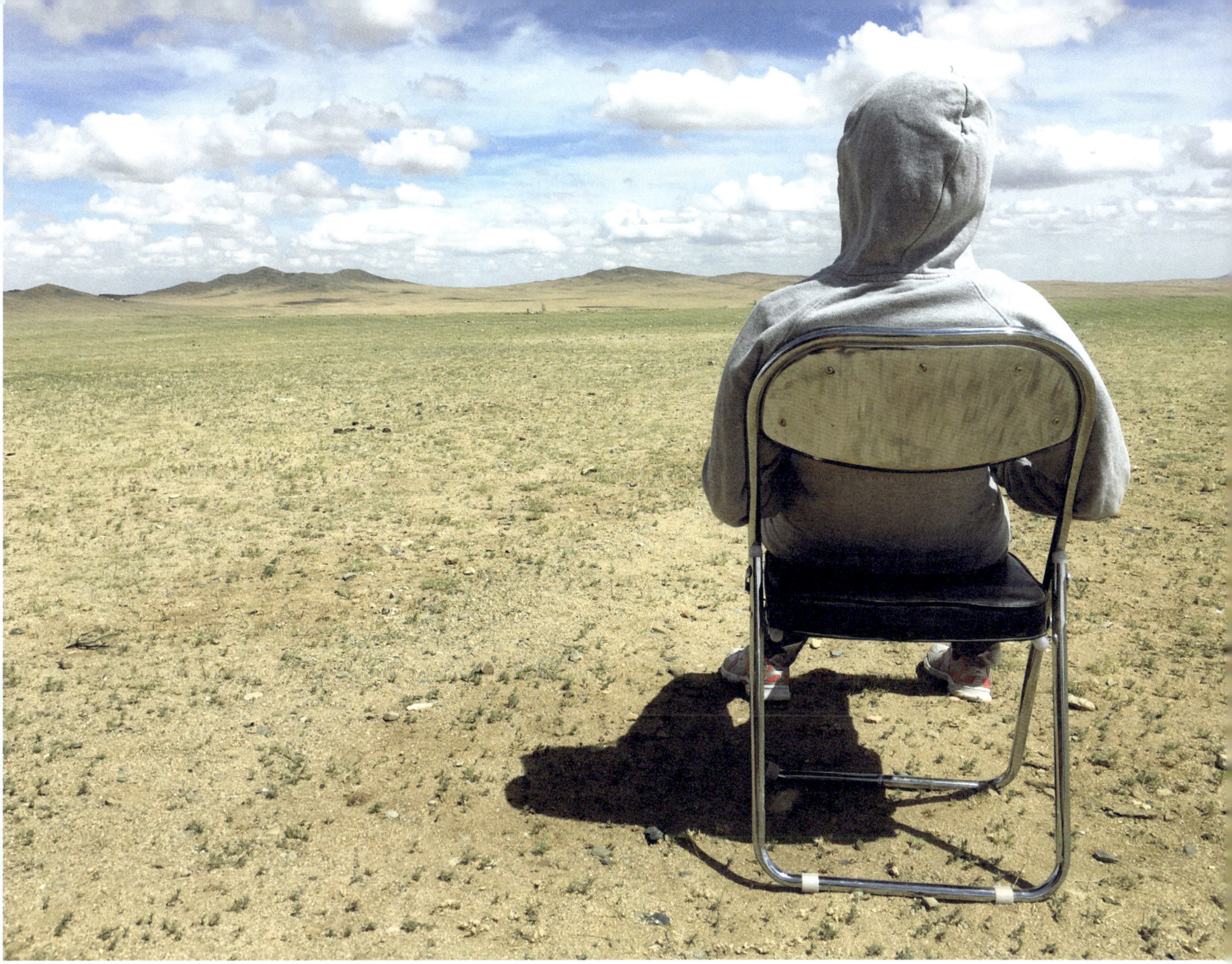

Fig. 28: A final gaze into the distance, enjoying the silence a last time – Mongolia we will miss you

Fig. 26: The yurt camp is dismantled

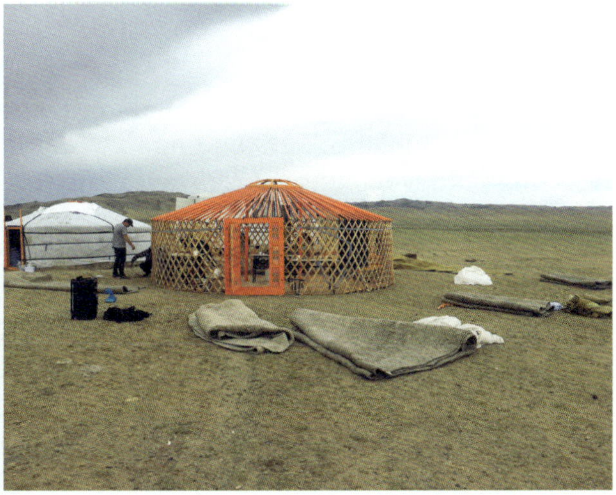

Marija: Last day on site: We finished everything we wanted to. We also thought about tasks for next year...we need to do some gluing on the peacock stone and think about how to get rid of the bird droppings. We have to do some research...

It is time to go...I am a bit sad. I enjoyed it here, more than I could have imagined. I like the silence, the emptiness and, last but not least, the lack of coverage. I enjoyed spending time with our colleagues and working with them. I hope I will come back and meet everybody again, drink a bit of vodka and learn some new knots. Until then: Goodbye Mongolia, hope you do well!!!

Experiences while Studying at the University of Applied Arts Vienna

GANZAM SUMBERRAZ

ULAANBAATAR, MONGOLIA
AUGUST 2018

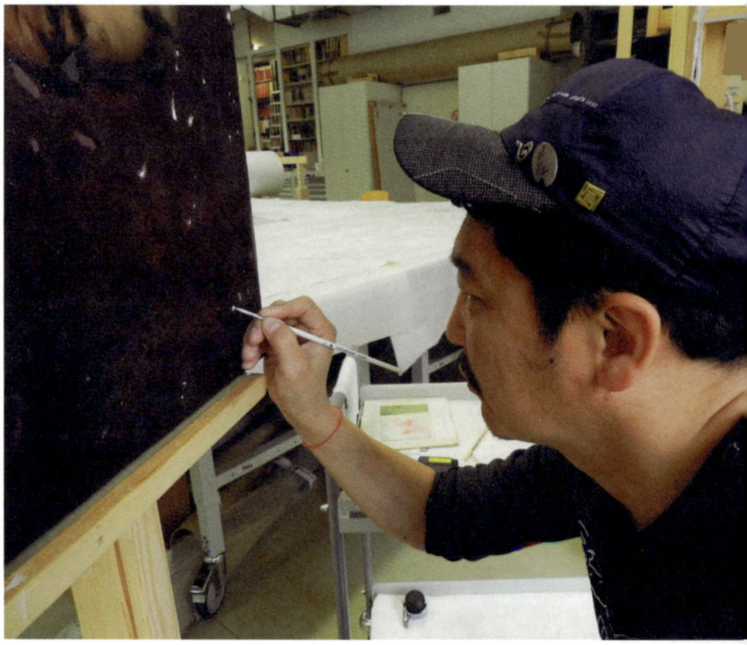

Fig. 4: Filling gaps in the paint layer with gesso

Mongolia has a very rich history and has many wonderful artworks, huge archaeological finds and a rich collection of treasures related to the past. The magnificent works of fine art and cultural heritage objects are not sufficiently preserved in Mongolia. There are cases where museums exhibit objects, damaged owing to inadequate treatment and poor storage conditions. Mongolia lacks professional specialists who define standards of conservation of works of fine art and historic objects. Besides, training environment and specialised instructors are not at hand. The Memorandum of Understanding between the Mongolian University of Culture and Arts, Eurasia-Pacific Uninet (EPU) and the University of Applied Arts Vienna has opened the gate to train specialised instructors to familiarise themselves with the conservation of fine art. In the framework of the collaboration, I was studying in the paintings department of the University's Institute of Conservation from 2 April 2017 to 7 July 2017.

I had several goals during the course of the study.

First, to get acquainted with the learning environment. It includes studying the curriculum and its special features, to familiarise myself with training equipment and work on it, and to study specialised literature.

Second, to explore the conservation at museums and galleries in Austria and visit conservation workshops.

Third, to study how to adapt the teaching methods in paintings and thangka conservation to practise in my country. In addition, to study Austria's art history and modern art development.

RESEARCH IN THE LEARNING ENVIRONMENT

The Institute of Conservation at the University of Applied Arts Vienna has four specialisations: paintings, stone, textiles and objects, and I have chosen the painting conservation workshop. With its years of history and experience, the Institute has a complete curriculum and provides a learning environment. All students have their own desks within the well-equipped workshop rooms, which are based on the requirements of the workshop's specialisation. The Institute provides training equipment and tools, and its safety is well-organised. A sufficient amount of various materials influences the quality of training. Conservation may cause larger amounts of dirt or require hazardous chemicals, so the students are well-equipped with safety equipment such as fume exhausters at each studio desk, protective masks, gloves and goggles.

The Institute has a small specialised library that consists of specialised literature and students' theses. It is placed adjacent to the paintings workshop, which makes the working environment more convenient.

The training process is based on art-training principles, where there is a focus on practical work in a workshop. The relationship between instructor and student is based on open discussion. There is a number of things that I observed, which I want to include in my future training methods:

The instructor does not answer the questions directly. If problems or questions occur, instructors and students discuss them and consider different approaches, before a solution is formulated. Students are encouraged to report on their work and discuss it. Instead of communicating in a strict way, the instructors give students the opportunity to think openly and give their advice as suggestions. Academic hours are used effectively and well.

Once a year, students and instructors attend an excursion where they visit museums, historical sites or conservation facilities in a certain city or area. The sites are presented by professionals. During the trip students give presentations and there are professional discussions between students and instructors.

On the trip, I visited Melk Abbey, which is registered as a World Historical Heritage Site in the Wachau area. Besides, I saw many churches and historical sites, and how Austria preserves its historical heritage. During my training period, two students graduated from the paintings department. Their research was carefully analysed from all possible points of views.

RESEARCH METHODS

I studied at the Institute of Conservation under the supervision of Gabriela Krist and assistant Caroline Ocks. During my studies, I mainly focused on the preservation, protection and conservation of two oil paintings – a portrait of *Gräfin Kufstein* from 1749 (Fig. 1) and a male portrait from 1970 – and a thangka depicting the god Namsrai. My studies started with the portrait of *Gräfin Kufstein*, its research (Fig. 2), condition assessment and development of a concept for conservation. The practical work focused on consolidation (Fig. 3) filling of gaps in the paint layer and retouching them. These measures I also carried out on the male portrait (Fig. 4). Additionally, I studied surface cleaning and the consolidation of paint layers.

At the end of the training, I focused on the conservation of the thangka that I had brought from my home country. After a condition assessment, I consolidated the paint layer, removed dust and dirt, and treated water stains with Gore-Tex® compresses. Gaps in the paint layer were filled and retouched. During my stay, I did various experiments on a variety of organic materials as regards how to use them. In the end, I also had the possibility to do a thangka-painting workshop for the students of the Institute (Fig. 5) and to instruct them in the basic techniques.

I have also attended the International Summer School that was organised by the Institute of Conservation and took place from 11-24 of July 2017. Participants came from China, India, Ukraine, Belarus and Mongolia. The goal of the course was to briefly describe the essence of the Vienna conservation of art and cultural assets, to present the training at the Institute and exchange experiences with other countries.

Austria is located in central Europe and its tourism and industry are highly developed. It was impressive to see how the historical and cultural heritage was conserved and made an economic value. In Vienna, I have visited a number of museums, such as Albertina, MUMOK, Leopold Museum, Belvedere Museum and 21er Haus, Schönbrunn Palace, the Kunsthistorisches Museum and the Natural History Museum Vienna. I also had an opportunity to travel to Berlin and visit the Alte Nationalgalerie, Archäologisches Zentrum, the Bode-Museum and historical sites.

Even though I have tried to study as much as I can, there is so much left to learn. Based on the knowledge I obtained, I have been developing courses on the technology of conservation and painting conservation courses. Different countries have developed and implemented different conservation methods and technologies. While Asian countries such as Japan, China and Korea have agreed on "direct" conservation with traditional methods, European countries are trying to protect and preserve as much original substance as possible. Thus, our country, Mongolia, needs to develop and implement its own technology in the near future and furthermore develop a training for future conservators

Fig. 3: Preparing cross-sections of paint layer samples in the chemistry laboratory

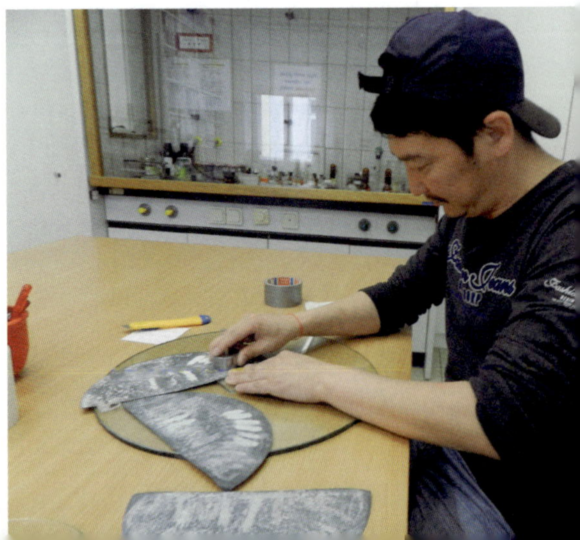

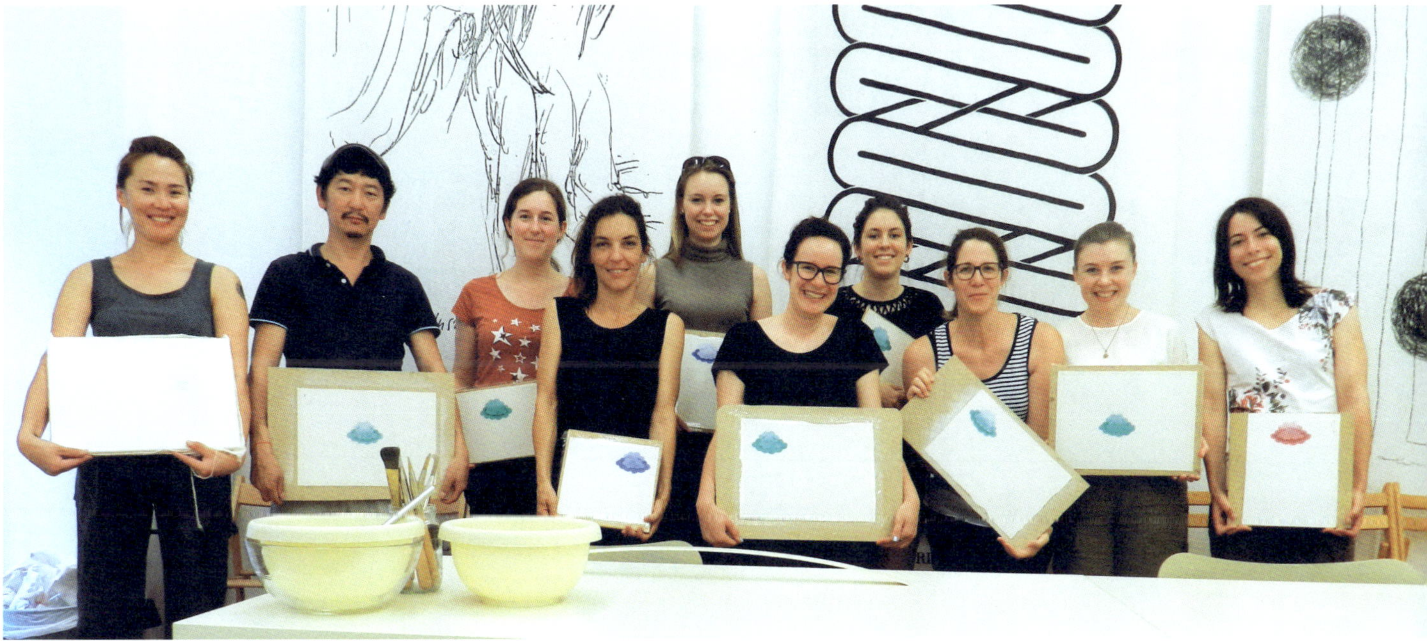

Fig. 5: Thangka workshop at the Institute of Conservation

Fig. 2: Consolidation of paint layer on the vacuum table

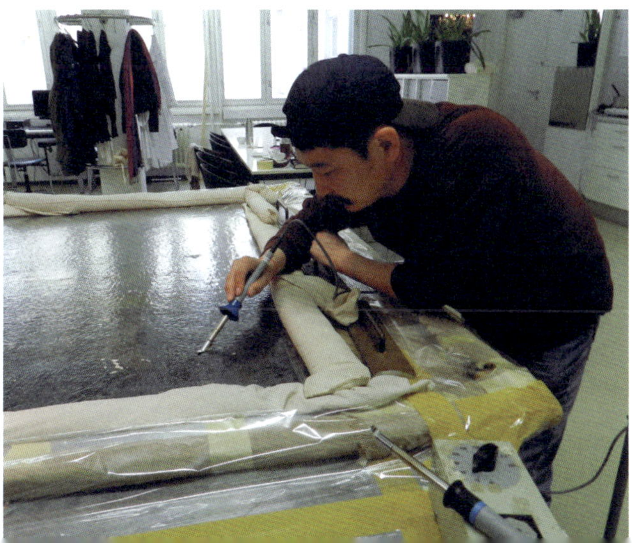

Fig. 1: With a fellow intern in the paintings workshop

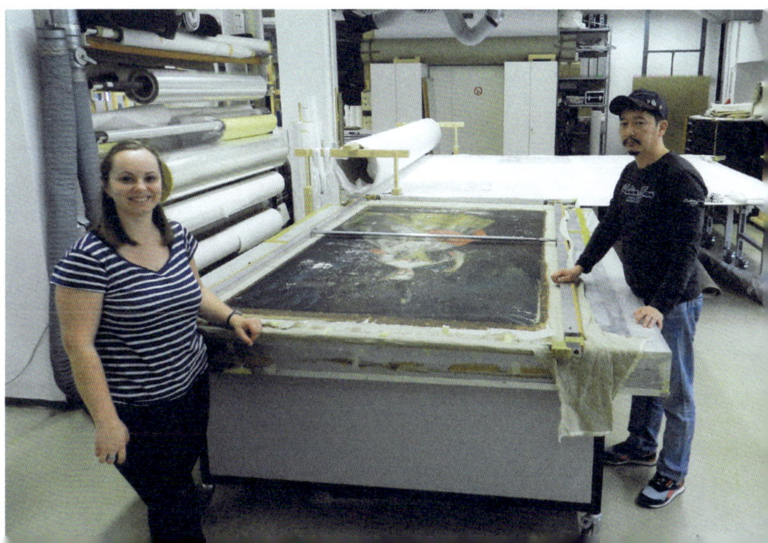

The Conservation and Re-Display of Metal Equestrian Armour

KHOSBAYAR NARANKHUU

from Bayan-Ulgii, Mongolia

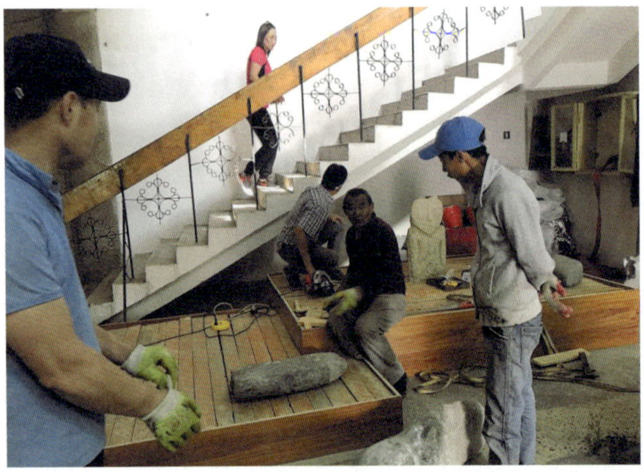

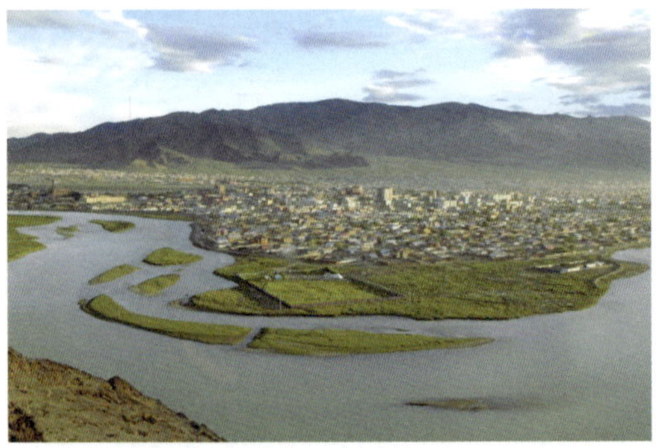

top: Fig. 1: Ulgii town after the flood
left: Fig. 6: Installation of sculptures in the entrance hall

INTRODUCTION

I had a great opportunity to attend a short-term training session at the Institute for Conservation at the University of Applied Arts Vienna in the winter term of 2016. Gabriela Krist, head of the Institute, had already started her collaboration with various institutions in Mongolia such as the National Center for Cultural Heritage, the University of Arts and Culture of Mongolia, and the Bogd Khaan Palace Museum in 2013. Since then, several workshops, seminars and scholarships were organized both in Mongolia and Austria. Ganzam Sumberraz and Chinbat Magsar, lecturers from the School of Fine Art and Design of the University of Arts and Culture of Mongolia were hosted by the Institute of Conservation with the Ernst-Mach Scholarship of the Austrian Exchange Service (OeAD) in 2016 and 2017. I hope for continued collaboration between the Institute of Conservation and Mongolian institutions, because the Institute's expertise and support are needed in Mongolia. My stay at the Institute allowed me to gain insights in conservation of different materials and objects. Back in Mongolia, I had the chance to work on the conservation of metal armour at the Bayan-Ulgii provincial museum in West Mongolia and apply the knowledge I got from my studies in Austria.

THE BAYAN-ULGII PROVINCE

Bayan-Ulgii is the westernmost province of Mongolia, 1700 kilometres from Ulaanbaatar, the capital city of Mongolia. It is located in the mountainous region of the Altai Mountains and the highest peak, the Khüiten Peak (4,374 m) in the Altai Tavan Bogd massif. The region is arid and dusty with a severe lack of precipitation. The climate is harsh, ranging from -40°C in winter to +35°C in summer. A couple of days after we arrived in Ulgii town, the capital of the province, there was heavy rain and a disastrous flood. The flood destroyed the homes of over 500 households and affected a total of 2,500 people (Fig. 2).

The population of the Bayan-Ulgii province counts 101,591 people, 80% of it being Kazakhs and only 20% Mongolians. Although the main economic resource is livestock husbandry, Bayan-Ulgii is in a good position for trade since its borders touch on both China and Russia. After the 1990 Democratic Revolution, almost half of the residents migrated to Kazakhstan, but many returned later. This is a province with a speciality for having many inhabitants and ethnic minorities.

THE BAYAN-ULGII PROVINCIAL MUSEUM

Bayan-Ulgii was established as an *aimag* (province), or an administrative unit of the People's Republic of Mongolia separate from Khovd province, by a decision of then-leader of the country, Marshall Choibalsan Khorloo, in 1940. In 1948 the provincial museum was founded as a cabinet for regional studies. By Resolution No. 461 of the Ministers' Council of the People's Republic of Mongolia, this cabinet was expanded into a provincial museum in 1962.

In the beginning, an official from the local administration was responsible for the museum collection. Some artefacts and objects kept in a destroyed mosque became the basis of the museum collection. The current three-storeyed museum building (Fig. 4) was built by a public *subbotnik* (a voluntary weekend campaign during the Soviet period) as part of the socialist development of the capital in the early 1960s. Local political party leaders such as Kh. Musakhan and M. Khurmankhan worked actively and organised raw bricks from the ruin of the Sagsai monastery in the Sagsai sum (district) of Bayan-Ulgii province.

The museums' exhibition halls are divided into three departments: nature, history and ethnography, which were a so-to-speak standard for provincial museums of the socialist state. The design of the museum exhibition and display was most recently changed in the late 1980s. Currently, the museum has 5,258 artefacts and objects and, with the support of local inhabitants during the last four years, has enriched its collection with a total of 300 objects. However, we were told that numerous objects and cultural monuments are being destroyed or sold to foreigners, because the museum does not have subsidies for acquisitions.

top row: Fig. 2: The Bayan-Ulgii museum building
Fig. 3: Our team
middle row: Fig. 4: Department of History of the Bayan-Uglii provincial museum
Fig. 5: Installation of sculptures in the entrance hall
bottom row: Fig. 8: The armour before conservation
Fig. 9: Detail of the armour before conservation

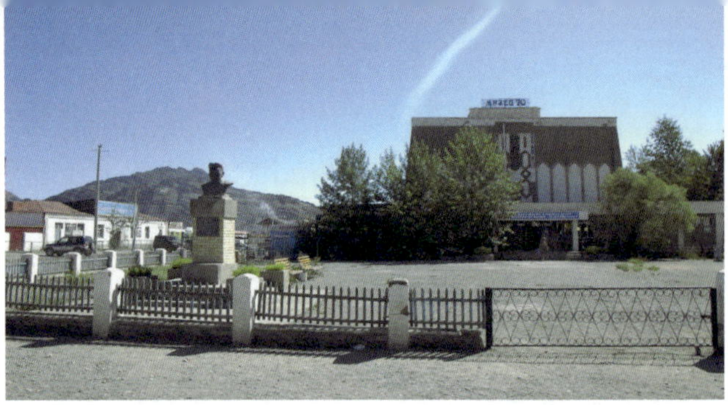

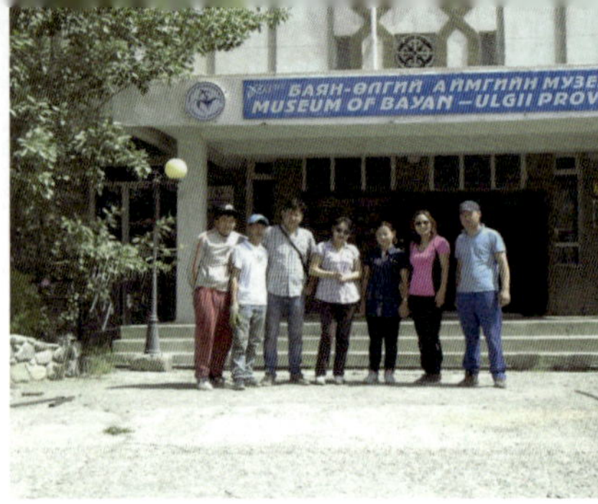

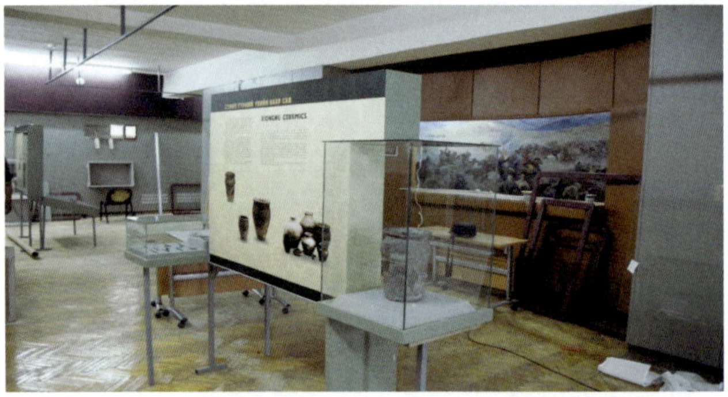

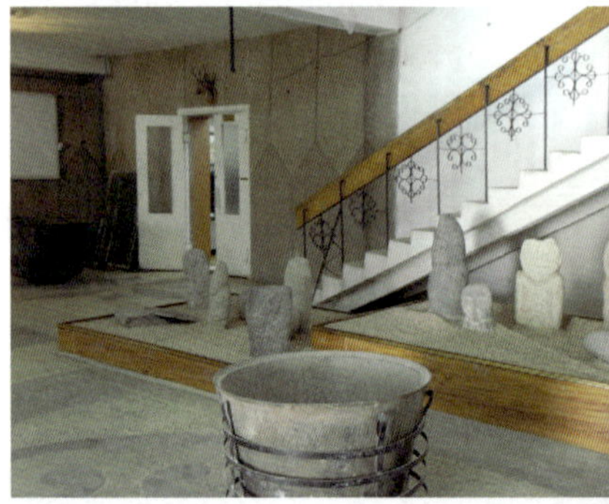

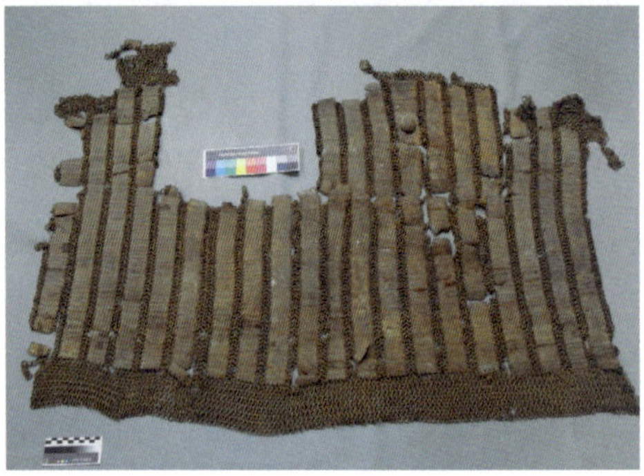

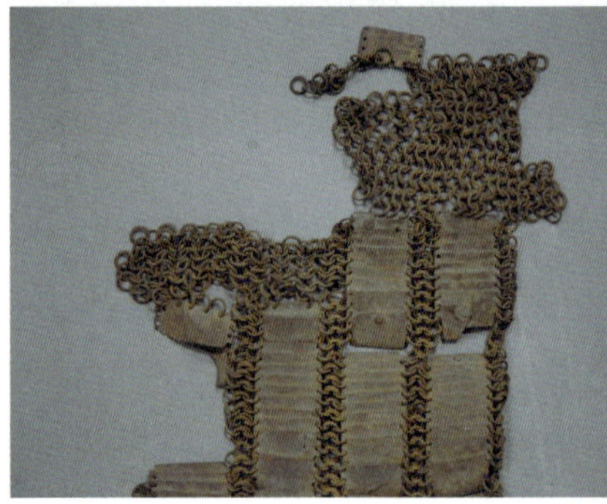

OUR CAMPAIGN

From 4 July - 5 August, 2018, I, together with Munkhtogoo and Erdmaa, curators from the National Museum of Mongolia, visited the Bayan-Ulgii provincial museum (Fig. 5). The aim of our visit was to re-design the exhibition and display of the museum, because it is the 70th anniversary of the museum this year. Our task was to re-design the Department of History and the entrance hall of the museum and to produce ten glass showcases of different sizes (Fig. 6). In the entrance hall we set up an arrangement of stone sculptures that had been kept outside the museum building (Fig. 7-8). Some of the sculptures were damaged and had to be conserved.

During our renovation work at the museum, we found one object of the Department of History very fascinating: a set of equestrian armour that had been kept in the museum since the late 1950s, exhibited in a 120 cm-long wooden-framed display cabinet (Fig. 9).

THE EQUESTRIAN ARMOUR

The armour (Fig. 10-11) is 115 by 75 centimetres and weighs 82 kilograms. Owing to its size and weight, researchers found it must have been for a horse. In Mongol it is called "tushimt garkhin khuyag", which translates to "armour of metal plates and chain mail". This type of armour was commonly used from the 15th to the 18th century in the vast territory from Central Asia to Turkey. However, the precise date of this equestrian armour could not be identified. In the museum registration list, it was recorded that Utnuu, an inhabitant of the Buyant *sum* of Bayan-Ulgii province, presented the equestrian armour to the museum in 1959. We were

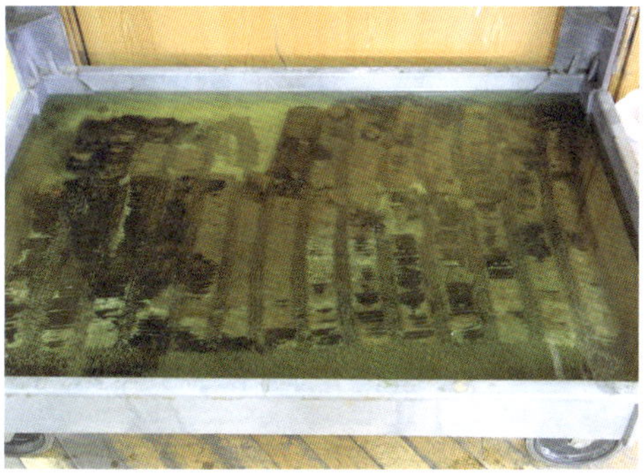
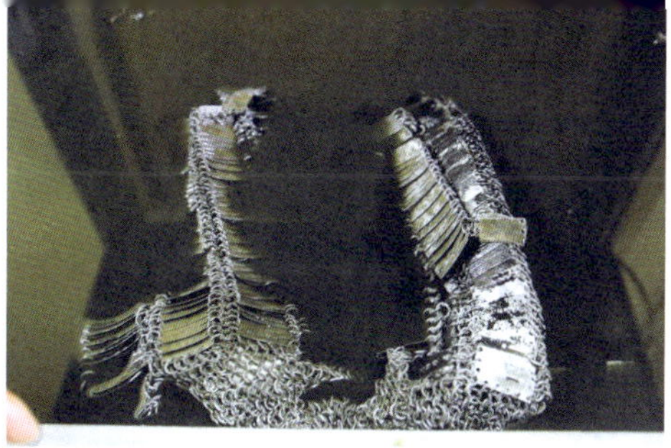
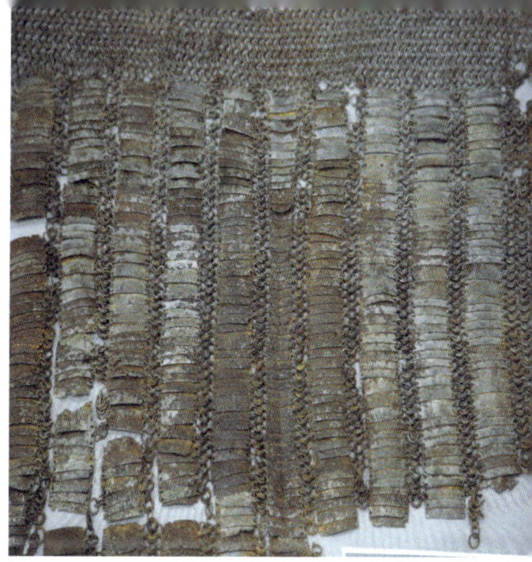
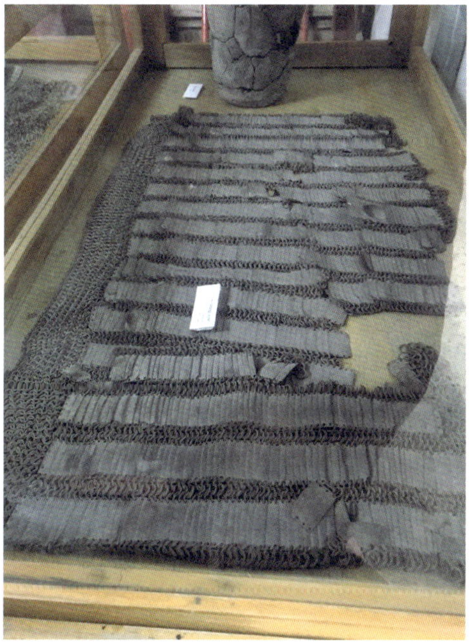
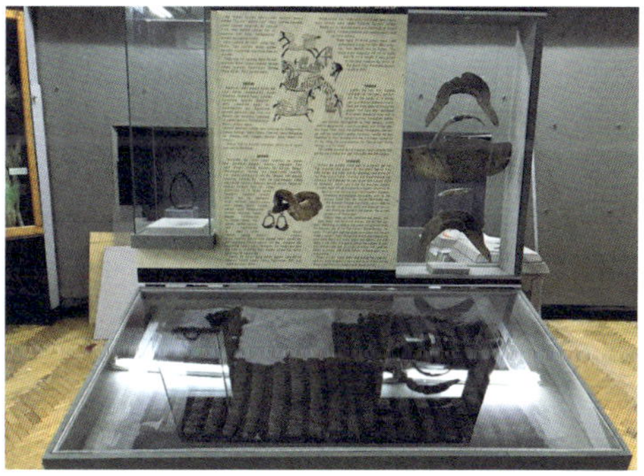
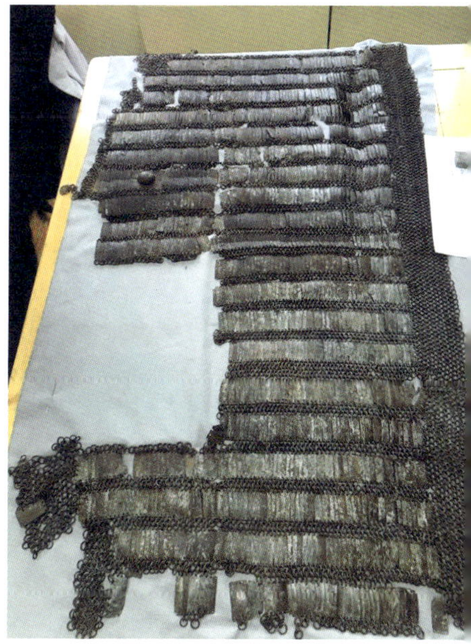

top row: Fig. 10: Water and lemon acid bath
Fig. 11: During the water and lemon acid bath
Fig. 12: Detail of the armour in between two water and lemon acid baths
bottom row: Fig. 7: The equestrian armour in the old glass cabinet before consolidation and conservation
Fig. 14: The armour on display
Fig. 13: The armour after conservation

fascinated by the armour and decided to conserve and re-display it in a new glass cabinet. In order to do the former, I took the armour and two other objects from the museum to the National Center for Cultural Heritage in Ulaanbaatar. The National Center, established in 1988, is the main institution for conservation in Mongolia. The conservation was carried out by a conservator from the Center, N. Bat-Erdene, whom I assisted.

CONSERVATION OF THE EQUESTRIAN ARMOUR

The armour was covered with thick layers of dust and severely affected by corrosion (Fig. 10-11). Some parts of the armour were broken and others were missing. We decided to re-connect departed parts and to perform both dry and wet cleaning and give it corrosion treatment. A total of 116 metal plates and chain parts could be reconnected. Afterwards, the surface was cleaned with a soft brush and a vacuum cleaner. However, layers of dirt, smoke residue and coal-black remained on the surface. Therefore we put the armour in a bath of a 10-percent solution of lemon acid in water for 24 hours (Fig.12) and afterwards rubbed it with a brush. This process was repeated four times (Fig. 13-14). The corrosion was treated with pure spirit and water. After cleaning, the armour was polished with a soft sponge and a suede cloth to dry it.

In order to prevent the conserved armour from friction, cracks and detachments during transport, we packed it up with thick layers of a suitable cloth (Fig. 15). Thus the armour and the other museum objects were brought back to Bayan-Ulgii. We made new glass cabinets for the objects and displayed them together (Fig. 16).

Myanmar Thailand

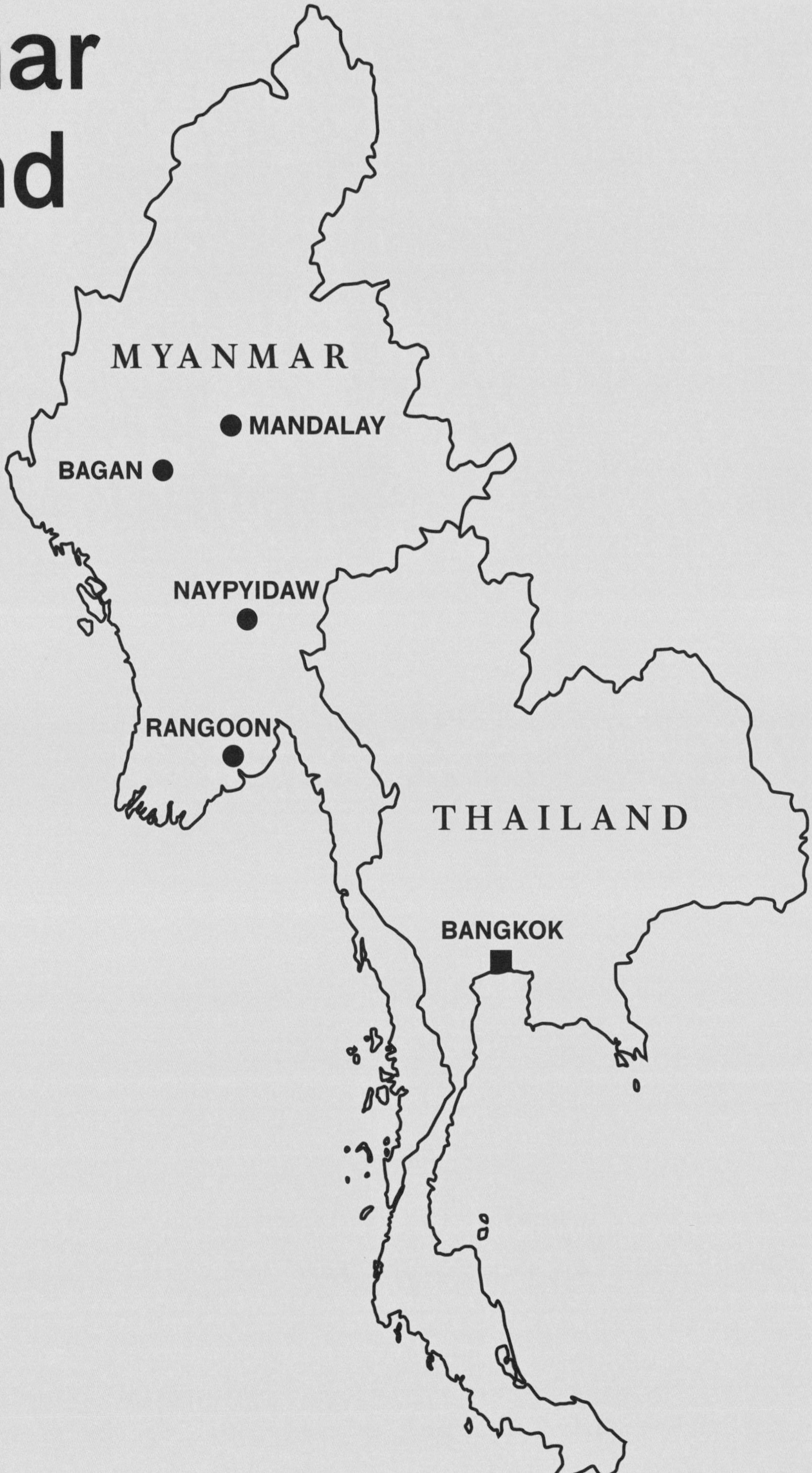

Burmese Travel Diary

GABRIELA
KRIST

FEBRUARY
2017

On Orwell's Trail and the Quest for the DG…

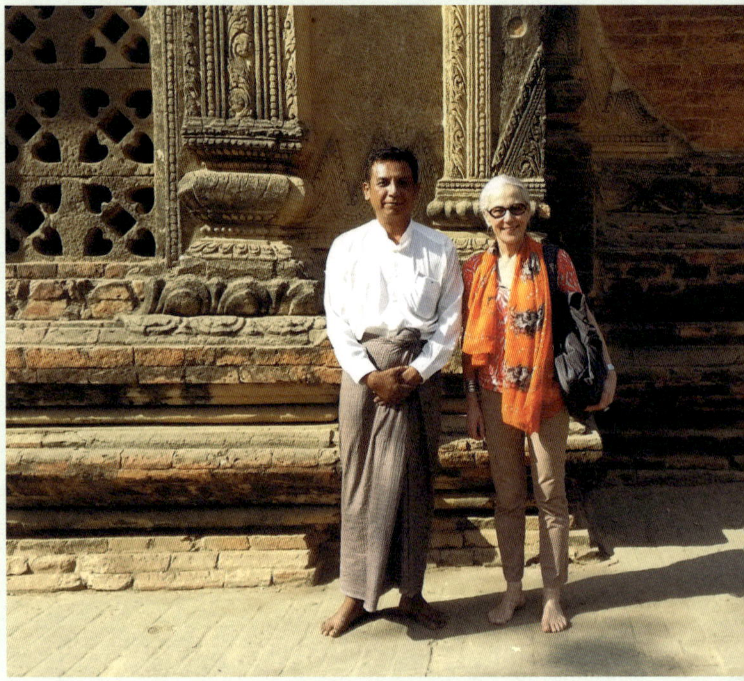

Fig. 21: Visit at Nanpaya Temple in Bagan

BACKGROUND HISTORY

At the request of the Austrian Embassy in Bangkok, which is also responsible for Myanmar, I accompanied the ambassador, Enno Drofenik, to Mandalay, Myanmar (Fig.1), for the first time in February 2015 to sound out a possibility of cooperation in the field of conservation. The Burmese Ministry of Culture, Department of Archaeology, proposed several monuments as possible projects that were in dire need of urgent conservation work; but, sadly, an appropriate partner for cooperation could not be found in Mandalay in 2015.

The fact-finding mission in 2015 was not really successful, so the Austrian Embassy in Bangkok endeavoured to sound out further contacts in Myanmar for possible conservation projects. Dates for talks with THE DG – the most important man in the country with regard to the conservation of cultural assets – were planned for February 2017. We arranged to meet him on 14 February in Nay Pyi Taw (Naypyidaw), the new capital of Myanmar. We bought flight tickets; at the DG's request I was to view Yangon (Rangoon) as well and above all Bagan in order to inspect possible projects.

Two days before my departure I received a mail from Mie Mie Khaing, the DG's assistant. The meeting planned for 14 February in Nay Pyi Taw had to be postponed. It was arranged for me to go the Archaeological Museum in Bagan. An important UNESCO meeting...So once more the trek to the travel agency: an attempt to change flights failed (much too expensive!) so I decided to keep mainly to my originally planned travel route; I only had to slot in an additional trip by car from Nay Pyi Taw to Bagan in order to meet the DG for the new date set in Bagan.

From Vienna to Bangkok on 11 February no problem; the embassy booked me a good hotel. I could look out over Bangkok from my room on the nineteenth floor, sunset, a riot of pink and red! The city has changed incredibly in recent years; it has truly become the centre of Southeast Asia!

On 13 February Enno picks me up at the hotel. We have quite a few appointments ahead of us. First of all a meeting with Ananda Chuchota, Fine Arts Department, Ministry of Culture. The Director greeted us with a friendly smile. We're in the Land of Smiles...

In Thailand there's a great need for conservators, but we're told that at present there are problems with the existing study courses. Conservation work is done by artists and craftsmen. An appropriate curriculum is being discussed at ministerial level, but there's not much clarity as to how this will be organised. The search is on for counselling and cooperation partners. Austria might be able to help here?!

Subsequently, we are scheduled to meet representatives of Silpakorn University.

Silpakorn is the leading university in Thailand, not only for the arts, and an ASEA-member as the University of Applied Arts Vienna. It offers a course of study in conservation, but this is trailing off since there are not enough candidates applying for it. The University of Applied Arts could give advice on setting up a new curriculum and help to raise standards in conservation!

Now we're invited to lunch in the university canteen, used by students of hospitality and catering as an opportunity for training. Here I met, for the first time, Prof. Sompid Kattiyapikul, Dean of the Silpakorn International College and Paramaporn Sirikulchayanout, Director of the Art Centre of Silpakorn University (Fig. 2). I had no idea what consequences this meeting had and what followed...all my thoughts focused on Myanmar, no plans for Thailand at this moment.

Now I have to say farewell to Enno. He's flying to Laos tomorrow, while I leave for Nay Pyi Taw and then on to Bagan to meet the DG.

On 14 February from Bangkok to Nay Pyi Taw. Pick up dollars at the airport, because there are certain things in Myanmar you can only buy with American currency. You never know!

I land in the early evening at the new airport of the new capital. A large and wonderful building, super clean, adorned with gigantic Burmese mosaics telling the history of the country (Fig. 3). I am much impressed. The airport is empty, totally died-out (Fig. 4). After customs checks I waited for my taxi, ordered by the Austrian Embassy. I'm alone in the huge, empty arrivals hall. Another person approaches me, a man, who is also waiting for his chauffeur. We wait together and exchange visiting cards. As we say good-bye, the German gentleman remarks you never know in this city, contacts might be useful?!

At last my chauffeur turns up. An hour late, Ommmm. Dressed in a chequered longyi, the traditional Burmese "trousers" – I like the green-and-blue checks most – and the compulsory plastic flip-flops. The best are made in Mandalay, I must buy some. They are velvety, have a rubber sole and are super comfortable. With me, they'll be in the best of hands...

Off we go in the XXL-sized black limousine to the hotel. It's dark, I try to orient myself on the landscape; but we're in the capital, no hope. We're alone on the four-lane motorway lined with oleander-type bushes. Alone, not a soul near or far. The drive in the dark lasts forty minutes until we get to the hotel. Is the driver really taking me to the hotel???? A gigantic new box in a freshly laid-out park, totally overstyled, and utterly deserted as well. My chauffeur briefs me, they only have new hotels here, mushrooming out of the ground for the new capital city. I'm quite curious as to what Nay Pyi Taw will be like tomorrow morning.

The car bringing me to Bagan is booked at 7.30 on 15 February. Five hours' drive apparently, maybe 8 hours? I'm looking forward to the landscape and golden pagodas and an English-speaking chauffeur in a chequered longyi!

It's raining this morning. I'm alone in the dining room, it's huge and very modern in design, very tasteful, with Burmese arts and crafts, huge old copper vessels and of course pagoda-like lacquered artefacts. There's toast and a whole plethora of warm dishes. Far too much, far too many staff. I soon finish my breakfast and pay – thank goodness, my visa card works! We set off. It's raining cats and dogs. Once again we are utterly alone on the four-lane highways. The chauffeur has to get petrol. Then we take THE motorway to Mandalay and Bagan. A new motorway, says the chauffeur, we're proud of it! Whizzing past fruit plantations as ox carts and goat herds wander along the hard shoulder (Fig. 5-6). We overtake them all, animals and people, but not a car in sight. Alone on the brand-new motorway for three hours. Then the motorway suddenly stops and the country highway starts. We pass villages and drive through an incredibly beautiful landscape, golden pagodas appear at regular intervals and all at once belong to the past again (Fig. 7-8). This country is beautiful, incredibly beautiful and original.

We get to Bagan around noon. A town? A village with dusty dirt roads, people walk everywhere or ride bikes. Women protect their skin, primarily their faces, against the sun with a clay paste applied to cheeks, chin and forehead. The miracle agent is called *thanaka*. Children wear this protection against the sun as well (Fig. 9-10). Where's the hotel? In New Bagan, says the chauffeur, he knows it. We turn into a side street and at the end of it we can already see the guesthouse...with an indescribably lovely view of the archaeological park with its countless temples and pagodas. I have never seen anything as fantastic in my life (Fig. 11-13).

The hotel is simple, the room OK, but the terrace, which also serves as dining room, looks onto an incredible view. As though out of nothing, the pagodas rise up from the lush, green deciduous forest, one more beautiful than the next, but many are damaged...In the early morning I must wait here for the hot-air balloons, I'll book a balloon trip the next time (Fig. 14).

I have to go on to the Archaeological Museum, the DG is expecting me.

So who is the DG? What does he look like? The Director General, Department of Archaeology and National Museum, Ministry of Religious Affairs and Culture, Mr Kyaw Oo Lwin, and the UNESCO Bangkok Office have extended invitations to the international conference "Proposed Programme of Bagan Monuments, Post-Earthquake Restoration and Preservation", taking place from 15-16 February in the museum (Fig. 15). I'm also invited.

On 25 August 2016 an earthquake measuring 6.8 on the Richter Scale shook Bagan and its archaeological park with its more than 3000 pagodas and temples dating from the 8th to the 13th centuries; more than a hundred monuments were massively damaged, some completely destroyed. The UNESCO immediately convened an expert committee and commissioned it to draw up an initial review of the situation. These results will now be presented at the conference and discussed. The first protective measures have already been initiated, the affected objects examined and secured as an interim measure; a master plan is to be set up for the conservation work.

A Chinese research and conservation team from Xi'an has won for the analyses and conceptual plan for an important and severely damaged temple. China immediately made 100 million dollars available after the earthquake and is now topping up its support by another million dollars. India, the Archaeological Survey of India (ASI), too, was assigned a site for analysis and conservation.

The inspection of the archaeological park in Bagan is planned for the afternoon. Special guided tours provide an overview of the massive damage and insights into the current analyses and protective measures. We were very impressed by the safeguarding and stabilising actions carried out by the local population with bamboo. Scaffolded pagodas look as though they're veiled in lace (Fig. 16)! The

UNESCO Bangkok Office supervises the works on site, an application as World Heritage Site is in preparation.

The next day, 16 February, more lectures are held, all high standard. Myanmar was able to react more swiftly than Nepal, which was hit by a catastrophic earthquake in 2015, but that's another story. The Burmese joined in the discussion as well. They are in traditional dress with their spotless white shirts and discreet longyis; I really like their outfit, looks very elegant. And I can also put my name under what the Burmese say, so much sense in their remarks. I keep quiet and let the others talk.

At last, after lunch, I am permitted to meet the DG, a meeting I've had to wait for almost throughout these past two years; at last I see the Director, a man I've been pursuing all the way across Myanmar. Kyaw Oo Lwin is a man of my age, thin, straight-backed and polite. He receives me in a side room in the museum and apologises that our meeting had to be postponed so often, but emphasised he would very much like to work together with Austria. "What about the stone temple, the Nanpaya, one of our most important monuments. Do you think you can get it into shape again?" Stone is a scarce resource in Bagan, most buildings are of brick. The country here hasn't any conservators either, they are all archaeologists, who are reluctant about conservation, they much prefer digging, researching, doing their own job. And there's a great deal to do in the museums as well. The care and cultivation of collections is one topic. I'll be meeting Daw Baby later, the museum director; she'll explain the situation to me. It would be wonderful, stressed the DG, if work could soon be started on the building. There's the danger of subsidence and collapse. We shall get support, local artisans; there's also a guesthouse where we can stay (I make a mental note of checking this out first!); archaeologists – we should train them – would help us in conservation stocktaking and documentation, but also work with them hands on – make conservators out of them, that would be excellent! Earthquakes happen time and again and then everything has to start all over again...this is the way things are, karma! No other country is permeated by Buddhist ritual as much as Myanmar. This is where Buddhism is a living force, it's everywhere (Fig. 17–20). But back to the temple. The question hangs over us; do we think we can take this on? I say, I'll have to see. Then I take my leave of the DG with the obligatory offering of Mozart Kugeln – Austrian chocolate balls – they've survived the long journey and make their usual impression.

An archaeologist takes me to the Nanpaya (Fig. 21). An imposing sandstone building with incredibly fine stone-cutting work (Fig. 22). Earlier earthquakes have left their marks, but also brutal old repairs, massive iron constructions in the interior in order to stabilise the vaulting, planned by archaeologists, massive, made for all eternity. Cornices totally degraded, the stone decaying. The conservation of the temple a huge challenge! Particularly because this monument, owing to its quality and art-historical significance, is in the direct spotlight of local and international attention. It needs the whole works, everything we are capable of, from static reinforcement to stone consolidation. Can we make it? Nothing's impossible. We'll make it!

2018: A year passed and...we didn't make it! All the efforts of recent years! We failed in that it wasn't possible to secure the necessary support from the local bodies. But...and this is our success story...we managed to get in closer contact with Silpakorn University in Bangkok. From Myanmar to Thailand, at least this has been achieved! More to follow!

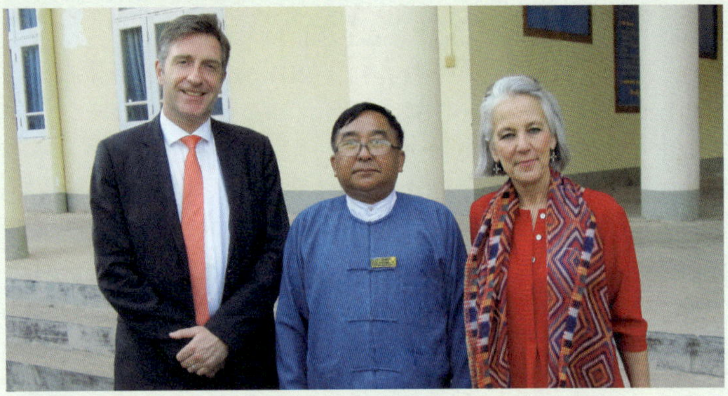

from top to bottom:
Fig. 1: With Enno Drofenik in Mandalay
Fig. 2: Meeting at Silpakorn University – Sompid Kattiyapikul (left) and Paramaporn Sirikulchayanout (right)
Fig. 3: Wall design in the Nay Pyi Taw International Airport
Fig. 4: Arrivals hall at Nay Pyi Taw International Airport

Fig. 9-10: Landscape and people in Bagan

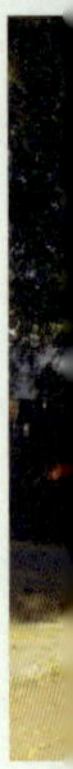

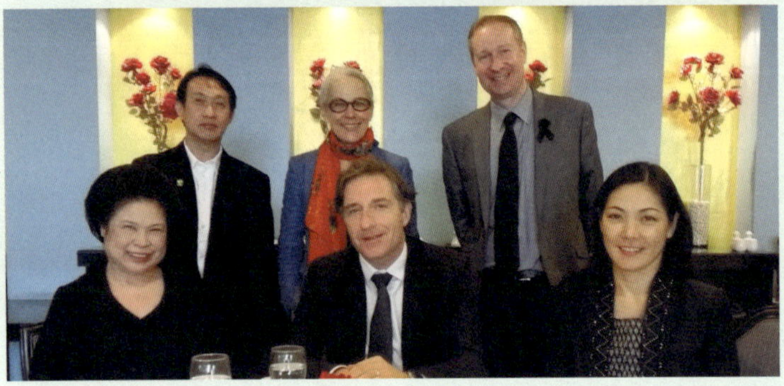

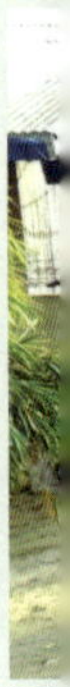

Fig. 5: Ox carts and cattle on the street to Bagan

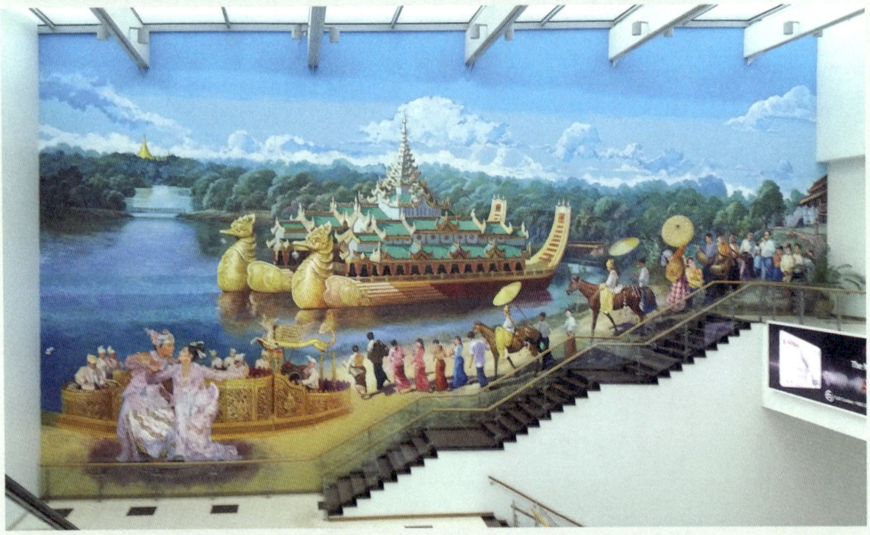

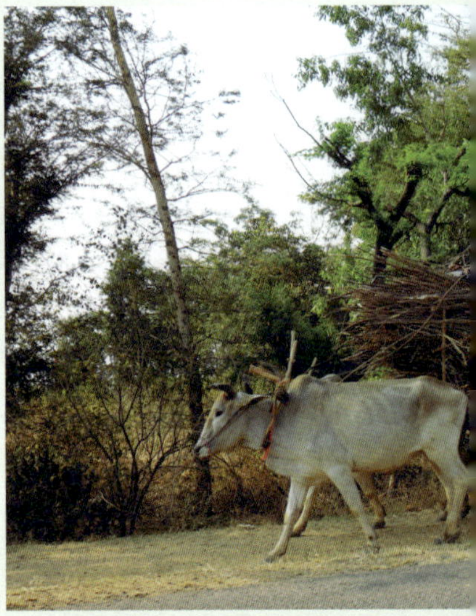

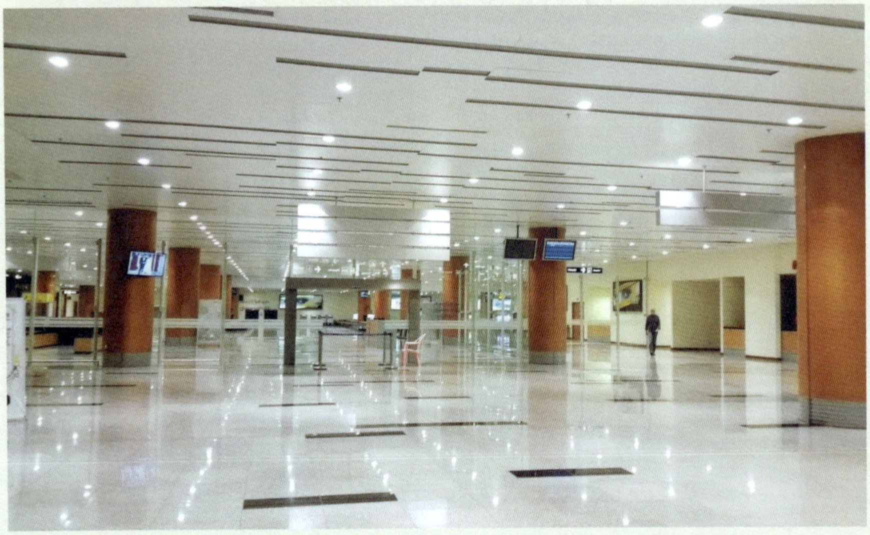

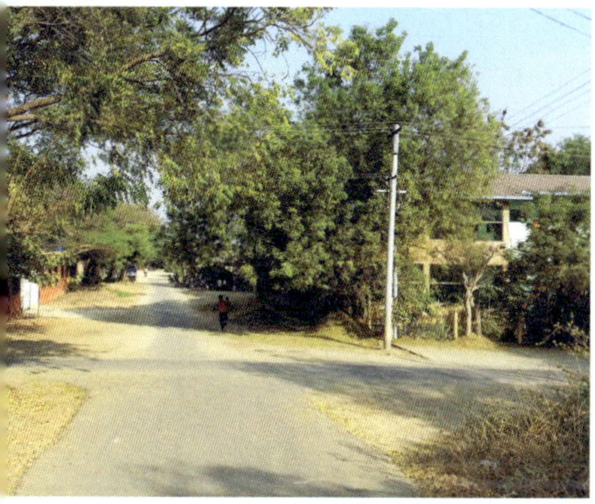

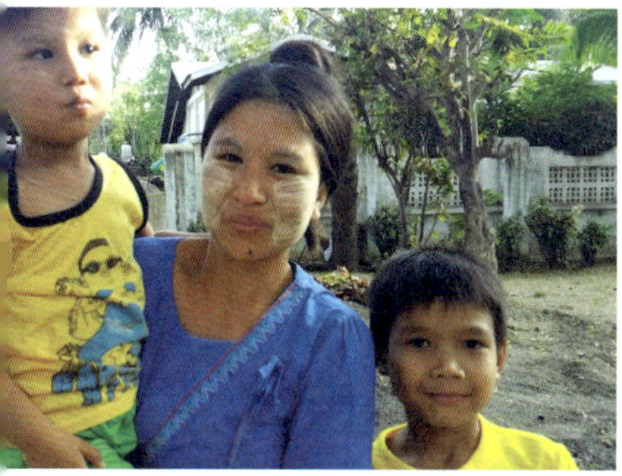

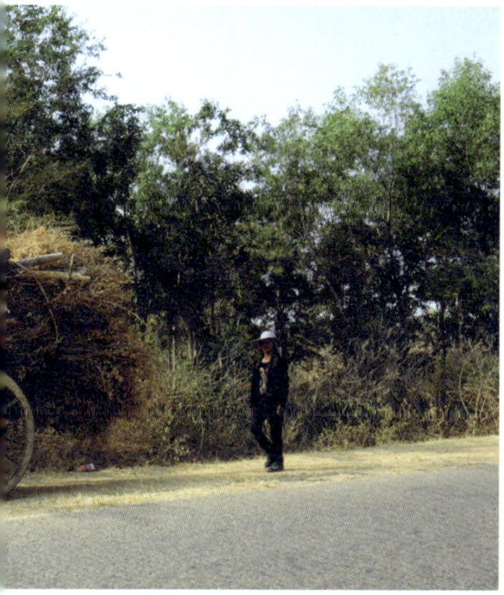

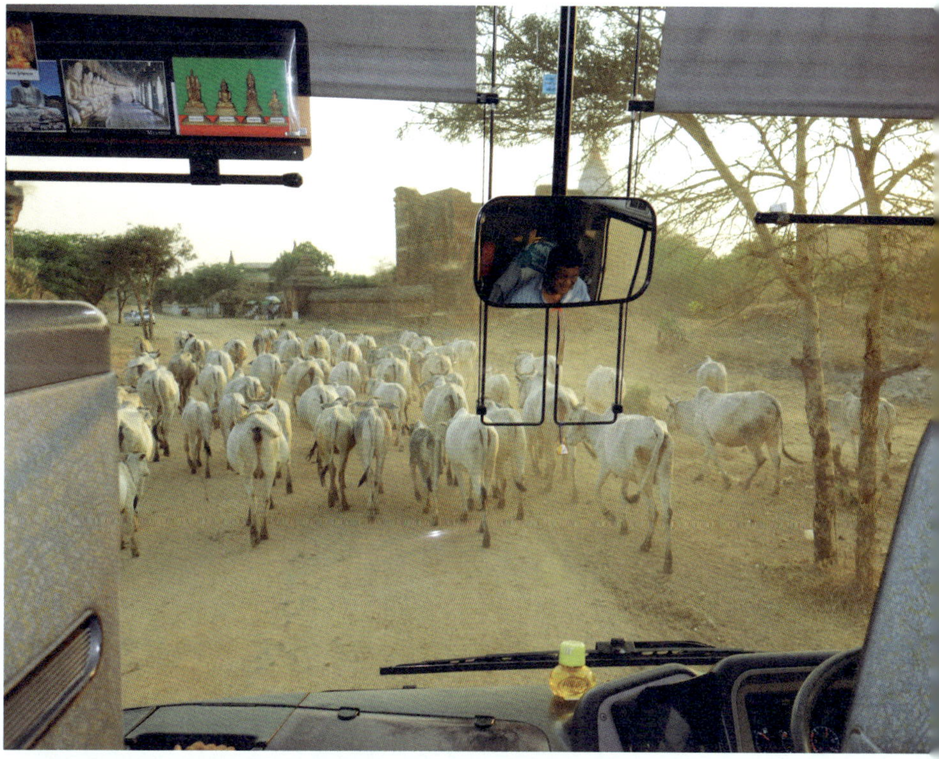

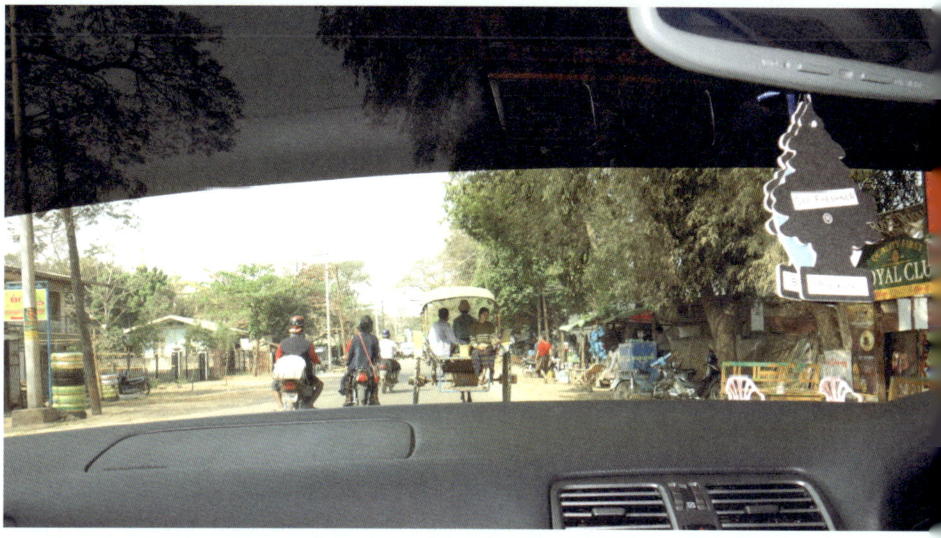

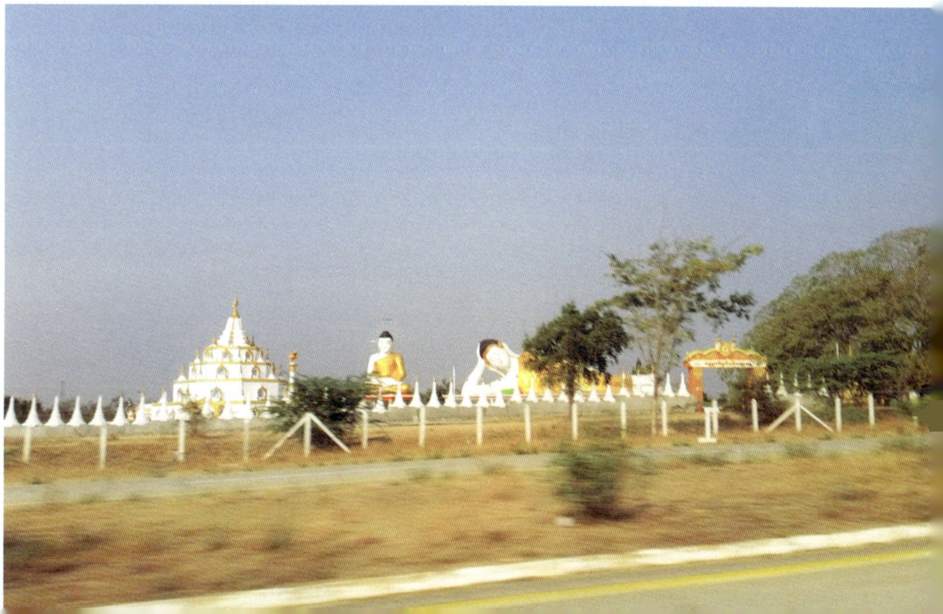

from top to bottom:
Fig. 6: Ox carts and cattle on the street to Bagan
Fig. 7-8: Passing by the street life and golden pagodas on the way to Bagan

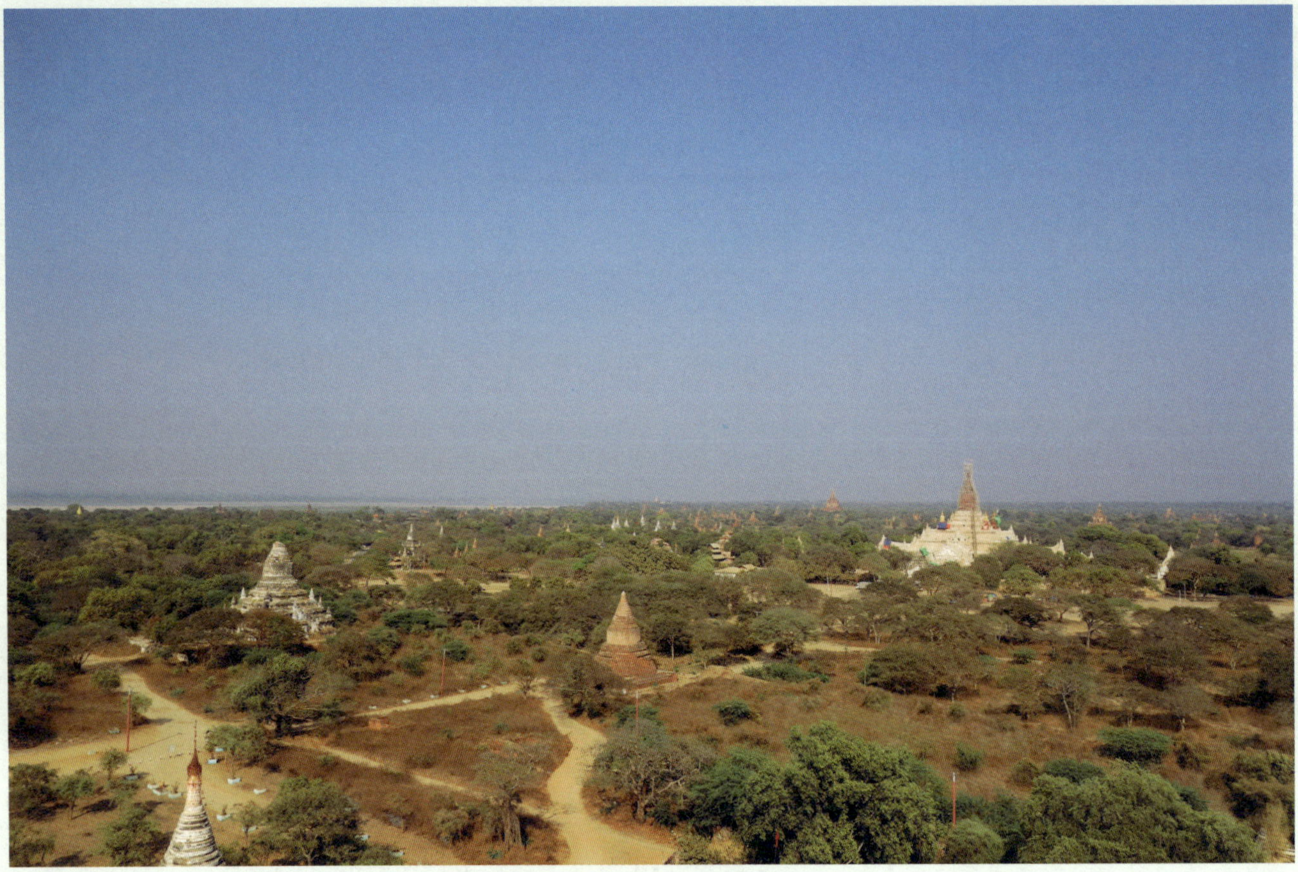

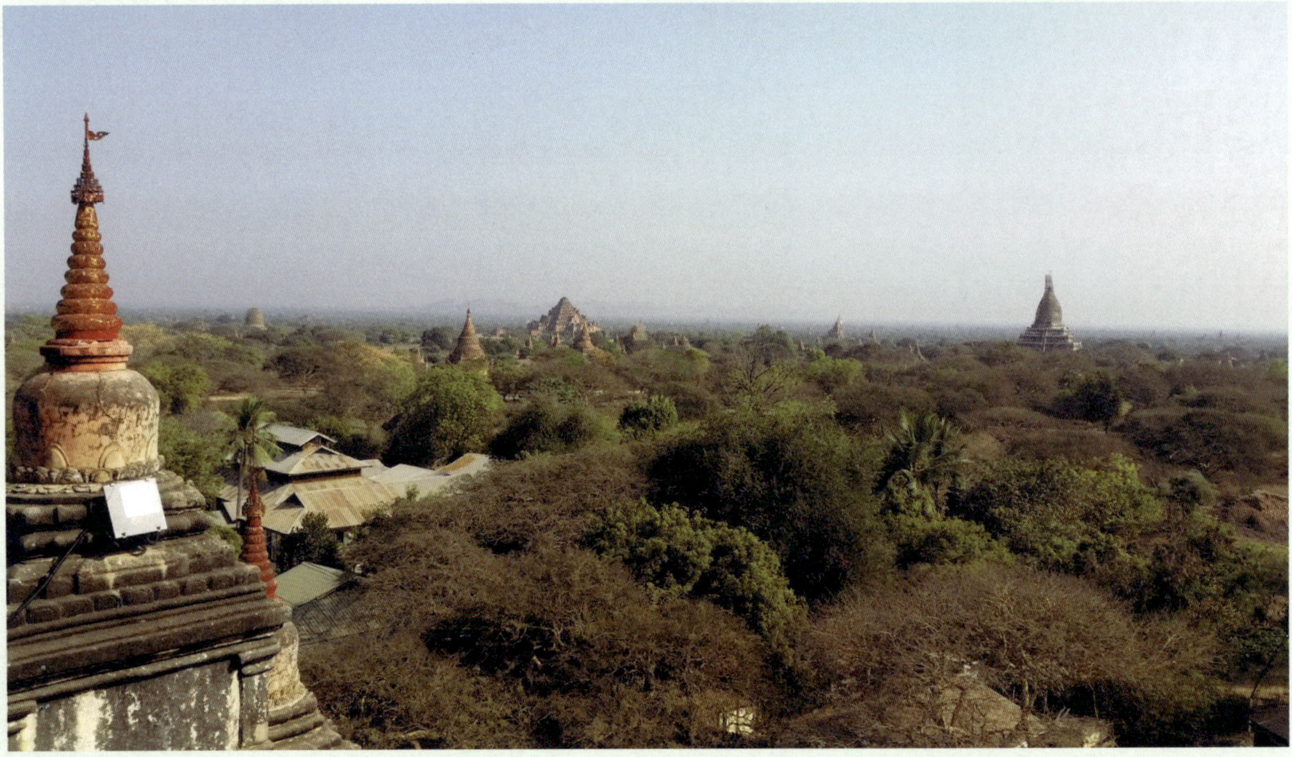

Fig. 11-13: Archaeological garden in Bagan with numerous Buddhist pagodas and temples

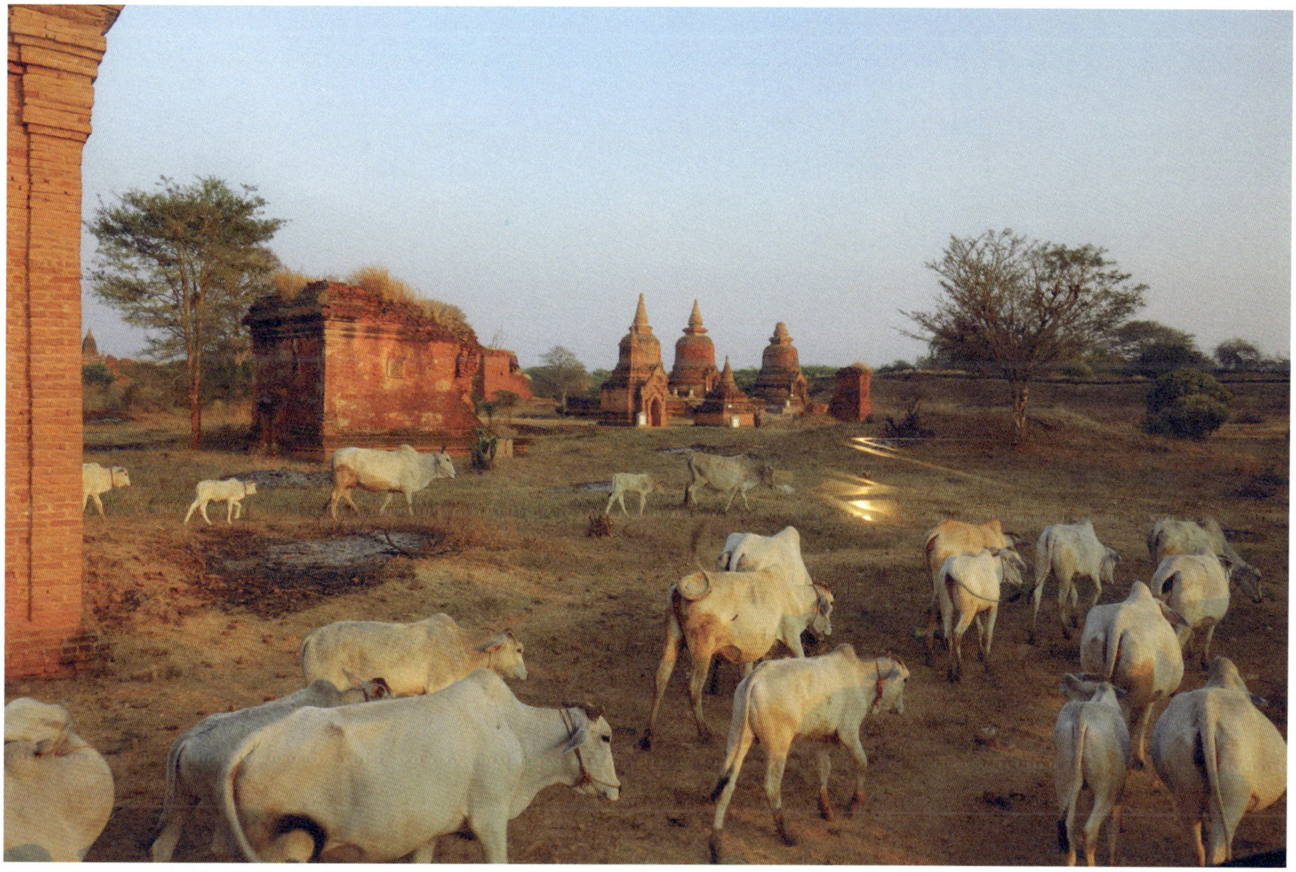

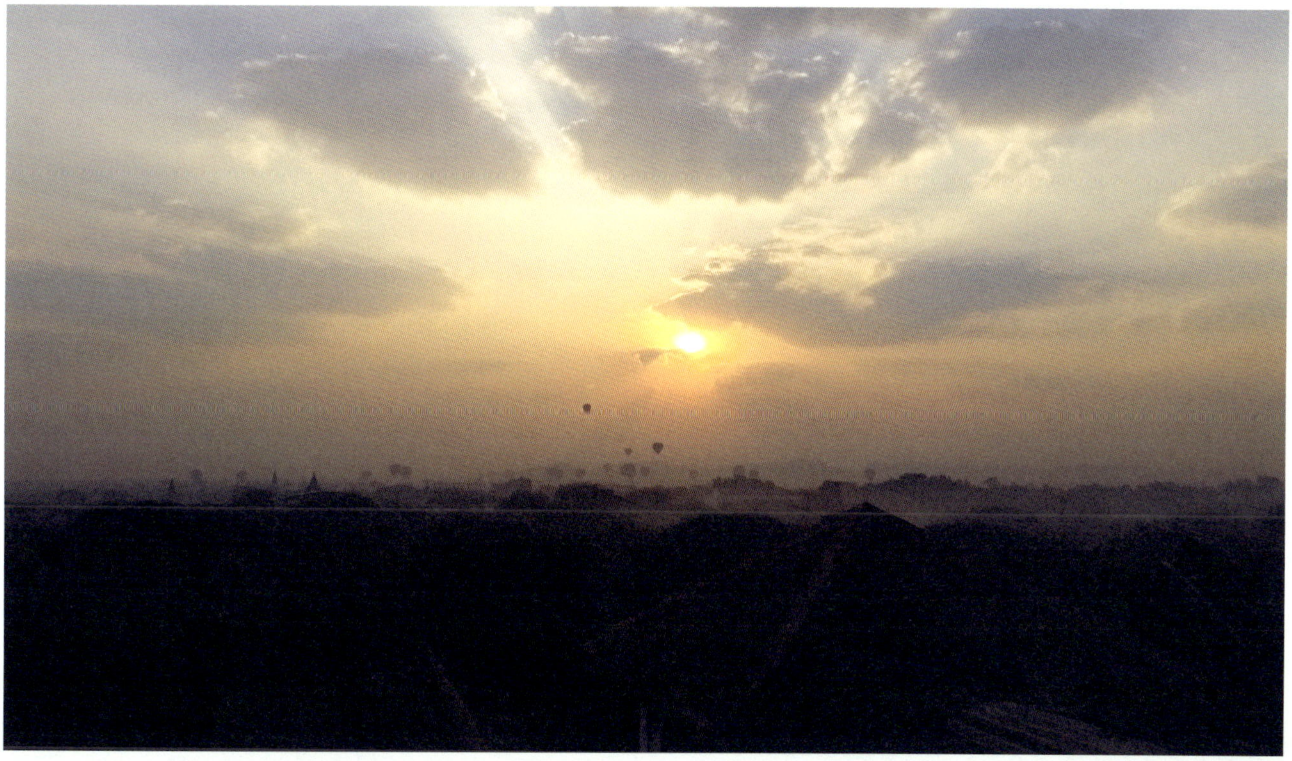

Fig. 14: Hot air balloons in the sun rise over the archaeological garden in Bagan

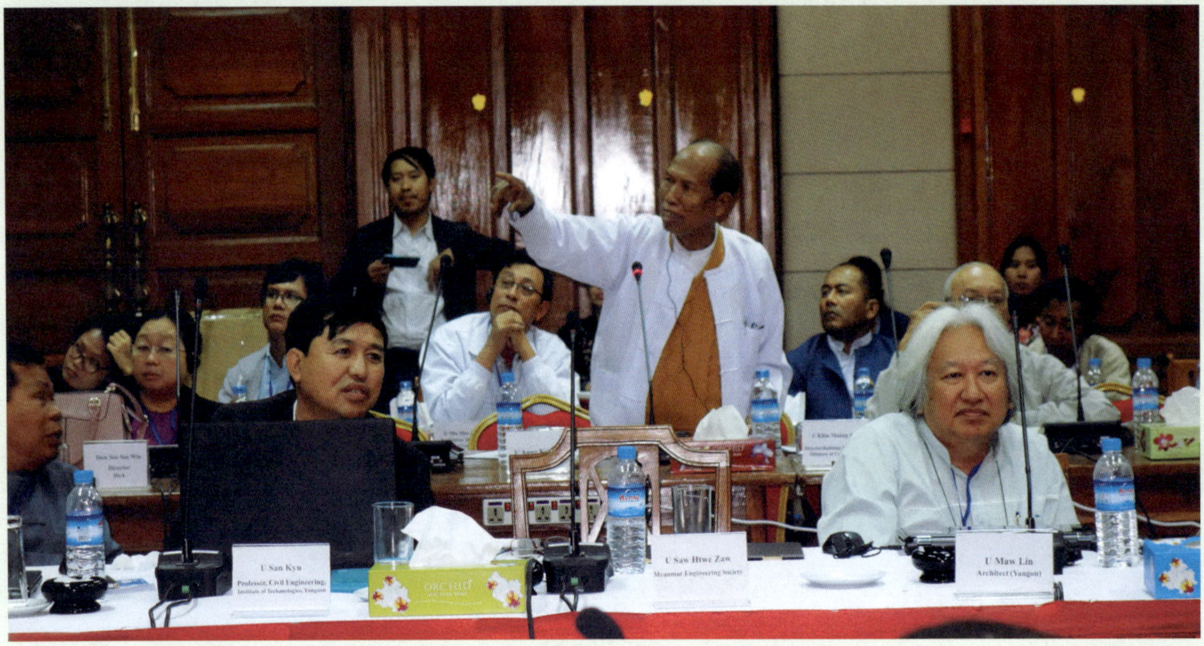

Fig. 15: Post-Earthquake Conference, Bagan, February 2017

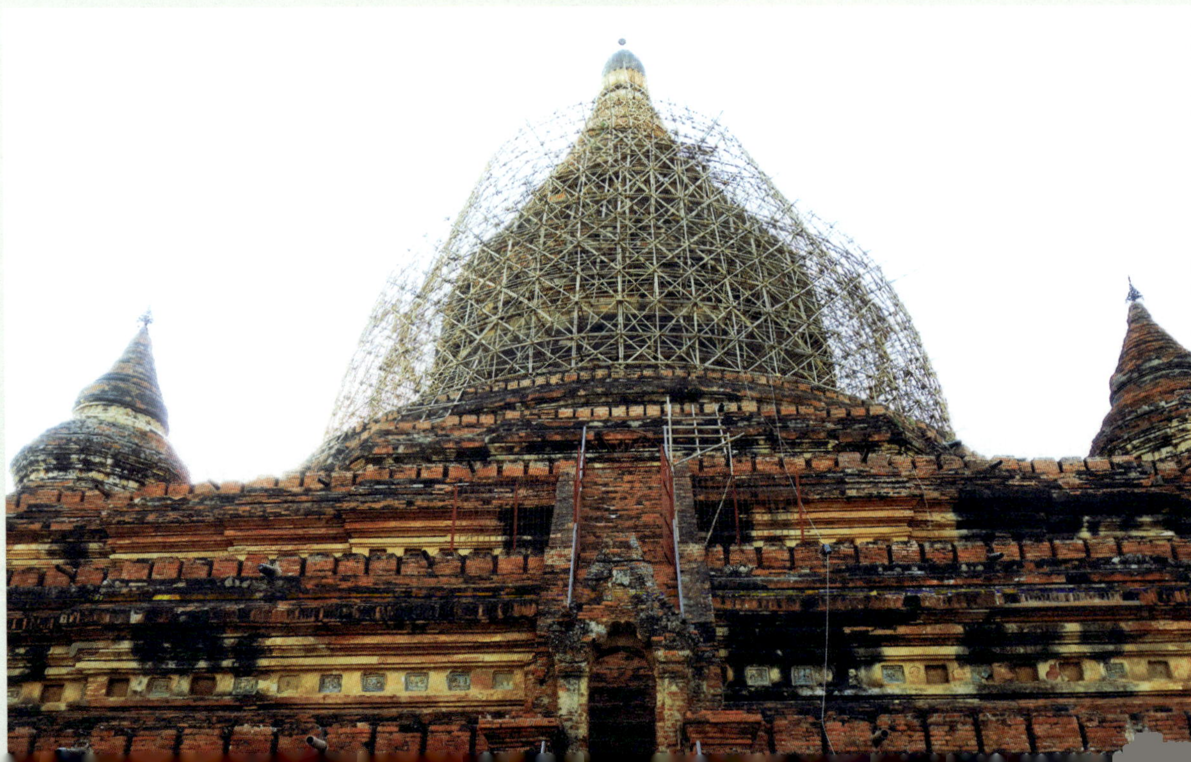

Fig. 16: Instable pagoda “veiled” in supportive bamboo scaffolding

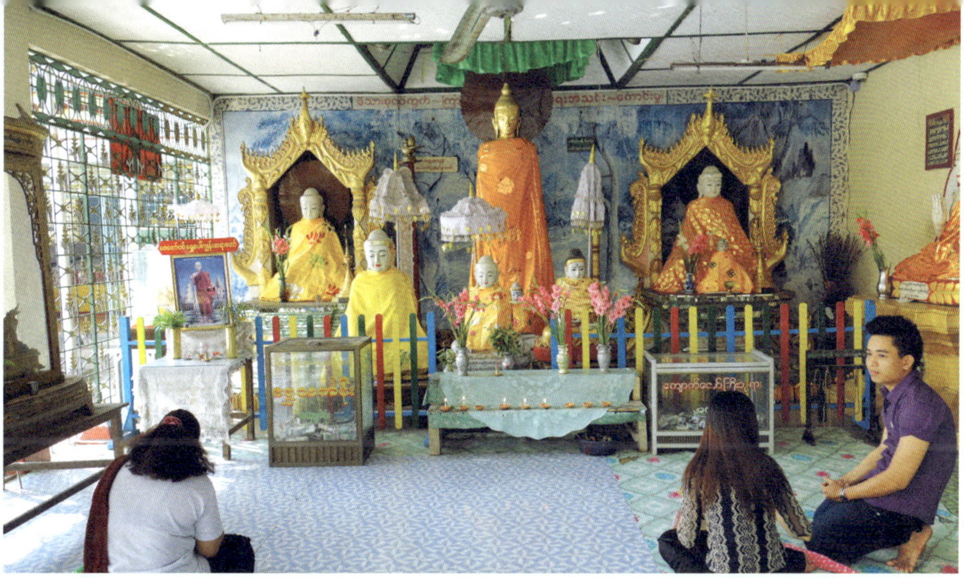

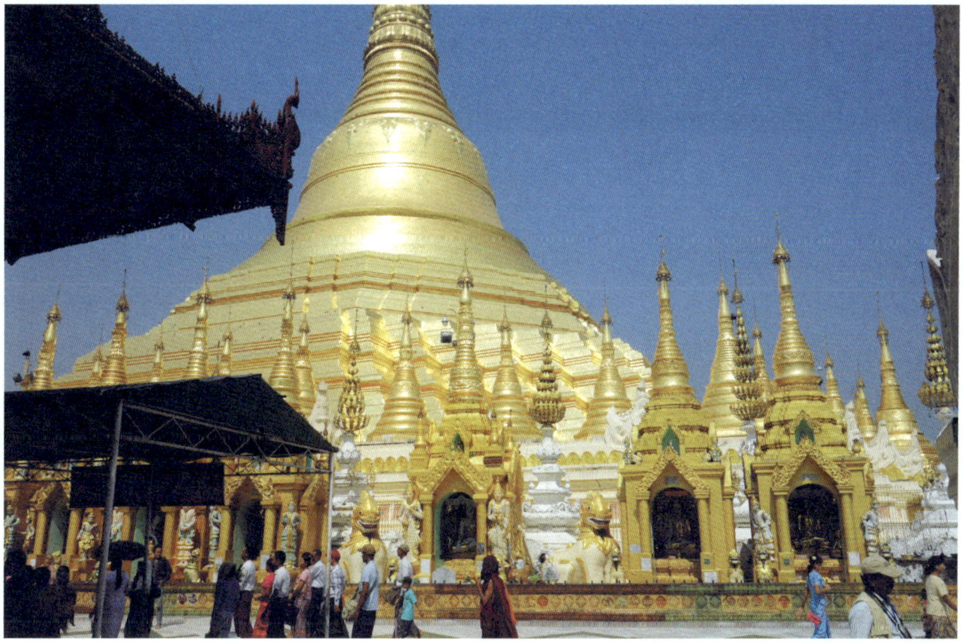

Fig. 17-18: Buddhist life in Myanmar, Yangon

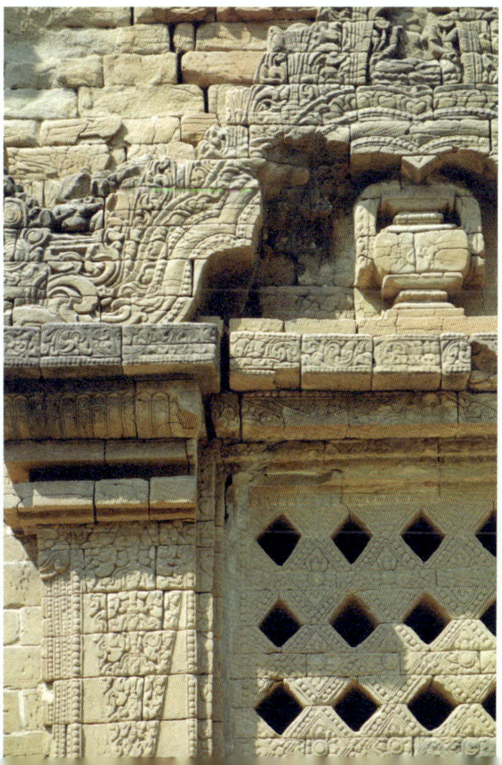

Fig. 22: Precious stone-cutting, Nanpaya Temple

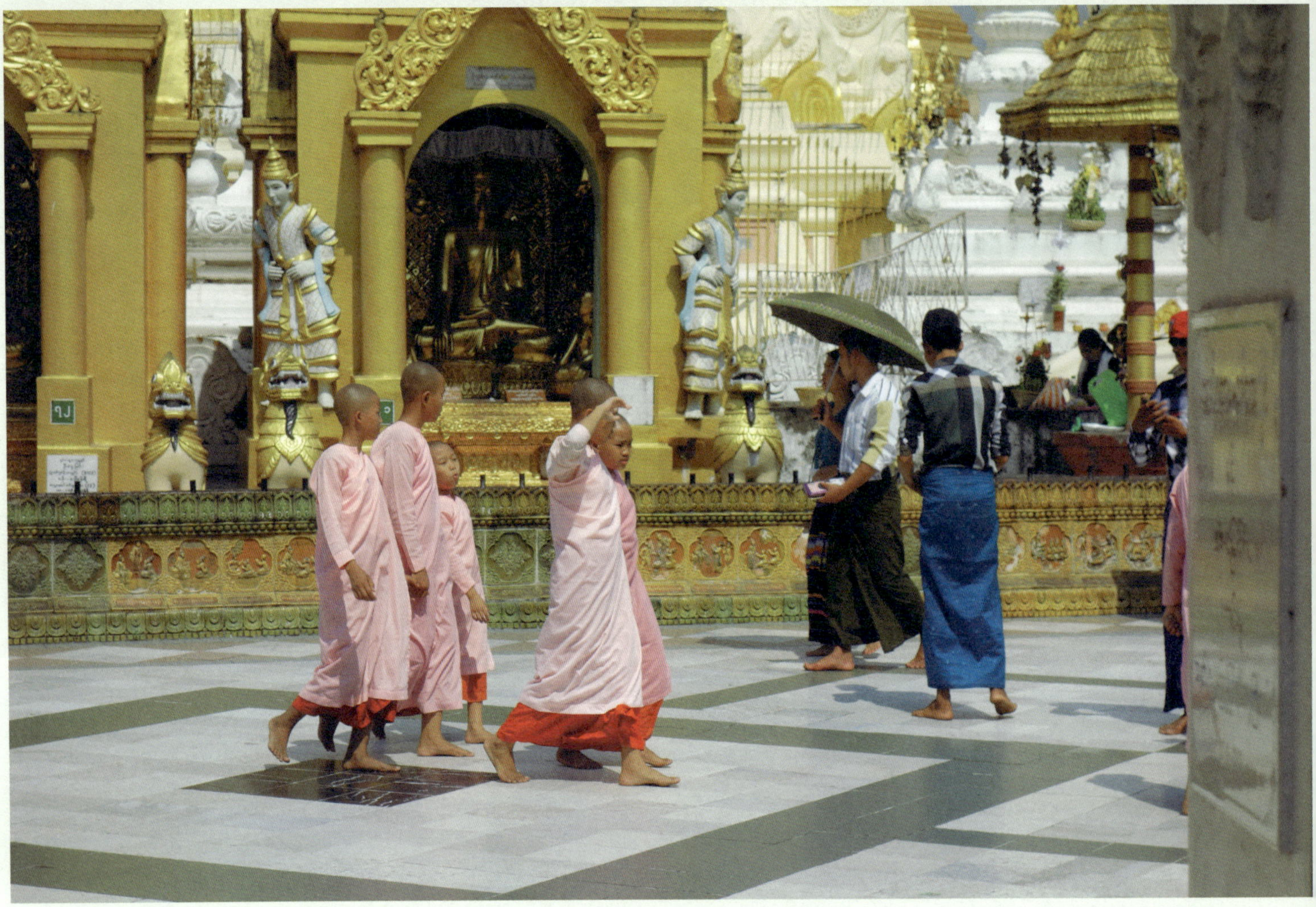

Fig. 19-20: Buddhist life in Myanmar, Yangon

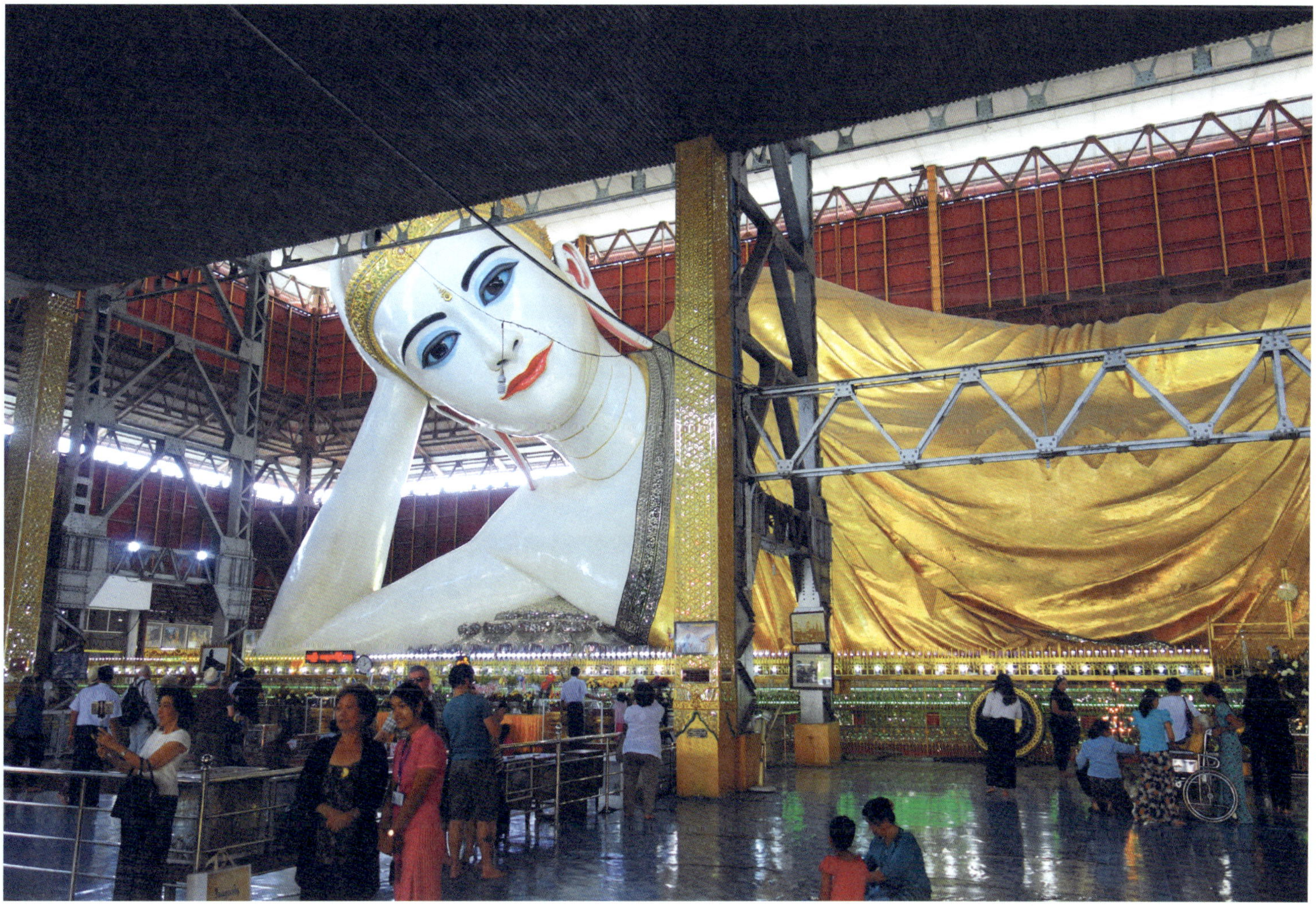

BY GABRIELA KRIST

Via Detours... From Myanmar to Thailand

GABRIELA KRIST

New Cross-Border Cooperation Opportunities in the Field of the Preservation of Cultural Assets

The Institute of Conservation of the University of the Applied Arts Vienna and the Silpakorn University in Bangkok

At the request of the Austrian Embassy in Bangkok, which is also responsible for Myanmar, I accompanied Ambassador Enno Drofenik to Mandalay for the first time in February 2015 in order to scout for potential partners in the field of conservation. However, during this mission it was not possible to find a suitable collaborative partner in Myanmar. Therefore the Austrian Embassy endeavoured to sound out further expert contacts in conservation in Myanmar and prepared a second fact-finding mission for 2017.

In 2016, the University of Applied Arts Vienna joined the ASEA-European Academic University Network, which is also active in Myanmar and Thailand. It supports projects there between Southeast Asian and Austrian universities. Now there was a concrete basis for carrying out the appropriate cooperative ventures in the region.

First of all, in February 2017 an initial fact-finding meeting was held at Silpakorn University in Bangkok, before the planned journey to Myanmar. There is a great need for conservators throughout the whole of Southeast Asia, but at the moment no functioning programme of study or training. Hence a search is underway to find consulting and cooperation partners, and Austria would be predestined to help.

A top-notch delegation from Silpakorn University headed by President Wanchai Sutananta, Sompid Kattiyapikul, Dean of the International College, and board member Chainarong Indhara-Meesup visited the University of Applied Arts Vienna in November 2017; also present were Rector Gerald Bast and Enno Drofenik, now working in the foreign office in Vienna. It was arranged to hold an initial training workshop in February 2018. Likewise a MoU was suggested as the basis for future cooperative ventures (Fig. 1).

WORKSHOPS AS PART OF CONSERVATION ACTIVITIES – "LEARNING" TOGETHER

From 12–16 February 2018, Veronika Loiskandl and Katharina Kohler, university assistants at the Institute of Conservation, organised the workshop "Structural Conservation of Canvas Paintings" at the National Gallery in Bangkok. The objective of this first educational session together with the Silpakorn was to introduce students, conservators, teachers and artists to the basic tenets of conserving canvas paintings. In addition, it aimed, through theoretical lectures and practical exercises, to sound out what knowledge could be expected from the participants, and where work still has to be done.

Taking part at the workshop opening were Vira Rojpojchanarat, Minister of Culture of Thailand, Eva Hager, Austrian Ambassador in Bangkok, also high-ranking representatives of Silpakorn University, and guests. The success of this event motivated other fruitful activities in further training and education (Fig. 2–3).

The next training workshop took place soon afterwards, from 3–7 September 2018. Tatjana Bayerová, chemist at the Institute of Conservation, University of Applied Arts Vienna, introduced the participants to the scientific basics in the analysis of paintings. The focus was on the specification of pigments and binding agents, also practical analysis procedures. Twenty-three participants attended the session and responded to it with great interest; it was financed by the ASEA-Uninet (Fig. 4).

DEVELOPMENT OF A NEW INTERNATIONAL CONSERVATION PROGRAMME AND A CONSERVATION CENTRE IN BANGKOK

Parallel to the analytical education session, the Director of the Department of Studies at the University of Applied Arts Vienna, Bernhard Kernegger, and the signatories held numerous talks with representatives of Silpakorn University on the development of a joint new curriculum on the preservation of cultural assets. In addition, pertinent institutions were visited in order to gain a picture of the status of conservation in Bangkok, including the Silpakorn Art Centre and the Conservation Science Division at the National Museum in Bangkok. Meetings were also organised with teachers and students of the current conservation programme in order to stake out the need of a new course of study and contents.

Silpakorn University has faculties teaching the sciences, technical and business and economics studies and is simultaneously the leading university of the arts in Thailand. But problems exist in conservation studies, which are conducted in the primary years as a bachelor of arts course and currently offered as a two-year master's degree for graduates of art studies. There are only limited job opportunities in Thailand for conservators; when vacancies crop up, they are not paid appropriately; artists earn better. In Thailand, conservation work is primarily done by private firms, which employ artisans and artists; the profession of the academic conservator – established in Austria for more than eighty years – is generally unknown. The main objective of conservation work is reconstruction; age, value, and the authenticity of monuments and cultural assets are disregarded.

There are no conservation workshops at the university, no objects that can be worked on. The current curriculum mainly addresses art technologies and recruits bachelor of art graduates for conservation studies. Another missing factor is a cooperation network for theoretical and practical educational projects, nor are there any contacts to museums and religious institutions for acquiring objects.

Great potential for worthwhile joint activities was generated in many preparatory talks and the initial joint workshops. Besides the concept of a joint master's degree course focused on conservation in intercultural cooperation, the University of Applied Arts will use its expertise to support the establishment of corresponding workshops – present aspirations include the planning and realisation of a conservation centre. Furthermore, the Institute of Conservation could help in the further training and education of teaching staff.

The potentials for a jointly planned curriculum are interesting and very promising: by appealing to students not only from Thailand but also from Myanmar, Laos, Vietnam and so forth, Thailand and Silpakorn could take on a trailblazing role for Southeast Asia in academic conservation training. Meanwhile, with this new programme of studies the University of Applied Arts Vienna could consolidate and sustain its intensive and long-lasting presence in Asia, and the Institute of Conservation could input its experiences in international cooperation and conservation work at World Heritage Sites. Moreover, the new curriculum for other partner universities of the applied arts could be a contact point in Mongolia, Nepal, India and China for fostering conservation specialists, who are lacking in these countries as well.

The new programme of studies is to be established at the Silpakorn International College – SUIC; here, all the university's English-language international programmes are on the curriculum. The SUIC was founded in 2003 and is celebrating its 15th anniversary this year.

The ceremonial signing of the Memorandum of Understanding on 6 September 2018, in the presence of Austrian Ambassador Hager, marked the creation of a contractual basis for further cooperation between the Silpakorn and the University of Applied Arts Vienna; both institutions will endeavour to implement the ambitious plans in the near future (Fig. 5).

The anniversary year 2018, when Thailand and Austria celebrate 150 years of diplomatic relations, provides an ideal opportunity for giving a common impetus to the international preservation of cultural assets, and the University of Applied Arts Vienna is happy to be making its contribution!

ACKNOWLEDGEMENT:

Projects reported in this contribution were supported by the ASEAN-European Academic University Network (ASEA-UNINET).

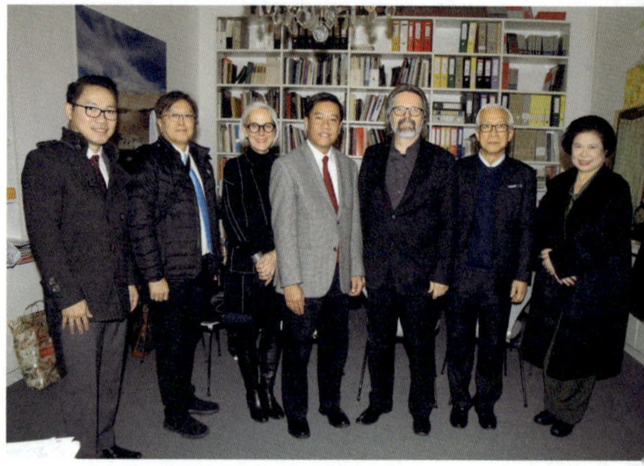

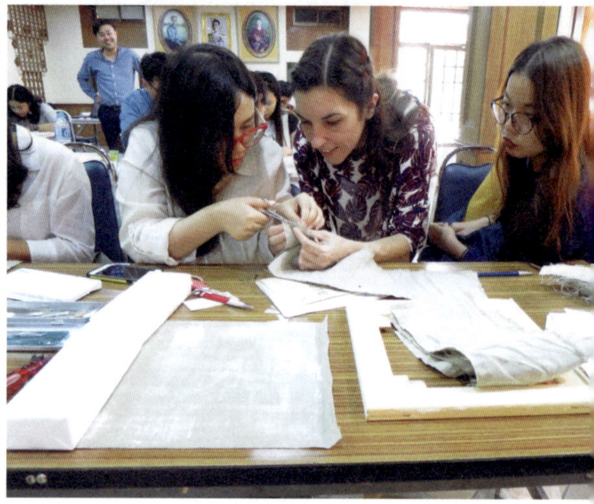

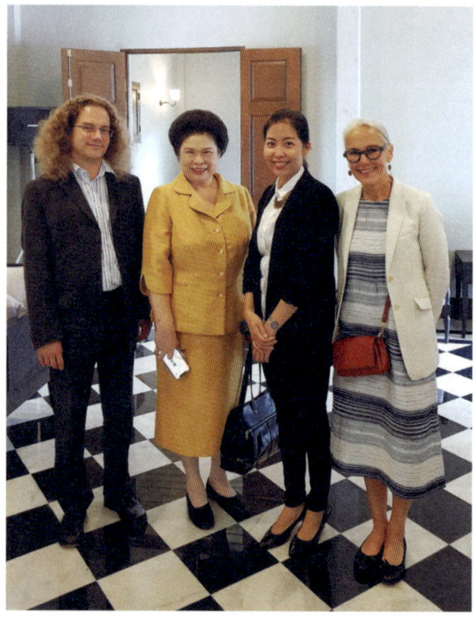

from top to bottom: Fig. 1: Delegation from Silpakorn University, Institute of Conservation, November 2017
Fig. 2: "Paintings Conservation Workshop", National Gallery in Bangkok, February 2018
Fig. 6: With Bernhard Kernegger, Sompid Kattiyapikul (Dean of the SUIC) and curator of Silpakorn University Art Gallery at House No 1, Bangkok, September 2018

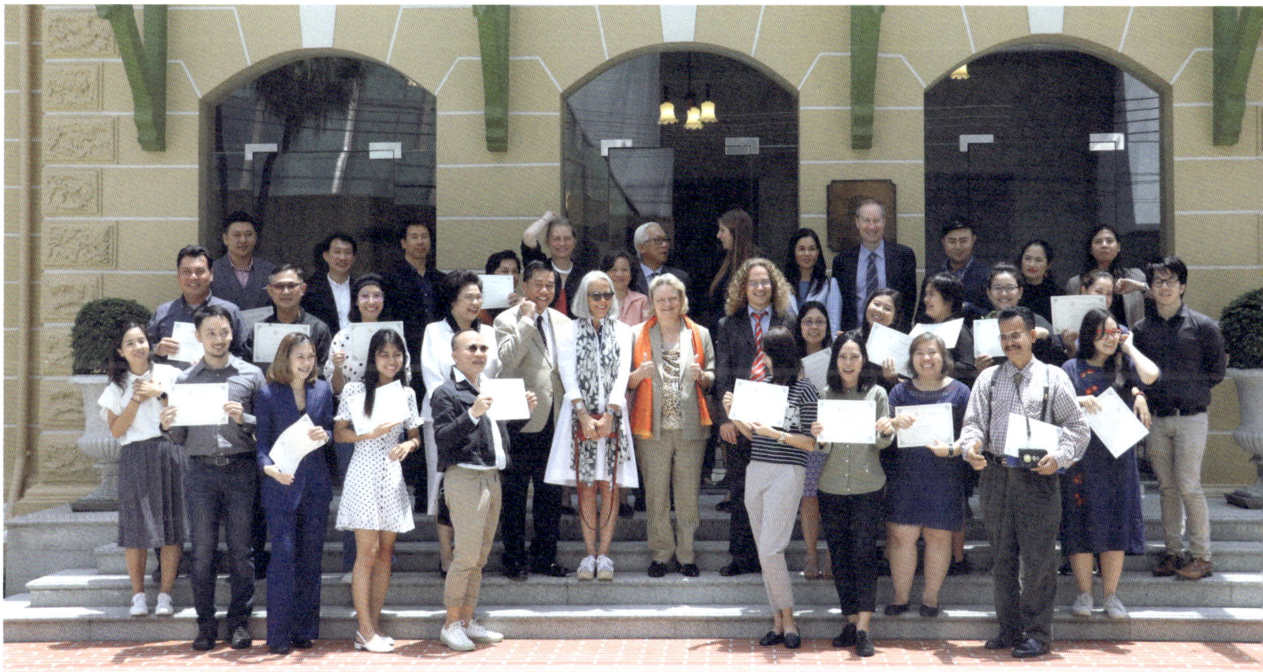

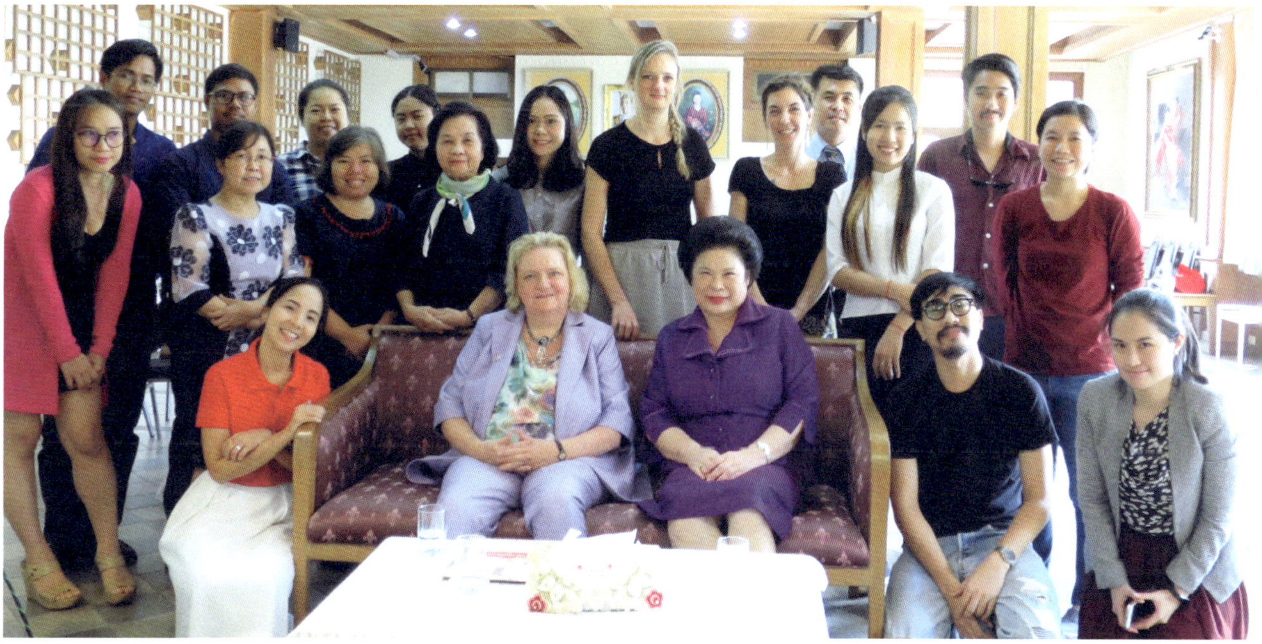

from top to bottom: Fig. 4: Workshop "Paintings Analysis", Bangkok, September 2018
Fig. 3: "Paintings Conservation Workshop", in presence of Austrian Ambassador Eva Hager and Sompid Kattiyapikul, Dean of the SUIC, National Gallery in Bangkok, February 2018

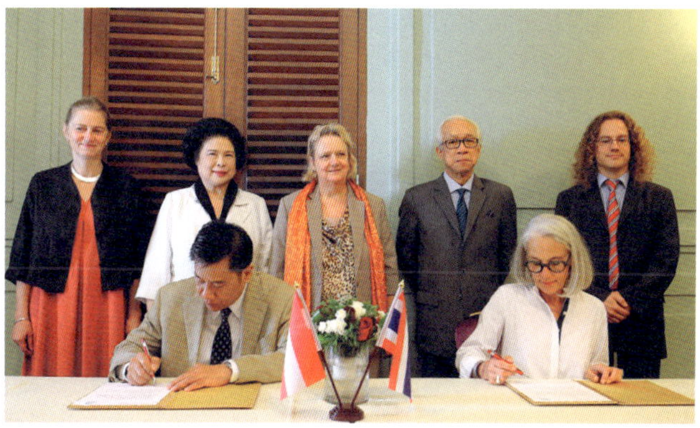

Fig. 5: Signing MoU between Silpakorn University and the Vienna University of Applied Arts, Bangkok, September 2018

Factsheet Workshops

PROJECT	Conservation Workshops in Thailand		
INITIATED BY	Gabriela Krist, Sompid Kattiyapikul	HEADED BY	Gabriela Krist
DURATION	12–16 February 2018 3–7 September 2018	COORDINATED BY	Martina Haselberger, Caroline Ocks
PARTNER INSTITUTIONS	Silpakorn University		
FUNDED BY	ASEA-UNINET Silpakorn University University of Applied Arts Vienna		
WORKSHOP ORGANISER	Gabriela Krist, Tatjana Bayerová, Bernhard Kernegger, Katharina Kohler, Veronika Loiskandl		
PARTICIPANTS	Apichai Piromrak, Chiraporn Aranyanark, Sopit Panyakhan, Yanisa Thongchay, Parichat Saengsirikulchai, Wanwisa Woraward, Nathamon Yudee, Guntima Tunjai, Pronpimol Duangkaew, Rawisara Trarakulngenthai, Thammarat Kangwankong, Suchat Khwanwan, Soun Sreyleak, Praewchompoo Chunha-Urai, Burin Pimmongla, Wanapol Saenkham, Sarayuth Phucharit		

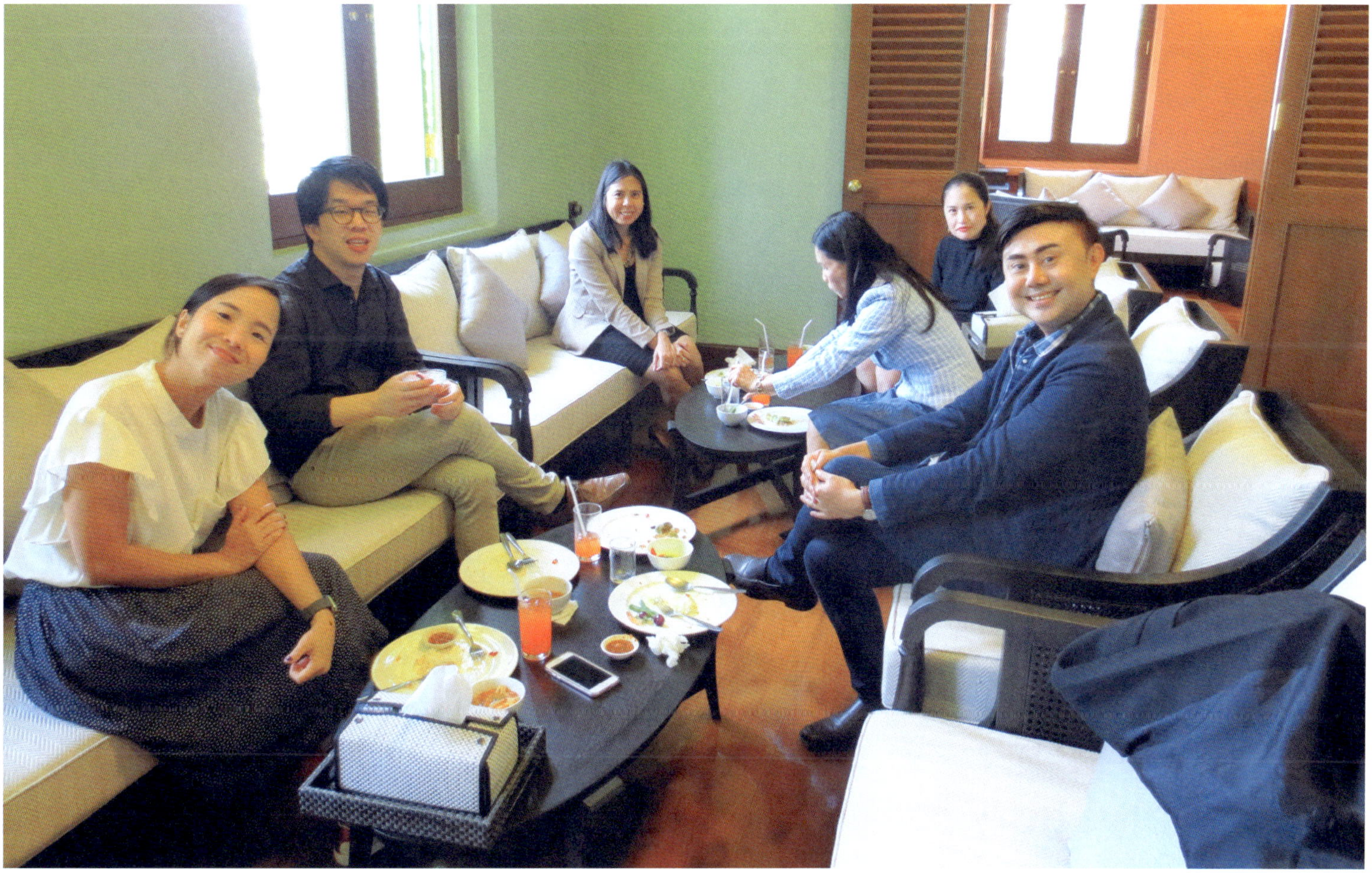

Fig. 19: Participants of the workshop during the break

Conservation Training in Thailand

VERONIKA LOISKANDL, TATJANA BAYEROVÁ

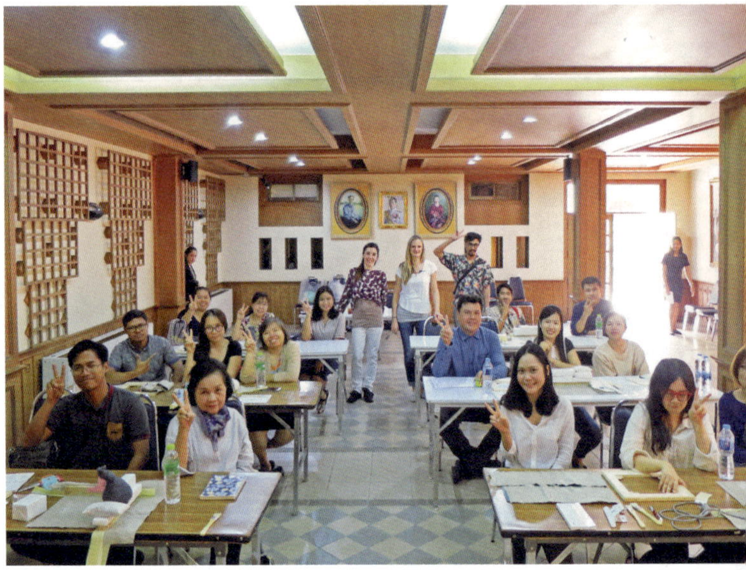

Fig. 5: Workshop room with all students, Katharina and Veronika

Building up Paintings Conservation

Everything started in February 2016 with Gabriela Krist's trip to Myanmar via Bangkok... even though Bangkok seemed to be just a stopover at the beginning, it was the starting point of an interesting collaboration in the aftermath. An unscheduled meeting with Sompid Kattiyapikul from Silpakorn University International College (SUIC) resulted in an unexpected surprise: Silpakorn University was looking for assistance in setting up a conservation training programme.

Their interest was further accentuated when a high-ranking delegation from Thailand visited our Institute of Conservation in Vienna in November 2017. During a guided tour around the Institute we were able to present our approach to imparting the appropriate conservation methods. The visit seemed to leave a strong impression on the Thai delegation, because we were invited to Bangkok in order to give a practical training workshop on site a short time later. Katharina Kohler and I were supposed to travel, and Caroline Ocks and Martina Haselberger took care of the travel organisation.

Since this was the first collaborative event between our Institute and Silpakorn University, we were invited to an opening ceremony and the following ceremony of signature of the Memorandum of Understanding (MOU) between Silpakorn University and the Ministry of Culture of the Kingdom of Thailand. Both ceremonies attracted the attention even of the highest administrational ranks; besides the representatives of Silpakorn University and other guests, the Minister of Culture of the Kingdom of Thailand, Vira Rojpojchanarat, was also present. After the ceremonies, several lectures were on the agenda. Vira Rojpojchanarat, who was active in the preservation of historic monuments before his ministerial office, gave an interesting overview of sites in Thailand and related international research activities. In a private conversation with the Minister, Katharina got an opportunity to talk about her dissertation topic concerning outdoor polychromy on wood. At the end we gave a small presentation about our university and studies at our Institute.

The five-day workshop took place in the meeting room of the National Gallery in Bangkok (Fig. 1), within walking distance of our hotel. The building was built in 1902 and originally used as a Royal Mint. In 1977, the Fine Arts Department's collection was accommodated there during a renovation and redesign campaign at the National Gallery. The collection consists of permanently displayed objects of local works of art from the 17th century; but there are also special exhibitions of contemporary art.

As we are convinced that practical hands-on training is an essential component of conservation courses, we decided to emphasise it in our workshop. However, there were still open questions for us...who would be the workshop participants? What would be their backgrounds? Based on experiences obtained from our institute's International Summer Schools with students from India, China, Ukraine and Belarus, and also on knowledge gained from working with several foreign exchange students during the semester, it was clear to us we should start with an introduction of our basic approach when viewing panel paintings – description of original, present and actual condition.

We introduced the workshop participants to the basics of stretching paintings, demounting and remounting canvases using strip lining, and the principles of tear-mending and inlays. Each topic started with a short theoretical introduction (Fig. 2) followed by practical sessions (Fig. 3–4). The participants could try all possible manipulations with the pre-prepared canvas dummies and gained their own experience when using different adhesives and tools. Continuous discussions led to an exchange of knowledge between both parties.

A total of seventeen participants (Fig. 5) with diverse professional backgrounds attended the workshop. There were both students and lecturers from the Graduate School of Silpakorn University and from the Faculty of Fine Arts. In addition, a curator and three art-teachers from the Rajini School in Bangkok participated. Seven of these participants were conservators of diverse specialisations – mainly paper, painting and wall painting conservation. It turned out that one of the participants, who was a paintings conservator, had attended numerous international courses and had decades of experience in various disciplines, from underwater archaeology to painting conservation. At present she is working as a painting conservator, and we got an opportunity to see her current conservation work at the Rajini School. The object was an oil painting from the 19th century, the full figure portrait of a member of the royal family. The painting's condition was very problematic. Most likely, several interventions had been carried out in the past, during which various substances were applied to the substrate. Unfortunately, these materials had aged unfavourably and led to further damage to the painting.

The main challenge for painting conservators in Thailand is the climate. The paintings that were shown to us or that we saw later in the National Museum were from the 19th century. All of them were painted using the common European materials and techniques, which, obviously, are not particularly suitable in the local climate. All the paintings showed repeated, thorough treatments. These interventions all resulted in extensively altered paintings; moreover, the use of not-exactly appropriate conservation materials led to even more damage. The visual appearance of most of the paintings was greatly impaired and unsatisfactory.

A frequent question of the workshop participants was: "What can be done when acrylic paints turn whitish?" It became clear to us that there was a lack of knowledge on traditional materials and techniques and currently readily available materials. Our recommendation here was to use *historically common techniques*, since, as we had observed, the climate in Thailand appeared to be highly unsuitable for acrylic paints.

Towards the end of our stay we had the opportunity to visit the National Museum (Fig. 6) and the Grand Palace (Fig. 7–8) – two places where conservation measures of completely different approaches have been adopted. The approach observed at the museum corresponded to our understanding of conservation of cultural heritage in the museum environment. This was in contrast to the palace, where aspirations are focused on complete renewals inspired by historical models. There we could observe that damaged murals were obviously not conserved, but that large areas were simply painted anew (Fig. 9). In this case it wasn't clear whether and to what extent the value of the original paintings was considered or not. However, based on the discussion with the workshop participants, it seemed quite doubtful that such considerations were entertained.

In the National Museum however, we quickly recognised the famous *tratteggio* retouching technique (Fig. 10) performed on the murals in the Buddhai Sawan Chapel dating from 1792.

The National Museum's collection dates back to 1862, when the museum association of King Mongkut (Rama IV) started collecting art objects. In the beginning, the royal collection was not accessible to the public. Over the years, it was moved several times, until it was brought to its current location during a renovation in the 1950s. We saw both air-conditioned exhibition spaces which were probably state-of-the-art in the mid-20th century (Fig. 11), also areas that have only recently been improved and adapted to the current museum standards (Fig. 12).

At the end of the workshop, the Austrian ambassador in Thailand, Eva Hager, visited us and we introduced her to our institute. She showed great interest in our activities and assured us of her support. The week in Thailand was extremely interesting for all of us. The feedback from the Thai participants was very positive and the wish was voiced in support of follow-up workshops.

Veronika Loiskandl

It was just four months after Veronika and Katharina's workshop when I got a short email from Gabriela Krist asking me to give the next workshop in Bangkok. "Hm, well, I'm a chemist, what should the workshop be about?" I responded. The answer came almost immediately: "about what you know, the role of natural sciences in conservation". Without hesitation I automatically replied, "Yes, why not?" But, the closer the date of the workshop, the more insecure I became. On the way to Bangkok I had the same questions in my mind as Katharina and Veronika a few months earlier: "Who would be the workshop participants? What would be their background? How would they benefit from a lecture of a chemist, when they do not know the essentials of painting materials technology?" But it was too late for these questions, we landed in Bangkok.

Despite the monsoon period, the Monday morning of the first workshop day on 3 September was sunny and warm. This time the venue was not the premises of the National Gallery, but a beautifully restored house on No. 1 Captain Bush Lane, just opposite our hotel. The house was constructed in the typical colonial style in the early 1900s by the French Distillery Company (Fig. 13). Thailand's Crown Property Bureau saved it from demolition in 2012 and, because of its architectural value, the villa has been listed as a protected monument by the Department of Fine Arts. House No. 1 is not open to the public, but since its restoration in 2016 it can be rented for special occasions, which Silpakorn University International College (SUIC) did in the week between 3-7 September for work meetings between Gabriela Krist, Bernhard Kernegger and authorities and for co-workers of Silpakorn University and SUIC, and for the workshop as well.

After the welcome and introductory words by our SUIC colleagues, both the meetings and the workshop could start. At first glimpse, I realised that most of the participants showed the same faces I knew from the first workshop photos. And when I saw that they had turned up again, I took it as an encouraging signal of the participants' interest. This fact made me more secure; talking about natural sciences among artists is not so popular. First I explained the general role of sciences in the process of conservation and presented the premises, equipment and methods used at our Institute. Then I went on to talk about paint layers. I clarified the basic terms and definitions, composition of paint layers and the reasons why it is necessary to make investigations of paint layers, and then we proceeded. In the afternoon of the second day, the first practical session started; Participants were trained how to take minute samples from painting mock-ups, they observed the taken fragments under three small portable microscopes and then started with cross-section preparation by mounting the samples into silicon moulds and covering them with epoxy resin. The whole third day was dedicated to practice; in the morning participants ground and polished their cross sections and observed them under the small microscopes (Fig. 14). In the afternoon, Gabriela Krist joined us and together we made the condition survey of paintings that had been brought by participants, and we also observed them under UV-light using the portable UV-light lamp. The inspection of the first paintings didn't bring any substantial results, but then we were "lucky"; one of the paintings that looked absolutely fine in normal light showed massive intervention from the past under UV-light. Once the participants had calmed down after the "wow effect" from the UV-light discovery, the fourth and last workshop day started. I briefly introduced the main artists' pigments and binders, and the afternoon was dedicated to case studies in combination with questions of participants and lively discussions, finished with short and very positive feedback (Fig. 15).

Friday morning was reserved for lectures by Bernhard Kernegger, who talked about the institutional profile of our university, and Gabriela Krist, presenting our institute. Besides workshop participants and colleagues from SUIC, honourable guests were present – Eva Hager, Austrian ambassador, Wanchai Sutananta, President of Silpakorn University, Sompid Kattiyapikul, Dean of SUIC and Board Member Chainarong Indhara-Meesup. When the applause after both lectures finally subsided, the time came for highlights of the whole week. The first was the ceremony of signature of the Memorandum of Understanding between the Silpakorn University and the University of Applied Arts Vienna. The second highlight was the awarding of the certificate, followed by the group photo of happy and certified workshop participants.

The fairly busy working programme described above was accompanied by two special semi-official events. The first was the dinner in the residence of the Austrian ambassador, where the embassy's chef prepared delicious Thai seafood soup and roasted lamb, and Eva Hager served excellent Austrian wine (Fig. 16). The second event, this time only in the presence of high-ranking Silpakorn University members, was the farewell dinner at Lyon French Cuisine, probably the best traditional French restaurant in Bangkok.

Writing this article, neither Veronika nor I can forget to mention and thank the management team of SUIC and our translator, who took care of us during both workshops, for their incredible hospitality and support. Our SUIC colleagues were always very friendly and considerate, and, despite being preoccupied with their own work and the organisational tasks of the workshops and meetings, they found time to spend some "private hours" with us. During the first workshop they took Veronika and Katharina for an evening trip to Chinatown (Fig. 17). On the occasion of the Chinese New Year, the girls were able to enter into the hustle and bustle of this special place in Bangkok. Our free afternoon spent with SUIC colleagues after the awarding ceremony of the second workshop was oriented more on sites of cultural heritage. We made a short boat trip (Fig. 18) on Chao Phraya River and visited two Buddhist temple complexes from the 16th and 17th century – Wat Pho and Wat Arun.

The genuine interest of the participants and their desire to learn something new, heightened by the – to us – exotic spirit of Bangkok, made both workshops an experience we will never forget.

Tatjana Bayerová

ACKNOWLEDGEMENT:

Projects reported in this contribution were supported by the ASEAN-European Academic University Network (ASEA-UNINET).

Fig. 2: Theoretical Session

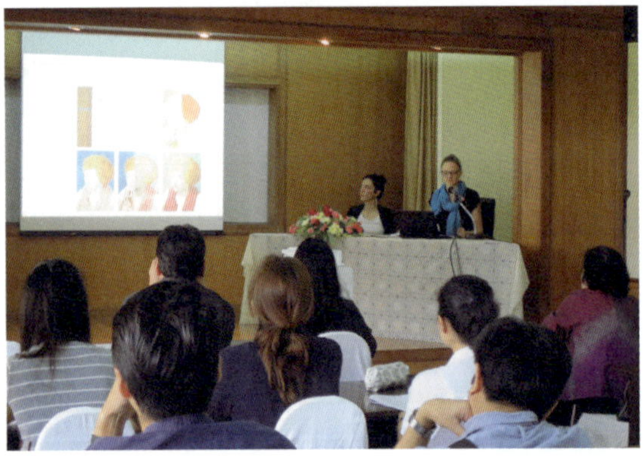

Fig. 3: Katharina teaching students

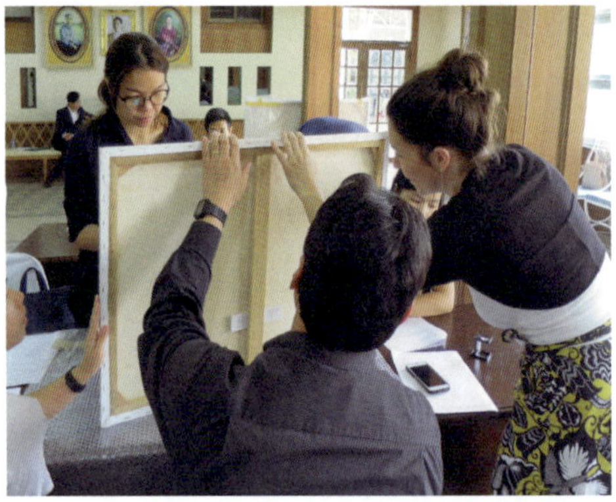

Fig. 4: Veronika teaching students

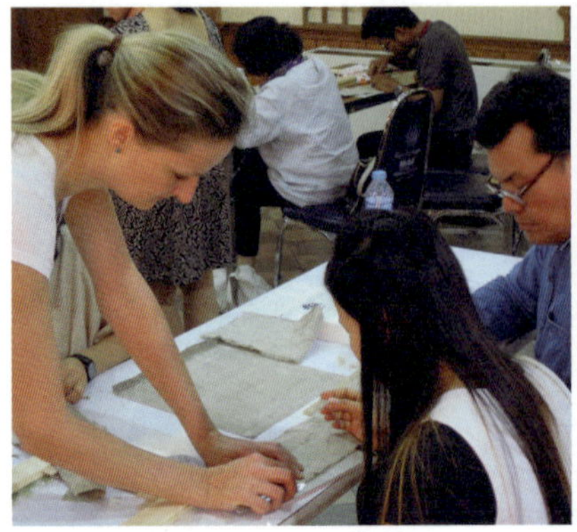

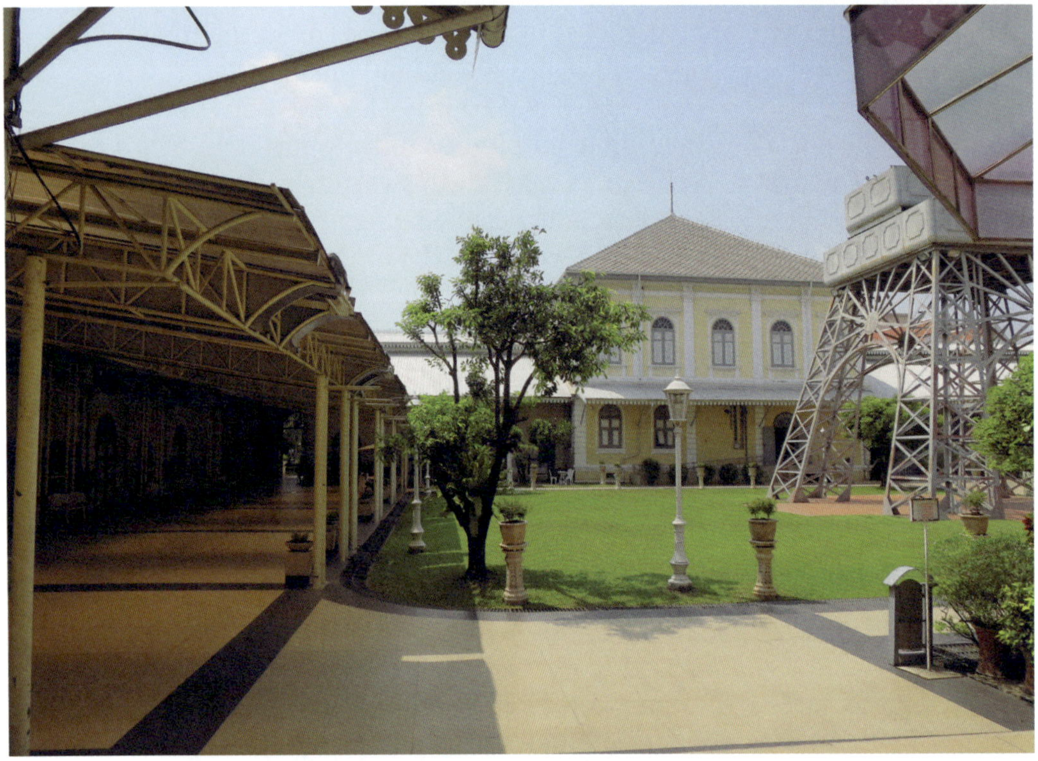

Fig. 1: National Gallery in Bangkok

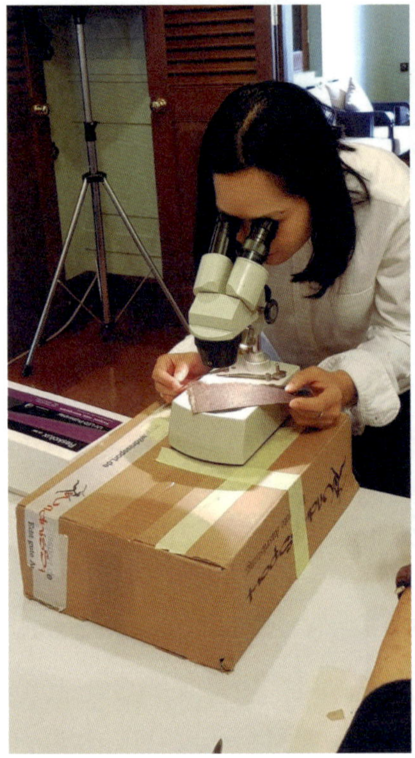

Fig. 14: Workshop participants practising optical microscopy

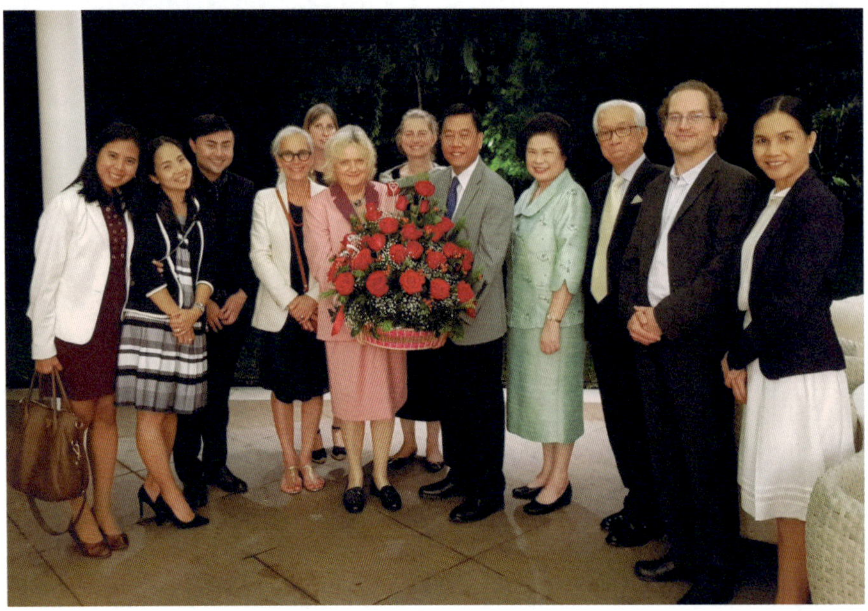

Fig. 16: Evening at the Austrian Embassy in Bangkok

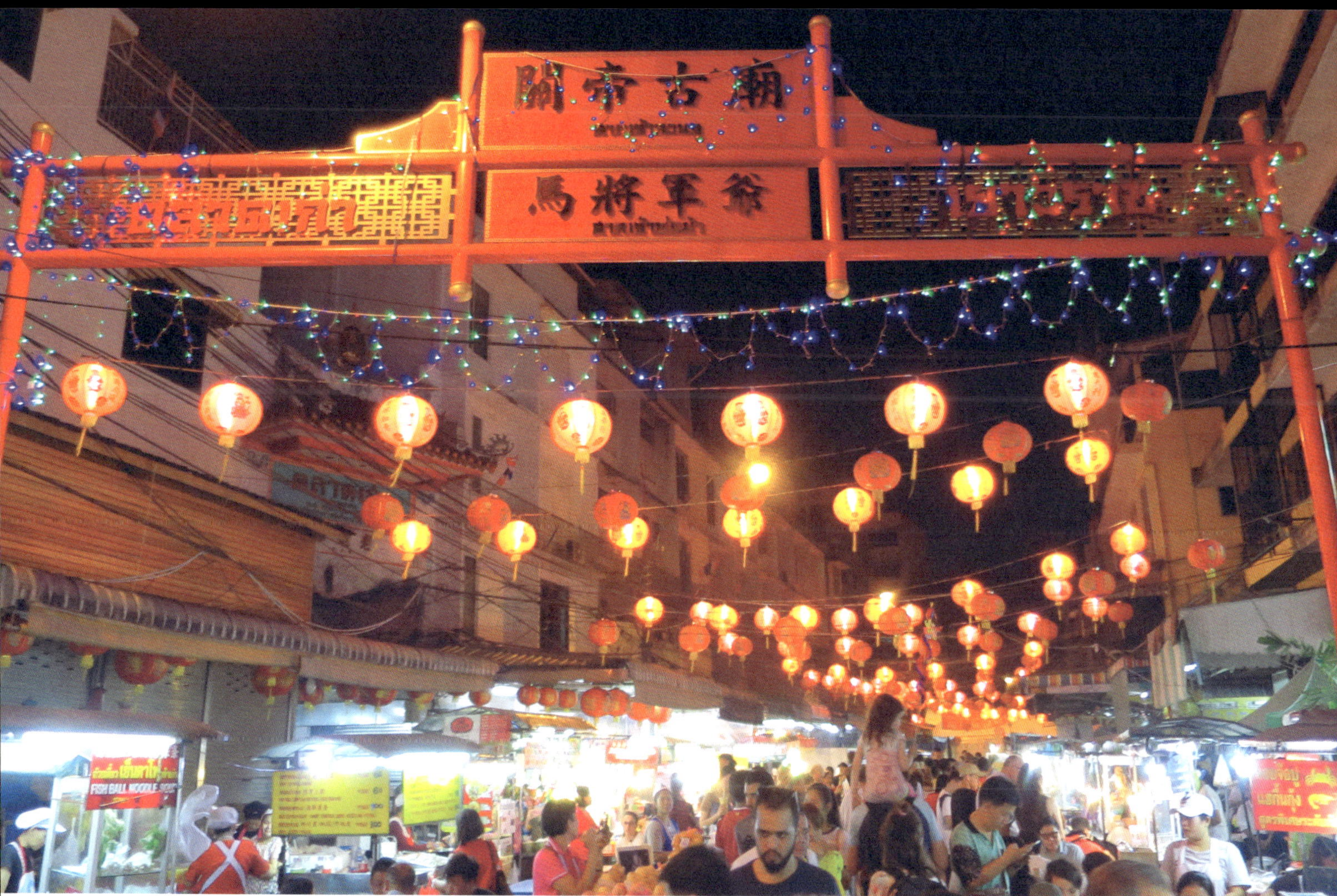

Fig. 17: Chinatown one day before Chinese New Year's festivities

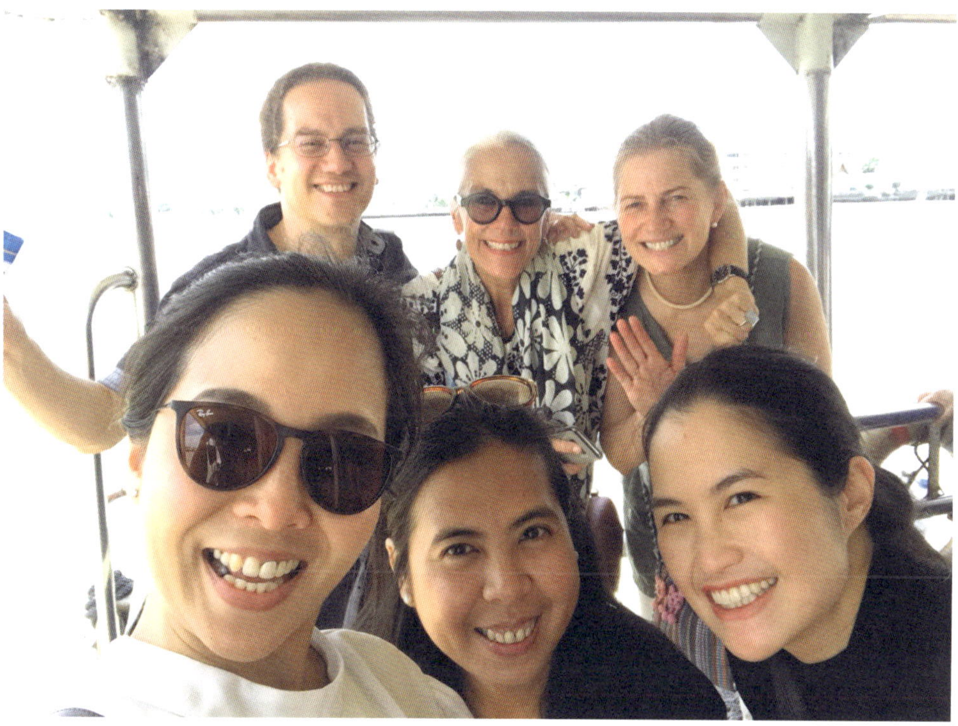

Fig. 18: Boat trip on Chao Phraya river

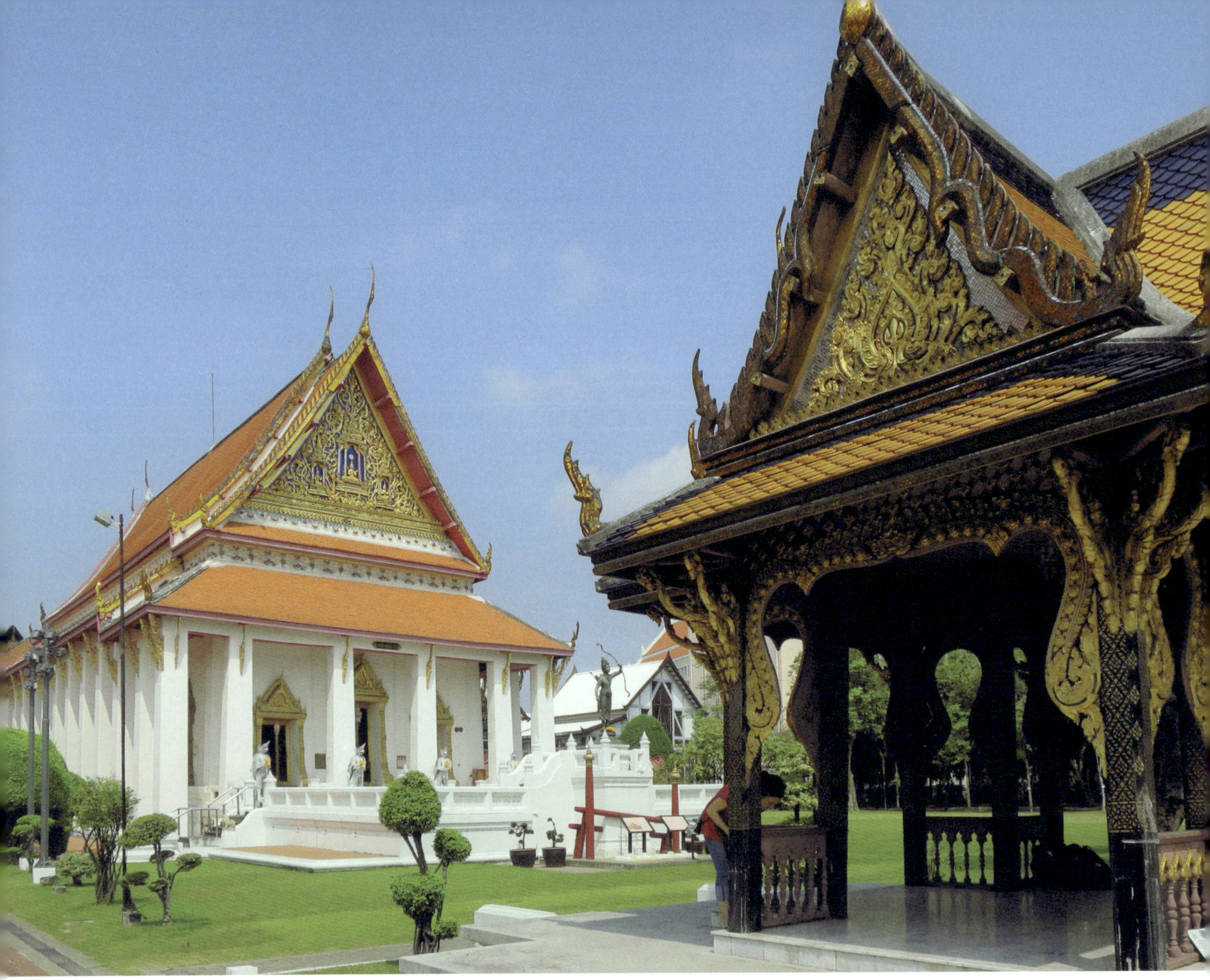

Fig. 6: National Museum Bangkok, Buddhai Sawan Chapel

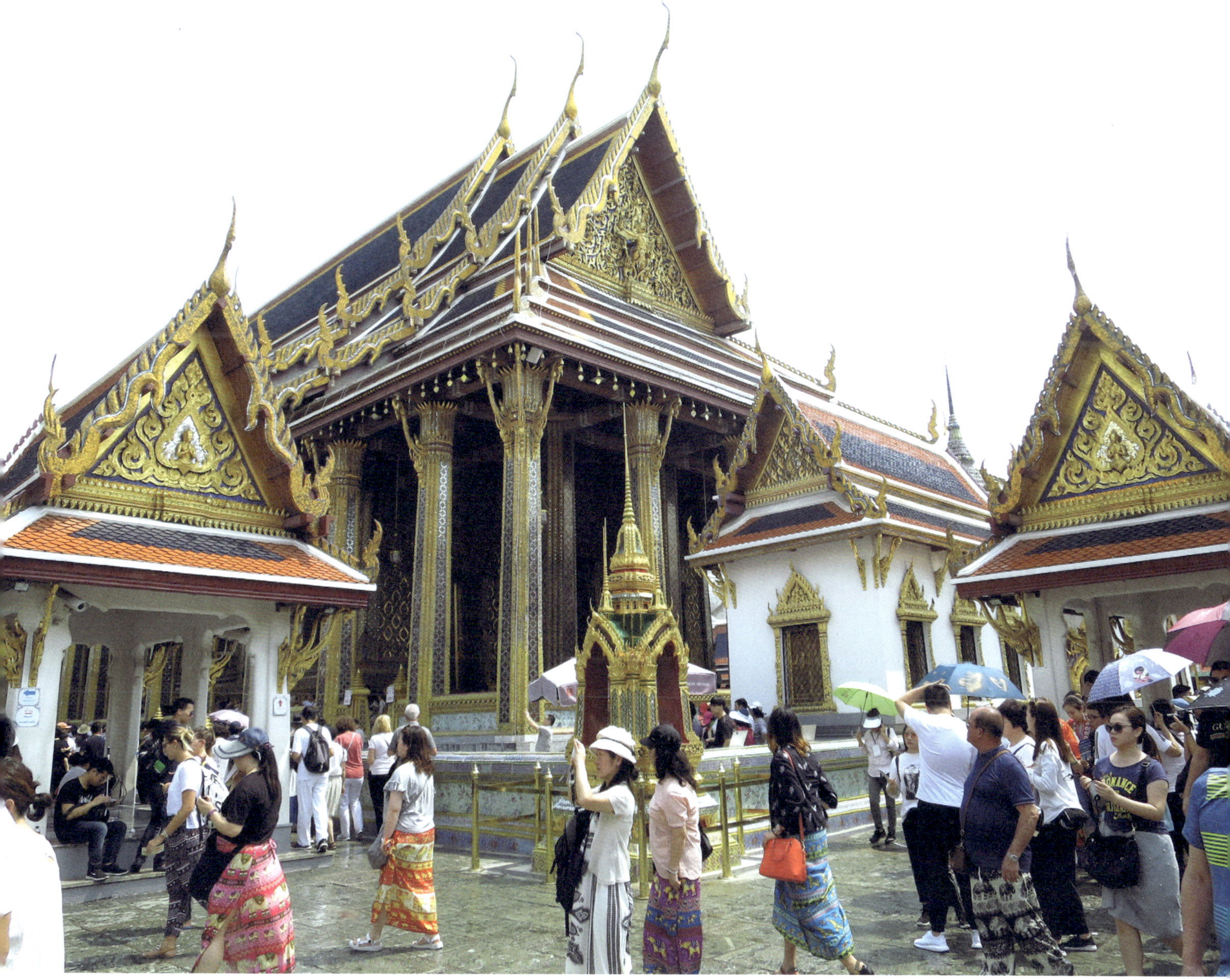

Fig. 7: Grand Palace Bangkok

below: Fig. 10: Buddhai Sawan Chapel, detail of Tratteggio retouching on mural paintings
Fig. 11: National Museum Bangkok, exhibition space with the technical state of the mid-20th century
Fig. 12: National Museum Bangkok, exhibition space recently adopted to current museum standards

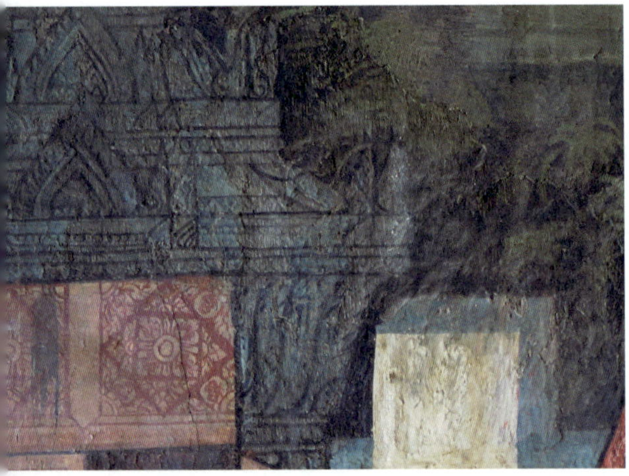

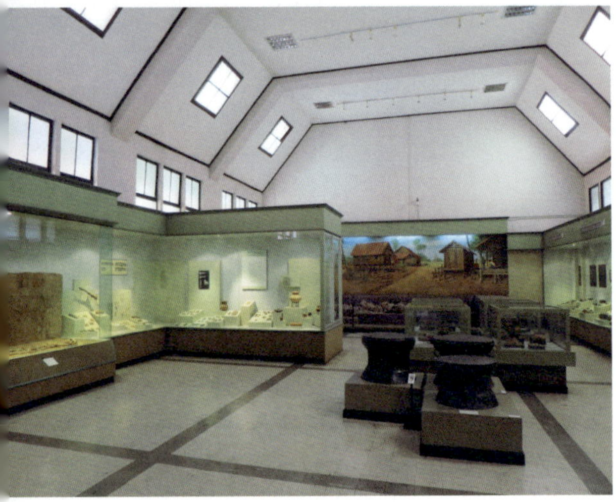

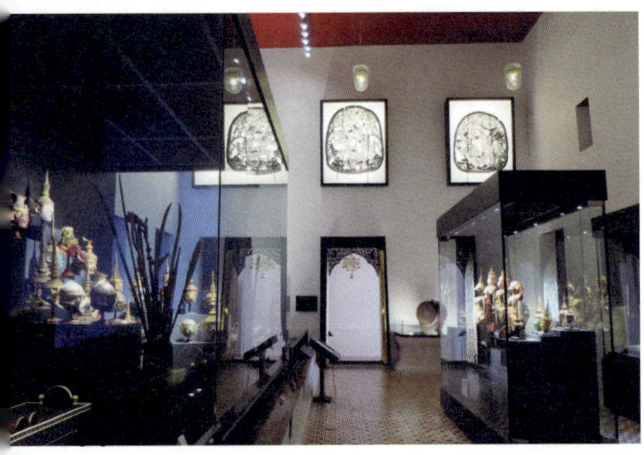

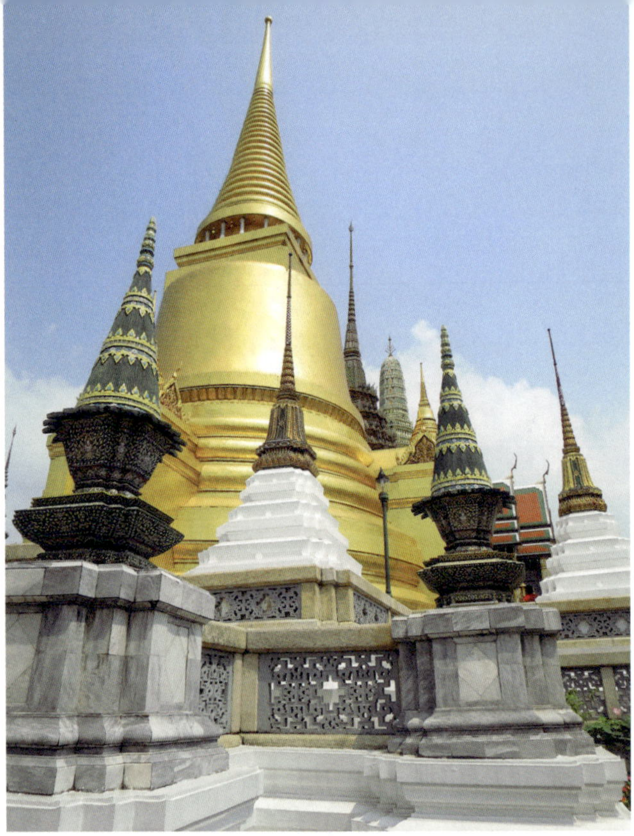

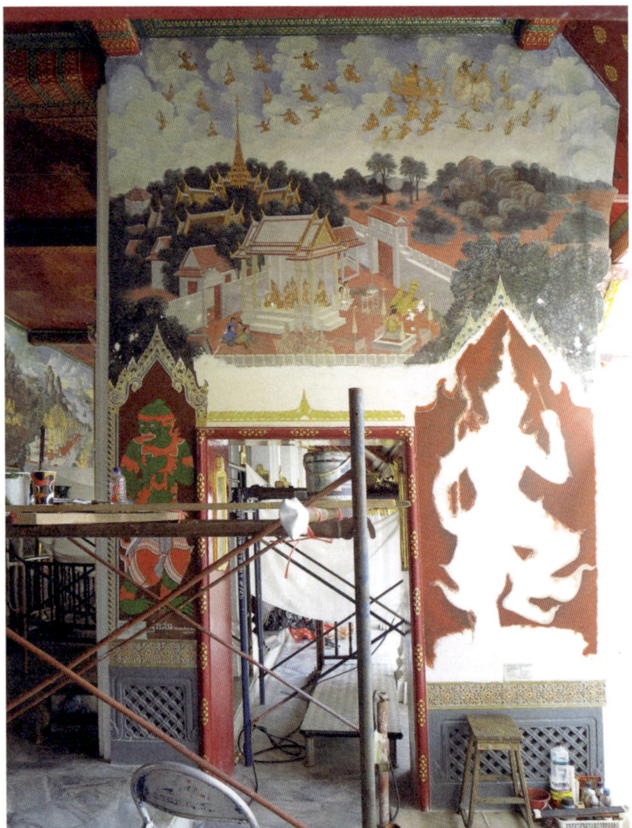

above: Fig. 8: Grand Palace Bangkok
Fig. 9: Grand Palace Bangkok, repainting of mural paintings

Fig. 13: House No. 1, the former seat of French Distillery Company, today listed as a protected monument; the venue of the second 'Paintings Conservation Workshop' in Thailand

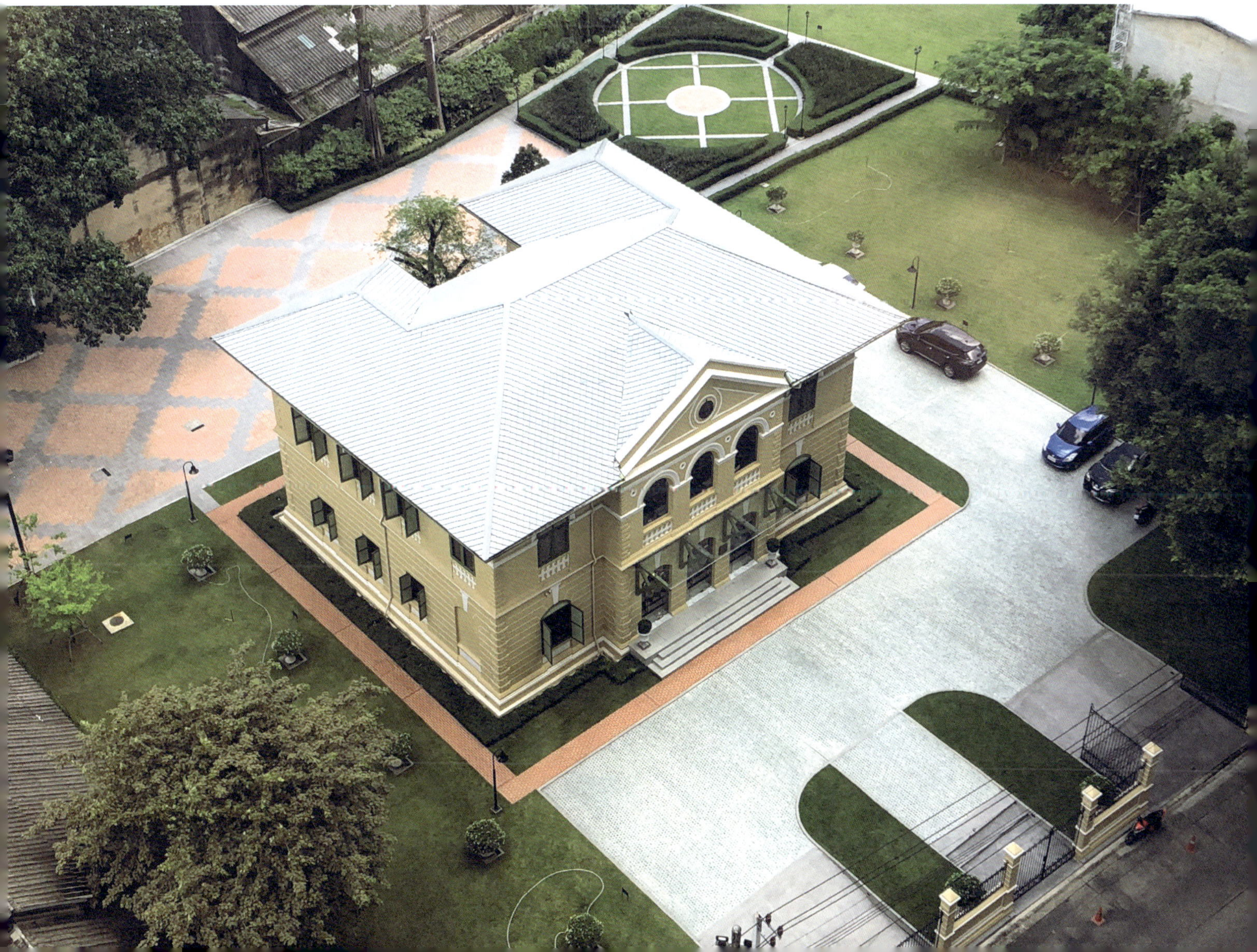

My Three Days in Thai Paradise

TATJANA BAYEROVÁ

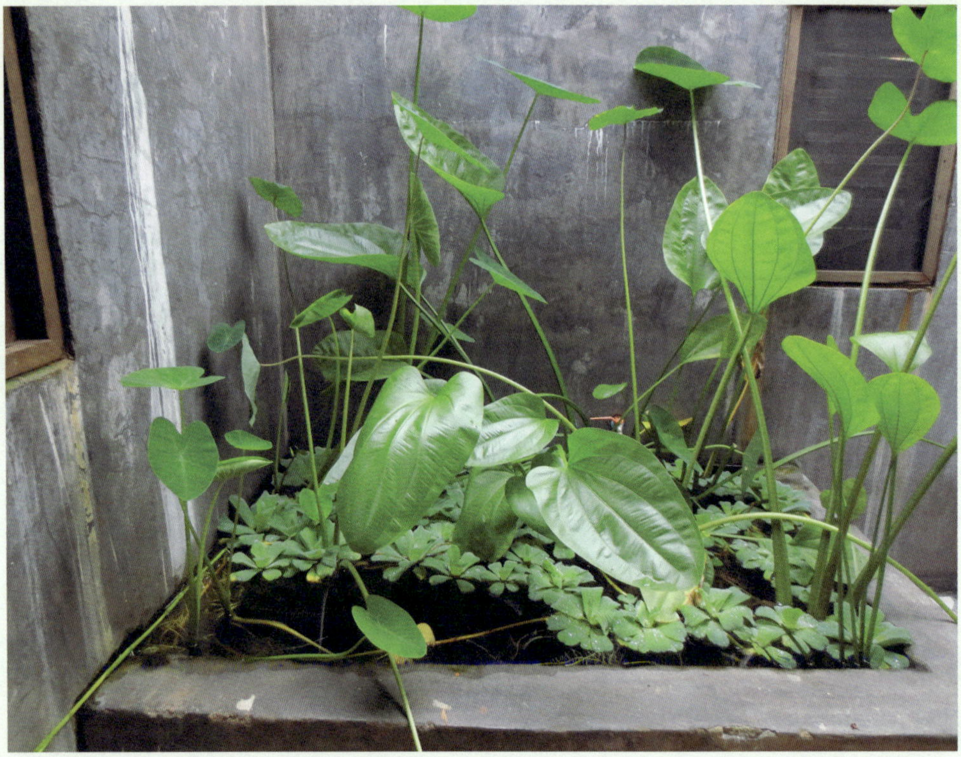

Fig. 1: Bali-style toilet

I woke up on Sunday morning with a strange feeling: “The workshop is over, I have nothing to do!” It took me a while till I realised it was true and I could start thinking about my holidays during the next ten days in Thailand. Weather outside did not look very friendly, heavy lead-grey clouds signalised that a thunderstorm would come soon. An ideal time to crawl with the laptop back to bed and start planning the next days.

One can get blinded by the imagination of white-sand beaches and islands, but Thailand is also a tropical wonderland of mountains, jungles and waterfalls. From the beginning it was clear to me I would love to see some exotic, genuine nature.

My first choice was the north of Thailand. Chiang Mai is not only the largest and the most important city of northern Thailand, but it is also surrounded by mountains, tribal villages and national parks; this might be something I would love to visit. After a closer look at the distance between Chiang Mai and Bangkok (700 km) I decided it was too far and I started to search again. I realised there were a few spectacular national parks to visit. And then I found it – Khao Yai National Park. The brief information about this place offered online was: "Khao Yai National Park is Thailand's oldest rainforest, only 4 hours from Bangkok. It is probably the best place to spot wildlife in Thailand. During your stay, you might see wild elephants, bears, porcupines, gibbons, snakes and parrots. One great option is a sunset visit to the eerie bat caves, when thousands upon thousands of bats fly up into the dusk. You can also take a dip in the waterfall that Leonardo DiCaprio dove into during a scene in his movie *The Beach.* After reading this text I immediately knew this is "my park" (the information about DiCaprio didn't play the key role in my decision, moreover, it wasn't DiCaprio jumping over the waterfall himself, but his stuntman). I booked the longest possible stay in a rainy season, which was a three-day, private wildlife tour at Tontan Travel, the agency registered by the Tourism Authority of Thailand.

Searching and booking activities took me almost the whole day, but I didn't mind since it was raining non-stop. And, moreover, I'm on holiday! I celebrated my first and next two free days by having a wonderful aromatic massage, sightseeing, delicious food and reading more detailed information about the place I planned to visit.

On Wednesday I took the long-distance train from the Hua Lamphong Railway Station, the central train station, direction northeast to Pak Chong, a small, sleepy and remote town about 180 km away from Bangkok, where I hailed a taxi that brought me to The Frog Khao Yai Resort in the vicinity of the national park. I was curious about what to expect from this place, since its critics on TripAdvisor differed a lot. But I was not disappointed, on the contrary. I found myself in an incredibly beautiful place in the middle of nowhere, with no tourists and no restaurants around, and, I was the only visitor. The accommodation was in a private Bali-style villa, also with a Bali-style toilet, from which I had such an amazing view as I have never had and probably never will from any other toilet in my whole life (see Fig. 1, it's a must!). Already the first evening I realised what the name of the resort meant: there were…dozens?…hundreds? of frogs of various sizes that made noises all night long (Fig. 2). Being the only guest in a fairly large area, where, except me, there was only one resort caretaker and his dog, accompanied by the omnipresent noise of frogs, I started to have doubts if I was really the most adventurous person. Nevertheless, I convinced myself that frogs were lovely, small and harmless animals, that the dog was the best protection, and I was in a paradise and needed to sleep.

Thursday morning, when I woke up, the sun was shining and frogs were silent. At eight o'clock sharp, my driver arrived, guide and walking encyclopaedia of flora and fauna in one person, Tata. He spoke perfect English, and although he had completed studies in economics because his mother wished to be proud of him on becoming a bank official, yet Tata dedicated his life to the park. Khao Yai National Park was established on 18 September 1962 as the first national park in Thailand and it is the third largest in area in Thailand. In 2005, the park, together with four neighbouring protected areas, was proclaimed a UNESCO World Heritage Site under the name "Dong Phaya Yen-Khao Yai Forest Complex" covering around 6,150 square kilometres (Fig. 3). The average altitude of the park ranges from 400 (1,312) to 1,000 metres (3,280 feet) a.s.l. with the highest mountain, Khao Rom, 1,351 meters high (4,432 feet). The vegetation includes rainforests, evergreen tropical forests and grasslands. Khao Yai is home to diverse wildlife – mostly mammals, birds and reptiles – and it is one of the few places in Thailand where wild elephants still survive.

No more than fifteen minutes drive from the resort, we crossed the national park´s border and reached the first viewing point, a terrace above the wide and deep abyss filled with rainforest. A great number of wildlife photographers was there, with professional equipment, and they were waiting – what they were waiting for? On the other side of the abyss there was an enormous fig tree with a lot of ripe fruits, and something yellow was moving there. And then I saw the yellow things through the Tata's telescope – the first real wildlife I saw with my own eyes. They were the massive yellow bills belonging to about eight great hornbills sitting on the tree and eating the fruits (Fig. 4). Tata told me that Thailand had one of the largest populations of hornbills, and the wildlife photographers waited the whole day for the best shots. After almost an hour of observing the birds I was finally ready to move further. We put on the anti-leech socks and flooded ourselves in the jungle for four hours. First we met a relatively large scorpion, which did not care about us at all. Then we saw all kinds of beautiful birds large and small, too many to list them all here, squirrels, spiders – here, the forest spider dominated with its large size, various lizards and ants, and bees flying from their spectacular chimney-shaped nest. I had absolutely no orientation as to which direction we were moving in, since all the orientation aids I remembered from childhood – the use of sun and watch, lichens on trees, position of stars or shape of anthills – did not work. There was sun but I had no watch, there were no stars since it was day, lichens were on all sides of trees, and the shape of anthills in Thailand is very different. Nevertheless, when I just had the feeling we were returning back to the Jeep, Tata stopped and whispered, "look there". "There" meant a branch of the liana in the shadow, where a beautiful, coiled, bright-green snake with a thin yellow line along its sides was sleeping (Fig. 5). I found out this was an adult female of the pit viper, one of several venomous snakes in Thailand. But at that moment the snake looked so unbelievably peaceful! It was probably still digesting its previous meal. When we were almost at the car, my guide suddenly stopped again, quickly mounted his telescope and focused it onto the tree crowns surrounding us. A couple of white gibbons were playing there, and we could watch them for another ten minutes before they disappeared in the jungle. After a late lunch, we had only two hours left, since the park closed at six o'clock in the evening. After this time nobody, except rangers, is allowed to stay there. Tata was in permanent contact with other guides and rangers, but nobody knew of the presence of a wild elephant. He sadly told me that probably I would not see any wild elephants because although it was an exceptionally sunny day, it was still the rainy season and it was difficult to see wild elephants during this season. I replied that it would be a great bonus to see a wild elephant, but I wished once in my life to see and experience the real jungle, and this was more than enough. Nevertheless, we waited at one of the many salt lakes – artificially made small ponds filled with salty water where elephants came and drink – when suddenly Tata got a message that one elephant was at the next pond. We immediately jumped into the Jeep and hurried to the spot – and then we saw him. He was a beautiful specimen, a great big adult male just performing his anti-insect cleansing using his majestic trunk (Fig. 6). Since it was almost closing time, we were the only people there, and my guide carefully drove the car forward and backward so I could observe and take pictures of this magnificent animal. What an amazing day no. 1!

The weather of the second day was definitely not nice. There were heavy rain showers throughout the day, and we were already completely wet after the first stop at the "hornbills tree". We went to see the best-known two of a total of 44 waterfalls in the park – Haew Suwat and Haew Narok (Fig. 7). The wonderful Haew Suwat waterfall cascades from a twenty-metres-high cliff, and it became world famous after the release of the movie *The Beach*. Haew Narok waterfall is the largest, most impressive and highest waterfall in the park with three levels, in total about two hundred metres high. Water from the first cliff flows about sixty metres down to the second and third level. Watching the incredible strength of the water, which is quite dangerous in the rainy season, it was difficult to imagine that in the dry season there is almost no water.

Since the rain became heavier and heavier, we tried to dry off a bit at the park's headquarters including visitor's centre. Looking from the window of the centre I noticed that a barking deer was standing outside. I was surprised by such behaviour from a wild animal, but my guide explained me that deer frequently come to the remote sides of buildings where they hide themselves from predators. Still wet, we returned to the jeep and saw a group of macaques on the platform at the back of the car, eating and playing with our lunch we had forgotten there. We drove along one of the rivers in the park and saw two water monitors, one of them a big adult male of imposing size measuring around eight feet. We slowly proceeded to the hornbill viewing point and arriving at the spot, we immediately noticed excitement among the wildlife photographers, who, as usual, were in their places. All their equipment was carefully protected against rain and they observed the side of the fig tree with no hornbills. We immediately installed our telescope and saw a big brown-black mass of roundish shape stuck to the thick branch of the tree. What a surprise also for the experienced experts on the park! This was a young bear that had found his peace and quiet under the fig's crown and, despite the rain, was sleeping there undisturbed. We spent the whole hour alternately observing hornbills and the bear, but he was in a deep sleep and did not move at all. We said good bye to the bear and birds and drove around forty minutes outside the park along its border and then turned off to a hilly area opposite the park. This was the place from which we could observe a "bat miracle". Luckily, we were the first car on spot between two pineapple fields; we prepared the telescope and two cameras and waited. Around five o'clock a faint trickle of small black bodies was discernible but soon a huge stream of bats bodies formed a cloud that waved over the fields. Carefully listening one could hear the whisper of thousands of bat wings reminiscent of the gentle rustle of wind. We could also observe some bat-hunting falcons emerging from the cave, but they were not skilled enough to catch any of them. The whole performance lasted around 65 minutes. During this time over two millions bats flew out from the cave and, in ribbon formation, they flew in the direction of the national park, where the next seven-to-nine hours they would catch insects; and then, being saturated they would return back to the cave. This spectacle is regularly repeated each day regardless of weather for 365 days a year. End of the unforgettable day no. 2.

The next morning was cloudy, but it was not raining. As usual, we first stopped to greet the hornbills and the bear, but its spot was already empty. We drove to the highest accessible point of the park, around 1,000 metres (3,280 feet) a.s.l., behind which a prohibited, military area was located. This day, butterflies were the focus. There were around twenty different species, one more beautiful than the other. So many colours, patterns, and their ability to mask and blend with their surrounding...again a miracle that can be created only by nature itself! Then we made a short inspection of the nearby jungle, which was crowned by watching a group of black gibbons, one of the many critically endangered species worldwide. Unfortunately, time couldn't be stopped, and the evening was rapidly approaching. The last time we stopped at the viewing point to wave to the hornbills and macaques, which immediately surrounded our car, Tata focused his telescope to the sky above us, and I could see the majestic eagle circling over the park and our heads. And this was my farewell to the wildlife. What a wonderful day no. 3!

Sitting in the plane back to Vienna, my mind full of exciting wildlife experiences, I briefly browsed through the current Austrian Airlines magazine, where I found an article about Chiang Mai, the place I originally wanted to go to. The article ended with words: "...anyone who hasn't been to Chiang Mai hasn't been to Thailand."

But this is not true, I WAS IN THAILAND!

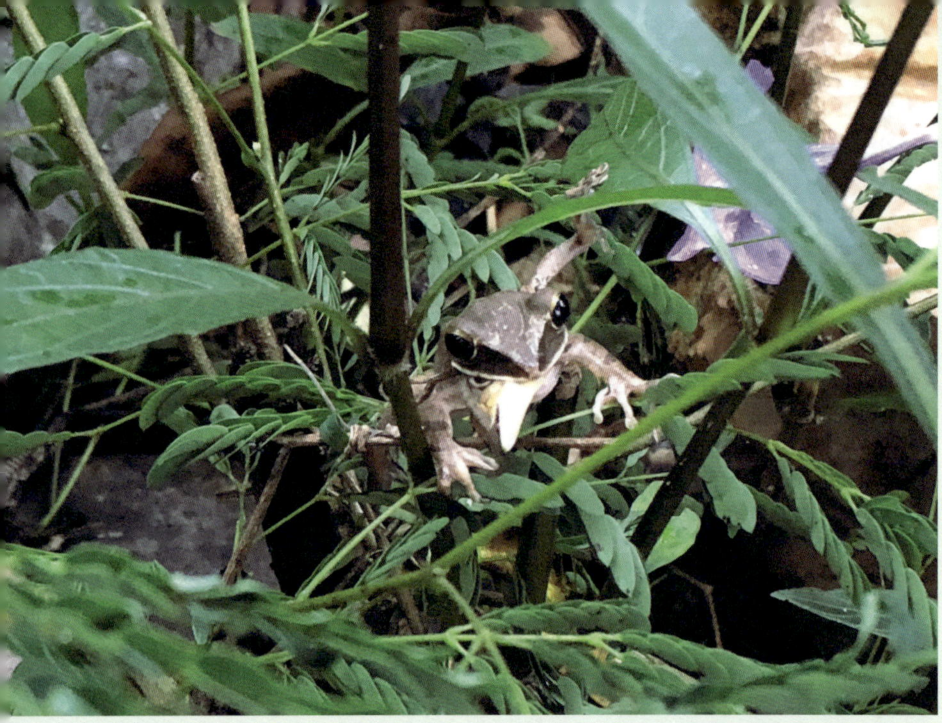

Fig. 2: Frogs in the Frog Khao Yai Resort

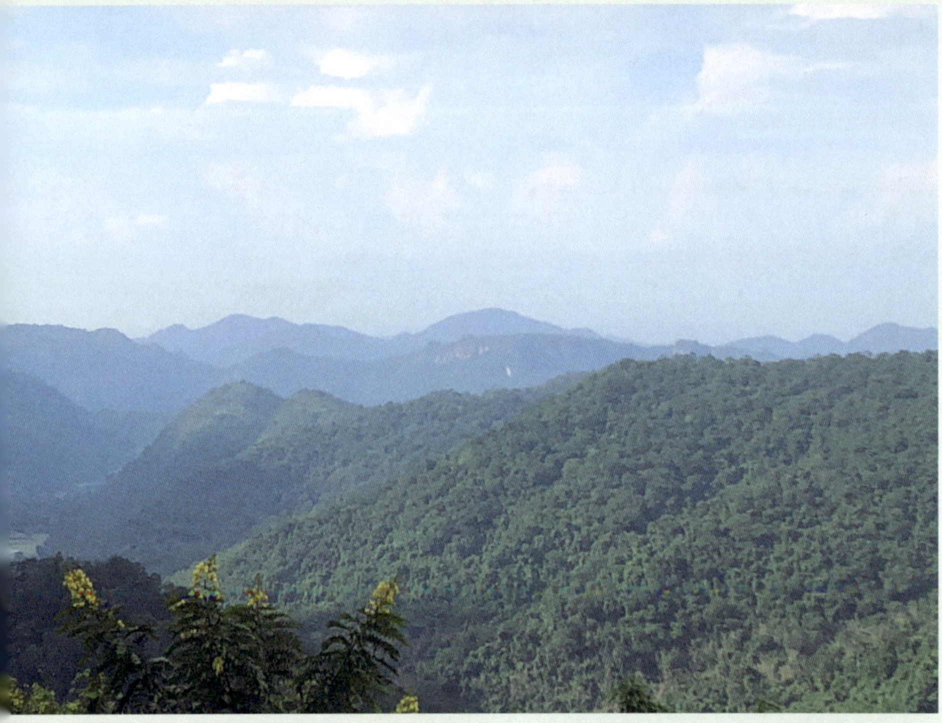

Fig. 3: Khao Yai National Park

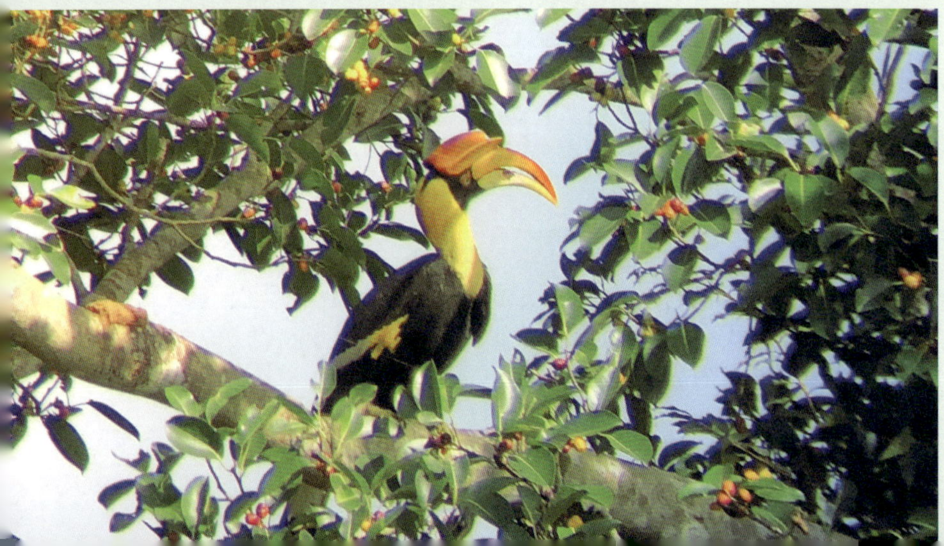

Fig. 4: Great hornbill on a fig tree

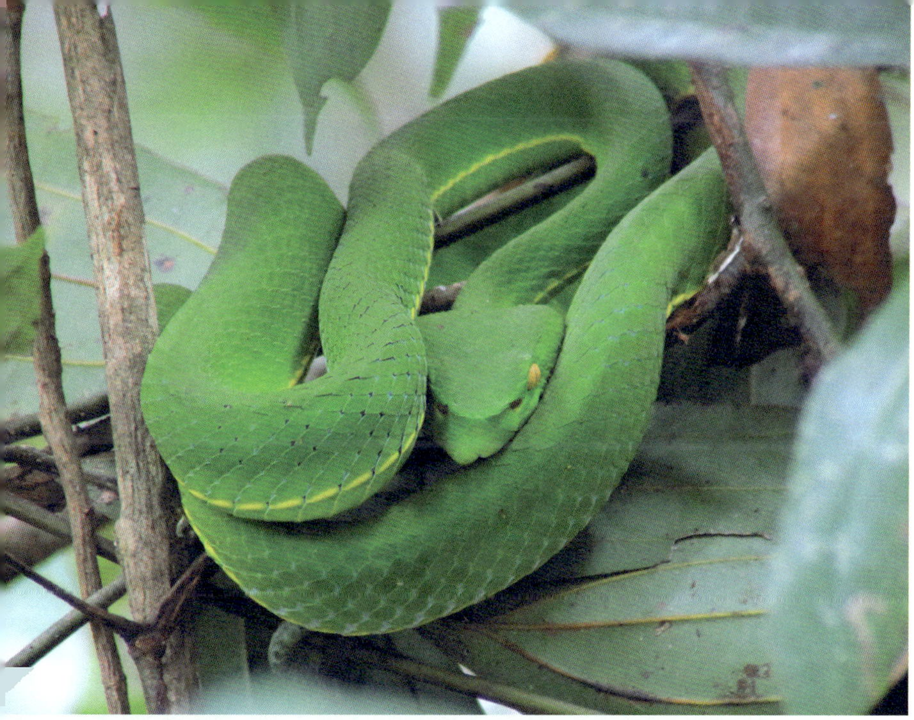

Fig. 5: Sleeping pit viper

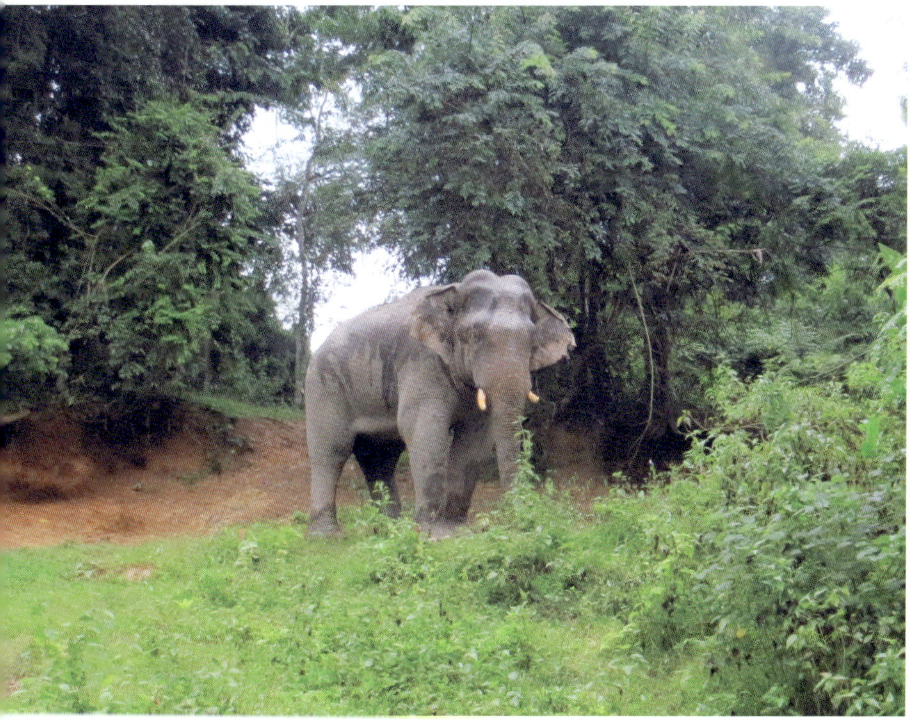

Fig. 6: Elephant at the salt lake

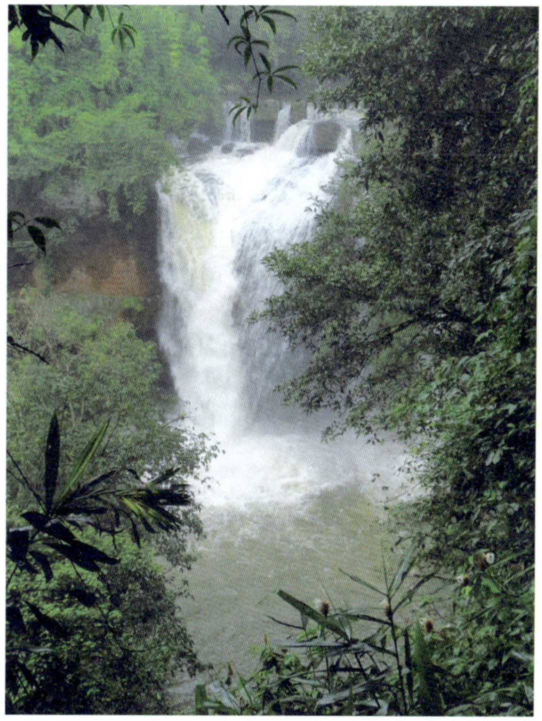

Fig. 7: Haew Narok and Haew Suwat waterfalls

China

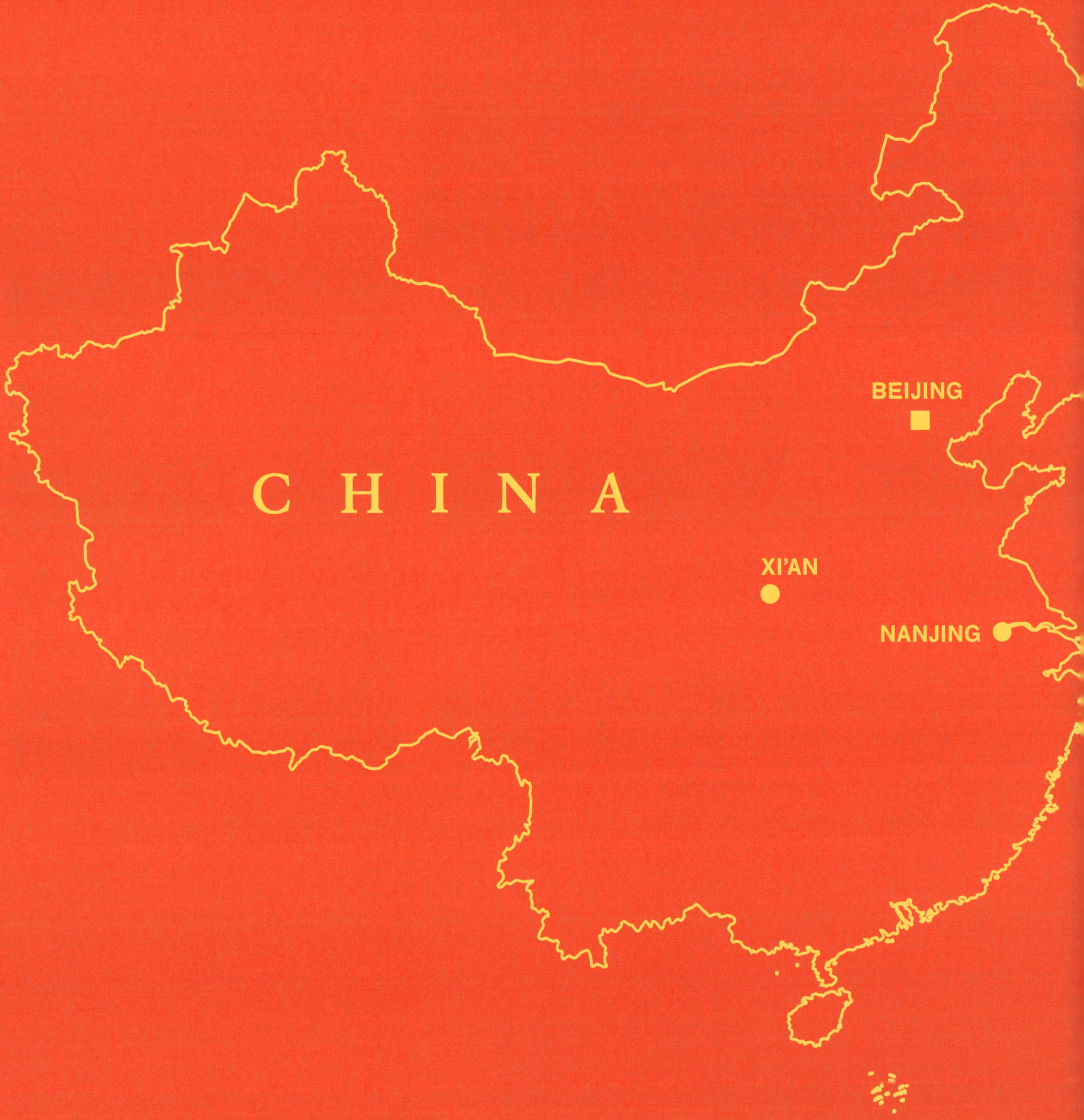

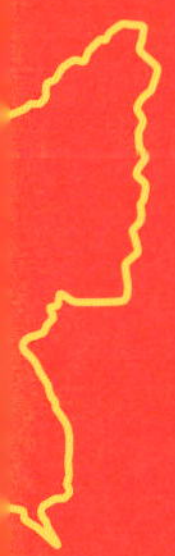

The Silk Road… Connecting Us

GABRIELA KRIST

CHINA 2012–2017

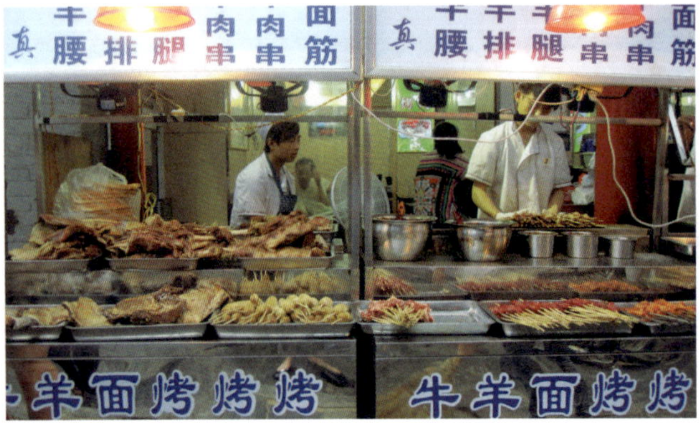

Fig. 6: Impressions from Nanjing, 2016

"Coined by Ferdinand von Richthofen, the term 'Silk Road' has become a handy concept for scholars who attempt to deal with the trans-continental cultural movements between Europe and Asia. Although much has been achieved in the field of history, archaeology and art history, a lot of potential of this concept remains to be explored. The One Belt 'The Silk Road Economic Belt' and the One Road 'the 21st-century Maritime Silk Road' Initiative, pushed by the Chinese government since 2013, albeit ignoring the historical complexity, appears to be a well-thought-out exploit of the historical Silk Road to address the contemporary political and economic challenges. The initiative, in return, has instigated Chinese research institutions, which have long shied away from the foreign land, to start research projects in Silk Road countries."

This introduction to the Silk Road concept comes from the preface of our postprints of the second Silk Road Conference, held in Nanjing in 2016, written by Liangren Zhang, our Chinese partner and the driving force of the Silk Road initiative.

All began in 2012, when Brigitte Winklehner, former President of the Eurasia-Pacific Uninet (EPU), invited Sabine Ladstätter, Director of the Austrian Archaeological Institute (ÖAI), and myself to come with her to Xi'an to investigate possibilities of cooperation with Northwest University (NWU). Her idea was to dock onto a previous Austrian initiative, the conference "The Importance of the Silk Road in Politics, Trade and Culture in the Past and at Present Times" in 1998, organised by herself, Northwest University, and the University of Salzburg, in Xi'an (Fig. 1–2).

After arrival in Xi'an we met for a dinner party organised by Brigitte's former project partners' dean at Northwest University, Li Changan, and with President Sun. We were introduced to the faculty of this prestigious university, especially to professors of archaeology and conservation, among those Liangren Zhang. The idea was to link experts in archaeology and conservation from China and Austria and to discuss how these two disciplines, often working on their own, can exchange and share experience.

The idea of a follow-up conference was born! Xi'an as the starting point of the Silk Road was to be the venue, and archaeology and conservation the focus of discussion. Why limit this opportunity to Austria and China only? We decided to open up and to invite international experts working on projects along the Silk Road.

The first international conference, "Archaeology and Conservation along the Silk Road", was held at Northwest University in Xi'an from 23–25 May 2014 (Fig. 3). Liangren Zhang, at that time Professor of Archaeology at NWU, and myself were appointed as the coordinators. His task was to identify speakers – archaeologists and conservators – mainly in China. Sabine Ladstätter and myself tried to find experts in Austria and beyond working on Silk Road projects and willing to contribute to the meeting.

Thirty presentations from 11 Asian and European countries were delivered at this most interesting and stimulating conference in Xi'an. The excursions to the Terracotta Warrior Museum, Qin Dynasty (Fig. 4), and the Yang Mausoleum, Han Dynasty, were the highlights for us foreigners, not yet familiar with the sophistication of Chinese culture and art (Fig.5–6).

At the second conference at Nanjing University (where Liangren Zhang had moved) from 20–22 May 2016, forty-eight participants from China, Austria, Germany, Switzerland, Iran, Russia, Italy, United Kingdom and the USA could be registered (Fig. 7). Again, Sabine Ladstätter and myself were at hand to suggest Silk Road topics and projects to be presented by Austrian scholars and experts from Europe. We are presently working on the postprints of the conference, which was again a success. The publication is again a joint venture – what concerns work and finances – between the University of Applied Arts Vienna and Nanjing University.

The Silk Road initiative was planned in such a way that it spun out the spirit of the Silk Road in the academic world. On the one hand, the term "Silk Road" has been a popular theme of conferences over the world, but many countries as Russia and Iran were not included. On the other, archaeologists and conservators, because of the often unfortunate separation of the two disciplines, have been sitting in different meetings without communicating with each other. Instead, these conferences brought them together in the hope of providing an opportunity to exchange questions and approaches and to work together.

The EPU was the umbrella of the events, all organising partners are members of the network. It was founded to unite universities of Austria, East Asia, Central Asia, South Asia and the Pacific Region. With a total of 157 member institutions today, the network has been fostering joint research centres, inter-institutional research projects, conferences, as well as faculty, staff, and student exchange. The timely marriage of the initiative of the former EPU-President Brigitte Winklehner and the rising interests of Chinese scholars towards archaeology of foreign countries gave birth to the Silk Road Conference Initiative, the next event will take place in Teheran, Iran in November 2018.

The cooperation with Liangren Zhang counts as the starting point of our work in China and the various projects which followed.

Apart from these two conferences, which also helped to illustrate and to make the important work of Austrian scholars and our universities in the fields of archaeology and conservation visible, it was also possible as yet to organise two International Summer Schools in Vienna in 2016 and 2017. Funded by the Impulse Programme of the Austrian Exchange Service (OeAD), it united teachers and conservation students of NWU in Xi'an together with Indian colleagues from National Museum Institute (NMI) as well as the Belarusian State Academy of Arts and the Lviv Polytechnic Institute in Ukraine.

We also started a student exchange programme and were happy that Jane, Zhenzhen Ma, doctoral student from NWU, spent twelve months with us. Jane was the first Chinese student at our institute and laid the foundation for others to come. At present we are working on a joint PhD study programme between Northwest University and University of Applied Arts Vienna. If finalised it would be the first programme of this kind at our university and a chance for doctoral students to carry out conservation research at two universities and in two countries.

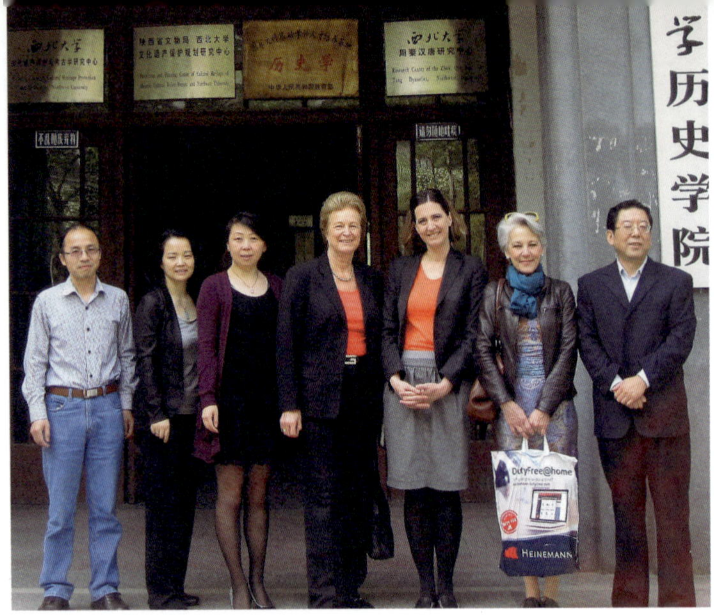

Fig. 1: With Brigitte Winklehner, Sabine Ladstätter and Liangren Zhang, first fact finding mission, Northwest University, Xi'an, 2013

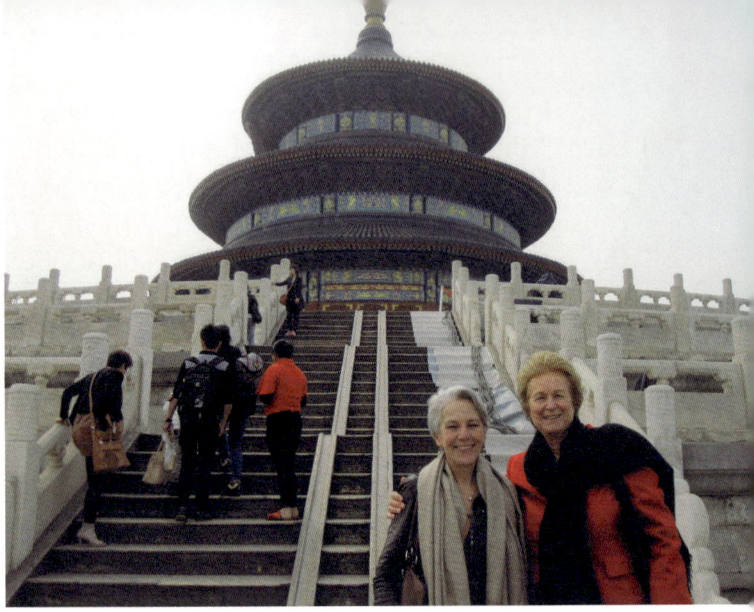

Fig.2: Sight-seeing with Brigitte Winklehner, Temple of Heaven, Beijing, 2013

Fig. 4: Qin Dynasty Terracotta Warriors at the necropolis complex of Emperor Qin Shi Huang, Xi'an

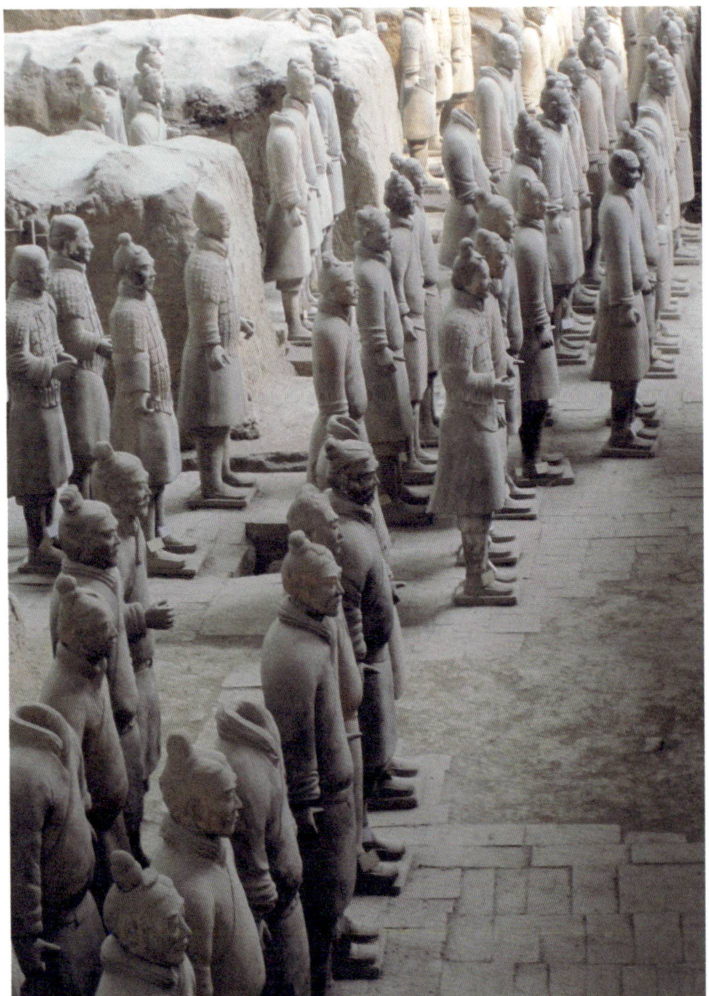

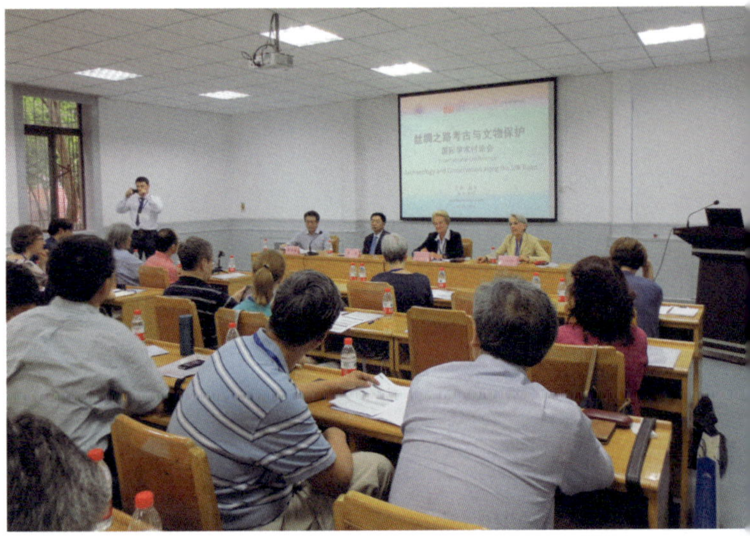

Fig. 3: First International Silk Road Conference in Xi'an, May 2014

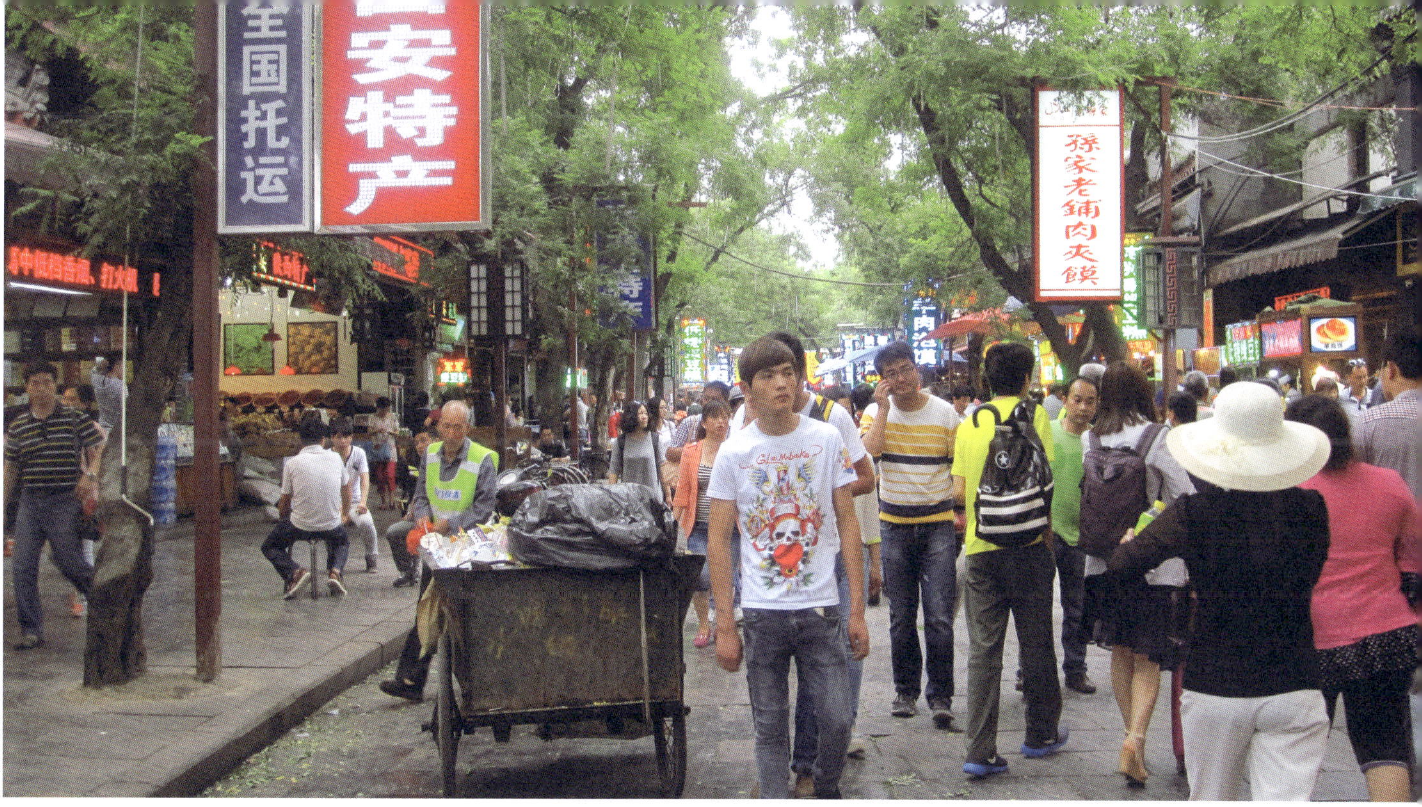

Fig. 5: Impressions from Nanjing, 2016

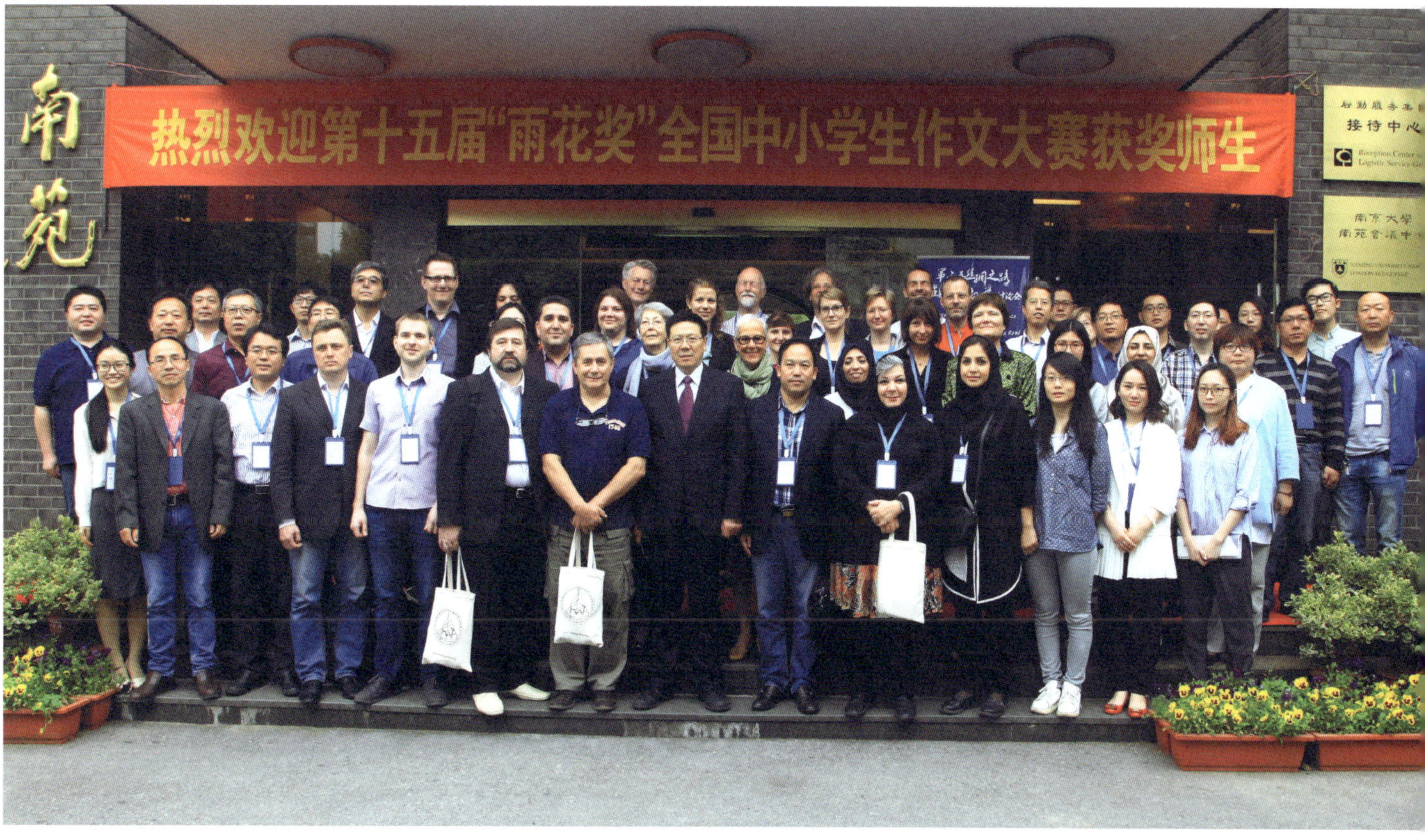

Fig. 7: Second Silk Road Conference in Nanjing, May 2016

Factsheet Silk Road

International Conference Series – East Meets West on the Silk Road

PROJECT	Archaeology and Conservation along the Silk Road
INITIATED BY	Brigitte Winklehner, Gabriela Krist, Sabine Ladstätter, Liangren Zhang
HEADED BY	Liangren Zhang, Gabriela Krist
COORDINATED BY	Martina Haselberger, Tanushree Gupta
DURATION	14-20 April 2013: Kick-off meeting, Xi'an, China 23-25 May 2014: First conference, Xi'an, China 20-22 May 2016: Second conference, Nanjing, China 14-16 November 2018: Third conference, Tabriz, Iran
FUNDED BY	Eurasia-Pacific Uninet (EPU) Northwest University, Xi'an (NWU) Nanjing University, Nanjing
PARTICIPANTS	Gabriela Krist, Tatjana Bayerová, Barbara Rankl

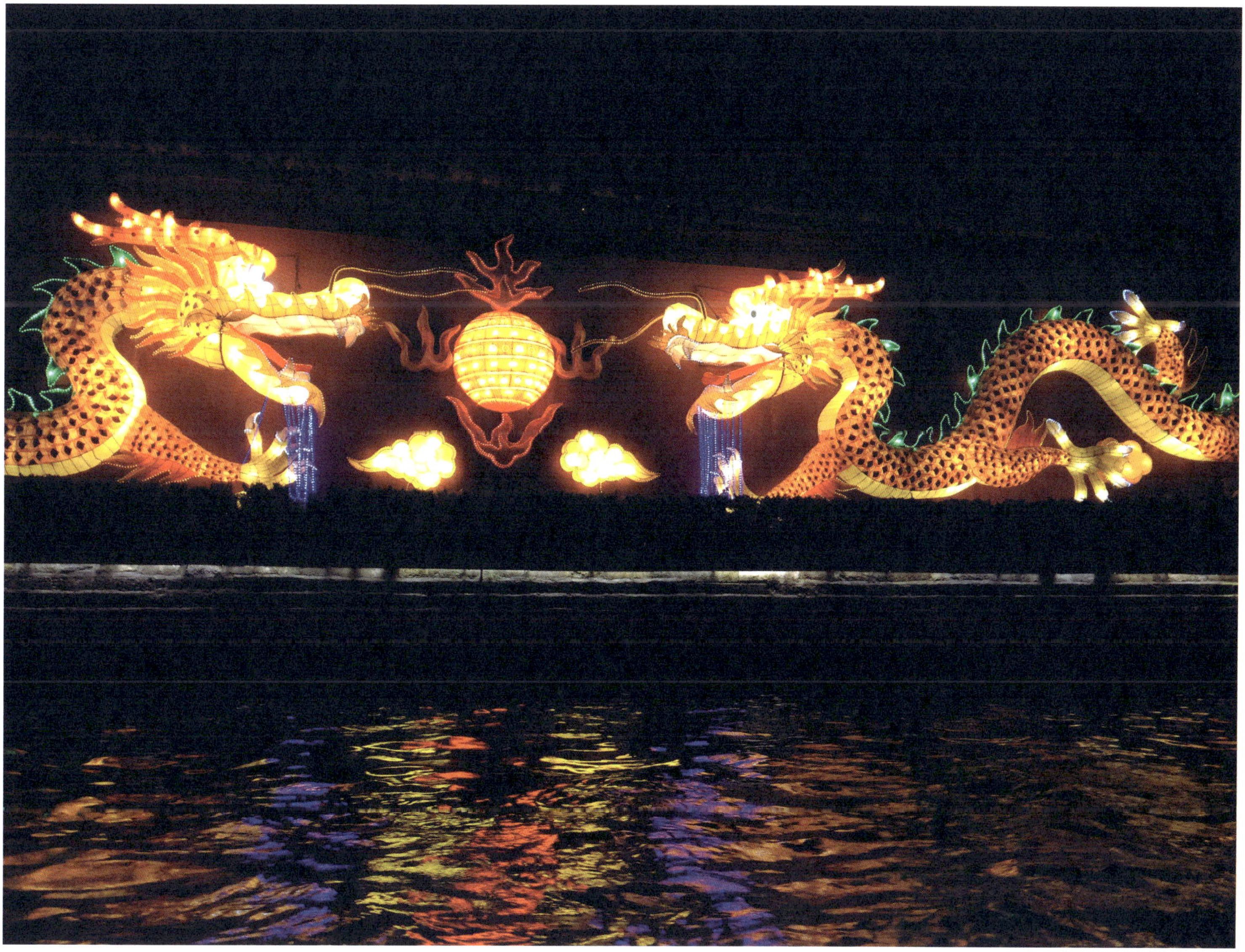

Fig. 9: Qinhuai River night view, Nanjing, China

The International Network in the Past, Present, and Future

TATJANA BAYEROVÁ, BARBARA RANKL

The Silk Road

> "The Silk Road was an ancient trade route that connected the Far East and the Mediterranean from around 114 BCE till 1400 CE. This network of routes, extending some 6,400 km, derived its name from the trade in silk and in addition to economic trade it was a route for cultural interaction between the regions along its network."
>
> *Marta Luciani, University of Vienna. The conference "Archaeology and Conservation along the Silk Road", 2014.*

The Silk Road connected civilisations and brought cultures from across the world into contact with each other for thousands of years. There were not only goods traded, but this transcontinental corridor with its extinctions provided an exchange of science and technology, cultural practices and religious beliefs. Due to a variety of outstanding values, some of the cultural heritage along this road is inscribed in the UNESCO world heritage list.

These trade routes were irregularly used already in the 7th century B.C., but greater exchange of goods between China, Central and West Asian countries, Africa and Europe started in the 2nd century B.C. and silk became the most important and valuable trade commodity. Due to this fact, in 1877 the German geographer Ferdinand von Richthofen named this famous trade route "Silk Road".

The main route (Fig. 1) originated in Chang'an (today Xi'an), followed the Great Wall of China to the northwest, bypassed the Taklamakan desert, climbed the Pamir mountain ranges and then led to Samarkand, Bukhara (both in today's Uzbekistan) and Merv (today Turkmenistan). On the territory of Iran, the route crossed Tehran and then continued via Bagdad to Syria to Palmyra and to the north passing Aleppo. The route went through today's Turkey until it finally ended in Istanbul. In all directions along the main corridor there were numerous extinctions, so the route also led to the African continent. In addition, other trade routes were linked to this huge transport network, including the Amber Road with its starting point at the Baltic Sea. After the fragmentation of the Mongol Empire and with the discovery of the sea routes to India, Southeast and East Asia, the transcontinental mainland route lost its economic importance in the early 16th century.

Aside from parts of the historical Silk Road in Pakistan and China that are still preserved as a paved highway today, there are a number of current efforts to reinstall the old Silk Road under economic and logistical aspects. In 2013, Xi Jinping, the president of the People's Republic of China, presented the establishment and expansion of a "Silk Road Economic Belt" (Fig. 1). This "Belt and Road Initiative" (BRI) is divided into a land route and a sea route.

A large number of infrastructure projects are intended to connect Asia, Africa and Europe on a economic, cultural and political level. In addition to trade routes generating new economic growth, also oil and gas pipelines should be built and economic corridors created with the help of free trade zones and the concentration of technology clusters.

In 2018, the BRI represents a conglomerate of existing, planned or envisaged projects which encounter a great international interest, since a "construction site" of this dimension could have an enormous impact on the constellations of a multipolar world order in the future.

As already mentioned before, science, arts and literature, as well as crafts and technologies were shared and disseminated along the lengths of Silk Road routes not only in antiquity, this process is still alive. The scientific community of archaeology and conservation forms an international network in which the Institute of Conservation plays an important role.

The conference entitled "Archaeology and Conservation along the Silk Road" has found its permanent position on the conference programme list of the recent years. Up to now, there were two conferences organised in 2014 and 2016, the third event is planned in autumn 2018.

As was described by Gabriela Krist and Brigitte Winklehner earlier in this publication, the idea of the "Silk Road" conferences was (re)born in 2012 and in 2013 there was the first meeting of the initiators of this project held in China. But the tradition goes back much further...

The Chinese-Austrian collaboration in this field started already in 1998, when the first joint conference "The Importance of the Silk Road in Politics, Trade and Culture in the Past and at Present Times" was organised at Northwest University (NWU) in Xi'an. Seven years later in 2005, there was another conference on the "Silk Road" issue organised, this time at the University of Vienna as the result of the joint effort of Wang Jianxin (NWU) and Falko Daim (then University of Vienna). Unfortunately, this collaboration between NWU and University of Vienna stopped when Daim moved from Austria to Germany. In 2005, the Chinese Government formulated a new law to stress the importance of the establishment of conservation and archaeological work in China. These legal steps supported the wishes of NWU for further international collaboration in the field of archaeology and conservation.

NWU was founded in 1902 and has been a leading university in the field of archaeology and conservation in China. Its conservation education programme is one of the earliest and most elaborated in China and the Faculty of Archaeology is considered one of the leading institutions in the country. It focuses on practical excavations in Shaanxi Province and on Silk Road sites in Central Asian countries. The collaboration and the strengthening of contacts with Central Asian countries have always been of high interest and priority, but in 2005 there were no funds available for joint research activities with Central Asian research institutions. It was hoped that the network of the Eurasia-Pacific Uninet would help set up relevant contacts and the planned Silk Road project was considered a tool of reinforcing the professional cooperation.

Finally, in April 2013 the first kick-off meeting took place in Xi'an, which is described in more detail in Gabriela Krist's introduction. As a result of the meeting a concrete working plan was established which focuses on three areas: "Organisation of workshops and conferences on Silk Road topic with the focus on archaeology and conservation and with the participation of Central Asian countries", "Student exchange in archaeology and conservation" and "Experts and teachers exchange in archaeology and conservation". For the mutual exchange of students, teaching staff and other experts, a bilateral agreement in the form of a Memorandum of Understanding (MoU) had to be established between NWU and the Austrian partners (Austrian Archaeological Institute, University of Applied Arts Vienna). The MoU with Northwest University, Xi'an, was signed in 2015.

Since the first Xi'an meeting, the Silk Road programme has become an important long-term project of renowned Austrian EPU-members and valuable Chinese partners. It focuses on international collaboration in the field of archaeology and conservation and the implementation of joint-research and joint-conservation projects. It also serves as an important meeting point and dialogue platform. Another aim is the incorporation of other interested institutions from Asian countries into the project and EPU-network.

The first international conference "Archaeology and Conservation along the Silk Road" was held from 23-25 May 2014 at the School of Cultural Heritage of the Northwest University in Xi'an. With its long and rich history, once being the capital of the Han Dynasty and the starting point of the legendary Silk Road, the city of Xi'an was an obvious choice for the conference.

The technical programme of the first two days was divided into eight sessions: "Silk Road", "Textiles – Technology, Conservation and Archaeology", "Food and Cultural Interaction", "Artistic Interaction", "Conservation and Archaeology", "Architecture", "Archaeological Science" and "New Perspectives into Chinese Material Culture". Good quality papers, vivid discussions, the opportunity to network with new colleagues, as well as the informality the conference had adopted, made it excellent. The overall satisfaction was reflected in the wish of all the participants to meet again at a follow-up conference two years later.

The third day was dedicated to excursions to the archaeological sites – undoubtedly the most outstanding part of the conference for many of us. We got the opportunity to visit the huge necropolis complex of Qin Shi Huang, the First Emperor of the Qin Dynasty (221 to 206 BC), known as the "Terracotta Army Museum" (Fig. 2-4) as well as the "Yang Mausoleum of Han" or the "Han Yang Ling Mausoleum" of Emperor Jing (Fig. 5), fourth emperor of the Western Han Dynasty (188 to 141 B.C.), and Empress Wang.

The second conference took place from 20-22 May 2016 at Nanjing University, China, which became a member of the EPU-network in 2015. The main goal of the conference was to continue, and intensify, the collaboration between Austrian and Chinese EPU members in the field of Cultural Heritage Conservation and Archaeology and to develop new collaborative projects. Forty-two participants from China, Austria, Germany, Switzerland, Iran, Russia, Italy, the UK and USA listened to more than forty lectures on different topics and research issues (Fig. 6-7). One emphasis was set on studies of migration, distribution of grain varieties as basis for human and animal consumption as well as bio-archaeological research on the dissemination of diseases and epidemics from East to West. Regarding conservation, lectures on scientific research on art technologies such as manufacture of glass and tiles, bronze casting and painting techniques were of special interest. Problems and challenges in the preservation and conservation of sites along the Silk Road were discussed as well. Postprints from the conference were published by Böhlau Publishing House in September 2018 as the 16th volume of the series "Konservierungswissenschaft. Restaurierung. Technologie", edited by Gabriela Krist.

The third follow-up conference is planned to be held in Tabriz, Iran, in November 2018. The Iranian Research Institute of Cultural Heritage and Tourism will host the event and will be coordinated by Nanjing University and the University of Applied Arts Vienna. As the previous conferences, this one will be highly multidisciplinary, bringing together international experts in the fields of conservation, archaeology and art history focusing on sites along the Silk Road.

The information gathered for the historical overview of the Silk Road in the first part of this article was collected from the publications listed below.

LITERATURE

Henß, R., *Seidenstraße. Highway der Geschichte: von Istanbul nach Xi'an*, München 2017.

Hoering, U., *Der lange Marsch 2.0. Chinas Neue Seidenstraßen als Entwicklungsmodell*, Hamburg 2018.

Höllmann, T., *Die Seidenstraße*, 2. Auflage, München 2007.

Schmeisser, W./ et.al., *Die neue Seidenstraße. Digitalisierung und strategische Herausforderungen*, München 2018.

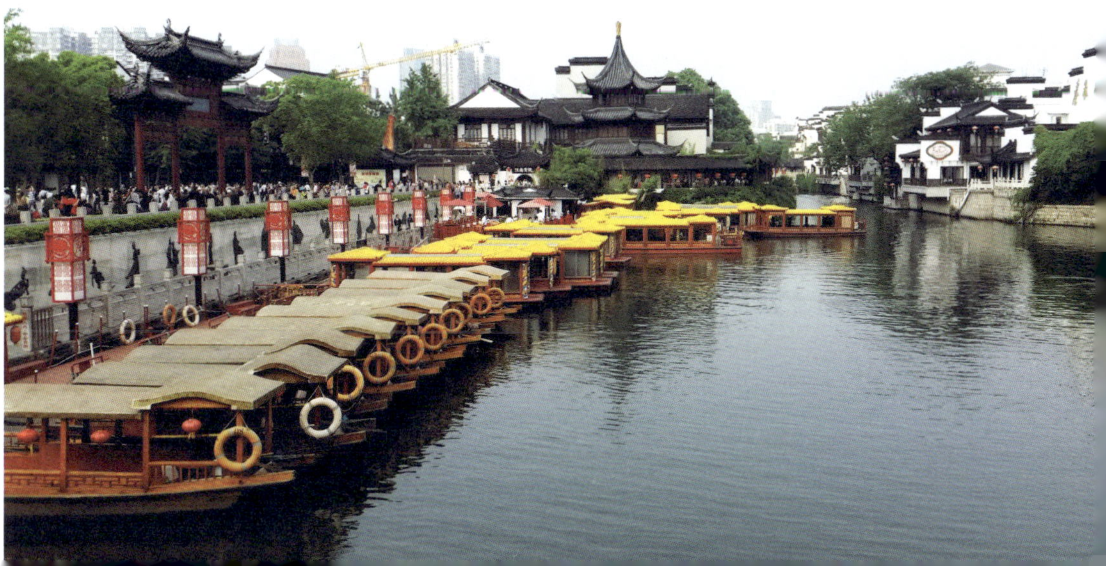

Fig. 8: View of Qinhuai River, Nanjing, China

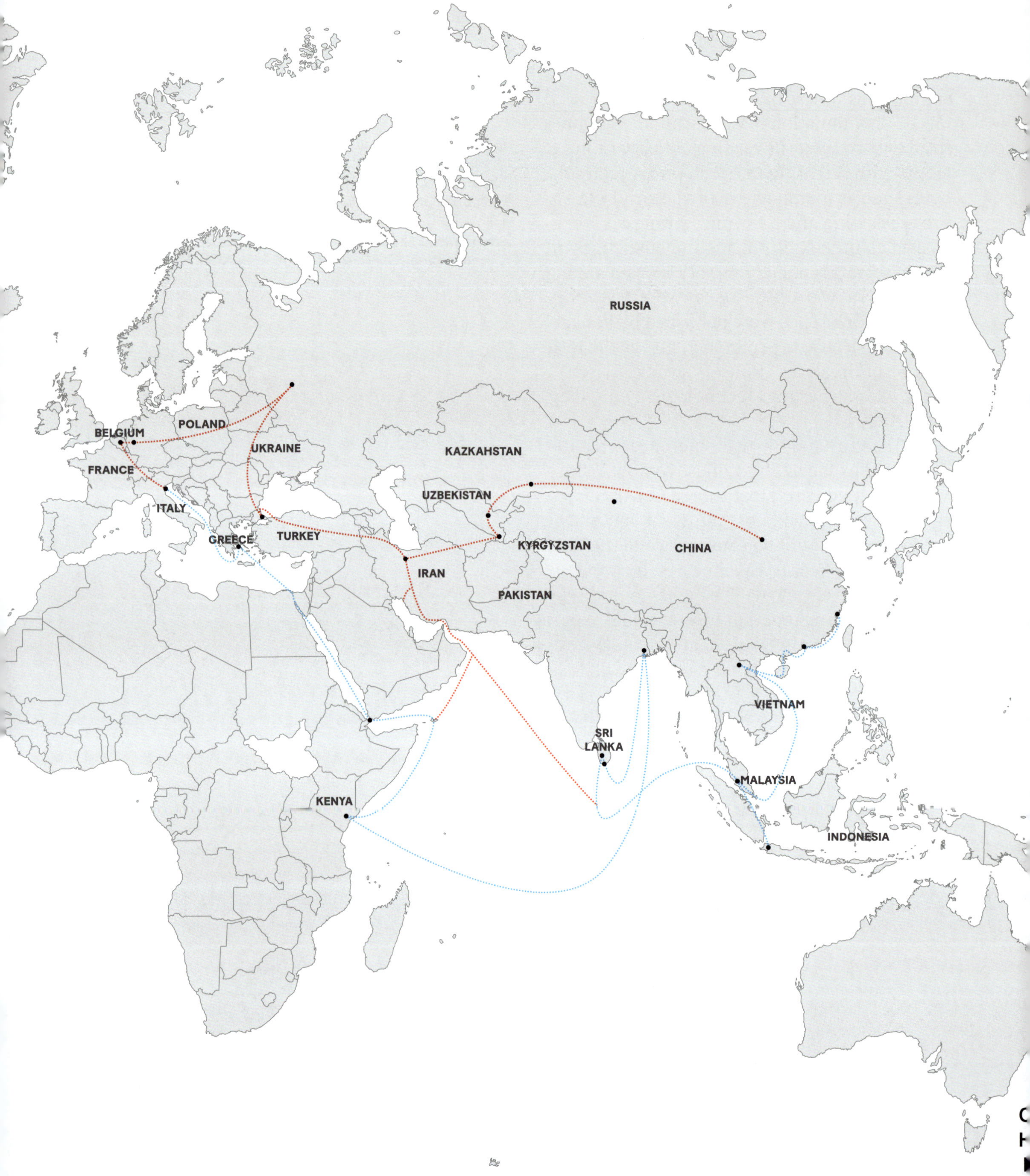

The Silk Road

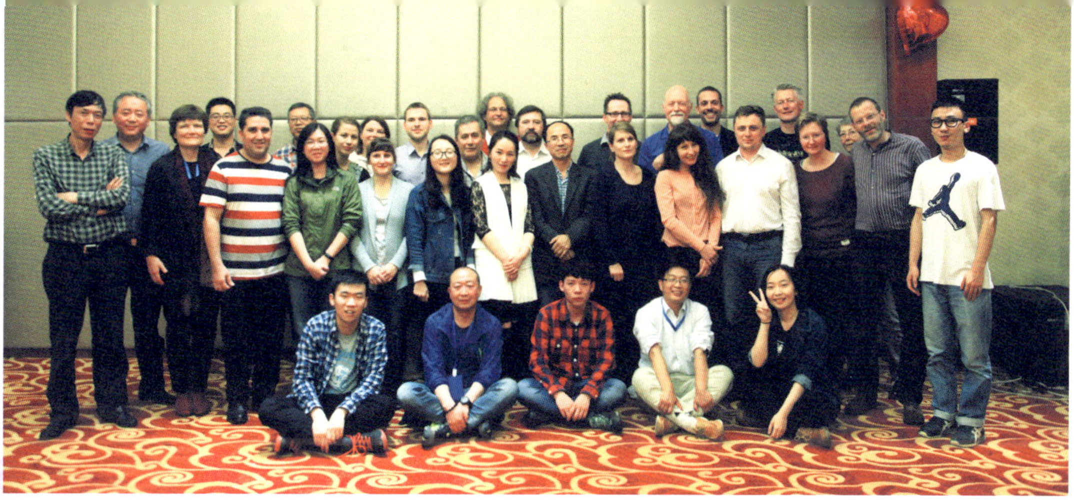

Fig. 6: The Second International Conference on Archaeology and Conservation along the Silk Road, May 2016, Nanjing, China

Fig. 2: "Terracotta Army Museum" in Xi'an, China

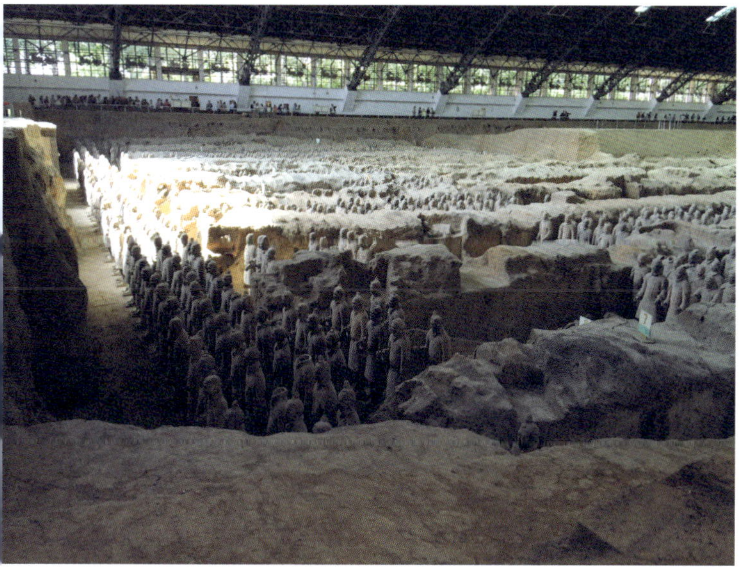

Fig. 3: In-situ conservation works, "Terracotta Army Museum", Xi'an, China

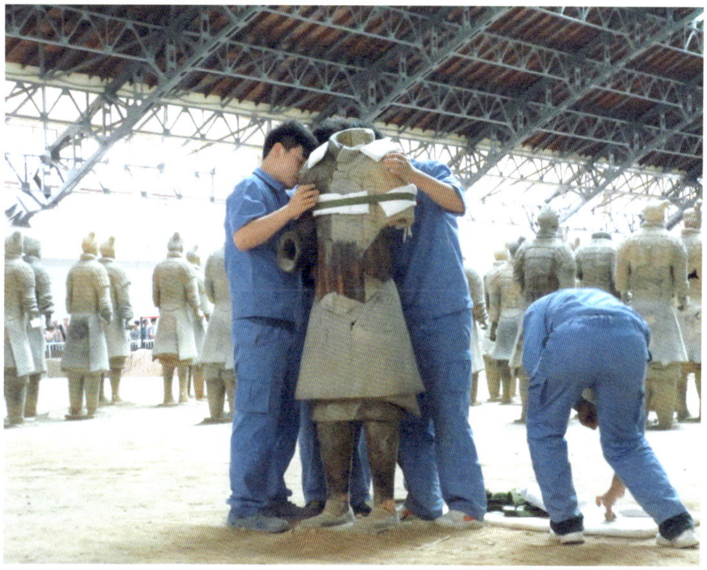

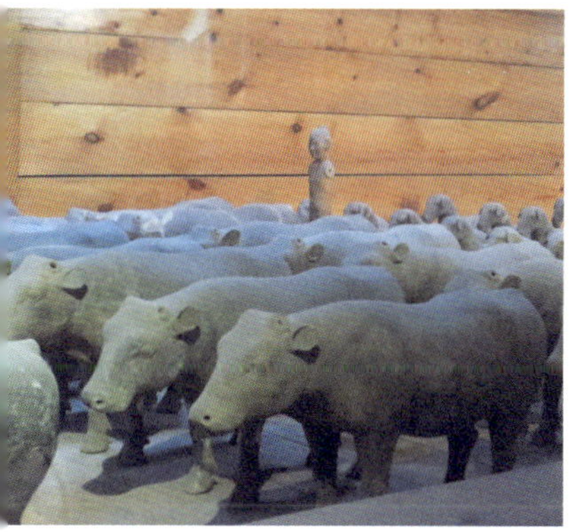

Fig. 5: Buried animal figurines, "Han Yang Ling Mausoleum", Xianyang, China

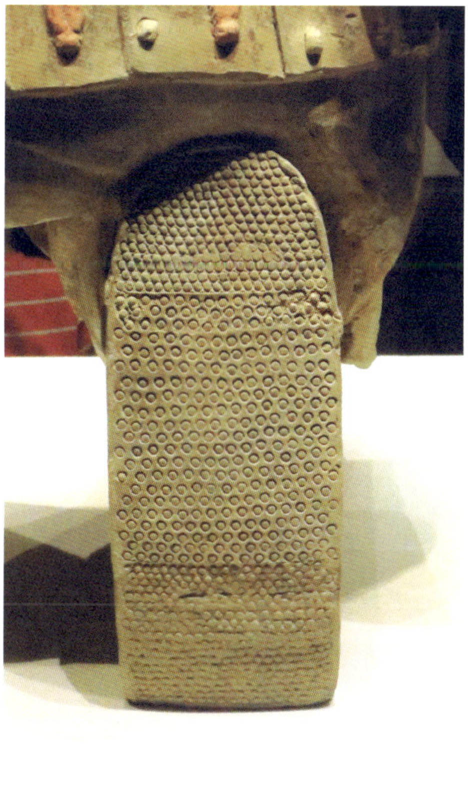

Fig. 4: Detail of the delicate work of the outsole of the kneeling archer, Pit 2, "Terracotta Army Museum", Xi'an, China

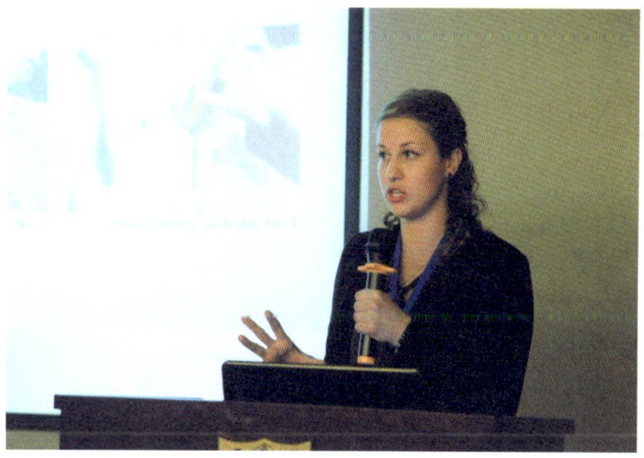

Fig. 7: Barbara Rankl presenting at the second international conference on "Archaeology and Conservation along the Silk Road", May 2016, Nanjing, China

More exchange is needed

INTERVIEW
LIANGREN
ZHANG

BY ROMAN
TRONNER

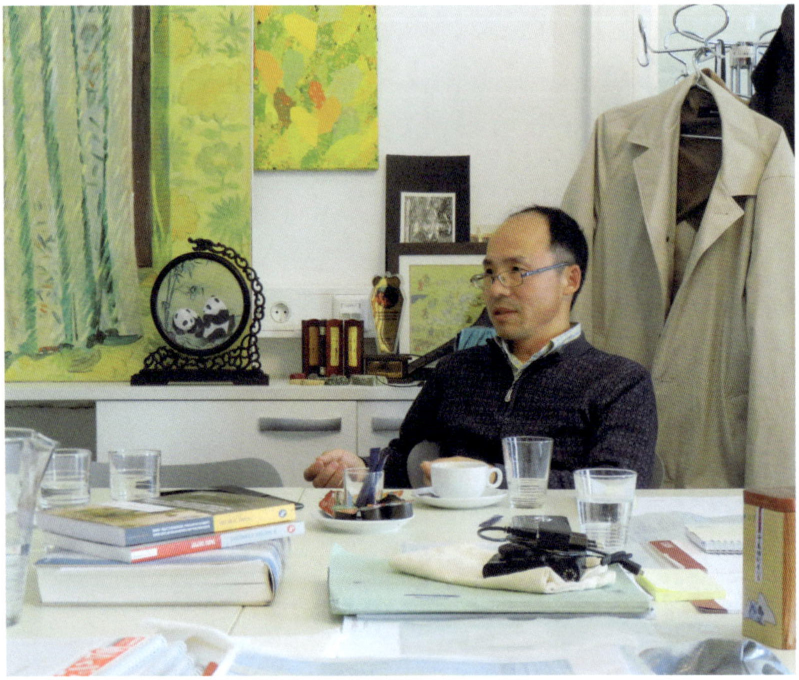

Fig. 1: Liangren Zhang, archaeologist and professor at Nanjing University

China's rich cultural heritage was largely neglected until the 1990s, but the country is rapidly catching up. The number of museums is growing and historical sites are being preserved. Despite the boom, conservation is still lagging behind. In March 2017, Roman Tronner asked the Chinese archaeologist Liangren Zhang from Nanjing University, during a visit at the Institute of Conservation, University of Applied Arts Vienna, how Europe and China can profit from fostering cooperation in the field of conservation.

Dr. Liangren Zhang got his PhD degree from University of California, Los Angeles. His PhD dissertation "Ancient Society and Metallurgy" was finished in 2007 and published in 2012. After returning to China in 2009, he was appointed as a professor first at Northwest University and then at Nanjing University. Since 2014, Zhang has been collaborating with the Institute of Conservation on the conference series "Archaeology and Conservation along the Silk Road".

China is a country of rich cultural heritage. What does this cultural heritage mean to the people in the past and today?

China has a long history, it's a large country and it has a lot of cultural heritage. The government and the people value their cultural heritage, but before the 1990s China didn't have the facility and personnel to protect and preserve this heritage. In the turbulent years before the 1990s, a big portion of cultural heritage was destroyed and lost forever. But nowadays the government and the people are investing in the facility and the personnel in the area of conservation and protection. Now a lot of conservation and protection projects are going on, not only conservation of objects but also protection of the pretty huge historical sites in China. This, by the way, means moving the inhabitants from the site area in some cases. This sort of preservation project is often combined with tourism.

So, cultural heritage and its protection have been put on the political agenda. How are cultural institutions like museums affected by this development?

Today in China there is a boom of museums, hundreds of new museums have appeared at the national, province and local levels. The problem is that these museums are short of artefacts; they don't have enough objects to put in the exhibition. So museums begin to exchange exhibitions with other institutions and sometime they even borrow exhibitions from Europe, from Egypt and so on. For instance, the National Museum in Beijing borrowed an exhibition from the British Museum; the Nanjing Museum borrowed exhibitions from other countries, like Canada.

There is another thing: in the past the museums always charged a fee to the visitors, but today more and more museums are free for visitors. Because of free admission the number of visitors is steadily growing and the people really love it! Nowadays museums are really crowded. So, we see more museums and more visitors going to museums. This results in higher investments in preservation projects by the government.

How much did these investments improve the infrastructure of conservation?

Several conservation centres have been established over China in the near past. There is a big one in Shanghai, several in Beijing and one in Nanjing. Our university doesn't have one, but we are planning to have one. Xi'an and many other museums have a conservation section themselves – so it's developing.

In this sense we owe gratitude to German, Italian, and US institutions because they helped develop conservation in the end of the 1990s. During that time, we didn't have the facilities, we didn't have the funding, and we didn't have the trained personnel to do the work. And then the German, Italian, and US institutions came to China and helped build laboratories. After ten years of learning, the Chinese conservators began to build more labs on their own.

What happened before the nineties, how strongly did China protect its cultural heritage?

Since the 1930s, the Chinese policy on cultural heritage says that all cultural artefacts belong to the state. So, when archaeologists find something in the field, they can't take it to their own homes, but it belongs to the state as all the cultural sites do. Only authorized personnel, archaeologists, can dig at these sites; otherwise the excavation is illegal. From the 1950s, we learned from the Soviet Union. A law established in the 1950s said that any construction must be preceded by survey and excavation and the constructor was legally bound to pay for the survey and excavation. In many cities when there was a big road construction, archaeologists were to be called in.

And what was the situation about conservation?

Conservation itself was lagging behind I should say. China has a long history of conservation, because its cultural heritage comprises a lot of paintings, paper paintings, and furniture. The large museums have had a conservation team ever since we had museums in the 1920s – admittedly very late. We know that in the imperial houses of the Qing dynasty, and the previous dynasties, they had their own personnel to take care of artefacts. However, scientifically trained personnel in the field of conversation came only after the 1990s and the training came from Germany, Italy, and the US.

The law on preservation was rewritten in 1982, which reinforced the earlier articles. The act is important for the protection of big sites, so for instance, a large settlement, a large capital site, will be protected from further destruction. In 2009, there was a new manual for archaeologists; it stipulates that archaeologists must invite conservators to the site, for the on-site conservation whenever it is necessary. Or at least they have in their mind what kind of artefacts are expected. If there are sensitive artefacts to be discovered they must call a conservator to do on-site conservation right away because now they understand that certain organic materials can vanish in a few minutes. Conservation must be done right away. Also, long-term conservation must be planned in advance – for instance pottery, clothing, for these sort of things we should plan. Without proper facilities or personnel, the excavation cannot be realised. So really we have to take care of the conservation issue. Nowadays, archaeologists really do that, so they plan the conservation ahead of the actual digging.

So despite all efforts, education in the field of conservation is lagging behind?

Large museums have a section of conservation, new museums and a lot of old museums don't have one. Of course, the conservators can train people, and they do that. A few universities have conservation programmes. The first university programme for conservation was started twenty years ago. But more and more conservation programmes are coming up. So yes, you are right; we are still lagging behind in education.

Who does the training in the museums?

Mostly it's done by the museum staff, they have their own conservators. The staff is trained in traditional fashion – the master-disciple pattern, you know – and they are trained by watching and doing. It takes many years. Sometimes a university conservator goes to help but it doesn't happen a lot. Very often we ask museum staff to come to the university to teach our students, because they have materials, they have experience and they have facilities. While training at the university is more based on scientific analysis and on technical equipment, like scanning electron microscopes, traditionally, the staff from the museum doesn't use that. They practice conservation by experience.

Does your university, Nanjing University, offer a conservation study programme?

We would like to have a conservation study programme at our university. We are planning to have one. But it will come years later. Our university is building up a lab of conservation and we are also building up scientific archaeology. So it's very similar to conservational science.

Regarding your cooperation with the Institute of Conservation here in Vienna, when did you get in contact for the first time?

Well, it just happened that I had the opportunity to get to know Prof. Gabriela Krist in 2014 on the occasion of a conference organized by the Eurasia-Pacific Uninet (EPU). This network proposed a conference on the Silk Road subject and at that time I was in Xi'an at Northwest University. EPU already had an agreement with this university. So that was where we met and we held a conference in Xi'an. Last year we had another conference at Nanjing University.

These conferences were different from the normal ones. You know, normally archaeologists sit together and talk about archaeology and the conservators sit together and talk about conservation. But in these conferences we brought archaeologists and conservators together so they share their knowledge and exchange with each other. That is something very new in China; it happens that archaeologists and conservators are separated from each other, so I think it is a good idea to bring the two groups of people together. Not only the two professions, but also people from different countries – so it is really about the Silk Road. During the two conferences we brought scholars from China, Europe and especially Austria, Russia and sometimes even Central Asia, Mongolia and America together.

Recapitulating these conferences, do you see any differences between China and Europe in dealing with the topic of conservation – culturally and technically?

In principle, they are the same. The only difference is that China has a set of cultural heritage. Austria has another set of cultural heritage. For instance, Austria has a lot of oil paintings, but we don't; we have a lot of lacquerware instead. Austria has a lot of glassware, but we don't; we have a lot of textiles, silk. So we have different strengths. A few museums do have European oil paintings and I don't think we have trained personnel to conserve those things. Of course silk is also available in Europe and Russia, but I think we have more experience with it. So it's very important to share these kinds of skills and experiences.

What was the major outcome of the Silk Road conferences?

Besides bringing together the disciplines, the conferences help us understand each other because both sides have their own concerns so they can work better with each other. Another thing is to share knowledge from different countries. The direct outcome of the two conferences is different. For the first Silk Road conference we didn't publish anything, but for the second we plan to publish proceedings. And of course, because of the two conferences we are interested in each other and for instance, Gabriela Krist and I continue the dialogue, the exchange and activities.

You are specialized in metal. What is the focus of your research?

I am not really a metallurgist. I am mainly an archaeologist, but I have interests in ancient metals. My dissertation is about the ancient metallurgy of Russia and China. And the theory is very anthropology oriented, how ancient society worked. What was the significance of metallurgy for the ancient societies in China and Russia? Metal is not only a medium of technology, but also a product; it's an economic thing. I was investigating the question how metal affected ancient societies in the two regions. And then after that, in 2010, I went to excavate a Bronze Age settlement, which resulted in a lot of metals, and then in 2011 I got a project to study ancient metals from Xinjiang and the project is still going on.

Is metal conservation a topic in China?

It is a big topic, it is well known that China has a lot of cast bronzes and ritual bronze vessels and when you visit China wherever you go you can see a lot of bronze vessels. They are vulnerable to weathering, so you can see a lot of them corroded and sometimes they get affected by bacteria. So a lot of ancient bronzes are in a bad condition and we don't have enough personnel to deal with them. There is another problem with the storage. Many museums don't have the proper storage facilities for them. But you can do nothing; you just can watch the bronzes deteriorating. So this problem is really specific to China. In Europe you have different kind of problems – of course you have cast bronzes, but the questions and problems are different. Our scientists are looking for matters to solve this problem. I don't know whether they have found a solution yet.

Besides paintings and objects, mainly metal, the Institute of Conservation in Vienna specialises in textile and stone conservation. How do you think your university could profit from the collaboration and vice versa?

My visit to the institute here in Vienna is a good opportunity to see how the institute organises conservation, and of course we are going to ask this institute for advice on how to design and how to plan the facilities in China, the central programme – all these sorts of things. Regarding metal: I know in Europe there are many regional bronzes coming from China and in China there are a few hammered metal artefacts from the Near East and Europe. So that's a field we can work together.

For my Viennese colleagues it's important to visit China to know, to find out what the institutes are doing, and they will be interested in having collaboration projects. We have plenty of these actually. For instance, we have Buddhist temples everywhere, we have mural paintings which need to be conserved, we have thangka paintings that need to be conserved as well, and we have various kinds of artefacts: bamboo slips, sometimes ivory, elephant tusks – so it depends on the discovery. But also furniture, we have plenty of furniture. If you plan to explore, you can find a lot of it.

To summarise, what are the most important results of that cooperation with Austria?

Well, it's important for us to know each other, to know what can be done, what kind of resources are available; that's the purpose of my visit to this institute. Prof. Krist has been to China several times and she knows the country well. We need to know each other first and then we can plan. I am very satisfied to see the labs here, the staff. We all would like to continue the collaboration; first of all we would like to continue the conference series. We will continue to discuss what can be done in terms of scientific research in conservation; we need to find a common ground or opportunities.

Was there anything striking for you during your visit here in Vienna?

The fact that here at the institute in Vienna the students can work on the original object itself – because of manifold cooperation with museums – is striking to me. Our students at Northwest University in Xi'an don't have such opportunities to work on the real object, so very often they are doing experiments only, because museums don't have confidence in them yet. But I think it is very important for the students to gain "real" experience, to have the chance to work on the real objects. So this is very good. Once we have students we can send them here.

IIC-ITCC Overseas Courses in Beijing

TATJANA BAYEROVÁ,
TANJA KIMMEL

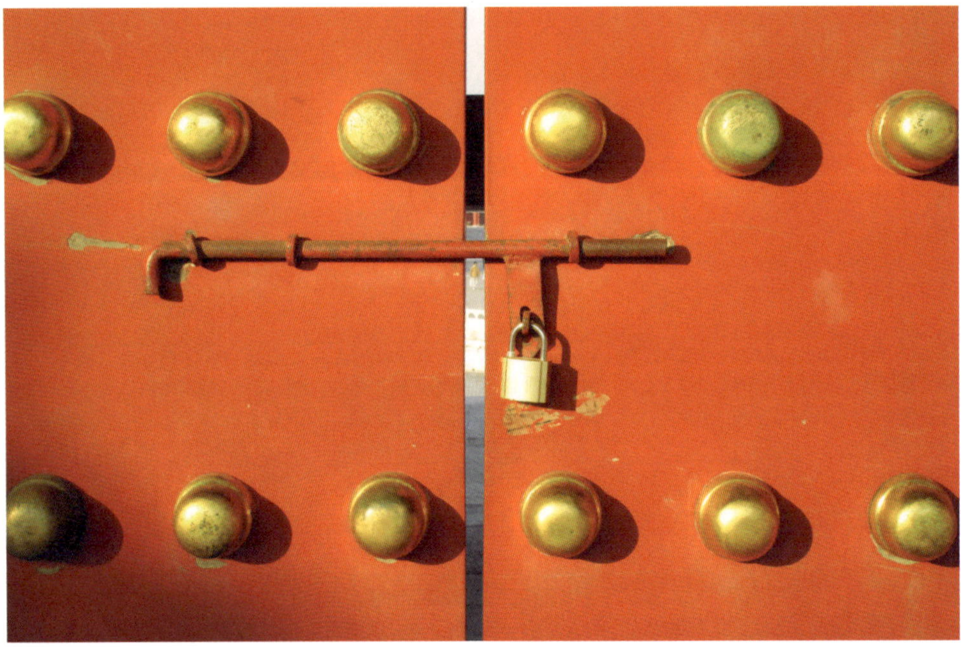

Fig. 1: Locked door of the Forbidden City, Beijing

In 2015, the International Institute for Conservation of Historic and Artistic Works (IIC) and the Palace Museum in Beijing established IIC's first overseas training institute – the IIC International Training Centre for Conservation (IIC-ITCC) in the Palace Museum in Beijing. Based on the joint effort of IIC's professional know-how and the immense cultural resources of Beijing's Palace Museum, every year the Training Centre offers a thematic training course for mid-career conservation professionals of different backgrounds from developing countries in Asia-Pacific and other participants from all over the world. Each course is dedicated to a particular topic of interest and based on theory lectures given by world-renowned experts, practical training, case studies presentations, discussions of attendees with the lecturers, and cultural site visits. Among the main objectives of these courses are: the dissemination of knowledge of the best theories and practice in conservation, the development of a professional network between the participants and their institutions, future collaboration, access to IIC teaching resources, and promotion of the IIC's objectives and ideas for the Asian professional conservation community. Up to now, three courses have been organised on the following topics: "Scientific Approaches to Preventive Conservation" (2015), "Non-Destructive Analysis in the Conservation of Cultural Heritage" (2016) and "Scientific Approaches to Textile Conservation" (2017). The upcoming workshop in late October 2018 will focus on paper and photograph conservation, followed by a symposium addressing the same topic.

Both Tanjas (Tatjana B. and Tanja K.) had the pleasure to be selected from approximately seventy candidates and participate at two of these courses – Tatjana B. in 2016, Tanja K. in 2017.

The 2016 IIC-ITCC course "Non-Destructive Analysis in the Conservation of Cultural Heritage" reviewed the current methods and approaches in this topic, which is of the highest importance and interest in the field of conservation science. The course took place at the Gugong Institute of the Palace Museum in Beijing from 13-18 November and welcomed 24 participants from different institutions from thirteen countries across the world (Fig. 3). The six-day extremely dense programme led by six renowned lecturers included theoretical and practical sessions, demonstration in the conservation laboratories, and museum visits and excursions (Fig. 4). In the theoretical lectures, for which the pre-course preparation was recommended, attendees were introduced to the principles, challenges and limitations of selected non-destructive analyses. The methods introduced were "Analytical Imaging and Microscopy", "Colour and Gloss Measurements" and "Multispectral Imaging" (David Saunders, British Museum, UK), "Optical Coherence Tomography" and "Spectral Imaging" (Haida Liang, Nottingham Trent University, UK), "Raman Spectroscopy" (Fig. 5) and "Infrared Spectroscopy" (Austin Nevin, Italian National Research Council, Italy), "X-ray Computed Tomography" and "X-Ray Fluorescence" (Lynne Lee, Getty Conservation Institute, USA) and "3D Imaging" (Cristiana Achille, Politecnico di Milano, Italy). Numerous case studies from the Palace Museum were presented by Jirong Song (Palace Museum, Beijing).

During the practical sessions, participants in small groups were trained in operating non-portable as well as portable analytical instruments and could compare various types of devices used for the particular method. The possibility of such a "hands-on training", the discussions with the lecturers and with the Palace Museum laboratory team: their explanation of the appropriate data interpretation as well as their tips and tricks were an absolutely invaluable highlight for many participants, me (Tatjana B.) included. The variety of instruments introduced and the possibility to touch and use them was really remarkable. Nevertheless, it is clear that not all facilities, especially the highly sophisticated ones (e.g. optical coherence tomography, 3D imaging, X-ray computed tomography), can be concentrated in one relatively small working place. On the other hand, there are still more methods which, thanks to the continuous development of new and user-friendly instruments, are becoming accessible for smaller institutions or museums and are used for daily routine analyses. One of these methods is X-Ray fluorescence (XRF), a technique I was especially interested in, since the purchase of a portable XRF device for our institute had been the subject of debate for quite some time. I greatly appreciated the possibility of seeing various XRF instruments and discussing with experts which of those devices, and with which parameters, would be the most versatile for work at our institute.

The third IIC-ITCC course, "Scientific Approaches to Textile Conservation" in 2017, hosted 23 fellows from twelve countries with a spectacular variety of backgrounds in textile conservation (Fig. 6). The workshop lasted from 13-23 November and took place for the first time in the newly established "Hospital for Conservation" at the Palace Museum in the Forbidden City, Beijing (Fig. 7). The "Hospital for Conservation" is a centre of conservation studios and also the largest scientific institution for heritage conservation in China.

During this nine-day workshop, the participants worked closely with instructors Sarah Staniforth (IIC President, UK) (Fig. 8), Dinah Eastop (UCL Institute of Archaeology, UK) (Fig. 9), Mary Brooks (University of

Durham, UK) (Fig. 10), Austin Nevin (Italian National Research Council, Italy), Diana Collins (Hong Kong) and the specialists from the Palace Museum. The workshop started with theory lectures presenting current approaches to preventive conservation and non-destructive analysis of textiles. Following practical sessions, demonstrations, case studies, group exercises and discussions, resulted in helping participants to understand the key principles and themes in the practice of textile conservation. Such profound understanding is an essential prerequisite for the formulation and execution of appropriate conservation treatments for textile objects. Some of the case studies focused on the comprehensive textile collections of the Palace Museum, an institution with a longstanding reputation for the care and research of imperial textiles in China. As an additional value to the whole workshop, there was also the exceptional opportunity to view the museum's major exhibitions as well as some textiles from storage and conservation studios with state-of-the-art equipment.

The workshop was very well-organised. I liked the subjects that were taught and the way the course was structured: from lecturing to small group work and recaps for the "participants homework". I gained so much from the lively and productive discussions that grew from these interactions, resulting in the exchange of knowledge and experience amongst the participants. Despite the programme's intensity, the participants had the opportunity to focus on issues and challenges they face each day as textile conservators or museum professionals. The workshop gave me good ideas for my own courses, and I am now questioning my work practice in a different way. I personally found the session about "non-destructive analysis of textiles" most useful, since it included a lot of new information for me. The same interests and common problems broke down cultural and language barriers among the participants. At the end, I not only got to know new colleagues from China and many corners of the world but also made new friends with whom I share unforgettable moments.

The course was also a precursor to the IIC-Palace Museum 2017 Hong Kong Symposium, an international forum themed "Unroll and Unfold: Preserving Textiles and Thangkas to Last" that took place in Hong Kong immediately after the workshop on 24-26 November 2017.

The symposium, jointly presented by IIC, Palace Museum and Leisure and Cultural Services Department in Hong Kong, enabled participants to develop a valuable professional network for advice and resources, as well as sharing knowledge and experience with hundreds of textile conservation specialists worldwide. Besides conservation issues, the symposium addressed the artistic and historical aspects of textile artefacts ranging over thangkas, embroideries, archaeological textiles along the Silk Road, and royal and ethnic costumes throughout the East and West. Eighteen distinguished textile specialists and scholars from across the world presented case studies and the latest research findings on the subjects. The technical sessions included a series of social events giving delegates a chance to establish a professional network for advice and resources, as well as sharing knowledge and experience with over 280 textile conservation specialists from 24 countries.

For both Tanjas it was a great honour to be selected from so many candidates and participate in a workshop led by the most distinguished international lecturers. The professionalism of all the teaching and IIC-ITCC staff, their easy-going and understandable manner of presentation with an interdisciplinary approach, was simply amazing. The workshops' organisation and structure of courses were excellent, and even though both of us have been in the conservation profession quite a long time, we have certainly learned a lot!

We would like to thank the IIC and IIC-ITCC for giving us the opportunity to be part of these great professional events. Our thanks also go to the Palace Museum for the perfect organisation, hospitality and wonderful workshop atmosphere. Thanks to the AXA Art Travel Scholarship, Tanja K. could attend the Symposium in Hong Kong. Last but not least, both Tanjas are grateful to Gabriela Krist who encouraged us to apply for the course and granted us the necessary time and opportunity to participate.

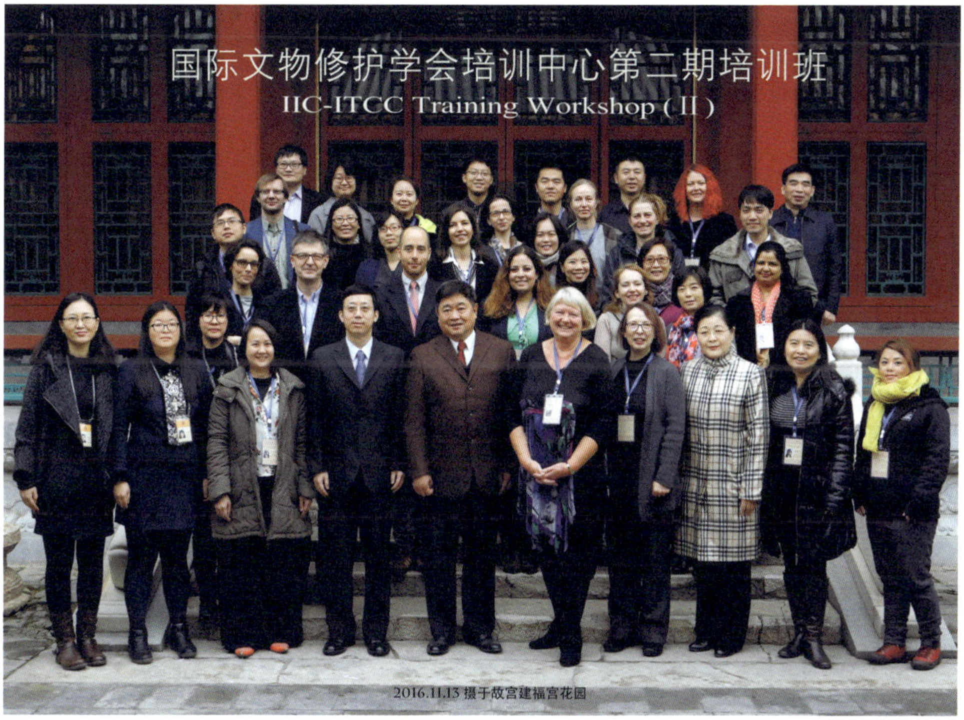

Fig. 3: The second IIC-ITCC course in 2016, group photo at Jianfu Palace Garden, Palace Museum, Beijing

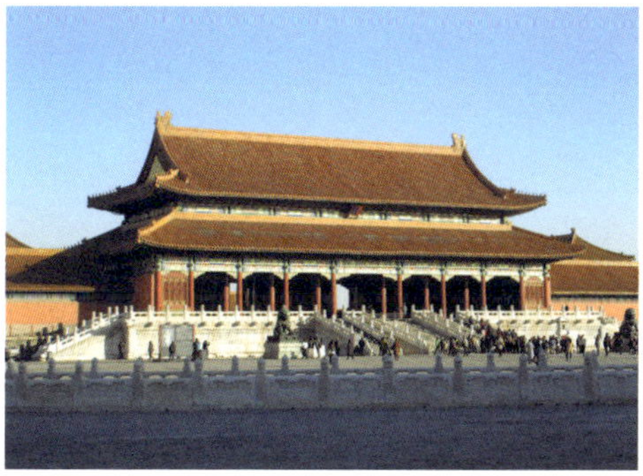

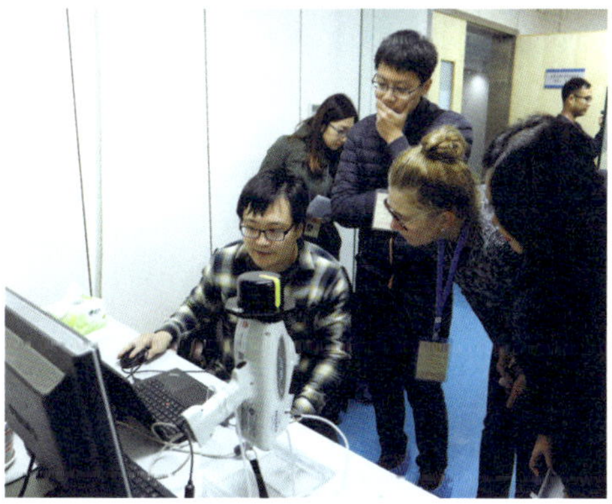

Fig. 2: The Gate of Supreme Harmony 'Tai He Men', the third gate of the Forbidden City, Beijing
Fig. 5: Participants working on Raman spectroscopy

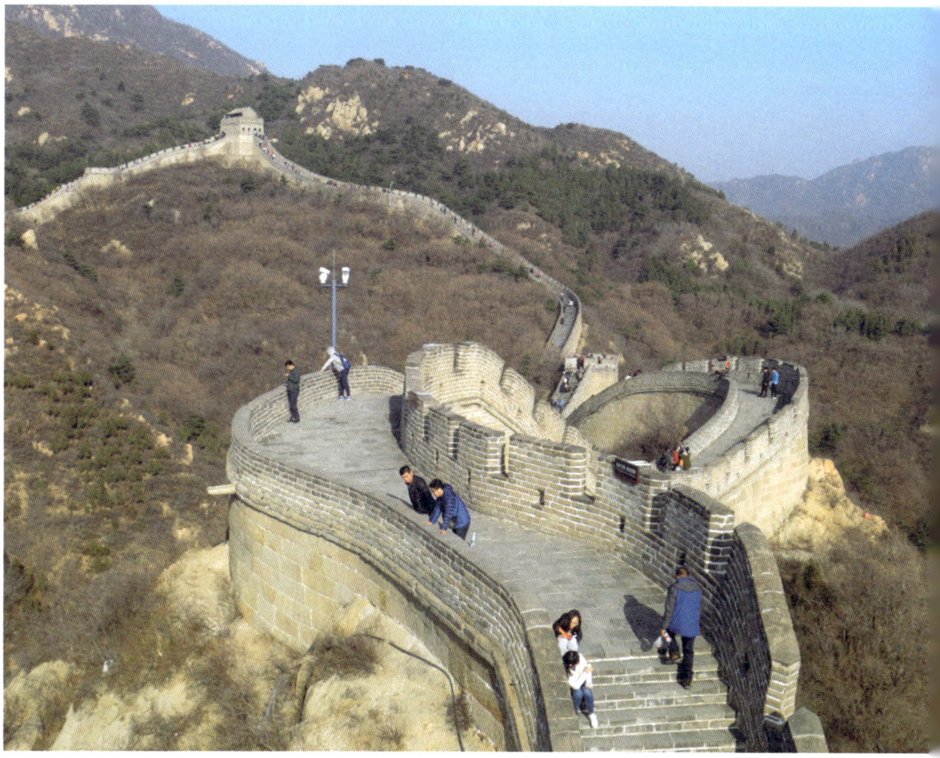

Fig. 4: Trip to the Great wall

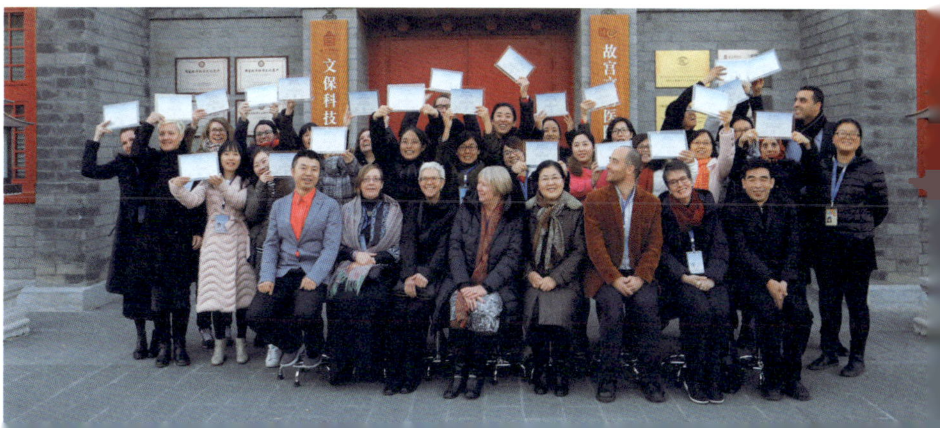

Fig. 6: The third IIC-ITCC course in 2017, group photo after the closing ceremony, Palace Museum, Beijing (from the following article)

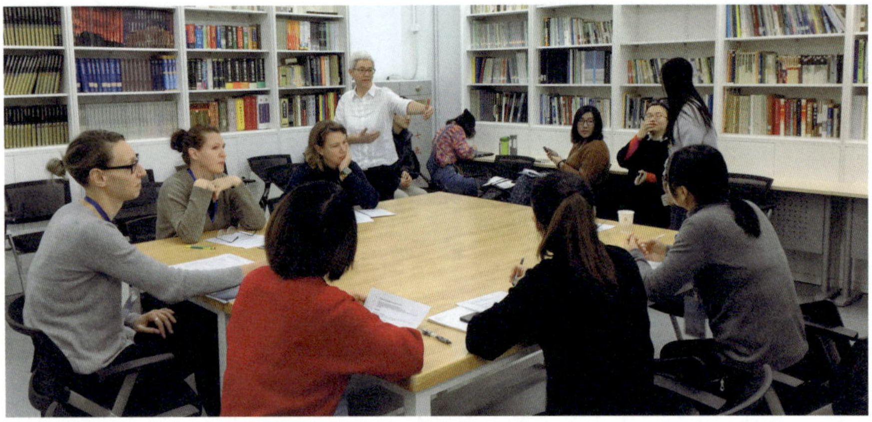

left side: Fig. 9: Group work with Dinah Eastop, UCL Institute of Archaeology (UK)
Fig. 10: Participants discussing with Mary Brooks, University of Durham (UK)
Fig. 11: Tourists in Forbidden City, Beijing

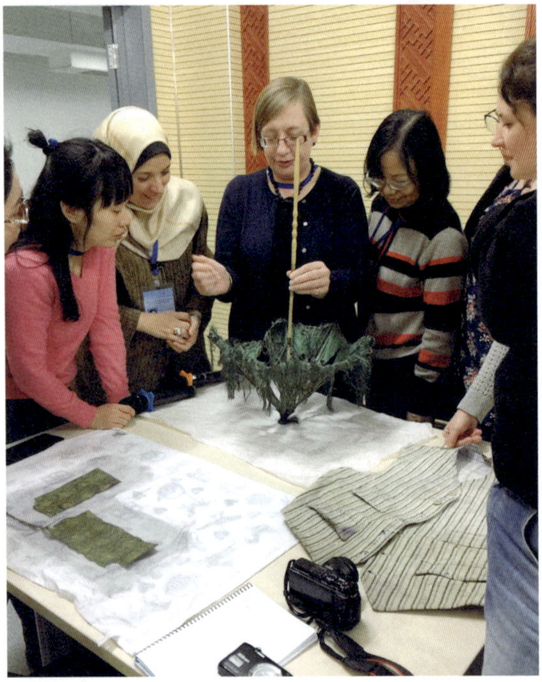

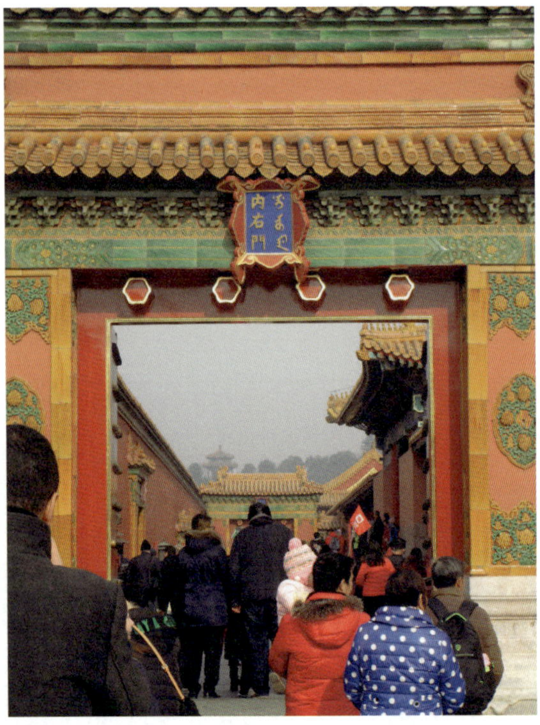

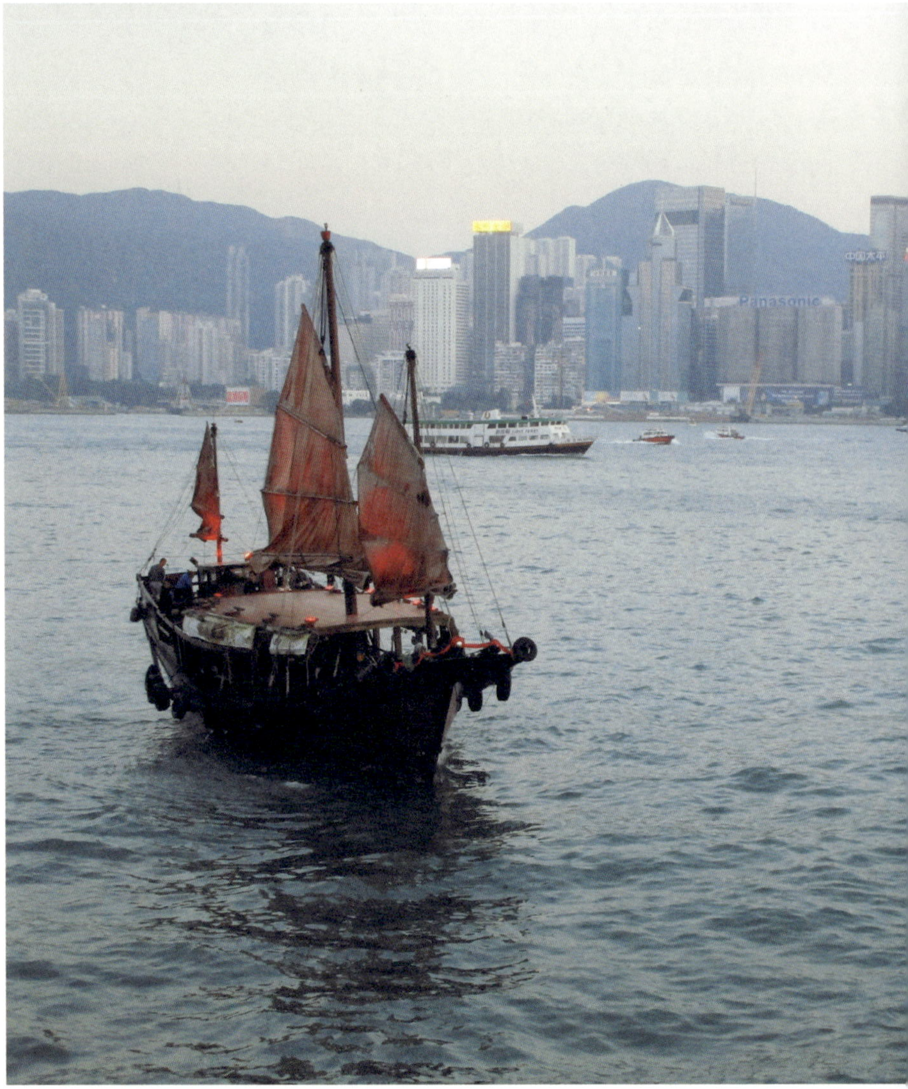

Fig. 12: Hong Kong Skyline

Fig. 13-14: "The Big Buddha" at Ngong Ping, Lantau Island, Hong Kong

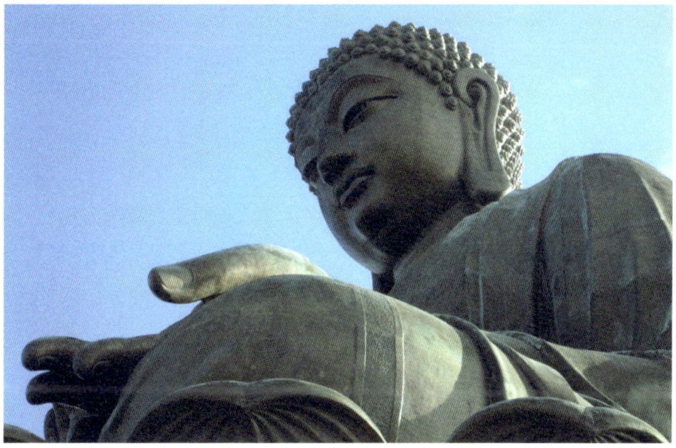

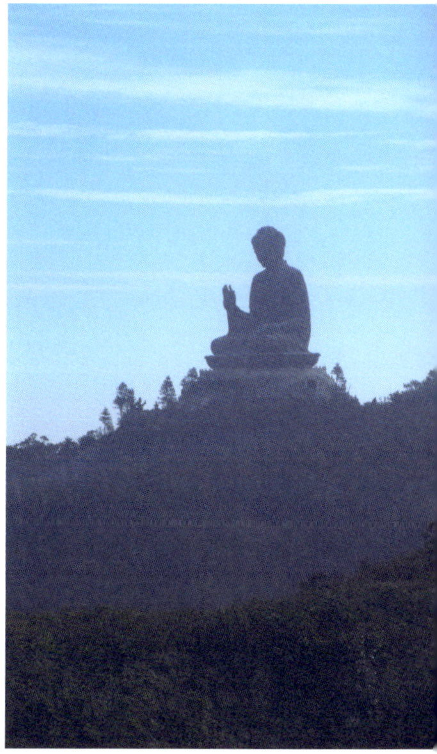

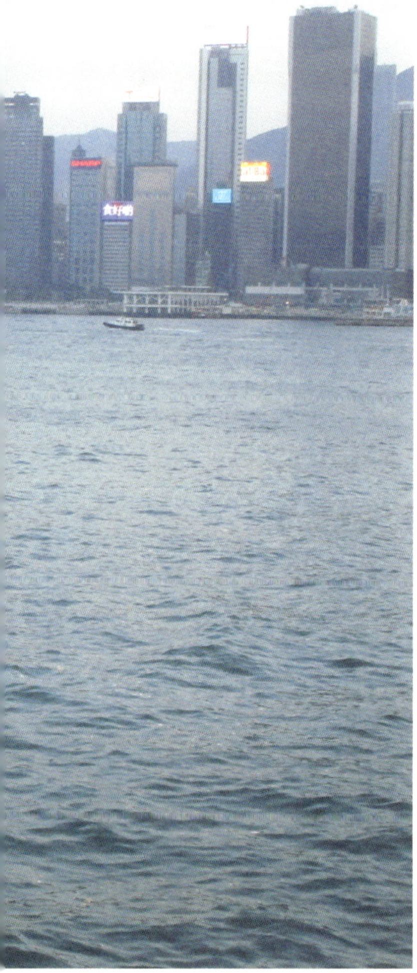

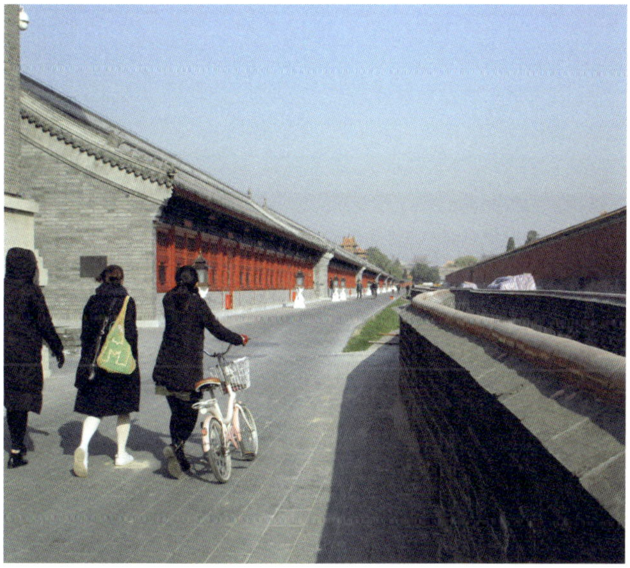

Fig. 7: "Hospital for Conservation" (exterior) at the Palace Museum, Beijing

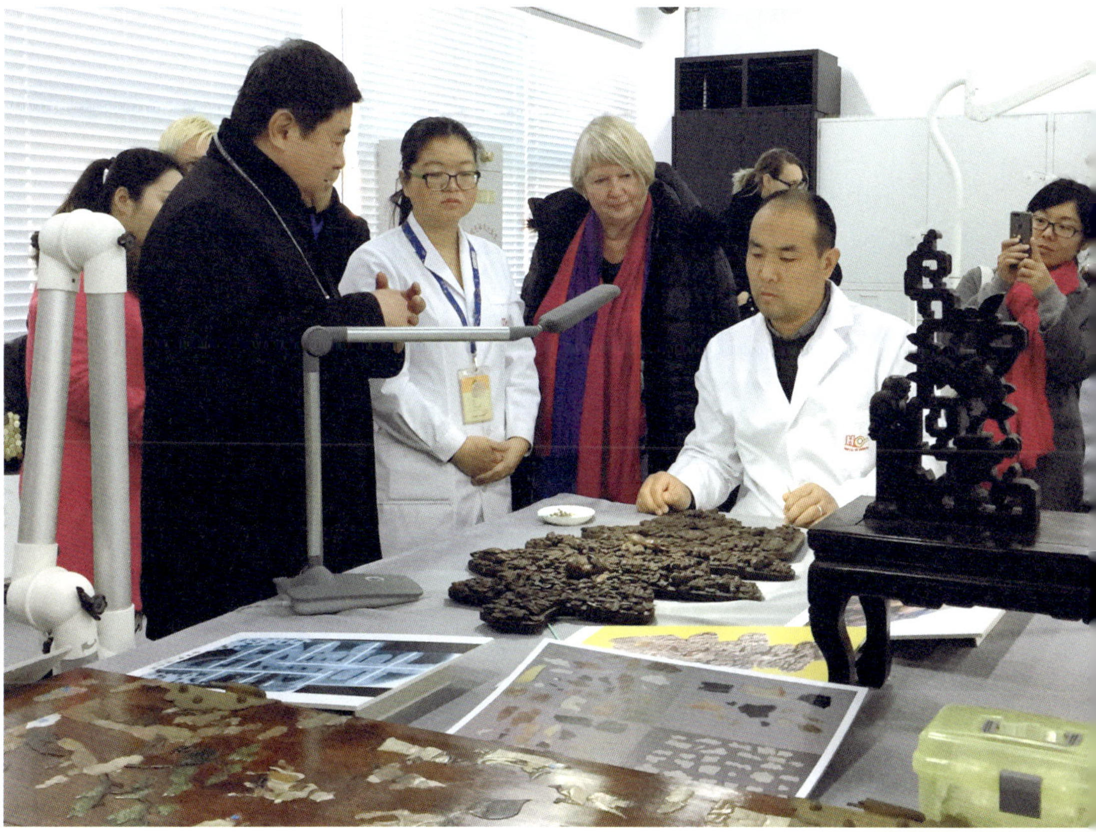

Fig. 8: Sarah Staniforth, President of IIC (UK), watching "doctors" restoring some of the museums artefacts

Nepal

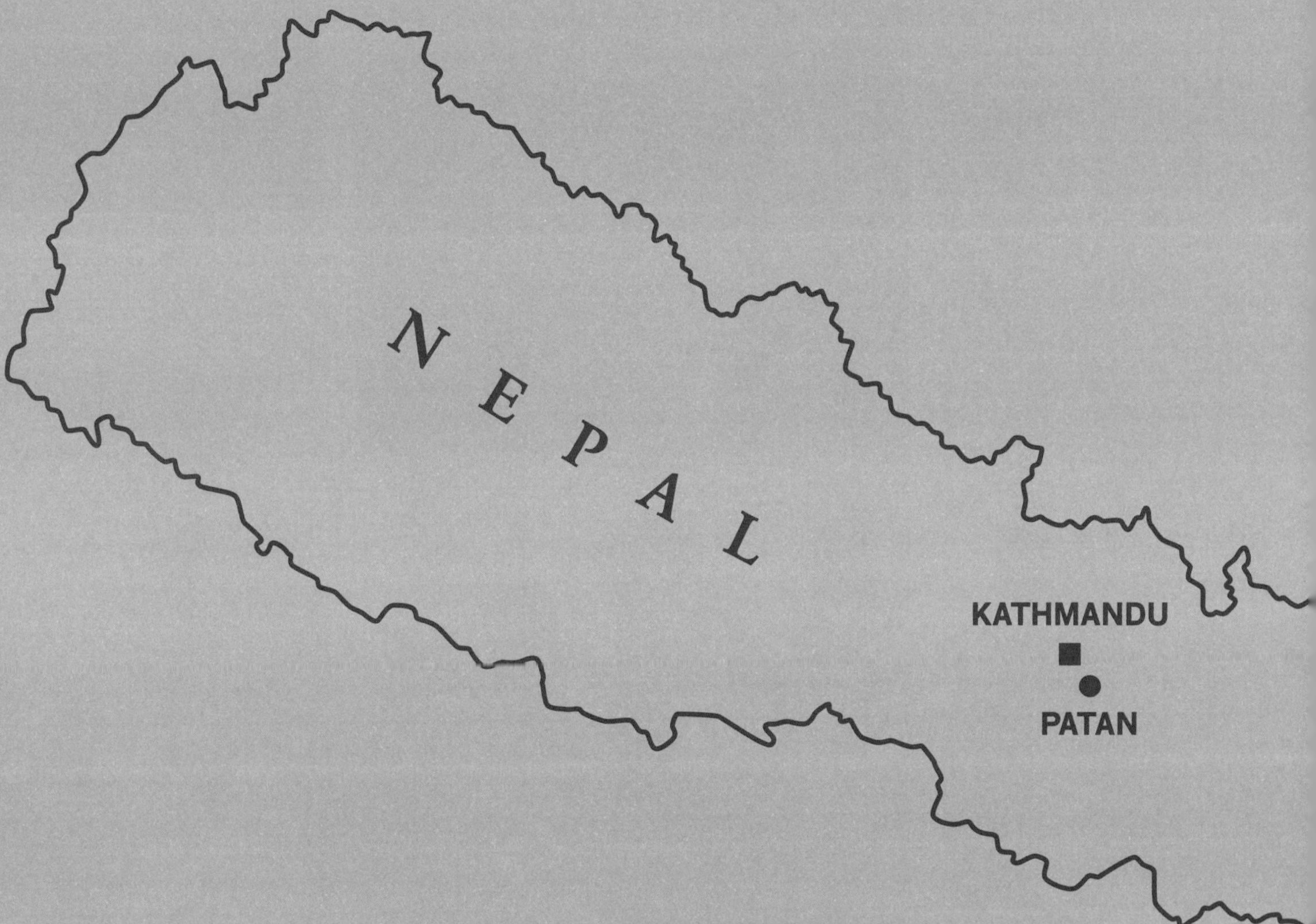

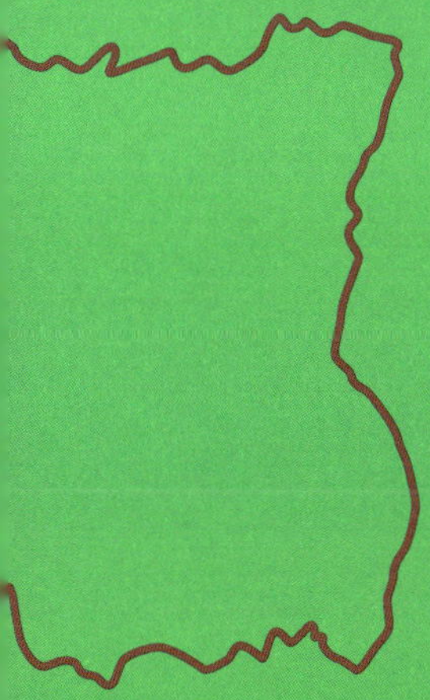

In the Footsteps of Important Austrian Scholars, Architects and Preservationists

GABRIELA KRIST

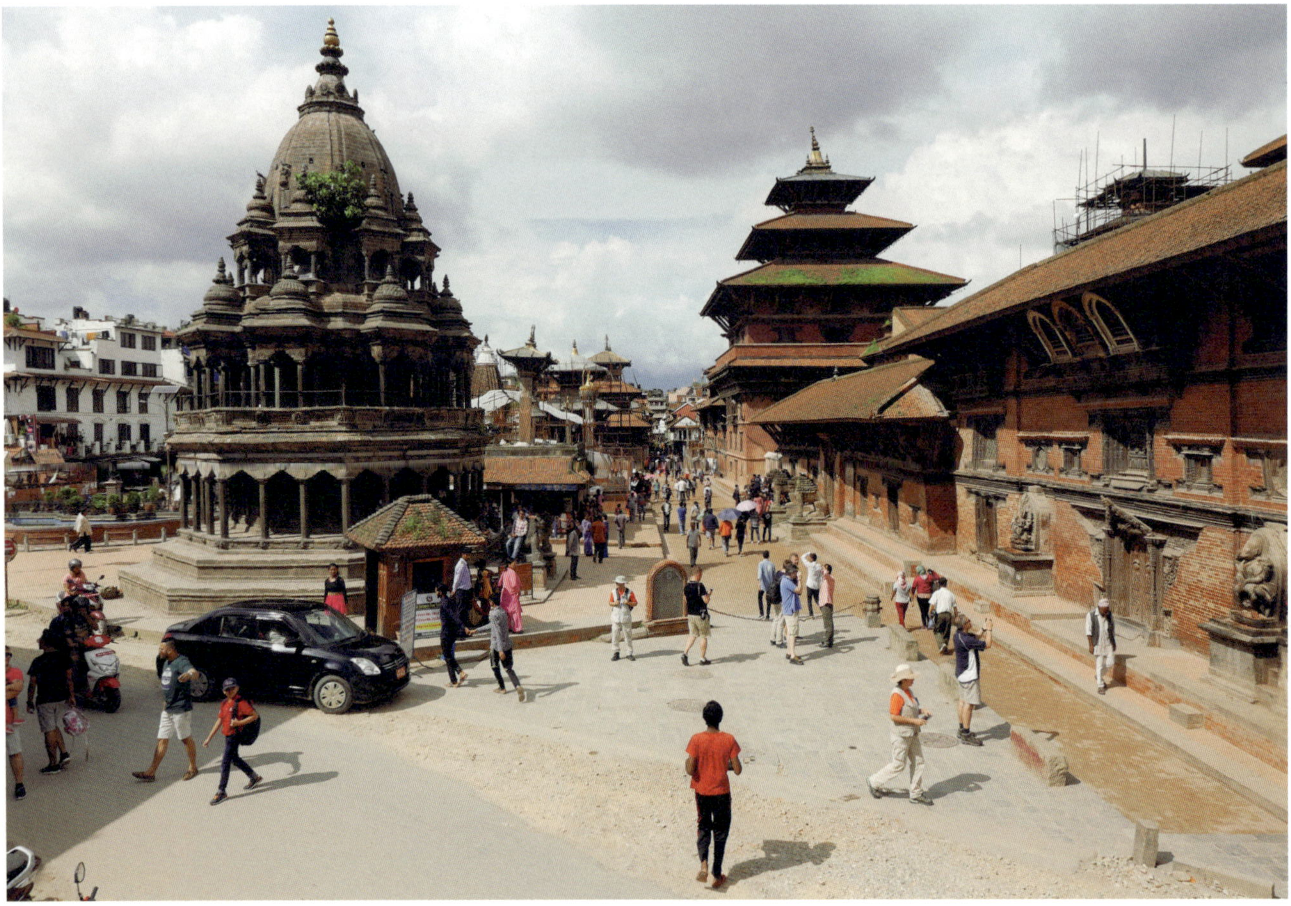

Fig. 1: Patan Durbar Square, 2017

The Institute of Conservation in Patan, Nepal

In 2009, Eduard F. Sekler contacted Manfred Trummer, chief conservator of the Austrian Museum of Applied Arts/Contemporary Art (MAK) and member of the teaching staff at our institute, to ask for help and assistance in the ongoing conservation of the Royal Palace and its surrounding monuments in Patan, one of the three historic capitals of the former Nepalese Kingdoms and today among the most attractive Nepalese tourist hotspots. Sekler, a professor at Harvard University, architect, art historian and Austrian citizen, had already established the first conservation master plan for the Kathmandu Valley in the 1960s; it has continued to be a sound basis for all ongoing preservation and conservation initiatives in the country down to the present day. His whole life was dedicated to the research and documentation of Nepalese monuments, which he considered to be of utmost universal significance. He was also one of the founding members of the Kathmandu Valley Preservation Trust (KVPT), a central organisation in Nepal for documentation, conservation and restoration. We are very proud that the KVTP has remained, through today, our main Nepalese partner. Eduard F. Sekler unfortunately died in May 2017 at the age of 96.

Following Sekler's plans, we – Manfred Trummer and myself – carried out a first preparatory mission to Patan in March 2010 to meet Rohit Ranjitkar from the KVPT, a close collaborator of Sekler, and Thomas Schrom, another pertinent Austrian designer and architect working in Nepal for many decades, and a staff member of the Nepalese UNESCO branch, to discuss possible involvement and cooperation of the Institute's team in running conservation projects.

As a next important step, a funding body for the planned cooperation had to be found. Gerald Bast, Rector of the University of Applied Arts Vienna, joined the Eurasia-Pacific Uninet (EPU), an Austrian university network also active in Nepal. This was, and still is, a basis for the Institute to partially finance missions and working campaigns in Nepal.

The Institute of Conservation has been active in the Himalayan region since 2004. Until 2010 the team was involved in the framework of an Austrian Science Fund (FWF) research project in the already mentioned conservation of the Buddhist temple complex in Nako, Himachal Pradesh, India, and this experience could be transferred to the Nepalese environment.

Since 2010, the Institute's team, senior conservators, alumni and students have undertaken one or two missions per year to Patan. In the first years, various important stone monuments could be investigated and conserved together with the KVPT and local craftsmen: the Tusha Hiti, the Bhandarkhal Tank Pavilion, the two stone relief gates at Nasal Chowk, two Stone Lions at the tank and the two Gatekeeper Lions at the Mul Chowk. The treatment of the fire-gilded Golden Doorway Ensemble at Mul Chowk was the first successful metal conservation project finalized in 2012. In addition, wall paintings in Sundari Chowk and the Ivory Window Ensemble were among the broad range of artworks treated by the Institute's team. Conservation work in Nepal is not as easy as in Europe, but much more comfortable than in Nako, which sits at an altitude of 4,000 m and is a two-to-three-day journey by Jeep from New Delhi. Of course, projects have to be prepared well in advance at home, materials have to be ordered and equipment brought along that is unavailable in Nepal. As the projects with which we were entrusted so far comprised mostly hands-on conservation work, there has never been enough time to study the monuments in depth before treatment, a procedure generally used in Austria. Nevertheless, five pre-diplomas and two diploma theses could be carried out on the study and conservation of selected monuments and artworks in Patan. In addition, several publications appeared in international conservation journals and books, and presentations at conferences were given.

In April 2015, a major earthquake and several aftershocks suddenly interrupted not only the daily life of the Nepalese population but also conservation work in the whole country. Apart from the human catastrophe (nearly 9,000 people died), cultural heritage suffered. A large number of important monuments have been destroyed or heavily damaged by the quakes (Fig. 3). Fortunately all our Nepalese colleagues survived, which was the first major concern. Gerald Bast and I immediately approached the

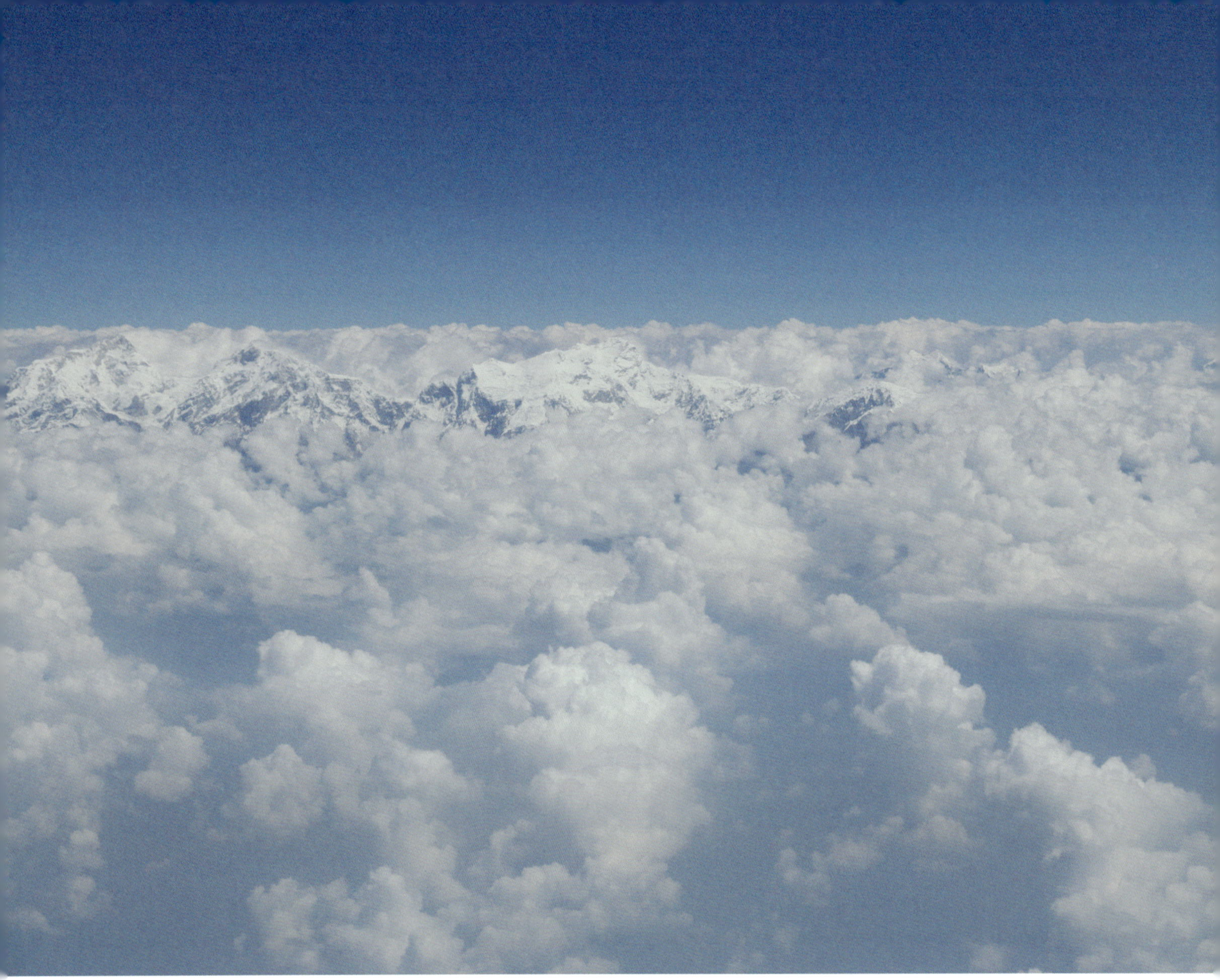

Fig. 2: Above the clouds – peaks of the Himalayan mountain range

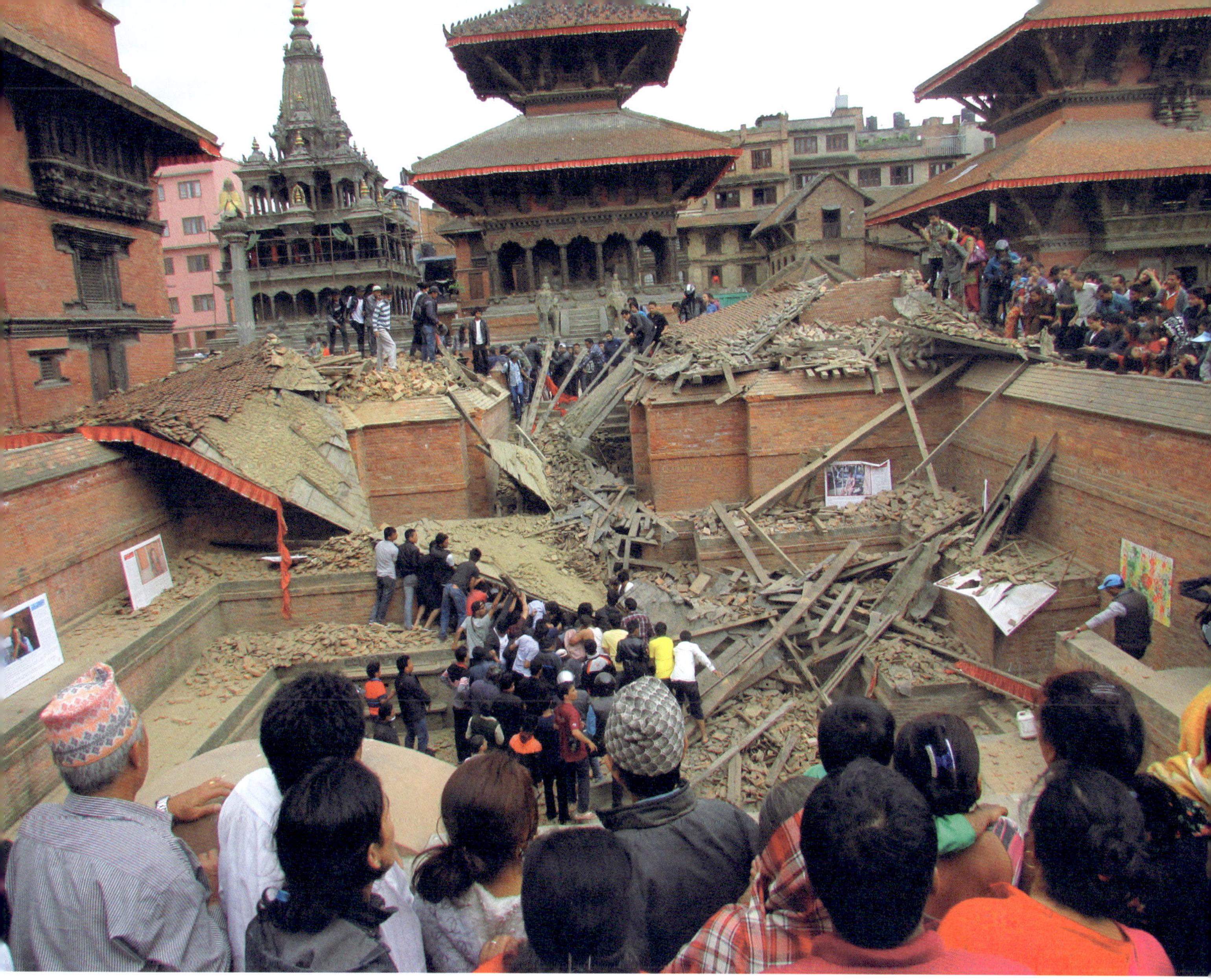

Fig. 3: After the earthquake, 2015

Austrian Federal Ministry for Europe, Integration and Foreign Affairs (BMEIA) and the Austrian Federal Chancellery, Arts and Culture Division (BKA), also the Austrian Development Agency (ADA) for assistance to help Nepalese colleagues to carry out first-aid stabilization and rescue measures. The Austrian authorities granted immediate sponsorship. The long-term involvement of Austria and Austrian experts in Nepal, especially in Patan, was the basis for the successful search for funds.

In June 2015, shortly after the natural disaster, staff members of the Institute – Manfred Trummer and Martina Haselberger – personally carried money to the KVPT to buy materials and construct shelters for architectural elements and artworks retrieved from destroyed temples and structures. This immediate help was necessary to store and protect treasures from vandalism and the approaching monsoon, and to save them for future conservation and reconstruction measures.

In summer 2015, the Institute's team joined forces with the KVPT to secure, conserve and restore several monuments damaged by the earthquake: the Lion Pillar in front of Bhimsen Temple, the sculpture of god Harishankara from the eponymous temple on Durbar Square, the King's throne (Naga Throne), the fire-gilded Taleju Temple roof pinnacles of the Royal Palace, which had collapsed. In addition, the work on the precious Ivory Window Ensemble from the façade of Sundari Chowk was continued and successfully concluded in summer 2016. The two original ivory windows were conserved within the framework of a diploma thesis. While they can now be admired at the Patan Museum, two reconstructions of these wooden windows embellished with ivory decoration were again re-inserted, together with the original conserved gilded metal window, on the façade of the Royal Palace. Not only the public but also the local press followed this event with interest during the whole period.

Under the leadership of the famous Austrian architect and designer Götz Hagmüller, who has lived in Nepal since 1979, and Manfred Trummer, a plan for a new lighting system for the showcases at the Patan Museum was set up in order to save energy and to be better prepared for power cuts. A solar energy system for the whole museum, now in the planning phase, will be sponsored by the Austrian authorities, which would allow the Patan Museum to become a model for other museums in the region. In addition, we started a collection care project in the galleries in 2016. Team members and students of the Institute, together with staff members of the museum, are continuously checking inventories and showcases, cleaning and securing objects, a measure contributing to the long-term preservation of the important collection.

The Patan Museum has already previously been closely connected with the name of Götz Hagmüller and the Republic of Austria. Following the design of the architect, and under his direction, the Patan Museum was renovated over a period of 15 years, generously funded by the Austrian government. It was finally inaugurated in 1997 and counts today among the most attractive museums in Asia. It displays a long span of Nepal's cultural history and its traditional sacred arts. The collection mainly consists of masterpieces of cast bronzes and gilt copper repoussé works of Hindu and Buddhist deities, traditional crafts for which the city of Patan is world famous. Hagmüller's sophisticated interior design carefully considers these traditional Nepalese craft techniques and materials. The revitalisation of the Garden of Dreams in Kathmandu from 2000 to 2007 is another of Hagmüller's masterpieces. The wonderful park with its pavilions in the busy capital became THE recreation spot, which attracts not only tourists but far more locals, who spend their precious leisure time there.

In 2016, 14 team members of the Institute, together with our local partner, carried out important conservation projects at the Durbar Square and the Royal Palace, which helped to overcome the earthquake shock and give the local community some of their monuments back so that normal life can re-start in the city centre (Fig. 6). The conservation and re-erection of the King's Stone Pillar on Patan Durbar Square constituted one of the major efforts of the summer campaign. Its fire-gilded metal sculpture of Yoganarendra Malla was conserved as well and placed back on his ancestral place on top of the pillar in February 2017 (Fig. 7–9).

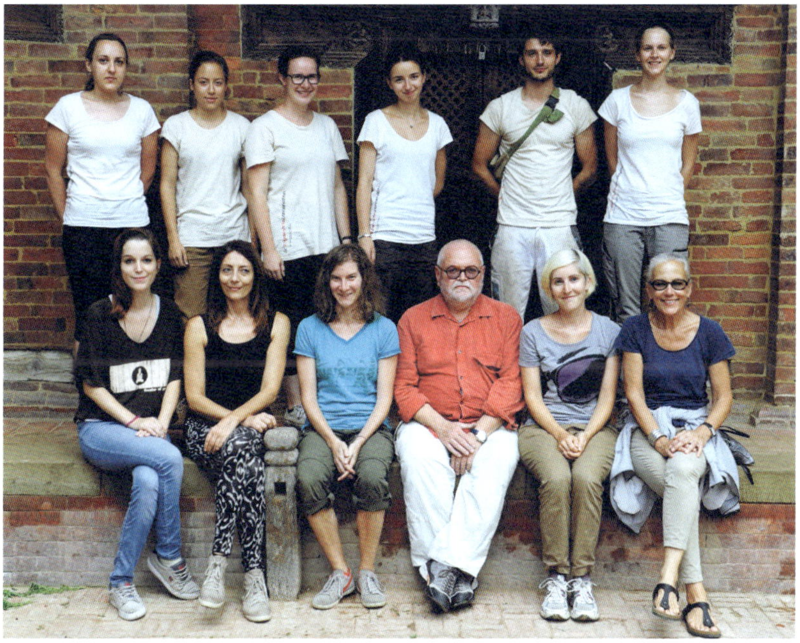

Fig. 6: Team, conservation campaign, summer 2016

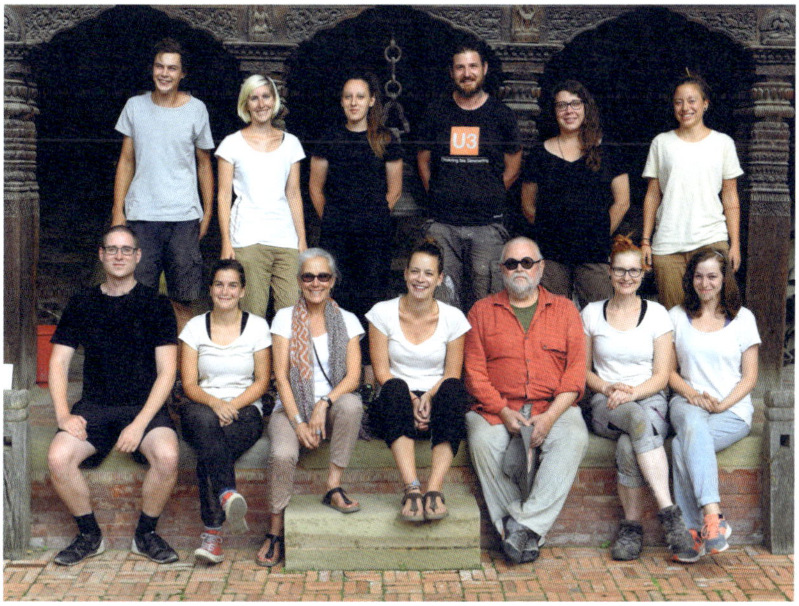

Fig. 10: Team, conservation campaign, summer 2017

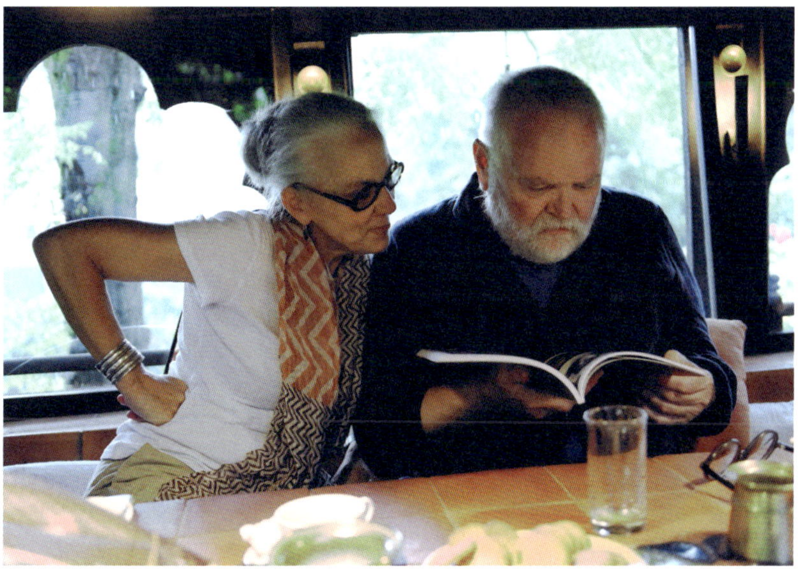

corner: Fig. 4: With Manfred Trummer on a visit at Götz Hagmüller's house in Bhaktapur

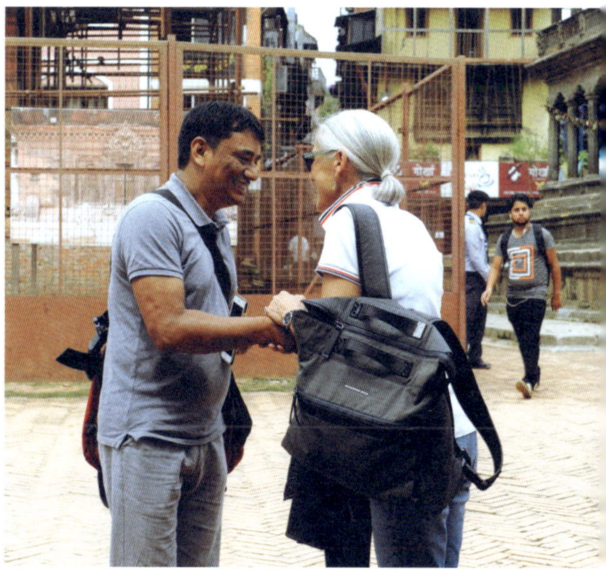

Fig. 5: Always a pleasure – meeting with our colleague Suresh Shrestha

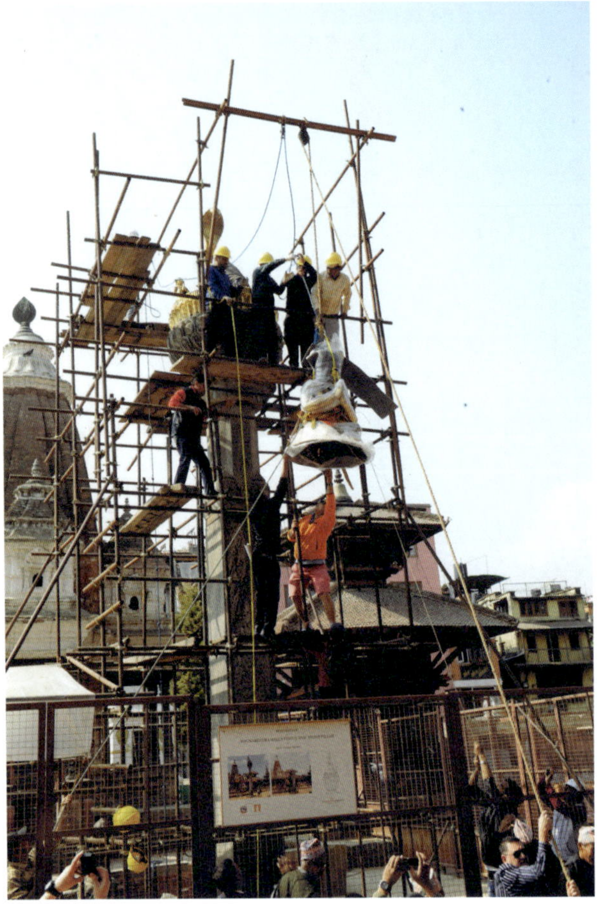

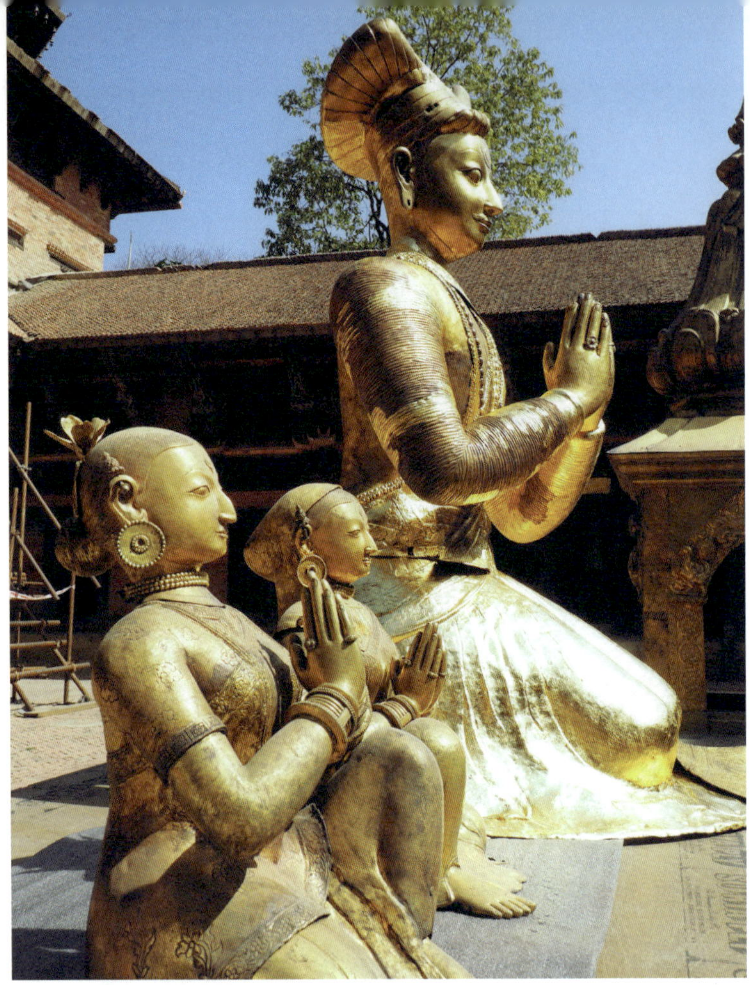

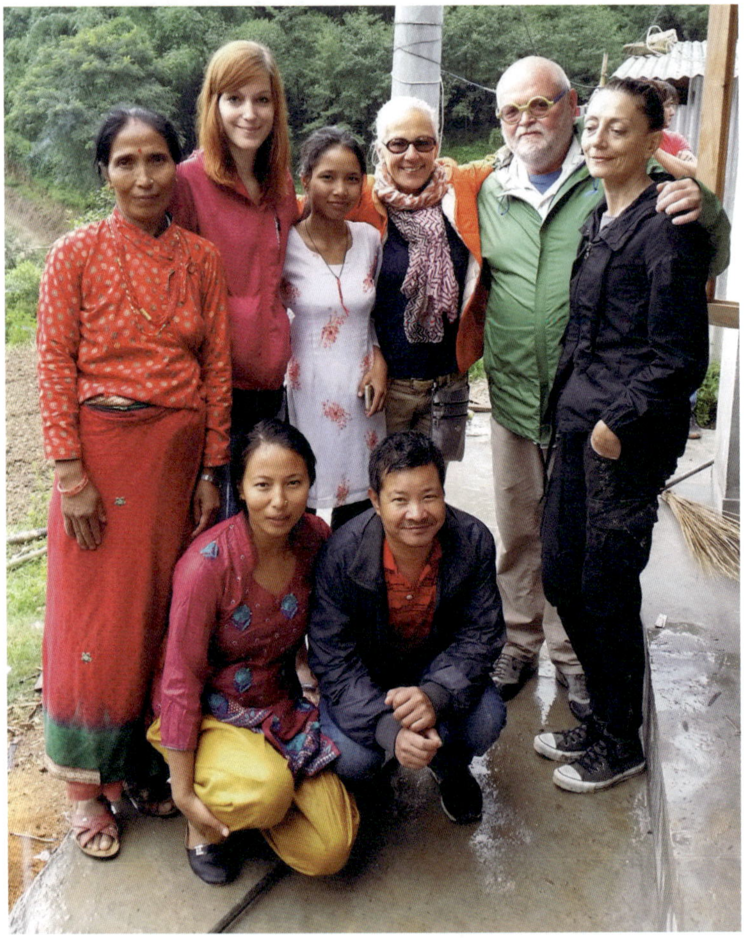

Fig. 11: Together with Manfred Trummer, Gundi Lamprecht and KVPT's cook Jagat and his family

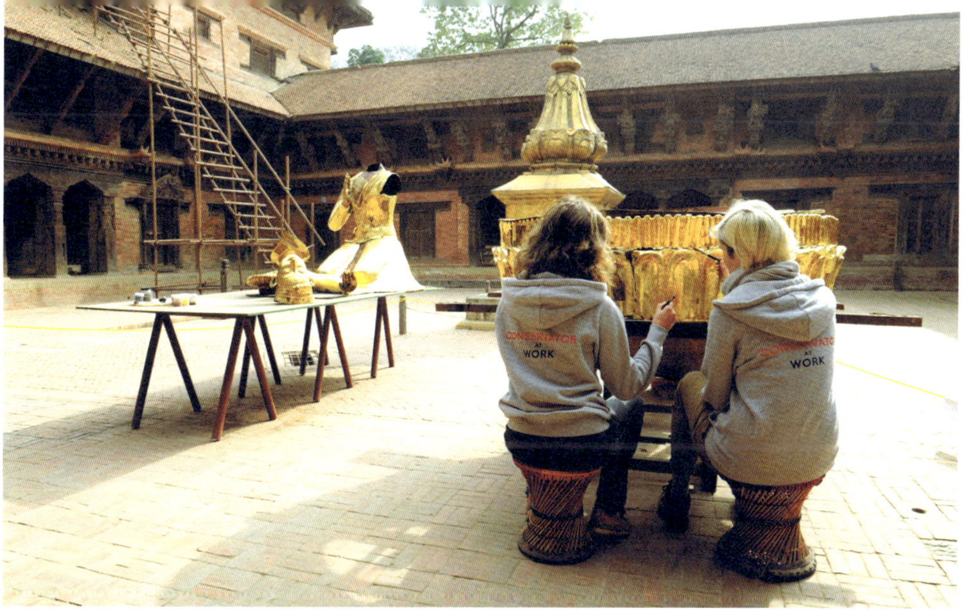

Fig. 7-9: Conservation and re-erection of the Pillar and Sculpture of Yoganarendra Malla, 2016-2017

In the following summer, emphasis was placed on the conservation of the stone base of the collapsed Harishankara Temple, an important precondition for the planned reconstruction. The metal conservators were also able to finish the conservation work at the fire-gilded pinnacle of the Taleju Temple, which could finally be re-assembled on its original location at the end of 2017 – a time-consuming project that accompanied our team since the earthquake (Fig. 10).

In February 2018, a small team from the Institute moved out again: this time for the treatment of the joints and fire-gilded pinnacles of the tallest stone temple at Patan Durbar Square, the Krishna Mandir. The work was urgent as the scaffolding, which was erected for the static restoration of the earthquake-damaged building, had to be used. Together with local craftsmen, our team was able to conclude the conservation work on the rooftop; the rest was finished by local craftsmen trained by us.

Architect Carl Pruscha, professor and former President of the Academy of Fine Arts Vienna, was also active in Nepal for many decades. Among his most important creations are the Center for Economic Development and Administration (CEDA) building at the Tribhuvan University for the Ford Foundation and the Taragaon hostel for a Nepalese women's organization. Pruscha's *Inventory of the Cultural Heritage in the Kathmandu Valley*, the first edition published in 1975, the second in 2015, is considered a standard work. It serves architects and conservators as a basis for the study of Nepalese architecture and its transformations over the time. It can also be seen as a "memory" of monuments frequently encounter earthquakes and which have to be re-built and reconstructed. A planned dissertation will use Pruscha's *Inventory* as a starting point for further research into the conservation and building history of built cultural heritage at Patan Durbar Square.

Presently we are preparing reports of the summer working campaign of 2018. The Institute's team returned from Nepal on 9 September – it was again a demanding campaign involving 12 senior and junior conservators. The conservation of the Golden Door of the Patan Museum (Fig. 12-13) and the stone base of Vishveshvara Temple at Durbar Square were the most important tasks of the year.

Since the start of the project, a team from Austrian State Television (ORF), with filmmaker Gundi Lamprecht, has accompanied the institute to Patan several times, also joining in summer 2018 (Fig. 15-16). Four documentary films have been produced so far: "Im Tal der tausend Götter – Die Tempelretter von Kathmandu" (2012), "Die Tempelretter von Kathmandu – die Rückkehr" (2015), "Die Tempelretter von Kathmandu" (2016) and "Hilfe für Nepal Kurzfilm" (2017). The latest film is currently in progress, which contributes to the visibility of the joint efforts and work of our institute and the KVPT before and after the earthquake.

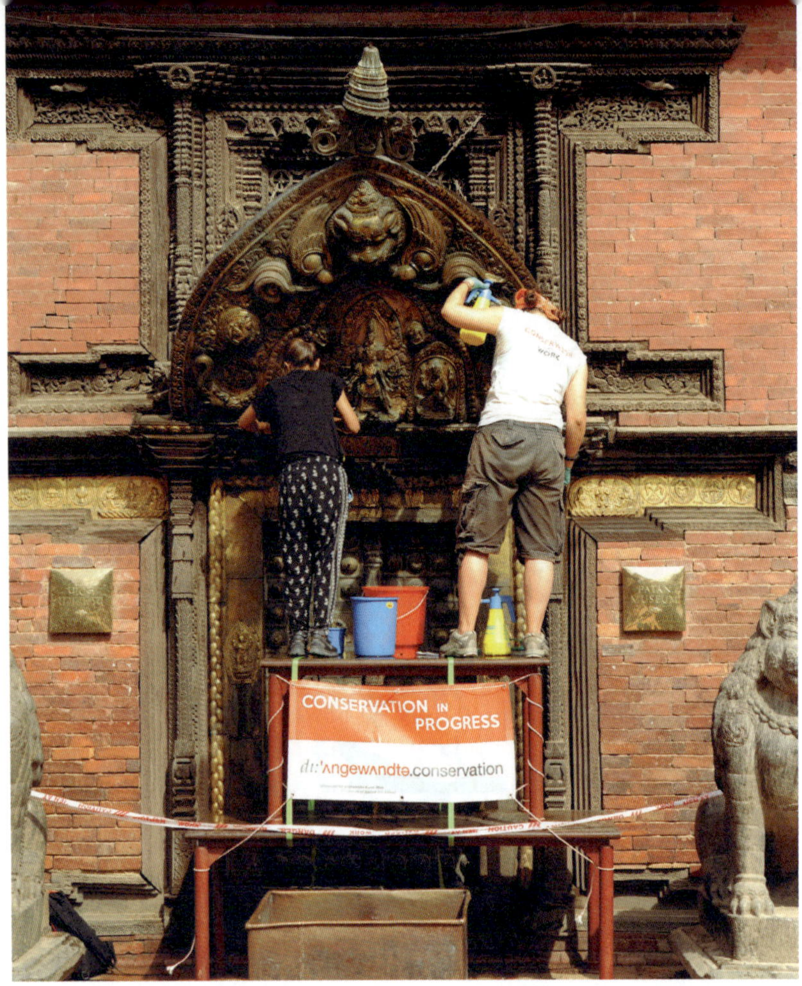

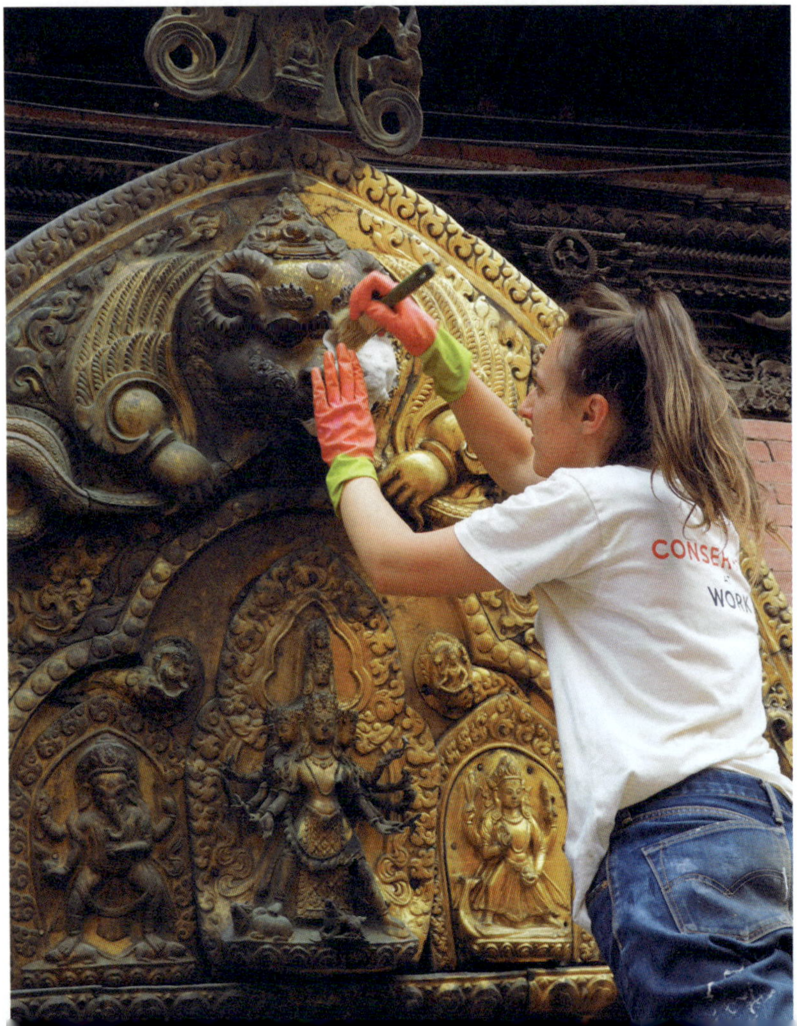

Fig. 12-13: Conservation of the Golden Door, 2018

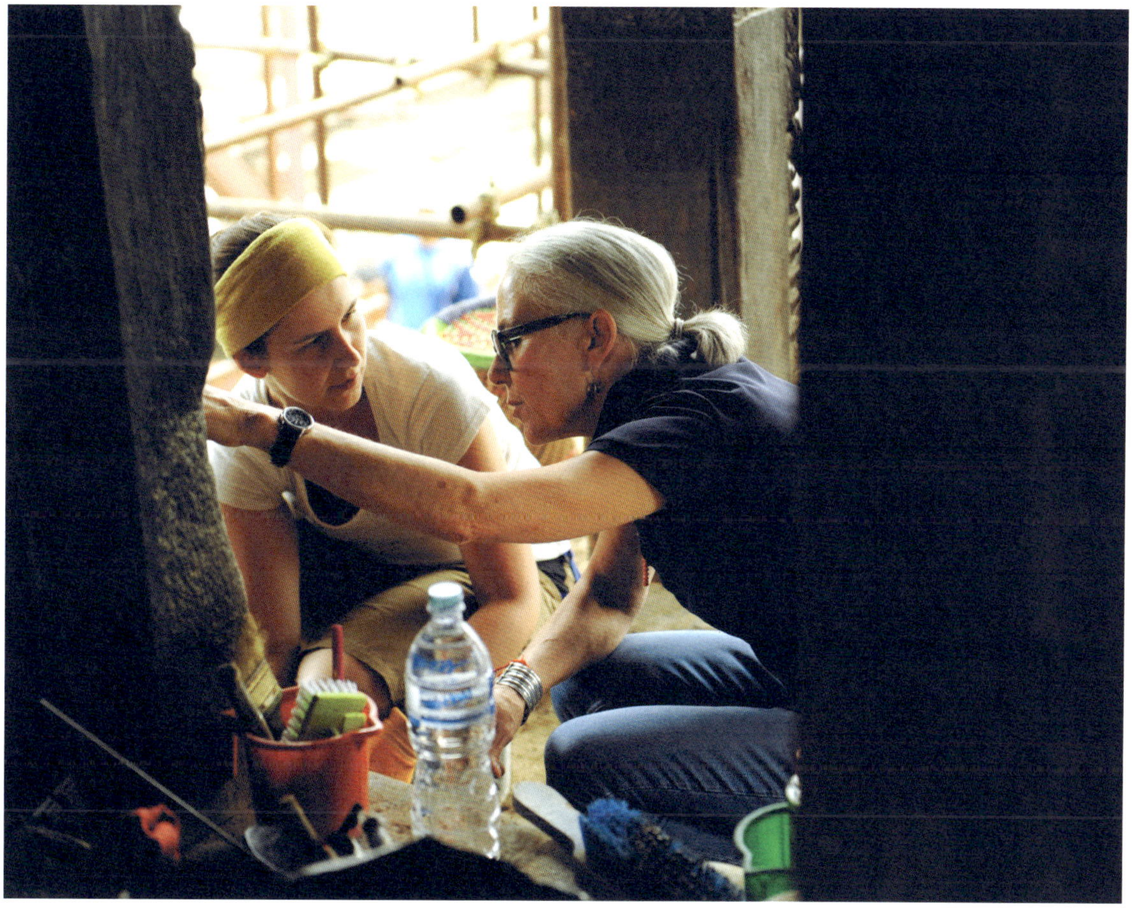

Fig. 14: At the work site

Fig. 15: With Gundi in front of the Patan Museum

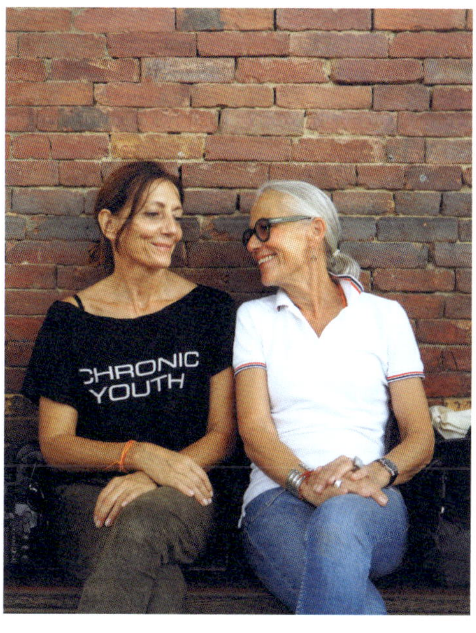

Fig. 16: With Gundi, between Nepalese gentlemen, in front of the Patan Museum

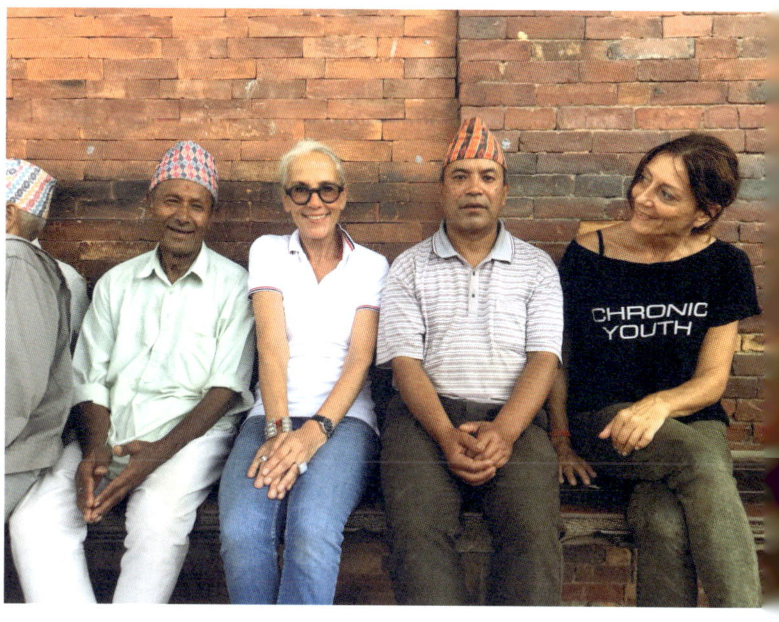

Factsheet Nepal

PROJECT	Conservation at the Patan Durbar Square and Royal Palace in Nepal		
DURATION	Since 2010 until now	HEADED BY	Gabriela Krist, Manfred Trummer
INITIATED BY	Eduard F. Sekler	COORDINATED BY	Martina Haselberger, Lisa Gräber, Marija Milchin
PARTNER INSTITUTIONS	Kathmandu Valley Preservation Trust (KVPT) Patan Museum Development Board UNESCO Office Kathmandu		
FUNDED BY	Austrian Development Agency (ADA) Federal Chancellery of Austria (BKA) Austrian Federal Ministry of Europe, Integration and Foreign Affairs (BMEIA) Eurasia-Pacific Uninet (EPU) University of Applied Arts Vienna		
TEAM MEMBERS	Tatjana Bayerová, Lisa Gräber, Martina Griesser-Stermschegg, Martina Haselberger, Veronika Loiskandl, Marija Milchin, Caroline Ocks, Christoph Schleßmann, Kathrin Schmidt, Marisa Laurenzi Tabasso (senior conservators & scientists of the Institute of Conservation, University of Applied Arts Vienna)		
STUDENTS AND GRADUATES INVOLVED	Amélie Bezard, Martin Bucher, Julian Cech, Elisabeth Delvai, Regina Friedl, Katharina Fuchs, Tanushree Gupta, Karoline Halbwachs, Magdalena Hopfensperger, Luis Kaipf, Sophie Krachler, Teresa Lamers, Sophie Langer, Stella Lattanzi, Susanne Leiner, Rupie Loghanathan, Severin Mair, Katharina Mendl, Malgorzata Mozdyniewicz, Bojana Novicic, Marina Paric, Barbara Rankl, Fabian Sever, Ana Stefaner, Magdalena Treml, Angela Vorhofer, Theresa Wagner, Thomas Weidinger, Georg Weninger, Benjamin Widtmann		

Projects

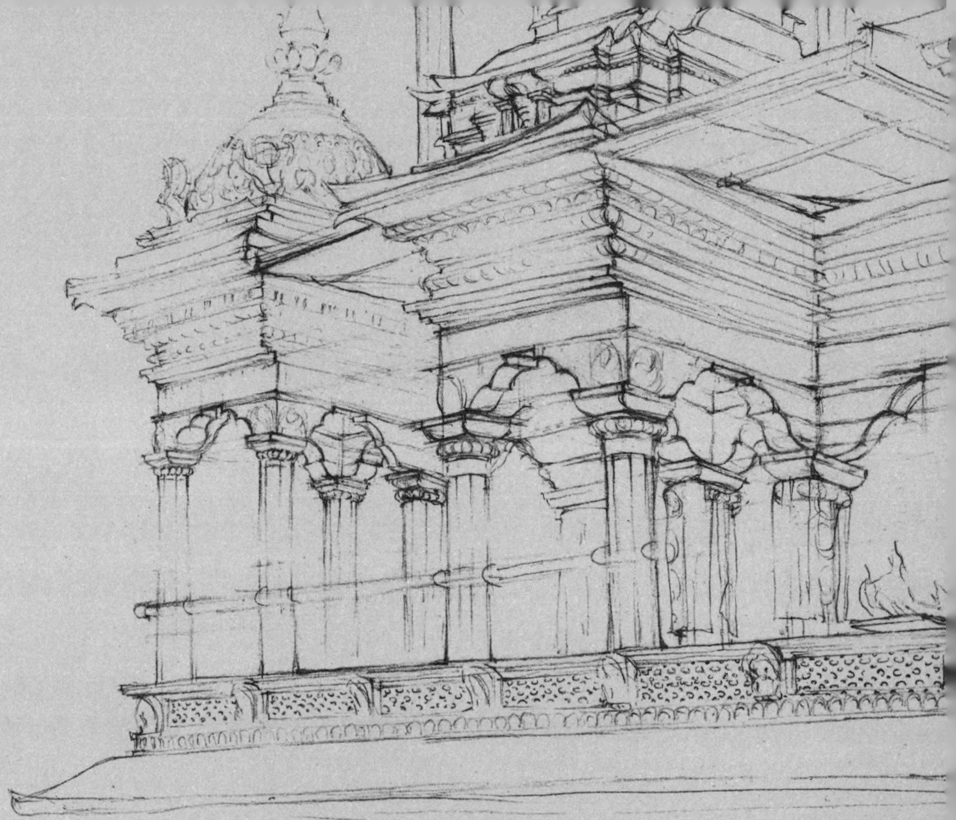

Captured in drawings by Mariia Bakhareva, 2018

Bhandarkhal Tank Pavilion, Royal Garden, Patan Royal Palace

Bhandarkhal Tank Lions, Royal Garden, Patan Royal Palace

Tusha Hiti, Sundari Chowk, Patan Royal Palace

Gatekeeper Lions, Mul Chowk, Patan Royal Palace

Golden Doorway Ensemble, Mul Chowk, Patan Royal Palace

Relief Stone Gates, Nasal Chowk, Patan Royal Palace

Wall paintings, Sundari Chowk, Patan Royal Palace

Lion Pillar and Sculpture, Patan Durbar Square

Pillar and Sculpture of Yoganarendra Malla, Patan Durbar Square

Naga Throne, Patan Durbar Square

Taleju Temples, pinnacles, Patan Royal Palace

Harlshankara Temple, stone base and sculpture, Patan Durbar Square

Ivory Window Ensemble, Sundari Chowk, Patan Royal Palace

Krishna Mandir, joints top level and pinnacles, Patan Durbar Square

Vishveshvara Temple, stone base and elephant sculptures, Patan Durbar Square

Garuda Pillar and Sculpture, Patan Durbar Square

Throne of the Kings of Patan, masterpiece collection Patan Museum

Golden Door, Patan Museum

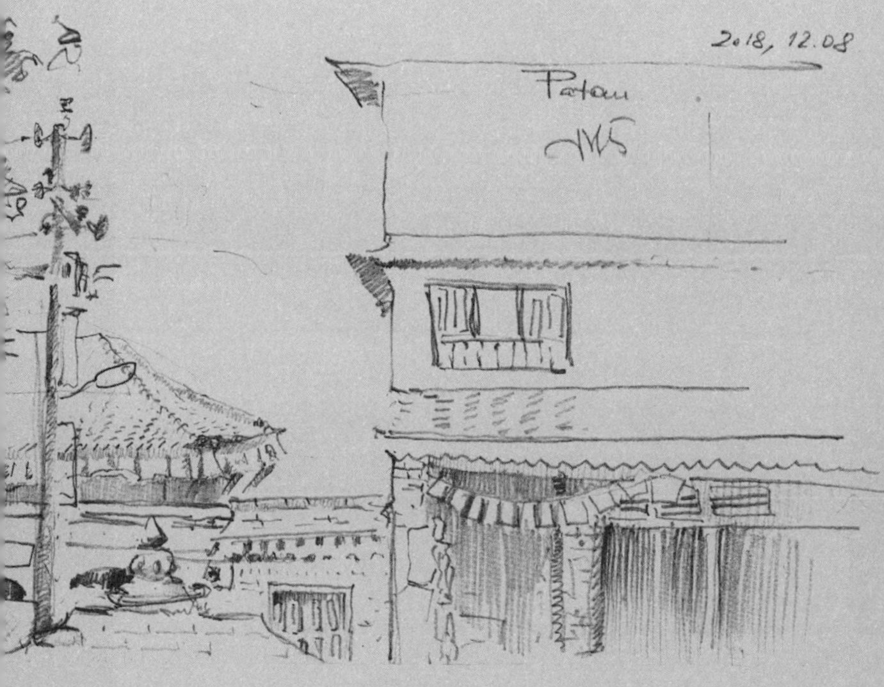

The Institute in Patan, Nepal

MARTINA HASELBERGER

Fig. 1: Patan Durbar Square, 2008

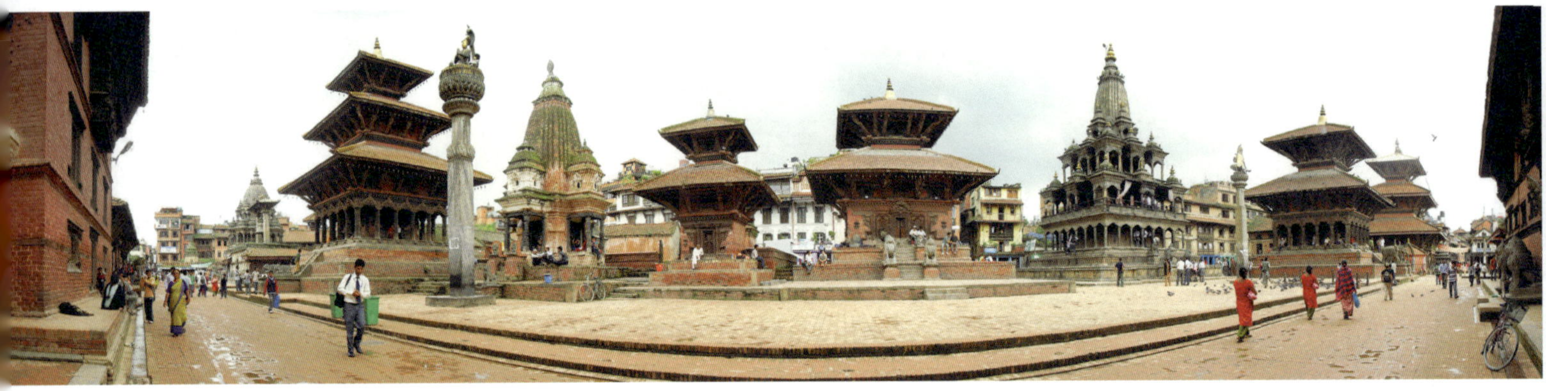

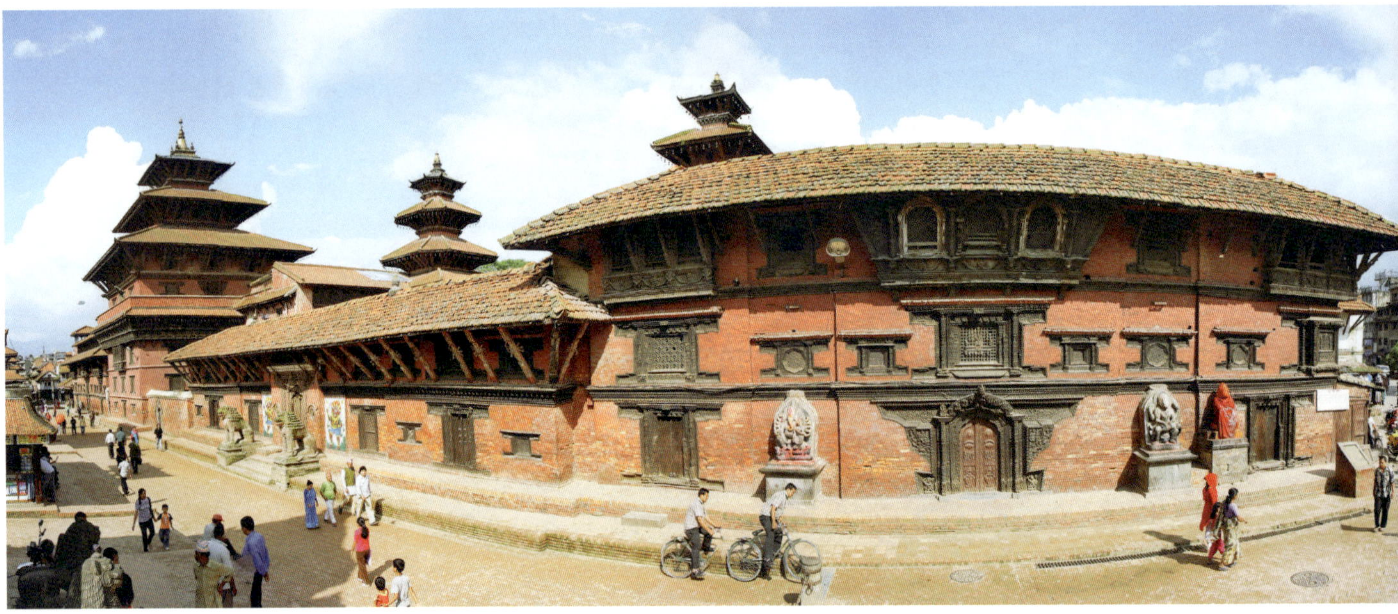

Fig. 2: Patan Royal Palace Complex, 2008

Working Missions and Experiences

"It's not your first time in Nepal, is it?"

Visa officer takes a closer look at the numerous tourist visas in the passport.

"No...not really."

Smile.

"You seem to like the country a lot?"

"Actually, yes."

Looking back on almost ten journeys to Nepal, I am already used to this kind of conversation at the airport in Kathmandu. It started during my conservation studies, at the age of 20, when I first entered this vibrant country of sacred cows, Hindu and Buddhist gods and goddesses, crowded streets and colourful festivals. I was privileged, together with three other students from the stone conservation class, to participate in a conservation campaign by the Institute of Conservation in Patan, today the third largest city in Nepal, next to its capital Kathmandu. It was only the second campaign ever.

In the previous year, in spring 2010, our institute's head, Gabriela Krist, together with senior lecturer Manfred Trummer, chief conservators of the Museum of Applied Arts/Contemporary Arts (MAK), travelled to the country for the first time in the Institute's history to sound out possible involvement and cooperation in running conservation projects at the request of Eduard F. Sekler, founder of the Kathmandu Valley Preservation Trust (KVPT). Discussion and talks were promising. The expertise and advice of the conservation professionals from Austria was in demand with regard to the long-term preservation of the cultural property on Patan Durbar Square. Rohit Ranjitkar, Director of the KVPT, welcomed the cross-border collaboration with the Austrian university. Then things really got going – the checklist was soon processed:

- A funding agency for the on-site missions was identified: Eurasia-Pacific Uninet (EPU)
- A first monument to be treated was chosen, the Bhandarkhal Tank Pavilion in the palace garden
- Three flights from Vienna to Kathmandu in summer 2010 were booked

The starting signal was given for another chapter in the international conservation activities of the Institute of Conservation, which has lasted until today.

"ISN'T IT LIKE A PIECE OF HEAVEN?"

Nepalese poet Kunu Sharma, 17th century

Patan Durbar Square is an impressive place indeed. Its outstanding universal value was recognised at an early stage by its inscription in the UNESCO World Heritage List in 1979 as part of the Kathmandu Valley World Heritage Site. It was the first cultural property in Asia to be listed! Apart from the square in Patan, the Durbar Squares (palace or audience square) in Kathmandu and Bhaktapur, the sacred Hindu districts of Pashupatinath and Changu Narayan, also the Buddhist stupa complexes Bodnath and Swayambhunath, rank among the protected monument zones. Although these sites are recognised as highlights, they present just a small part of the altogether 888 historic cultural monuments and zones embedded in the Kathmandu Valley – a striking number considering the valley measures approximately 33 x 24 km, more or less the length of the World Heritage Wachau Valley in Austria.

But now, back to Patan Durbar Square: on a relatively small area – only 167 x 70 metres – it boasts an impressive range of tangible heritage of high artistic and cultural value and also living culture, noticeable and perceptible every day. The harmonious co-existence of Hindu and Buddhist buildings and lifestyle is unique. One can hardly imagine this without having ever set foot on Patan's soil. Architectural highlights, ranging from temples of pagoda and sikhara-style, free-standing pillars, bells and mandapa to sunken water wells line up next to each other and face the even more impressive Royal Palace (Fig. 1-2). In its three inner courtyards, the so-called *chowks*, the palace houses not only important Hindu temples, such as those of Taleju, the main Goddess of Patan, but also the Royal Bath Tusha Hiti, the precious fire-gilded Doorway Ensemble and the well-known Patan Museum, ranking among the finest and most attractive museums in South Asia. The majority of the monuments on the square is built in brick-wood or stone and dates from the 16th to the 18th century. Their intricate ornamentation and sculptural elements exhibit the outstanding craftsmanship associated with local Newars in brick, stone, timber and bronze. It is one of the most highly developed crafts in the world and still vivid in the Kathmandu Valley!

Altogether, Patan Durbar Square conveys not only an impressive image of the wealth and prosperity in Patan under the reign of the Malla dynasty, but is also a testimony of the sibling rivalry between the three former kingdoms, Kathmandu, Patan and Bhaktapur. Because of constant competition, palaces were enlarged and temple buildings erected on their forecourt – a golden period of art from which we still profit today. Unlike Kathmandu, Patan has not been used as a residence since the beginning of the 18th century. Thus structural adaptions were limited to a minimum. The Royal Palace partly fell into a deep sleep.

With all this in mind, it becomes more and more evident why this place has attracted international scholars since the 19th century – among them many Austrians, architects and conservation experts, active in Patan since the 1960s.The opening of the country in the 1950s, and the inscription of the Patan Durbar Square and Royal Palace as a UNESCO World Heritage site, finally moved them into the centre of global attention and interest.

CITY WITH MANY NAMES

Each time I cross Bagmati River, enter the city of Patan and arrive at Mangal Bazar, my appreciation of this place increases. Slowly but steadily, I also get used to the chaos, the masses of people and the missing traffic rules. Walking on the crowded roads is an "art" and I am still wondering how pedestrians, cyclists, vehicles and cows manage to occupy the same space without a fatal collision (Fig. 5). My personal rules to get ahead: first, you always have to walk with the traffic flow, no abrupt stops or changes of direction, second, don't spend too much time on searching for pedestrian crossings, and third, act like a real "jaywalker".

For me, one endearing feature of Patan are its many names. Depending on whether you search for a place in Patan on Google Maps, look in the travel guide or talk with a merchant, you will hear different titles – Patan, Lalitpur or Yala. Being one of the oldest inhabited areas of the Kathmandu Valley, dating back to the Licchavi period (3rd to 8th century A.D.), the city was historically called "Patan". This is also the most commonly used name. Its modern name, "Lalitpur", was mentioned first in 920 A.D. and means "beautiful city", very fittingly I would say. Its Newari name "Yala", probably a derivation of the Newari word for "village of the sacred pillars", is more or less used in everyday language.

WORLD HERITAGE IN DANGER

Since I work at the Institute of Conservation I have been in the fortunate position not only to work in Nepal, but also join projects in India and Mongolia. Besides, I always follow the activities of my colleagues in Thailand, Myanmar and China. I think I can say that one phenomenon is particularly common and widespread in all these Asian countries: the aspiration for modernisation – the preference of the new over the old.

Nepal has not been spared from this attitude. Newly built, reinforced-concrete constructions with obtrusive glass façades harass the historic buildings and considerably impair their surroundings. The spread of modern construction patterns and materials in the 20th century and their use to beautify monuments also adversely affected the historical substance itself – the outcome: old temples with tiled cladding, marble facings, metal lattice and fluorescent lightning. Furthermore, the sudden availability of cement resulted in an unreflected use of generous amounts of the new material, often in pure form, for repair and restoration work on historic structures. Rising tourism is a blessing and curse at the same time: on one hand it constitutes an important source of income for the local communities, on the other, tourist shops, restaurants and high-rise hotels are shooting up like mushrooms in the neighbourhood of monument zones. Although plans for sustainable urban development and a protective inventory were compiled by Austrian scholars Eduard F. Sekler and Carl Pruscha in the 1970s, overall urban growth seems somewhat uncontrolled.

Another major risk for any building in Nepal certainly arises from the perennial earthquakes. The Kathmandu Valley is located in one of the most highly vulnerable seismic zones of the world – the most recent one hit the area in 2015 – future quakes are anticipated. Besides, ravages of time and decay of cultural heritage are especially compounded in Nepal by the local climate with its heavy rainfalls during monsoon period, and rampant vegetation.

FILLING THE GAP

We can't change the weather or stop the earth from shaking, but as conservators we can contribute something to the preservation of tangible cultural heritage: share and pass on our expertise.

As in many countries in Asia, professional education and training in the field of conservation is still missing in Nepal. "Conservation" work is largely done by craftsmen or artisans, of which the country has excellent ones – wood carvers, metal workers, stone masons and carpenters. They are able to produce excellent copies and work in the traditional style.

Nevertheless, the idea of preserving "original substance" arrived late in the Kathmandu Valley. Here "conservation" mainly follows the idea of replacing damaged elements and making things new. Replicas are more appreciated than the age-affected original. Particularly in sacred buildings it has even been desired to apply new materials and more richly decorated components on behalf of the client, in order to increase his religious merit.

We attempt to fill this gap, increase awareness and appreciation for the original, for the old, and make our knowledge and experience available to preserve it. It is our obligation to help where help is needed, where our expertise is needed. In this context I fully share the view of my tutor, Gabriela Krist.

This does not necessarily mean that active craftsmanship and conservation are mutually exclusive. Skills and knowledge of craftsmen are included in the conservation process, for instance they support our conservation work in the creation of stone indents and replacements, in the reshaping and repair of deformed metal artworks (Fig. 6–8). They reproduce missing attributes or sculptural and decorative elements. Their knowledge helps us to understand local craft techniques and building constructions. Ever since the beginning, we have thus closely collaborated with local craftsmen. This is also our contribution to the preservation of traditional crafts in the sense of intangible heritage.

At the same time, we constantly address another factor of damage: the lack of maintenance and care. In Austria, it is recognised that these measures help to avoid frequent and costly interventions and slow down deterioration. Our institute made efforts to impart these ideas in Patan as well. In 2014, our graduate Katharina Fuchs, elaborated a maintenance concept in the framework of her diploma thesis, including possibilities to lower the rate of spreading biological colonisation. In any case, it will take time to raise awareness of this issue.

CONSERVATION IN NEPAL – A PIECE OF CAKE?

> "In 1985 I took my first photograph of a small ruinous Shiva sanctuary next to a Sattal (resthouse) on the road to Panauti. Here, as on so many occasions, unhampered plant growth had ruined it. When I came again that way in 1991, I was happy to discover that the little building had been restored, although plant growth had set in again. By 1994 the plant growth had become a real menace once more. Three years later, all that remained of the building were wall fragments and the sacral Shiva lingam, freshly painted as evidence of ongoing worship despite the lack of the built sanctuary. Its functional, religious authenticity was untouched by the loss of its shelter, the formal and material authenticity of which was gone. "But we can rebuild it," the then-director of the Archeology [sic!] Department said to me as we gazed at the scene."

Eduard F. Sekler, "Sacred Spaces and the Search for Authenticity in the Kathmandu Valley", in: *Historic Cities and Sacred Sites: Cultural Roots for Urban Futures*.

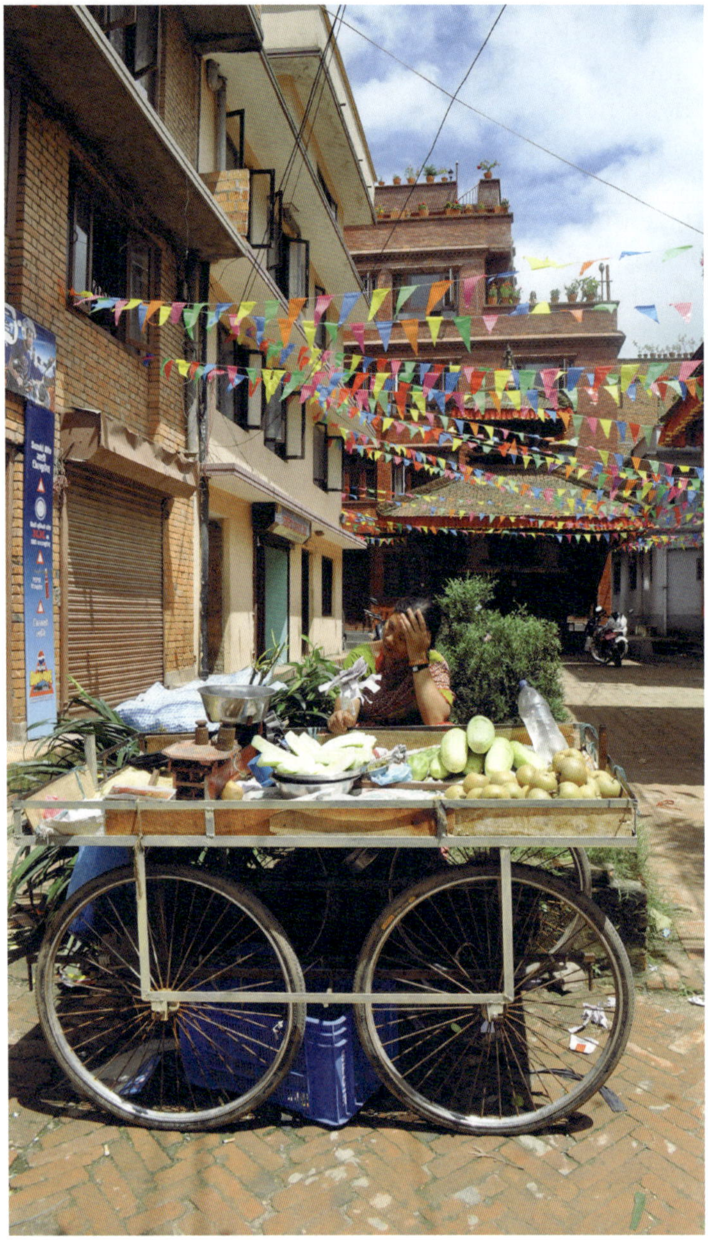

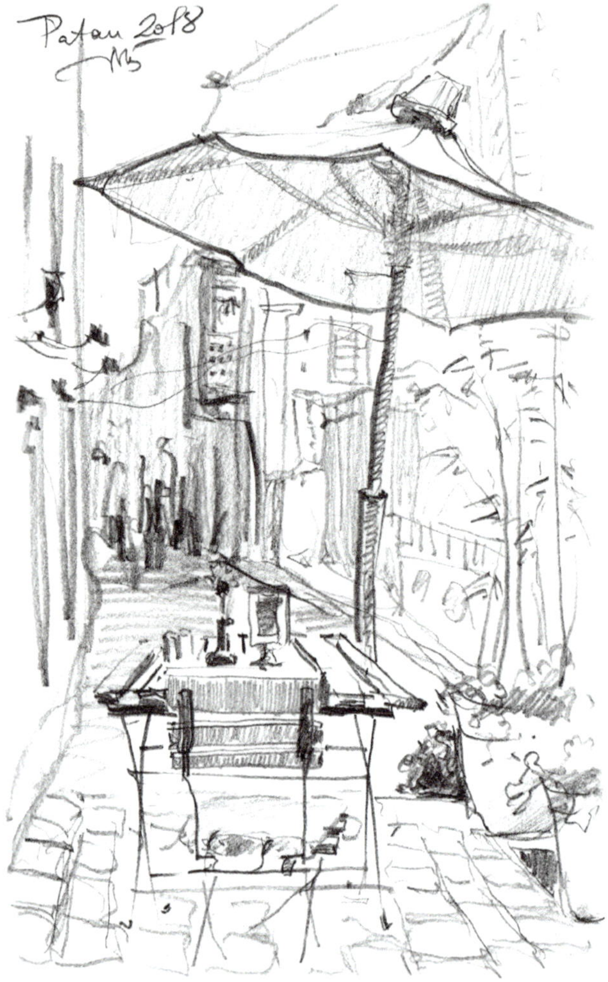

Fig. 3: Impression on the way to Patan Durbar Square – food vendors at every corner

Captured in a drawing by Mariia Bakhareva, 2018

corner: Fig. 4: Grocery shop in Patan

Fig. 6: Conservators and craftsmen jointly re-install the Ivory Window Ensemble

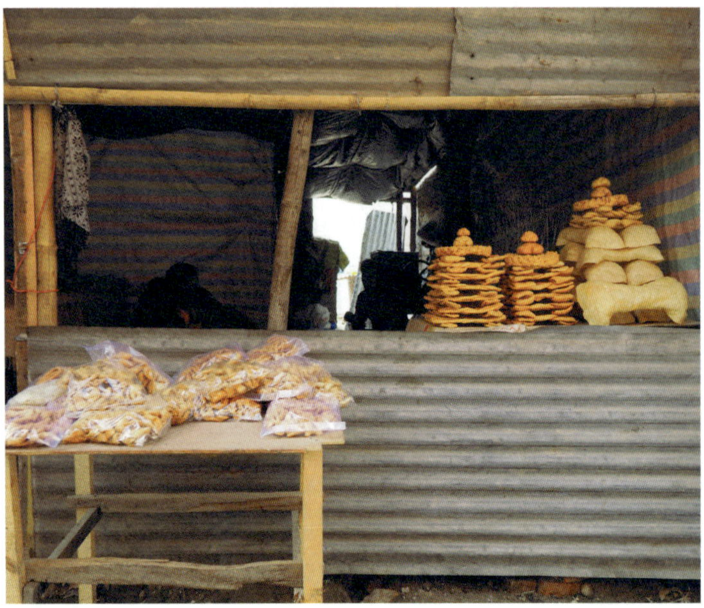

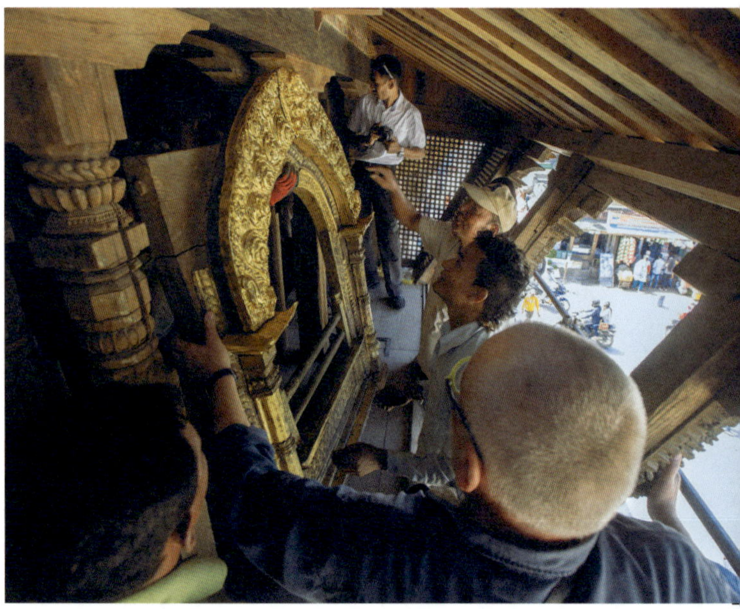

Fig. 8: Woodworker making copies

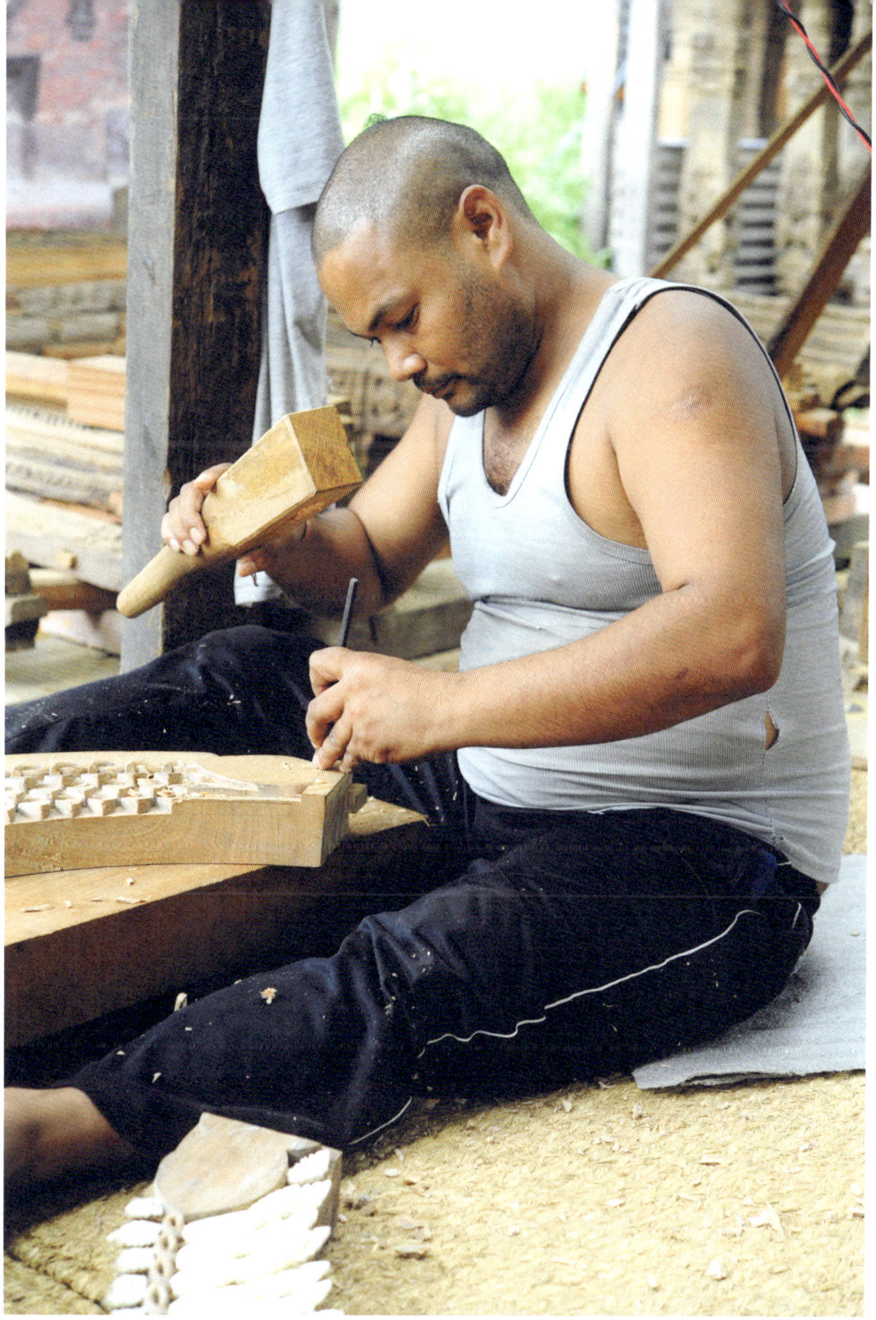

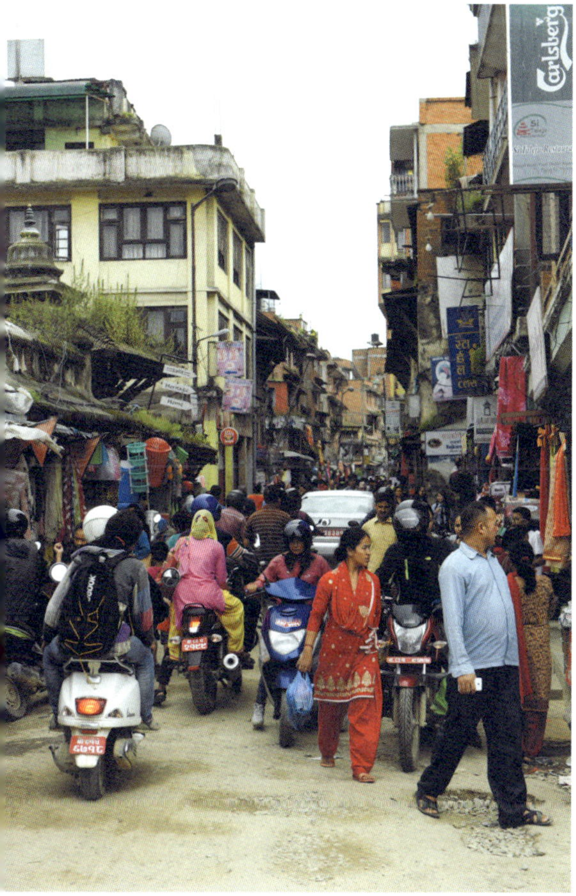

Fig. 5: Crowded street in Patan

Fig. 7: From the beginning on, Surya, a stonemason, supported us in the creation of stone indents

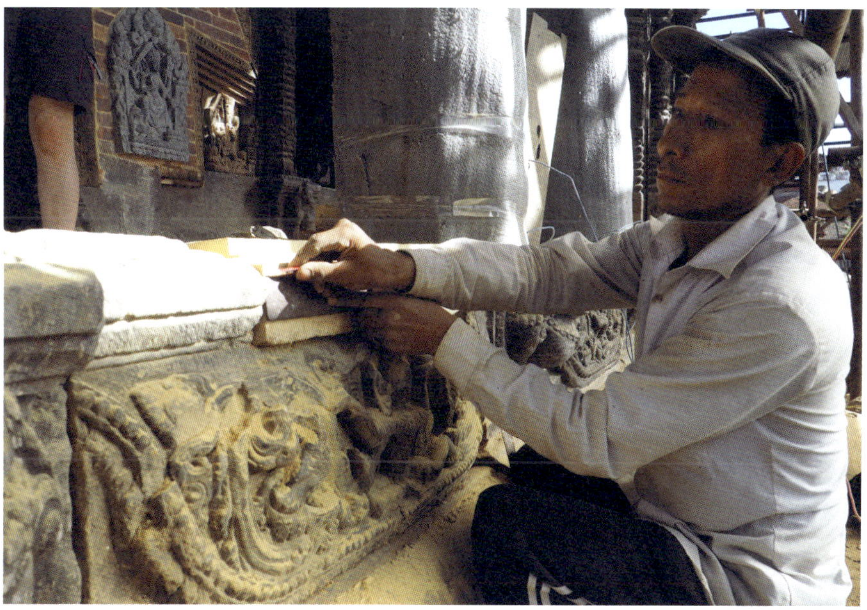

While reading this field report of Eduard F. Sekler, I feel strengthened in my view that, even forty years later, conservation was, and still is, a challenging task in Nepal.

You are confronted with varying views and beliefs, a different cultural background and another aesthetic sensitivity. Worship and religious practice still enjoy high priority in Nepalese culture. Cultural lives thereby revolve around the monuments and tangible cultural heritage is actively used (Fig. 9-10). It's not turned into a "museum piece" (as may be the case in Europe) – it is a part of daily life. You "can't" stop people worshiping their sculptures, touching them, bringing votive offerings, carrying them through the entire city on holidays (Fig. 11). During the festivities of Jyeshtha Purnima, the Throne of the Kings, the masterpiece of the Patan Museum collection, is carried out of its protected environment and positioned directly in front of Krishna Mandir (temple) at Durbar Square – exposed to wind and weather. In Austria it's hard to imagine the Imperial Crown and the insignia of the Holy Roman Empire on display on St. Stephen's Square in Vienna. As Sekler already witnessed, religious authenticity is sometimes more valued than material or formal authenticity. Historic structures and original substance might decay noticeably while people continue to make offerings to their gods. This rating of values sometimes contradicts what we as conservators feel is our obligation: the preservation of original substance, historic structures and surfaces.

Also the aesthetic expectations of Nepalese people differ from what we are used to in Central Europe. Integrity plays a decisive role. Gods and goddesses have to be complete and unscathed to be worshipped, minimal conservation without reconstruction of missing parts would sometimes infringe the religious belief of the locals.

We have to keep all this in mind to balance conservation and usage correctly, respect the authenticity of the monuments, and respond to the interests of all parties involved.

But not only the common attitude; also the given environment forces us to break new ground. You have to tailor your conservation concepts and approaches to the Nepalese context, consider the applicability of materials and methods on the available building materials and in the given climate; to take into account material availability and local bureaucratic procedures to be followed in conservation work, and at the same time consider the individual requirements of each monument or work of art. Sometimes you have to be spontaneous and creative. Sometimes you have to communicate with gestures, hands and feet.

In this demanding and stimulating environment not only the staff of our institute, but also our students who accompany us to Patan each year, are constantly learning and developing further, both on a professional and personal level. Personal qualities are built and refined. I am thinking of flexibility and solution-orientation, which are not only advantageous as a conservator but in everyday life; further, understanding and respecting otherness, openness and willingness to try new things, which are, in my opinion, among the most valuable qualities in this era of globalisation.

HANDS-ON CONSERVATION IN NEPAL – AN OPEN-AIR EVENT

Looking back, the teams from our institute have implemented more than eleven working campaigns in Patan so far – sometimes annual, sometimes biannual, each ranging from two to five weeks.

The first thing I needed to get used to in Nepal is the six-day working week. Only on Saturday can you sleep in before rushing to a shopping or sightseeing tour. The second thing concerns the working conditions. An equipped workplace or a laboratory as we know it from Austria is not available. The most basic things like electricity and water supply have to be organised. So, each year we set up anew our temporary workplaces, either directly at the monuments or in the courtyards of the Royal Palace. Both are open-air and in the public space. In the meantime, I already know that two things are indispensible: a rain cover and a barrier tape. June to September – exactly when we are on site – is monsoon period in the Kathmandu Valley. Almost 390 mm of precipitation come down from heaven in one month. A blessing for farmers, it hampers the work of conservators (Fig. 12). Objects have to be covered or sheltered and protected from literally being "swept away". And, we are not only exposed to the weather, but also to a curious audience. Our workplaces are often on the route of tourists and guided tours. Besides, Nepali have a particular interest in watching other people working. Therefore barrier tapes or fences are needed: first, to discourage people from touching objects or intervening in the conservation work, and second, also to protect our privacy (Fig. 13–15). At the same time, we don't completely exclude them from the process; they still have the opportunity to follow the conservation work – an occasion that is often not possible under regular conditions.

Another thing one should have is a hard head…or a hard hat…especially when working on the scaffolding in Nepal (Fig. 16). Each year anew we become painfully aware that Nepalese are slightly smaller than Europeans and scaffold levels are accordingly lower. Work in bent-over or kneeling position is on the agenda (Fig. 17–18).

Despite this, at least the purchase of material and equipment in Patan is significantly easier than, for instance, in Nako, over 13,000 feet up in the remote area of Himachal Pradesh the Himalayas: this is due on one hand to the fact that Patan is a vibrant metropolis in the largest urban agglomeration of Nepal, the Kathmandu Valley. On the other hand, our eight years of working experience confer an advantage; nevertheless, it is still challenging from year to year. To search for the right brush, a bucket, a pair of pliers or wrapping tape you have to know which of the thousand small stores to approach. They all look the same. We obtain sand for our mortars directly from the palace garden. The same applies to slaked lime, which is available in the KVPT's own lime pit. Since last year, also larger amounts of natural hydraulic lime (NHL) from the French company LaFarge have been available in Patan, extending the range of material which could be used for our stone conservation work. All these materials were already tested and investigated by us in our laboratories in Vienna. It revealed that they are of fairly good quality, although the NHL is a little more inhomogeneous than the one from Europe.

We bring tools like drilling machines, angle grinders and cutting tools from Austria. After several deformed drill bits and torn saw blades owing to the mostly inadequate quality of the Chinese imports available in Nepal, we rely on our products. The same applies to adhesives, consolidants and more specific conservation materials, which are not available in Nepal. All of them are transported in our luggage, distributed amongst the whole team. So far only lead paint caused considerable problems at the airport in Delhi. The laser, which was brought from Italy and applied in our conservation campaign in 2013, was a comparably easy task.

STONE CONSERVATION IN PATAN

At first glance, one might think that stone plays a tangential role in the handicraft and building trade in Nepal. The number of brick-wood temples and monuments is huge. But closer scrutiny reveals that appearances are deceptive. Stone has been used equally for the construction of whole temples, particularly sikhara-style temples like Krishna Mandir, but also for fountains and *ghats* (stepped tanks) for water provision, steles and pillars, *chaityas* (small commemorative stupas) and gates. There is an incredible amount of statuary, reliefs and sculptural work, made of stone, representing animals and mythological figures. They flank the entrance to temples and embellish their façades and bases.

The range of monuments and artworks made of stone, which we conserved in recent years, was similarly varied: from the waist-high sculpture of god Harishankara to the base of the eponymous pagoda temple on Durbar Square, from the small Lion Pillar to the Pillar of King Yoganarendra Malla, from the intimate Royal Bath Tusha Hiti to the Pavilion of the Bhandarkhal Tank in the Palace Garden, from stone lions at Mul Chowk to the multi-part relief gates of Nasal Chowk – all different in size and shape, function and meaning, all facing different problems that required tailor-made solutions.

Stone sculpting still comprises an important branch of crafts in Patan, although not as popular as metal crafts. Besides the traditional sculpting that follows old guidelines on how to sculpt and portray religious idols, increasingly modern imitations and artistic creations of stone are available for purchase in tourist shops. Nevertheless, today's sculptors, like their fathers and grandfathers, strive to endow life to their works. And as long as "stone sculpting rests in able hands and [...] as long as there are rocks, and people who see the potential in a rock to become God", it will live on in Nepal. Hereby I agree with the author of this statement, Kapil Bisht.

KNOWLEDGE IS POWER

What are the physical and chemical properties of the stones used in Patan. How were they processed and how were historic structures built? What is causing damage to the stone monuments? Climate, environmental surroundings, human interventions, stone intrinsic properties? Over the years, senior conservators of the Institute explored these questions together with several students, who dedicated their pre-diploma or diploma theses to these issues. We studied and surveyed the monuments, took samples of the stones and mortars and analysed them in our laboratories in Vienna – together with conservation scientists of the Institute of Art and Technology at the University of Applied Arts Vienna, and our own chemists, we spend hours in front of optical and scanning electron microscopes and the FTIR spectometer. We studied the conservation history of the monuments and consulted art historians and architects on site, experts in the field of Nepalese art and architecture. We now know a lot more than eight years ago, although there are still unanswered questions.

For the monuments on Durbar Square mainly two stones were used: on one hand, a siliceous sandstone with whitish-to-ochre colour. It is fine-grained and relatively soft, which enables fine workmanship. Surfaces of this stone show elaborate carved features and detailed depictions. On the other hand, we face a weakly metamorphic stone, a kind of schist, greyish in colour. Its density and hardness make it difficult to hew and carve fine details. At the same time, its stability makes it a suitable building material for static and load-bearing elements. The two stones vary not only in their scope of use, but also in their physical and chemical properties resulting in different mechanisms of deterioration.

The low water uptake of the schist extensively prevents it from decay mechanism traced to the influence of water, such as microbiological growth, salination and solution processes. In contrast, porous sandstone absorbs water like a sponge. The schist is vulnerable to cracks and breakage mainly caused by mechanical stresses or impact. Instead, the sandstone tends to more or less crumble away and disintegrate (Fig. 23). This knowledge helps us not only to explain damage patterns and identify their causes, but also to define adequate conservation treatments.

PLANTS

In Nepal you don't need to have green fingers – every plant grows and flourishes without great effort. The high availability of water during the monsoon period, combined with mild winters, provides an extremely favourable habitat for algae, bacteria, moss and higher plants. While in Austria a kind of "natural" inactivation or elimination of biological colonisation is caused by frost in winter or by periods with little rainfall and hot temperatures in summer, in Nepal these limitations hardly exist. The result: overgrown and unintentionally "greened" objects. Particularly the sponge-like sandstone offers perfect conditions here for biological growth – a constantly moist substrate. But the biological colonisation is not only an aesthetical problem. As conservators, we also have to consider harmful substances released from microorganisms like acids, the root pressure of higher plants that causes cracks and distortion of the surrounding stone, and the formation of compact biological crusts on the stone surface.

Thus, while on my balcony in Vienna I struggle to keep my plants alive, I combat them in Nepal. For cleaning purposes we avoid taking water from the tank in the garden, which

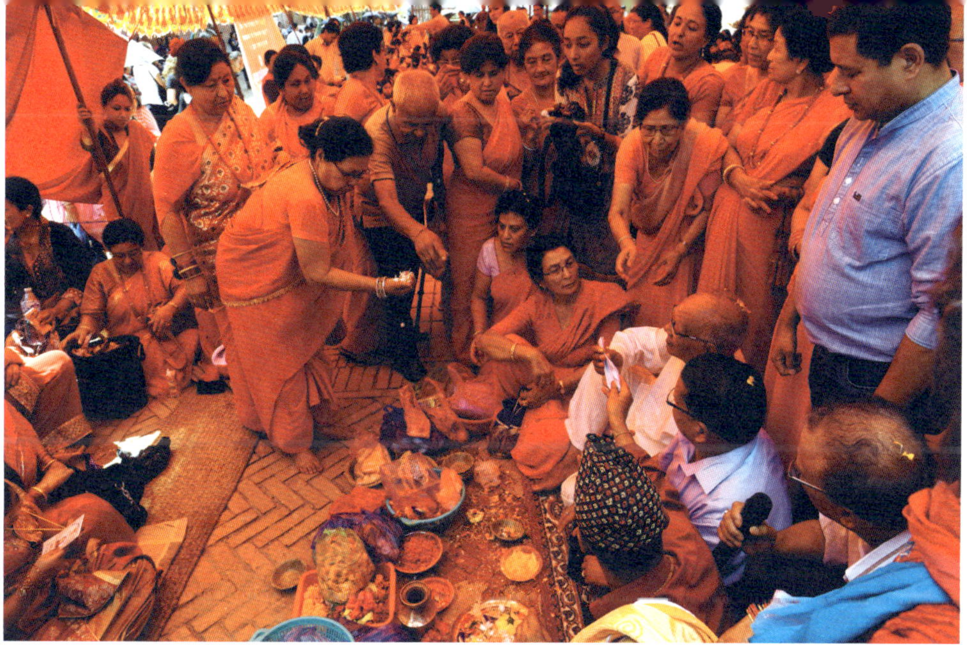

Fig. 9: Worship and religious practice are closely linked to Nepal's daily life

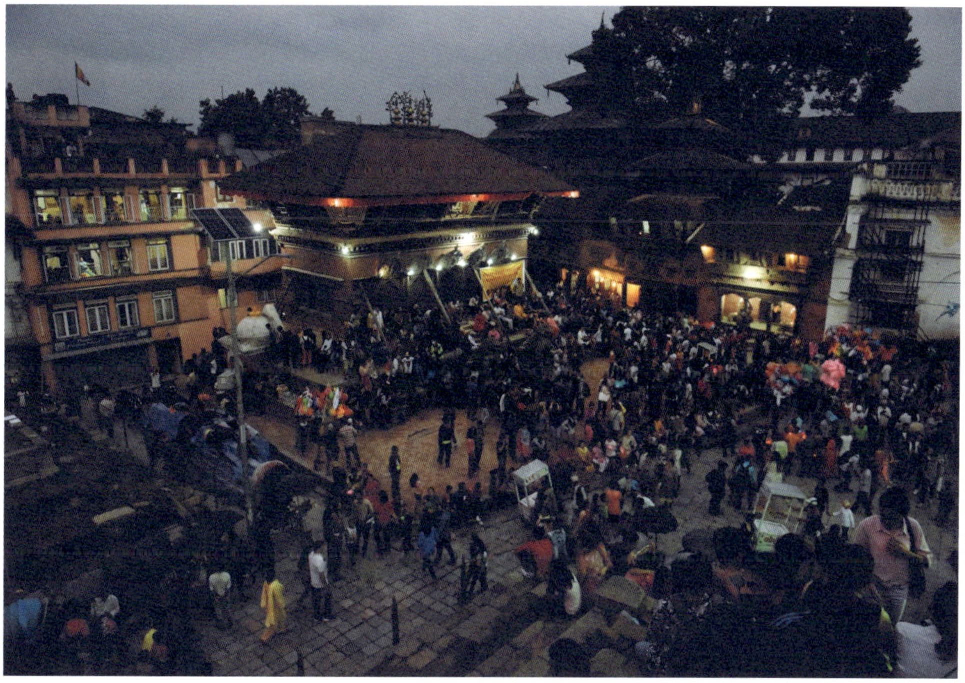

Fig. 10: Cultural life revolves around the monuments

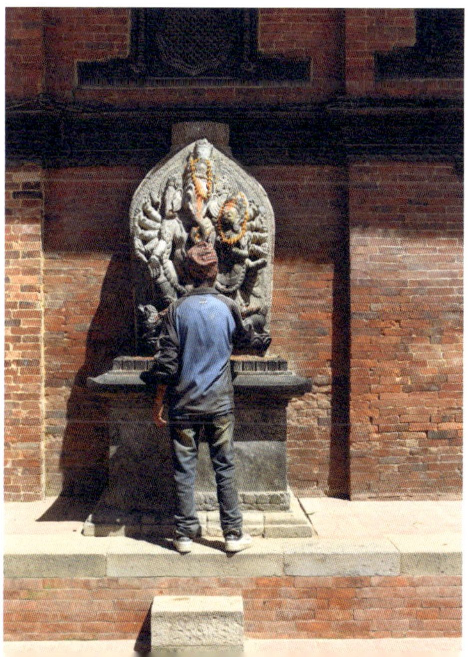

Fig. 11: Worshipping, bringing votive offerings and touching their gods – common sights in Nepal

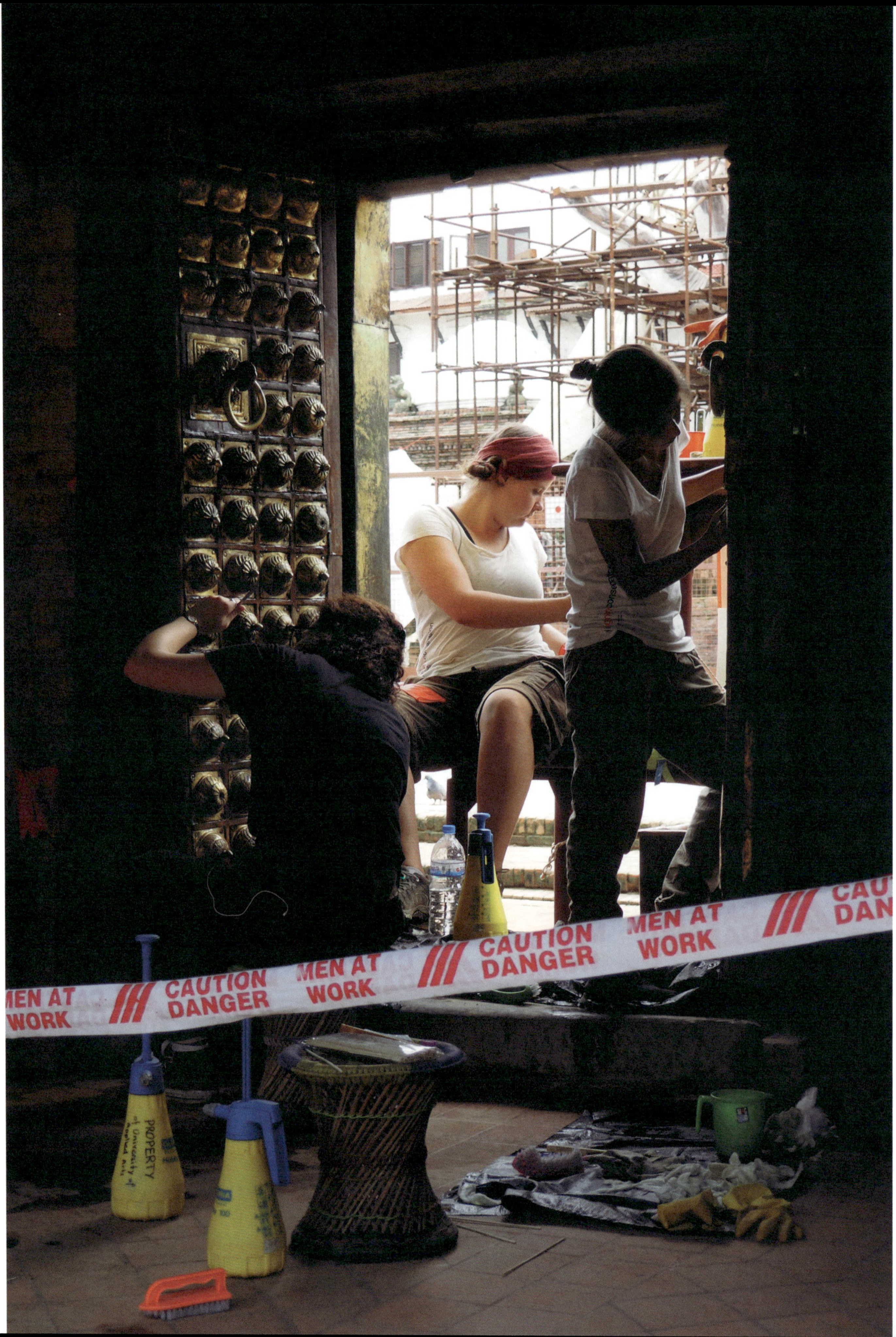
CAUTION
DANGER
MEN AT
WORK
PROPERTY

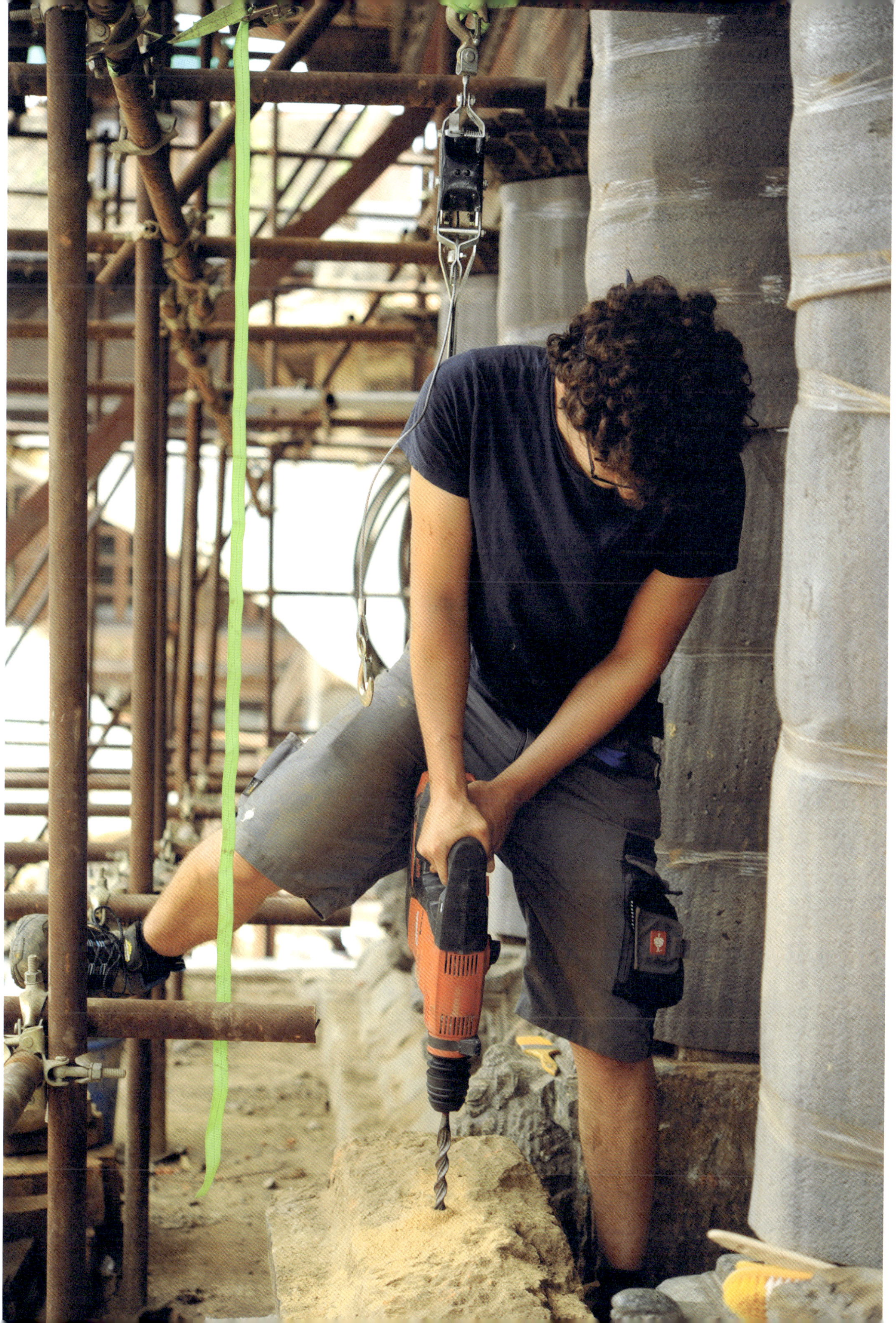

BY MARTINA HASELBERGER

previous pages:
Fig. 14: Barrier tapes keep viewers at a distance while allowing them to follow the conservation work
Fig. 19: Stone conservation – pinning and gluing of broken parts

Fig. 12: Heavy rain is forcing us to take a break

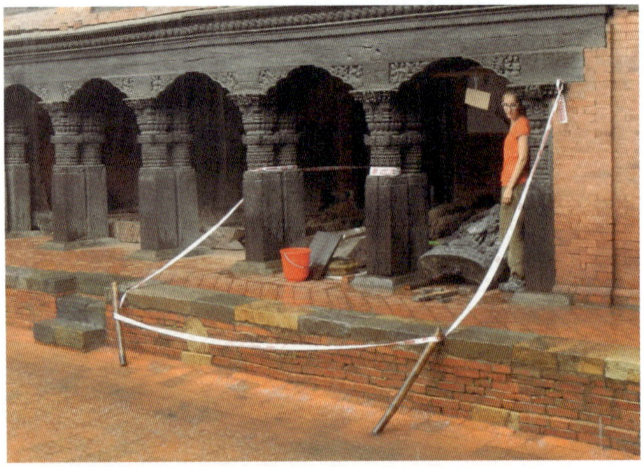

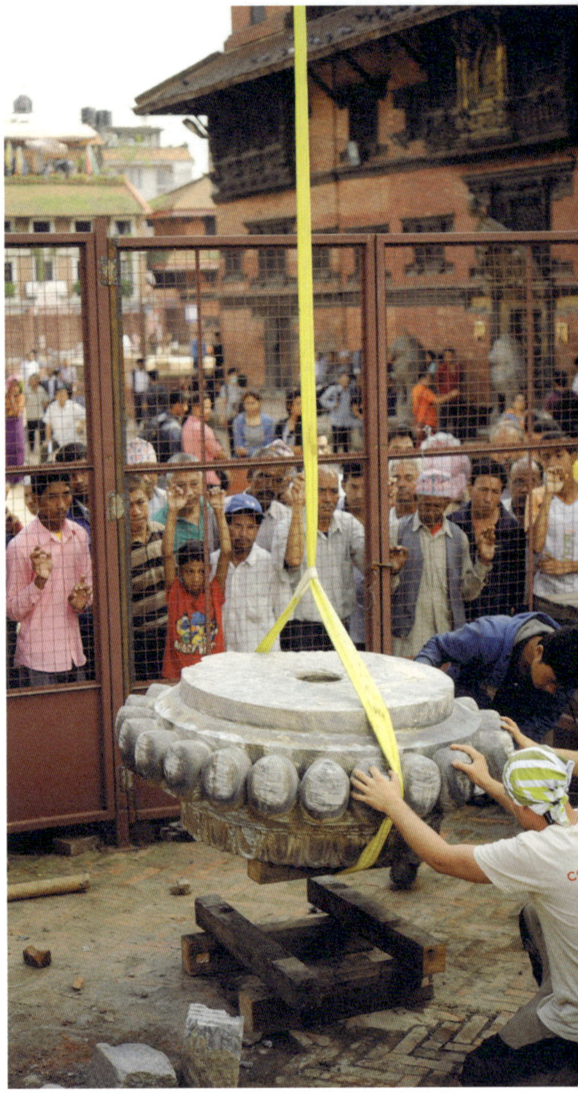

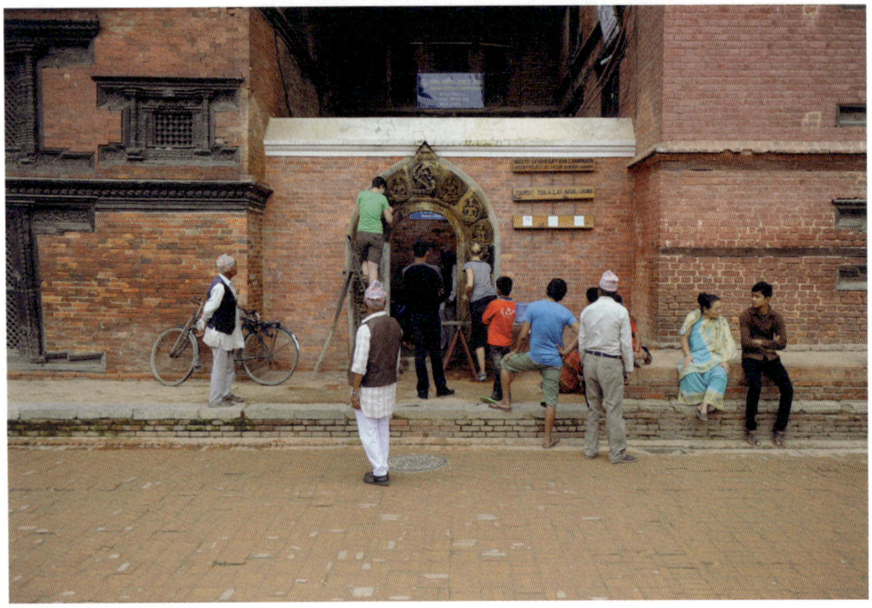

Fig. 13: Conservation in public space without barriers results in a "close-up" audience

Fig. 15: Sometimes fences are needed to maintain the required distance between audience and site

Fig. 16: Scaffoldings in Nepal – hard hat areas

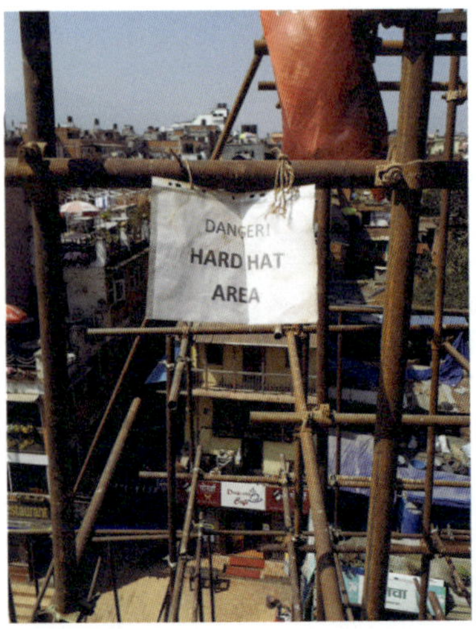

Fig. 17-18: Nepalese scaffoldings demand working in a bent-over or kneeling position

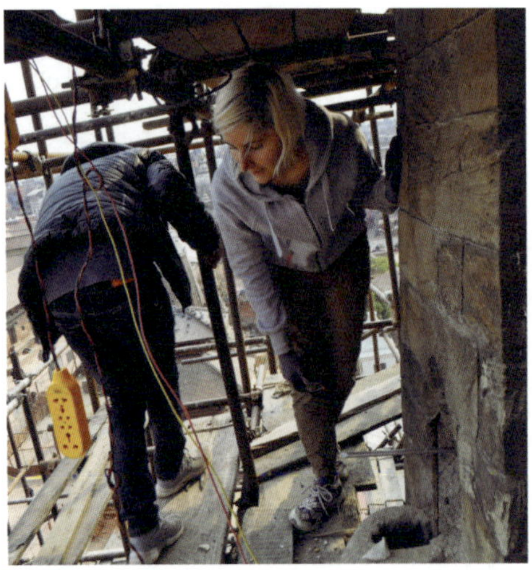

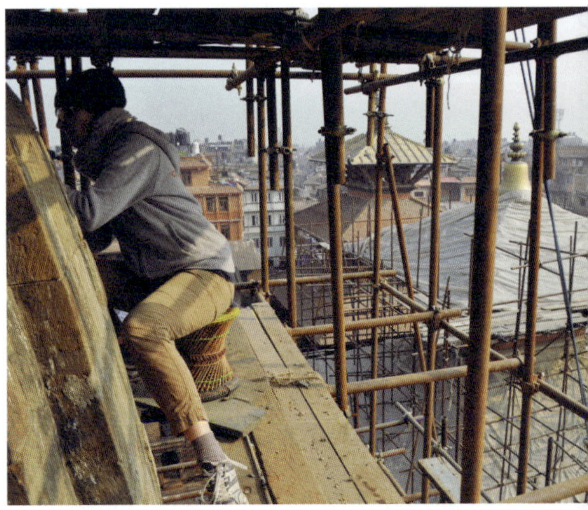

Fig. 20: Stone conservation – dry cleaning

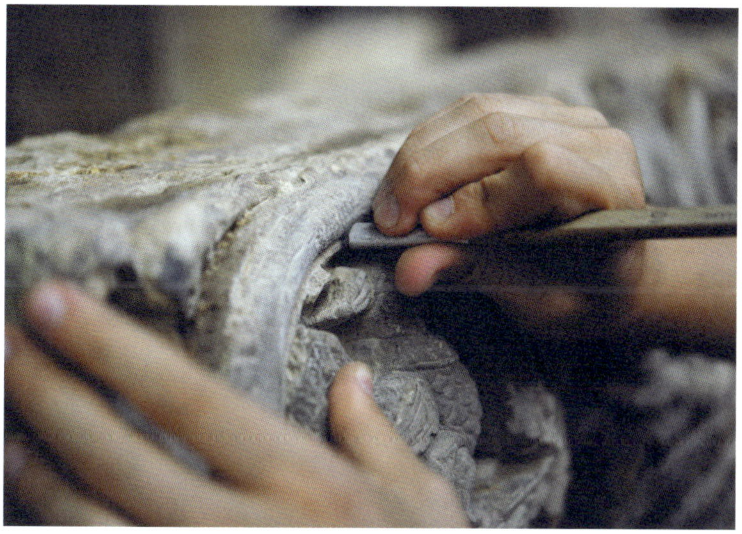

Fig. 23: Heavily deteriorated surface of the local sandstone

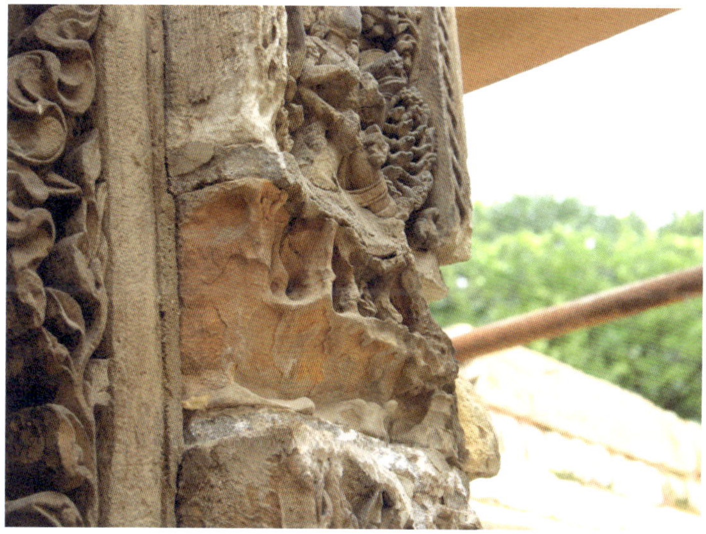

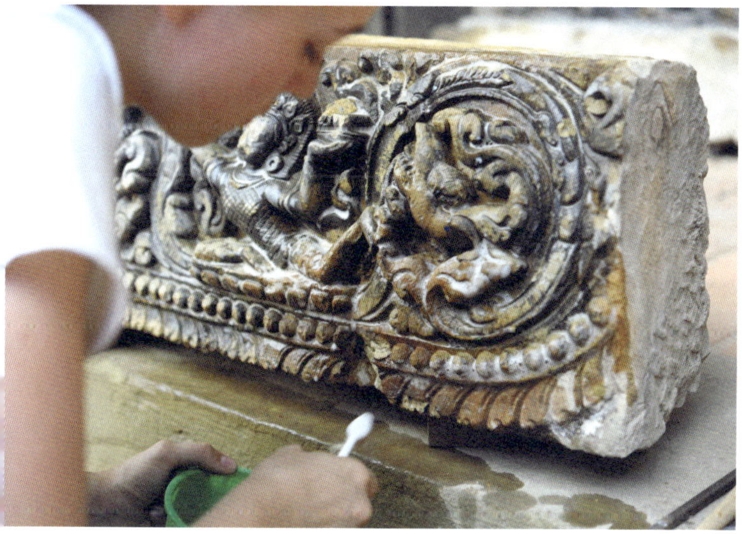

Fig. 21: Stone conservation – cleaning with water and surfactant

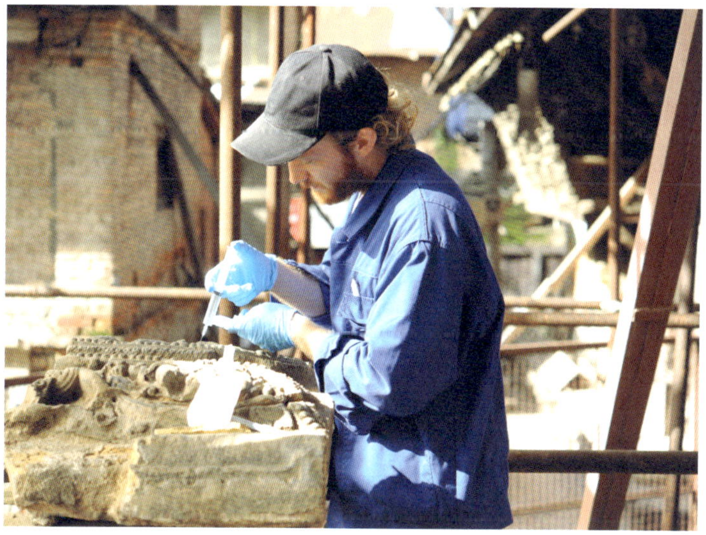

Fig. 24: Consolidating the sandstone

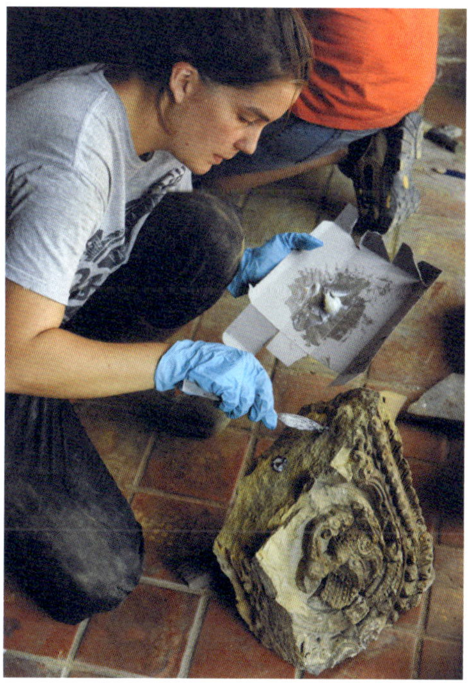

Fig. 22: Stone conservation – gluing of broken parts

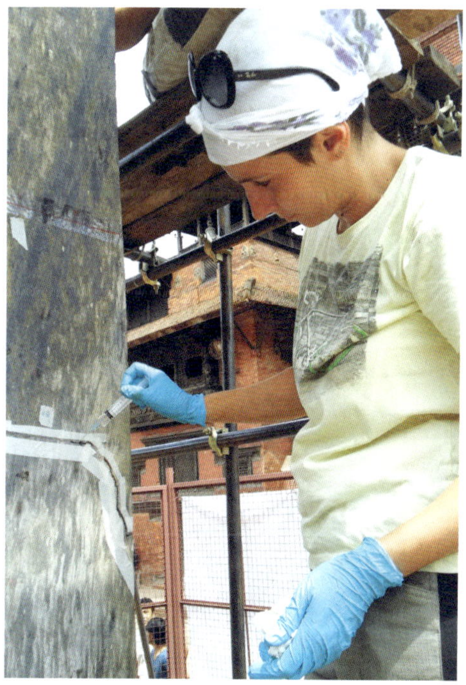

Fig. 25: Injecting cracks in the schist

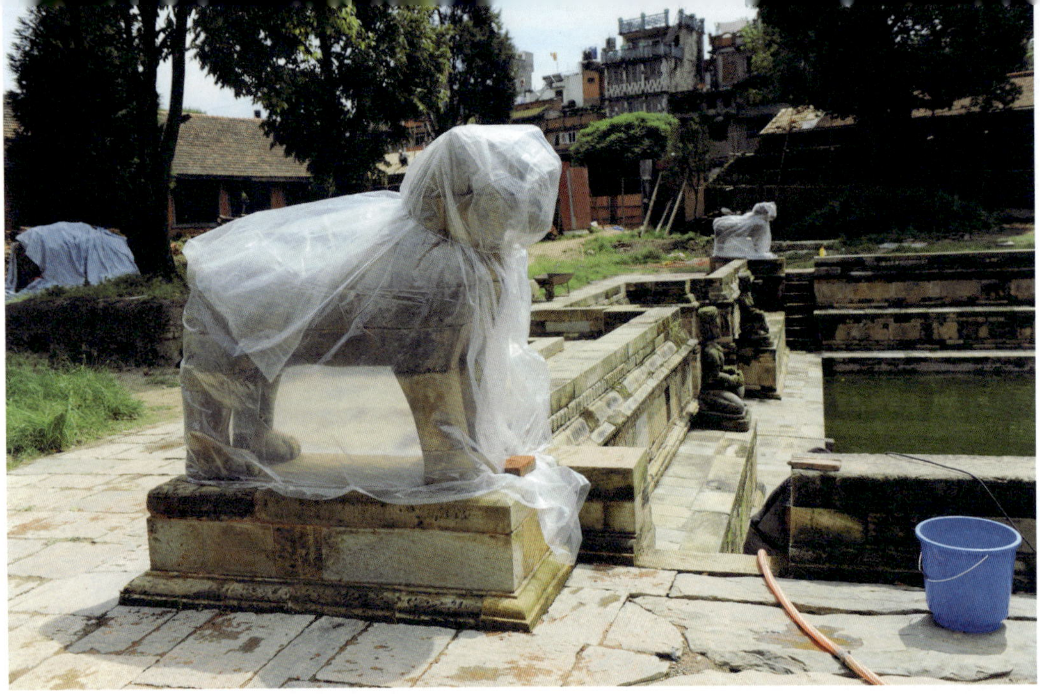

Fig. 26: Biocide treatment

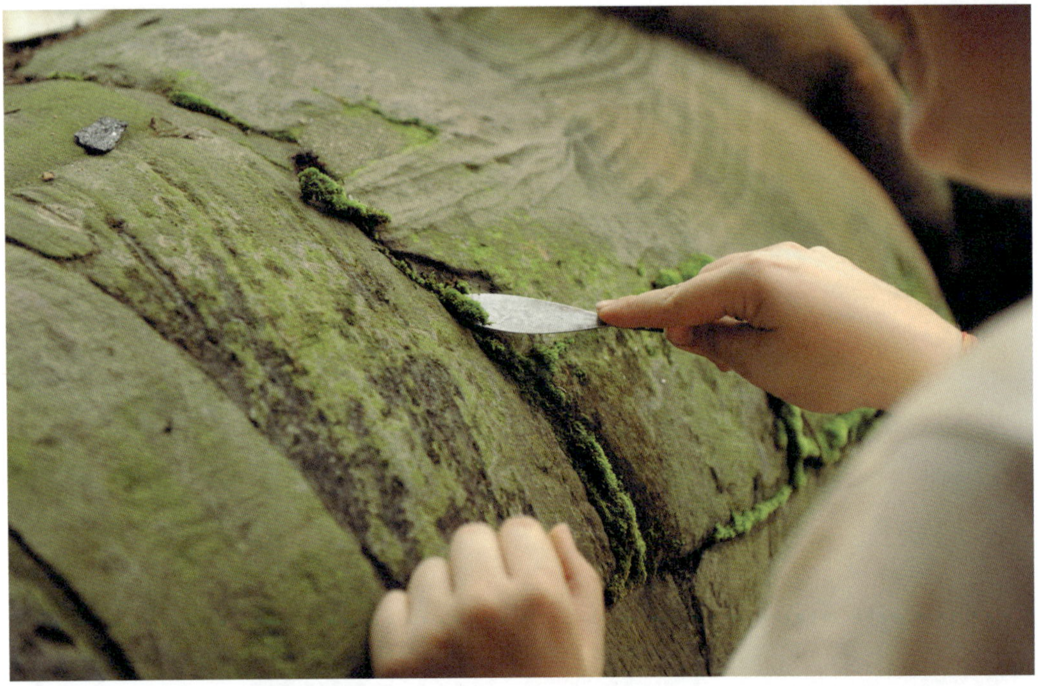

Fig. 27: Removal of moss on monuments

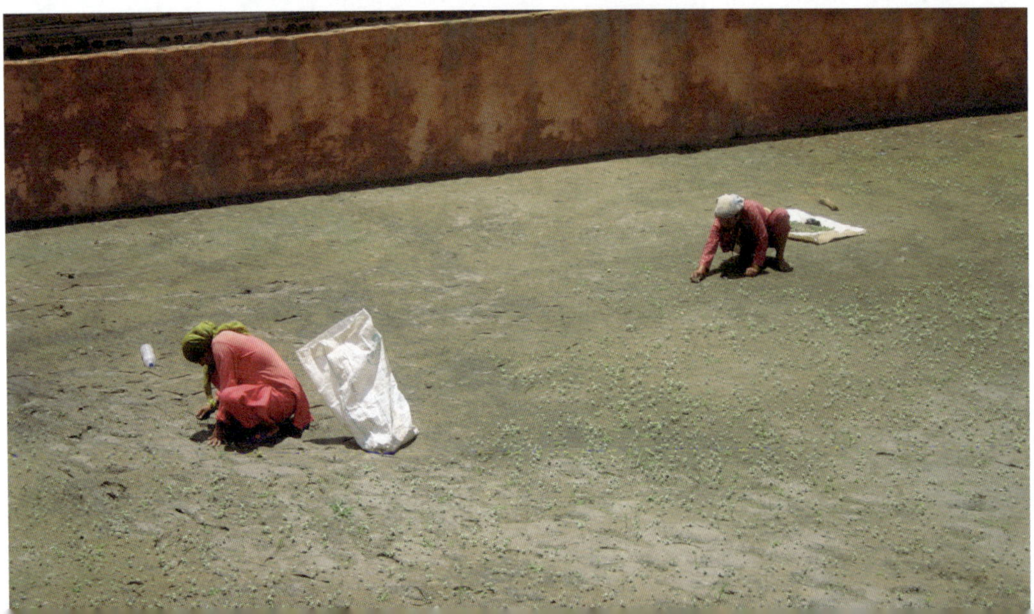

Fig. 28: Plucking of seedlings in the Bhandarkhal Tank

contains algae and bacteria. An application of the already "green" water on the stone objects would only accelerate biological growth. Instead we use water from the tap or drinking water (for very sensitive objects). In some cases we use biocides to kill the microorganisms to enable other conservation measures such as gluing, consolidation, backfilling and filling (Fig. 26). In any case the best way to avoid rapid biological growth in Nepal is frequent cleaning and maintenance. Seedlings are to be plucked as soon as apparent, roots are to be pulled out, biofilms are to be removed before forming thick, crust-like layers (Fig. 27–28). Dust and dirt can be nutrients for bacteria and fungi and have to be equally removed. Altogether a time-consuming but effective way to avoid extreme biological colonisation and rapid growth of plants.

BUILDING BACK BETTER

We quickly realised that beside external factors and human activity, the construction of the monuments themselves constitutes another potential weakness. Historic structures made of sandstone often consist of small blocks that were simply placed one above another. Only a natural resin, so called silay, was used to stick them together. We already detected it deep inside joints and between single stone blocks. Dowels, clamps or mortar as used in Europe were hardly applied. In contrast, the monuments made of schist often have stone tenons and recesses to keep the single blocks in the right position. Considering the much bigger size of these blocks, anything else would be negligent. The problem is that in most cases the tenons are too small in scale, bedding mortar is not present either.

All these facts simplify our job – dismantling for example is easier – but have detrimental effects on the stability of the monuments. Both constructions are vulnerable to the lateral movement during earthquakes. Severe distortions or complete collapse are the result.

In any conservation effort we thus try to improve resilience and strengthen the structures as far as possible. A tricky task as the interventions should be hardly visible for the observer, but hidden inside.

On one hand, we keep originally applied plug-in systems but modify (enlarge) them by inserting vertical pins; this decreases the danger of tipping.

On the other, we insert new clamps to connect blocks on a horizontal level and thus form "rings" to prevent edges or single blocks from bursting. Vertically added pins connect superimposed blocks or the aforementioned "rings" with each other to avoid movement or drop downs. Stainless steel is used for the clamps and pins to avoid corrosion and resulting bursting.

Particularly in the aftermath of the recent earthquake and the current phase of rebuilding, the main principle is: building back better. To be earthquake-resistant, monuments have to be strengthened in such a way that they are rigid enough to avoid extreme whipping back and forth and at the same time flexible enough to sway. This we learnt from our Nepalese colleagues and from consultations with Austrian engineers. Thus we avoid too stiff connections to allow a certain and especially lateral movement. Applying this principle allows the buildings to "dance" during earthquakes, as we know it from the skyscrapers in Japan.

Another negative constructive peculiarity of some monuments is the too-close contact with water-storing materials, as well as missing rear ventilation. The two gatekeeper lions in front of Mul Chowk and the two lions flanking the tank in the palace garden for instance had brick cores. The stone Relief Gates at Nasal Chowk were in direct contact to the surrounding brick-earth wall. The same applied to the finely-carved stone blocks of the base of Harishankara Temple, which were in contact with the brick-earth core and the blocks of the sunken step-well Tusha Hitit. Both brick and earth retain moisture and slowly release it. The result: the stones also remain wet for a long time. The fact that the sandstone described before was used for all these monuments compounds the situation. It tends to get very soft and sandy under these circumstances. You can even scratch it with your fingers.

The solution: we removed brick cores, reassembled the structures with an air draft behind to prevent water penetration from the back or inserted damp-proof foils such as at Tusha Hiti.

WELL-MEANT IS NOT ALWAYS GOOD

"Those who don't know history are doomed to repeat it" Edmund Burke once stated.

There is truth in this statement also for conservators. We can learn valuable lessons by knowing the conservation history of monuments. And we can avoid failures from the past.

Although our predecessors worked to the best of their knowledge and beliefs, some former restoration measures applied at Patan Durbar Square have considerable negative impact.

The use of too-dense pointing mortar containing more or less pure low-quality Portland cement and little aggregate in the joints affected the water balance of the stone.

Normally, the purpose of joints is that water should evaporate through them, which means that deterioration problems also happen inside the joints while the stone is preserved. If the joints are too hard or dense the deterioration process continues inside the stone.

Therefore we usually remove overly dense or cracked grouts and mortar fillings, mainly mechanically with hammer and chisel (Fig. 29-30). For new fillings and re-pointing of joints we currently stick to lime-based mortars, whether air lime or natural hydraulic lime. Based on test series, monitoring and results of scientific investigations, we know that they work well in the climate of the valley and have performed satisfactorily with the building stones. Furthermore, we try to use locally available materials, sand from the heap and lime from the own lime pit in the palace garden.

Beside overly dense mortars, also coatings can negatively impart the water balance of stones. This also applied to two secondary surface coatings, which we detected on some monuments: one bitumen-based found on the Relief Gates and one acrylate-based on the Bhandarkhal Tank Pavilion. Both seemed to be applied to inhibit water infiltration. Although well-meant, they instead prevented the water inside the stone from evaporating properly.

In our working missions we have tried as far as possible to remove or replace these inappropriate materials, which were applied during former restoration and caused decay.

We reduce surface coatings to allow the stone to "breathe" again and restore its original permeability (Fig. 31). From time to time, this results in real solvent orgies and the sometimes funny view of conservators breathing in the acetone a little too deeply.

Or it means that a laser is used on Durbar Square for the first time in history. This was the case in 2013 and 2014 when Italian expert Alessandro Zanini, together with his laser, accompanied the team in order to remove the bitumen coating on the Relief Gates (Fig. 32).

METAL CONSERVATION IN PATAN

A walk through the streets of Patan is always accompanied by an impressive background noise. Honks, birds, merchants loudly touting their wares, tinkling bells...beside all these noises one sound particularly attracts your attention: the rhythmic, more or less meditative beating of hammers on metal. You follow the sound and end up in a small workshop or a courtyard, curiously watching one of the numerous craftsmen in Patan processing their artworks.

The city of Patan is particularly famous for its long and still vital tradition in metalworking crafts, which is among the most highly developed in the world. Newar craftsmen have produced masterpieces of art out of copper, bronze, gold and silver – sculptures, bells, pinnacles, door and window embellishments. Today many of them are in dire need of conservation. Our first metal conservation project was scheduled in 2013: the Golden Doorway Ensemble in Mul Chowk, one of the courtyards of the Royal Palace. Flanked by the two sculptures of the River Goddesses Yamuna and Ganga, its main doorway comprises the entry to the Shrine of goddess Taleju. She is a form of the Goddess Durga and chief patron of the country, her worship thus has a special place in Newar society. Although more suave and gentle than Durga, she thirsts after blood from time to time. Animal sacrifices in her shrine in the Royal Palace are on the agenda.

While working in Mul Chowk each year, we are "fortunate" to observe this event in the first row. Students who are in Patan for the first time are, for a moment delighted when goats are guided in the courtyard and lashed in front of the shrine. They feed and stroke them. After being informed of the animal's destiny, first rescue attempts are considered. In the end, we can only leave the courtyard when the slaughter takes place – although for us incomprehensible – it is part of the local religious practice.

CONSERVATION AND CRAFTS

In Patan, metal conservation goes hand in hand with metal crafts.

First, the artworks often consist of numerous single copper sheets fixed and connected with rivets or nails – altogether a quite complicated plug system. I remember the more than a hundred individual parts of the Taleju pinnacles and the multi-part sculptures of the River Goddesses Ganga and Yamuna and Yoganarendra Malla. We had to dismantle them to enable wet cleaning and reshaping. During the re-assembling we were grateful for the help of the coppersmith (Fig. 34).

Second, the aforementioned single metal sheets are often mounted on wooden supports, as it is the case with doors, windows and pinnacles, or have an iron substructure, as we found inside statues. Both materials easily decay in the given climate – wood rots, iron corrodes. To ensure the safe mounting of the objects, the substructures thus have to be renewed in some cases, which is often done by local blacksmiths or carpenters.

Third, the relatively thin copper sheets are often deformed or impressed, partly resulting in cracks and voids. However, the worst deformed sculpture I ever assessed was the one of King Yoganarendra after the earthquake in 2015 (Fig. 35). After having survived the earthquake in 1934 relatively unscathed, the sculpture and the upper three parts of its stone pillar fell in 2015, with only the lowest shaft left standing. Compressed in bent posture, the king was only a mere shadow of his former self. In this case the coppersmiths did a really good job. The whole sculpture could be reshaped – with some cut-backs from the conservator's point of view.

The deformations were so severe that a "cold" forming with simple hammering was not possible but the coppersmith had to heat the copper up considerably (hot forming) to bring it into the correct shape (Fig. 36). This procedure is accompanied by the loss of the valuable original gilded surface.

Thus we normally try to find possibilities in close consultation with the craftsmen and the KVPT to avoid this hot forming. Sometimes a deformation can be left untreated, sometimes a crack or gap can be bridged by a metal sheet applied on the bottom side.

Altogether, it is always a mutual learning process – as conservators we built up our knowledge on metal processing and craft techniques, while craftsmen become more aware of preserving the original surfaces and "gentle" handling.

GOLD

The majority of the metal artworks we conserved so far are made of fire-gilded copper sheets, mainly repoussé work, where sheet metal is hammered into relief. Besides, casting techniques are applied in Patan, also known as "lost wax", where bronze is cast into a clay mould that previously contained a wax model, which melts away in the casting process.

The practice of both techniques has been continually pursued in Patan. The same applies to fire-gilding, forbidden in Europe because of its toxicity for human and environment, it is still used in the Kathmandu Valley.

Original fire-gilded surfaces are quite resistant also in the given challenging climatic conditions of Nepal – I already held century-old sculptures in my hand with still-preserved original surfaces. Nevertheless, usage and people devotionally touching the surfaces result in worn-down gilding. This is not a peculiarity of Nepal – also metal sculptures elsewhere have brightly polished and shiny toes, fingers or breasts caused by people in search of some luck. The problems arise when the protective gold is completely gone and the bare copper is shining through, as copper is more susceptible to weathering and corrosion.

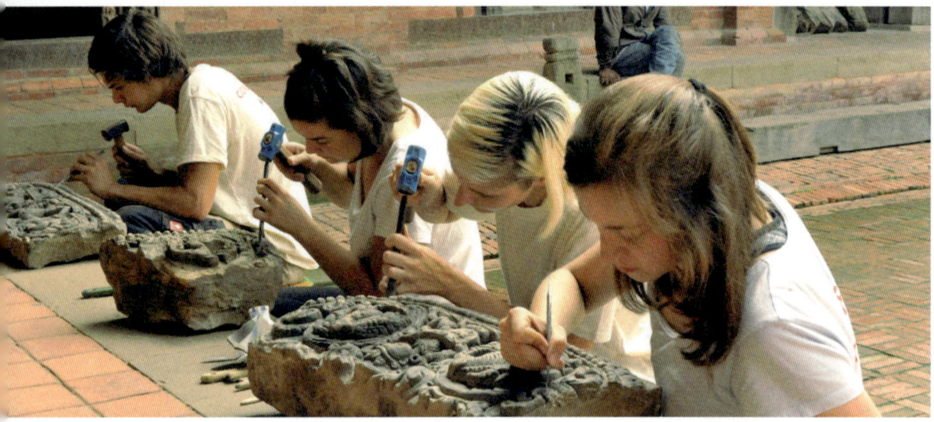

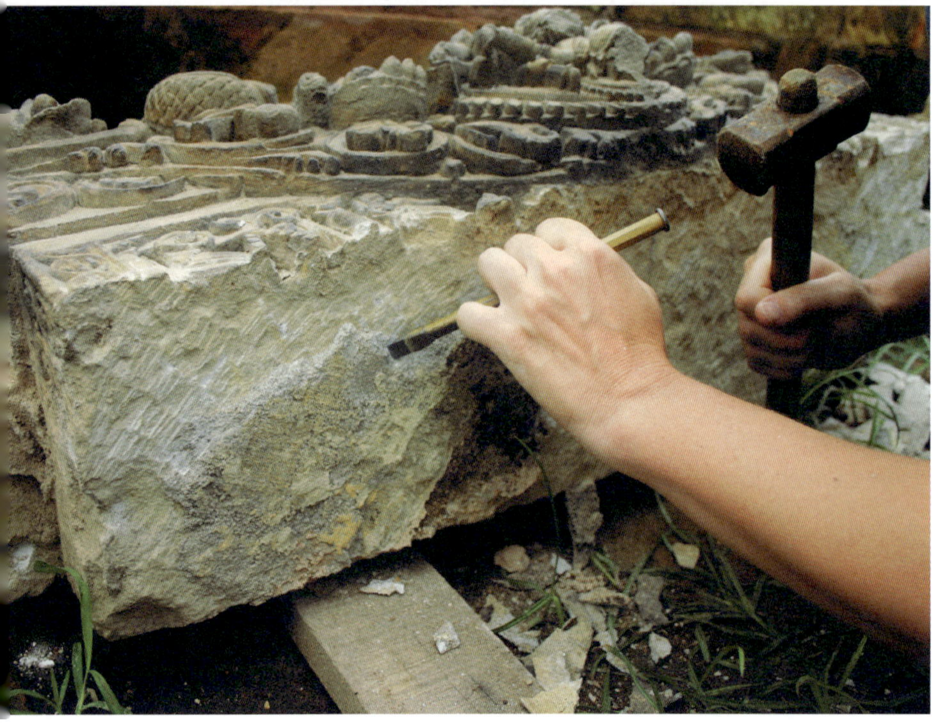

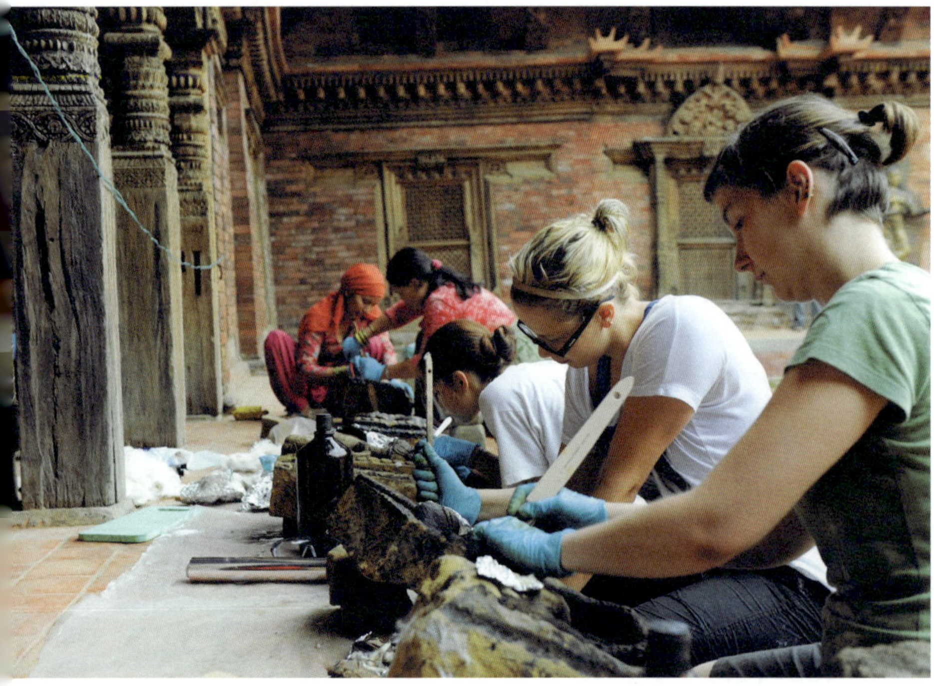

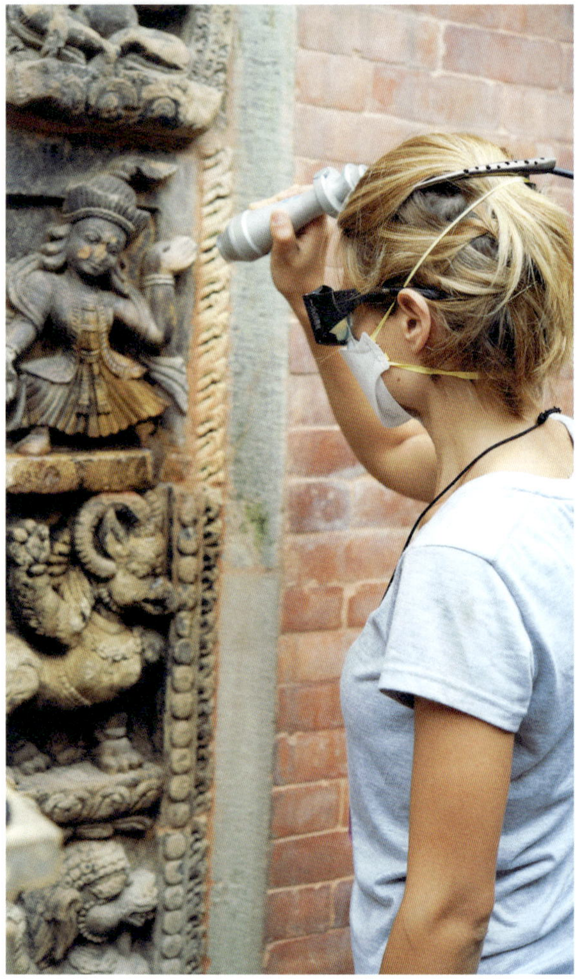

Fig. 29-30: Removal of remnants of old cement mortar

Fig. 31: Reducing surface coatings with acetone

Fig. 32: Cleaning of stone surfaces with laser

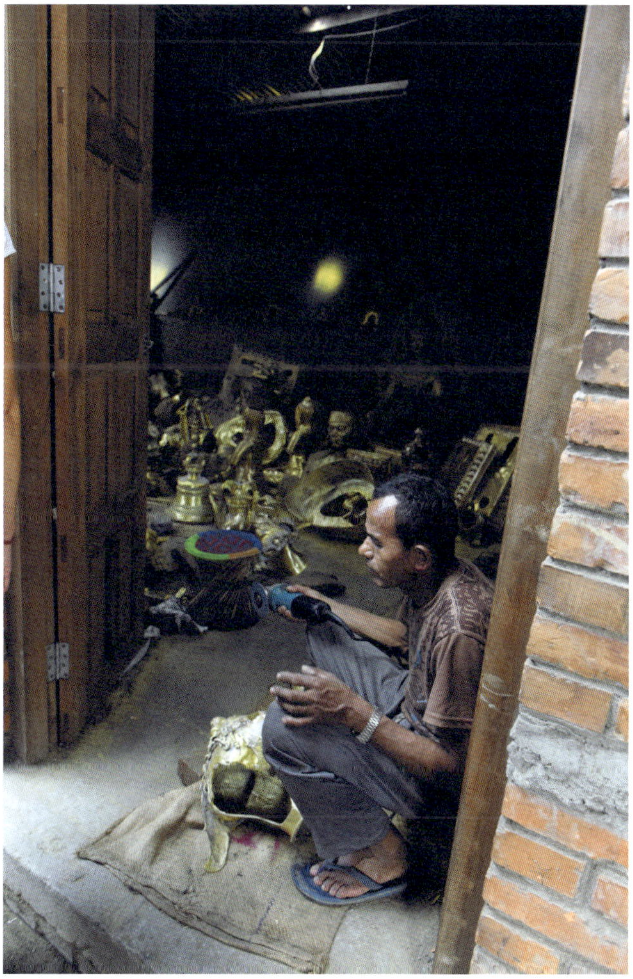

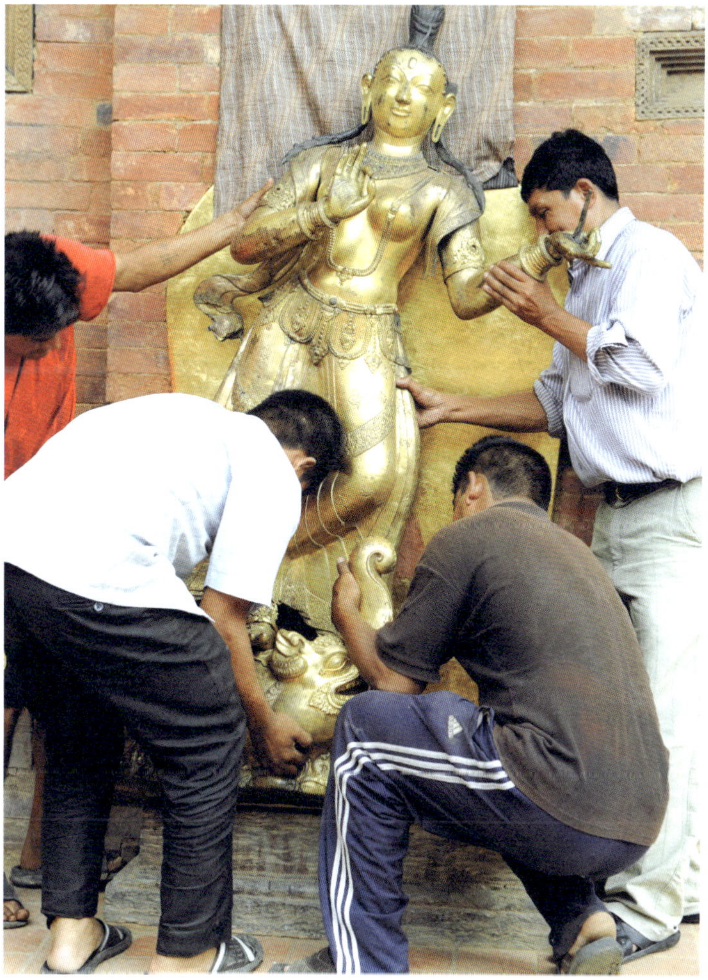

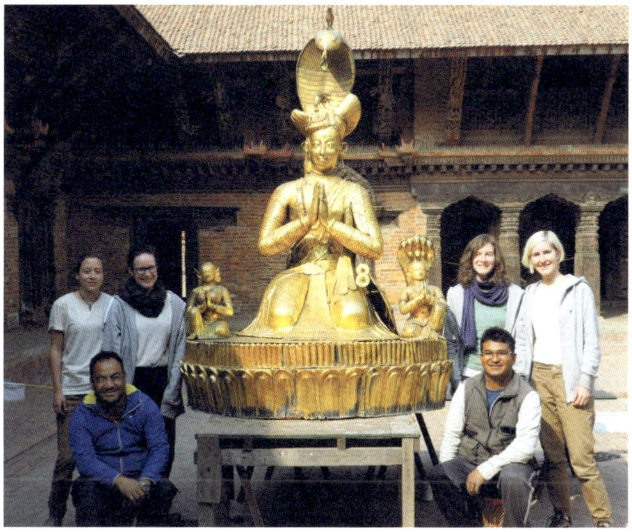

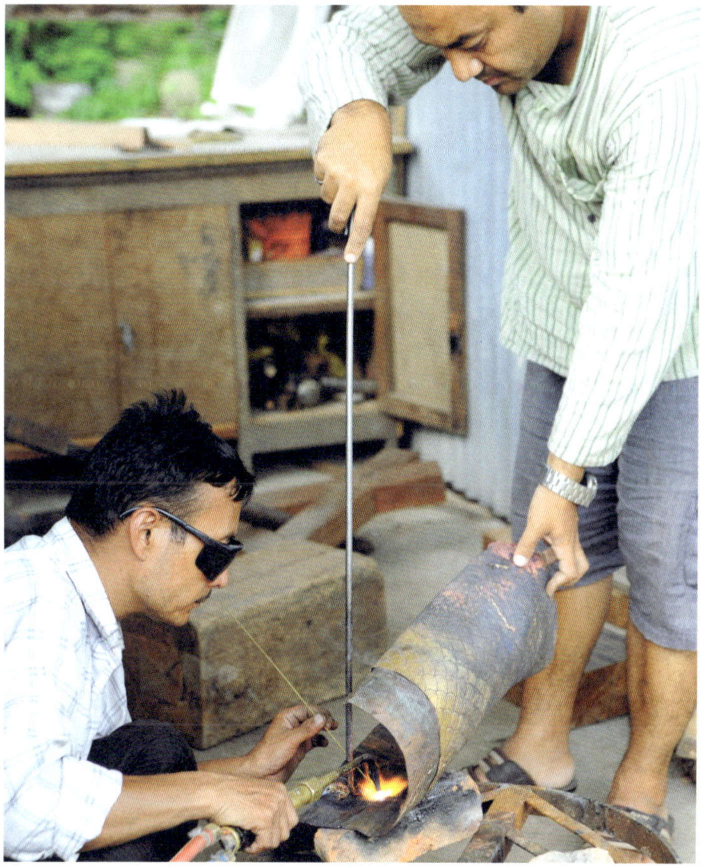

top left: Fig. 33: Metal worker in Patan's backyards
top right: Fig. 34: Dismantling the River Goddesses
left: Fig. 35: Conservation of the earthquake-damaged sculpture of Yoganarendra Malla – possible through the collaboration between conservators and craftsmen
right: Fig. 36: Rectification of the deformed sculpture was only made possible by hot forming

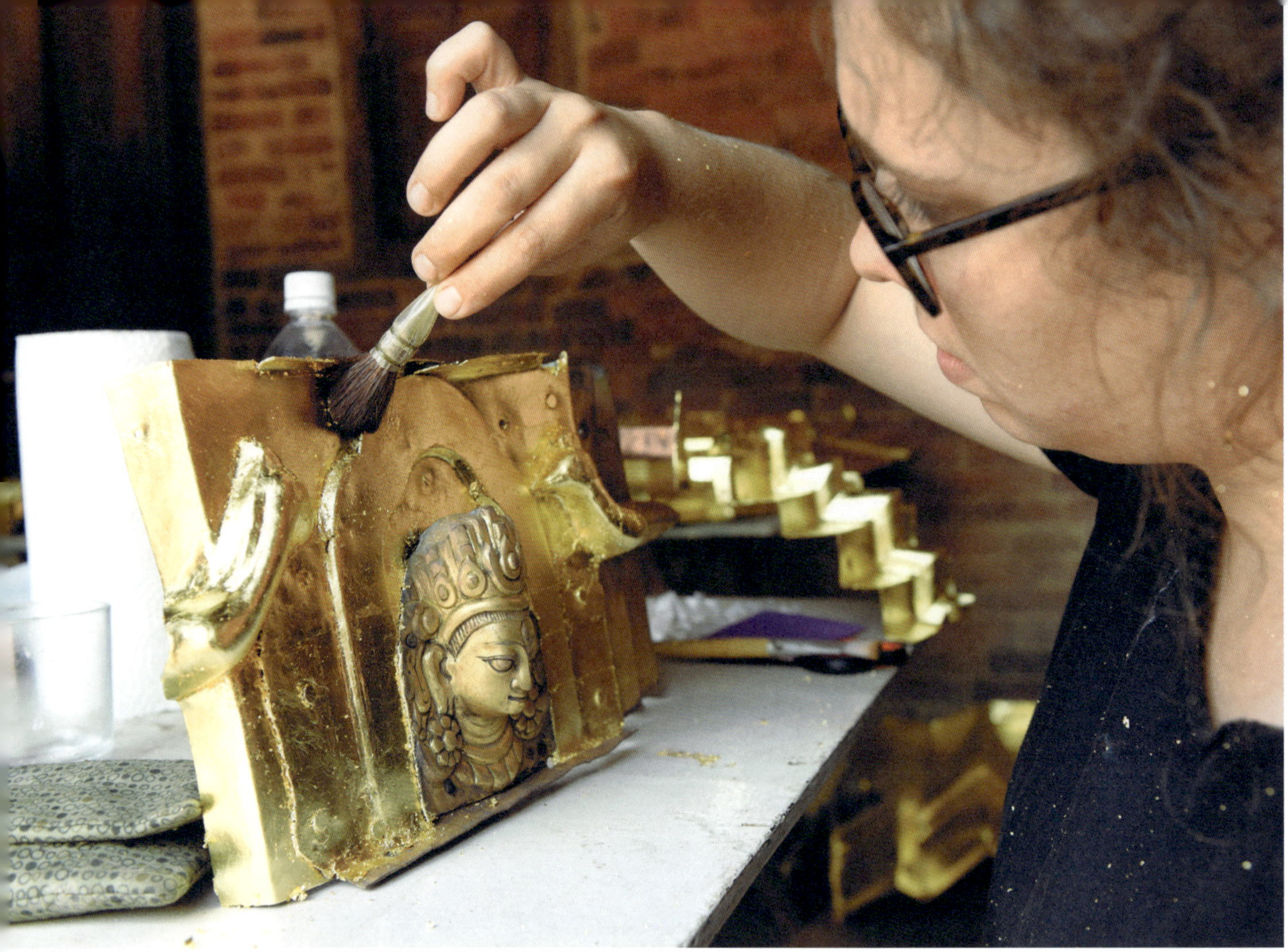

Fig. 37: Re-gilding of pieces of the Taleju Pinnacles

Fig. 38: Partial re-gilding of the sculpture of Yoganarendra Malla

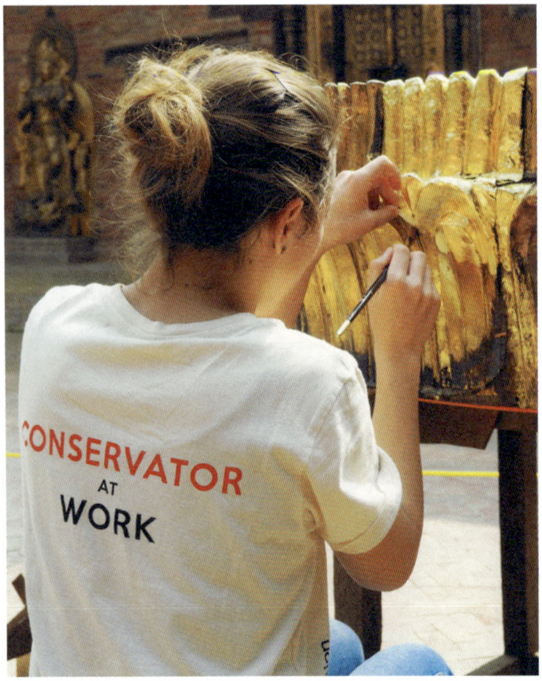

Fig. 41: Application of cotton soaked with citric acid to prolong reaction time

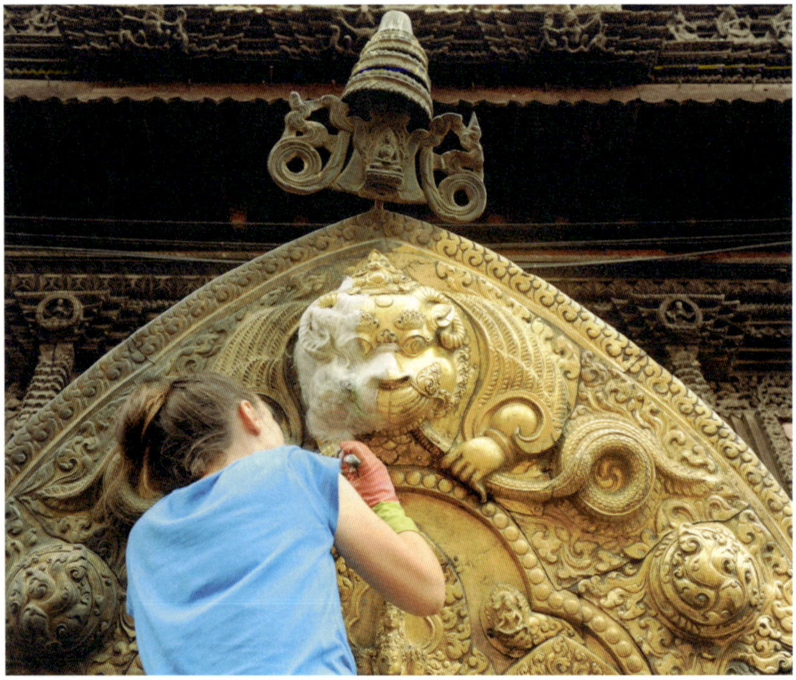

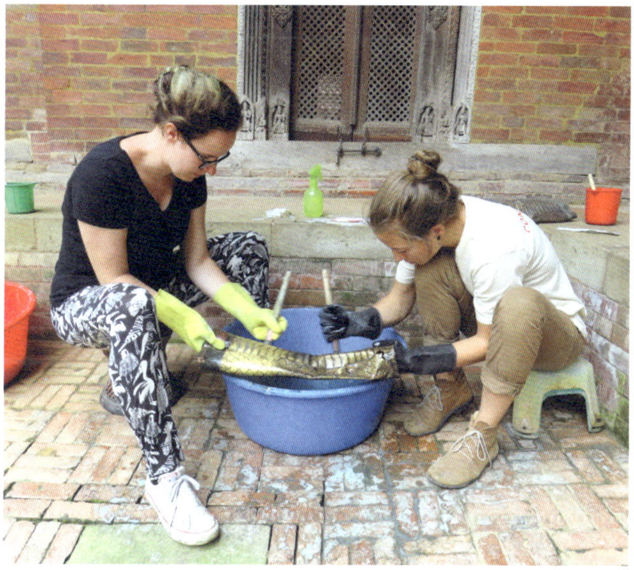

Fig. 39: Cleaning of fire-gilded copper with citric acid diluted in water

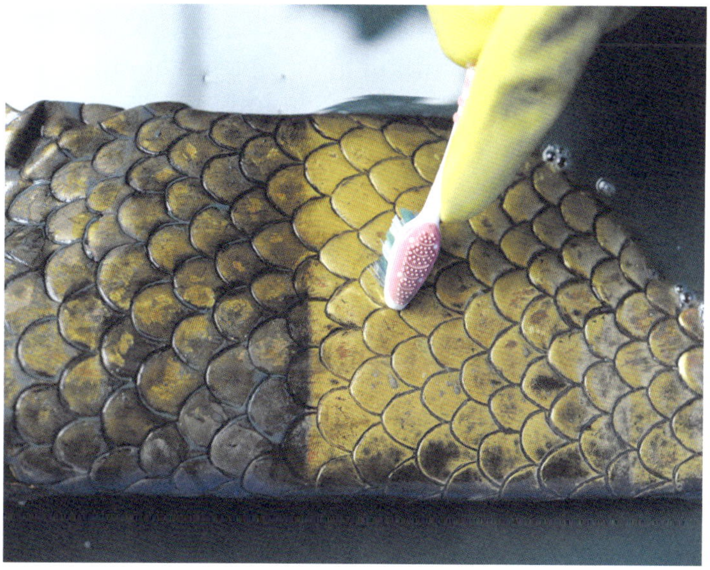

Fig. 40: Visible cleaning success.

Fig. 42: Squeezing real lemons to receive the “precious” citric acid

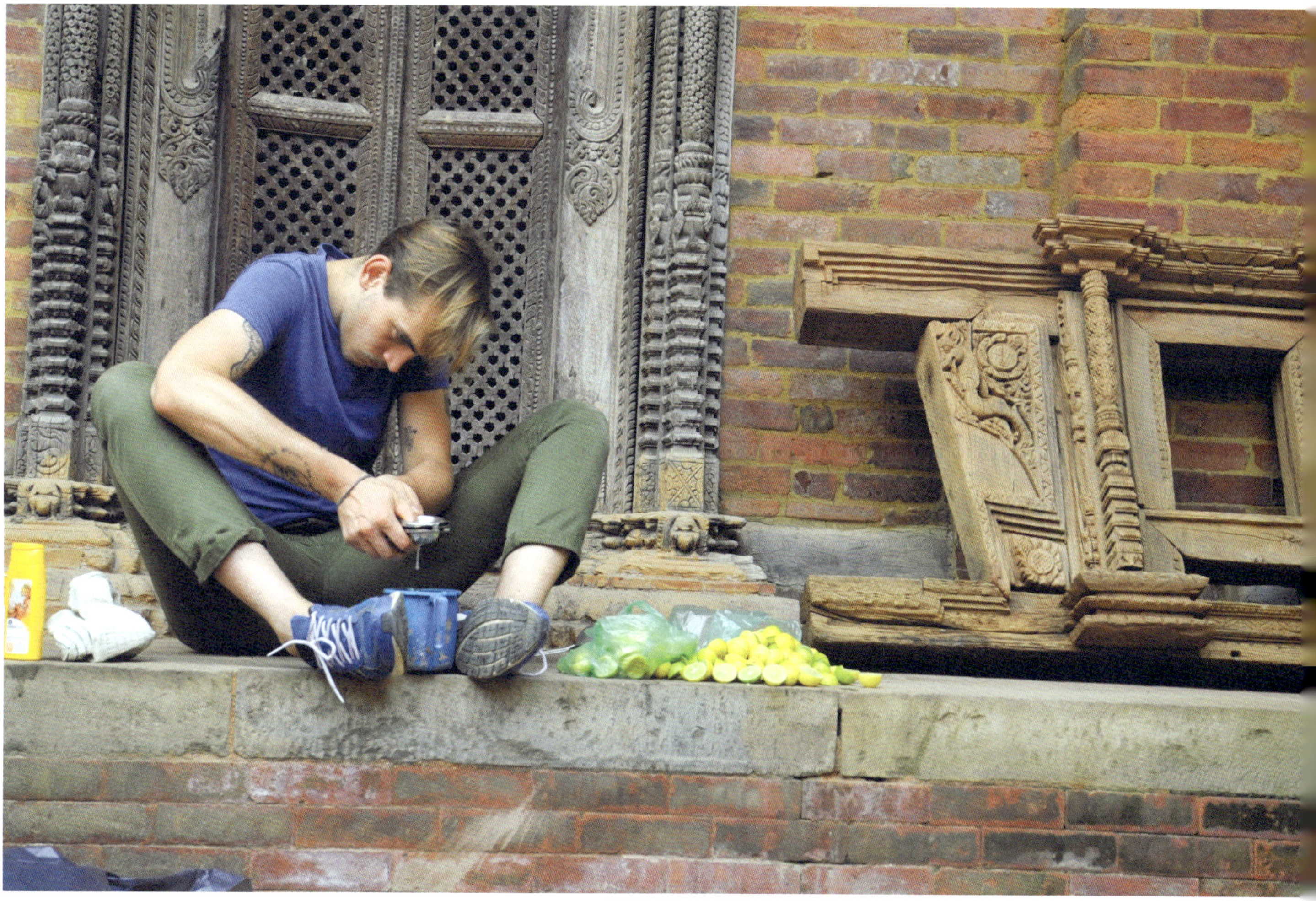

To replace these losses, we use a gilding technique, common in Europe but completely unknown in Nepal: leaf gilding (Fig. 37–38). In doing so, a steady hand and reduced breathing is obligatory when lifting the micrometre-thick gold leafs. A previously applied adhesive guarantees that the gold sticks to the surface.

Our gilding job regularly attracts both locals and tourist, although most of them have to be convinced that we are not painting with gold paint but using real gold.

WHEN LIFE GIVES YOU LEMONS... USE THEM FOR CLEANING

A recurrent task for us is the cleaning of fire-gilded surfaces. Not only remnants of worship, but also compacted crusts of dust and dirt, pigeon droppings and corrosion layers have to be removed or considerably reduced.

When water, surfactants and scalpels reach their limit, we fall back on our old remedy: citric acid. It is not only easily available, cheap and friendly to human and environment, but is a suitable complexing agent for removing corrosion products and hard crusts. At the same time it has a lower reactivity than other chelating agents, why the cleaning progress is easy to control and the gilded surface not damaged.

We use the acid diluted in water, a low percentage is sufficient, and apply it with brushes or cotton buds to extend contact time (Fig. 39–41). Sometimes we also bathe bigger objects in the diluted acid. In the first years we were highly motivated and squeezed real lemons. “Sour makes you happy”, the marketer probably thought when we left with 10 kg of fruits (Fig. 42). After recurring cramps in our hands we switched to ready-made crystalline citric acid which we still use.

...AND THEN THE EARTH QUAKED...

Only once in my life have I experienced a fairly strong earthquake – it was in Nepal in 2011. I was just in the apartment at the top floor of KVPT’s office, when I heard an unfamiliar sound...similar to trampling, like children playing on the roof terrace. Then, from one second to another, the cabinets, the chairs, the glasses on the table, the picture frames on the wall, everything started swinging. My first reaction: I started to search for my passport and the keys of the apartment. In retrospect not the best reaction but, well, I am Austrian with little earthquake experience. Finally, I was obviously the last person who left the building and headed to the square, which was already crowded with locals.

From today’s viewpoint, I can certainly say that this was a short and rather harmless earthquake, especially compared to the one that hit the Kathmandu Valley three years ago.

On 25 April 2015, a call from Patan reached us. That’s where there was a great earthquake! We made sure our colleagues and friends in Patan were alright. Luckily, the 25th was a public holiday, when most of them spend their free day in a park or the countryside. Then the first photos and further news arrived (Fig. 43). The earthquake measured 7.8 on the Richter scale, its epicentre was 82 km northwest of the capital, Kathmandu. In the aftermath, the region was haunted by several aftershocks, the major one on 12 May.

The sad statistics after the earthquakes: almost 9,000 dead, more than 2,900 buildings of cultural value, including property within the seven UNESCO World Heritage Sites, severely affected or completely destroyed.

In June 2015, my colleague, Manfred Trummer, and I headed out to Patan. Our mission: personally to hand over cash, an advance payment from Rector Gerald Bast to the KVPT to buy urgently needed material and start with the construction of temporary shelters for salvaged works of art, get a clear picture of the situation on site, and set conservation priorities together with KVPT.

A journey has never been more depressing for me. The plane from Delhi to Kathmandu was almost empty but our joy about plenty of free seats was tempered. The exceptionally heavy thunderstorm we had to cross during landing approach did the rest.

Arriving in Kathmandu, the first impression was not too bad – numerous houses still standing, the streets were passable. We arrived in Patan and started our fact-finding tour. The longer we walked through the inner city and narrow streets, the clearer the dimensions and full extent of damage became. The majority of the buildings was temporarily shored up with beams, damaged roofs covered with tarpaulins. We had to overcome heaps of rubble and debris, always with a scrutinising look along the façade if something was falling down (Fig. 44).

Patan Durbar Square, once so vibrant and impressing, was a picture of misery. The earthquakes caused the complete destruction of some of its oldest historic structures, including the Charnarayana Temple (1565), ranked among the most significant examples of typical Newar architecture, two mandapa resthouses from the 16th and 17th centuries and the Harishankara Temple (1706). The fire-gilded sculpture of the 17th-centruy king Yoganarendra Malla, formerly surveying the square on top of his stone column, was buried under the partly collapsed shaft and lotus of the column. The Lion Pillar in front of Bhimsen Temple could also not withstand the shaking and partly collapsed.

Besides, the earthquakes also left a trail of devastation at the Royal Palace: one exterior façade of Sundari Chowk facing the garden was destroyed, gilt roof structures of the Taleju Temples partly collapsed or had to be dismantled.

GOOD PLANNING IS HALF THE WORK

The state of shock did not last long in Patan after the April 2015 earthquake. The KVPT moved rapidly and launched its emergency response to salvage cultural heritage property. Its long-term presence on site enabled this immediate action. Within days after the earthquake, staff of the KVPT, under direction of Rohit Ranjitkar, coordinated military, police and local groups to protect and rescue historic building elements (Fig. 45–46). Damage to historic structures was assessed, unstable structures shored up, temporary storage for salvaged decorative components of collapsed temples erected, and a temporary working place established to study and repair works of art (Fig. 47–48).

In order to tackle the practical conservation of the numerous earthquake-affected artworks and monuments, the KVPT joined forces with us. But how to proceed in this completely new and adverse situation?

First, we needed to find sources of funding – it was clear that the annual project budget granted by the Eurasia-Pacific Uninet in the previous years would not be sufficient.

Gabriela Krist and our rector made great efforts – professional and personal contacts up to the highest political levels were tapped, letters were written, presentations were given. In the end the Austrian Development Agency (ADA), which already co-funded our project in Nako, the Austrian Federal Chancellery and the Austrian Federal Ministry for Europe, Integration and Foreign Affairs allied and confirmed their support. Austria's strong ties with Nepal in the field of cultural heritage preservation, which go back to the 1960s, should be continued! With lightning speed our institute prepared an official project proposal, time schedules and budget plans. I was involved from the start. In December 2015 the grant agreement was signed! I never experienced a more rapid project application.

Second, we needed to set priorities. The number of earthquake-damaged monuments was simply incredible! Together with our funding partners we decided to concentrate our efforts on monuments and sites with an "Austrian background" – where Austrian scholars had been active in the past or restoration and conservation work had been funded by Austria. Furthermore, close communication, exchange and consultation with Rohit Ranjitkar were important in making a choice. He knows exactly what is required and how our capacities can be best exploited! Our joint conclusion:

We tried to focus strategically on objects or monuments that can be successfully treated in a foreseeable period due to clear extent of work.

We prioritised artworks which are broken in pieces or could suffer further damage if left untreated.

We selected artworks or monuments which required conservation measures as precondition for reconstruction or rebuilding.

LIKE A PHOENIX FROM THE ASHES – NEPAL WILL RISE AGAIN

Today, almost four years after the earthquake, a return to normality is noticeable.

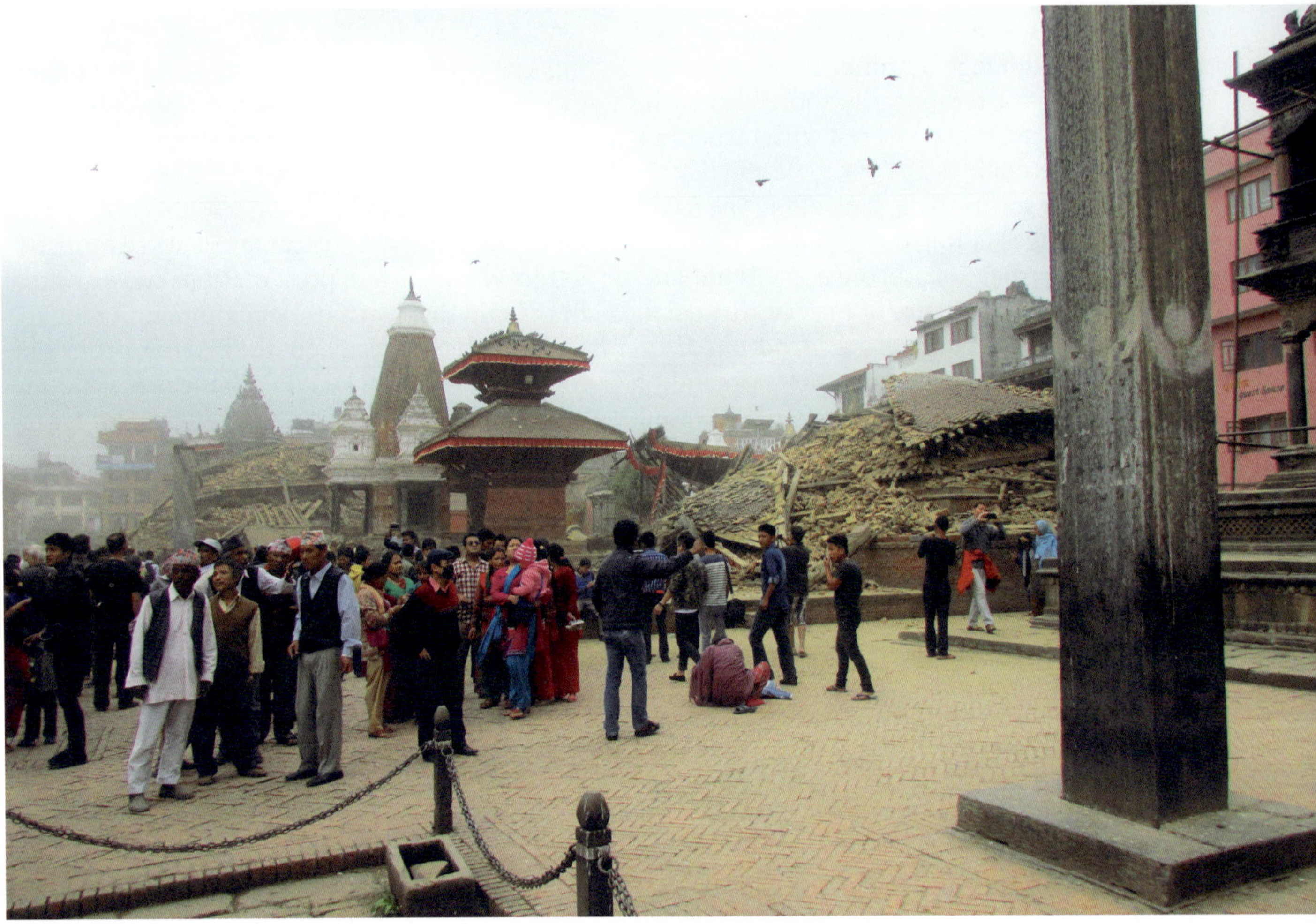

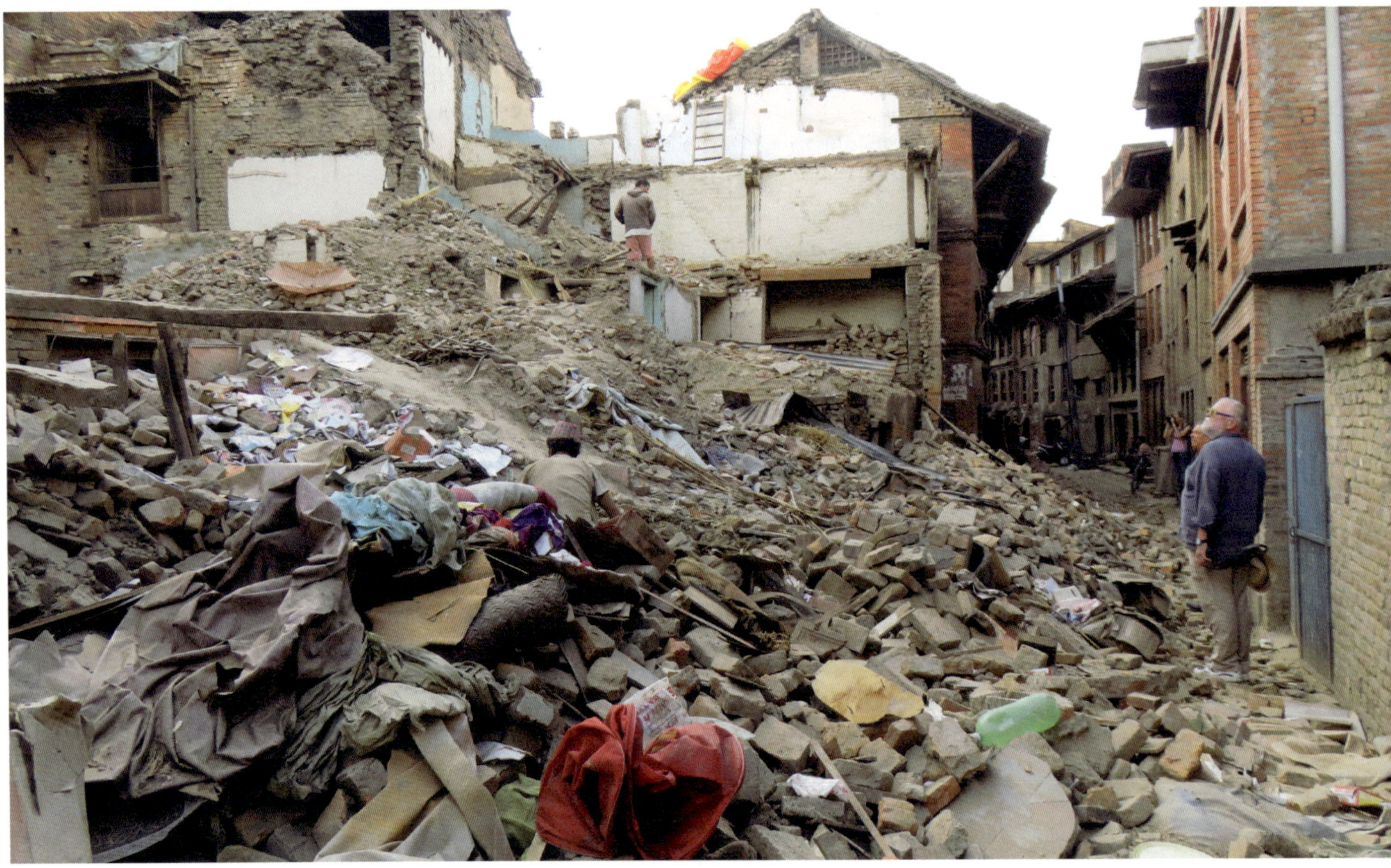

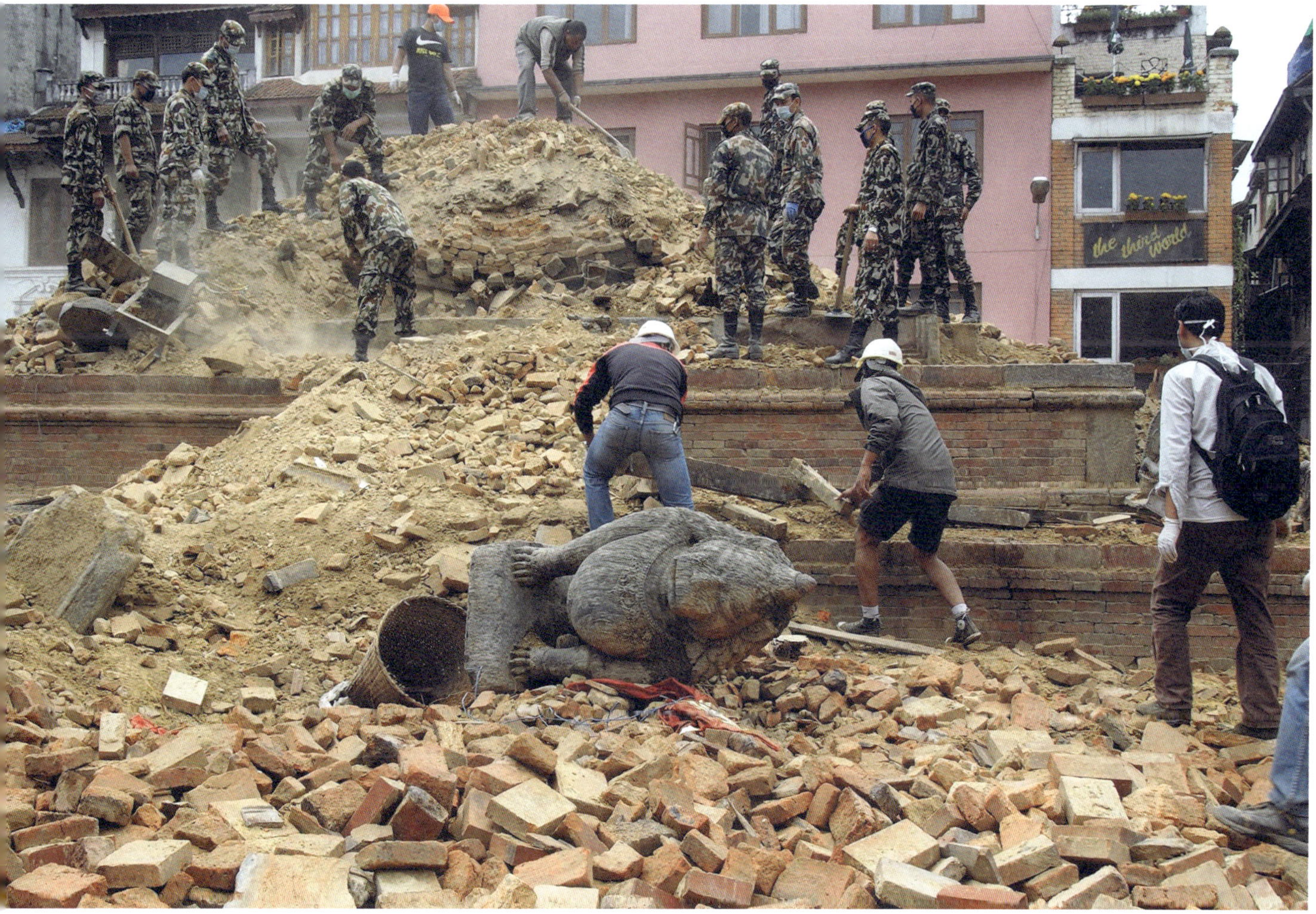

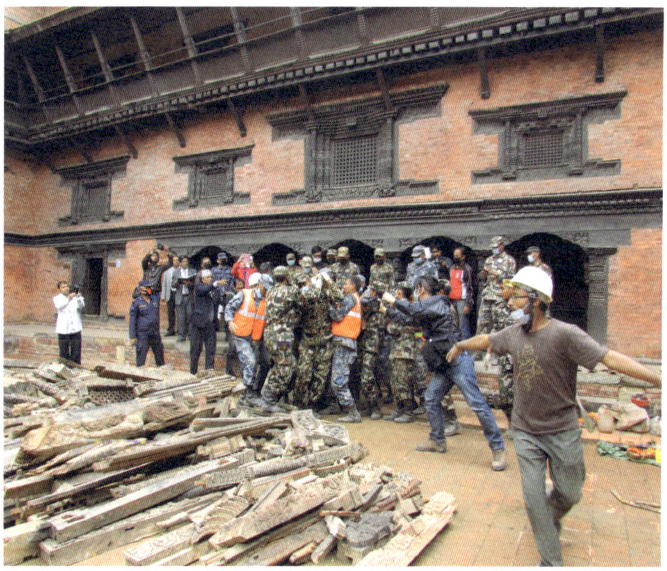

top left: Fig. 43: Patan Durbar Square, only minutes after the earthquake on 25 April 2015
left: Fig. 44: With Mandred Trummer on the Fact Finding Mission in June 2015
top: Fig. 45: Salvage and safeguarding of decorative and structural components of collapsed monuments out of the piles of rubble
right: Fig. 46: Transfer of salvaged components to the museum courtyard

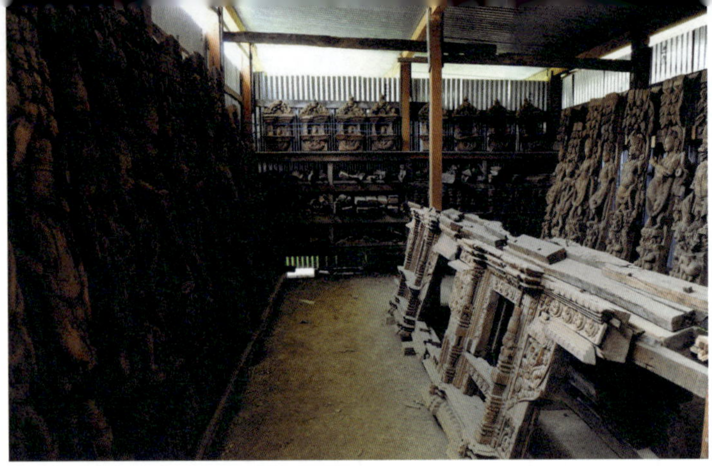

Fig. 47: Temporary storage for salvaged decorative components, erected with financial support from Austria

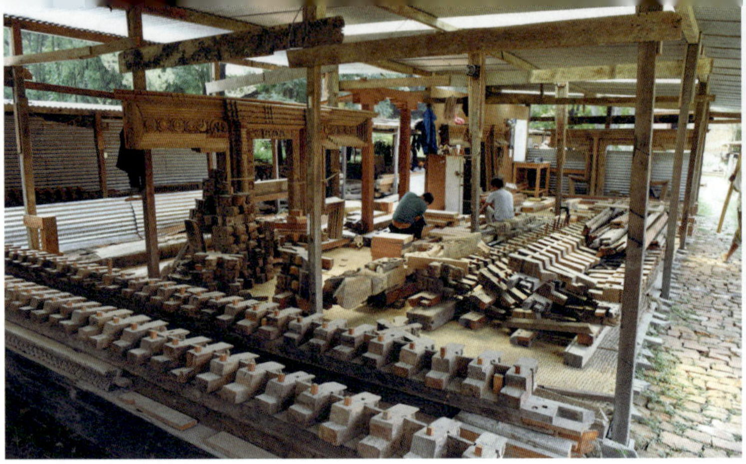

Fig. 48: Temporary working place for carpenters and woodworkers

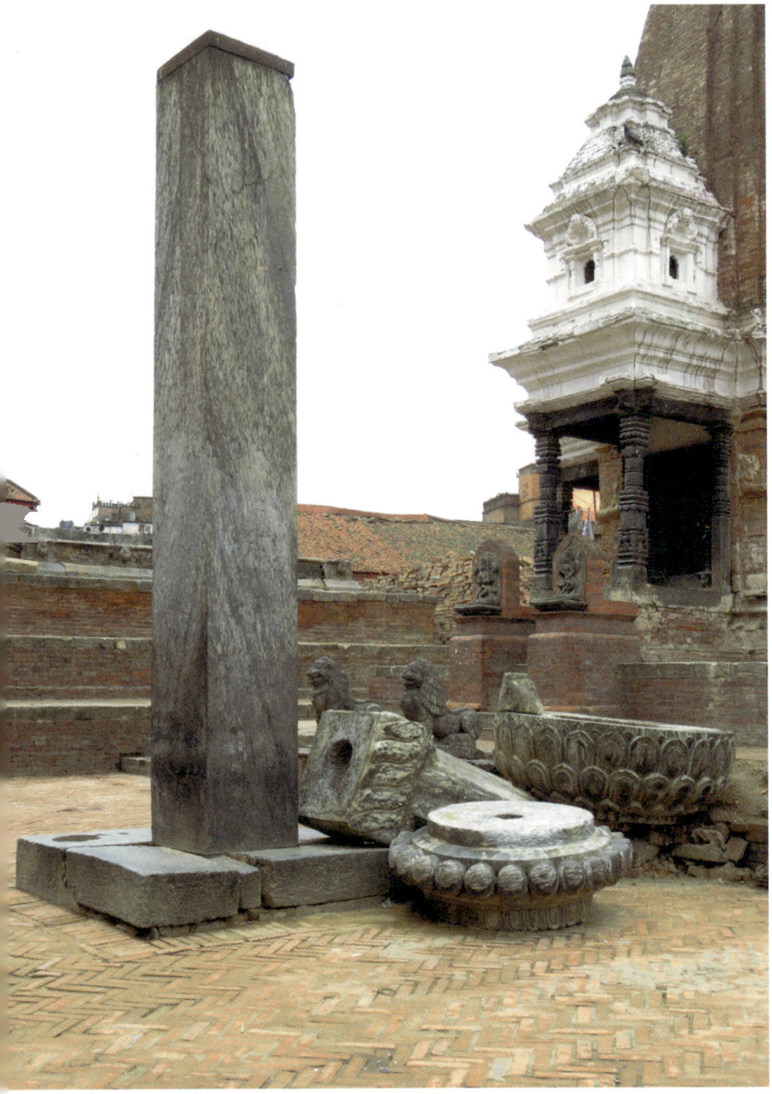

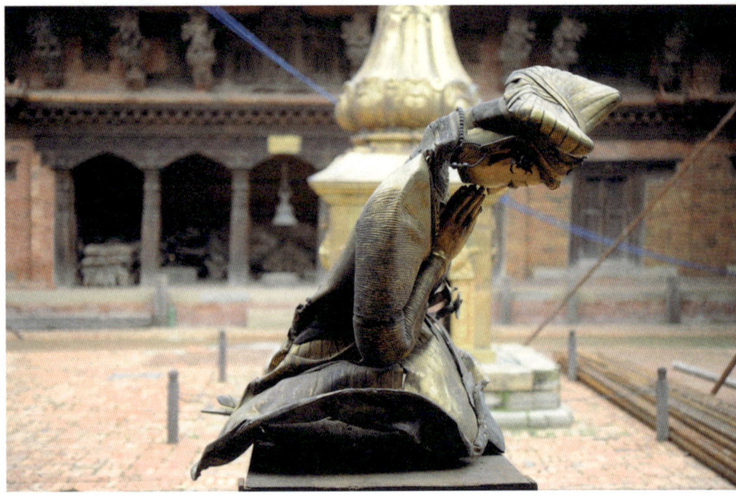

Fig. 49-50: Earthquake-damaged pillar and sculpture of Yoganarendra Malla

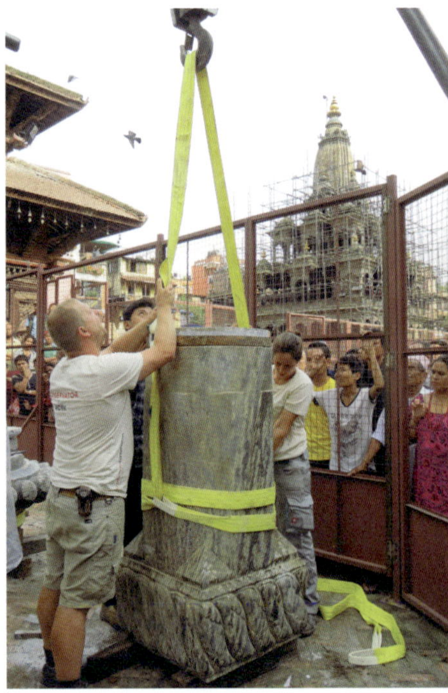

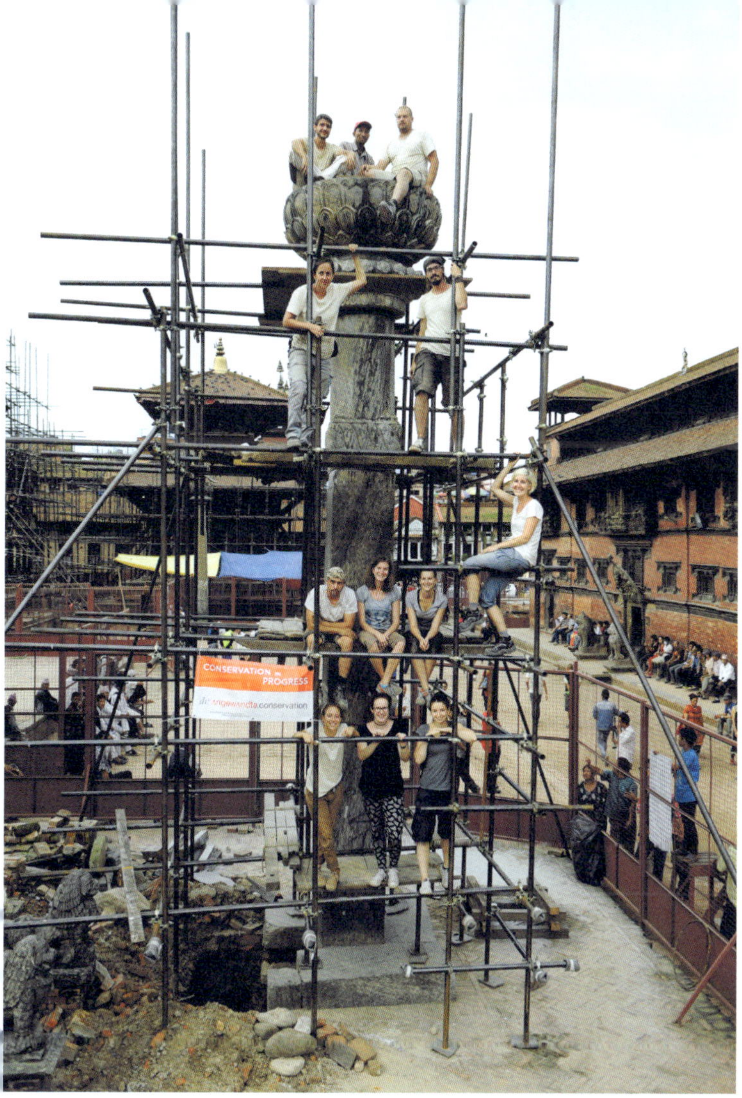

Fig. 53: Team of the conservation campaign 2016 at the re-erected pillar of Yoganarendra Malla

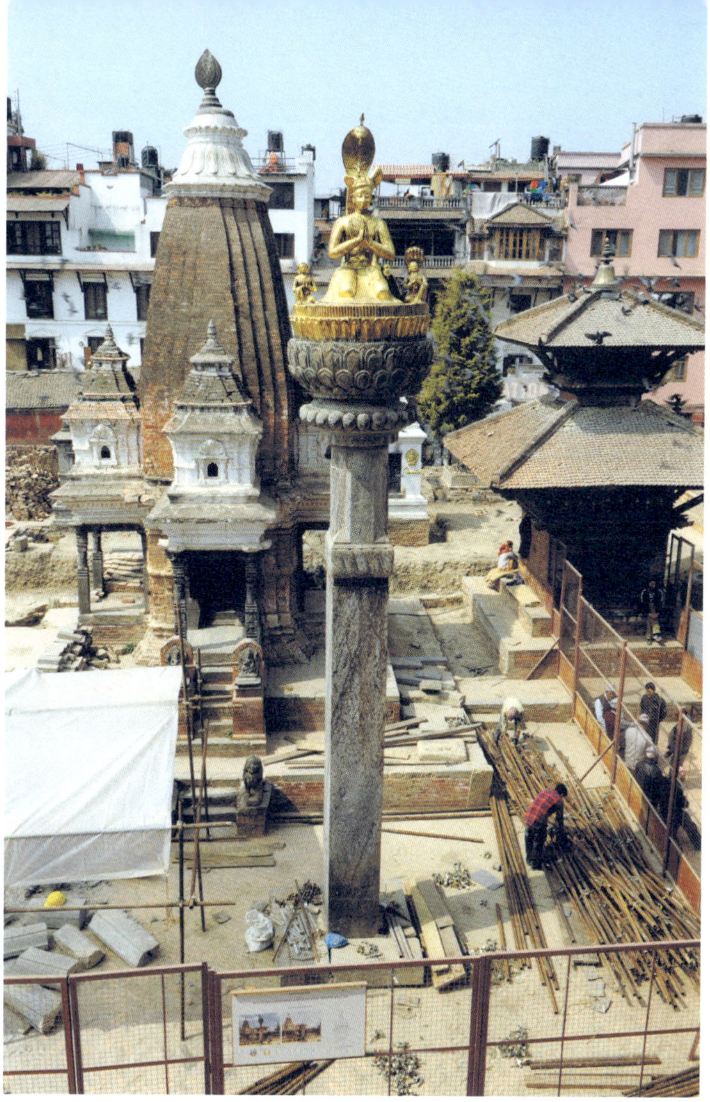

Fig. 54: Pillar and sculpture of Yoganarendra Malla after conservation in 2017

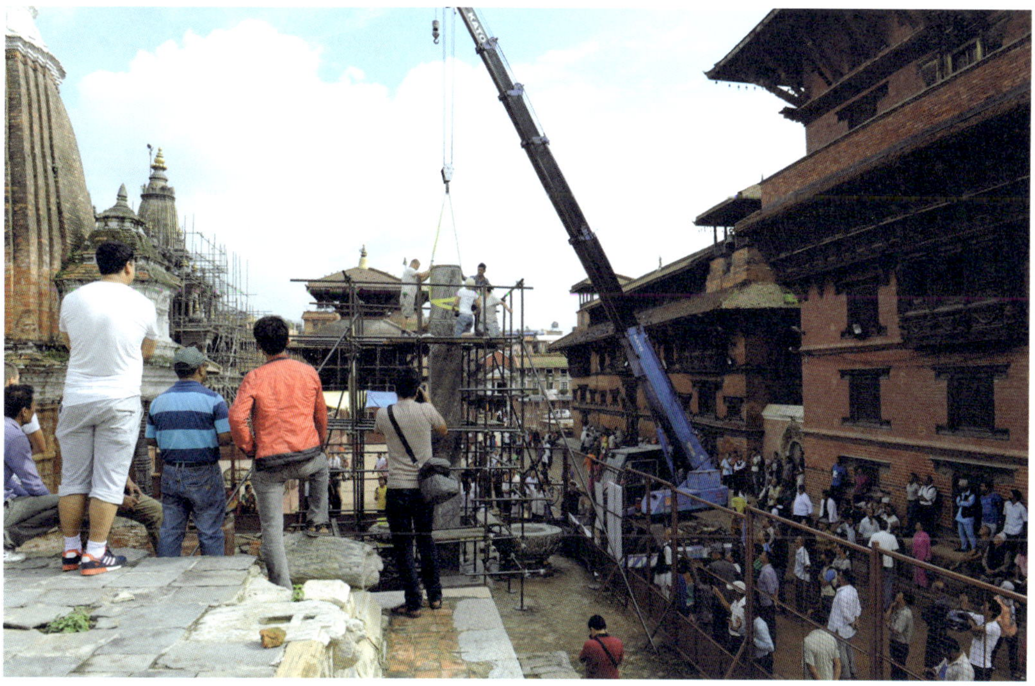

Fig. 51-52: Re-erection of the pillar

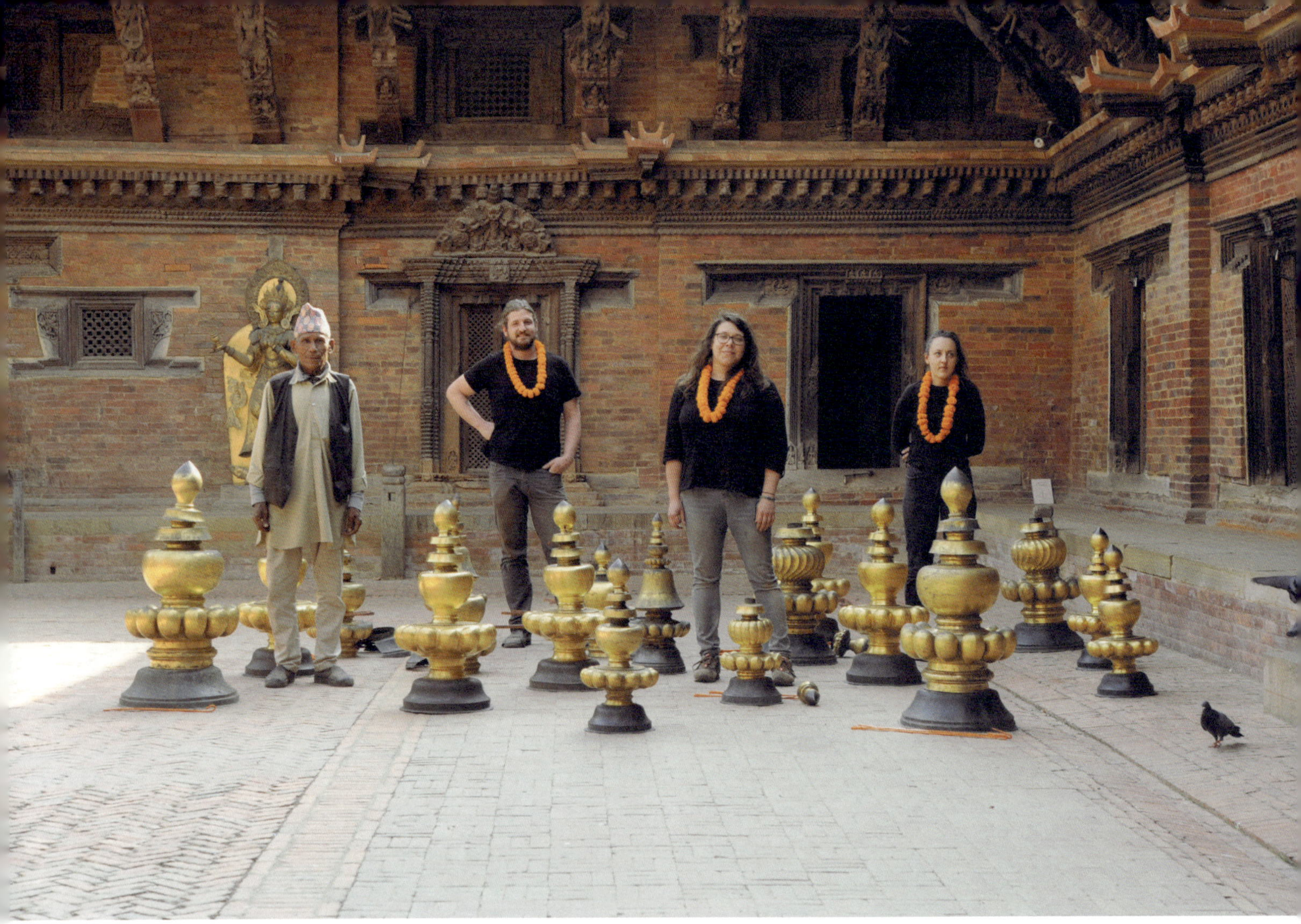

Fig. 55: Metal conservation team of the 2018 campaign together with the conserved pinnacles of Krishna Mandir

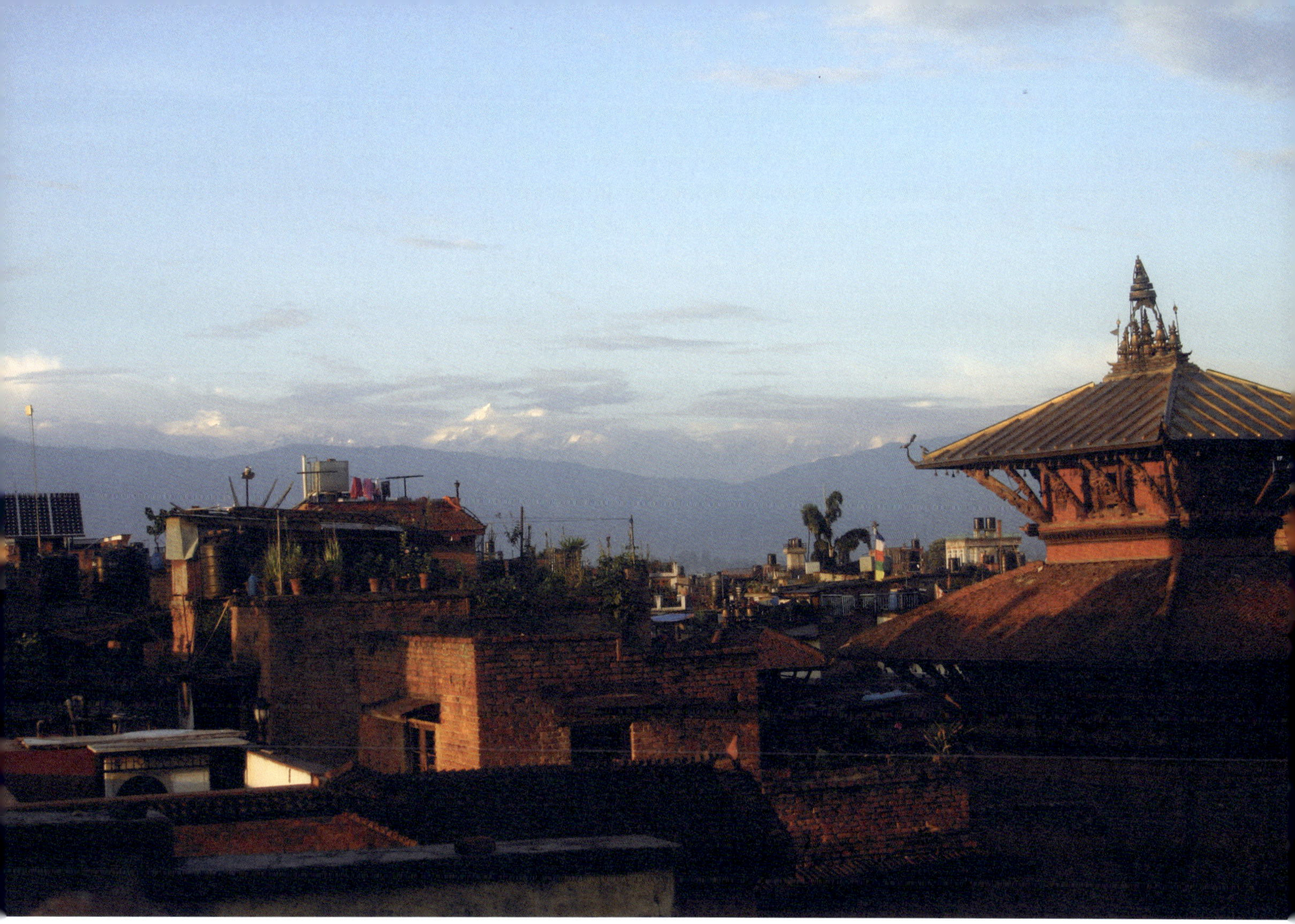

Fig. 56: Above the rooftops of Patan

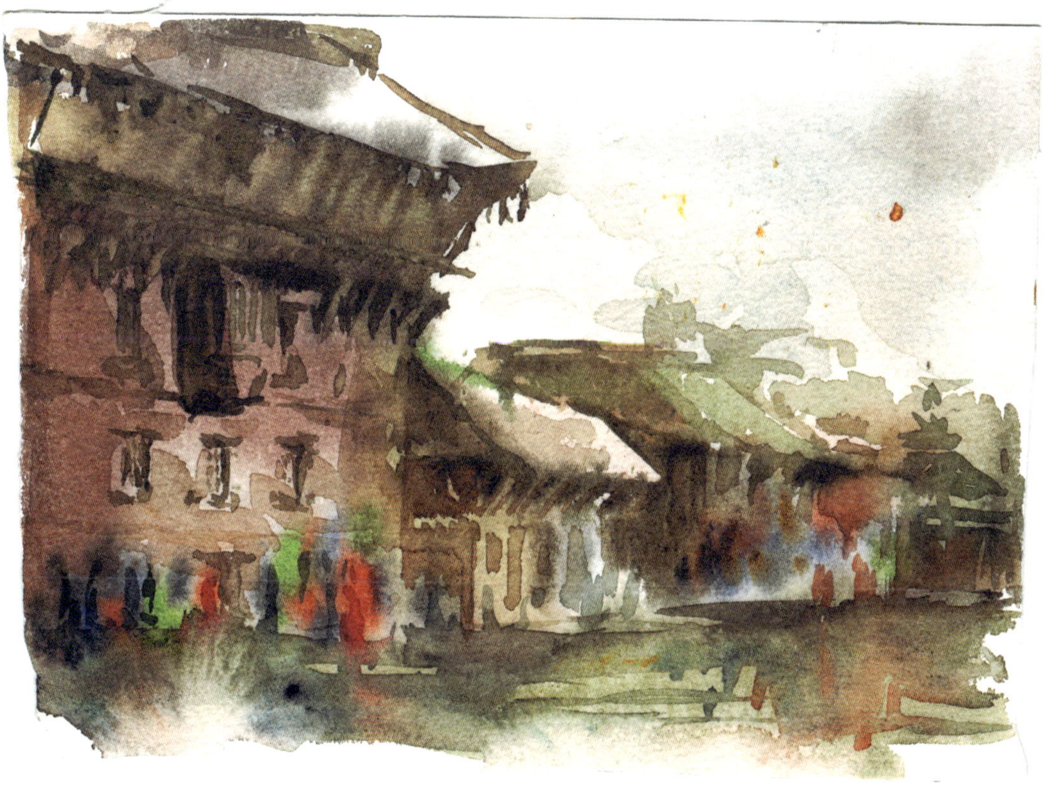

Captured in a drawing by Mariia Bakhareva, 2018

Durbar Square is again crowded by tourist groups. Hotels are well booked; I am forced to hurry up with the hotel booking for summer as our accommodation is receiving inquiries from spring on.

Looking back at the results of our work missions, they sometimes astound me: we were able to conserve and re-erect the partly collapsed Pillar of Yoganarendra Malla (Fig. 49–50) – the King's Pillar – and the Lion Pillar. Stone surfaces were cleaned, visible cracks assessed and closed, broken elements re-adhered and missing ones reconstructed. The severe deformations of their crowning fire-gilded sculptures were successfully eradicated through rectification and welding by the local craftsmen. By cleaning, re-gilding and retouching of the sculptures, a well preserved condition could be achieved. Then, witnessed by masses of curious locals, tourists and journalists, the pillars were re-erected: the smaller pillar by pure "manpower", the bigger by use of a crane. Both times we adhered to the original method of construction with only minor adaptions to improve seismic resistance. Being focal elements on Durbars Square, their re-erection was of great importance for the locals and constituted a tangible sign of progress (Fig. 51–54).

We assessed and treated the stone blocks comprising the base of the collapsed Harishankara Temple. Gluing of broken pieces and backfilling were done where necessary. These measures pave the way for now being able to re-use most of the original blocks in the planned reconstruction of the temple, which will be able to carry the weight of the building. The salvaged main sculpture of the temple was likewise treated, the broken pieces re-adhered and thus prepared for re-assembling in the reconstructed temple.

The so-called Naga Throne, an artwork of regular worship and great historical significance for the history of Patan, was conserved and only re-erected last year on the square under the protective roof of the rebuilt mandapa.

Also the multi-piece fire-gilded pinnacles, which were treated by us over three campaigns, are already reassembled on top of the Taleju Temples.

The opportunity offered by the erected scaffolding at Krishna Mandir was taken to repoint the joints at the top roof area of this most significant stone sikhara temple. Condition survey combined with test series and scientific analysis in Vienna built the base to develop an adequate pointing mortar. In addition, the 21 fire-gilded pinnacles embellishing the temple could be conserved (Fig. 55). In the last mission we treated the stone base of Vishveshvara Temple and the Golden Door at the Royal Palace, the entrance to the Patan Museum.

But we were not only working practically in Patan. My colleague Marija Milchin and I also had the possibility to raise awareness for our efforts and present our conservation projects at international conferences – from Glasgow to Montreal, from Czech Litomyšl to Reykjavík.

Nevertheless, obstacles have also been put in our way: ranging from closed borders to India and resulting riots, lack of fuel and rising prices for building materials, then the lack of labourers and material, and finally to frequent staff turnovers in ministries and month-long waiting for official permits. Flexibility and patience were of the utmost importance in these situations, and we have been grateful for the considerable concessions of our Austrian funding partners. And, well…sometimes bureaucratic obstacles can be best solved with a letter from the Austrian Embassy.

Currently, I am preparing the forthcoming work mission in spring 2019, probably the last as our project funding is coming to an end. I am slightly wistful. Patan has almost become a second home. Not only because of the many familiar faces: Rohit, Raju, Jagat and the team of the KVPT, the museum employees Paritosh and Krishna, the old man in Mul Chowk, shop owner Lalita (her small shop is our place to go for buying groceries), the staff of our hotel, the coffee shop owner and gift seller next door, the tourist guides on Durbar Square. Also, because I already know the city well and know where to get the best momos and dal bhat. The stresses of organisation and the rush in Vienna are quickly forgotten when I sit on the rooftop terrace, taking the first sip of chai tea and watching the sunset over the Himalayan mountain range (Fig. 56). Somehow, I come to rest and become much calmer about certain issues. Perhaps it is due to the Buddhist spirit. Or the long waiting times, which sometimes condemn you to idleness but which you have to accept in Nepal. Or it is just because of the enormous amount of sugar in the chai tea.

At the same time I am inspired anew each year by the Nepali, how they look ahead confidently even after a devastating catastrophe. Only a few months after the earthquake, shops in the valley were packed with shirts, mugs and flags with the slogan "Nepal will rise again". I am grateful to be able to contribute to this movement, contribute as a conservator to the "rise" of Patan Durbar Square, which was, and still is, integral part of the peoples' daily lives, ritual activities and local traditions, as well as a major tourist attraction.

Much has already been achieved – much more still needs to be done.

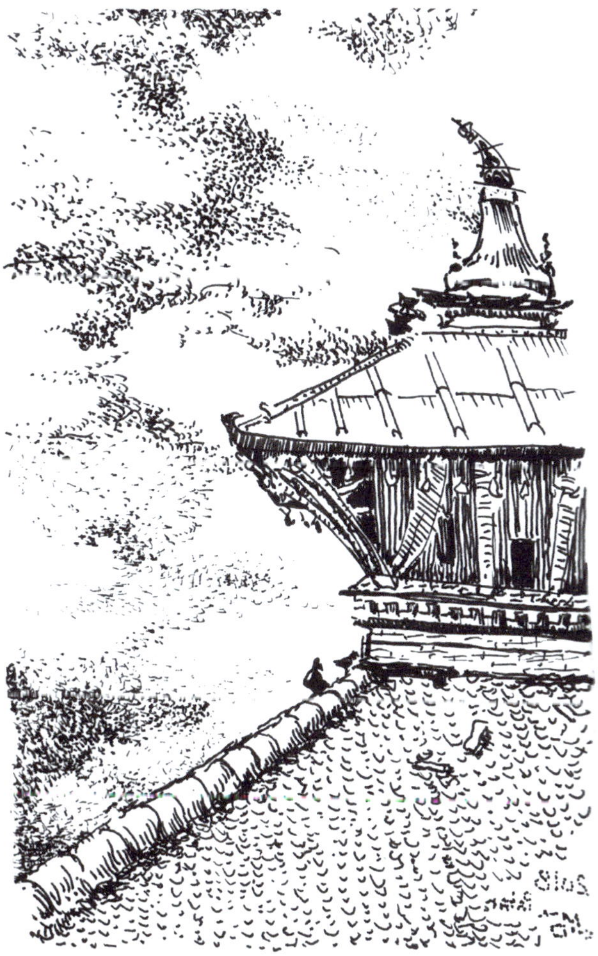

Captured in a drawing by Mariia Bakhareva, 2018

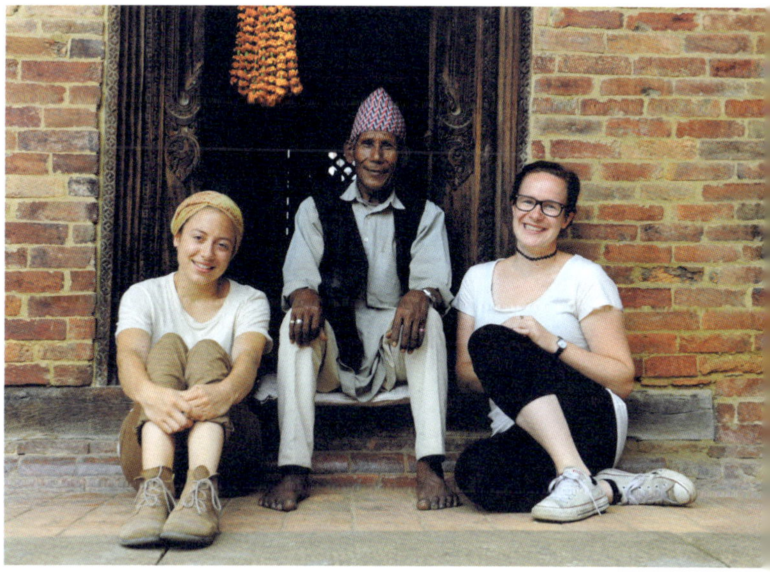

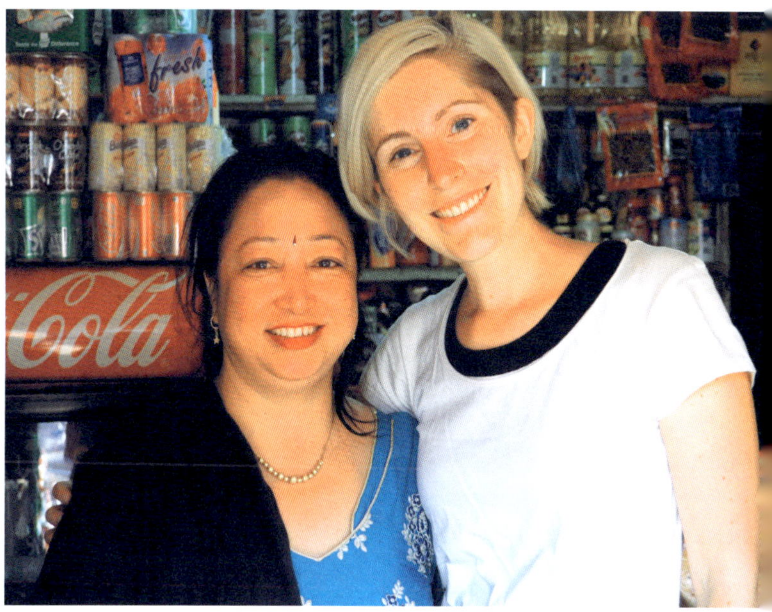

Fig. 57-58: Friends and familiar faces in Patan

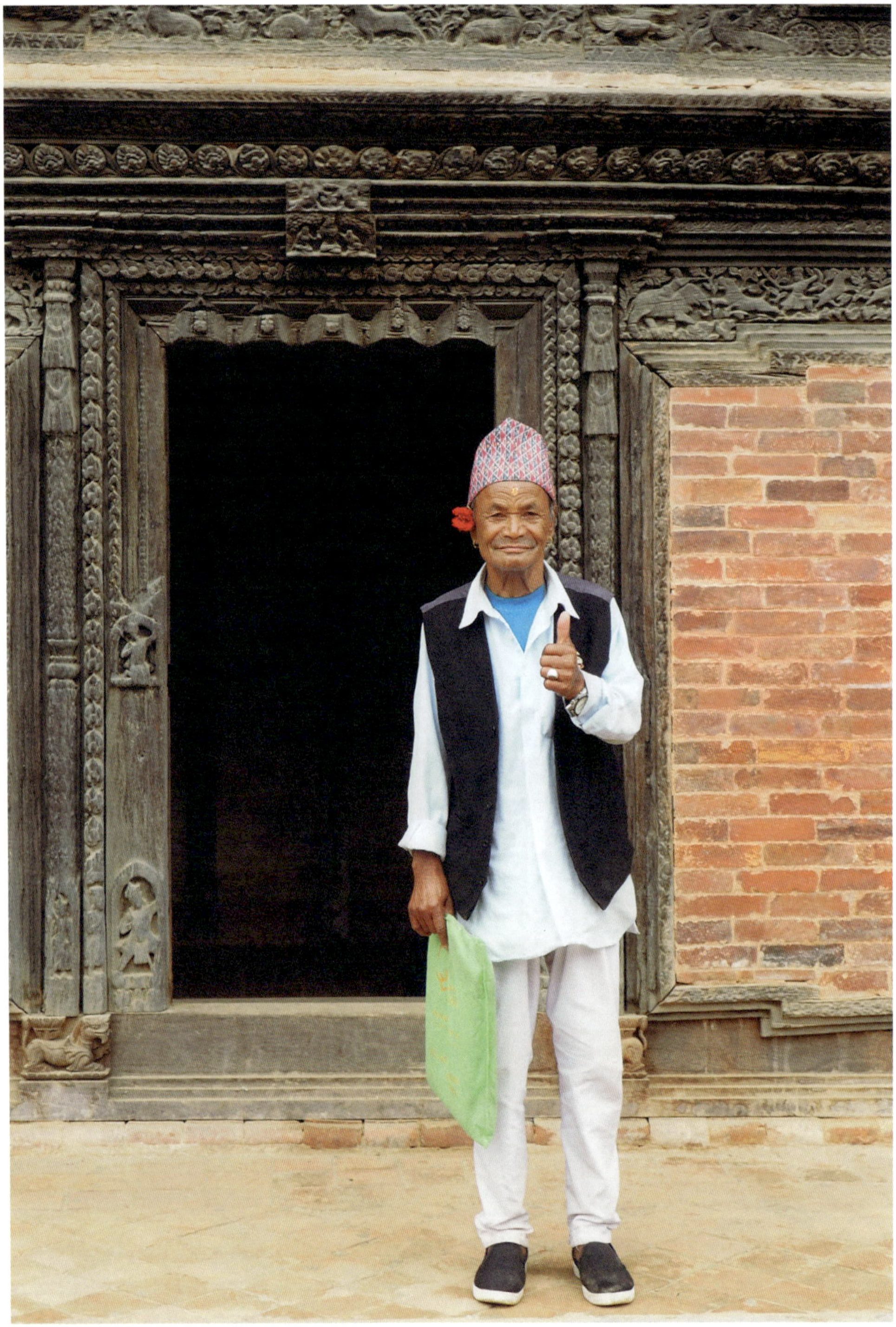

Fig. 59: Thumbs up for Nepal

next page: Captured in a drawing by Mariia Bakhareva, 2018

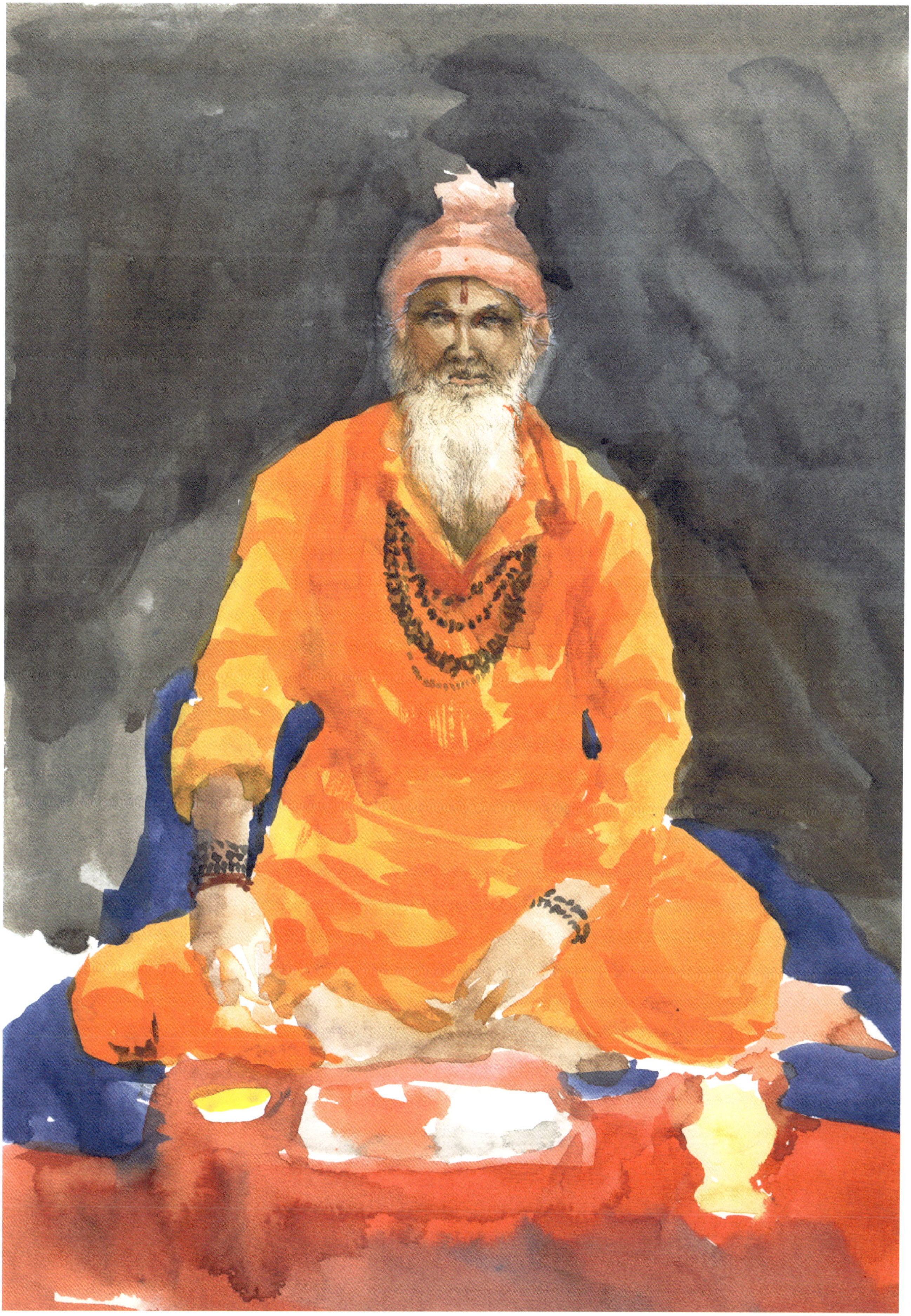

BY MARTINA HASELBERGER

A Photographer's Impressions

CHRISTOPH SCHLESSMANN

Daily Life in Nepal and the Conservation Campaign of the Institute of Conservation in Summer 2017 in Pictures

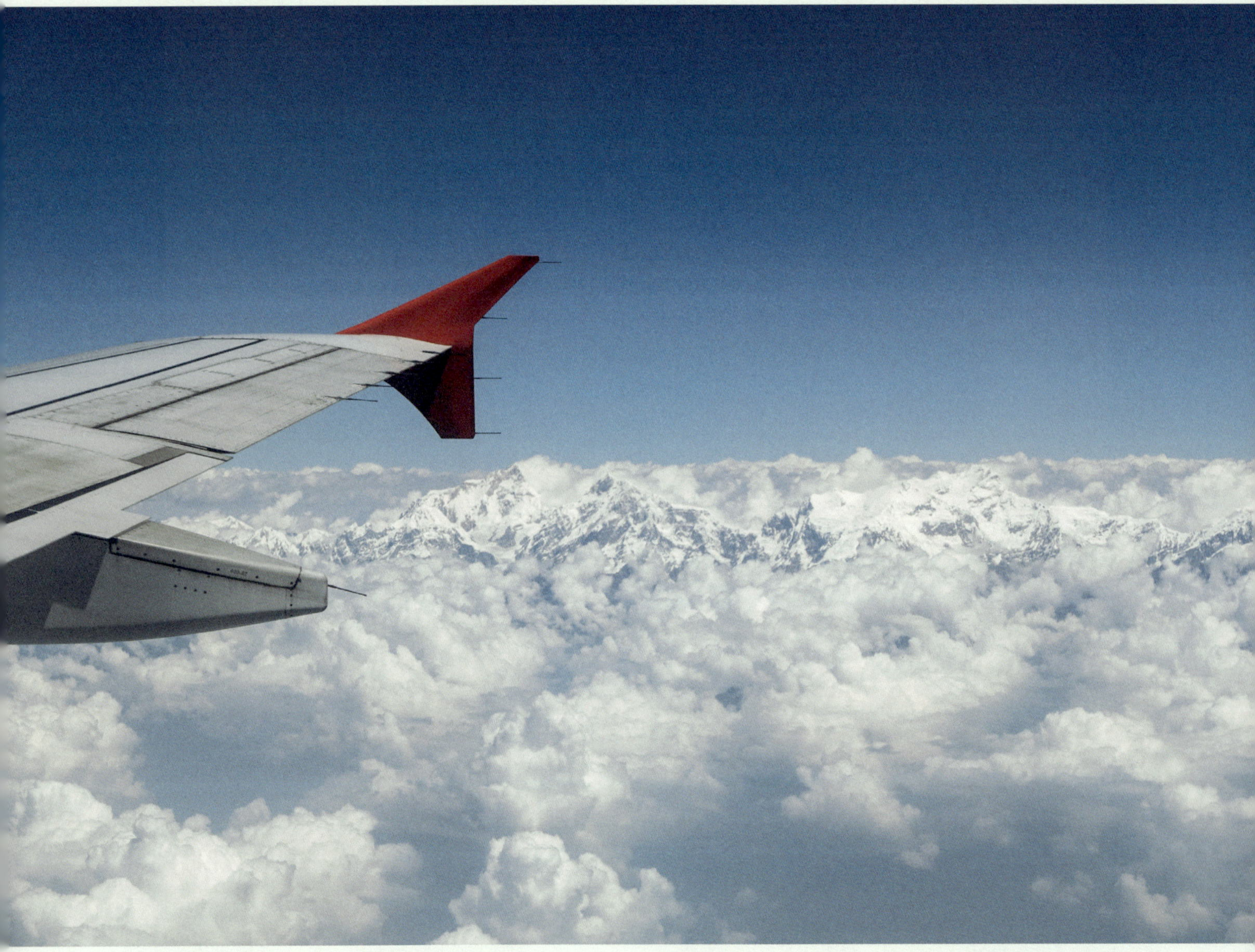

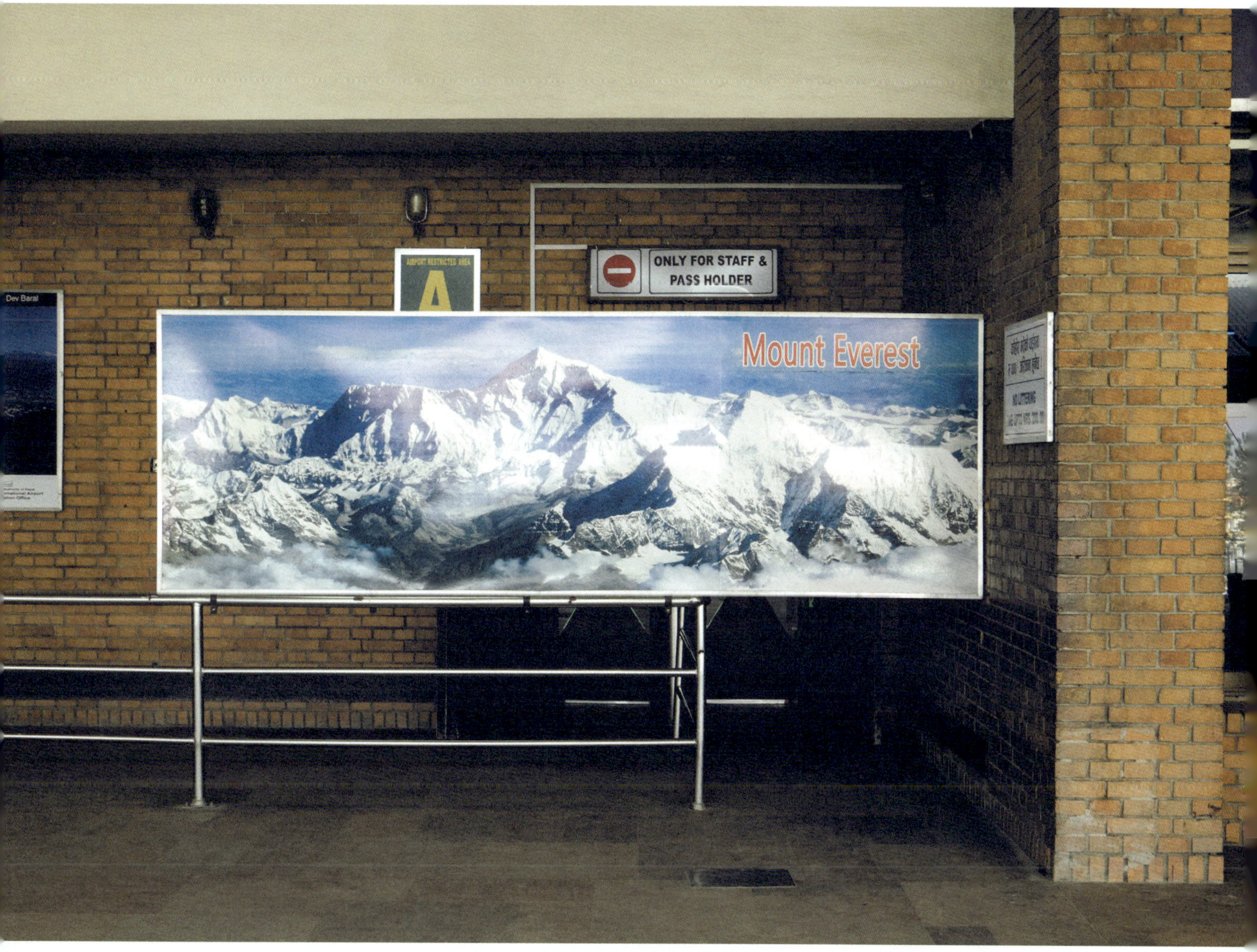

View of the Himalayas, because of smog only possible in a roundabout way

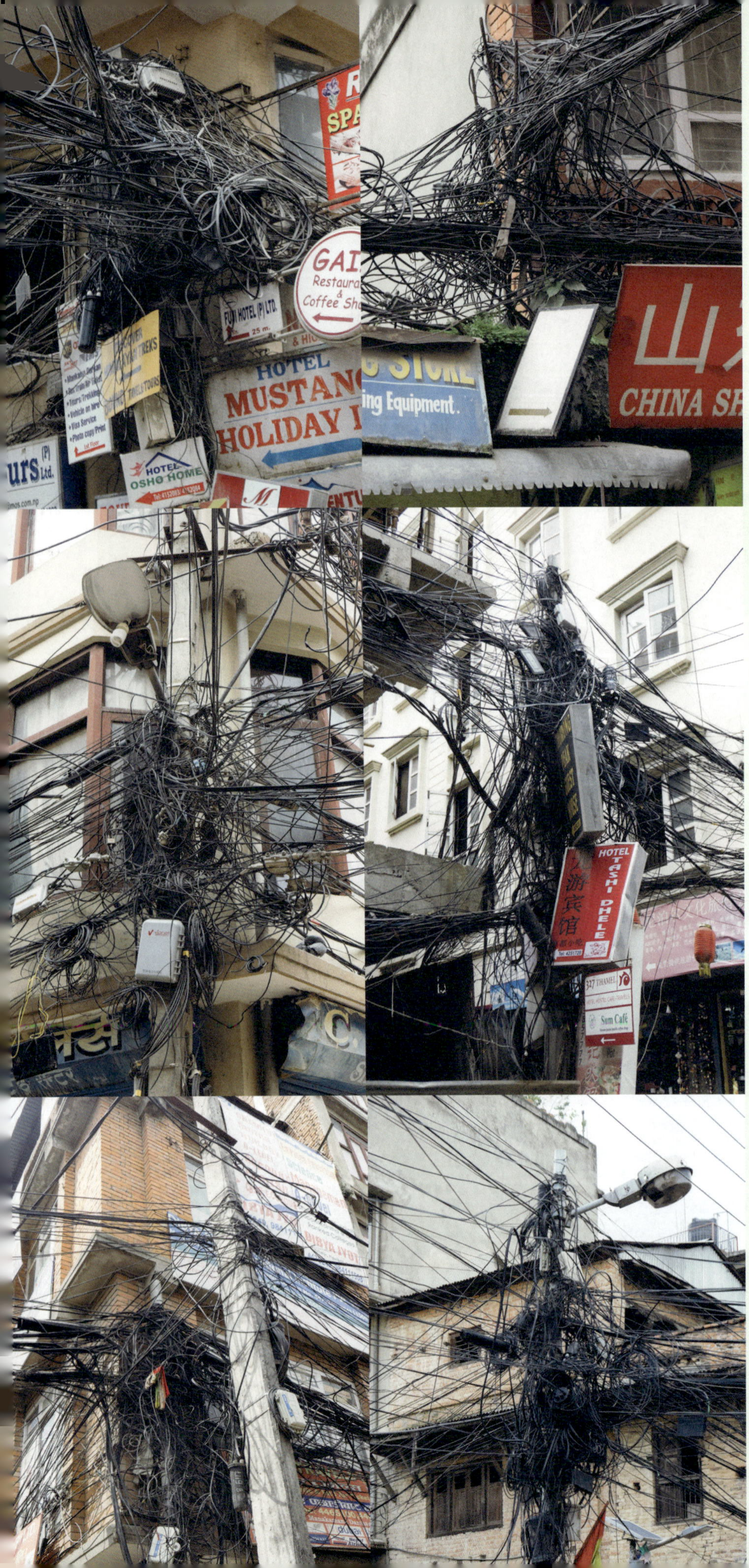

Cable tangles

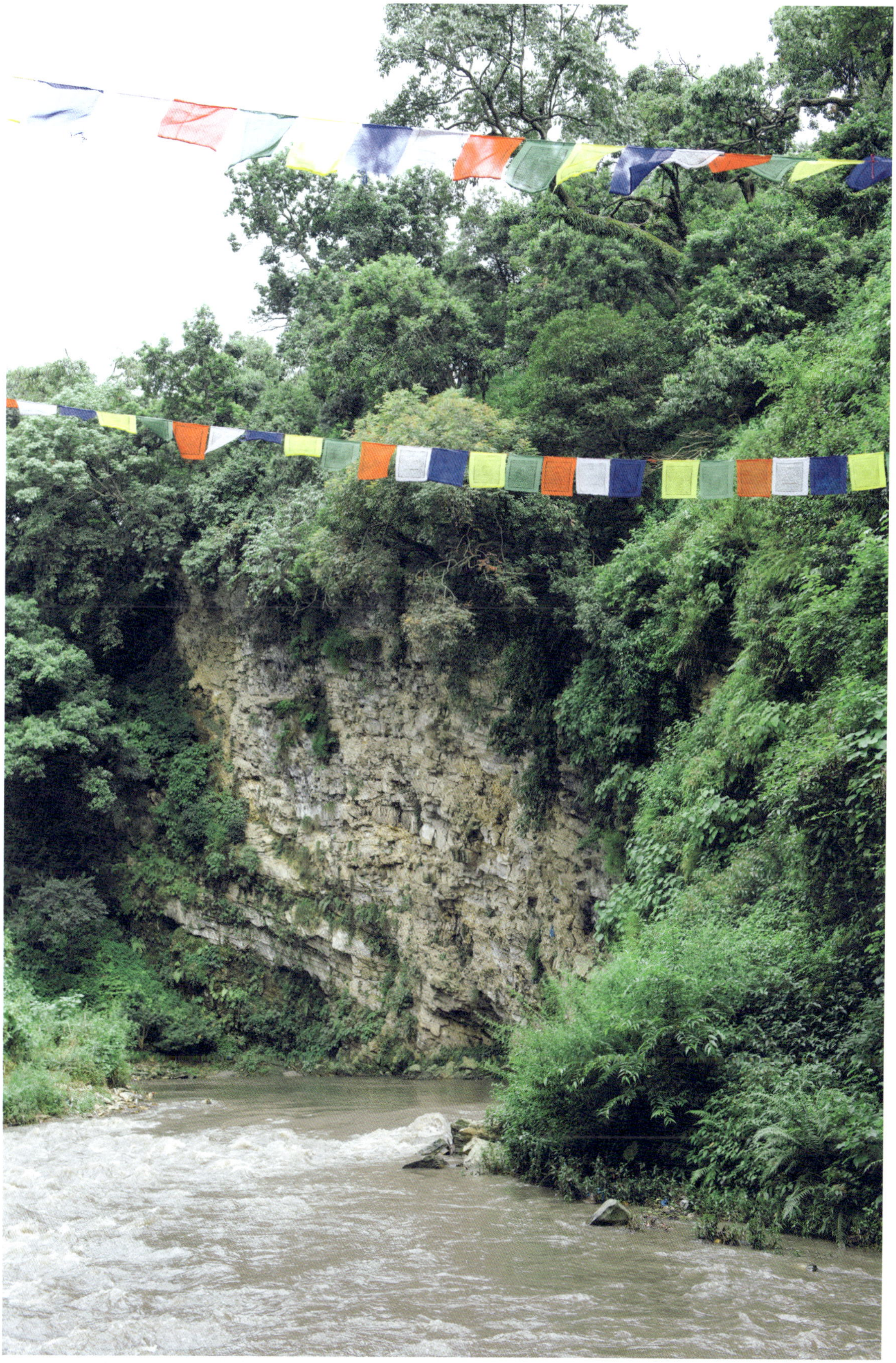

Tibetan prayer flags

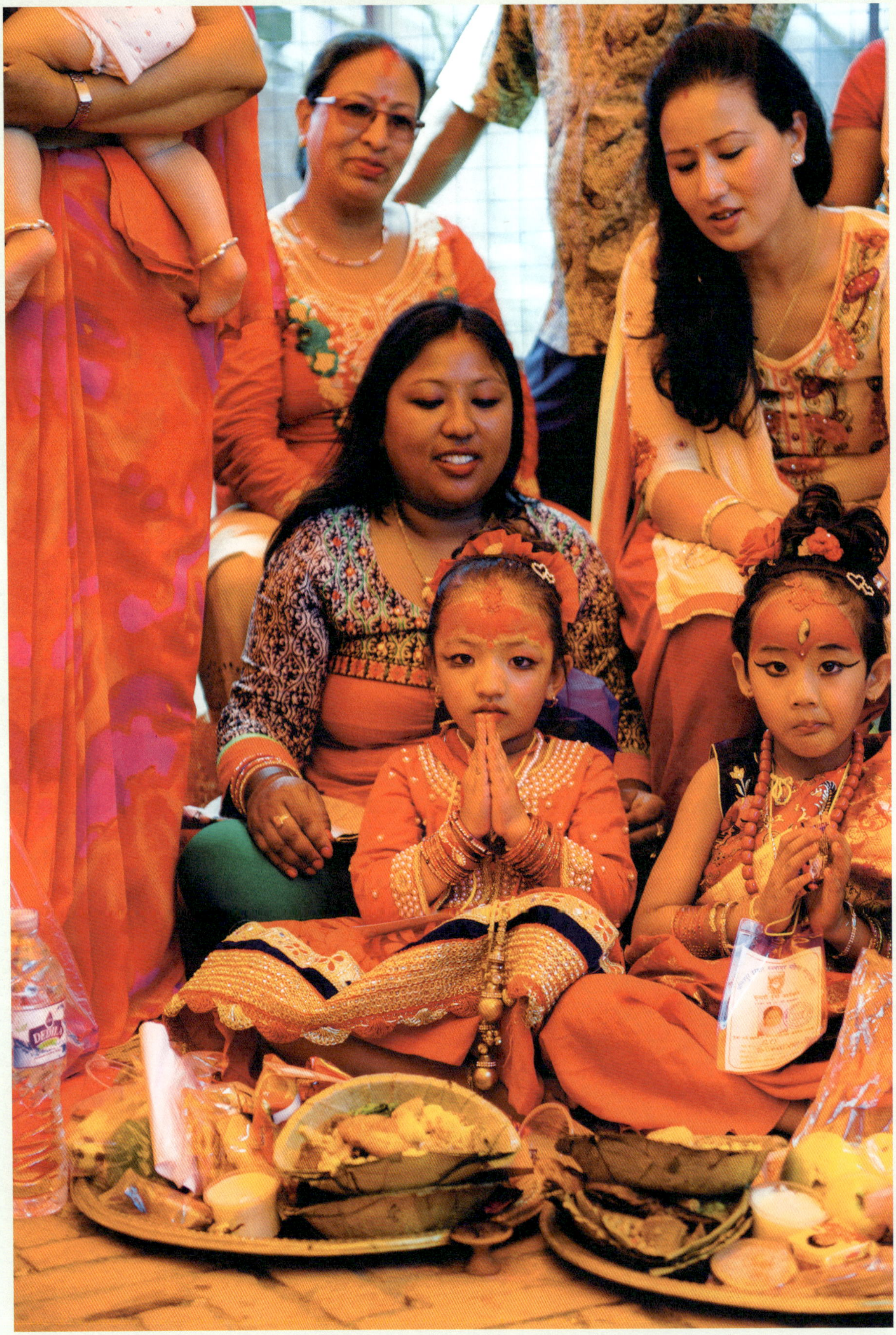

Prospective child goddess in Patan

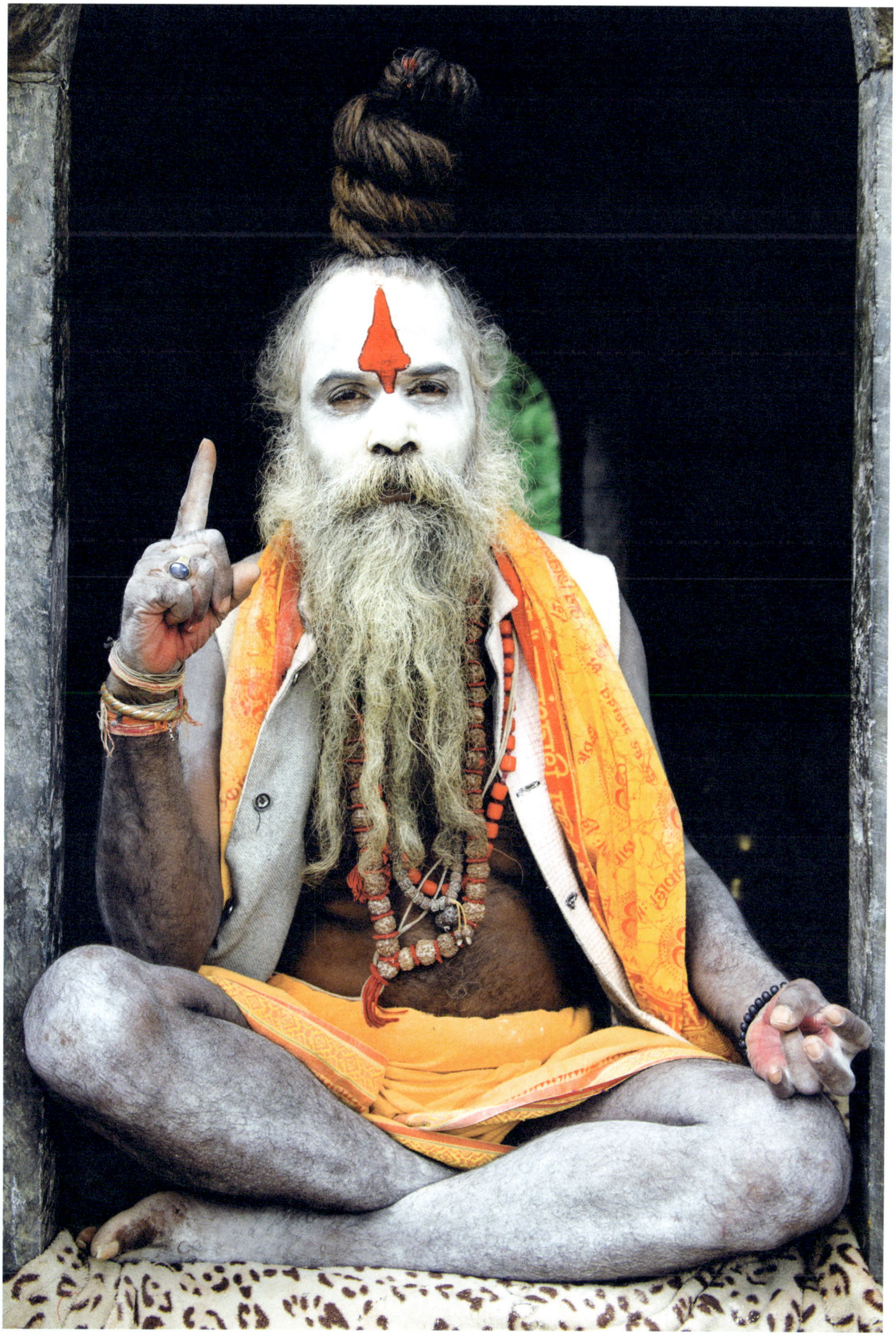

BY CHRISTOPH SCHLESSMANN

Sadhu in Pashupatinath

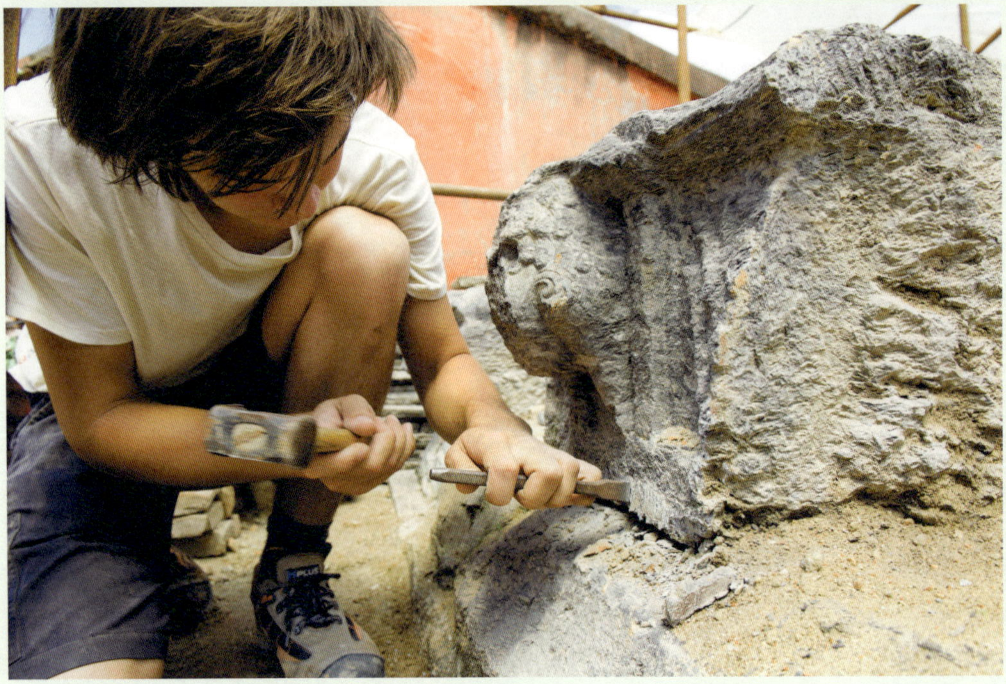

Conservator of the Institute of Conservation working at Harishankara Temple

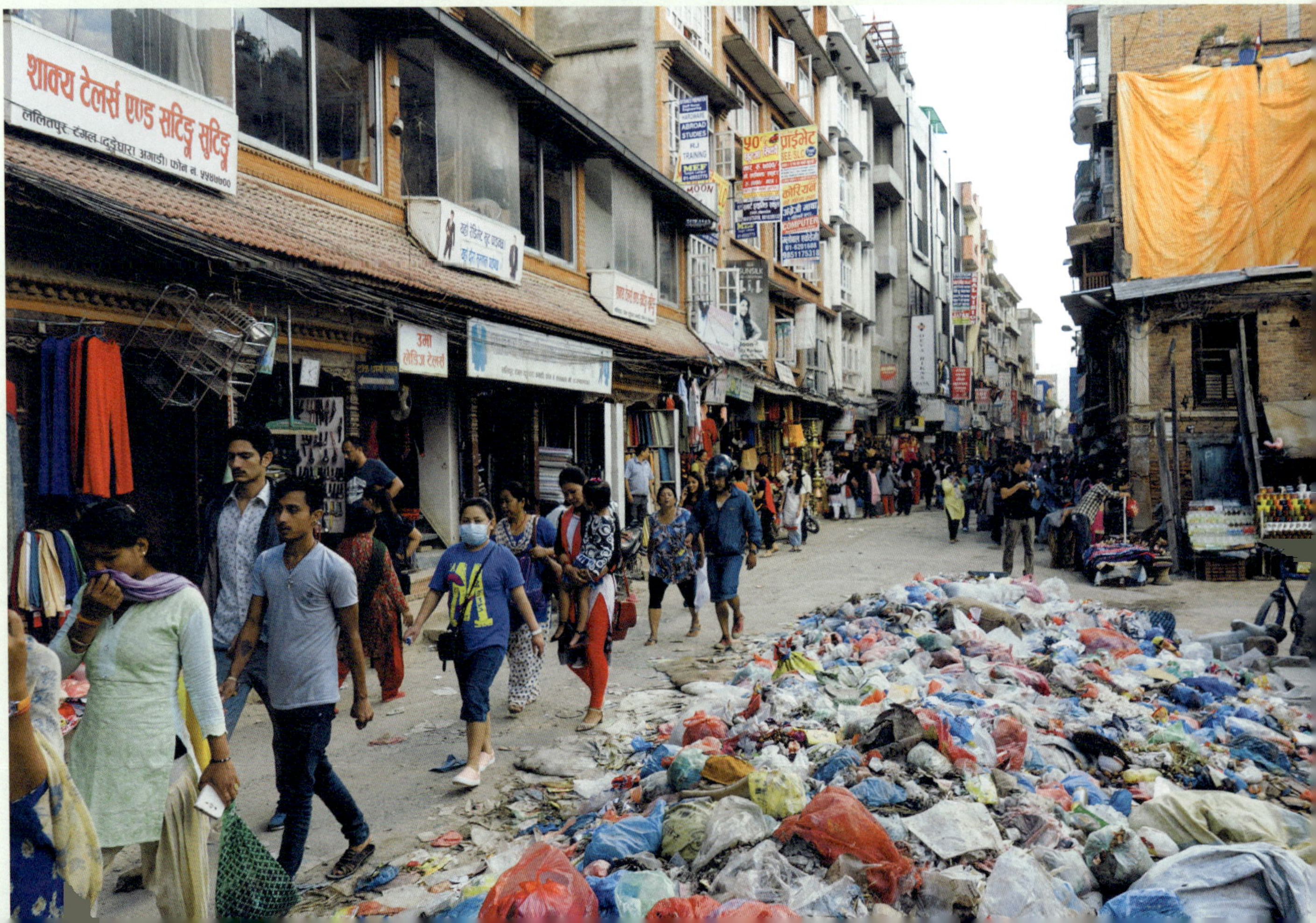

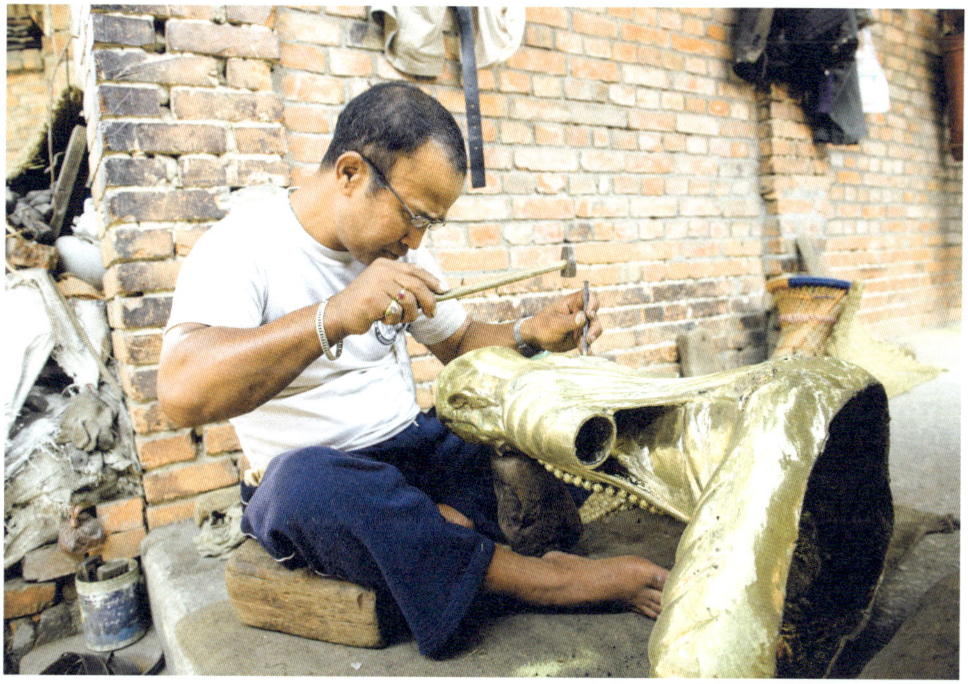

Traditional crafts in Patan

Streets of Nepal: traffic, festivals, rubbish

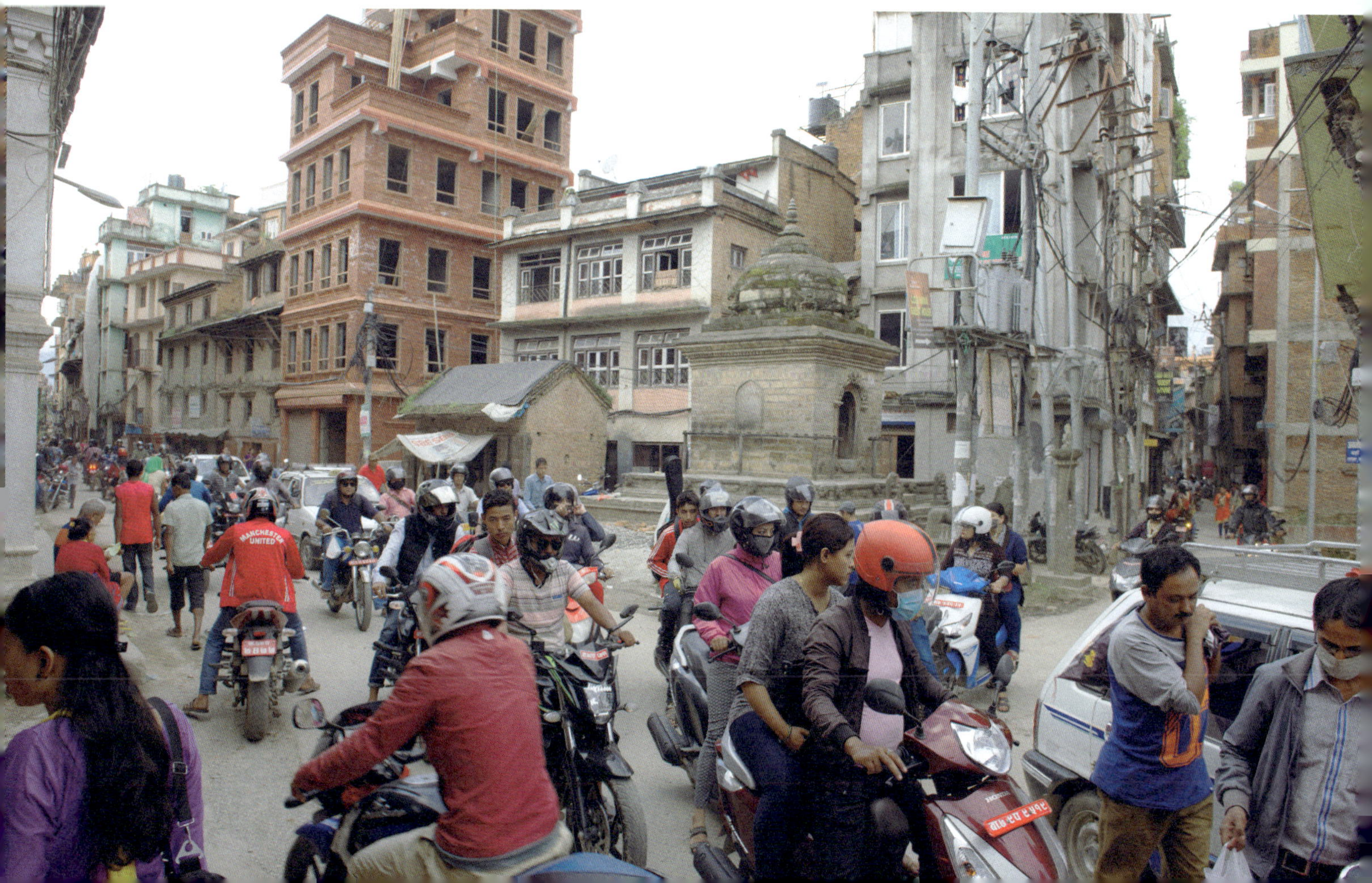

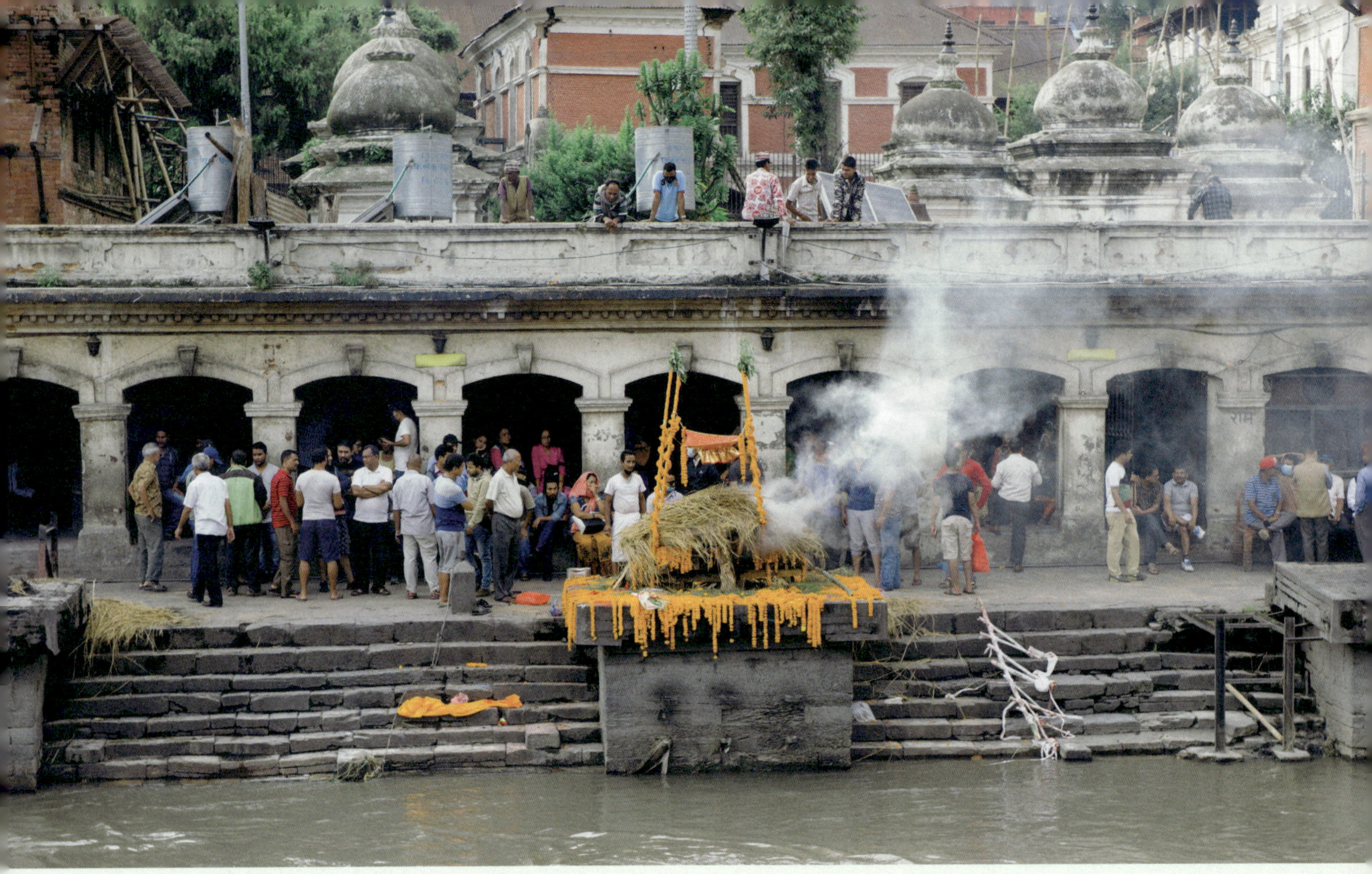

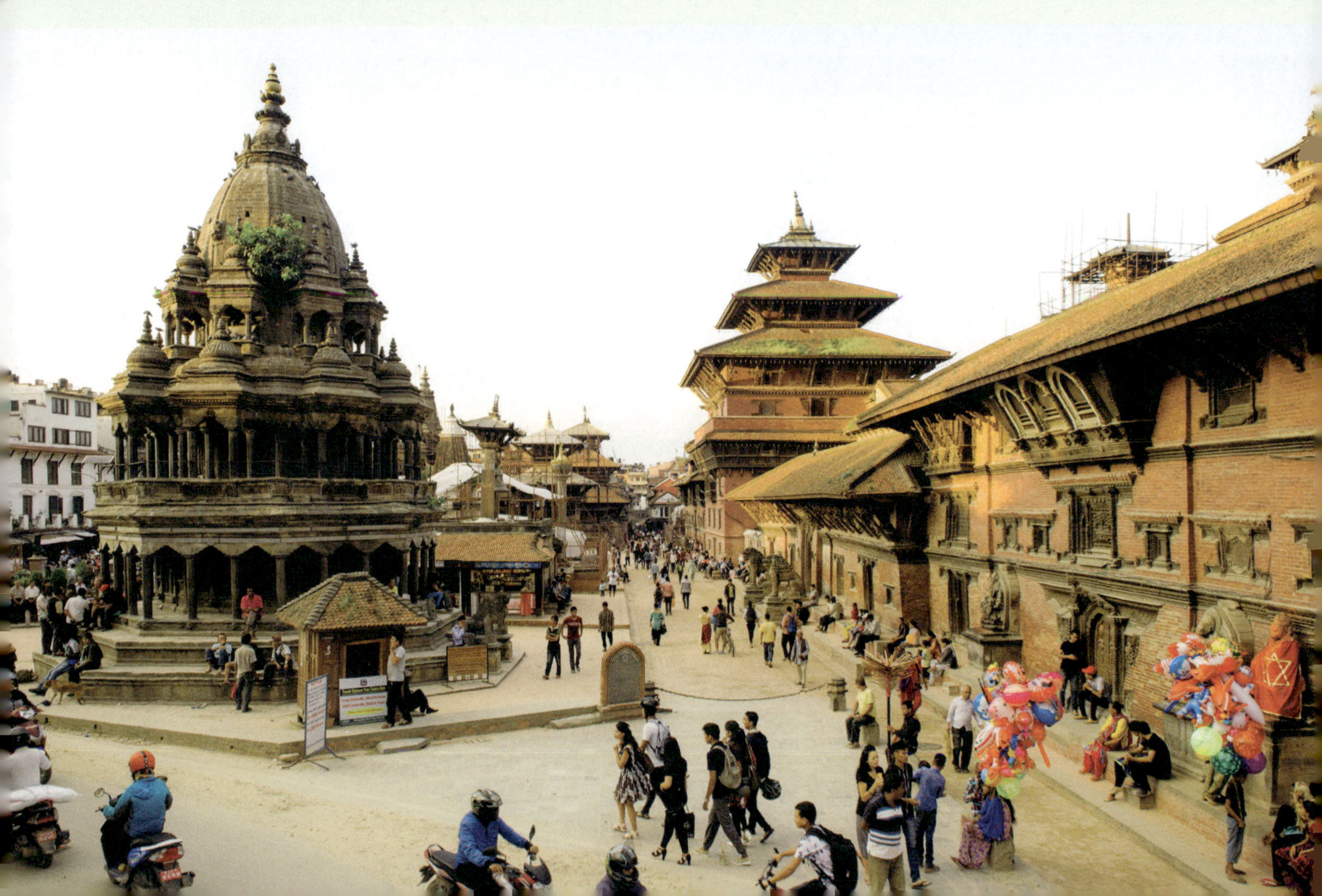

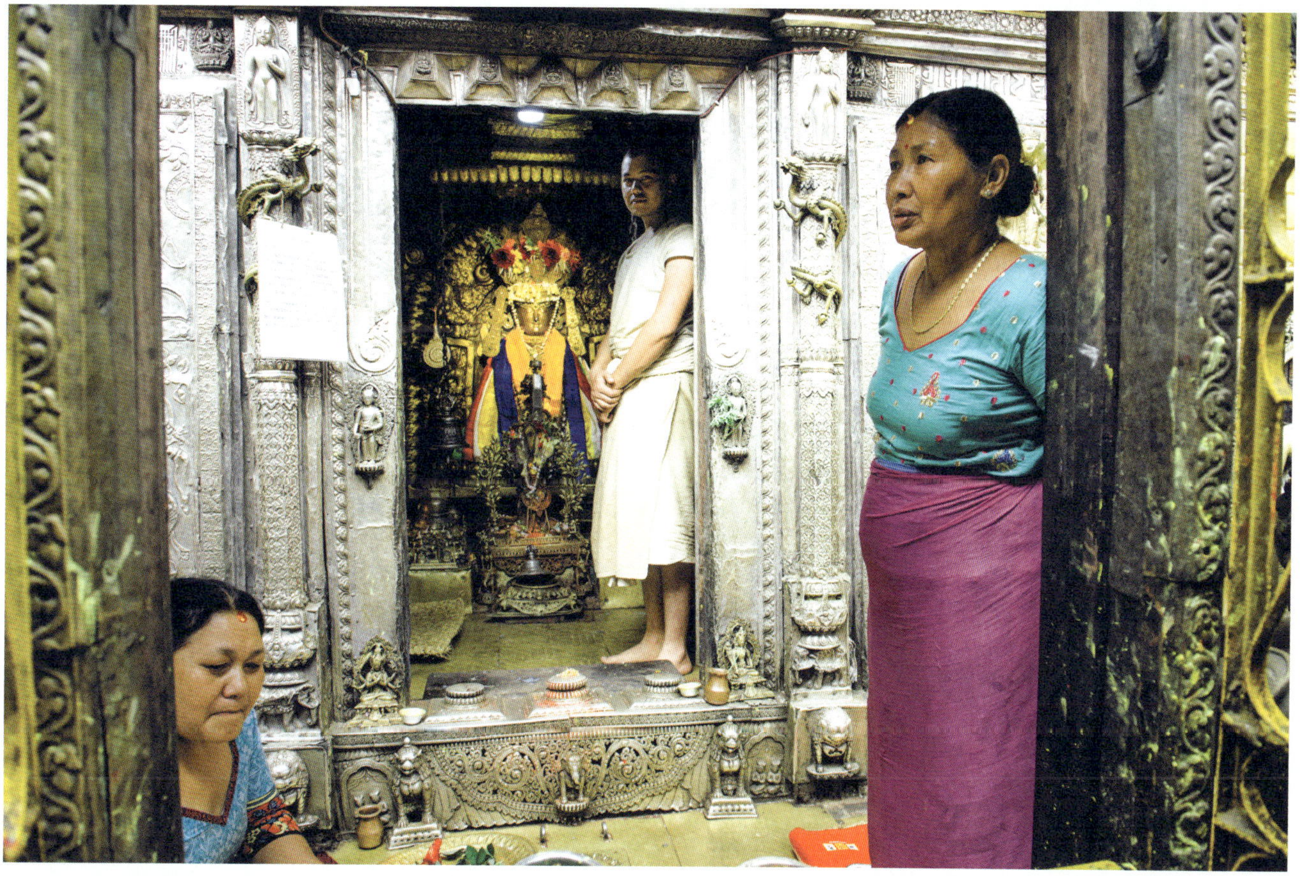

top left and next page:
Temple district Pashupatinath
left: Patan Durbar Square
above: Daily worship

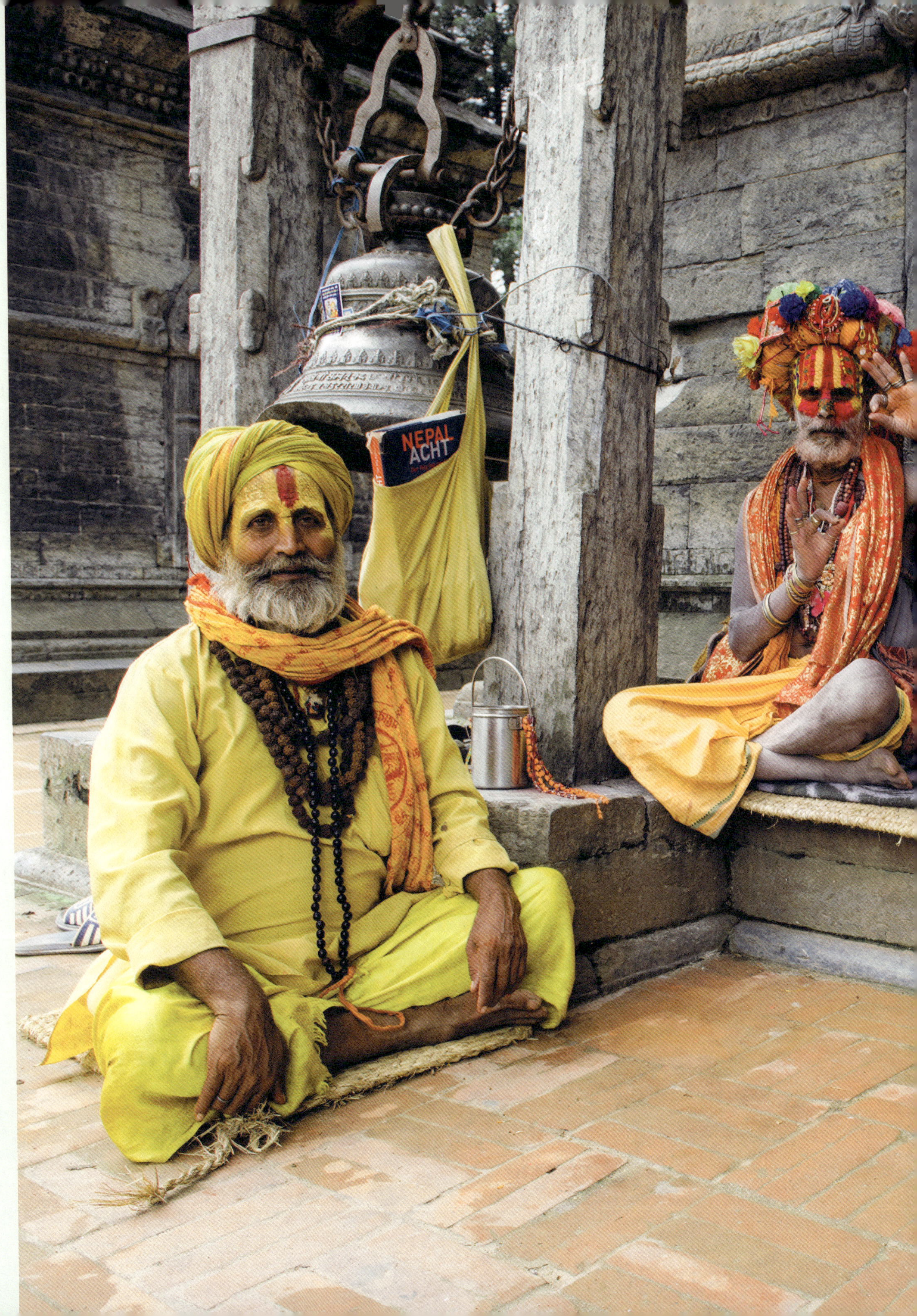
NEPAL
ACHT

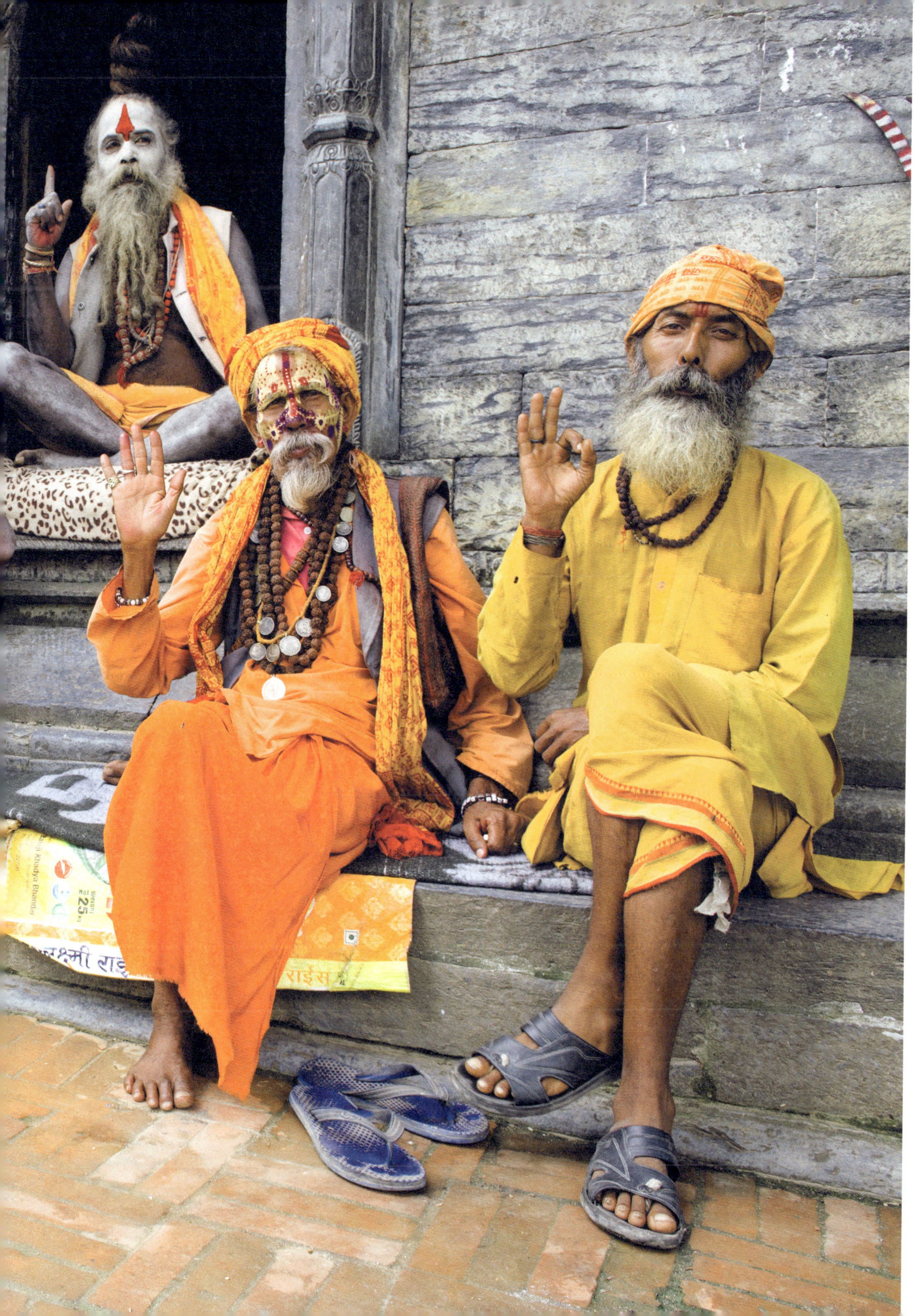

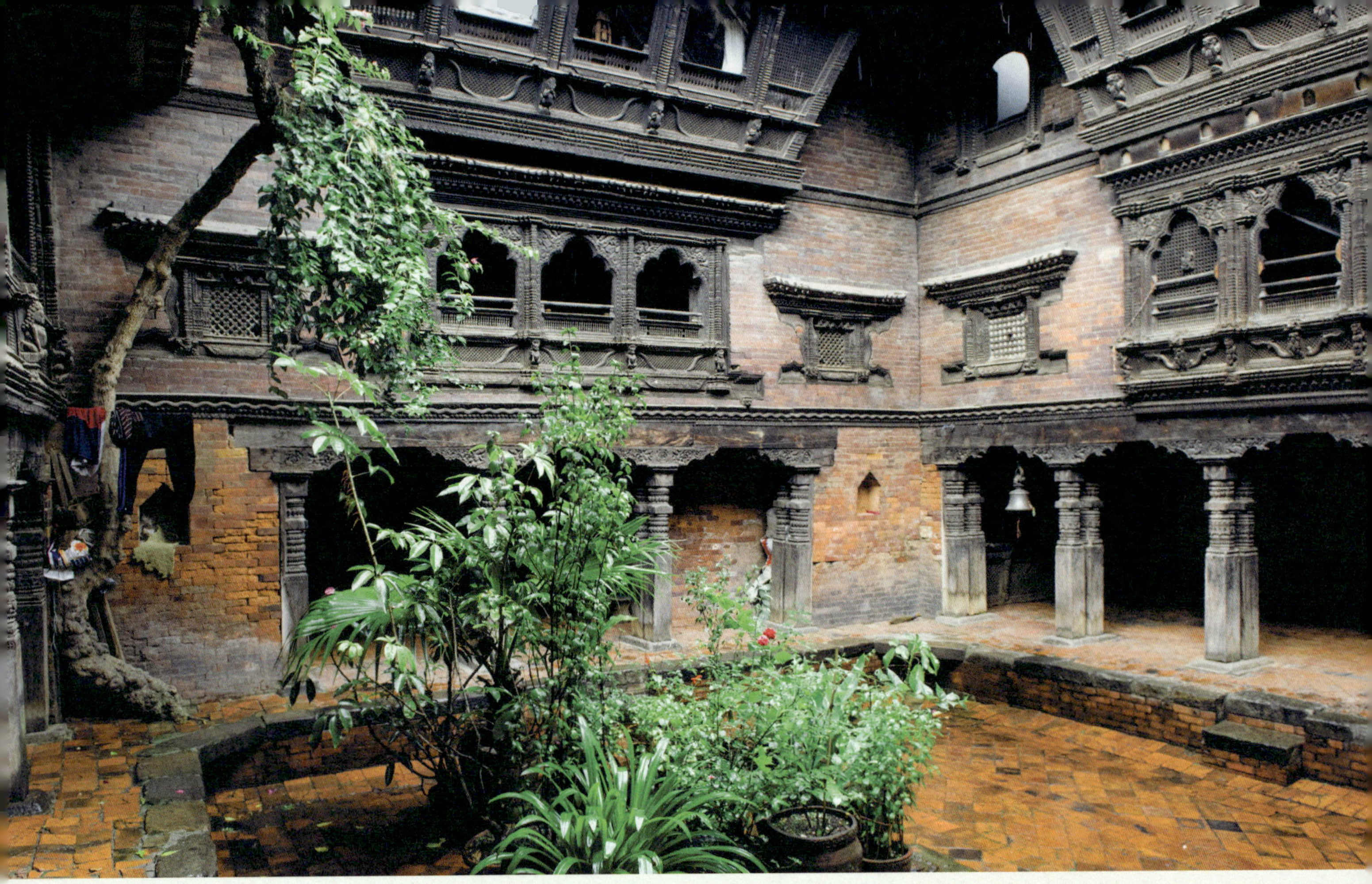

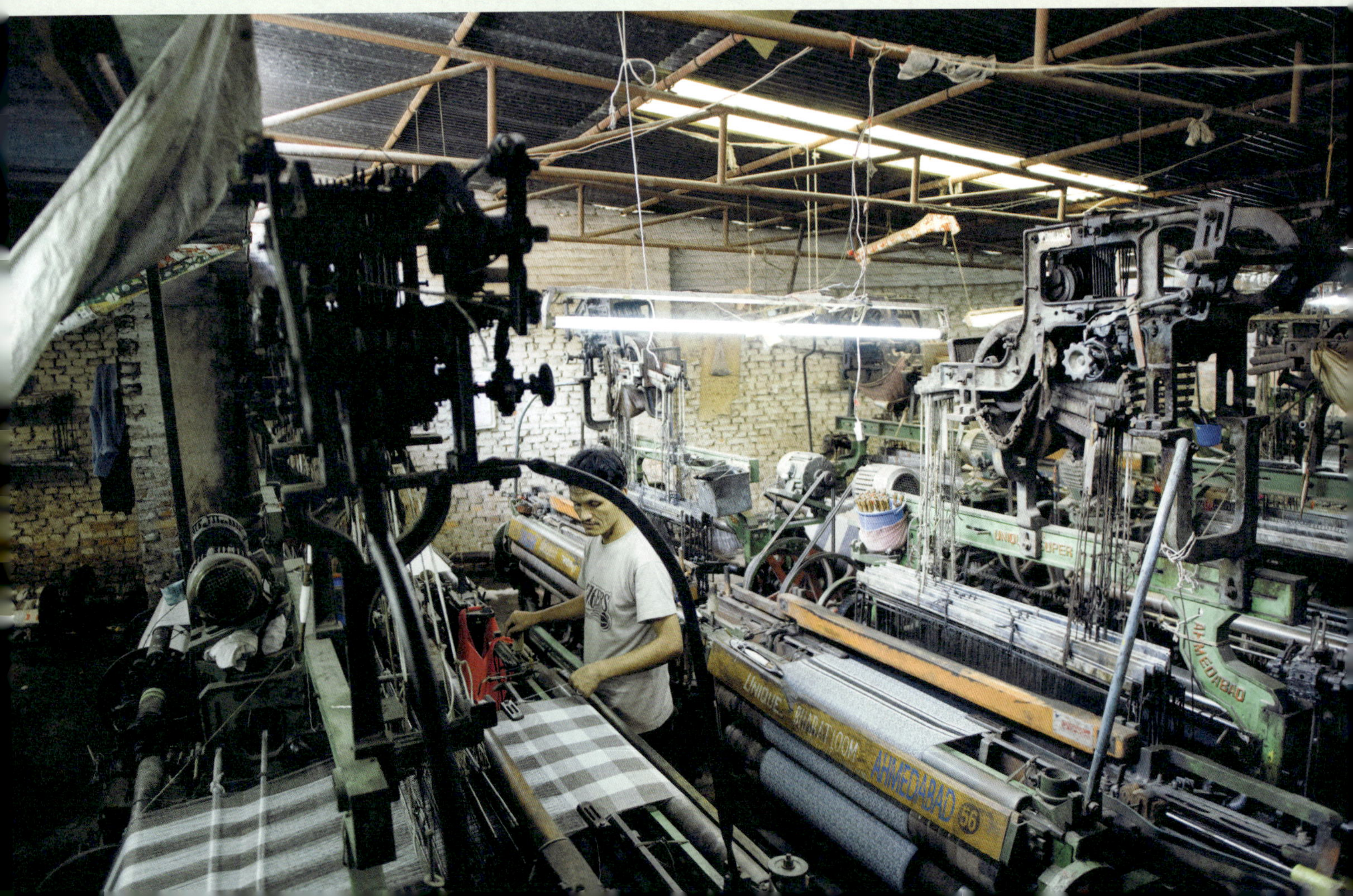
AHMEDABAD
56

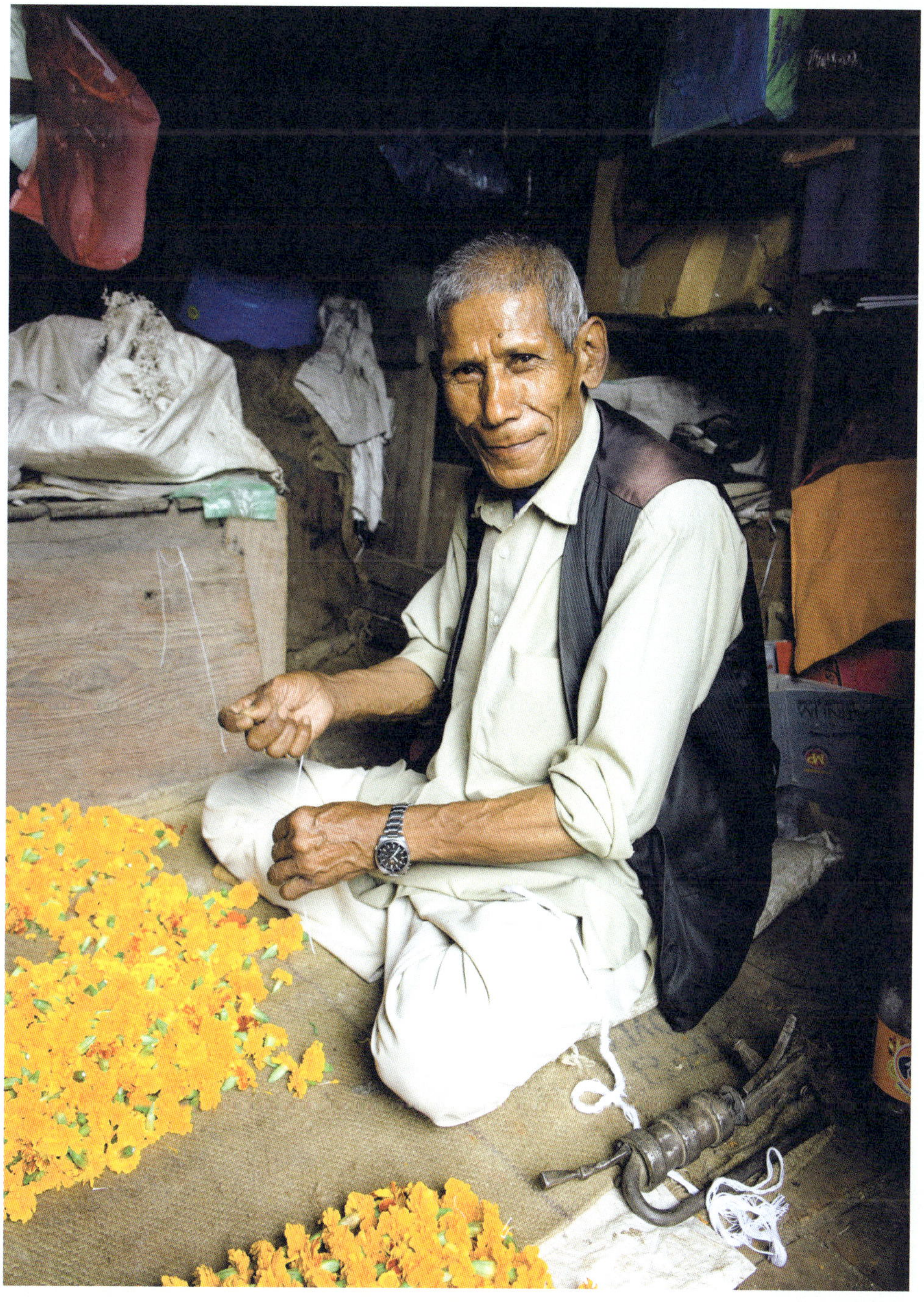

Preparation of sacrificial offerings

top left: Typical Newari house in Bhaktapur
left: Traditional crafts in Patan

Nako and Patan

MANFRED TRUMMER

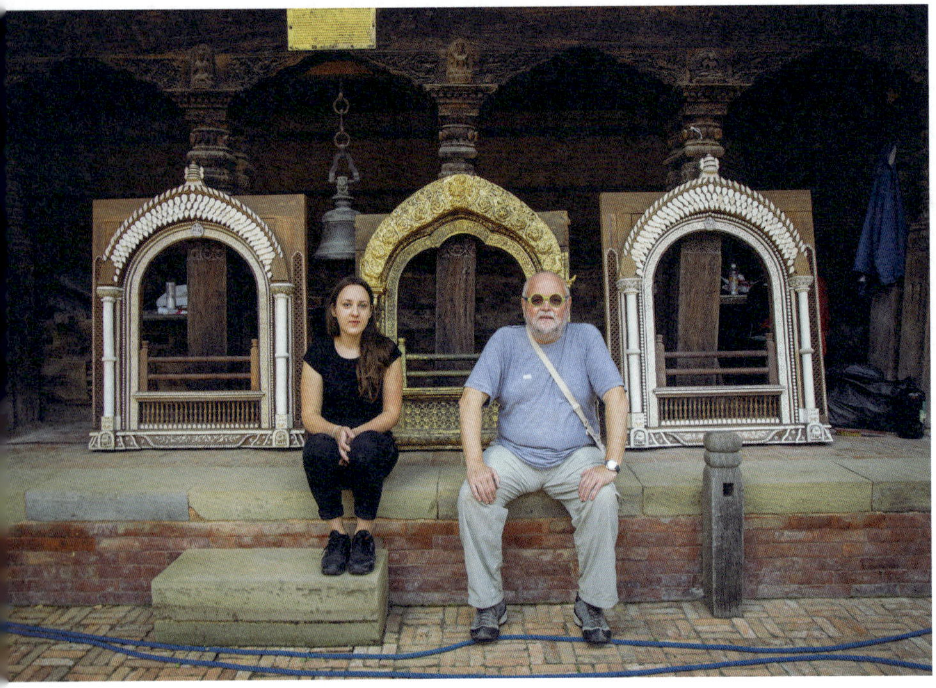

Fig. 9: One of my main projects: the conservation and reconstruction of the Ivory Window Ensemble done in collaboration with students of the Institute of Conservation and local craftsmen (2014 and 2017)

Personal Memories

The first contact I had with Nepalis, that I am aware of, was in the small village of Nako in the Indian Federal State of Himachal Pradesh in the Province of Kinnaur. I worked for several years in this small village on the Tibetan-Chinese border with a team from the Institute of Conservation, University of Applied Arts Vienna, on the preservation of early wall paintings in four small temples. In the first year I wasn't really aware of the Nepalese farm labourers; I was so preoccupied with myself at an altitude of 3,660 metres (12,008 feet) above sea level and with what was sometimes physically strenuous work.

It was only in the second year during a longer stay that I often noticed small children, ragged and dirty, who lingered on the large square in front of the temples, while the locally resident children were at school or did their lessons directly on the square in groups, wearing school uniform. The Nepalese children made a piteous impression on me – no shoes, utterly dirty, and with constant colds and running noses. It was on my Sunday walks that I first came across the slum housing with their improvised shelter of blue tarpaulins and plastic sacks set up on the outskirts of the village by itinerant Nepalese workers. The shacks were mostly built of layered stones arranged in several rows around a flat well in which the Nepalis stowed away their few goods and chattels. They worked on the vegetable and corn fields of the local farmers, tended and harvested the peas that were the main crops. The farmers told us the peas were the best in the whole of India and very much in demand in Delhi and other cities.

In the following year – my longest sojourn in Nako – nearly all of us stayed in the sole hotel in town, a half-finished, two-storey concrete building, first built a few years before. The entrance was on the upper floor on the north side in which some of the available rooms and a common lounge were located. The windows of the very simply appointed rooms on the upper and lower floors all looked south towards a pea field encircled by stones, and we could also see part of the adjacent main road. This is where a portion of village life took place mornings and evenings, and a small open stream supplied by a lake situated higher up and irrigating the lower-lying field served as laundry and body-care facility.

On some days the trickling stream running downhill at the edge of the main road was the scene of an ad hoc market for travelling pedlars and farmers from the next village, selling vegetables and cheap household goods.

One day, already at the start of my stay, I noticed a man who had arrived on the service bus from the much lower-lying Rampur. He wasn't selling the usual wares, but had several hand-knotted carpets in his baggage.

With the assistance of our hotel boy Manesh, who acted as interpreter, I bought a small rug sized about 2.8 metres long and 80 cm wide. During the bargaining, it turned out that the travelling tradesman also came from Nepal and sold carpets from his home village.

The carpet has a yellowish-orange field framed by a stripe of blue wool 2 cm wide and shows a stylised female figure at the top and a male figure at the bottom end, each with a domestic animal, a sheep or goat.

It is very densely knotted and has a fairly long pile; it certainly made my bare accommodation a lot cosier.

Even today, every time I walk over the rug or use it as an underlay for my mattress roll I often think of Nako, the purchase, and the carpet vendor.

At the time, I had no idea what significance Nepal would have for me several years later.

My first journey to Nepal was in 2009 – I flew to Nepal through Eduard F. Sekler as intermediary, who arranged contact with Thomas Schrom, an associate of the Kathmandu Valley Preservation Trust (KVPT) with headquarters in Patan. Sekler asked me to have a look at a stone fountain, the royal bath Tusha Hiti (Fig. 1), in the former Royal Palace of Patan next to Durbar Square, and gauge what conservation action could be taken.

My first stay, as in Nako, was taken up by my work (Fig. 2), and I didn't go on many trips in the vicinity. On my second stay I began to roam through the streets surrounding Patan Durbar Square. Mostly I went on my walks early in the morning before work started, when the vegetable vendors and farmers came into town from the surroundings and peddled their agricultural products along the main road, which led to a large bus station located in the south. All kinds of of goods were spread out in baskets or on mats and cloths, directly available to the customers (Fig. 3).

The street market is always cleared away by 9 am, when the shops in the buildings open their shutters. The concentration of shops is extreme and every available inch is used, from cellar to first floor (Fig. 4).

Of special interest for me were the tradesmen, still very numerous in Nepal, who sell wares made of coloured metal (Fig. 5). Here you can find household goods from plates to large storage vessels, simple religious figures, oil lamps, candle holders, wind chimes with bells usually made of copper and zinc alloy (brass). There is a wide range of goods on offer, and the items are paid for by weight. Some of the pedlars also sell metal architectural components, such as step-shaped tower pinnacles made of brass that can be also found crowning the many temples on the main square.

During my evening explorations I soon noticed that most of the items on offer were made in the vicinity in small workshops, often

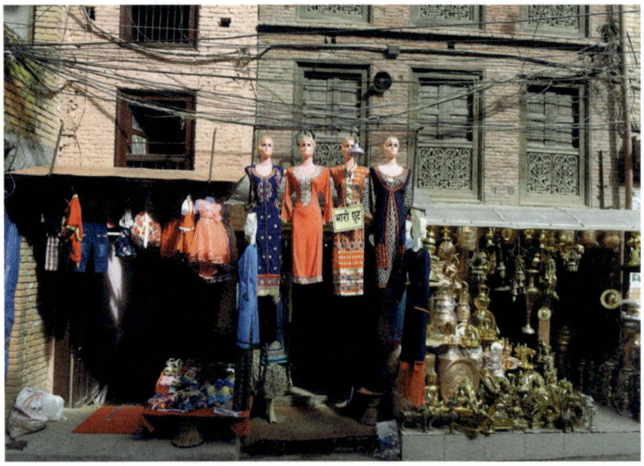

Fig. 5: Clothing shops alternating which metal vendors

in the backyards. You can't avoid hearing the hammering of coppersmiths and the less intrusive sound of chiselling, and you can follow the noises and find the workshops even if they are located in the very back of a house; their activity always betrays them. (Fig. 7)

One of the most important handicraft skills in Patan is the fabrication of a great variety of bronze and brass figures. These are mainly produced, after modelling, in lost wax processes or the lost mould technique. Once the sand mould is knocked off, the figures are subjected to a work-intensive finishing process. The still-adhering sprues or casting channels have to be removed, the individual parts of complicated figures have to be cast separately, and, after the first finishing stages, any occurring casting flaws are soldered and closed up. The intensive fine work on the figures starts only after these steps and is reserved for the chasers or chisellers, who finish off the figures with fine sculptural details and grind and polish the surfaces. (Fig. 8) Then the metal surfaces are frequently patinated in order to integrate the soldered areas into the overall surface. The figures with the best quality of casting may also be wholly or partially gilded. The tradespeople's shops often have sculptures on offer that are wrapped in cotton bindings under which a gilding or special patinating process is in progress. A very beautiful and illustrative example of this casting technique can be seen in the Patan Museum; here the individual work steps are shown through the example of a head, demonstrating the various phases in production.

There's no problem if you wish to buy one of the figures because the whole town teems with shops selling a multifarious range of mostly religious figures, such as the various Buddha interpretations of the Mahayana and the Vajrayana, and the vast world of the Hindu gods.

On one of the side alleys, often very narrow, in the direct vicinity of Durbar Square you can find the workshops of carpenters, turners, woodcarvers and so forth. The shop fronts open up directly onto the alleyway, and you can watch the craftsmen producing their wares with their simple tools. I have commissioned bespoke items several times, such as ventilation grates made of wood and with variously carved decorations. The grates can still be found on the many windows of the former royal palaces in the Kathmandu Valley, but also on the stock of historical buildings that are still threatened by decay.

The list of craftsmen who really do still ply their eponymous "craft" could be extended many times over.

During our conservation work, transcending all language barriers, we have worked closely together with excellent local stonemasons, carpenters, woodcarvers and coppersmiths (Fig. 9).

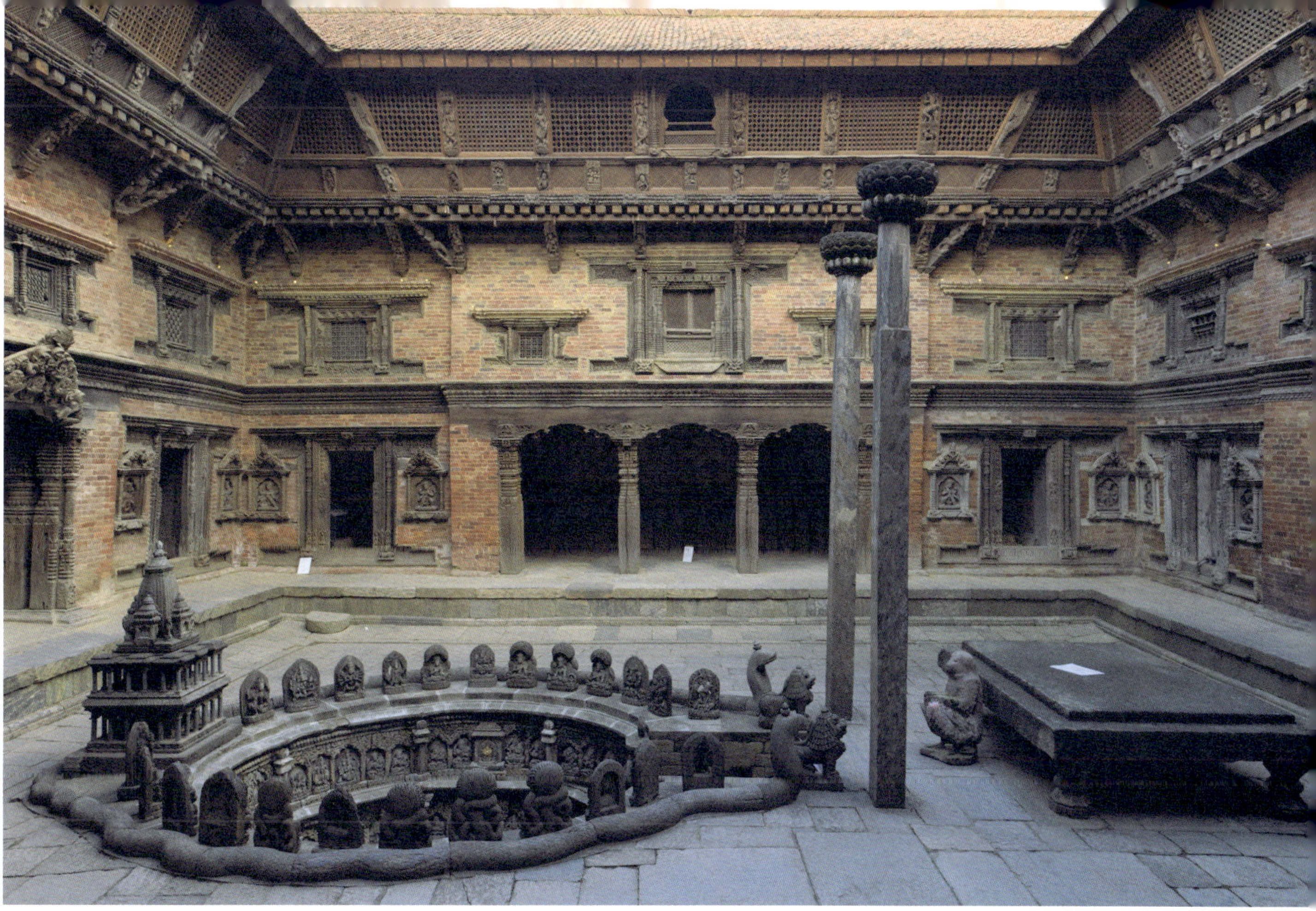

Fig. 1: Tusha Hiti, Royal Palace, after conservation, 2017

Fig. 7: In the coppersmith's workshop

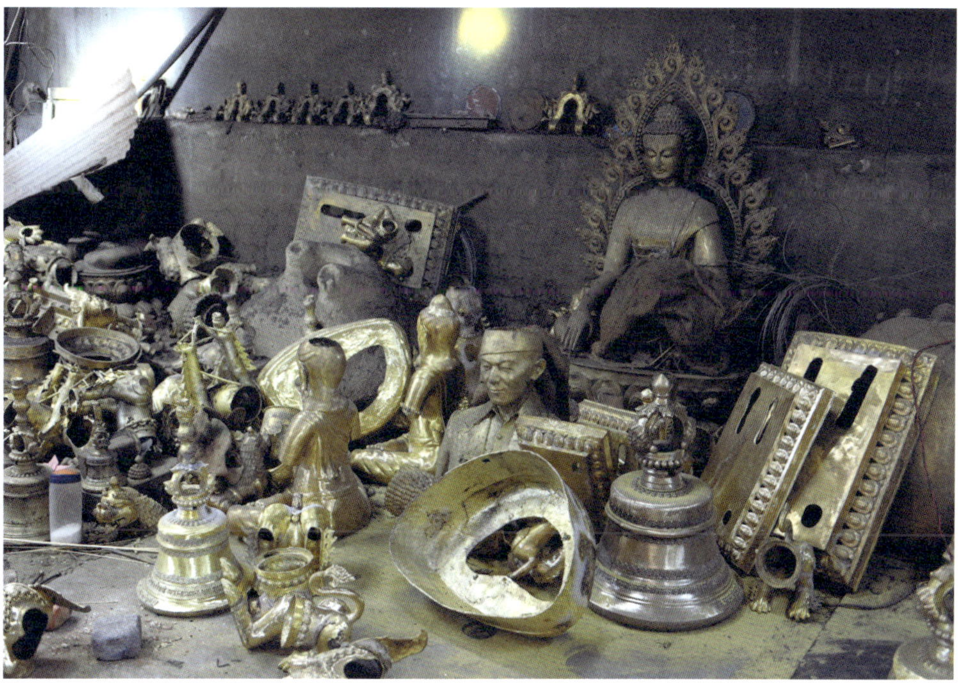

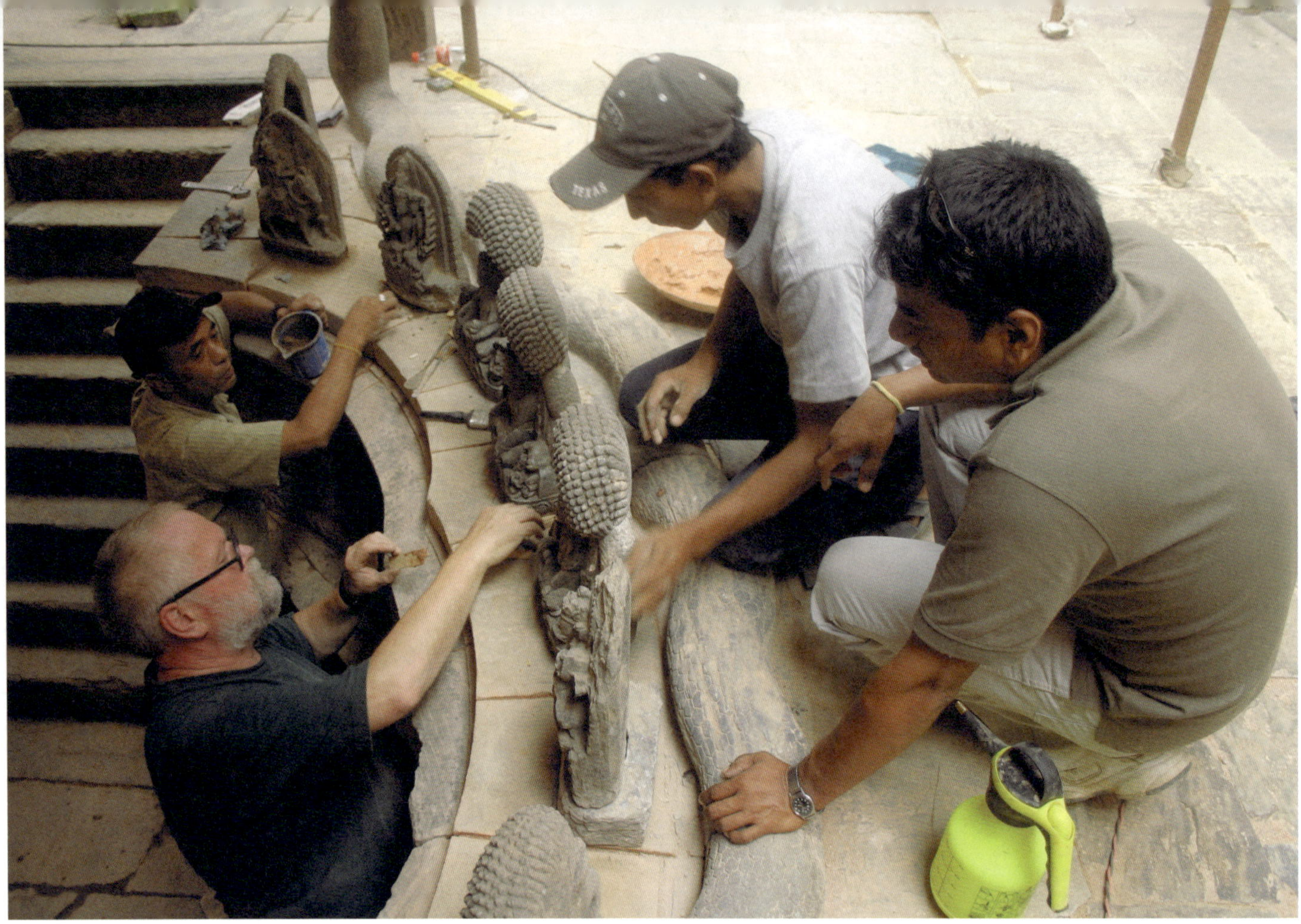

Fig. 2: Conservation work at Tusha Hiti

Fig. 8: Sand moulds

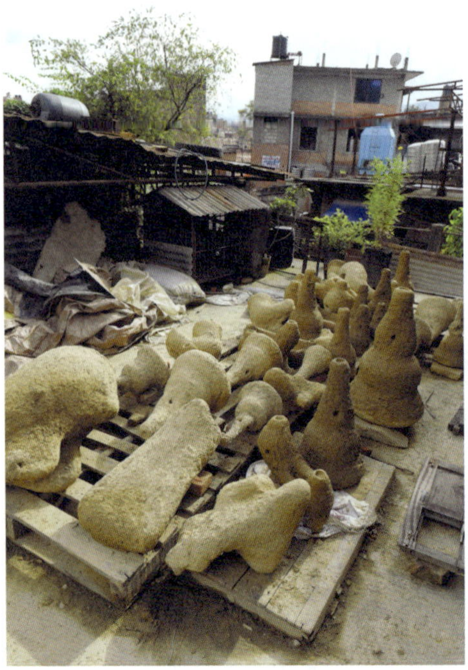

Fig. 6: Basketware and wickerwork vendor

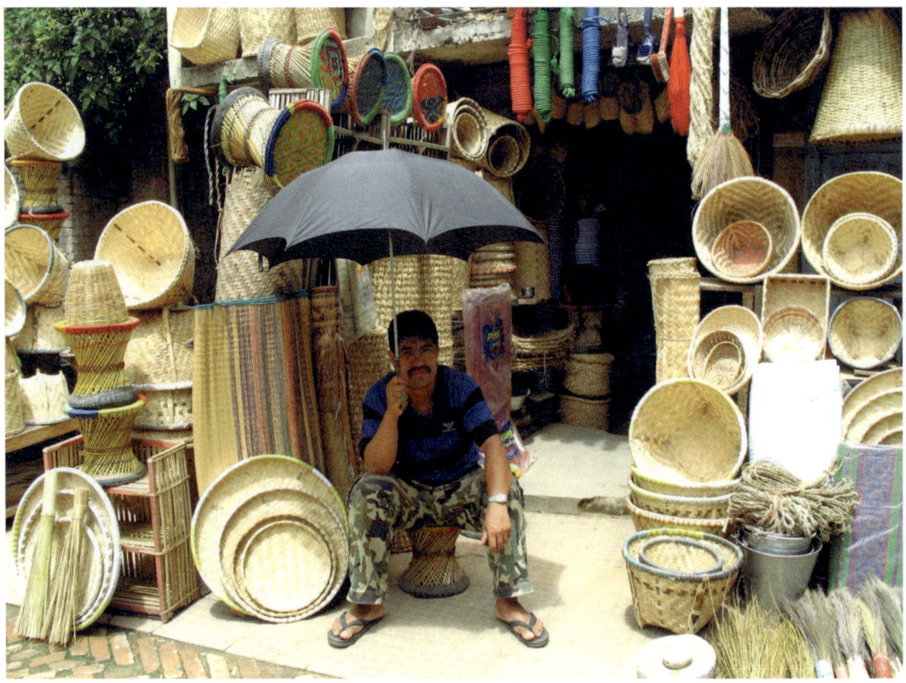

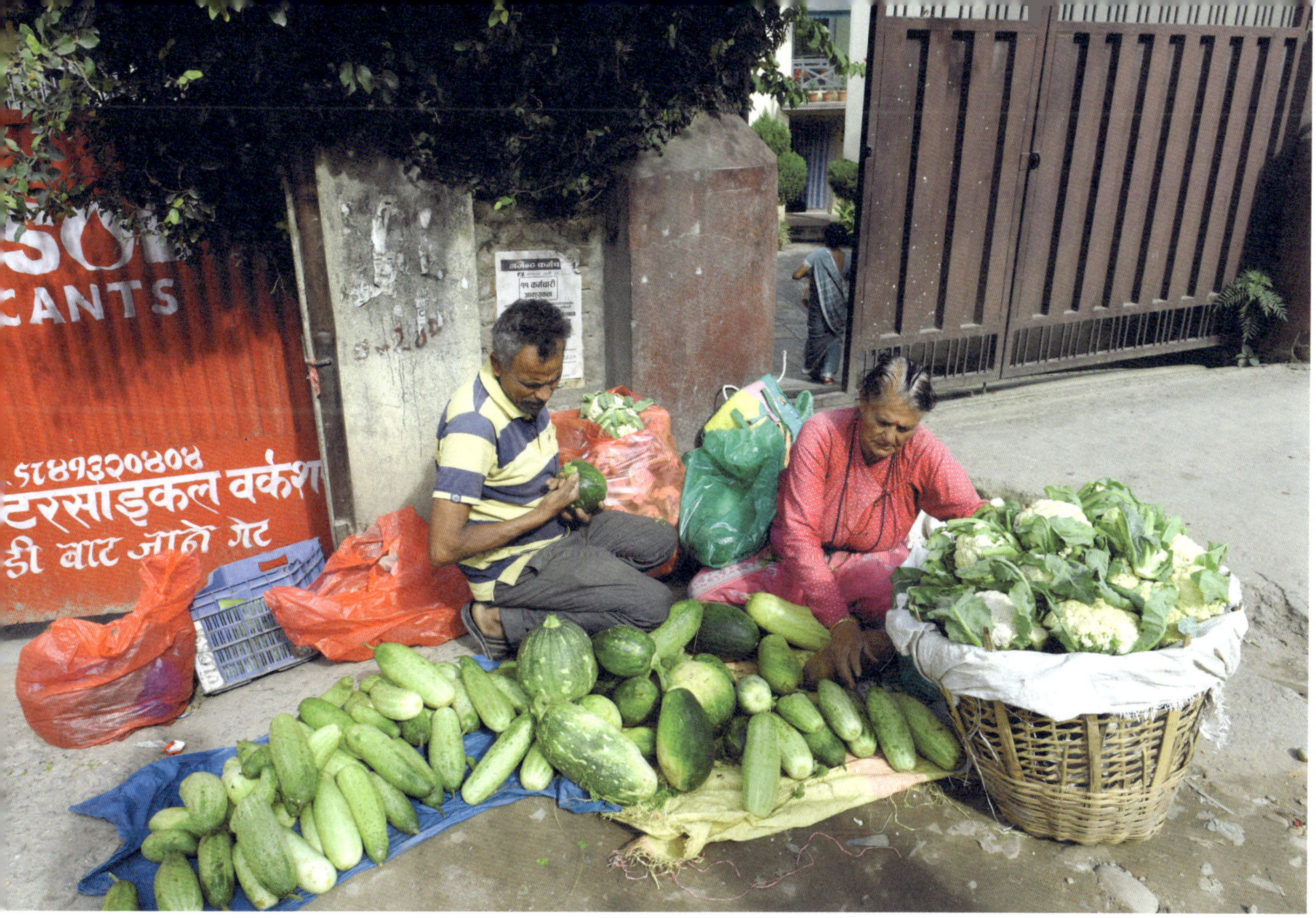

Fig. 3: Vegetable vendors

Fig. 4: Shops all over the streets of Patan

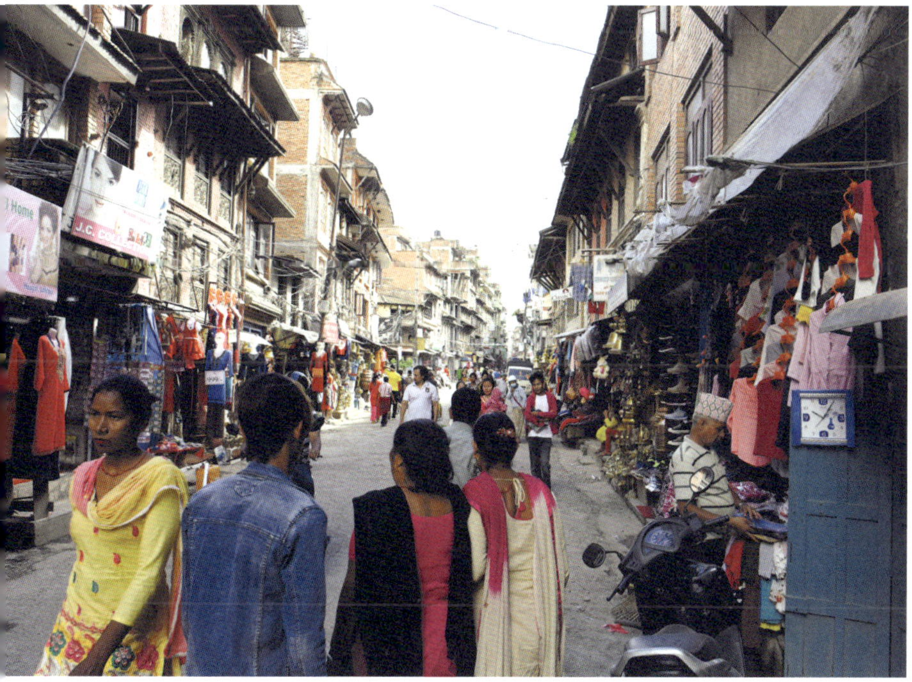

Captured in a drawing by
Mariia Bakhareva, 2018

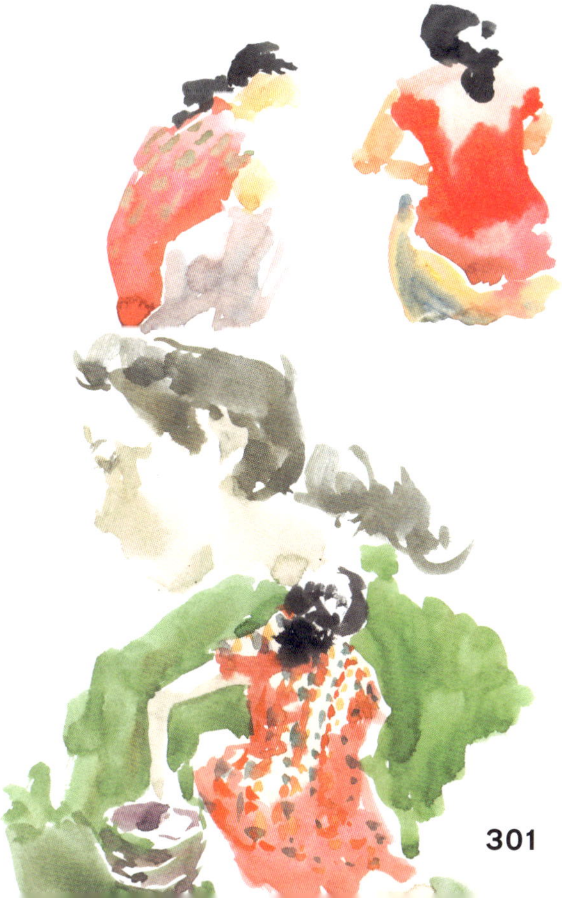

Nepal – A Journey to Adventure

REGINA
FRIEDL

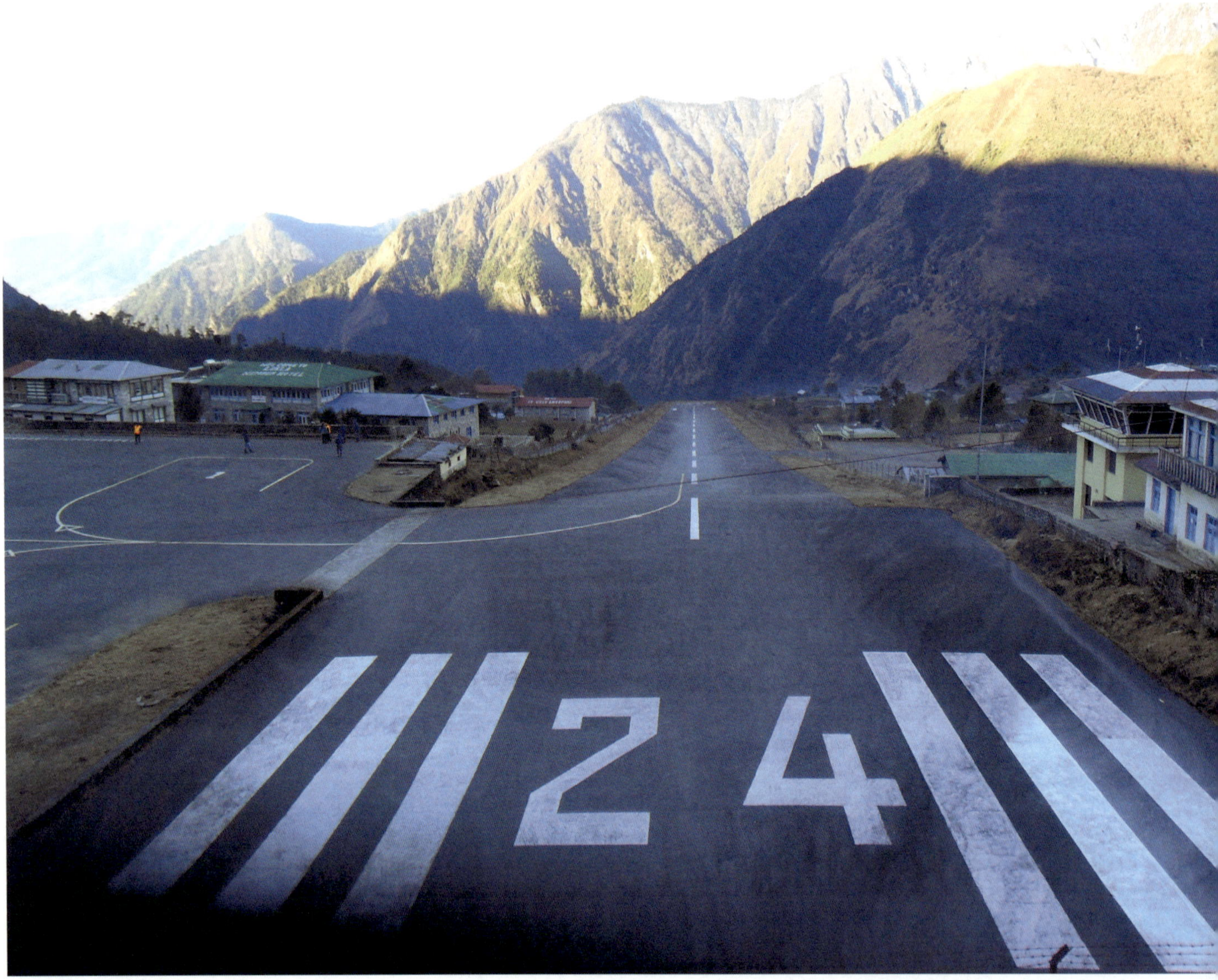

Fig. 3: The runway in Lukla

Stories from the Roof of the World

I came to love and admire Nepal on my first trip in 2012. I was there for a total of six weeks, four of them spent working for the conservation campaigns of the Institute of Conservation; the remaining days offered me the time and opportunity to explore this wonderful country more closely.

Among other things I did a two-day trekking tour round Kathmandu Valley and travelled by bus to Pokhara, a very exciting journey, fatiguing, somewhat bumpy, but absolutely beautiful.

Start was very early in the morning – departure from Thamel, Kathmandu's tourist centre! The suburb, otherwise so wide awake, was still fast asleep. The streets with their countless souvenir shops seemed dead and empty. No one was to be seen on the streets when we tramped to the Kantipath bus station around six o'clock in the morning. By the time we got to the bus station peace and quiet had suddenly fled; chaos ruled on the pavements. We caught sight of dozens of tired tourists with puzzled but also rather frantic expressions. Countless vendors were bustling among them, urging customers to buy water, snacks, pastries and so on.

The planned departure of the bus was shortly before seven; but we were to be at the bus already at half past six. This is because of the cheap fare for the bus journey, when converted about six euros for a return trip, around 200 kilometres each way – an offer the locals also jump at. We climbed into the bus and got seats in the last row. Not really the cosiest of places, it's true, but at least we had a little more leg room during the long journey. The bus filled up in no time, and shortly after seven the bus trundled off. Traffic in Kathmandu was already in full swing, and even the sleepiest passenger was woken up by the permanent honking of horns. Headway was pretty sluggish at first, only after about an hour's driving did we at last move out of the densely populated city.

Now the road led through the valley alongside very steep slopes. This route is the only land connection from Kathmandu to Pokhara. The mountain road is so narrow that two buses just about find enough room to pass each other, so traffic jams are pre-programmed here as well. Thus the greatest precision was demanded of the bus driver when confronted with opposing traffic in the form of lorries and touring buses; he wound his way at walking pace past the other vehicles, always keeping his eye on the deep abyss on the right. The road was in a bad state in parts and in some spots strewn with holes because of landslides or strong rainfall. We were intensely aware of every detail – the choice of seats on the back row had its revenge. We were shaken to the bone and our heads constantly banged on the bus roof. I grew sleepy; the temperature in the bus rose continuously – of course there was no air conditioning. The compensation for this was a breathtaking view; we drove uphill and down dale, we wove our way through curves and along rock faces, through deep gorges, past rapids, countless rice terraces and in the background the Himalayas with their peaks towering over everything. The wonderfully green natural countryside was truly a contrast to the hectic capital of Kathmandu. The landscape changed yet again during the last hour of the bus journey, and we drove along a road that was even worse. When we finally arrived in Pokhara we all took a deep breath of relief, glad to be able to leave the bus at last. Despite the arduous eight-hour bus journey, I actually did enjoy individual moments, overwhelmed by the ever-changing landscape.

Pokhara was much quieter and wasn't dominated by the hectic bustle we knew from Kathmandu. We could see the famous holy mountain Machapuchare, also called "Fishtail" because of its shape (Fig. 1). We had time at last to relax on the shore of the Phewa Lake in the heart of Pokhara and we spent a few relaxing days there before returning to Kathmandu and then to Austria. I already knew very well that I would miss Nepal. But I didn't have to wait long for the next time.

I started out on my second Nepal trip already in February 2013, and this visit was to be something quite special! In 2012 I had thought about going on what was retrospectively to be a short trekking tour in Kathmandu Valley, so, while still in Austria, I contacted the trekking guide of my choice, Narendra: whatever happened, this time the trip was to last longer than two days. I had set my mind on visiting the

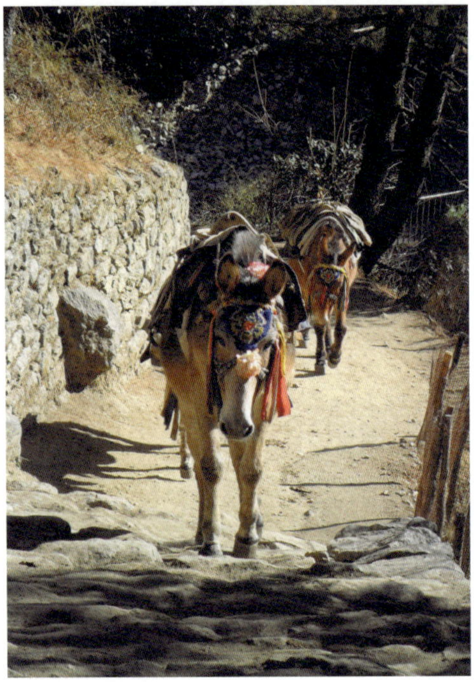

Fig. 10: The so-called "mountain taxis"

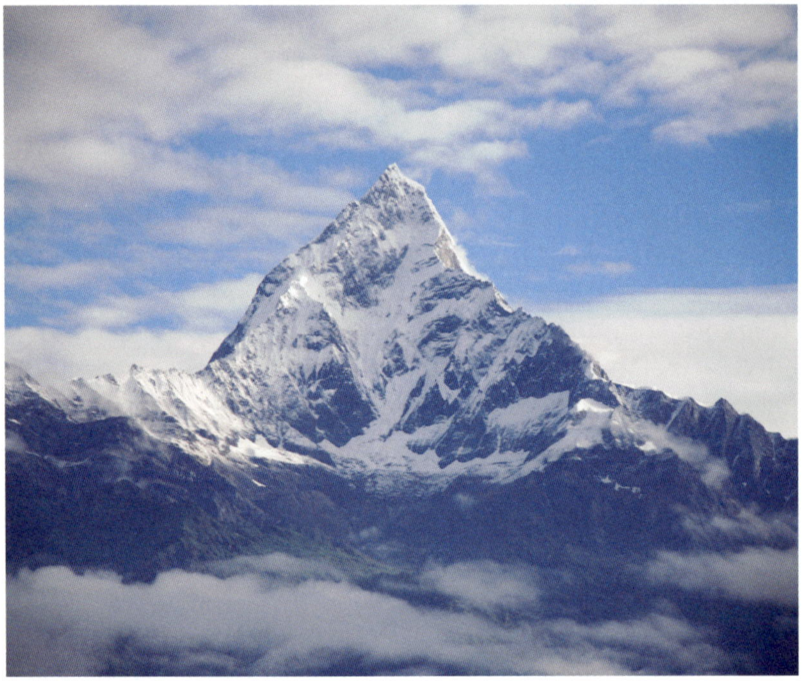

Fig. 1: The holy mountain Machapuchare, also called "Fishtail"

Fig. 7: The stage in our trek took us through many small villages

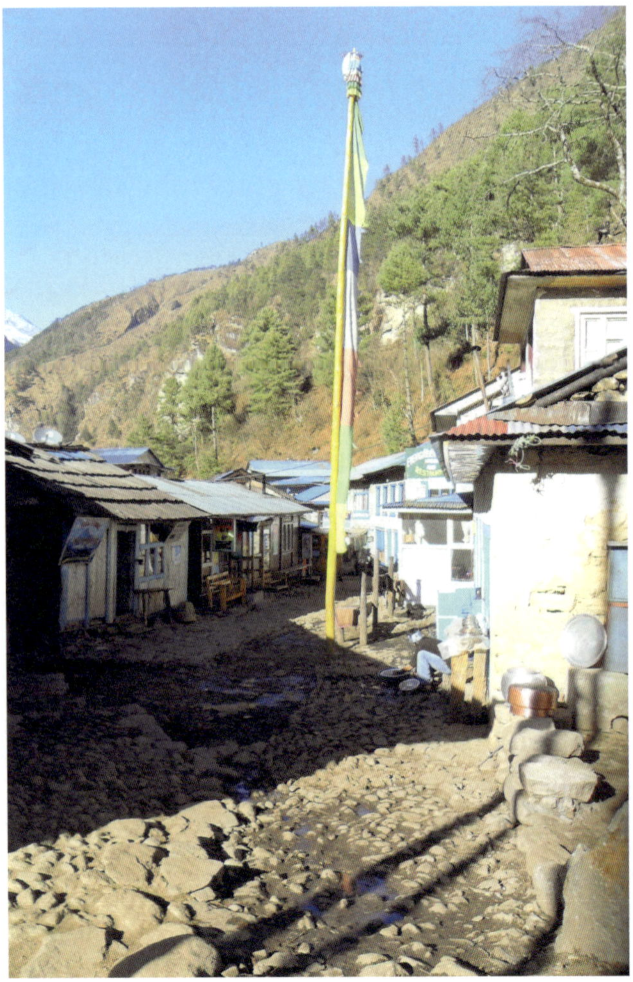

Fig. 5: On the way to Phagding, the villages with innumerable fields in the valley

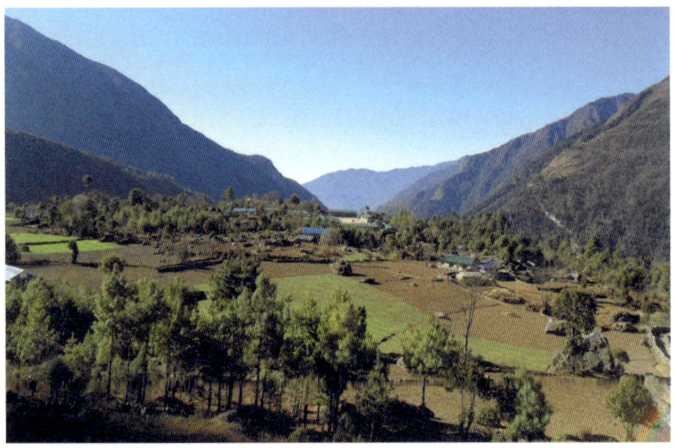

Fig. 4: Reinvigorated and ready for our trekking tour (from left to right Andrew, Claudia, Doris, me and our guide Narendra)

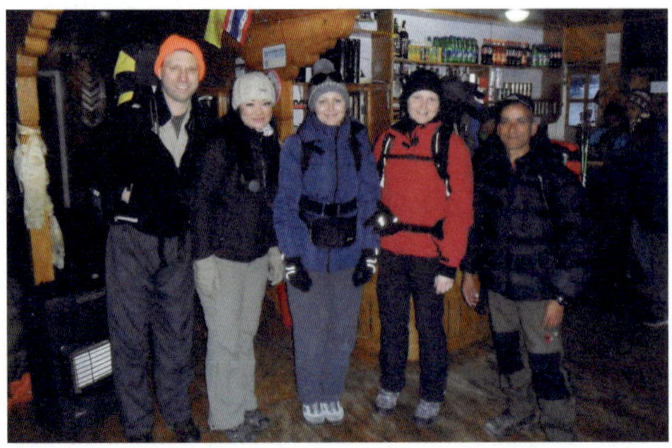

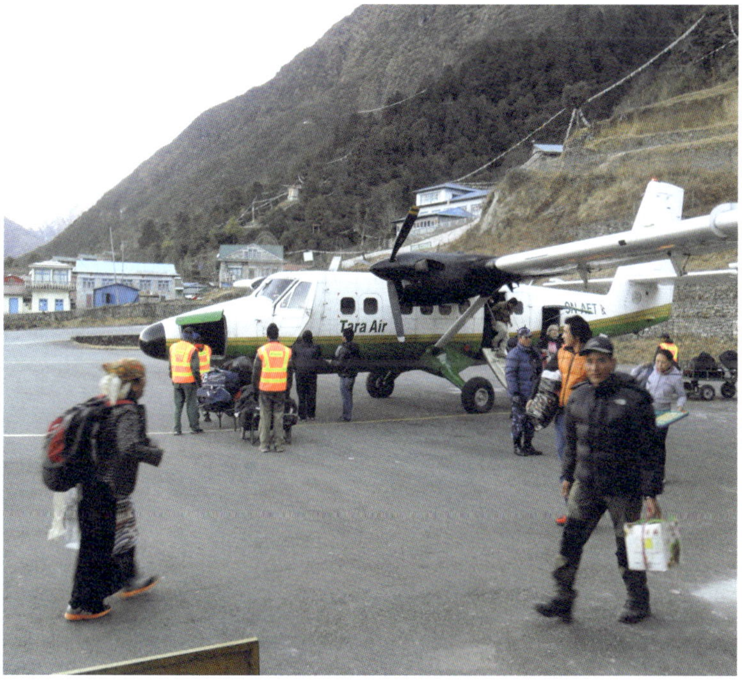

Fig. 2: Safe landing in Lukla

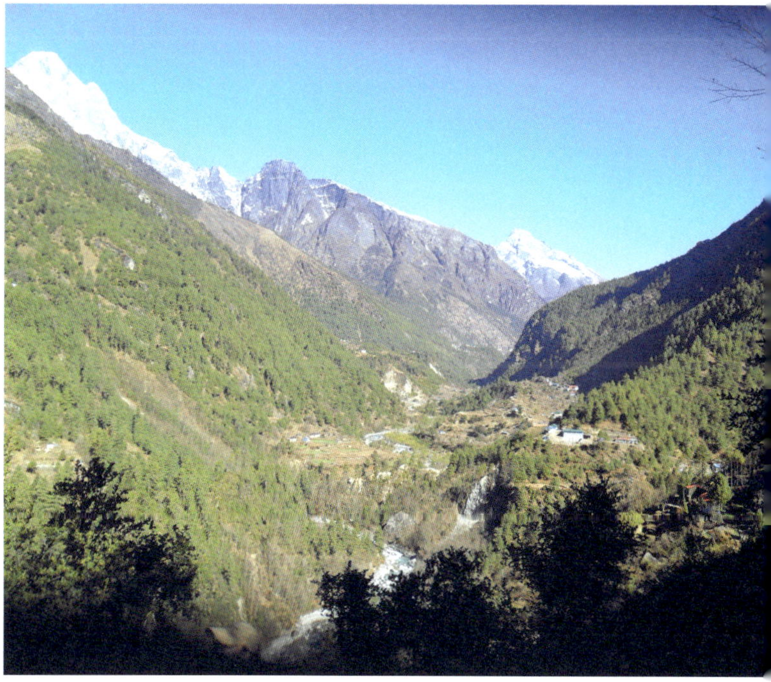

Fig. 6: Forests, rivers, mountains, in between an occasional house

Fig. 8: Our first hanging bridge with the colourful prayer flags; we would cross quite a few of them on our trip

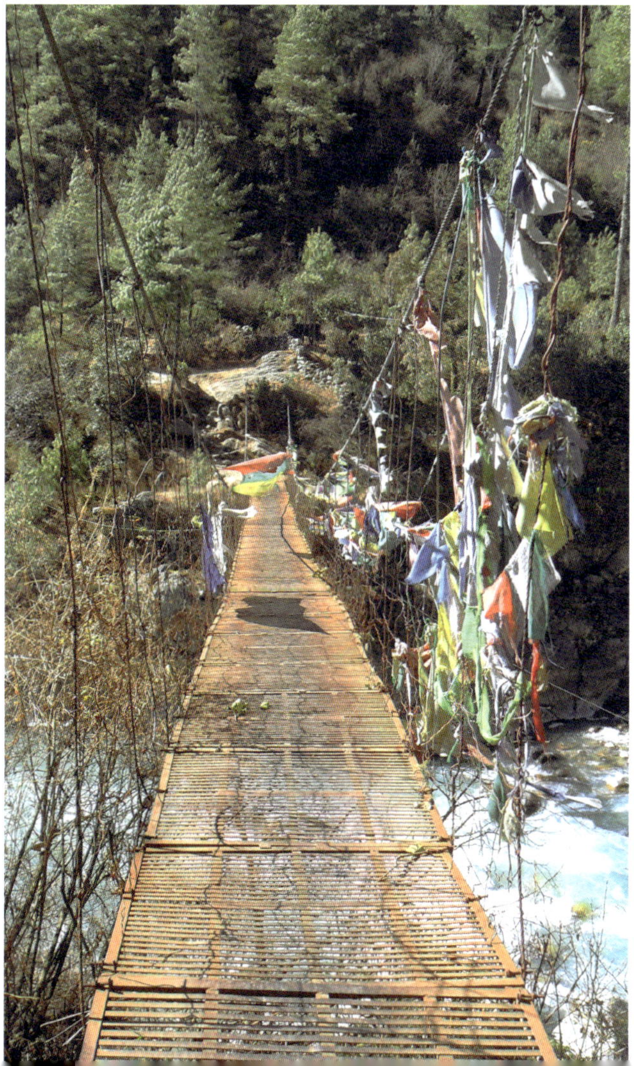

Fig. 9: Heavy loads are carried nimbly uphill

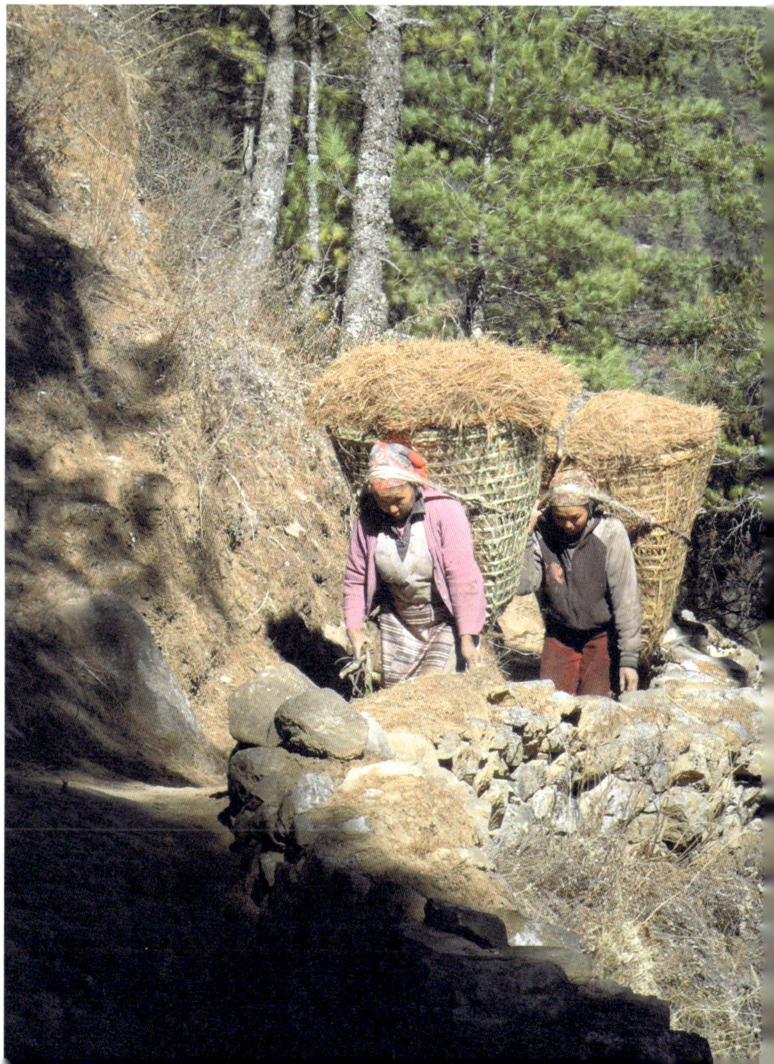

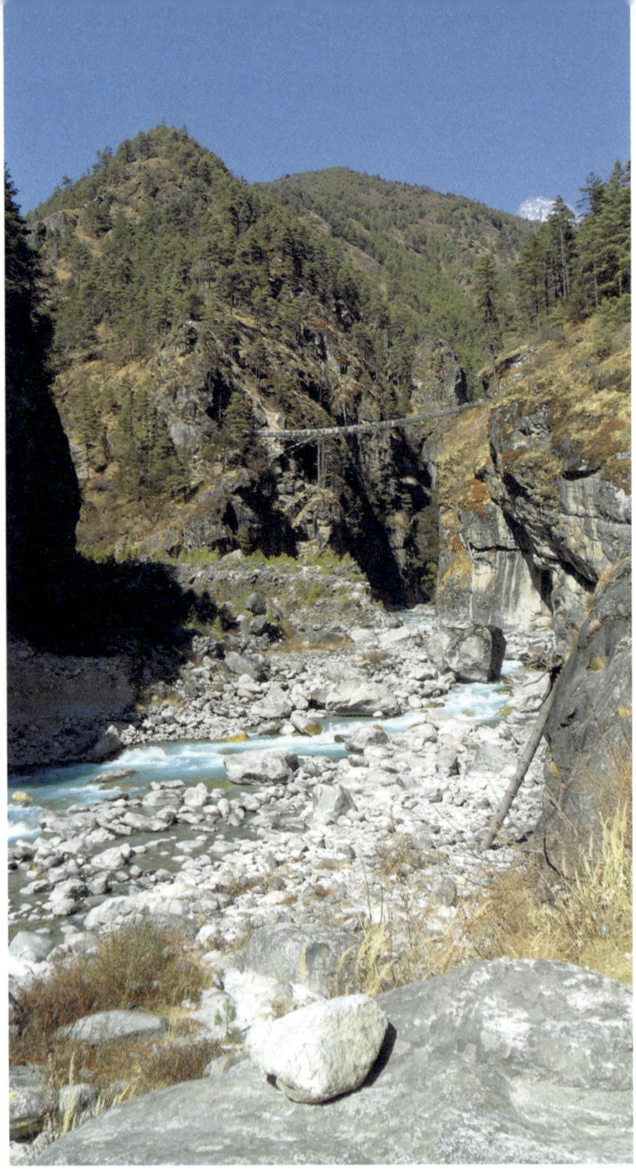

Fig. 11: Another hanging bridge shortly before the steep climb to Namche Bazaar

below: Fig. 13: Starting to feel the low temperatures
bottom: Fig. 12: View onto Namche Bazaar

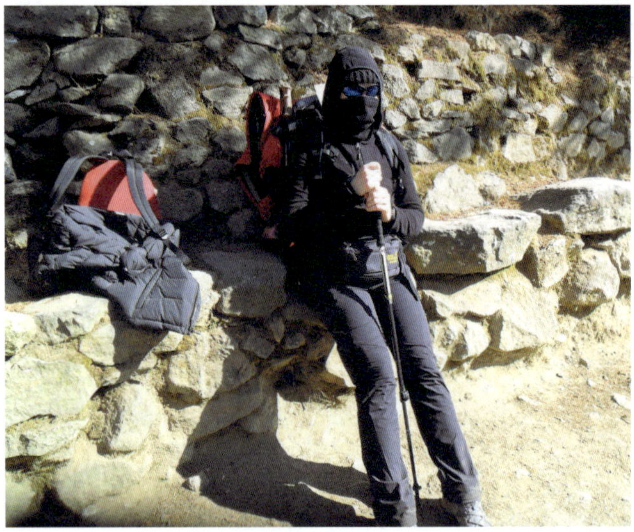

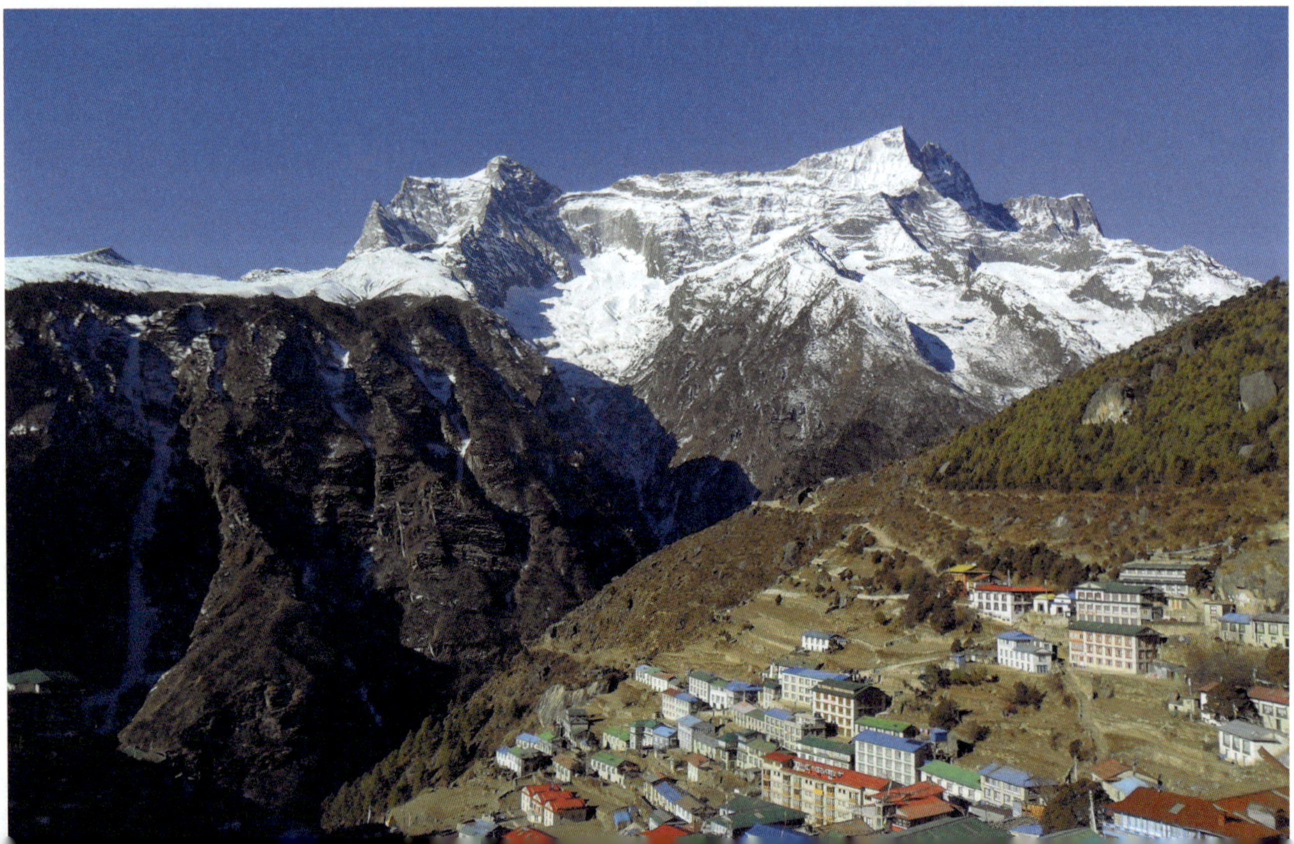

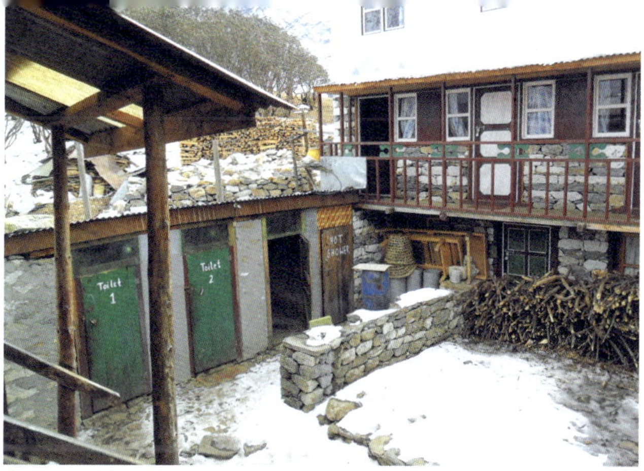

Fig. 15: Toilets and "hot shower" outside in the icy cold

below: Fig. 16: The monastery in Tengboche
bottom: Fig. 17: View onto Tengboche

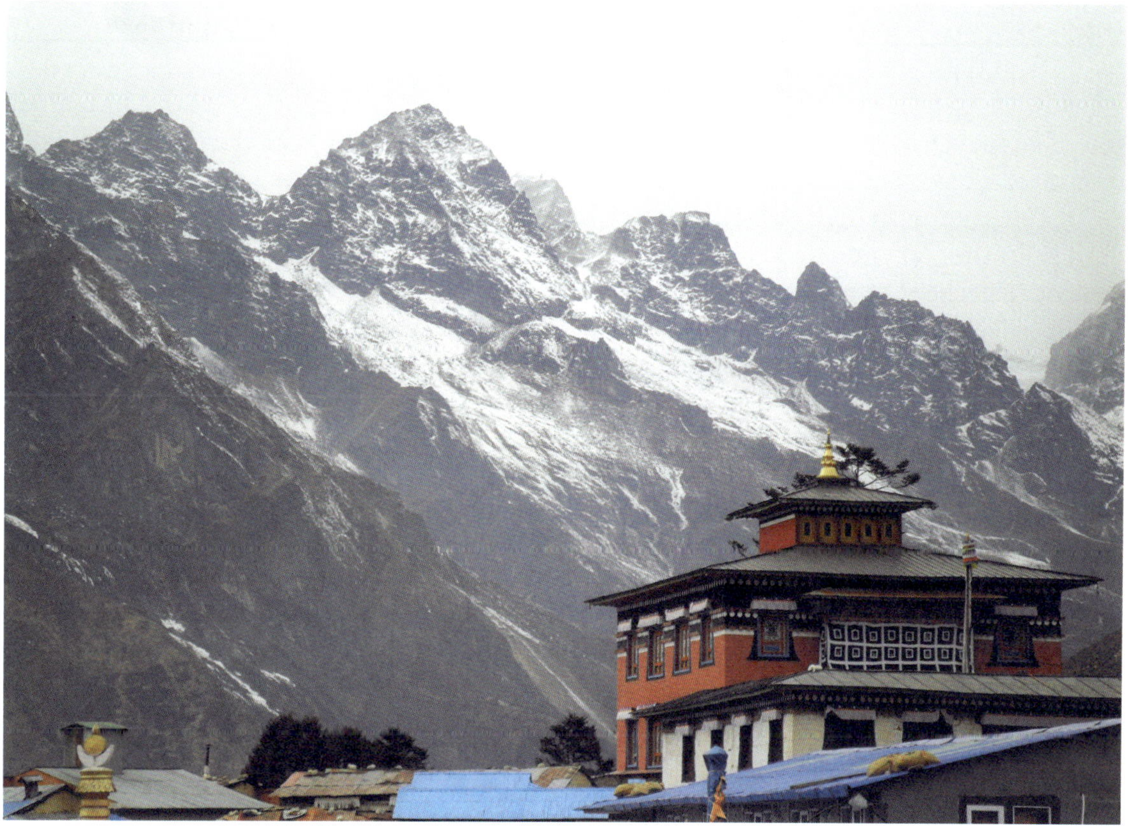

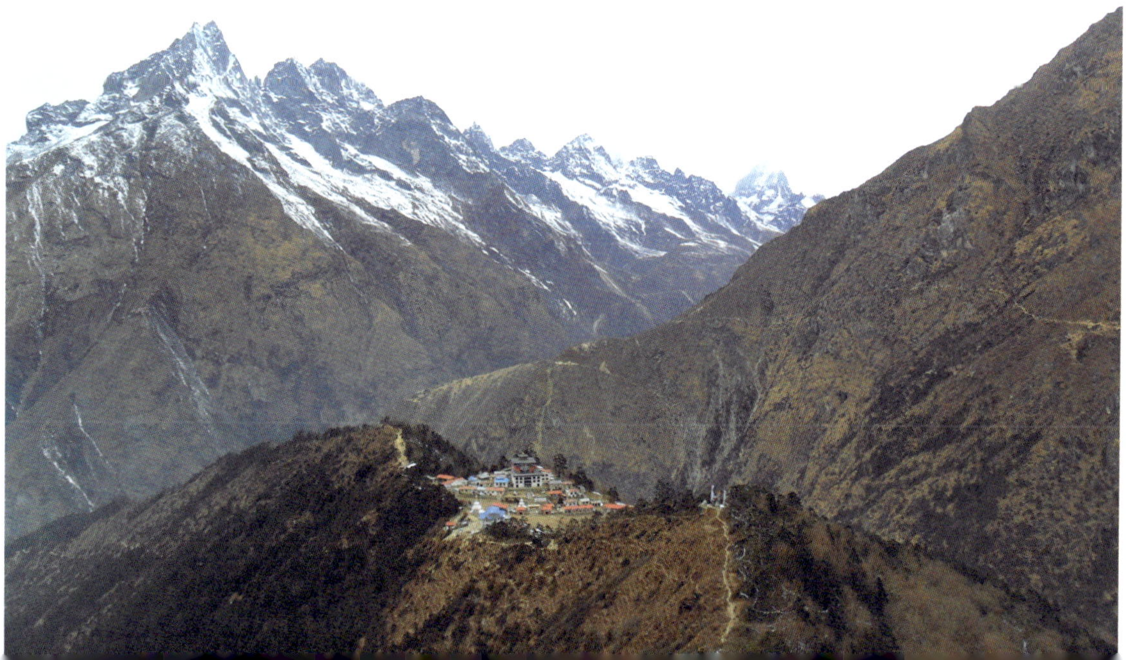

Everest Base Camp with my sister. But Narendra advised us not to do this on account of the low temperatures – they can drop down to minus 25°C or lower at night, clearly a little too bracing! But our guide immediately had an alternative at hand, also a great idea; the so-called "Mount Everest View" trekking tour. This took about seven days; you start out from Lukla; lots of breathtaking views awaited us during the tour. We thought this suggestion sounded very good and we decided to go on the said tour around the 9th of February. Narendra organised the inland flights and accommodation. Our tour was booked, I was simultaneously excited yet full of suspense as to what the land and people would be like outside the tourist season.

Together with my sister I arrived in Kathmandu in the morning of 8 February 2013, and Narendra greeted us at the airport with beautiful floral garlands. We all went by taxi to our hotel. The taxi ride was also a gripping experience because the action on the roads in Nepal's capital has to be seen to be believed. They teem not only with people, rickshaws, mopeds, countless cars, but also dogs and holy cows. It seems utter chaos, but thanks to the permanent honking of horns and our skilful driver it worked astonishingly well. In Nepal, honking horns seems to be a form of communication between the individual road users; you get accustomed to the noise, the extreme traffic and the crowds, fairly quickly.

On arrival at the hotel we first of all drank some Masala tea, typical of Nepal, a wonderfully aromatic tea made with milk and spices such as cardamom and cinnamon and lots of sugar. Now reinvigorated but still very fatigued from the long flight, we packed our things together for the tour. We quickly realised that we should only take the most essential stuff for our seven-day tour since we didn't intend to hire a sherpa as porter. We wanted at all costs to have the experience and find out what it's like to tramp around with baggage, sleeping bag and thermal mat on mountain passes and at unaccustomed altitudes. As we packed we also realised we would have to put up with quite a few privations during the tour. The equipment really did include only the most essential items: warm clothing, sleeping bag, toothbrush and -paste, soap and water. When we finished packing, we set off on a walk through Thamel. One souvenir shop after another lines the streets, in between we found several shops selling the final utensils for the trekking tour. The top floors are where night life is at home in Thamel, one bar or restaurant after the other. Besides the innumerable tourists, rickshaw drivers and mopeds, the streets also teemed with stray dogs in all this hustle and bustle.

We fortified ourselves for the coming days with a wonderful Buddhist meal, went back to the hotel, and so to bed.

The night was short and punctuated with the barking of dogs; at night the street belongs to the dogs, they mostly sleep during the day. But it may also have been the excitement that made the night seem so short because the next morning we were, after all, scheduled to land on the most dangerous airport in the world – Lukla. The alarm clock woke us at five o' clock and we readied our rucksacks. Soon we rode to the airport with Narendra. The flight was scheduled at seven o' clock, the airport didn't open until six.

The twin-engine propeller aircraft was ready and waiting. A few men wearing mouth masks and high-visibility waistcoats were stowing away all kinds of stuff, like food and other containers, in the tiny hold of the aircraft, then everything was crammed, non-slip, full of colourful trekking rucksacks. The two pilots with thick sunglasses and black leather jackets made some curt announcements to the ground crew and meanwhile checked the TARA AIR plane.

We boarded together with Narendra, our two trekking companions Claudia and Andrew from Hong Kong and seven other passengers – the plane only seated twelve passengers. The engines were already running; the flight attendant told us to wear earplugs against the deafening noise and gave us a sticky boiled sweet to suck. The flight from Kathmandu to Tenzing-Hillary Airport takes only 27 minutes. The ancient royal city of Kathmandu stretched out under us, veiled in smog, many buildings, a conglomeration of huts and settlements and thousands of motorbikes and cars. The city was waking up below us. After a short time the landscape changed to mountains, and we held our breath, because only a few metres separated wings and rock faces, at least that's the way it felt for us at that moment. The first, mighty, snow-capped mountains came into view – I couldn't believe I was really in a plane on the way to Lukla. A short time later, a little village came into view – Lukla. The short asphalt strip – only 527 metres long – was the runway with a twelve percent gradient. The pilot activated switches and pressed the buttons. He brought the aircraft down and with one hop we landed; in the same instant the end of the runway was in sight, a stone wall that zoomed nearer and nearer. The pilot throttled down the propellers, the plane slowed down and turned 90 degrees. We came to a stop and got out; we had arrived at last, at an altitude of 9,337 feet; it was cold, we were hungry but happy and curious as to what we would encounter in the next few days. Lukla is a pretty little tourist town where you can buy all kinds of souvenirs. It lies on the shadow side of a mountain, which is why it is somewhat cooler here and the wind blows ill, as Narendra explained to us. We boosted our energy with breakfast in Lukla before we were ready to take on the first stage of the trek (Fig. 2–4).

We hiked for about three hours without a break to Phagding (8,562 feet). This doesn't sound all that long, but one shouldn't forget the altitude, which we had to get used to. The difference in altitude of 5,905 feet between Kathmandu and Lukla, overcome in 27 minutes, was after all a minor shock for the body. The hike to Phagding offered wonderful views, the paths were lined with small stupas and stone houses, most of which had blue window frames (Fig. 5–7).

We arrived around midday and had time in the afternoon to explore the village and the surroundings. We went to the river with its beautiful, bright blue water, and to the hanging bridge gaily festooned with colourful prayer flags. The first night in the mountains was incredibly cold; luckily, we had packed enough warm things and had suitable sleeping bags. But we still slept in our hats and jackets.

The night was short and uncomfortable. I had to get used to the unheated rooms and simple plank beds with thin mattresses. Reinvigorated by breakfast, we started out from Phagding for Namche Bazaar (11,286 feet), one of the largest and prettiest mountain townships.

The way wasn't particularly difficult at the start, it was an easy route downhill and led alongside the river through patches of woodland and villages till we came to Sagamatha National Park. The people in the small villages spent most of the time outside, children sat next to elderly people in front of the houses and smiled at us. They placed their hands together in front of their chests and, with broad grins, wished us "namaste". We heard this greeting time and again, and it accompanied our entire journey.

The hiking paths were also used by the Nepalese – in contrast to us, they usually carried heavy baskets filled to the brim with food and all kinds of stuff they needed for their everyday life in the mountains. They attach their heavy load to their heads with a strap (Fig. 9). Narendra told us that up to a hundred kilograms of wares could be transported this way. Wearing light trainers or even only sandals, the Nepalese nimbly negotiate the stony paths with their heavy burdens. We also had to dodge nimbly when bells announced oncoming traffic on the paths – horses, cattle, donkeys or yaks, also heavily laden, would come at us. The Nepalese drove the animals with sticks and wore a scarf at their mouths against all the dust swirling up from the animals' progress. Narendra charmingly entitled the pack animals as "mountain taxi" (Fig. 10).

After the entrance gate to the national park, the way led downhill again for a short time, past a waterfall, then went steeply uphill. The highlight of this stage in the trip was certainly the Hillary hanging bridge. It took quite a bit of pluck, however, to cross it at this dizzying height. But since hundreds of heavy yaks, too, are driven across the bridge every day, we could trust its stability.

Now our first view of the roof of the world, Mount Everest (29,029 feet), opened up before us, the Nuptse (25,679 feet) at its left and the Lhotse (27,940 feet) at the right, which to us seemed somewhat higher than the famous Mount Everest. Only now did I become really aware of the dimensions in which we were moving. Surrounded by the highest mountains in the world, we were ourselves situated at an altitude of 11,482 feet; it was an indescribable feeling (Fig. 12). We hiked on for another two hours and arrived at last in Namche Bazaar in the early afternoon. The name Namche Bazaar means "Common Market". The Tibetans came here along countless paths across the mountains to sell their wares. A sea of buildings, mostly used as hotels and lodges, spread out across the entire valley, surrounded by giant mountains. You really can buy almost everything in Namche Bazaar, besides souvenirs you can find European food here as well, even at this altitude (Fig. 12–13).

Over our evening meal together we discussed the plan for the following days. An acclimatisation day was on the agenda in order to accustom our bodies and circulatory system to the altitude. So the next morning we set off on a cosy little hike around Teng Boche. The temperatures were distinctly more unpleasant than in Lukla; we tramped along wearing hoods and hats again, and this time with a scarf before our mouths to protect ourselves from the cold air – we had no desire to catch the so-called "Khumbu cough", which is caused by the ice-cold air.

First of all we hiked around Namche Bazaar. We made our way to a vantage point from where we could see Mount Everest, Ama Dablam, Lhotse and other giants. We spent a long time lingering at this point. The view was breathtaking, and it was absolutely impossible to capture and absorb the impressions. Overwhelmed by this panorama, we set out again and treated ourselves to coffee and tea in the Everest Panorama Hotel, a café with genuinely the best view you can imagine. Back in Namche Bazaar, we explored the village and ended up in a bar. Since we were touring outside the usual tourist season, we were the only guests. We enjoyed the peace and quiet, before we met again for supper in our digs and, again at an early hour, went to our cold beds – we wanted to set off again early in the morning (Fig. 14).

After an opulent breakfast, Narendra, my sister, and I set off again, this time to Tencboche (12,664 feet). Our two companions from Hong Kong had to spend another night in Namche Bazaar because they were feeling the first symptoms of mountain sickness. This manifested itself, among other complaints, as headache, nausea and dizziness. During our hike of around six hours we went uphill, down dale, through forests, along rocky paths past little stone houses, yaks and the locals resting on benches. We noticed the temperature dropping more and more. Soon we saw the famous Buddhist monastery of Tengboche. The small village of Tengboche lies at the foot of the north wall of Thamserku and extends over a broad saddle covered with grass. It is surrounded by a half-moon-shaped ridge covered in rich woodland. Although Tengboche seemed so close, we had a two-hour hike in front of us. Having finally arrived, we were glad of the well-deserved rest and looked forward to exploring the village and the monastery. We left our luggage in the very plain and simple room and had a look around. The toilets and showers were only accessible across the snow-covered hotel courtyard. One thing we were already sure of: once again we would have to face a very cold night (Fig. 15).

We were allowed to view the monastery prayer room and also marvel at the daily prayers and ceremonies. The monks wore modern trainers and thick down jackets under their familiar wine-red habits. A monk gave us warm tea during the prayers, which we gladly drank; it was just as cold inside the monastery as outside. Afterwards, my sister and I roamed around the village and discovered another hiking path. We followed it, just a section of it at first, then on and on, always upwards. At around 13,780 feet we took a break and had a short rest. We could hardly tear our eyes away from the wonderful panorama and spent what seemed like an eternity there at this height until our tummies rumbled and we returned to our digs. For supper there was warm soup and tea; the only heating was a small fireplace in the middle of the room. Tired, happy and replete, we went to our rooms. We got ready for the cold night; we needed everything we had brought with us to wear. Under bedcover, sleeping bag and several layers of functional clothing we spent probably the coldest night of our lives at around -15° C (Fig. 16–19).

For breakfast there was wonderfully warm porridge and hot tea; we were already on the

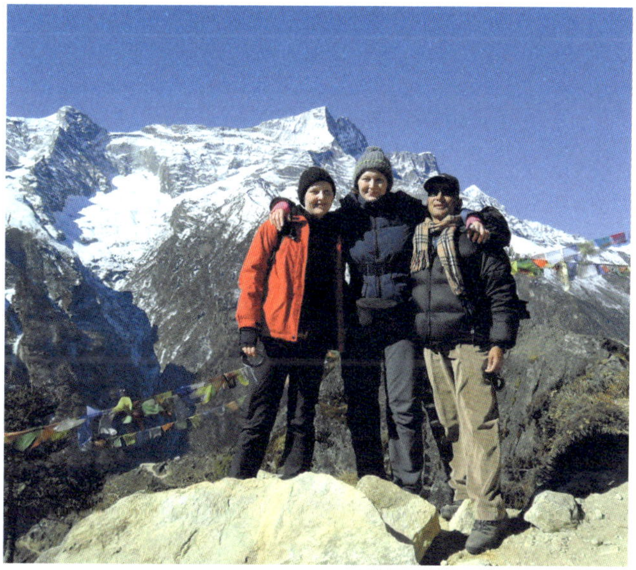

Fig. 14: Together with our guide Narendra

road again at seven o' clock in the morning. We hiked through Khumjung (12,401 feet), which is likewise renowned for its Tibetan monastery. The famous Hillary School is also located in this small and quiet township, surrounded by snow-covered mountains and hills. Our group was reunited back in Namche Bazaar. Together we made our way down to Phagding. The way was easier now, despite the innumerable herds of donkeys, yaks and horses in the retinue of singing herdsmen whom we met on the way. We spent another night in Phagding before returning to Lukla (Fig. 20-21).

After a three-hour, easy ramble, we were back at our starting point in Lukla. We still had enough time to explore the area; our flight was scheduled to leave at seven the next morning. The alarm went off already at five o' clock. Looking forward to our return but also feeling sad at leaving, we fell on our breakfast and got ready for the flight. But Lukla didn't want us to leave. It had snowed in the night and the runway was covered in snow. Because of the weather and bad visibility, planes were not permitted to start from Kathmandu in the direction of Lukla; so there was no plane in Lukla either. We were stranded. So we spent the day lazing around in our digs and passed the time playing cards and going for walks. The next day was the same routine all over again. The alarm went off at five o' clock. We were all ready to leave, everything was packed. Full of hope we set off. But it wasn't meant to be. There was still snow on the runway, bad weather was forecast. Another day in cold and windy Lukla, in the cold digs, no hot water, only boredom. Once again we strolled through the surroundings and hoped the weather would improve. With lots of hot tea and thick blankets we could withstand the rigours of our stay until we fell into bed in the evening, tired again from hanging around and doing nothing. And the alarm went off again at five in the morning and yet again we packed our things together in the hope of a flight. All good things come in threes. We waited, full of suspense. And then, at last, at nine in the morning, we got the go-ahead for the longed-for flight. We were over the moon with joy and while still at the airport we dreamed of a hot shower in the hotel (Fig. 22-23).

Back in Kathmandu we had to get used to the noise and bustle all over again. We were so satiated with the wonderful views in the mountains, from the peace and quiet and the many impressions we had been so privileged to experience during the last nine days.

It was a tour full of privations, lots of laughter, fatigue, happiness, but also, and most of all, a great deal of cold. Nevertheless, I shall never forget the breathtaking landscapes, the life in the lodges and the unique culture, also the view of the highest mountain in the world. And as I left the country I thought yet again how much I would miss Nepal and its people, the landscape, the friendliness and the smiles.

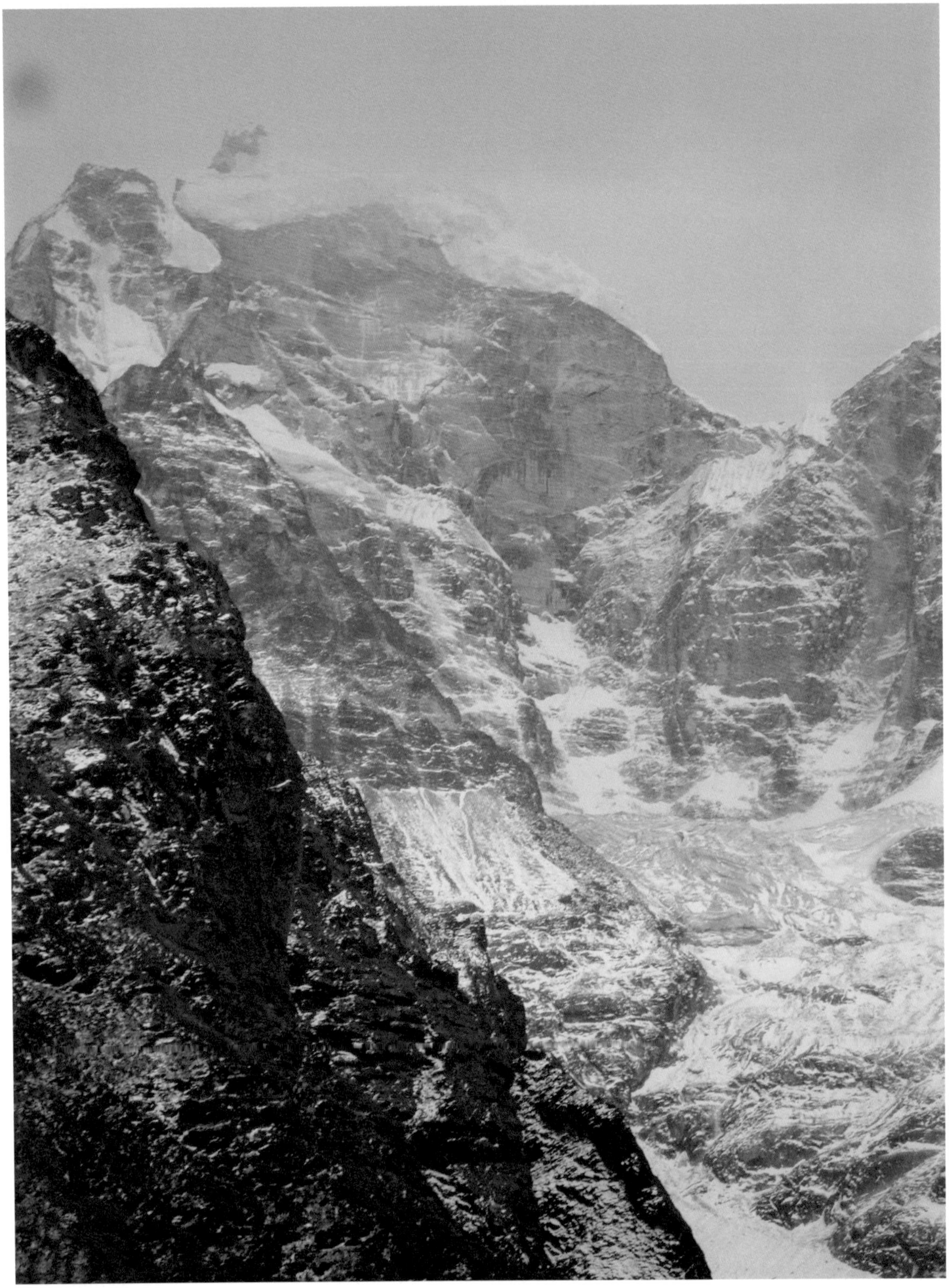

Fig. 18: Incredible mountain formations and icy cold

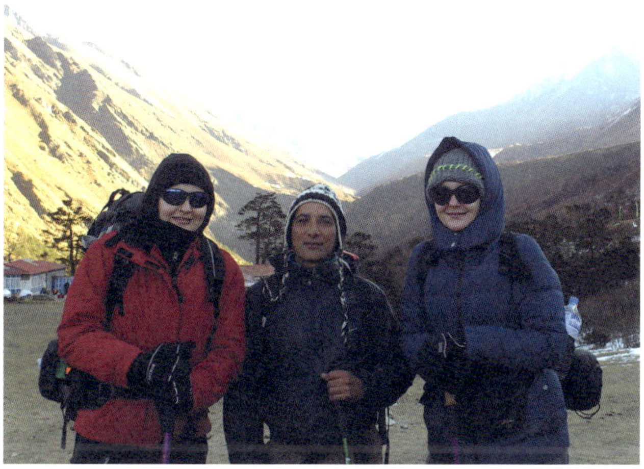

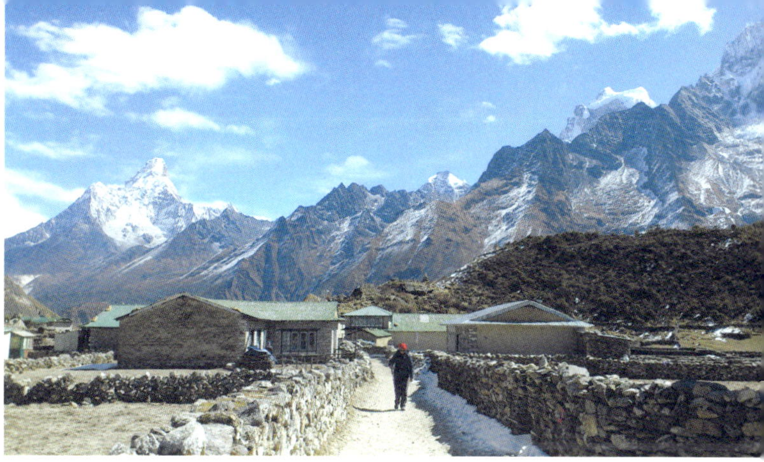

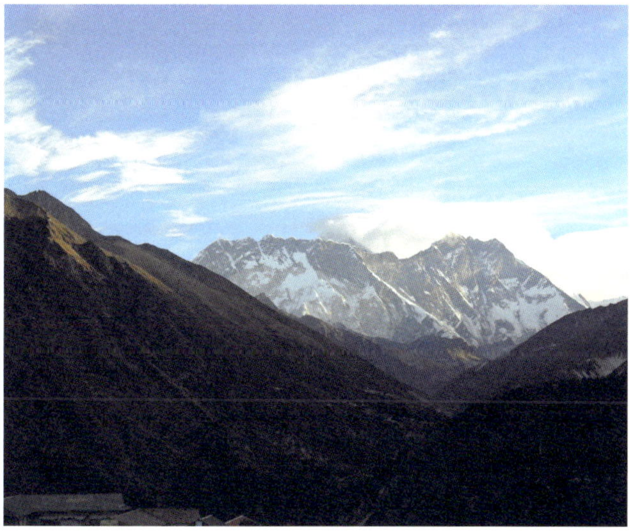

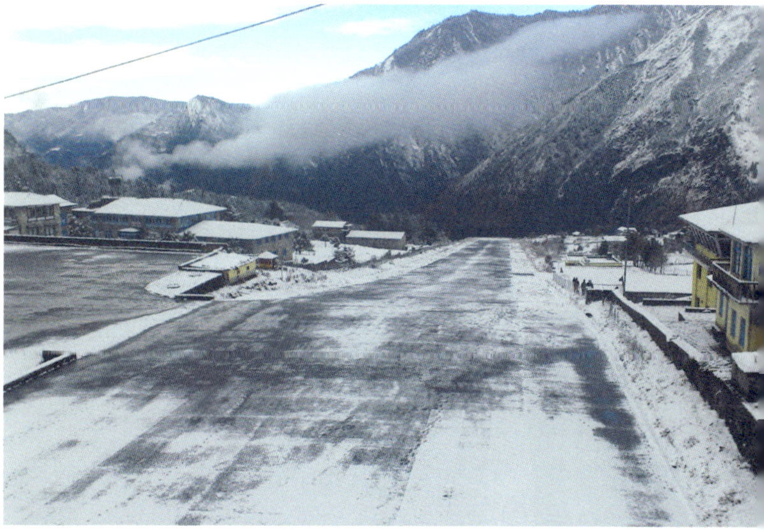

above: Fig. 20: Before going back to Namche Bazaar we enjoyed the wonderful view once more

Fig. 19: Mount Everest in a shy mood

above: Fig. 21: The way through Khumjung

Fig. 22: The snowed-up runway in Lukla

Fig. 23: At last, sitting in the plane on the way to Kathmandu

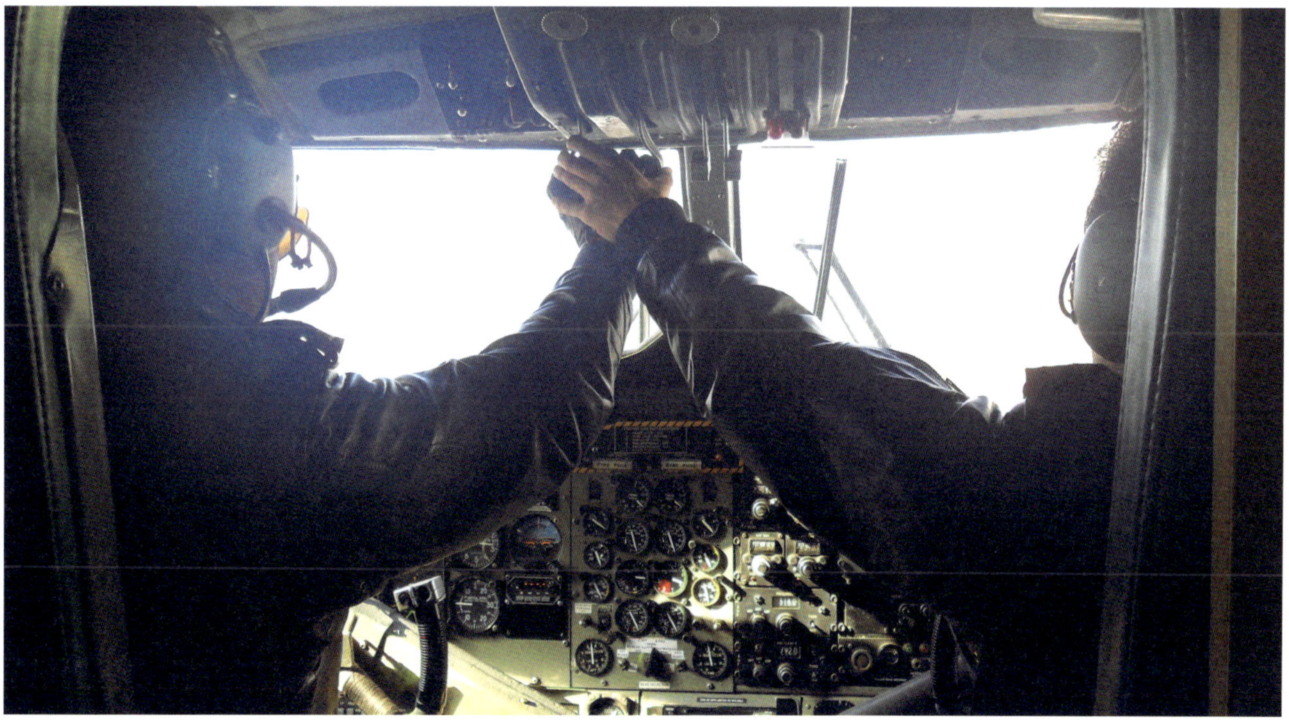

My Very Own Nepal

KATHARINA
FUCHS

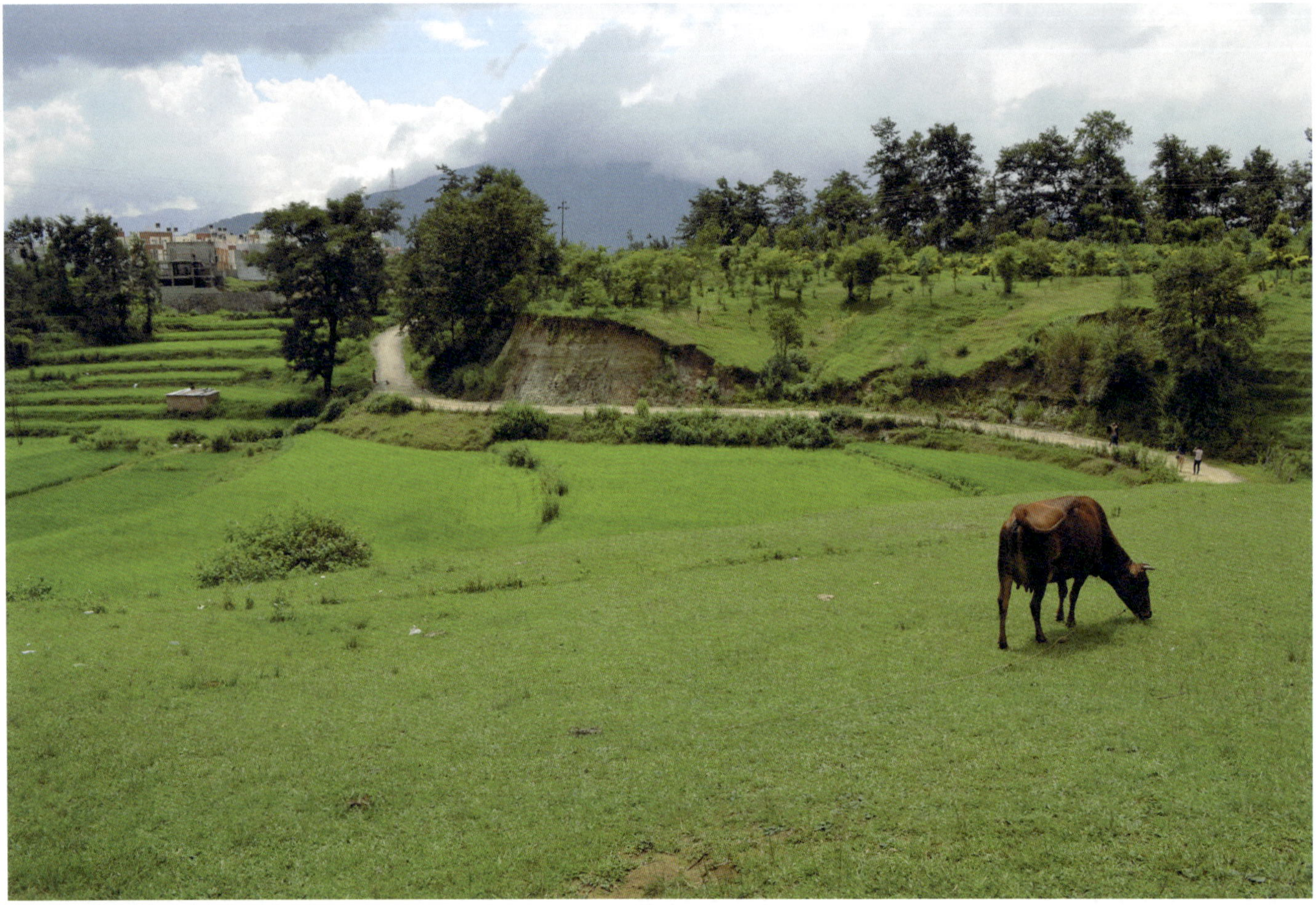

Fig. 1: Outskirts of Kathmandu

Whenever I hear anything about the country of Nepal my heart beats faster. Ever since my first trip to the country between the two giants, India and China, it has had an important place in my life.

During my studies, I had the good fortune of being involved – and not only once – in the preservation of important cultural assets. In fact, I was even able to take part, four times, as a student in the conservation campaigns of the Institute of Conservation at the World Heritage Site on Patan Durbar Square. Besides this extraordinary experience of working with local people on a still-living cultural site, my second stay gave me the chance to gather some other impressions.

Helene, a friend of many years who, apart from her activities as an expert in her profession, is enthusiastically committed to social work, gave me a very different view of the everyday life of children in this cultural environment. By chance, Helene and I were in the land of the high mountains at the same time. When I arrived in summer 2012, Helene had already been living in Kathmandu for six months and was working in a social project as a teacher and carer of children of various ages. For our first meeting I invited her to our construction site in Patan. She didn't want to miss the chance to watch us at work. Meeting someone I know from my immediate family circle so far away from our home country did seem somewhat bizarre. Nevertheless, I was overjoyed to show her our work in more detail and to be able to explain everything, which she followed with great interest.

We decided even before this first meeting that after the conservation campaign I would come and stay with her for a few days and get to know her current day-to-day life before setting out on a short trip. But as simple as this sounds, things can turn out just as complicated. Taxi and bus strikes are relatively common in the conurbation of Kathmandu, and so, as fate would have it, also on the day I wanted to set out to see my friend. She had lived in Kathmandu quite a long time, so she was quite cool about everything and immediately sent me an alternative means of transport. The other students were all having to wait for some kind of transportation to the airport, when a young man, who I would say looked more like a lad of around thirteen, picked me up on a purple motorbike. There I was, cram-packed with my huge trekking rucksack, supposed to climb onto the motorbike with this young man, who was probably half my size? No way. But what other options did I have? As is usual in Nepal, he naturally didn't have a helmet, and one for me even less. But what could happen after all; you can't drive faster than 60 km/h on these roads in any case. On one hand, the road is only maintained to an improvised degree; you often encounter potholes and a lack of asphalt paving; on the other, this is because the roads are multifunctional spaces. Besides the chaotic commotion of a motley variety of transport vehicles, pedestrians also wander along the road; in between, you come across a dizzying array of vendor booths being surveyed by man, woman and beast. Also, any rubbish or waste products land directly on the carriageway, which is often a favourite spot for a cow to have a doze.

Awkwardly – because of the weight on my back – I heaved myself onto the chugging vehicle, which immediately sagged down under my weight. My colleagues watched, highly amused, and wished me a good time, and I wished them bon voyage. Then we were off. Despite the strike, the roads were jam-packed with other motorbikes and cars – naturally, they all had to get from A to B off their own bat. Because the school where Helene worked was located on the north side of Kathmandu, we had to cross through the entire city. During the journey I felt the dry air and the dust on my skin. All kinds of smells – petrol, fried food, the mouldy smell of the Bagmati River, kept rising into my nose. I was happy when I had terra firma under my feet again and even more so when Helene greeted me.

Scarcely arrived, I immediately noticed how green this district was. Nature was tangible again for the first time for ages; my colleagues and myself had lived and worked directly on Patan Durbar Square, so we hardly ever got out of town. Here, on the outskirts of the city, the lush green of the surrounding jungle merged with the brick-red of the buildings into a fascinating new landscape.

Arriving in the "Hostel", as the school where Helene worked was called, the first

Fig. 2: Children from the hostel, volunteers and me

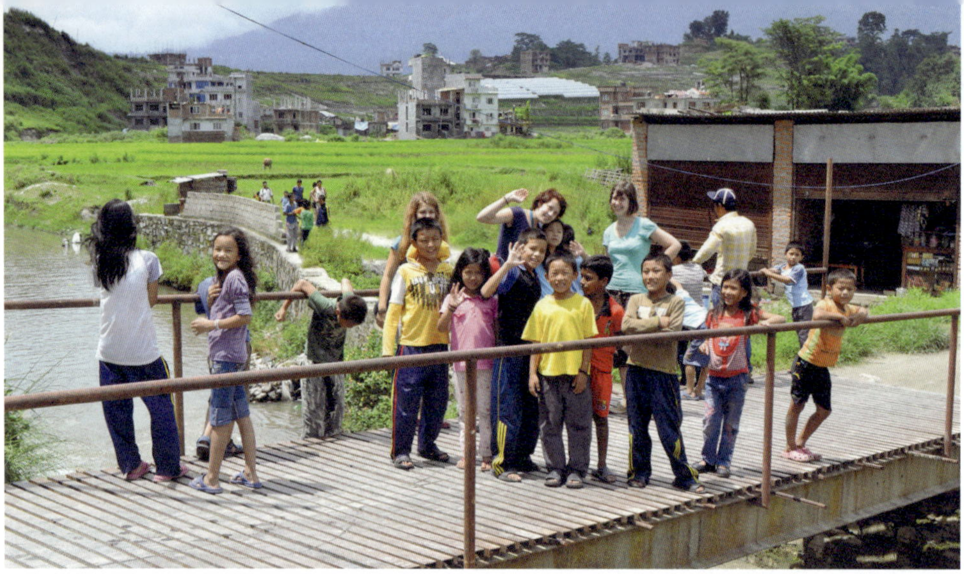

Fig. 3: Nepalese with their goats in the suburbs of Kathmandu

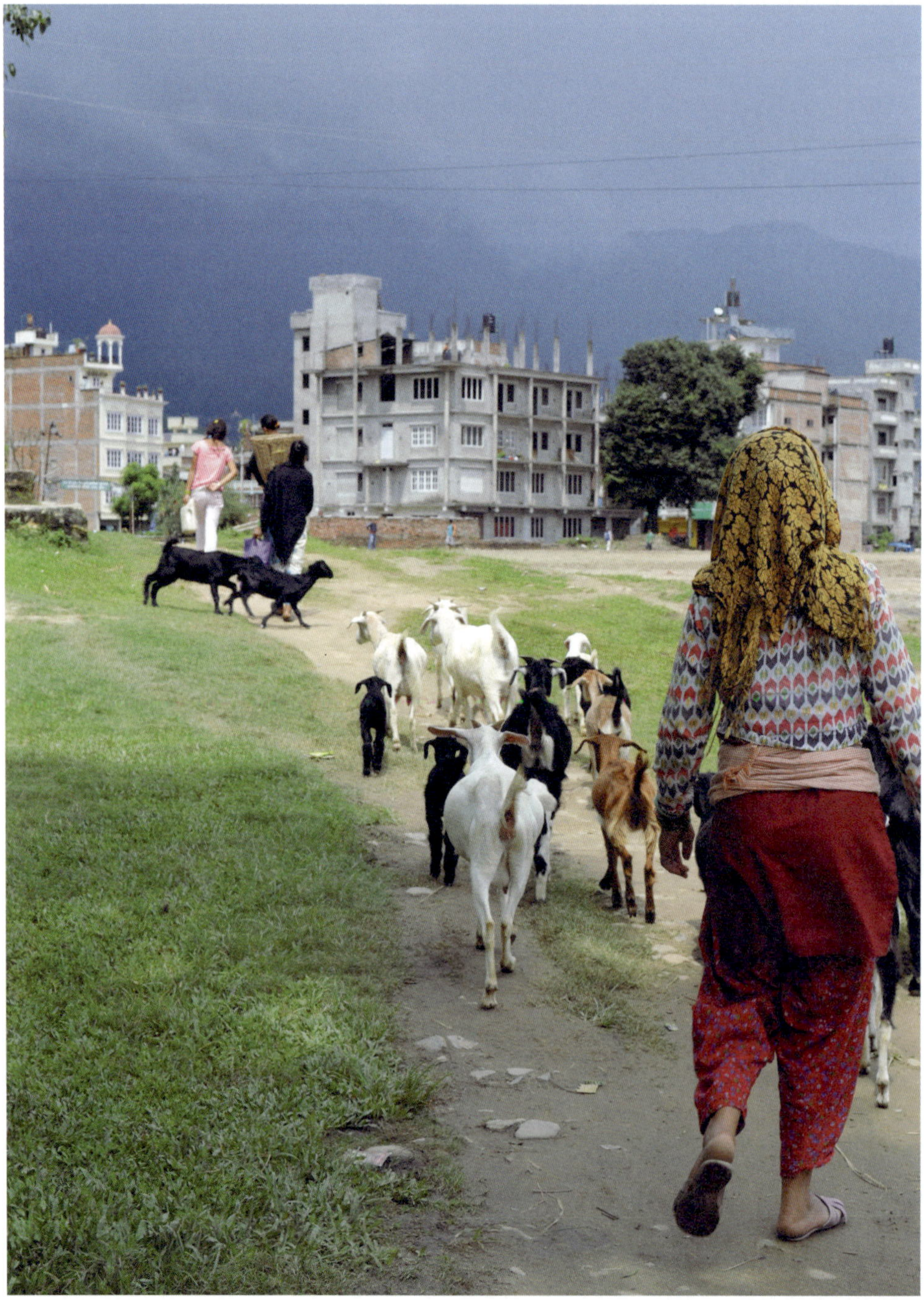

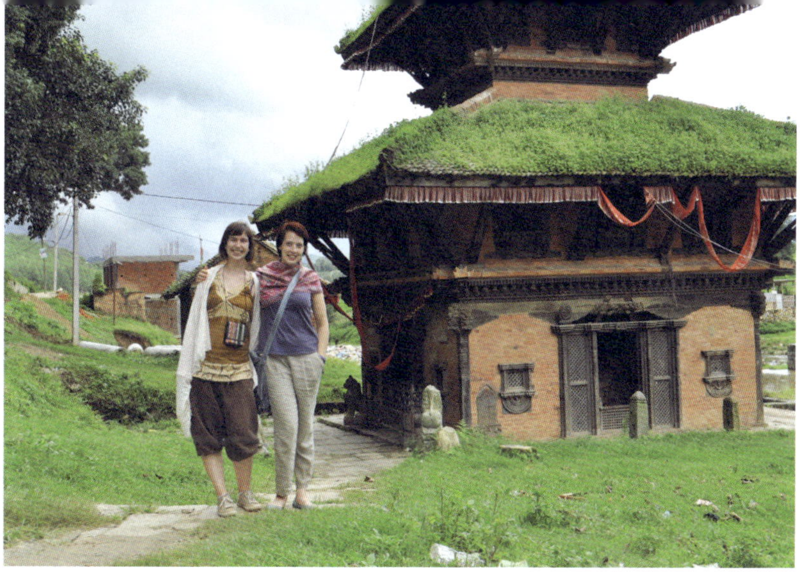

Fg.4: Heli and me during the trekking tour in the city of Panauti

Fig. 5: Monastery Namo Buddha

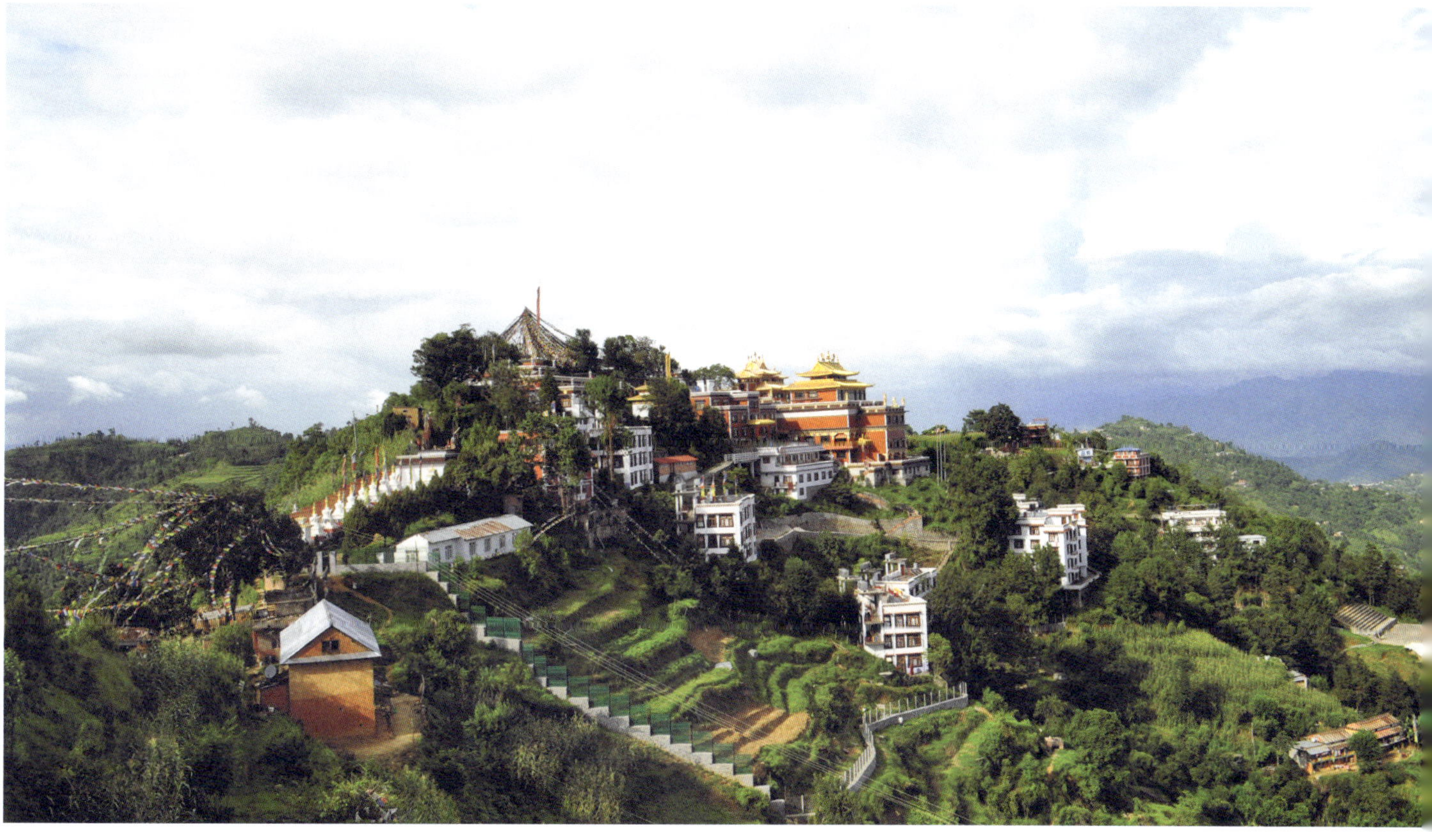

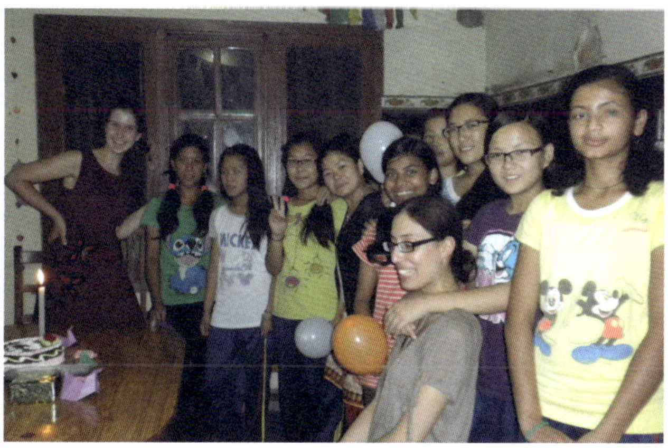

Fig. 7: Birthday party at the Hostel

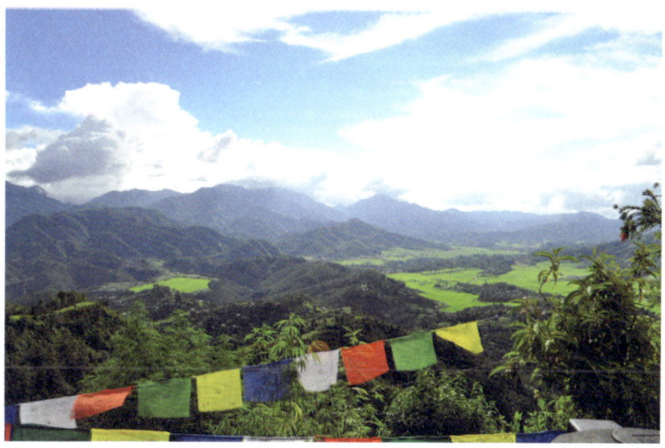

Fig. 6: View from Namo Buddha monastery

thoughts came into my head as to how I would at all imagine what a Nepalese orphanage/ boarding school/school would be like, since I also went to a boarding school. The building used by the social organisation was not at all how we would imagine a traditional boarding school in Austria. Not only children lived here, but also teachers and in some cases even the children's parents. The building complex was flanked by two higher concrete buildings at each end of the grounds. The children's living and common rooms were at the right. As in most new buildings in the Kathmandu Valley, the living rooms are painted turquoise. During my arrival a film was being shown; it was probably the only television in the building complex, in the children's common room. It was a documentary about elephants, watched with thrilled intensity by countless children's eyes in a sweaty, clammy room, also painted turquoise.

The connection to the other concrete building on the left side accommodating the school and the canteen led past tiny corrugated iron huts jostled together. Several elderly people stared out of doors or from behind curtains. Among all these corrugated iron huts I noticed a dripping tap; I can no longer remember its appearance, but nevertheless, it remained strongly impressed in my mind. I immediately asked myself whether it was the only water main connection for all the huts. At the end of the way, I arrived at an area of concrete, the back courtyard of the school building where the youth of the Hostel played football and basketball.

As a newcomer it's difficult to remain undiscovered, and the children and young people wanted to show and tell me about all kinds of things. The girls especially were fascinated by a new woman. As I soon noticed, the separation of the sexes that occurred to me in Nepal is already firmly anchored in the children's heads. Many young couples in public places seemed more remote from each other than close and often met secretly in quieter places. Groups of friends likewise tend to split up according to gender. This traditionally characterised social behaviour was confirmed for me even more when on the next day I got to know a young pair from Germany who were doing voluntary work here for a year. The young Nepalese girls well-nigh swooned over the tall, blond young man with blue eyes and kept asking if he was engaged already and when the wedding would be. The romantic dream of the great love of one's life is no different here from the rest of the world.

On the same day we decided to go on a walk along with a group of children to a small shrine near the building complex. Tradition and the modern age collide on the outskirts of a cosmopolitan city of a million inhabitants. Next to countrywomen in the paddy fields surrounded by cows and goats, high-rise towers are pounded up out of nothing. Landscape and urban planning seem non-existent. Nevertheless, the free-and-easy life of the country is already the rule here; laughing children romped through the meadows, women looked up briefly to see where the noise was coming from and then went on with their work. Some children simply loved for us to pick them up while we chatted in the shade about this and that; among the things we talked about was how most of the children in the Hostel seem to come from the Solokhumbu region south of Mount Everest. The villages are difficult to access, and accordingly the access to education, therefore they come to school here on the outskirts of the city of Kathmandu. Families from the region join the social project and move into the capital to make a new start.

In the next few days Helene and I made our way along the edge of the Kathmandu Valley. We started out from Panauti in the direction of the Namo Buddha Monastery (Fig. 5). It was only when we arrived at the monastery that we were told we had started our hike in the wrong direction. In Buddha's native country care should be taken always to walk in a clockwise direction. We should have started our tour in the completely opposite direction. Despite our faux pas, we had a wonderful trip. I don't think Buddha would have been displeased with us because of this. From then on, I made sure I planned my trips and hikes in Nepal in a clockwise direction.

The first impressions of the monastery – the landscape, the view, the building and the busy activities of monks and visitors – were fascinating (Fig. 6). Opposite the monastery there was a kind of grocer's shop with a small café. Here we found a mixed crowd, not only tourists but also young people and monks. Since it was again a hot day, we decided to make the most of the terrace and, over chilled drinks, watch everything going on around us. My idealistic imaginings of the life of a monk in the Himalayas were put into proper focus here. With an enraptured smile, I realised how much these people in this little shop were enjoying life. Their activities – besides relishing sweet things and meat products – consisted as well in a rapid initiation into the World Wide Web via the WIFI available here. Here, reality showed up my naiveté for what it was. Why shouldn't people who are committed to the teachings of Buddha pursue the enjoyments and activities of the present day as well?

I enjoyed the stay in the monastery very much, although we were awakened with the monks at five o'clock for the two hours of morning prayer. The communal praying was very meditative, although my thoughts always wandered to the pain in my legs, which weren't accustomed, and never will be, to remain in a lotus position for any length of time. Breakfast consisted of the typical steamed dumpling, called Thingmo, and the traditional butter tea. It also took place in the temple and was served by younger monks. The butter tea is topped up until you cover the cup with your hand. We didn't know anything about this at first, and so we were served oodles of tea, although I had had quite enough after one cup of this salty-tasting drink. The monastery only has vegetarian food, which I, as a vegetarian, was very pleased about. Yet the monks are not obliged to do without animal products. Time and again, I saw notices exhorting people to vegetarianism.

During the stay I noticed parallels to the Hostel. Despite strict discipline, seen already in the youngest monks, some of those dwelling here were children. Probably the times they ran around in the grounds laughing and having fun were in the breaks between learning and prayer. This short stay at the monastery remains in my memory even now as one of the most wonderful private experiences I ever had in Nepal.

We hiked around for several days and then came to Kathmandu for the birthday of a voluntary worker. The Hostel children wanted to organise a birthday party for her. The Hotel girls wanted to make every effort for the party; besides decorations, henna and sweets, they planned to serve the coveted prawn chips as a snack. Our Central European gastronomic counter-offensive took the shape of Kaiserschmarren – "Emperor's Nonsense" – cut-up pancakes (more or less). During the preparations, everyone sang and danced to blaring local pop music. Of course, you can't have a party without a birthday cake and small presents. The Kaiserschmarren was a flop with the Nepalese children and was thrown aside. As soon as the oven was free, the boys leaped over to fry the prawn fritters. After the cake was cut I got to know a new tradition. When you congratulate the birthday girl or boy, you have to shove a piece of cake into his or her mouth. Thank goodness it wasn't my birthday! I could never have stomached so much cake. But it was fun to watch how they all stuffed something into the birthday girl's mouth. Afterwards, the many henna packets were opened and the mood quietened down somewhat as they all concentrated on painting skin. My hands and arms were covered completely with all kinds of floral tendrils and volutes. The party came to a sudden end, typical of a country feast, because of a power cut.

I can no longer say exactly whether this was the last evening of this particular visit to Nepal. It was certainly shortly before my journey home. My flight was in the early afternoon, so Helene and I went for breakfast together in town. We spent our last morning together in Kathmandu in the "1905", the historic building named after the year it was built. Besides saying goodbye to Helene, I also encountered some faces I already knew who also work for the preservation of cultural heritage in Kathmandu. I felt as if these people, who had come to Nepal decades ago, had made something out of this restaurant that corresponded to the Western lifestyle, an occasional escape from the hurly-burly of the city. At any rate, the breakfast and setting of the restaurant already put me in the mood for my everyday life, which would soon overtake me in Vienna. Despite looking forward to my own four walls and the feeling of cleanliness you always have after an extended stay in Nepal, I soon felt my nostalgia and wanderlust welling up, and I felt the yearning for a little bit of Nepali chaos.

Temple elements were just turned into rubble

INTERVIEW
ROHIT
RANJITKAR

BY MARTINA
HASELBERGER

Fig. 1: Rohit Ranjitkar visiting the Institute of Conservation in Vienna

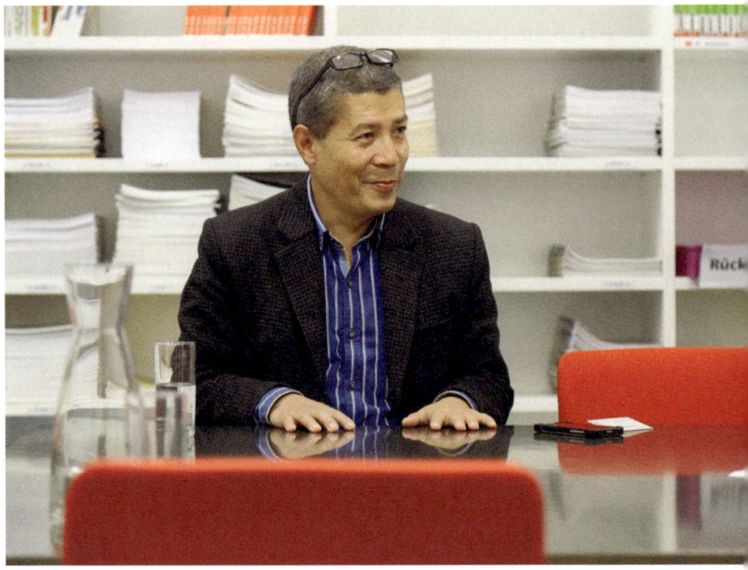

In spring 2015, a great earthquake hit Nepal. Large parts of the Royal Palace in Patan, a UNESCO World Heritage site, collapsed. The architect Rohit Ranjitkar from the Kathmandu Valley Preservation Trust Nepal talks about the challenges rescuers and conservators are facing after the earthquake.

Dr. Rohit Ranjitkar, architect and preservation consultant, serves as the Nepal Program Director of the Kathmandu Valley Preservation Trust (KVPT). His research includes the documentation and study of conservation practices in Nepal. Dr. Ranjitkar has worked in the field of architectural conservation with the KVPT since its establishment in 1991. KVPT is an international not-for-profit organization dedicated to safeguarding Nepal's extraordinary architectural heritage. Dr. Ranjitkar is responsible for the selection, design, and implementation of the restoration projects as well as fundraising, the training of local professional craftsmen and negotiations with local officials and involved community groups. He also implements new architectural projects, primarily the adaptive reuse of old houses into luxury facilities, which are renovated in the traditional style.

Furthermore, he is involved with the UNESCO World Heritage Centre, and German Technical Cooperation as a conservation consultant. He is author of the *Heritage Homeowner's Manual for the Kathmandu Valley World Heritage Sites,* which provides information on how to maintain and repair old homes, as well many other technical publications.

The Durbar Square and Royal Palace in Patan, a UNESCO World Heritage site, were heavily damaged by the earthquakes in spring 2015. What happened after the first earthquake? How did you react?

After the earthquake I came here to Durbar Square in the evening. Everything was a big mess, everything broken, people going here and there, it was very sad. What I saw in the morning of that day and what I saw after the earthquake – the contrast is almost unbelievable. First and foremost, we had to think about theft. So I talked with the people of the local community and they were very helpful. They guarded day and night, until police and armed forces came to guard after three days.

We then had meetings with the local community, with the municipality, with the Department of Archaeology and with the police on how to rescue all elements from the piles of rubble to save these artefacts. We were quite lucky as we had no casualties, and also there were no people trapped inside the buildings on Durbar Square. This has not been the case in Kathmandu where many people were trapped in monuments.

On the fourth or fifth day, army troops arrived with big trucks and bulldozers. I was right there when they were about to run the bulldozer to clean the square and the area around the monuments. I understand their task was to make or clear access for the public. Since they don't know the value of the artefacts, they are not trained to rescue the elements of the collapsed monuments, it was not easy to make them understand. I heard from many people what happened at the Kathmandu Durbar Square: many structural and decorative elements of collapsed monuments were still in the piles of rubble when the bulldozers started clearing work. Elements were just turned into debris, turned into dust. Many wooden elements broke due to the bulldozers. And even today if you go and see some of the timber pillars, you can see the marks of the bulldozer-blades. That was very sad.

I had a conversation with the team leader and made a few phone calls to my army friends, and finally they agreed not to use the bulldozer in Patan immediately. I asked the officers if they could help us rescue all the timber elements as well as all the reusable materials in order to restore and re-install them later. Finally, there were about 350 police, army and armed police forces lining and taking out all the pieces from the rubble.

For security reasons, we transferred the fragments to the museum courtyard. There were four monuments totally collapsed on the square, so I thought we could use the troops and keep all the elements in four different corners of the courtyard. That would make it easier to sort them out later and elements would not get mixed. The task turned out to be impossible with 350 people carrying, putting inside, and so on. I was happy at least pieces are safe, not missing. Even if they are mixed up I could always sort it out, I was pretty sure, it might take few extra hours. But many people disagreed with me. "How can you sort out when everything is mixed up?" they asked me. Anyway, we rescued everything. In about ten or eleven days, all the timber elements were already inside the museum. First preference was given to all the carved elements, which we rescued in five to six days, after that other plain timber elements were rescued as well. We sorted out all bricks that are re-usable, and one day we allowed the bulldozer to clean the rubble. So it took about two weeks to complete this process. We did almost all that actually before the second earthquake which hit the valley on 12 May.

A few days later a second earthquake occurred. How did you experience that? What happened?

During the second earthquake I was actually in the courtyard of Keshav Narayan Chowk. I was trying to sort out carved wooden pieces and assemble some of the windows with our craftsmen. Just a few minutes before the earthquake I saw a few people erecting scaffolding on North Taleju Temple to rescue the dislodged top roof, but after the earthquake I didn't see anybody any more. I was quite worried. I ran over there and I was happy that they had come downin time. They were quite lucky, because just before the earthquake occurred they had finished with the scaffolding material, so they all came down to take another bunch of material. Everybody was on the ground. No casualties. They were really lucky. From that day on, everybody was scared. Nobody wanted to climb up the scaffolding. I had to stop work. They came back slowly. So it was not easy in a way. We had a lot of small earthquakes, aftershocks, the work was very difficult. Everybody was scared. But we were all very enthusiastic because we saved all the pieces and we thought we could make it. Many people came to support us not only from the local community but also from different neighbouring communities, and school children too. We assembled the pieces; we started to sort them out and assign them to the four different collapsed temples. So it was an experience like assembling a huge jigsaw puzzle, I have to say.

Now after three years, some monuments are already standing again, many more are currently under reconstruction. What in fact has been achieved in these three years?

Our goal in the beginning was not rebuilding. That was our second priority, because you can do that anytime later, after you save the artefacts properly. The main task was to preserve those buildings that were in a bad condition, which might suffer from more damage due to aftershocks. For example, the Vishveshvara Temple was the most affected, it was already tilting, all the brick walls were bulging out on the ground level. It was quite amazing that the building was still standing, only on its timber columns. We immediately added supports and props, shored up the temple, so that it could not collapse. If it had collapsed, we would have lost many historical elements and it could have caused more casualties. So we moved quite fast.

That does not mean we ignored monuments which collapsed; we started repairing damaged wood-carved elements from the collapsed monuments and making new pieces to replace those that were damaged beyond repair. Much work was done parallel on many monuments, depending on what funds were raised and the availability of craftsmen and conservators. Since we have so many monuments in need of conservation, we asked the Austrian team from the University of Applied Arts to also come in winter; they have supported us each summer since 2010. Thanks to the Austrian team we were able to re-erect the Bhimsen Lion Pillar already on the first anniversary of 2015 earthquake. King Yoganarendra's pillar was restored by the team with local artists and erected in summer 2016, the king's sculpture was erected in spring 2017. Besides these projects, most of the stone and metal conservation was done with the help of the Austrian team. If I talk in numbers, a total of 18 monuments has already been completed by the KVPT after the 2015 earthquake up to now. These include some of the rebuilding, but most of them were partially collapsed or structurally damaged.

When do you think reconstruction and rebuilding work at Patan Durbar Square and the Royal Palace will be finished?

We are planning to finish what we have under construction and restoration now by the end of 2019. But not everything affected by the earthquake will be completed then. There are still a couple of temples in dire need of action, like Bhimsen Temple, which is still in a bad condition. That one will take another two years to be completed if we start soon, I hope within the next month.

We are currently negotiating with the government and the donors who are supposed to fund the work. Sorting out all these political issues is the precondition. The restoration of this temple will be implemented by local communities with the technical help from the KVPT. Besides this, there are a couple of other monuments affected by the last earthquake that still need to be worked out.

This is very fast in comparison to Bhaktapur and Kathmandu, the other two former royal cities in the valley. However, an earthquake can come again. How do you prepare in terms of conservation measures for a next natural hazard?

I do not want to say we are only preparing for the next earthquake because that is not the only threat. We always have problems with old buildings, for example damp proof barriers have never been used traditionally. I heard from older people that in earlier days we used to renew monuments from time to time as the problems cropped up. Now such practice is no longer in use due to lack of resources and many other factors. In the old days, people worked in the field for five to six months a year, and in the remaining time they did some community work, some kind of maintenance of the monuments, now that part is lost. This is one of the main reasons why we face so much damage after the last earthquake. When you do conservation and restoration work, it has to extend the monument's life. Today you cannot restore a former state only, because it was a different period, a different lifestyle, different quality and availability with regard to materials and skilled craftsmen.

In our current situation we have to think about what we can do better for the building. And we were already thinking of all these issues before the earthquake in 2015. Even before that, we integrated many small structural improvements in the buildings, like using steel pins. There is an ongoing controversial debate about using the modern materials. I myself believe that at the end of the day you have to think about human safety. During the earthquake I saw people first rushing to save people, not the historic elements. So I thought, this is it. I will never say I can make the monuments earthquake-proof. This is maybe not possible. What I can say is, whatever building we restore we have to think about how we can make it safer for people, so that there is enough time to escape. I don't mind if the building has some cracks, some tilting, some problem, we can fix that. But if the building comes down and people die, we cannot fix, we cannot bring back life. So I think all improvements that prevent the building from collapsing should be done wherever possible with minimal intervention.

What is the contribution of the Austrian team here and how can we help you in your overall efforts to care for the cultural heritage here in Patan?

We started the Kathmandu Valley Preservation Trust in 1991. Our founding chairman, Prof. Eduard Sekler, was from Vienna. He was very keen on the historical preservation of Nepalese cultural assets because he did a great deal of research and studies in Nepal in the 1970s. Throughout much restoration work we realized we were doing a straightforward job as restorers. But there is a gap in the proper conservation of particular things, like metal, stone, wood, bricks, which is why we are always looking for experts in material conservation. So this is how the Austrian connection came to life through Dr. Sekler, who helped us to connect with the University of Applied Arts Vienna. Since 2010 we have had the Institute of Conservation from the University of Applied Arts Vienna here. I am very grateful to its team for helping us, especially with all the metal and stone conservation. We lack such professionally trained people in our country, therefore it is adding value to our historical preservation projects. We would do the job without this, but something would be missing.

Photo credits

Brigitte Winklehner – Foreword
Fig. 1: Gabriela Krist, Institute of Conservation, University of Applied Arts Vienna

Gabriela Krist – Incredible India!
Fig. 1-4, 7-8: Stefan Oláh, Institute of Conservation, University of Applied Arts Vienna
Fig. 5-6: Institute of Conservation, University of Applied Arts Vienna
Fig. 6: Institute of Conservation, University of Applied Arts Vienna

Tatjana Bayerová – The Nako Story
Fig. 1, 4-7: Tatjana Bayerová, Institute of Conservation, University of Applied Arts Vienna
Fig. 2-3: Stefan Oláh, Institute of Conservation, University of Applied Arts Vienna
Fig. 8: Edgar Skomorowski, Institute of Conservation, University of Applied Arts Vienna

Martina Griesser-Stermscheg – The Nako Museum
Fig. 1-2: Martina Griesser-Stermscheg, Institute of Conservation, University of Applied Arts Vienna
Fig. 3-9: Institute of Conservation, University of Applied Arts Vienna
Fig. 10-11: Stefan Oláh, Institute of Conservation, University of Applied Arts Vienna

Gundi Lamprecht – This All Belongs to Tibet
Fig. 1-2: Stefan Oláh, Institute of Conservation, University of Applied Arts Vienna

Stefan Oláh – A Wild and Wonderful Journey
Fig.1-9: Stefan Oláh

Johanna Runkel – International Summer Schools in Vienna
Fig. 1: Tanja Kimmel, Institute of Conservation, University of Applied Arts Vienna
Fig. 2: Gabriela Krist, Institute of Conservation, University of Applied Arts Vienna
Fig. 3-5, 9: Agnes Szökrön-Michl, Institute of Conservation, University of Applied Arts Vienna
Fig. 6: Shivananda, participant of the Summer School.
Fig. 7-8: Institute of Conservation, University of Applied Arts Vienna
Fig. 10: Caroline Ocks, Institute of Conservation, University of Applied Arts Vienna

Johanna Runkel – Conservation Workshops
Fig. 3: National Museum Institute, New Delhi
Fig. 1, 2: Martina Griesser-Stermscheg, Institute of Conservation, University of Applied Arts Vienna
Fig. 4: Institute of Conservation, University of Applied Arts Vienna

Tanushree Gupta, Noor Jahan – Research in Vienna
Fig. 1: Institute of Conservation, University of Applied Arts Vienna, Caroline Dalhed
Fig. 2, 5: Indira Gandhi National Centre for the Arts, Nitin Kumar
Fig. 3: Institute of Conservation, University of Applied Arts Vienna, Tatjana Bayerová
Fig. 4: Institute of Conservation, University of Applied Arts Vienna.
Fig. 6: Institute of Conservation, University of Applied Arts Vienna, Gabriela Krist
Fig. 7: Institute of Conservation, University of Applied Arts Vienna, Tanushree Gupta
Fig. 8-9: Institute of Conservation, University of Applied Arts Vienna, Marta Anghelone
Fig. 10: Indian Embassy, Vienna, Martin Pegritz

T. Gupta, G. Krist, M. V. Nair, J. Runkel – India and Austria
Fig. 1, 3: Subhash Kowdiar, Napier Museum, Trivandrum
Fig. 2, 5, 9-10: Tanushree Gupta, Institute of Conservation, University of Applied Arts Vienna
Fig. 4, 8: Johanna Runkel, Institute of Conservation, University of Applied Arts Vienna
Fig. 6-7: Mohamad Gasnafar, Napier Museum, Trivandrum

Johanna Runkel – Kerala
Fig. 1-3, 6-7, 10, 30, 32: Johanna Runkel, Institute of Conservation, University of Applied Arts Vienna
Fig. 4, 9, 13, 15-16, 20-26: Subash, Napier Museum, Trivandrum
Fig. 5, 18, 29, 31: M. Gasnafar, Napier Museum, Trivandrum.
Fig. 8, 19: Napier Museum, Trivandrum
Fig. 11: Tanja Kimmel, Institute of Conservation, University of Applied Arts Vienna
Fig. 12: Gabriela Krist, Institute of Conservation, University of Applied Arts Vienna
Fig. 14, 17: Institute of Conservation, University of Applied Arts Vienna
Fig. 27-28: Tanushree Gupta, Institute of Conservation, University of Applied Arts Vienna

Roman Tronner – Interview Velayudhan Nair
Fig. 1: National Museum Institute, New Delhi
Fig. 2: Stefan Oláh, Institute of Conservation, University of Applied Arts Vienna

Gabriela Krist – The Dog Who Travels Comes Back with the Bone
Fig. 1, 9: Galmandakh Amarsanaa, Mongolian State University of Arts and Culture, Ulaanbataar
Fig. 2-3, 7: Gabriela Krist, Institute of Conservation, University of Applied Arts Vienna
Fig. 4-5: Britta Schwenck, Institute of Conservation, University of Applied Arts Vienna
Fig. 6, 8, 10-13: Institute of Conservation, University of Applied Arts Vienna

Katharina Kohler – Workshops on Cultural Heritage Conservation at Bogd Khaan Palace in Mongolia
Fig. 1-6: Katharina Kohler, Institute of Conservation, University of Applied Arts Vienna, 2017
Fig. 7, 10-11: Katharina Kohler, Institute of Conservation, University of Applied Arts Vienna, 2018
Fig. 8-9: N. Enkh-Manlai, Bogd Khaan Palace Museum, 2018

Marisa Laurenzi Tabasso – My Mongolian Experience in 2016
Fig. 1-10: Galmandakh Amarsanaa, Mongolian State University of Arts and Culture, Ulaanbataar, 2016

G. Enkhbat, E. Batjargal, Ts. Tsolmon – Joining Forces in the Field of Cultural Heritage Preservation
Fig. 1-3: National Center for Cultural Heritage, Mongolia

Martina Haselberger, Marija Milchin – Cultural Heritage Conservation in Mongolia: Stone Monuments
Fig. 1, 4-6, 8, 10-13, 15, 18-19, 23, 26, 28: Martina Haselberger, Institute of Conservation, University of Applied Arts Vienna
Fig. 2-3, 9, 14, 16, 17, 20-22, 24-25: Marija Milchin, Institute of Conservation, University of Applied Arts Vienna
Fig. 7: Johannes Weber, Institute of Art and Technology, University of Applied Arts Vienna
Fig. 27: Ts. Tsolmon, National Center for Cultural Heritage, Mongolia

Ganzam Sumberraz – Experiences while Studying at the University of Applied Arts Vienna
Fig. 1-5: Institute of Conservation, University of Applied Arts Vienna

Khosbayar Narankhuu – The Conservation and Re-Display of Metal Equestrian Armour
Fig. 1-7, 9: Khosbayar Narankhuu
Fig. 8, 10-14: N.Bat-Erdene, National Center for Cultural Heritage, Mongolia

Gabriela Krist – Burmese Travel Diary
Fig. 1-23: Gabriela Krist, Institute of Conservation, University of Applied Arts Vienna

Gabriela Krist – Via Detours...From Myanmar to Thailand
Fig. 1: Institute of Conservation, University of Applied Arts Vienna.
Fig. 2-3: Veronika Loiskandl, Institute of Conservation, University of Applied Arts Vienna.
Fig. 4-6: Silpakorn University

Veronika Loiskandl, Tatjana Bayerová – Conservation Training in Thailand
Fig. 1-14: Veronika Loiskandl, Institute of Conservation, University of Applied Arts Vienna
Fig. 15-18, 20: Tatjana Bayerová, Institute of Conservation, University of Applied Arts Vienna
Fig. 19: Veronika Loiskandl, Institute of Conservation, University of Applied Arts Vienna

Tatjana Bayerová – My Three Days in Thai Paradise
Fig. 1-7: Tatjana Bayerová, Institute of Conservation, University of Applied Arts Vienna

Gabriela Krist – The Silk Road...Connecting Us
Fig. 1-2, 4, 7: Institute of Conservation, University of Applied Arts Vienna
Fig. 3: Tatjana Bayerová, Institute of Conservation, University of Applied Arts Vienna
Fig. 5-6: Gabriela Krist, Institute of Conservation, University of Applied Arts Vienna

Tatjana Bayerová, Barbara Rankl – The International Network in the Past, Present, and Future: The Silk Road
Fig. 1, 6-7: Institute of Conservation, University of Applied Arts Vienna
Fig. 2-5: Tatjana Bayerová, Institute of Conservation, University of Applied Arts Vienna
Fig. 8: Gabriela Krist, Institute of Conservation, University of Applied Arts Vienna
Fig. 9: Barbara Rankl, Institute of Conservation, University of Applied Arts Vienna

Roman Tronner – Interview Liangren Zhang
Fig. 1: Martina Haselberger, Institute of Conservation, University of Applied Arts Vienna

Photo credits

Tatjana Bayerová,Tanja Kimmel – IIC-ITCC Overseas Courses in Beijing
Fig. 1-2, 7, 12-15 : Tanja Kimmel, Institute of Conservation, University of Applied Arts Vienna
Fig. 3, 5-6, 9-11: IIC-ITCC/Palace Museum
Fig. 4: Tatjana Bayerová, Institute of Conservation, University of Applied Arts Vienna

Gabriela Krist – In the Footsteps of Important Austrian Scholars, Architects and Preservationists
Fig. 1-2, 4, 10: Christoph Schleßmann, Institute of Conservation, University of Applied Arts Vienna
Fig. 3: Kathmandu Valley Preservation Trust
Fig. 5-9, 11-16: Institute of Conservation, University of Applied Arts Vienna

Martina Haselberger – The Institute in Patan, Nepal – Working Missions and Experiences
Fig. 1-2: Stanislaw Klimek, Kathmandu Valley Preservation Trust, 2008
Fig. 3, 7-8, 16: Martina Haselberger, Institute of Conservation, University of Applied Arts Vienna
Fig. 4: Katharina Fuchs, Institute of Conservation, University of Applied Arts Vienna
Fig. 5, 11-15, 17-19, 22-24, 26-32, 34-42, 44, 47-59: Institute of Conservation, University of Applied Arts Vienna
Fig. 6, 43, 46: Kathmandu Valley Preservation Trust
Fig. 9-10, 20-21, 33: Christoph Schleßmann, Institute of Conservation, University of Applied Arts Vienna
Fig. 25: Gabriela Krist, Institute of Conservation, University of Applied Arts Vienna
Fig. 45: Thomas Schrom

Christoph Schleßmann – A Photographer's Impressions
Fig. 1-23: Christoph Schleßmann, Institute of Conservation, University of Applied Arts Vienna

Manfred Trummer – Nako and Patan
Fig. 1, 3, 4, 5, 7, 8: Christoph Schleßmann, Institute of Conservation, University of Applied Arts Vienna
Fig. 2: Institute of Conservation, University of Applied Arts Vienna
Fig. 6: Manfred Trummer, Institute of Conservation, University of Applied Arts Vienna
Fig. 9: Kathmandu Valley Preservation Trust

Regina Friedl – Nepal – A Journey to Adventure
Fig. 1-26: Regina Friedl

Katharina Fuchs – My Very Own Nepal
Fig. 1-7: Katharina Fuchs 2012

Martina Haselberger – Interview Rohit Ranjitkar
Fig. 1: Peter Kainz, University of Applied Arts Vienna

Imprint

Gabriela Krist has been a university professor at the University of Applied Arts Vienna, Institute of Conservation, since 1999. She studied conservation at the Academy of Fine Arts Vienna, as well as art history and archaeology in Vienna and Salzburg. For many years she worked for ICCROM in Rome and at the Austrian Federal Office for the Care of Monuments (Bundesdenkmalamt).

Library of Congress
Control Number: 2019933222

Bibliographic information published by the German National Library
The German National Library lists this publication in the Deutsche Nationalbibliografie; detailed bibliographic data are available on the Internet at http:// dnb.dnb.de.

Translation and Editing: Scott Evans, Abigail Prohaska, Martina Haselberger, Johanna Runkel

Graphic Design: Theresa Hattinger

Printing: Holzhausen Druck GmbH, Wolkersdorf, Austria
Printed in Austria

Project Management "Edition Angewandte" on behalf of the University of Applied Arts Vienna: Anja Seipenbusch-Hufschmied, A-Vienna

Project Management and Production on behalf of the Publisher: Angela Fössl, A-Vienna

ISSN 1866-248X
ISBN 978-3-11-060289-0

www.degruyter.com